DB2 Universal Database v8.1 for Linux, UNIX, and Windows Database Administration Certification Guide

ISBN 0-13-046361-2

9 780130 463616

95999

IBM DB2 Certification Guide Series

DB2 SQL Procedural Language for Linux, UNIX, and Windows
  by Yip, Bradstock, Curtis, Gao, Janmohamed, Liu, and McArthur

DB2 Universal Database for OS/390 v7.1 Application Certification Guide
  by Lawson

DB2 Universal Database v7.1 Application Development Certification Guide
  by Sanyal, Martineau, Gashyna, and Kyprianou

DB2 Universal Database v8 for UNIX, Linux, and Windows Administration Certification Guide, Fifth Edition
  by Baklarz and Wong

DB2 Universal Database in Application Development Environments
  by Shirai, Barber, Saboji, Naick, and Wilkins

DB2 Universal Database v6.1 Certification Guide, Third Edition
  by Cook, Harbus, and Shirai

DB2 Universal Database in the Solaris Operating Environment
  by Shirai, Michel, Wilding, Logan, and Bauch

DB2 Cluster Certification Guide
  by Cook, Janacek, and Snow

DB2 Universal DRDA Certification Guide
  by Brandl, Bullock, Cook, Harbus, Janacek, and Le

DB2 Replication Certification Guide
  by Cook and Harbus

DB2 Universal Database and SAP R/3, Version 4
  by Bullock, Cook, Deedes-Vincke, Harbus, Nardone, and Neuhaus

The Universal Guide to DB2 for Windows NT
  by Cook, Harbus, and Snow

DB2 Universal Database v8.1 for Linux, UNIX, and Windows Database Administration Certification Guide

GEORGE BAKLARZ

BILL WONG

International Technical Support Organization
Austin, Texas 78758

PRENTICE
HALL
PTR

PRENTICE HALL PROFESSIONAL TECHNICAL REFERENCE
UPPER SADDLE RIVER, NEW JERSEY 07458
www.phptr.com

Library of Congress Cataloging-in-Publication Data available

Editorial/production supervision: *Kathleen M. Caren*
Cover design director: *Jerry Votta*
Cover design: *Anthony Gemmellaro*
Manufacturing buyer: *Alexis Heydt-Long*
Acquisitions editor: *Jeffrey Pepper*
Editorial assistant: *Linda Ramagnano*
Marketing manager: *Kate Hargett*
IBM Consulting editor: *Susan Visser*

 Published by Pearson Education, Inc.
Publishing as Prentice Hall Professional Technical Reference
Upper Saddle River, NJ 07458

Prentice Hall books are widely used by corporations and government agencies for training, marketing, and resale.

For information regarding corporate and government bulk discounts please contact:

Corporate and Government Sales (800) 382-3419 or corpsales@pearsontechgroup.com

Printed in the United States of America

10 9 8 7 6 5 4 3

ISBN   0-13-046361-2

Pearson Education LTD.
Pearson Education Australia PTY, Limited
Pearson Education Singapore, Pte. Ltd.
Pearson Education North Asia Ltd.
Pearson Education Canada, Ltd.
Pearson Educación de Mexico, S.A. de C.V.
Pearson Education — Japan
Pearson Education Malaysia, Pte. Ltd.

Table of Contents

Part THREE   DB2 UDB Administration 447

Part FIVE Appendices 849

DB2 UDB V8.1
Certification Test Objectives 851

CD-ROM Installation 861

Foreword

*A*n ongoing challenge for today's computer professionals is reserving the time to develop new skills to keep up with changes in technology. Our value as technology professionals is increased as we learn and develop new skills with industry leading products. One of the most technologically advanced products in the industry is DB2 Universal Database which is also the market leader on popular environments such as Linux.

More than 20 years ago, Relational database technology was invented in IBM Research delivering the first commercially available database in the early 1980s. This invention created the unique ability to represent data in a simple tabular form, access it through the powerful SQL query language, and make it readily available to the business community. Today, tens of thousands of businesses all over the world rely on DB2 databases to store their key corporate data assets and run their business both traditionally and over the Web.

DB2 provides virtually unlimited scalability, industry leading performance, reliability, and availability. DB2 continues to lead the industry by focusing on autonomic computing that will make DBAs more productive and allow our customers without a DBA staff to manage their database environments effectively with a minimum of effort.

The demand for DB2 skills continues to grow. Certifications were awarded in over 60 countries around the world, more than 3000 institutions worldwide are teaching DB2-related courses, and over 100,000 download requests have been made from DBAs and Developers who have wanted to extend their skills from Microsoft, Sybase, and Oracle to DB2 UDB.

This Certification Guide is an excellent way to learn about DB2, to develop new skills, and to provide new opportunities for yourself in the computer industry. This book includes a trial copy of DB2 and a demo that will give you an opportunity to develop skills using hands-on experience. I hope you use this Certification Guide in advancing your skills and enjoy the benefits of being a certified DB2 professional.

Janet Perna
General Manager, IBM Data Management
IBM Software Group

Preface

This book is a complete guide to the IBM's relational database servers, known as DB2 Universal Database Version 8.1. DB2 Universal Database (DB2 UDB) Version 8.1 is available on many operating systems, and the book has been written with this in mind. Any significant differences in the implementation of DB2 UDB on various operating systems are highlighted. If you are planning to become certified, or you would simply like to understand the powerful new DB2 UDB database servers from IBM, then read on. Those interested in becoming an IBM Certified Professional will want to review the information found in Appendix A at the end of this book.

The book is divided into four parts:

- Part 1 - Introduction to DB2 UDB (Chapters 1–4).
  Installing and configuring DB2 UDB servers and clients are covered in Chapters 1, 2, 3, and 4.
- Part 2 - Using SQL (Chapters 5–8).
  The Structured Query Language (SQL) is discussed in Chapter 5, 6 and 7. Database concurrency is discussed in Chapter 8.
- Part 3 - DB2 UDB Database Administration (Chapters 9–12).
  Creating a DB2 UDB database and its related table spaces is covered in Chapter 9. The common administration tasks are discussed in Chapters 10 and 11. Database monitoring and performance considerations are discussed in Chapter 12.
- Part 4 - Developing Applications with DB2 UDB (Chapters 13–14).
  An introduction to application development for DBAs is given in Chapter 13. Chapter 14 deals with some of the DBA activities that are related to application development. SQL used in a programming environment is discussed in chapter 15.

This book can be used as a self-study guide to help you prepare for the DB2 Universal Database V8.1 certification exams 700 and 701, or as a guide to DB2 Universal Database V8.1. Experience with DB2 Universal Database Version 8.1 is the best way to prepare for any of the DB2 UDB V8.1 certification exams!

Exam 700 covers DB2 V8.1 Family Fundamentals, while exam 701 covers DB2 V8.1 for Linux, UNIX, and Windows Database Administration.

A number of companion books are available for exams 703 and 704:

- Exam 703 - DB2 V8.1 Family Application Development

    DB2 UDB v8.1 Application Development Certification Guide, 2/e, Steve Sanyal, Kevin Gashyna, David Martineau, Mike Kyprianou, 0-13-046391-4

- Exam 704 - DB2 V8.1 for Linux, UNIX, and Windows Advanced Database Administration

    Advanced DBA Certification Guide and Reference for DB2 UDB v8.1 for Linux, UNIX, and Windows, 1/e, Snow / Phan, 0-13-046388-4

If you plan to do a lot of work with the SQL Procedural Language, the *DB2 SQL Procedural Language for Linux, UNIX and Windows*, 1/e, Paul Yip, et al, 0-13-100772-6 book from Prentice Hall would also be a good reference.

 Note: More information about DB2 UDB certification can be found at http://www.ibm.com/certify and in "DB2 UDB V8.1 Certification Test Objectives" on page 851.

Conventions

Many examples of SQL statements, DB2 commands, and operating system commands are included throughout the book. SQL statements are usually displayed within a shaded box, and any of the mandatory sections of the statements are shown in uppercase letters. An example of an SQL statement is shown:

```
SELECT lname, fname FROM candidate
  WHERE lname = 'WONG' OR
        LNAME = 'BAKLARZ'
```

SQL is not a case-sensitive language, so the above query would provide the same result regardless of the case of the SQL keywords or the database object (table names or column names). Of course, the data in the database is stored *exactly* as it was entered (including case). Therefore, the above query would only find the candidates with the last name of 'WONG' or 'BAKLARZ'. If the data were stored as 'wong', it would not be part of the result table.

If SQL keywords are referred to in the text portion of the book, they will be shown as a monospaced font. For example, the SELECT statement is used to retrieve data from a DB2 database.

DB2 commands will be shown using the same method as SQL keywords. For example, the CREATE DATABASE command allows you to define the initial location of database objects. DB2 commands are issued from the Command Line Processor (CLP) utility. This utility will accept the commands in upper- and lowercase letters. The CLP program itself is an executable called db2. In some operating systems, such as AIX, the program names are case sensitive. Therefore, be careful to enter the program name using the proper case.

There are a few operating-system-specific commands in this book. If the commands must be in lowercase they will be shown as such. For example, the UNIX command to create a user is the mkuser command.

Occasionally, notes are provided to highlight a particular point or features that are new to DB2 UDB Version 8.1:

Note: A note may be used to explain a minor operating system difference or it may be used to summarize a concept.

Note: DB2 Version 8.1-specific features are highlighted with this note format.

There are a few syntax diagrams shown in the book. We recommend that the Command Line Processor or the *DB2 UDB V8.1 Command Reference* be used to verify the syntax of DB2 UDB commands. The *DB2 UDB V8.1 SQL Reference* should be used to verify the syntax of SQL statements. To emphasize a term or concept, the term is shown in **bold** type or emphasized with *italics*.

Contributions

The DB2 Universal Database Certification Guide was updated for Version 8.1, making this the fifth edition. We would like to thank the many customers, colleagues, and technical support personnel we have worked with for their ongoing efforts to improve DB2 and their feedback on this book.

In particular, we would like to thank:

- Susan Visser, for her continued encouragement and support in updating this book
- Blair Adamache, Ken Chen, Jose Cuan, Jason Gartner, Bob Harbus, Juliana Hsu, Leo Lau, Mark Leitch, Dale McInnis, Serge Rielau, Jim Stittle, Carmen Wong, Paul Yip, and Paul Zikopolous for reviewing earlier drafts
- Thomas Chu and John Botsford for providing us beta code
- Bert Nicol for scheduling us to be in the office for more than a day
- Judith Escott for her management support and constant focus on providing DB2 skills support around the world
- The DB2 development team for their continued support of this book

Acknowledgments

I'm always thankful that I have an understanding family (and dog and cat!) that could deal with the late nights and busy weekends when I was updating this book. Needless to say, I couldn't have done this without their help and patience! Thanks, Katrina, Geoff, and Andrew!

George

I would like to take this opportunity to thank my family; Shirley, Dana, and Austin. Any measure of success that I have accomplished is due their support and understanding. They have also taught me how to take a vacation without me working on a book.

Bill

P A R T 1

Introduction to DB2 UDB

CHAPTER 1

Product Overview

- ◆ **DB2** UNIVERSAL DATABASE
- ◆ **DB2** CONNECTIVITY
- ◆ **DB2** APPLICATION DEVELOPMENT
- ◆ **DB2** ADMINISTRATION

*I*n this chapter, you will be introduced to the DB2 Universal Database (DB2 UDB) family of products for UNIX and Intel platforms. DB2 has the ability to store all kinds of electronic information. This includes traditional relational data as well as structured and unstructured binary information, documents and text in many languages, graphics, images, multimedia (audio and video), information specific to operations like engineering drawings, maps, insurance claims forms, numerical control streams, or any type of electronic information. This chapter will illustrate some of the ways to access data in a DB2 database using some of the interfaces provided with the products. A description of each of the DB2 products will be provided to illustrate some of the features and functions.

The DB2 database is an important part of IBM's e-business software portfolio. The e-business Application Framework provides an open blueprint on how to build e-business applications. Popular IBM e-business tools include WebSphere Studio for developing Java programs or components and Tivoli software for distributed systems management. As for application server software, IBM offers several types of servers depending on the business requirement, from WebSphere Message

Queuing software to Java-based transaction processing with Websphere Application Server. The most popular IBM software servers are its database servers, specifically the DB2 Family.

Fig. 1–1 *IBM Application Framework for e-business*

The DB2 Family executes on pervasive devices, Intel, UNIX, iSeries, and mainframe platforms. Supported operating environments include: Linux, Windows 2000/NT/XP/2003, AIX, HP-UX, Sun Solaris, OS/400, VSE/VM, and OS/390. For the Windows 2003 environment, DB2 is certified for the Standard Edition, Enterprise Edition, and Datacenter Edition products.

The DB2 code base is optimized for each platform to ensure maximum performance. The SQL API is common to all platforms, which allows applications written on one platform to access data on any platform. Internally, DB2 running on the OS/400, VM/VSE, or OS/390 environments differ from DB2 on the Intel and UNIX platforms, but it is the common SQL API that enables applications to work together. The DB2 code base on Intel and UNIX platforms are identical.

DB2 V8.1 for Linux, Windows, and UNIX provides seamless database connectivity using the most popular network communications protocols, including NetBIOS, TCP/IP, Named Pipes, and APPC.

DB2 and e-business

As a core component of IBM's e-business Application Framework, DB2 is a catalyst for delivering applications that change the way a company performs its operations. The transformation process of taking a business to an e-business, often centers around applications that impact the entire operations of a company, they can include: electronic commerce, Enterprise Resource Planning (ERP), Customer Relationship Management (CRM), Purchasing and Logistics Management (PLM), and Supply Chain Management (SCM). It is the process of re-engineering the company to integrate these new applications that enables a company to leverage these applications to their fullest potential..

Fig. 1–2 *e-business demands for information*

DB2 and Linux

Many companies are investing on Linux platforms because of the platform independence this environment provides. Today, the most popular hardware platform that is being used for Linux is the Intel platform in a server-based environment, however, many companies are also using Linux to consolidate workloads onto more powerful hardware, including IBM's largest enterprise zSeries servers which can run both DB2 UDB and DB2 Connect. Accompanying the major hardware vendors supporting Linux, are the major software vendors, who are also porting their applications to support Linux.

Fig. 1–3 *DB2 UDB and Linux*

DB2 Universal Database

In the distributed environment, DB2 offers several packaging options:

- **Enterprise Server Edition** - This offering is often used to build e-business applications and support departmental applications to large enterprise data warehouses. It offers the most connectivity options and can share data with third-party databases and DB2 on heterogeneous platforms.

- **Workgroup Server Edition** - This offering is often used in smaller departmental applications or for applications that do not need access to remote databases on the OS/400, VM/VSE, or OS/390 platform.

- **Express Edition** - DB2 UDB Express edition is a specially tailored full feature relational database for small and medium business.

- **Personal Edition** - This full-function database offering is for single-users and will not accept remote database requests. This offering is available on Linux and Windows.

- **Everyplace** - This is a mobile computing offering that gives mobile workers access to DB2 data sources in the enterprise through handheld devices such as personal digital assistants (PDAs) and handheld personal computers (HPCs). DB2 Everyplace can be run on a number of pervasive operating environments, including: Palm OS, Linux, Windows CE, Neutrino, PocketPC and Symbian.

 Note: DB2 Enterprise Server Edition is a merge of the products previously known as DB2 UDB Enterprise Edition and DB2 UDB Enterprise-Extended Edition. The product previously known as DB2 Satellite Edition has been merged into the new release of DB2 Personal Edition.

DB2 Enterprise Server Edition

DB2 Enterprise Server Edition is a relational database management system that is the foundation of many mission-critical systems and the primary focus of this certification guide. It is fully web-enabled, scalable from single processors to symmetric multiprocessors and to massively parallel systems; it supports unstructured data such as image, audio, video, text, spatial, and XML with its object relational capabilities.

Applications for DB2 Enterprise Server Edition can scale upward and execute on massively parallel systems or can scale downward with applications executing on single-user database systems.

Fig. 1–4 *DB2 Universal Database*

DB2 Enterprise Server Edition provides an option that enables DB2 to partition data across clusters or massively parallel computers. To the end-user or application developer, the database appears to be on a single system. SQL statements are processed in parallel, thus increasing the execution speed for any given query.

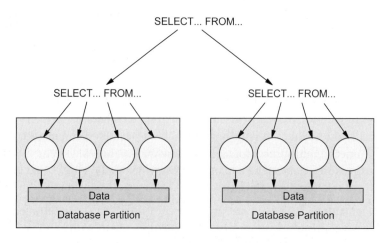

Fig. 1–5 *DB2 processing a query in parallel*

This option is often selected to support large database applications such as data warehousing applications. By providing for inter and intra-parallelism, databases can scale to multiple terabytes.

DB2 Enterprise Server Edition is available on the Linux, UNIX, and Windows platforms. This product is covered in detail in the *Advanced DBA Certification Guide and Reference for DB2 UDB V8 for Linux, Unix and Windows.*

 Note: The Database Partitioning Feature (DPF) allows DB2 Enterprise Server Edition to partition workloads on a single physical server or across a cluster of servers.

DB2 Workgroup Server Edition

DB2 Workgroup Server Edition is designed for use in a LAN environment. It provides support for both remote and local clients. A server with DB2 Workgroup Server Edition installed can be connected to a network and participate in a distributed environment as show in Figure 1–6.

Fig. 1–6 *DB2 Workgroup Server Edition with remote clients*

In Fig. 1–6, App1 and App2 are local database applications. Remote clients can also execute App1 and App2 if the necessary setup has been performed. A DB2 application does not contain any specific information regarding the physical location of the database. DB2 client applications communicate with DB2 Workgroup Server Edition using a supported distributed protocol. Depending on the client and server operating systems involved, DB2 Workgroup Server Edition supports the TCP/IP, NetBIOS, Named Pipes, and APPC protocols.

DB2 Workgroup Server Edition is available on the Linux, UNIX, and Windows platforms.

DB2 UDB Express Edition

DB2 Universal Database (UDB) Express Edition V8.1 is specially tailored to meet the needs of small and medium businesses (SMBs) by offering a database that is:

- Easy to install and deploy: Includes an option for a silent install from within an application
- Simple to manage: Autonomic (self-management) features reduce the skills and resources required to manage the solution by eliminating complexity
- Affordable: Competitively priced to address the needs of SMBs
- Open: Based on open industry standards and portable across pervasive operating platforms (such as Windows and Linux) to avoid vendor lock-in
- Scalable on demand: Features the full-function DB2 UDB engine to allow seamless transition to other DB2 UDB editions as businesses grow
- Extensible: With IBM Software Group middleware, includes LotusÆ for collaboration, TivoliÆ for management, and WebSphereÆ for dynamic e-business

DB2 UDB Express easily integrates with applications and results in faster deployment and faster time to market for partner applications. DB2 UDB Express is available on 32-bit Windows and Linux platforms, and supports up to two processors in a machine.

DB2 Personal Edition

DB2 Personal Edition is a full-function database that enables a single-user to create databases on the workstation on which it was installed. It can be used as a remote client to a DB2 server, since it also contains the DB2 client components. Applications written to execute on the Personal Edition offering can also be used to access a DB2 Server, with no programming changes.

The DB2 Personal Edition product is often used by end-users requiring access to local and remote DB2 databases or developers prototyping applications that will be accessing other DB2 databases.

Fig. 1–7 shows an example of a DB2 Personal Edition installation. In this example, the user can access a local database on his or her desktop machine and access remote databases located on the database server. From the desktop, the user can make changes to the database throughout the day and replicate those changes as a client to the remote database on the DB2 server.

DB2 UDB Server

DB2 UDB Personal Edition

Fig. 1–7 *DB2 Personal Edition*

DB2 Personal Edition includes graphical tools (via the DB2 Administration Client component) that enable a user to administer, tune for performance, access remote DB2 servers, process SQL queries, and manage other servers from a single workstation.

The Satellite Administration Center provides utilities that minimizes the cost of managing a large number of systems by administering collections of systems running the same application and database in groups. Scripts stored at a central administration control point are used to accomplish administrative tasks on the systems in a group. This model also allows for centralized problem determination.

This product is available on Linux and Windows.

DB2 Everyplace

DB2 Everyplace is a tiny "fingerprint" database of about 180K. It is designed for low-cost, low-power, small form-factor devices such as personal digital assistants (PDAs), handheld personal computers (HPCs), or embedded devices. DB2 Everyplace runs on devices that use the Palm Computing® Platform, Linux, Windows CE, PocketPC, Symbian, and QNX Neutrino. DB2 Everyplace provides a local data store on the mobile or embedded device for storing relational data from elsewhere in the enterprise. Relational data can be synchronized to the handheld device from other DB2 data sources such as DB2 Universal Database for Linux, UNIX, Windows, DB2 for OS/390, and DB2 for OS/400. DB2 Everyplace with DB2 Everyplace Synchronization Server will also synchronize data from other JDBC-compliant data sources such as Oracle and Microsoft.

The DB2 Everyplace Sync Server mobilizes professionals with e-business information anywhere, anytime. It extends the power of DB2 to a wide range of handheld devices, such as those running the Palm Pilot.

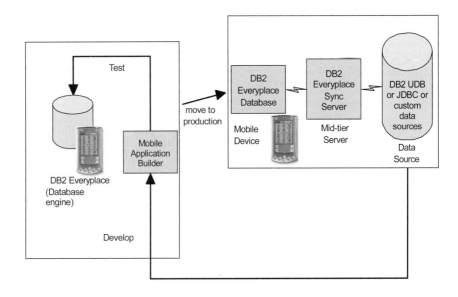

Fig. 1–8 *DB2 Everyplace*

The DB2 Everyplace Mobile Application Builder supports building applications for small handheld devices that access DB2 Everyplace databases. Some of its capabilities include:

• Supports visual construction of forms for different devices
• Supports the lightweight DB2 Everywhere database on the device
• Provides scripting capabilities for user-defined logic
• Integrates with other tools for application testing and debugging

DB2 Connectivity

DB2 provides a variety of options for connecting to other DB2 and non-DB2 databases.

- **DB2 Clients** - Client code is required on workstations for remote users to access a DB2 database.

- **DB2 Connect** - This product provides support for applications executing on UNIX and Intel platforms to transparently access DB2 databases on the OS/400, VM/VSE, and OS/390 environments. Note that DB2 Connect is not required to access DB2 for any of the UNIX or Intel platforms.

- **DB2 Replication** - This product provides replication capabilities for DB2 databases and is integrated in DB2 on the UNIX and Intel platforms.

- **DB2 Information Integrator** - This product extends the integration functions of DB2 UDB to support additional relational sources such as Oracle and Microsoft SQL Server, as well as non-relational sources using the SQL API.

- **DB2 Information Integrator for Content** - This product delivers an information integration solution that integrates diverse, distributed, unstructured data using IBM Content Manager interfaces and object-oriented API's.

- **WebSphere Application Server** - This Application Server is shipped with DB2 Universal Developer's Edition and allows developers to use Java as platform in a transaction processing environment.

The *DB2 UDB Quick Beginnings* manual for each platform provides operating system requirements for implementing DB2 distributed configurations.

DB2 Universal Database Clients

A DB2 client can be configured to establish communications with a DB2 server using various communication protocols. The supported protocols vary according to operating system:

- TCP/IP - used in all environments
- NetBIOS - used in Windows environments
- APPC - used in IBM operating environments
- Named Pipe - used in Windows environments

A DB2 client has a number of options for what client code needs to be installed, which will be depend on the requirements of the client. The options include:

Product Overview

- DB2 Runtime Client
- DB2 Administration Client
- DB2 Application Development Client
- DB2 Thin Client

Once a DB2 application has been developed, only the DB2 Runtime Client component needs to be installed on each workstation executing the application. Fig. 1–9 shows the relationship between the application, DB2 Runtime Client, and the DB2 database server. If the application and database are installed on the same system, the application is known as a *local client*. If the application is installed on a system other than the DB2 server, the application is known as a *remote client*.

Client Workstation   DB2 Database
Server

Fig. 1–9 *DB2 Universal Database - Runtime Client*

The Runtime Client provides functions other than the ability to communicate with a DB2 server or DB2 Connect server machine. For example, you can do any of the following:

- Issue an interactive SQL statement on a remote client to access data on a DB2 server or DB2 Connect server.
- Run applications that were developed to comply with the Open Database Connectivity (ODBC) standard or OLE DB.
- Run Java applications that access and manipulate data in DB2 databases using Java Database Connectivity (JDBC) or SQLJ.

If you need to graphically administer and monitor a DB2 database server, then you should install the DB2 Administration Client. It includes all the graphical DB2 administration tools in addition to all of the functionality of the DB2 Runtime Client.

If you need to develop applications, then you should install the DB2 Application Development Client. This is a collection of developer's tools that are designed to meet the needs of database application developers. The DB2 Application Development Client includes all of the graphical DB2 administration tools and the DB2 Runtime Client functionality.

The DB2 client product that you should install depends on your requirements and the operating system on the client machine. For example, if you have a database application developed for AIX, and you do not require the DB2 administration or application development tools, you should install the DB2 Runtime Client for AIX.

Some installations prefer having the DB2 Runtime Client reside remotely on another server. Remote workstations then need to access the DB2 Runtime Client code remotely, before getting access to DB2. Alternatively, DB2 can support a Java client, and with the use of the Type 4 JDBC driver, where the client code is accessed from the server. In this case, the DB2 Runtime Client code would not be required.

DB2 Connect

The DB2 Connect product allows clients to access data stored on database servers that implement the Distributed Relational Database Architecture (DRDA). The target database server for a DB2 Connect installation is known as a *DRDA Application Server.*

 Note: The most commonly accessed DRDA server is DB2 for OS/390.

DB2 Connect supports both the TCP/IP and APPC communication protocols. The protocol supported depends on the DRDA application server being connected to and the version of the host software being run. For instance, a DB2 Connect server acting as a DRDA Application Requester to a host DRDA Application Server can connect to DB2 for OS/390 at version 5.1 and higher. Any of the supported network protocols can be used for a DB2 client to establish a connection to the DB2 Connect server.

Some of the major capabilities provided by DB2 Connect include:

- Support for ODBC, OLE DB, CLI, JDBC, and SQLJ applications
- Distributed Join across all DB2 databases
- Distributed Join with heterogeneous databases (via Relational Connect)
- Connection Pooling
- zSeries Sysplex Exploitation for failover and load balancing

  Some of the common uses of DB2 Connect are:

- Web-enabling DB2 OS/390 by providing browsers direct access
- Leveraging Microsoft applications written using ADO, ODBC, or OLE DB can transparently access DB2 on mainframe platforms
- Offloading mainframe development cycles

The database application must request the data from a DRDA Application Server through a DRDA Application Requester.

 Note: The DB2 Connect product provides the *DRDA Application Requester* functionality.

The DRDA Application Server accessed using DB2 Connect could be any DB2 Server on OS/390, VM/VSE, or OS/400. If TCP/IP is the protocol of choice, then the following are prerequisites:

- DB2 for OS/390. Only version DB2 5.1 or higher supports TCP/IP in a DRDA environment.
- DB2 for OS/400. Only OS/400 version 4.2 or higher supports TCP/IP.
- DB2 Server for VSE/VM. Only version DB2 6.1 or higher for VM supports TCP/IP.

DB2 for OS/390,
VM/VSE, OS/400

DB2 Connect

Fig. 1–10 *DRDA application flow*

DB2 Connect is available as a server (Enterprise Edition) and a single-user package (Personal Edition). The DB2 Connect Enterprise Edition product provides the ability for multiple clients to access host data. A DB2 Connect server routes each database request from the DB2 clients to the appropriate DRDA Application Server (Figure 1–10). The remote client communicates with the DB2 Connect server using any of the supported communication protocols. DB2 Connect Personal Edition is available on Linux and the Windows platform. It provides access to host databases from the system where it is installed.

DB2 Replication

DB2 Replication allows for data to be propagated from one location to another. It supports a wide variety of databases including DB2, Oracle, Microsoft, Sybase, Informix, IMS, Lotus Notes, and flat files. Replication is also a core technology that enables mobile users to keep their data synchronized with corporate data residing on a DB2 server.

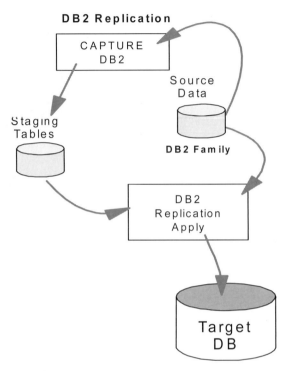

Fig. 1–11 *DB2 replication environment*

DB2 Information Integrator

DB2 Information Integrator allows you to access all data as a single virtual database. A single SQL statement can transparently access or join data located across multiple data sources. For example, you can join data that is located in a DB2 database, an Oracle database, and from an XML file with a single SQL statement. DB2 Information Integrator allows you access to several data sources, including relational databases (Oracle, Sybase, Microsoft SQL Server, Teradata, and ODBC sources) and non-relational sources (XML, BLAST, Documentum, Entrez, HMMER, Excel, flat files, and Lotus Notes databases using Extended Search).

 Note: DB2 has built-in capability to access federated relational data from other DB2 UDB and Informix IDS database servers.

Fig. 1–12 *DB2 Information Integrator*

DB2 Information Integrator for Content

DB2 Information Integrator for Content provides access to IBM's Content Manager sources, as well as other content repositories and relational sources. This product has text mining and text analysis capabilities.

Documents can be categorized into a customer-specific taxonomy and can be grouped based on the content. An integrated workflow function is available so that any data retrieved can be part of a workflow process.

DB2 Information Integrator for Content
- Define integrated views across diverse and distributed data
- Search federated unstructured data
- Mine additional metadata from text documents
- Define workflows

Fig. 1–13 *DB2 Information Integrator for Content*

IBM WebSphere Application Server

IBM WebSphere Application Server is built on an open Java-based platform that enables applications to leverage existing application resources and access various databases, including DB2. Some of the capabilities of WebSphere Application Server include the use of Java servlets, Java Server Pages, and XML to quickly transform static Web sites into vital sources of dynamic Web content. Enterprise Java Beans (EJB) can also be used for implementing EJB components that incorporate business logic. WebSphere Application Server is packaged with DB2.

DB2 Application Development

DB2 offers a rich application development environment that allows the developer to build databases supporting requirements from e-business and business intelligence applications. Many of these tools are integrated with the database; the major tools will be reviewed.

- **DB2 Universal Developer's Edition** - provides the tools for developers to build database applications, and includes: Personal Edition, Workgroup Server Edition, Enterprise Server Edition, DB2 Connect, Relational Extenders, all database clients, and WebSphere Application Server.

- **DB2 Development Center** - enables the creation of stored procedures and user-defined functions (UDFs). Also provides integration with WebSphere Studio Workbench and Microsoft Visual Studio.Net, Microsoft Visual Basic, and Microsoft's Visual Interdev.

- **DB2 Relational Extenders** - enables the SQL API to access unstructured data types including: text, image, audio, video, XML, and spatial data.

- **DB2 Data Warehouse Center** - provides the ability to build data marts/warehouses by automating the processes involved in managing, refreshing, moving, and transforming data, including the ability to define star schema model.

- **DB2 Data Warehouse Manager** - provides all the capabilities of the Data Warehouse Center, but includes support more data sources and includes the Information Catalog.

- **DB2 Data Links Manager** - DB2 offers supports for all popular programming languages and supports the latest Java-based application programming APIs, including: JDBC, SQLJ, ODBC, OLE DB, and CLI.

DB2 Universal Developer's Edition

The DB2 development environment can be installed either on a DB2 server or on a DB2 client. The installation provides all of the necessary data access tools for developing database applications. There are two offerings:

- DB2 Personal Developer's Edition (PDE) - for Linux and Windows platforms.
- DB2 Universal Developer's Edition (UDE) - for all server platforms

The application development environment provided with both product packages allows application developers to write programs using the following methods:

Product Overview

- Embedded SQL
- Call Level Interface or CLI (compatible with the Microsoft ODBC standard)
- DB2 Application Programming Interfaces (APIs)
- DB2 data access through the World Wide Web
- Java applets or applications using JDBC or SQLJ.

The programming environment also includes the necessary programming libraries, header files, code samples, and precompilers for the supported programming languages. Several programming languages, including COBOL, FORTRAN, C, C++, and Java are supported by DB2.

An application developed using the Developer's Edition can be executed on any system with the same operating system that has the DB2 Run-time Client installed. To run the application on another operating system requires the application be rebuilt on the target operating system.

DB2 Personal Developer's Edition (PDE) includes:

- DB2 Personal Edition
- DB2 Connect Personal Edition
- DB2 Run-time, Administration, and Application Development Client
- DB2 Extenders
- WebSphere Studio, Entry Edition

DB2 Universal Developer's Edition (UDE) includes these components:

- DB2 Enterprise Server, Workgroup Server, and Personal Edition
- DB2 Connect Personal and Enterprise Edition
- DB2 Run-time, Administration, and Application Development Client (all platforms)
- DB2 Extenders
- WebSphere Studio, Professional Edition (Windows)
- Websphere Studio Websphere Application Server, Standard Edition

DB2 Universal Developer's Edition is supported on all platforms that support DB2 Enterprise Server Edition. It is intended for application development and testing only. The database server can be on a platform that is different from the platform on which the application is developed.

DB2 Development Center

The Development Center is a graphical environment that supports the rapid development of DB2 SQL and Java stored procedures, SQL scalar and table user-defined functions (UDFs). This can be launched as a separate application from the DB2 program group or from the integrated development environments such as WebSphere Studio or Microsoft VisualStudio. The Development Center can be used to create stored procedures on local and remote DB2 servers and test, execute, and debug stored procedures.

Fig. 1–14 *DB2 Development Center*

 Note: The Development Center replaces the tool previously known as the Stored Procedure Builder and provides additional development enhancements such as the ability to build user-defined functions and structured data types.

DB2 Relational Extenders

DB2 Relational Extenders offer the ability to manipulate data outside of conventional rows and columns to include the manipulation of these types of data: text, image, audio, video, and XML. The DB2 Relational Extenders encapsulates the attributes, structure, and behavior of these unstructured data types and stores this information in DB2. From the developer's perspective, the DB2 Relational Extenders appear as seamless extensions to the database and enable the development of multimedia-based applications. The following DB2 Relational Extenders are provided by IBM:

- Net Search Extender
- Image Extender
- Audio Extender
- Video Extender
- Spatial Extender
- XML Extender

 Note: The new Net Search Extender is a merge of the products previously known as Net.Search Extender and Text Information Extender.

SOLD	ONHAND	RATING	ARTIST	TITLE	COVER	VIDEO	MUSIC	SCRIPT
1212	64	G	Shirley	Inner Light				
39	60	R	Bill	Relics				
73	95	PG-13	Dana	All Good Things				
286	97	PG-13	Austin	Generations				

Mix traditional relational data with unstructured data

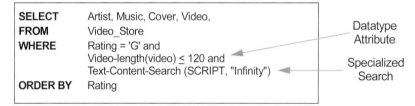

SELECT	Artist, Music, Cover, Video,
FROM	Video_Store
WHERE	Rating = 'G' and
	Video-length(video) ≤ 120 and
	Text-Content-Search (SCRIPT, "Infinity")
ORDER BY	Rating

Datatype Attribute

Specialized Search

Fig. 1–15 *DB2 Relational Extenders*

The purpose of the DB2 Relational Extenders is to provide for the management of unstructured data through the SQL API. By preserving the current investment in relational applications, new nontraditional applications can be introduced by leveraging existing skills. This open environment enables developers and independent software vendors to develop and introduce their own extenders as extensions to DB2.

The XML Extender is provided with DB2 and allows you to store eXtensible Markup Language (XML) documents as a new column datatype. You also have the ability to decompose and store XML in its component parts as columns in multiple tables. In either case, indexes can be defined over the element or attribute of an XML document for fast retrieval. Furthermore, text search and section search can be enabled on the XML column or its decomposed part via DB2 Net Search Extender. You can also formulate an XML document from existing DB2 tables for data interchange in business-to-business environments.

Fig. 1–16 *XML Extender*

 Note: The new XML Extender now supports Web services with the Web Services Object Framework (WORF), a set of tools for implementing Web services with DB2. WebSphere MQ Series applications can also use the XML Extender.

The DB2 Net Search Extender combines in-memory database technology with text search semantics for high-speed text search in DB2 databases. Searching with it can be particularly advantageous in Internet applications where performance is an important factor. Net Search Extender can add the power of fast full-text retrieval to JDBC and CLI applications. Its features let you store unstructured text documents of up to 2 gigabytes in databases. It offers application developers a fast, versatile, and intelligent method of searching through such documents.

 Note: The new integrated DB2 Net Search Extender can be managed from the Control Center and includes built-in federated support to index and search text data stored in other DB2 or Informix Dynamic Server (IDS) databases.

DB2 Data Links Manager

DB2 Data Links Manager can be used to build applications that need to combine the search capabilities of SQL with the advantages of working directly with files to manipulate raw data. A reference is stored for each external file, along with metadata that describes the contents of each file.

Fig. 1–17 *DB2 Data Links Manager*

DB2 Data Links Manager uses the DATALINK data type, which points to an external file, and the DB2 Data Links Manager components.

You use the DATALINK data type, just like any other data type, to define columns in tables. The DATALINK values encode the name of the Data Links Server containing the file and the file name in terms of a Uniform Resource Locator (URL).

Using DB2 Data Links Manager means that external files can be backed up with the database and SQL Data Control Language statements (GRANT and REVOKE) can be used to control permissions to those files.

Examples of applications that can use the DATALINK data type are:

- Medical applications, in which X-rays are stored on the file server and the attributes are stored in the database.
- Entertainment industry applications that perform asset management of video clips. The video clips are stored on a file server, but attributes about the clips are stored in a database. Access control is required for accessing the video clips

based on database privileges of accessing the meta information.

- World Wide Web applications to manage millions of files and allow access control based on database privileges.

- Financial applications, which require distributed capture of check images, and a central location for those images.

- CAD and CAM applications, where the engineering drawings are kept as files, and the attributes are stored in the database. Queries are run against the file attributes.

Even though the DATALINK column represents an object that is stored outside the database system, you can use SQL queries to search metadata to obtain the file name that corresponds to the query result. You can create indexes on videos, images, text (and so on), and store those attributes in tables along with the DATALINK column. With a central repository of files on the file server and DATALINK data types in a database, you can obtain answers to questions like "what do I have?" and "find what I am looking for."

DB2 Data Warehouse Center

This product brings together the tools to build, manage, govern, and access DB2 data warehouses. The DB2 Warehouse Center simplifies and speeds warehouse prototyping, development, and deployment. It helps satisfy user requirements for finding, accessing, and understanding information. It provides flexible tools and techniques for building, managing, and accessing the warehouse. And it meets the most common reporting needs for enterprises of any size.

Fig. 1–18 *Data Warehouse Center*

DB2 Warehouse Manager

The DB2 Warehouse Manager adds to basic warehouse and analytical functions available in DB2 Universal Database by providing:

- Additional warehouse scalability through warehouse agents co-located with the database. Warehouse agents manage the flow of data between warehouse sources and warehouse targets.
- Advanced transformations using Java stored procedures and user-defined functions including cleaning data, pivoting tables, and generating keys
- An integrated business information catalog to guide users to relevant information that they can use for decision making.
- Query report that satisfies the common reporting needs of most enterprises.
- An integrated business information catalog to guide users to relevant information that they can use for decision making.

> **Note:** The Data Warehouse Manager extends the functions of the Data Warehouse Center by providing support for additional data sources, additional warehouse and statistical transformations, and an Integrated Information Catalog.

Information Catalog Center

The Information Catalog Center is a tool for end-users to help easily find, understand and access available information in the corporation. This graphical tool uses a Business View Model, built by the Data Warehouse Administrator, that can be used by the business user to navigate through the data in an enterprise. It allows users to:

- Populate the catalog through metadata interchange with the Data Warehouse Center and other analytical and reporting tools
- Directly register shared information objects
- Navigate or search across the objects to find relevant information
- Display the metadata about the object
- Launch the tools used to render the information for the end-user

> **Note:** The Information Catalog Center keeps metadata on data that end-users need to access. This tool automates the exchange of metadata with the Data Warehouse Center.

Product Overview

DB2 Data Warehouse Edition

DB2 Data Warehouse Edition is a powerful business intelligence platform that includes a collection of database engines and tools to build data warehouses and analytic applications, bundled together at an attractive price for the large enterprise customer.

It includes federated data access, Data Partitioning, integrated Online Analytical Processing (OLAP), advanced data mining, enhanced Extract Transform and Load (ETL), workload management, and support for Microsoft Excel. DB2 Data Warehouse Enterprise Edition combines the strength of DB2 with essential business intelligence features, enabling real time information integration, insight and decision-making. It forms the foundation for building an Information on Demand infrastructure, delivering everything needed by customers to deploy, and partners to build, next generation business intelligence solutions.

DB2 Data Warehouse Enterprise Edition

The DB2 Data Warehouse Enterprise Edition includes a number of useful tools for building and using a data warehouse. The tools provided include:

- DB2 UDB Enterprise Server Edition with Data Partitioning Feature
- DB2 Cube Views
- DB2 Intelligent Miner Scoring/Visualization/Modeling
- DB2 Query Patroller
- DB2 Warehouse Manager
- Office Connect
- DB2 Information Integrator

DB2 Cube Views is a new feature available with the DB2 Data Warehouse Editions that simplifies query entry, helps minimize data integrity issues, and may enhance query performance. The data analyst can use DB2 Cube Views to design metadata models once and share them across all applications, saving administrative time. DB2 Cube Views can analyze the resulting model and recommend aggregates that improve Online Analytical Processing (OLAP) performance. This results in faster cube loads, drill through, and hybrid analysis, enabling enterprises to support a growing number of business users more efficiently.

DB2 OLAP Server

The DB2 OLAP Server is a scalable, industrial-strength Online Analytical Processing (OLAP) software that enables you to build sophisticated decision support, planning, and analysis applications for your enterprise. DB2 OLAP Server provides a fast path to turn your warehouse data into business insight. It delivers "speed of thought" query performance to a large set of online users. It is built for e-business with tools to help you quickly deploy Web-based analytical applications.

Note: DB2 OLAP Server provides DB2 integrated OLAP capabilities. Also, included to build OLAP solutions are: Integration Server to pull data from DB2, an OLAP spreadsheet plug-in for Excel and Lotus 1-2-3, and an Administration Manager.

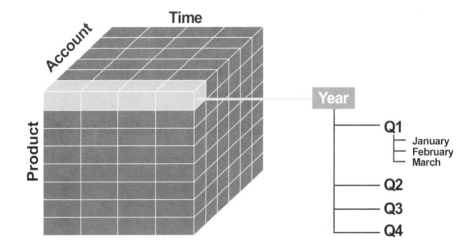

Fig. 1–19 *Multidimensional cube*

Flexibility in storage is extended to the application level. Depending on individual application needs, the cube can be stored in either DB2 for added flexibility of SQL access or multidimensional storage for optimal performance.

DB2 Administration

Database administrators have a number of graphical-based tools they can use to manage and administer DB2 databases. Alternatively, a DBA can also use script-based tools to administer the database environment. The main tools available with DB2 will now be examined.

Control Center

The Control Center is the central point of administration for DB2. The Control Center provides the user with the tools necessary to perform typical database administration tasks. It allows easy access to other server administration tools, gives a clear overview of the entire system, enables remote database management, and provides step-by-step assistance for complex tasks.

Fig. 1–20 *DB2 Control Center*

The Systems object represents both local and remote machines. To display all the DB2 systems that your system has cataloged, expand the object tree by clicking on the plus sign (+) next to Systems. The left portion of the screen lists available DB2 systems (local and remote). From this example, the system LOCAL contains a DB2 instance, DB2, in which the database SAMPLE is located. When Tables is highlighted, details about each table is shown in the Contents Pane. A number of the existing tables in the SAMPLE database are displayed.

The main components of the Control Center are:

- Menu Bar - Used to access Control Center functions and online help.
- Tool Bar - Used to access the other administration tools.
- Objects Pane - This is shown on the left-hand side of the Control Center window. It contains all the objects that can be managed from the Control Center as well as their relationship to each other.
- Contents Pane - This is found on the right side of the Control Center window and contains the objects that belong or correspond to the object selected on the Objects Pane.
- Contents Pane Toolbar - These icons are used to tailor the view of the objects and information in the Contents pane. These functions can also be selected in the View menu.

Hover Help is also available in the Control Center, providing a short description for each icon on the tool bar as you move the mouse pointer over the icon.

Replication Center

The Replication Center ia a graphical tool that allows the administrator to set up and adminster a data replcation environment. Replication subscription definitions are stored in a central control server as scripts. The main functions in setting up a replication subscription can be performed with this tool, including:

- Registering replication sources
- Monitoring the replication process
- Operating the Capture and Apply programs
- Defining alerts

Fig. 1–21 *DB2 Replication Center*

Other Tools Available from the Control Center

By using the Control Center Tool Bar, you can access other administration tools to help you manage and administer databases in your environment:

- Satellite Administration Center - Used to manage multiple DB2 Personal Edition or Workgroup Server installations.

- Data Warehouse Center - Used to build the data mart/warehouse.

- Command Center - This provides an interactive window that allows input of SQL statements or DB2 commands, the viewing of execution results, and explain information. The graphical command utility is the preferred method for text commands as it provides enormous flexibility and function; interacts with the Script Center.

- Task Center - Used to create, schedule, and manage scripts that can contain SQL statements, DB2 commands, or operating systems commands.

- Journal - This keeps a record of all script invocations, all DB2 messages, and the DB2 recovery history file for a database. It is used to show the results of a job and, contents of a script and also to enable or disable a job.

- License Center - Used to manage licenses and check how many connections are used.

- Development Center - This tool enables the creation and testing of DB2 stored procedures or user-defined functions.
- Tools Settings - Allows you to configure the DB2 graphical tools and some of their options.

The graphical tool set provided with DB2 is full functioned and very powerful, allowing you to administer and access your DB2 system from graphical interfaces.

The DB2 Web Tools allows the administrator to use an HTTP client to remotely execute:

- SQL statements against a DB2 database
- DB2 commands against a DB2 instance
- operating system commands against a DB2 server
- Stored Procedures through JDBC calls and DB2 administration server API

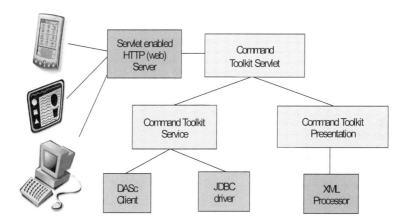

Fig. 1–22 *DB2 Web Tools*

Health Center

IBM has an autonomic computing initiative that is focusing on creating an IT infrastructure that can self-manage, self-diagnose and self-heal itself. DB2 provides a variety of tools to enable the database to manage itself. Self-managing and resource tuning (SMART) database technology allows greater automation with respect to configuring, tuning, and managing database operations. The Heath Center is a server-side tool that can monitor the health of a DB2 instance, even without user interaction. When defined thresholds are exceeded (i.e. log space not sufficient) alerts are activated. Alert notifications can be sent using e-mail or to a pager system, alternatively a preconfigured set of actions can be taken that has been defined in a script or task.

Fig. 1–23 *Health Center*

The graphical user interface allows the administrator to select database objects and drill-down on its details, current alerts, and the recommended actions described to resolve the alert.

Additional Administration tools

IBM has developed a number of system management tools to make adminstrators more productive in managing DB2. These tools include:

- DB2 Recovery Expert - users can obtain intelligent assistance when determining the most efficient technique for a recovery solution. Built-in self-managing and resource tuning (SMART) features provide intelligent analysis of a recovery situation and automate the rebuilding of the database environment, as well as the ability to generate undo SQL.

- DB2 Performance Expert - recommends changes on DB2 performance-related information. Also provides recommendations for system tuning to gain optimum throughput.
- DB2 High Performance Unload - rapid unload table spaces of all types with various options.
- DB2 Table Editor - a tool that provides direct DB2 access to users creating, reviewing, or updating data.
- DB2 Web Query Tool - enables easy access to DB2 data.

All of the above tools run on multiple platforms.

Advisors and Wizards

Wizards are tutors that help you create objects and perform specific database operations. Each Wizard has detailed information available to help the user. The DB2 Wizards are integrated into the administration tools and assist in a variety of administrative tasks. For example, the Add Database Wizard is used to set up communications between a DB2 client and a DB2 server, and is invoked from the Configuration Assistant.

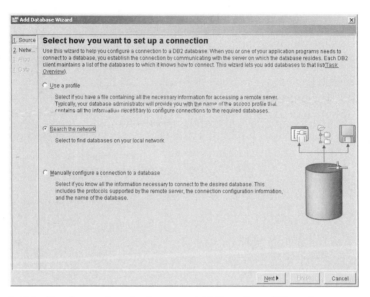

Fig. 1–24 *Configuration Assistant - Add Database Wizard*

Fig. 1–24 shows that there are a number of ways to add a remote database. You do not have to know the syntax of commands or even the location of the remote database server. One option searches the network, looking for valid DB2 servers.

 Note: The Client Configuration Assistant has been renamed to the Configuration Assistant and significant enhancements have also been added.

Invoked from the DB2 Control Center, the wizard extracts information from the system and asks questions about the database workload. It then runs a series of calculations designed to determine an appropriate set of values for the database and database manager configuration variables. You can choose whether to apply the changes immediately or to save them in a file that can be executed at a later time.

DB2 Wizards include:

- Create, Add, Backup, Restore Database
- Load
- Create Table
- Create Table Space
- Configure Database Logging
- Add Partitions

The Configuration Advisor (Fig. 1–25) can be used to get a database system up and running quickly. This can also be invoked from the Control Center, and gathers data about the hardware and application environment at your installation. The suggested configuration parameters can either be applied immediately or be used to ccreate a script to be cxccuted later.

This script also provides a list of the most commonly tuned parameters for later reference.

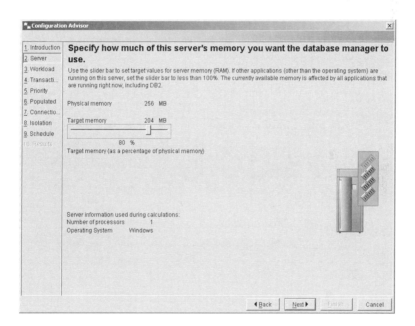

Fig. 1–25 *Configuration Advisor*

The Design Advisor replaces the tool formerly known as the Create Index Wizard.

The Command Line Processor (CLP)

The Command Line Processor (CLP) is a component common to all DB2 products. It is a text-based application that is used to execute SQL statements and DB2 commands. For example, you can create a database, catalog a database, and issue dynamic SQL statements from the CLP.

Note: The commands and statements issued through the DB2 CLP can also be issued through the DB2 Command Center, which is a preferred graphical interface.

```
db2 => list db directory

 System Database Directory

 Number of entries in the directory = 1

Database 1 entry:

 Database alias                     = DB2CERT
 Database name                      = DB2CERT
 Local database directory           = G:\DB2
 Database release level             = a.00
 Comment                            =
 Directory entry type               = Indirect
 Catalog node number                = 0
```

Fig. 1–26 *Command Line Processor*

Fig. 1–26 shows a command and its output as executed from the Command Line Processor. The Command Line Processor can be used to issue interactive SQL statements or DB2 commands. The statements and commands can be placed in a file and executed in a batch environment or they can be entered in interactive mode.

The DB2 Command Line Processor (CLP) is provided with all DB2 Universal Database, DB2 Connect, and DB2 Developer's products and Clients.

All SQL statements issued from the Command Line Processor are dynamically prepared and executed on the database server. The output, or result, of the SQL query is displayed on the screen by default.

All of the DB2 commands are documented in the *DB2 UDB V8.1 Command Reference*.

Visual Explain

Other graphical tools can be used for tuning or monitoring performance. Visual Explain is a graphical utility that provides a visual representation of the access plan that DB2 uses to execute an SQL statement.

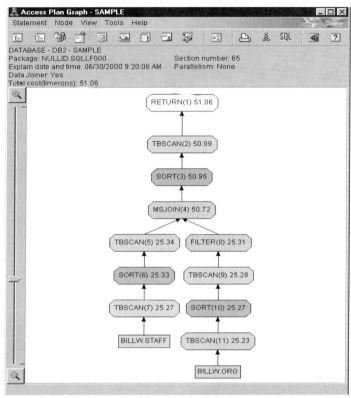

Fig. 1–27 *Access Plan Graph in Visual Explain*

Visual Explain can be invoked from the Control Center or from the Command Center. Fig. 1–27 shows the type of information that is displayed. This example shows that two tables are being accessed and an approximation of the cost of the query is also provided in the Visual Explain output. The estimated query costs represent the complexity and resource usage expected for a given SQL query. More details on the usage of Visual Explain are provided in "Monitoring and Tuning" on page 659.

DB2 Query Patroller

DB2 Query Patroller controls, monitors query execution and works with queries to prioritize and schedule user queries based on user profiles and cost analysis performed on each query. Large queries can be put on hold and scheduled for a later time during off-peak hours. Queries with high priority (based on user profiles) are promoted to the top of the schedule. In addition, DB2 Query Patroller monitors resource utilization statistics to determine which CPUs are the least used. It can use this information to determine load distribution of the system, which can allow it to balance the number of users allowed to submit queries at any given time.

DB2 Query Patroller greatly improves the scalability of a data warehouse by allowing hundreds of users to safely submit queries on multi-terabyte class systems. Its components span the distributed environment to better manage and control all aspects of query submission.

DB2 Query Patroller acts as an agent on behalf of the end-user. It prioritizes and schedules queries so that query completion is more predictable and computer resources are efficiently utilized. DB2 Query Patroller obtains the query cost from the DB2 Optimizer and then schedules and dispatches those queries so that the load is balanced across the installation-specified nodes.

DB2 Query Patroller sets individual user and user class priorities as well as user query limits. This enables the data warehouse to deliver the needed results to its most important users as quickly as possible. If desired, an end-user can choose to receive notice of scheduled query completion through electronic mail.

DB2 Query Patroller consists of components running on the database server and end-users' desktops. DB2 Query Patroller is made up of several components, each having a specific task in providing query and resource management.

Fig. 1–28 *DB2 Query Patroller Center*

The Server is the core component of DB2 Query Patroller. It provides an environment for storing user profiles, setting up system parameters, maintaining job lists, and storing node information. The DB2 Query Patroller system administrator has an interface to the Server to perform these tasks. The Server component executes on a node within the Database Management System (DBMS) called the Management Node.

The Administrator component gives a DBA or system administrator the tools needed to manage the DB2 Query Patroller environment. This tool allows for the management and viewing of queries. The administrator provides menus to display job lists and history, user profiles, node information, and system parameters. It also provides for the display of utilization graphs.

Database Monitoring

The *Snapshot Monitor* captures database information at specific intervals. The interval time and data represented in the performance graph can be configured. The Snapshot Monitor can help analyze performance problems, tune SQL statements, and identify exception conditions based on limits or thresholds.

The *Event Monitor* captures database activity events as defined by the event monitor definition. Event Monitor records are usually stored on disk and then analyzed after the data has been captured. The *Event Analyzer* graphical tool provided with DB2 can be used to analyze the captured data. More details on the usage of the DB2 monitors are provided in "Monitoring and Tuning" on page 659.

The DB2 folder is created on the desktop for environments such as Windows. This DB2 folder is typically used to invoke the graphical tools provided with DB2. Fig. 1–29 shows some of the components of the DB2 product as they appear in the DB2 folder. A component usually relates to an executable application or utility.

Fig. 1–29 *DB2 desktop folder (Windows)*

The graphical tools integrated with DB2 support these functions:

- Create, alter, and drop databases, table spaces, tables, views, indexes, triggers, schemas, users, user groups, and aliases
- Load, import, export, and reorganize data and gather statistics
- Schedule jobs to run unattended
- Back up and restore databases
- Monitor and tune performance
- Tune queries using access path analysis
- Manage data replication

The following are also available in the DB2 desktop folder:

- Information Center - Provides the user with quick access to the DB2 product documentation. Information is available about common tasks, problem determination, DB2 online manuals and the sample programs provided with DB2.

- Configuration Assistant (CA) - This is a graphical tool that is used to configure access to remote databases. It can be invoked from the DB2 Desktop folder or from the command line with the DB2CCA command.
- Command Line Processor (CLP) - The CLP is a text-based program that allows you to enter DB2 commands or SQL statements.
- Command Window (Windows platform).
- Command Center - a graphical tool that allows you to enter one or more DB2 commands and statements, store the commands as scripts, view the explain information for a statement, and schedule scripts via the Script Center.
- Control Center - The central point of administration for DB2 Universal Database. This tool allows you to access other tools such as the Command Center and the Journal.
- Event Analyzer - This allows you to access information on database activities collected by event monitors.
- Event Monitor - This allows you to work with DB2 event monitors including creating, starting, stopping, and removing event monitors.
- First Steps - This allows you create the SAMPLE database, view sample contents, and access the on-line DB2 library.
- Start/Stop HTML Search Server - This enables (or disables) the searching of a topic in the online books.
- Development Center - assists with the creation of stored procedures and user-defined functions that run on DB2 servers
- SQL Assist - a graphical online tool that can be used to build Select, Insert, Update, and Delete statements

Summary

This chapter discussed the DB2 Version 8.1 products for Linux, Windows, and UNIX. There are a number of offerings available:

- DB2 Enterprise Server Edition
- DB2 Workgroup Server Edition
- DB2 Personal Edition
- DB2 Everyplace Edition
- DB2 Connect Enterprise Edition
- DB2 Data Warehouse Manager
- DB2 Query Patroller

These products provide the flexibility to execute database applications running on pervasive devices up to multi-node clusters. DB2 provides support for the commonly used communication protocols and can access data from heterogenous database systems. DB2 replication is integrated in the databse and can be used to transform data from other DB2 and non-DB2 database systems. DB2 Connect is used to access DB2 data from DRDA servers, typically DB2 running on the zSeries platform.

DB2 V8 has introduced a number of application development enhancements, including the Development Center, which can be integrated with popular tools such as WebSphere Studio and Microsoft VisualStudio. The DB2 Warehouse Manager and integrated Information Catalog provides a graphical interface to building data-marts and data warehouses.DB2 Query Patroller provides query and resource management for decision support systems.

Significant new features have been added to make DB2 easier to manage. SMART technology (Self-managing and Resource Tuning) has been integrated into a number of DB2 components, including: installation, configuration, utilities, problem determination and resolution, and availability. This is part of IBM's autonomic computing initiative and new features will continue to be added to make the DBA more productive.

This chapter also introduced some of the graphical and command line tools available in DB2. The Command Line Processor (CLP) is a text-based application that allows you to enter DB2 commands and SQL statements and is found in all DB2 products. From the desktop, an administrator can configure remote and local systems, administer instances and databases, and create database objects. In the remaining chapters, additional DB2 functions and tools will be examined in how they assist the end-user, application developer, and administrator.

CHAPTER 2

Getting Started

* INSTALLING DB2 SERVERS
* USING THE COMMAND LINE PROCESSOR
* CREATING INSTANCES
* SETTING UP THE ENVIRONMENT
* INSTANCE ADMINISTRATION

*T*his chapter provides an overview of the first steps in getting started with setting up a DB2 database server. A few steps are required before the creation of a DB2 database and accessing the database using SQL. First, the installation process for DB2 in various operating environments will be examined. Specifically, the installation of DB2 servers on Linux, UNIX, and Windows.

A distributed installation will also be reviewed. If you are planning to install DB2 products across your network, a network based distributed installation can be significant. Rolling out multiple identical copies of DB2 products is possible with this method.

Once the DB2 products have been installed, the environment that is created by the installation process will be examined. This requires understanding the different levels of managing the DB2 environment from a global, instance, and user perspective. DB2 databases are created within an instance on a DB2 database server. The management of multiple instances including administration commands will also be reviewed.

Product Installation

This section discusses installation of DB2 Universal Database on Linux, Windows, and UNIX. There are some differences between the platforms, but once the DB2 product is installed, the administration is very similar within the DB2 Family of database servers.

The installation process detects the active communication protocols on your system and configures them to work with DB2. One DB2 instance is created and the DB2 Administration Server (DAS) service process is created to enable the use of various management tools including: Configuration Assistant, Control Center, Replication Center, and Development Center.

Windows Installation

This section discusses installing DB2 on the Intel platform; our example is Windows 2000.

Before beginning the installation on a Windows machine, make sure that the user account that will be used to perform the installation is:

- Defined on the local machine
- A member of the Local Administrator's group defined for the DB2 installation
- Given the *Act as part of the operating system* advanced user right

To install, insert the CD-ROM into the drive. The auto-run feature automatically starts the setup program. The setup program will determine the system language and launch the setup program for that language. If the setup program failed to auto-start, execute the following command from an operating system window:

```
x:\setup.exe
```

x represents the CD-ROM drive.

Fig. 2–1 *Welcome to DB2 Screen*

Fig. 2–1 shows the Welcome window. Click on **Install Products** to continue.

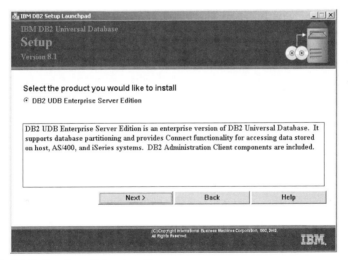

Fig. 2–2 *DB2 Product Selection Screen*

Fig. 2–2 Click on **Next** to continue.

Fig. 2–3 *Welcome to the DB2 Setup wizard*

Fig. 2–3 Click on **Next** to continue.

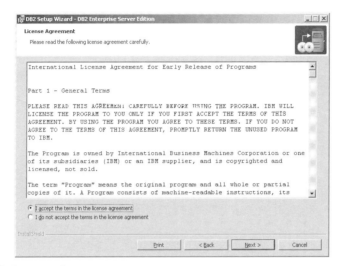

Fig. 2–4 *License Agreement*

Fig. 2–5 *Select the installation type*

There are three types of installation:

- **Typical** installs those DB2 components that are used most often including all required components, ODBC support, and commonly used DB2 tools such as the Control Center and the Configuration Assistant. The DB2 Setup wizard creates and customizes the DB2 instance using the communications protocols that are detected on the computer.

- **Compact** installs only the required DB2 features and ODBC support. The DB2 instance is created and customized to use the communication protocols detected on the computer.

- **Custom** installs only the components that you select. You are given the option of which administration tools, application development tools, replication tools, DB2 client, and when to start the DB2 instances as part of the Custom installation process.

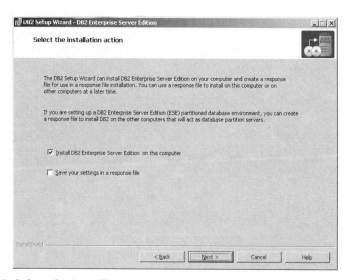

Fig. 2–6 *Select the Installation action*

The response file generator utility (available on Windows 32-bit and 64-bit operating systems) creates a response file from an existing installed and configured DB2 product. It can be used to recreate the exact setup on other machines later, using a different user ID.

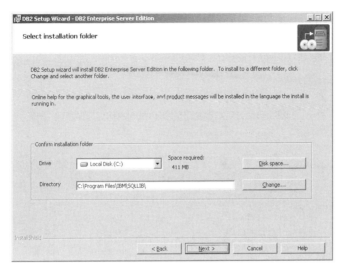

Fig. 2–7 *Select the Installation Folder*

The products will be installed in the `C:\Program Files\IBM\SQLLIB` directory. You can change the drive and the install directory from this window.

Fig. 2–8 *Set user information for the DB2 Administration Server*

The DB2 Administration Server (DAS) is a special DB2 administration service used to support the GUI tools and assist with administration tasks on local and remote DB2 servers. Only one DAS is allowed on a computer and it is configured and installed to start when the operating system is started.

It is recommended that the user ID has SYSADM authority on each of the computers within the environment so that it can start or stop the other instances if required.

You can create a new user or use an existing one. To create a new domain user you must be logged on as a user with authority to administer domain groups and users. Click **Local authentication** or **Domain authentication** to specify the type of user. After a **User name** and **Password** is provided, confirm the password by typing it again in the **Confirm password** field. DB2 will use this user name and password to log on when DAS is started as a Windows service. (DB2 user names can be up to 30 bytes long)

Note: For DB2 V8.1, the DB2 Administration Server is no longer an instance, it is a special DB2 administration service used to support the GUI tools and assist with administration tasks on local and remote DB2 servers. The DB2 Setup wizard automatically creates the DAS user during the installation.

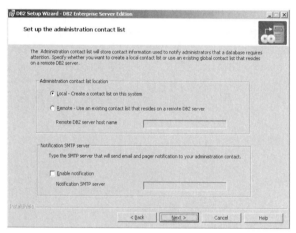

Fig. 2–9 *Set up the administration contact list*

The DAS can store a contact list that is used to notify administrators by email or pager when certain conditions occur. The contact list can be stored locally on each server, or a global contact list can be maintained by the DAS on a particular server. Remote or local lists can be used for global notification.

Here is a brief description of the options for this screen.

- Click **Local** to store the Administration contact list on the local system. This list will be used by all instance-owning partitions on the computer. This local list can be used by other servers.

- Click **Remote** to store the Administration contact list on a different system. For example, if this is a new partition in a partitioned environment, it is recommended that the contact list on the instance-owning partition be used as the global list by the other systems in the environment.

- Type the **Remote DB2 Server host name** of the system that contains the contact list you want to use.
- Select **Enable notification** to specify that you want an SMTP server to send email and pager notifications to your administration contact.
- Type the TCP/IP host name of the SMTP server to use in the Notification SMTP Server name field. You can choose to enable notification later. For information about enabling notification after installing DB2, refer to the **UPDATE ADMIN CONFIG** command in the *DB2 Command Reference.*
- Click on **Next** to continue (without enabling notification).

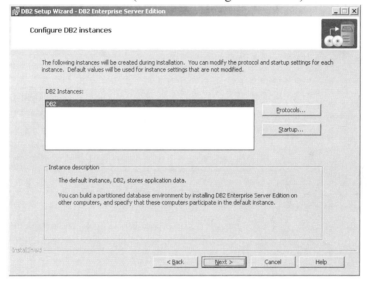

Fig. 2–10 *Configure DB2 Instance*

Fig. 2–10 shows an instance named DB2 will be created. The DB2 Setup wizard automatically detects the communication protocols installed on the computer, selects them for use, and generates default values for the instance to use for each detected protocol. You can override the selections and generated values. Highlight the DB2 Instance and Click **Protocols**; the following window appears:

Fig. 2–11 *DB2 Instance communication protocols (TCP/IP)*

The DB2 installation utility examines your system to see what communication protocols are installed and configured to use with the DB2 instance. If the DB2 Setup wizard does not detect a protocol, the **Do not configure at this time** radio button will be selected and you will want to configure the protocol at this time. If TCP/IP is not yet installed, the DB2 Setup wizard will not be able to update the services file.

The DB2 Setup wizard generated default values for the TCP/IP Service name and Port number parameters.Both must be entered and unique on the computer. It is recommended to use the default values unless they will conflict with other services on your computer.

- The Port number designates the particular TCP/IP port on which the server listens for requests from DB2 clients.
- The Service name is the name that is associated with the port number.

Fig. 2–12 *DB2 Instance communication protocols (NetBIOS)*

Fig. 2–12 shows that NetBIOS has been detected as well. DB2 uses the **Workstation name** entry as the workstations service name. The DB2 instance is known by this name on the network. This name must be unique among all NetBIOS nodes on a domain the network.

The **Adapter number** is the logical LAN adapter number that is used for the NetBIOS connection.The values shown in Fig. 2–12 will be used for NetBIOS settings with the DB2 instance unless changed at this time.

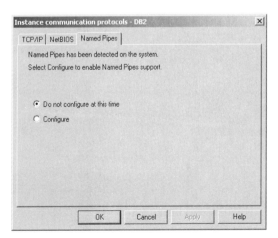

Fig. 2–13 *DB2 Instance communication protocols (Named Pipe)*

For completeness, the Named Pipe screen will be presented, but not configured at this time. Click **OK** to go back to the previous window (Fig. 2–10).

Getting Started

Fig. 2–14 *DB2 Instance startup options*

Click **Startup** and you are given the option of automatically starting the DB2 instance at system startup time. This eliminates the need to manually start the instance after starting your system. Click **OK** to go back to the previous window (Fig. 2–10) and the click **Next**.

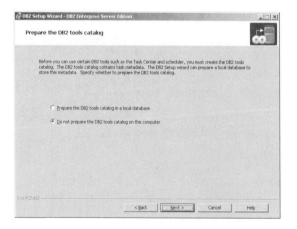

Fig. 2–15 *DB2 Tools catalog options*

The DB2 Task Center, scheduler and Information Catalog Center use the DB2 tools catalog to store metadata. For full functioning of the administration tools, it is recommended that scheduling be enabled, but it is not required.

Fig. 2–16 *Specify a contact for the DB2 health monitor notification*

The Health Monitor runs by default on the instance you are setting up It watches all DB2 related data within the instance. The Health Monitor automatically tracks performance in the database environment. When a health indicator is breached, at either alarm or warning level, an alert can be sent to a predefined contact. You can use the Health Center or the Command Line Processor (CLP) to view Health Monitor data.

Fig. 2–17 *DB2 Component Summary*

You can now review the **Current settings** to see a summary of the installation choices made. If you have chosen to perform the installation now, the DB2 Setup wizard will begin copying files when you click **Install**.

Fig. 2–18 *Setup Complete*

The DB2 products are now installed on your system with a list of recommended steps to follow after the installation, such as installing the documentation. Click **Finish** to exit setup.

Fig. 2–19 *DB2 First Steps*

This final screen gives you the option to create your first database (Sample), work with a number of DB2 tutorials, view the documentation, or exit First Steps.

Using the Command Line Processor

The Command Line Processor (CLP) was introduced in Chapter 1. This section discusses how the CLP is used in the DB2 environment, especially, to make changes at the session level. It is important to note that all commands can also be issued from the DB2 Command Center and if available on your platform, the DB2 Command Window.

When using the Command Line Processor, be careful that the operating system does not parse your SQL statements. If you enclose any SQL statements or DB2 commands within quotation marks, it will ensure that they are not parsed by the operating system. Within the Command Line Processor (CLP) you can issue operating system commands by prefacing them with an exclamation mark (!). For example:

```
db2 => !dir c:\
```

If the command exceeds the limit allowed by the operating system, use a backslash (\) as the line continuation character.

The complete syntax and explanation of all commands is documented in the *DB2 UDB V8.1 Command Reference*. You can obtain syntax and information for all of the DB2 commands from the Command Line Processor:

DB2 ?　　　　　displays a list of all DB2 commands

DB2 ? command displays information about a specific command

DB2 ? SQLnnnn displays information about a specific SQLCODE

DB2 ? DB2nnnn displays information about a DB2 error

To examine the current CLP settings, issue the following command:

```
db2 => LIST COMMAND OPTIONS
```

```
Command Line Processor Option Settings

Backend process wait time (seconds)      (DB2BQTIME) = 1
No. of retries to connect to backend      (DB2BQTRY) = 60
Request queue wait time (seconds)        (DB2RQTIME) = 5
Input queue wait time (seconds)          (DB2IQTIME) = 5
Command options                          (DB2OPTIONS) =

Option Description                                    Current Setting
------ ---------------------------------------------- ---------------
  -a   Display SQLCA                                        OFF
  -c   Auto-Commit                                          ON
  -e   Display SQLCODE/SQLSTATE                             OFF
  -f   Read from input file                                OFF
  -l   Log commands in history file                        OFF
  -o   Display output                                      ON
  -p   Display interactive input prompt                    ON
  -r   Save output to report file                          OFF
  -s   Stop execution on command error                     OFF
  -t   Set statement termination character                OFF
  -v   Echo current command                               OFF
  -w   Display FETCH/SELECT warning messages              ON
  -z   Save all output to output file                      OFF
```

Fig. 2–20 *Command Line Processor Option Settings*

Fig. 2–20 shows the default settings. These settings can be updated globally or for each CLP session using the DB2OPTIONS profile variable.

```
db2 ? UPDATE COMMAND OPTIONS
```

This command displays all the available options, the possible values for each option, and the usage of the UPDATE COMMAND OPTIONS command.

```
db2 UPDATE COMMAND OPTIONS USING OPTIONS...
```

This command changes the value of one or more options for a CLP session.

The Command Line Processor has two parts: a front-end process and a back-end process. The front-end process is called db2 and the back-end is db2bp. The back-end process will maintain a connection to the database. To release this connection, use the TERMINATE command. To end an interactive CLP session, issue the QUIT command (this does not release the database connection).

DB2 for Windows CLP Considerations

Windows does not allow the DB2 Command Line Processor to be used in every operating system window. A DB2 command window or the DB2 Command Line Processor program itself, must be used to issue any CLP statements. A command window can be started by clicking on **Start** and selecting **Programs → IBM DB2 → Command Line Tools → Command Window** or by executing the command DB2CMD. As indicated earlier, the DB2 Command Center can also be used and is the suggested method as it allows entry of multiple commands/statements, saving of these to a script and viewing the EXPLAIN output of a statement. The Command Center window can be seen as shown in Figure 2–21.

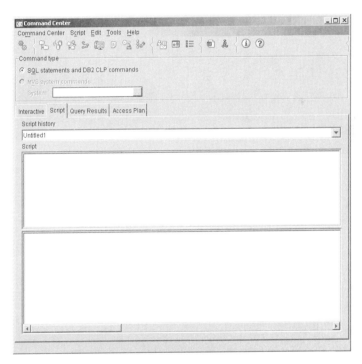

Fig. 2–21 *Command Center window*

Windows Install Directory Structure

It is useful to understand where the DB2 products are installed. Some of the directory structure is displayed below:

```
\sqllib          - Readme file, etc.

\sqllib\adsm     - ADSTAR Distributed Storage Manager files
       \bin      - Binary executable files
       \bnd      - Bind files for utilities
       \cfg      - Default system configuration files
       \conv     - Code page conversion table files
       \DB2      - Default instance directory
       \doc      - On-line Books
       \function -Default location for UDFs
       \function\unfenced -Default location for unfenced
        UDFs
       \help     - On-line help files
       \java     - Java programs
       \misc     - DB2 tools and utilities
       \msg      - Message files
       \samples  - Sample programs, sample scripts
```

Fig. 2–22 *Windows Install Directory Structure*

The files and directories in Fig. 2–22 are created under the sqllib directory on the drive where DB2 is installed (C:\SQLLIB, for example). Do not attempt to delete or modify any of these files. The actual directory structure may be different than the one displayed depending on the DB2 products installed. You can choose a directory different than SQLLIB.

Linux and UNIX Installation

The DB2 Setup wizard is also available on Linux and UNIX platforms and replaces the previous db2setup text-based utility. Additional GUI installation tools include the DB2 Launchpad and the DB2 Instance Setup wizard. Finally, Linux and UNIX platforms can also use response files to enable distributed installations. Response files store the same values and parameters that were selected during the initial installation of DB2 on the local system

The administrator can select from the following installation methods:

- The db2setup utility - this program is supplied with the DB2 product and is the recommended installation method. It is similar to the setup program for Windows in that it detects and configures communication protocols to use with the DB2 instances. The other methods require you to manually configure your system.

- The db2_install script is available for UNIX-based operating systems for manual installations. The db2_install script does not perform instance creation or configuration. This method may be preferred in cases where greater control over the installation process is required.

- The install command found in your operating system environment. For example, in AIX, the installp command will install the DB2 products. Using this command requires you to know the complete syntax.

- Response file installation - the response file is an ASCII file that contains setup and configuration values. The file is passed to the db2setup program and the installation is performed according to the values that have been specified.

- There may be an installation utility available in your operating system environment. For example, in AIX, the System Management Interface Tool (SMIT) is available to install software. This is a better choice than using the install command. However, there is no communication detection and configuration performed. Also, the DB2 instance is not created.

 Note: Red Hat, United Linux (previously known as Caldera Open Linux, Turbo Linux, SuSE Linux, Conectiva), and a variety of local Linux distributors have been tested with DB2.

To run the db2setup utility, perform the following steps:

1. Log in as a user with root authority.

2. Mount the CD-ROM file system.

3. Change to the directory where the CD-ROM is mounted by entering the cd / cdrom command where cdrom is the mount point of your product CD-ROM.

4. For Linux, AIX, and HP-UX, enter the ./db2setup command to start the DB2 Setup wizard. For Solaris, you will need to copy *product*.tar.Z, where *product* represents the product you are licensed to install, to a temporary file system. Then enter:

```
zcat product.tar.Z | tar -xf - ; ./product/db2setup
For Enterprise Server Edition or ese, the command becomes:
zcat ese.tar.Z | tar -xf - ; ./ese/db2setup
```

 Note: The DB2 Setup wizard is a graphical installer. Xwindow software capable of rendering a graphical user interface for the DB2 Setup wizard is required. Ensure that you have properly exported your display. For example, export DISPLAY=9.26.163.144:0.

Linux and UNIX Install Directory Structure

The directory for installation of the DB2 products will vary depending on your UNIX environment. For example, in AIX, DB2 products are installed in the /usr/opt/db2_vv_rr directory where vv represents the version of DB2 and rr represents the release. The directory structure created under /usr/opt/db2_08_01 will be similar to the following:

```
Readme            - Readme file, etc.
adm               - System administrator and executable files
adsm              - ADSTAR Distributed Storage Manager files
bin               - Binary executable files
bnd               - Bind files for utilities
cc                - Control Center files
cfg               - Default system configuration files
conv              - Code page conversion table files
doc               - On-line Books
function          - Default location for UDFs
function/unfenced Default location for unfenced UDFs
install           - Installation program
instance          - Instance scripts
java              - Java programs
lib               - Libraries
map               - Map files for DB2 Connect
misc              - DB2 tools and utilities
msg/$L            - Message catalogs
samples           - Sample programs, sample scripts
```

Fig. 2–23 *Linux and UNIX Install Directory Structure*

Depending on the products you are installing, some of these directories may not exist. When an instance is created, symbolic links are created under the home directory of the DB2 instance owner. These links point to the directory where DB2 was installed.

DB2 software registration is handled automatically if you installed your DB2 product from a CD-ROM using the DB2 Installer program. If you installed DB2 using the operating system's native installation tools, you must use the DB2LICM Licensed Management Tool command. This command lets you add, remove, list, and modify licenses and policies installed on the local system, refer to the DB2LICM command in the *DB2 Command Reference.*

```
db2licm -a /cdrom/db2/license/filename.lic
```

/cdrom represents the CD-ROM mount directory and FILENAME.LIC represents the file containing valid license information.

It is possible to install different versions of DB2 products on the same UNIX server because the product files will be installed on a different path.

Distributed Installation

Distributed installation is an installation method to make rolling out multiple identical copies of DB2 products possible. If you are planning to install DB2 products across your network, a network-based distributed installation can be significant.

Before starting an installation of DB2 products, you need to prepare an ASCII file called a response file that can be customized with the setup and configuration data that will automate an installation. The setup and configuration data would have to be entered during a normal install; however, with a response file, the installation can proceed without any intervention.

A response file specifies such configuration and setup parameters as the destination directory and the products and components to install. It can also be used to set up the following settings:

- Global DB2 registry variables
- Instance variables
- Instance database manager configuration settings

You can use a response file to install an identical configuration across every system on your network or to install multiple configurations of a DB2 product. For example, you can customize a response file that will install a DB2 Administration Client. You can then distribute this file to every system where you want this product to be installed.

You can create a response file by:

- Modifying a provided sample response file.
- Using the response file generator for Windows.
- Using the DB2 Setup Wizard

Getting Started

Sample Response Files

The DB2 CD-ROM includes a ready-to-use sample response file with default entries. The sample response files are located in: db2/*platform*/samples, where platform is one of the following:

- hpux
- aix
- solaris
- linux
- linux64
- linux390
- windows

You can use the following sample response files to install DB2 products on supported workstations:

- db2adcl.rsp   DB2 Application Development Client
- db2admcl.rsp   DB2 Administration Client
- db2conee.rsp   DB2 Connect Enterprise Edition
- db2conepe.rsp DB2 Connect Personal Edition
- db2ese.rsp   DB2 Enterprise Server Edition
- db2pe.rsp   DB2 Personal Edition
- db2rtcl.rsp   DB2 Run-Time Client
- db2wse.rsp   DB2 Workgroup Server Edition

A part of DB2ADMCL.RSP file is shown in Fig. 2–24.

```
* General Options
* ----------------
PROD                = ADMIN_CLIENT
*FILE                = C:\SQLLIB
*TYPE                = 0,1,2   (0=compact,1=typical,2=custom)
*COMP               = APPC
*COMP               = NAMED_PIPES
*COMP               = NETBIOS
*COMP               = TCPIP
*COMP               = ODBC_SUPPORT
*COMP               = JDBC_SUPPORT
*COMP               = SQLJ_SUPPORT
*COMP               = IBMJRE
```

Fig. 2–24 *Sample Response File*

You can copy a sample response file onto a hard disk drive and modify each parameter. See the manual *Installation and Configuration Supplement* for more information about available parameters for a response file.

Response File Generator (Windows only)

The response file generator utility creates a response file from an existing installed and configured DB2 product. You can use the generated response file to recreate the exact setup on other machines.

For example, you could install and configure a DB2 Run-Time client to connect to various databases across your network. Once this client is installed and configured to access all the database that your users must have access to, you can run the response file generator to create a response file and a profile for each instance.

To generate a response file, execute the following command:

```
db2rspgn -d x:\path
```

A response file is generated in the path you specify with the -d option. The file name is fixed depending on which product has been installed. For example, the DB2ADMCL.RSP file is generated for the Administration Client. In addition to the response files, instance profiles are generated in the same path for all instances in this machine. Each instance profile has the settings of DB2 registry variables, database manager configuration parameters, node directory, database directory, and so on. If you are planning to set up and configure identical DB2 products, you only need to specify the installation response file when you perform the installation. The

installation response file that was created by the response file generator will automatically call each instance profile. You only need to ensure that the instance profiles are located in the same drive and directory as the installation response file.

Distributed Installation with a Response File

With a response file, the installation can proceed without any intervention. You can
configure a CD-ROM drive or a hard disk drive to be shared and make the DB2
install files and response files accessible to the machines where the DB2 product
will be installed. To use a response file, you use the same installation program as
the normal installation with the option to specify a response file. For Windows or
UNIX, execute the following command:

```
db2setup -r response_file
```

The -r option performs specifies that the installation configuration information will
come from a response file. The response_file is the full path and file name of the
response file to use, see additional options for DB2SETUP in the Command Reference.

The DB2 Environment

Before creating and working with databases, you need to understand the DB2 environment. The DB2 environment controls many database-related factors, such as what protocols may be used for accessing remote databases, what paths should be used by applications when searching for database-related files, how much memory will be allocated for various buffers that databases and applications use, and how the system will behave in certain situations. This complex environment is controlled by several different mechanisms including:

- DB2 Profile Registry
- Environment variables
- Configuration parameters

This section discusses the DB2 Profile Registry and Environment variables. Configuration parameters are discussed throughout the remainder of this book.

DB2 Profile Registry

Much of the DB2 environment is controlled by entries stored in the DB2 Profile Registry. The objective of the Profile Registry is to consolidate the DB2 environment; so key controlling factors are centrally located and easily managed. Many of the Registry values control DB2 interfaces or communication parameters; so the variables that are set in the registry may vary by platform.

The DB2 Profile Registry is divided into four registries. They are:

- DB2 Instance Level Profile Registry - The majority of DB2 environment variables are placed within this registry. The environment variable settings for a particular instance are kept in this registry. Values defined in this level override their settings in the global level.
- DB2 Global Level Profile Registry - If a variable is not set for a particular instance, this registry is used. This registry contains the machine-wide variable settings.
- DB2 Instance Node Level Profile Registry - This registry level contains variable settings that are specific to a partition (node) in a multi-partition environment. Values defined in this level override their settings at the instance and global levels.
- DB2 Instance Profile Registry - This registry contains a list of all instance names recognized by the system. You can see the complete list of all the instances available on the system by running DB2ILIST.

The following are some of the parameters that may be set in the DB2 Registry:

- DB2CODEPAGE - This applies to all platforms. If not set, DB2 will use the code page set for the operating system.
- DB2DBDFT - The default database for implicit connections.
- DB2COMM - This applies to all DB2 servers that participate in a distributed DB2 environment. It specifies which DB2 communication listeners are started with DB2.
- DB2NBADAPTERS - This applies only to DB2 for Windows specifying which local adapters to use for NetBIOS communication.

Note: You do not have to reboot your system after making changes to the DB2 Registry.

For a complete list of parameters and values, refer to the *DB2 UDB V8.1 Administration Guide*.

Environment Variables

There are some environment variables that may or may not be stored in the DB2 Profile Registry (depending on the operating system). They are system environment variables used by DB2 that must be stored in a location where the platform stores its system variables. The following are examples of DB2 system environment variables:

- DB2INSTANCE - Specifies the active DB2 instance
- DB2PATH - Specifies the path for the DB2 executables

A summary of the location of these DB2 environment variables is shown below DB2. For further details on environment variables and on which operating system platforms you may see them or need them, please refer to the *DB2 Administration Guide*.

Table 2–1 *DB2 Environment Variables*

Operating System	Location of DB2 Environment Variables
Windows	System Environment Variables, specifies the system within the System icon from the Control Panel.
UNIX	Within a script file called db2profile (Bourne or Korn shell) or db2cshrc (C shell) depending on the UNIX platform. Incorporated with the user's initialization file (.profile or .login).

Declaring registry and environment variables

The registry information is stored in files containing variable names and values. However, these files should not be edited or manipulated directly. To update registry and environment values, use the DB2SET command. Any changes made to the values in the registry are applied dynamically, and you do not need to reboot your system for the changes to take effect. The DB2 registry applies the updated information to the DB2 applications started after the changes are made. For example, if changes are made at the instance level, you must issue a DB2STOP to stop the instance followed by a DB2START.

Using the DB2SET command with the -all option, you can see the list of all of the profiles variables set for your environment.

```
DB2 CLP                                              _ □ x

C:\>db2set -all
[e] DB2PATH=C:\Program Files\IBM\SQLLIB
[i] DB2ACCOUNTNAME=BAKLARZ\db2admin
[i] DB2INSTOWNER=BAKLARZ
[i] DB2PORTRANGE=60000:60003
[i] DB2_GRP_LOOKUP=LOCAL
[i] DB2INSTPROF=C:\PROGRA~1\IBM\SQLLIB
[i] DB2COMM=TCPIP
[g] DB2_GRP_LOOKUP=LOCAL
[g] DB2SYSTEM=BAKLARZ
[g] DB2PATH=C:\Program Files\IBM\SQLLIB
[g] DB2INSTDEF=DB2
[g] DB2ADMINSERVER=DB2DAS00

C:\>
```

Fig. 2–25 *The db2set -all command*

The output of the DB2SET command with the -all option is shown in Fig. 2–25. Notice that the instance-level settings are preceded with an [i] and the global settings are preceded with a [g].

The following are some examples of usage of the DB2SET command:

To set a parameter for the current instance:

```
db2set parameter=value
```

To set a parameter's value for a specific instance:

```
db2set parameter=value -i instance_name
```

To sct a parameter at the global level:

```
db2set parameter=value -g
```

To view a list of all variables that can be set in the profile registry:

```
db2set -lr
```

Hierarchy of the DB2 Environment

Since there are multiple places where a variable can be set, DB2 uses a hierarchy to determine where it will look to determine a variable's value. It uses the following search order:

1. Environment variables set with the DB2SET command. (or the export command on UNIX platforms).

2. Registry values set with the instance node level profile (using the DB2SET -i <instance name><nodenum> command).

3. Registry values set with the instance level profile (using the DB2SET -i command).

4. Registry values set with the global level profile (using the DB2SET -g command).

Although most DB2 environment settings can be set either in the DB2 Profile Registry or in the operating system environment, it is strongly recommended that the DB2 Profile Registry be used whenever possible. If DB2 variables are set outside of the DB2 Registry, remote administration of those variables is not possible and any changes made mean that the Windows system must be rebooted for any changes in the value of the variables to take effect.

The DB2 Instance

A DB2 instance is defined as a logical database server environment. DB2 databases are created within DB2 instances on the database server. The creation of multiple instances on the same physical server provides a unique database server environment for each instance. For example, you can maintain a test environment and a production environment on the same machine.

Each instance has an administrative group associated with it. This administrative group must be defined in the instance configuration file known as the *database manager configuration file*. Creating user IDs and user groups is different for each operating environment.

The installation process creates a default DB2 instance. This is the recommended method for creating instances. However, instances may be created (or dropped) after installation.

The instance directory stores all information that pertains to a database instance. The location of the instance directory cannot be changed once it is created. The directory contains:

- The database manager configuration file
- The system database directory
- The node directory
- The node configuration file (db2nodes.cfg)
- Other files that contain debugging information, such as the exception or register dump or the call stack for the DB2 processes.

DB2 Instances on Windows

The default instance created during the installation of DB2 for Windows is called DB2. The DB2 environment variables are set during install. If you want another instance, you can create the additional instance using the command DB2ICRT. The instance name is specified at creation time and does not have to directly correspond to a user ID as it does in UNIX environments.

DB2 Instance Considerations on Windows

When installing DB2 on Windows, the DB2 instance is defined as a Windows service. Therefore, the DB2 instance name must adhere to any naming rules for Windows services. The DAS is defined as a Windows service as well. You can configure these services to start automatically. Click the **Services** icon located in the Windows Control Panel to verify the existence and status of these services.

Fig. 2–26 *Windows Services*

Fig. 2–26 shows the Control Panel for Windows Services. The instance can be started from this control panel or from an operating system window using the command NET START DB2. The DB2 Security service can be started with the command NET START DB2NTSECSERVER.

DB2 Instances on Linux and UNIX

If the DB2 installation was done manually, the following tasks must be completed before the DB2 server can be used:

1.   Create group and user IDs for a DB2 installation.

Three users and groups are required to operate DB2.

Table 2–2   *Required users and groups*

Required user	Example user name	Example group name
Instance owner	db2inst1	db2iadm1
Fenced user	db2fenc1	db2fadm1
DB2 administration server	db2as	db2asgrp

- The i*nstance owner* home directory is where the DB2 instance will be created.
- The *fenced user* is used to run user defined functions (UDFs) and stored procedures outside of the address space used by the DB2 database.
- The *user ID* for the DB2 administration server is used to run the DB2 adminis-

tration server service on your system.

The commands to create the required groups and user IDs for DB2 will depend on the operating system, this example is for AIX:

```
mkgroup id=999 db2iadm1
mkgroup id=998 db2fadm1
mkgroup id=997 db2asgrp
```

To create users for each group (AIX example):

```
mkuser id=1004 pgrp=db2iadm1 groups=db2iadm1 home=/home/db2inst1
db2inst1 passwd mypasswrd
mkuser id=1003 pgrp=db2fadm1 groups=db2fadm1 home=/home/db2fenc1
db2fenc1 passwd mypasswrd
mkuser id=1002 pgrp=db2asgrp groups=db2asgrp home=/home/db2as
db2as passwd mypasswrd
```

Note: You must have root authority to create users and groups and you may specify your own user and group names as long as they adhere to system naming rules and DB2 naming rules, refer to "Naming Rules" in the *DB2 UDB V8.1 Quick Beginnings* manual.

2. Create a DB2 Administration Server (DAS).

For AIX, issue this command to create the DAS:

```
/usr/opt/db2_08001/instance/dascrt -u DASuser
```

3. Create an instance using db2icrt.

Log on as a user with root authority and issue the following command (AIX example):

```
DB2DIR/instance/db2icrt -a AuthType -u FencedID InstName
```

- DB2DIR is the DB2 installation directory, on AIX it is /usr/opt/db2_08_01
- -a AuthType is the authentication type for the instance: SERVER, CLIENT, SERVER_ENCRYPT. This parameter is optional, and SERVER is the default.
- -u FENCEDID represents the name of the user which fenced user defined functions (UDFs) and fenced stored procedures will run.
- INSTNAME is the name of the DB2 instance. The name of the instance must be the same as the name of the instance owning user. Specify the name of the instance owning user you created. The instance will be created in the instance owning user's home directory.

4. Set up communications for the instance.

The DB2COMM registry variable allows you to set communication protocols for the DB2 instance. The variable can be set to any combination of the following keywords, separated by commas:

- APPC   starts APPC support
- NETBIOS starts NETBIOS support
- NPIPE   starts NAMED PIPE support
- TCPIP   starts TCP/IP support

For example, to set the database manger and DAS service to start connection managers for TCP/IP, enter:

```
db2set DB2COMM=tcpip
db2set DB2DAS00 DB2COMM=tcpip
db2stop
db2start
```

The database manager configuration file has a parameter SVCENAME that is assigned as the main connection port name for the instance and defined in the etc/services file. For example, if the name defined in the services file is db2c_DB2, the command to update the database manager configuration file is the following:

```
update dbm cfg using svcename db2c_DB2
```

the corresponding entries in the /etc/services file would be:

```
db2c_DB2     5000/tcp
```

5. Update the product license key.

Refer to the DB2LICM command in the *DB2 Command Reference.*

 Note: Remember that all commands are case sensitive in UNIX environments. For more information on manual installations, refer to the *Installation and Configuration Supplement.*

Starting the DB2 Instance

Now that a DB2 instance has been created, it must be initialized or started. The process of starting an instance is similar to starting a network file server; until the instance is started, the clients will not be able to access the databases on the server.

The command to start a DB2 instance is called DB2START. This command will allocate all of the required DB2 resources on the server. These resources include memory and communications support.

```
db2start
SQL1063N DB2START processing was successful.
```

On Windows, you may also start an instance with the command:

```
net start instance_name
```

Stopping the DB2 Instance

The command to stop the current database manager instance is DB2STOP. Messages are sent to standard output indicating the success or failure of the DB2STOP command.

```
DB2STOP
SQL1064N DB2STOP processing was successful.
```

On Windows, you may also stop an instance with the command:

```
net stop instance_name
```

Instance Administration

This section discusses how to administer DB2 instances, both locally and remotely. Certain tasks in DB2 can only be performed at the instance level, such as creating a database, forcing users off databases, monitoring a database, or updating the database manager configuration. Other tasks require a database connection, such as issuing SQL Data Manipulation Language (DML) statements, using the LOAD utility, or using the BIND command.

Both remote and local administration of instances can be done using the Control Center. The ATTACH command can be used from the command line for both local and remote administration tasks.

To attach to an instance, you can use the ATTACH command. The syntax of the ATTACH command is as follows:

```
ATTACH [TO nodename] [USER username [USING password]]
```

If the ATTACH command is executed without arguments, the node name you are currently attached to is returned. If you attempt to attach to an instance while attached to another instance, the current instance will be detached and the new attachment is attempted. In other words, you can only be attached to one instance at a time.

Note: The currently active instance can be identified using the GET INSTANCE command, which returns the value of the DB2INSTANCE environment variable.

Database connections are independent of instance attachments. A single application can maintain several database connections at the same time it has an instance attachment, but it can only maintain a single instance attachment at any one time. The database connection can be implicit or explicit. An implicit database connection will connect to the database specified by the DB2DBDFT registry variable. An explicit database connection can be made using the CONNECT TO DATABASE statement.

The local instance is determined by the value contained in the DB2INSTANCE variable. When attached to a second instance, you are using the directory services of the local instance. You cannot make catalog changes or list, update, or reset catalogs for database, node, or DCS directories (used only if DB2 Connect is installed) in the second instance.

Local Instance Administration

After DB2 has been installed on a server and an instance created, a user can access this instance in one of two ways:

- By setting the DB2INSTANCE environment variable to the name of the instance. The DB2PATH environment variable must be set to the location of the DB2 executables. This is known as an *implicit attachment*.

- By cataloging a local instance and issuing the ATTACH command. This is known as an *explicit attachment*.

Instance Attach Scenario

This scenario examines a situation in which a local user wants to access two instances on the same database server without changing the environment when the user logs into the system.

The two local instances are called DB2TEST and DB2. They are located on an AIX database server. The user, Dana, is a local user on the database server. Dana has set the DB2INSTANCE and DB2PATH variables to allow access to the DB2TEST instance. In AIX, Dana would edit her profile to include the following entry:

```
. /home/db2test/sqllib/db2profile
```

Dana also wants to access the DB2 instance on the same server. To do this, she catalogs the DB2 instance as a local node by using the following command:

```
catalog local node mydb2 instance db2
```

In this example:

- LOCAL identifies that this is a local instance.
- MYDB2 is the local alias for the node to be cataloged.
- DB2 is the name of the local instance to be accessed.

The contents of the node directory can be examined using the LIST NODE DIRECTORY command:

```
Node Directory

Number of entries in the directory = 2

Node 1 entry:

  Node name                    = MYDB2
  Comment                      =
  Protocol                     = LOCAL
  Instance name                = db2
```

To access a database in the instance named DB2, Dana must catalog the local database using the following command:

```
catalog db db2cert as mycert at node mydb2
```

In this example:

- DB2CERT is the name of the database as it exists in the instance on the database server.
- MYCERT is the alias that user Dana will use when connecting.
- MYDB2 is the local alias given to the local instance by Dana in the CATALOG NODE command.

If Dana issues the LIST DB DIRECTORY command, the output is similar to the following:

```
System Database Directory

Number of entries in the directory = 1

Database 1 entry:

  Database alias               = MYCERT
  Database name                = DB2CERT
  Local database directory     = /home/db2test
  Database release level       = a.00
  Comment                      =
  Directory entry type         = Remote
  Catalog node number          = 0
```

Notice that the entry is a REMOTE type. The database has been cataloged via the MYDB2 node. This is, in fact, a local node on the same workstation. A local node is essentially another DB2 instance. In this case, the instance is called DB2 as shown above.

Attaching to an Instance Using the Control Center

So far, DB2 commands have been used to attach to an instance. This can also be done using the Control Center. To do this, right-click on the required instance and select Attach from the menu as shown here:

Fig. 2–27 *Attaching to an instance*

An attachment being made to the JEREMY instance is displayed. To be able to perform administrative tasks at a remote instance, you should log on to the instance as the DAS user.

DB2 Administration Server (DAS)

The DAS must be running on every DB2 server that you want to administer remotely or detect using the client configuration search method. The DAS provides remote clients with the information required to set up communications to access the DB2 server instances. You can create only one DAS for each machine. When the DAS is created, the DB2 global-level profile registry variable DB2ADMINSERVER is set to the name of the DAS user.

The DB2 Administration Server assists the Control Center and Configuration Assistant when working on the following administration tasks:

- Enabling remote administration of DB2 servers.
- Providing the facility for job management, including the ability to schedule the running of both DB2 and operating system command scripts. These command scripts are user-defined.
- Defining the scheduling of jobs, viewing the results of completed jobs, and performing other administrative tasks against jobs located either remotely or locally to the DAS using the Task Center.
- Providing a means for discovering information about the configuration of DB2 instances, databases, and other DB2 administration servers in conjunction with the DB2 Discovery utility. This information is used by the Configuration Assistant and the Control Center to simplify and automate the configuration of client connections to the DB2 databases.

In order to start administration from a remote client, the user must have SYSADM authority in the DAS. Once the instance and the databases are registered, the user must also hold the appropriate authorities and privileges for each administration task.

The following are some of the commands used to administer the DAS service:

- DB2ADMIN START - Starts the DB2 Administration Server.
- DB2ADMIN STOP - Stops the DB2 Administration Server.
- DASICRT - Creates the DAS in UNIX.
- DASIDROP - Drops the DAS in UNIX.
- DB2ADMIN CREATE - Creates the DAS in Windows.
- DB2ADMIN DROP - Drops the DAS instance in Windows.
- DB2 GET ADMIN CFG - Displays the database manager configuration file of the DAS.
- DB2 UPDATE ADMIN CFG - This command allows you to update individual entries in the database manager configuration file for the DAS.
- DB2 RESET ADMIN CFG - Resets the configuration parameters to the recommended defaults. The changes become effective only after the DB2ADMIN START command is executed.

Getting Started

Summary

In this chapter, the process of installing DB2 on various platforms was demonstrated. The creation of a DB2 instance and the role of the DB2 Administration Server (DAS) in a DB2 system were described.

The DB2 Setup wizard is a graphical installation utility available on Linux, UNIX, and Linux environments. The DB2 Setup wizard provides an easy-to-use interface for installing DB2 and performing initial setup and configuration tasks. The DB2 Setup wizard can also be used to create instances and response files.

The DB2 Setup wizard can be used to create a response file. The selections you make as you proceed through the DB2 Setup wizard are recorded in a response file that you can save to a location on your system. For your convenience, the DB2 Setup wizard allows you to create a response file without performing an installation. This feature may be useful in an environment where a DBA does not have the authority required to perform an installation. The DBA can create a response file for the installation and provide it to the system administrator who will install the product on the DBA's behalf.

A DB2 instance can be defined as a logical database server environment. For each environment, the instance creation process including any special user ID and group setup required, was reviewed.

The DB2 environment variables, including DB2INSTANCE and DB2PATH, were discussed, specifically that they are defined on every DB2 system. The location of the DB2 environment variables differs by platform. Also discussed, were the DB2 profile variables and the DB2 Profile Registry and how the various levels of the registry can contain different levels of information and how searching through these levels can affect your system.

Throughout this chapter, DB2 commands were demonstrated through the Command Center or the Command Line Processor. The Command Line Processor has default settings that can be modified for each session or changed globally using the DB2OPTIONS profile variable. Lastly, examples of how to execute DB2 commands were demonstrated using the Command Line Processor.

Instance management, including starting and stopping a DB2 instance, was reviewed. DB2 for Windows is integrated with the Windows services environment, and each DB2 instance is a Windows service. The commands used to start and stop an instance are DB2START and DB2STOP.

Getting Connected

♦ CLIENT OVERVIEW

♦ CLIENT INSTALLATION

♦ AUTOMATING CONFIGURATIONS

♦ MANUAL CONFIGURATIONS

♦ BINDING DATABASE UTILITIES

DB2 databases can be accessed by applications that run on the same machine as the database or from a remote machine by using a distributed connection. In addition to providing client access to a centralized database running on a server, distributed connections can also be used to perform administrative tasks on the database server by a Database Administrator using a client workstation.

DB2 Client Overview

In the last chapter, the installation of a DB2 Server on Windows, Linux, and UNIX has been demonstrated. The installation and configuration of the DB2 clients will now be examined.

The DB2 client provides a runtime environment that is required for DB2 applications to access database resources. The DB2 client contains the communications infrastructure to communicate with remote database servers. You can also execute SQL, bind packages, use data manipulation utilities (Import/Load/Export), and catalog remote nodes and databases. Most of the database administrator tasks can be performed from a DB2 client.

These are the types of DB2 clients you can install:

- **DB2 Run-Time Client** provides the ability to access DB2 databases and a basic application execution environment.
- **DB2 Administration Client** provides all the features of the DB2 Run-Time Client and includes all the DB2 Administration GUI tools, documentation, and support for Thin Clients.
- **DB2 Application Development Client** provides all the features of the DB2 Administration Client and also includes libraries, header files, documented APIs, and sample programs to build character-based, multimedia, and object-oriented applications.

Installing the DB2 Client

The DB2 client installation for either Intel or UNIX workstations is similar to the server installation. The easiest method for installation is to use the DB2setup wizard. The DB2 Administration Client will install the DB2 Run-Time Client, the Administration tools, and the Thin client. The components installed will include support for:

- CLI, ODBC, OLE DB
- JDBC, SQLJ
- System Bind Files
- GUI tools

Note: In Windows you must make sure the user account used to install the product is defined on the local machine, belongs to the Local Administrator's group and has the *Act as part of the operating system* advanced user right.

A thin client refers to a DB2 Administration Client that runs its applications from a code server across a network. A thin client can be set up by installing a DB2 Adminstration client or DB2 Connect Personal Edition on a workstation running a Windows 32-bit operating system. This workstation can then act as a code server that allows the application to run with only the immediately necessary modules at the client.

The following diagram illustrates in more detail a remote client connecting to a DB2 server:

Fig. 3–1 *Remote client flow to DB2 server*

All remote clients use a communications product to support the protocol the client uses when accessing a remote database server. This protocol support is either part of the client's operating system or available as a separate product.

The protocol stack must be installed and configured before a remote client can communicate with a remote DB2 server.

DB2 provides many different methods for configuring a remote client that wants to access a DB2 database server. Though the methods may differ, the steps are basically the same:

- Make sure that the communication product is installed and configured on the client workstation. The following protocols are supported: TCP/IP, NetBIOS, Named Pipes, and APPC.

- Perform the communication-specific steps. For example, if using TCP/IP, update the services file on the server with the port number(s) that the database server is listening on.

- Catalog the remote node. This is the database server to which you want to establish the connection.

- Catalog the remote database. A DB2 database server can support both local and remote clients concurrently.

The easiest way to configure a remote client for communication with a DB2 server is by using the Configuration Assistant.

 Note: Normally, the communication settings for the DB2 server are configured during installation.

Roadmap to Distributed Communications

There are several methods to set up communications between a DB2 client and a DB2 server. The methods will be introduced to help you decide which is the most suitable for your requirements. The following ways of connecting a client to a DB2 server will be reviewed:

- Automated Configuration using Discovery
- Automated Configuration using Access Profiles
- Manual Configuration

DB2 Discovery

DB2 Discovery is a helpful concept to understand before attempting to set up distributed connections.

DB2 Discovery allows you to automate the configuration of remote clients connecting to DB2 databases. You can easily catalog a remote database from a client workstation without having to know any detailed communication-specific information. From the client, DB2 Discovery requests information from DB2 servers to return to the client issuing the discovery request. A discovery message is sent to the DB2 servers, and if the servers are configured to support the discovery process, data is returned to the client.

The returned data includes:

- The instances on the DB2 server that have discovery enabled and information about the protocols that each instance supports for client connection
- The databases defined within these instances that have discovery enabled, including the name and description for each available database

Both the database server and the client have control over DB2 Discovery. Using configuration parameters, the user can control:

- Whether discovery is disabled or enabled, and if enabled, the discovery method that will be used
- The protocols that DB2 Discovery uses
- If an instance can be discovered
- If a database can be discovered

See "Configuring DB2 Discovery" on page 93 for more details.

Getting Connected

Fig. 3–2 *Search and Known Discovery*

The search discovery method searches the network for valid DB2 database servers that a client workstation can access. You do not need to provide specific communication information. The remote client, using the Configuration Assistant, searches the network to obtain a list of valid servers.

In the known discovery method, you must provide information about the server that you want to access, specifically the server name.

Automated Configuration Using Discovery

If you use this type of *automated configuration*, you do not need to provide any detailed communications information to enable the DB2 client to contact the DB2 server.

As mentioned earlier, discovery works in one of two ways:

- *Search discovery* - the DB2 client searches for DB2 servers on the network.
- *Known discovery* - one particular server is queried for information about the instances and databases defined there.

You can use either the Configuration Assistant or the Control Center to exploit discovery-based configuration, and this method is normally used to configure small numbers of clients.

Step-by-step examples of using discovery are given in "Configuring DB2 Clients" on page 96.

Configuring DB2 Discovery

As well as needing to have the communication protocols installed and configured, various parameters need to be correctly configured for Discovery to work. As mentioned previously, as long as DB2 is installed after the communications protocols have been installed and configured, these Discovery-related parameters should be set automatically. However, if you add a new communications protocol after DB2 is installed, or if Discovery is not working, you may need to check the parameter settings.

Restricting Discovery

As well as enabling discovery for either the search and known methods, it is also possible to disable discovery so your DB2 server cannot be located on the network. This is achieved by setting the DAS parameter DISCOVER to DISABLE. It is also possible to configure discovery on a DB2 server in a hierarchical manner. You can disable or enable at the DB2 server level, instance level, and database level. This provides you with the ability to enable discovery of your DB2 server while hiding certain instances and/or databases (Fig. 3–3).

Getting Connected

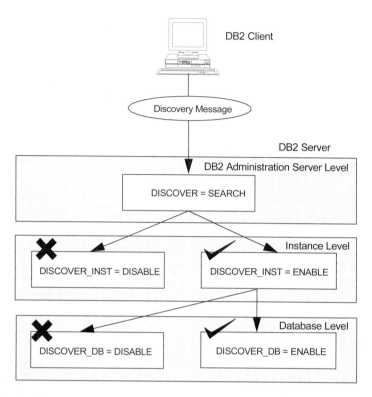

Fig. 3–3 *Discovery hierarchy*

To set the discovery parameters for the DAS service on the server, you can use the Command Center or CLP. For example, to set the DISCOVER parameter to SEARCH and the DISCOVER_COMM parameter to TCP/IP, enter the following commands:

```
update admin cfg using discover search
update admin cfg using discover_comm tcpip
```

To view the parameter values currently set for the DAS service, enter the following command:

```
get admin cfg
```

To set the discovery parameters for the DB2 instance or a database on the server, you can use the Control Center. Select the object, right-click on the mouse and select **Configure Parameters**.

To set the discovery parameters for the DB2 client, you can use the Configuration Assistant. Click on the **Client Settings** button and go to the Communications tag. Alternatively, you can use the `update dbm cfg` command from the CLP or Command Center, or if you choose, you can use the graphical interface of the DB2 Control Center to update configuration parameters.

 Note: The DAS service must be configured and running on each DB2 server you wish to locate in this manner.

Configuring DB2 Clients

DB2 provides several different methods for configuring a remote client that needs to access a DB2 database server, as detailed in "Roadmap to Distributed Communications" on page 91. In this section, more details and examples of using these methods will be reviewed.

Automated Configuration Using Discovery

You can use the discovery function of DB2 to automate the addition of remote databases. This can be done in one of two ways:

- Enter the name of the machine on the network (e.g., the hostname if using TCP/ IP and then use discovery to automatically return the instances and databases on that machine (*known discovery*).
- Search the network for machines, and then use discovery to automatically return the instances and databases on each machine (*search discovery*).

You can use either the Configuration Assistant or the Control Center to perform automated configuration. This is an example of using the CA to perform known discovery.

Known Discovery Using the Configuration Assistant (CA)

You can access the CA from the desktop or from the command line using the DB2CA command.

Fig. 3–4 *Configuration Assistant (CA) - Add Database Using Wizard...*

If no databases are yet cataloged on the client, the Welcome panel is displayed (Fig. 3–4). Otherwise, the databases that are cataloged on your client workstation are displayed under Available DB2 Databases in the main CA panel. To add another database, click on the **Add** button (or the **Add Database** button from the Welcome panel). The Add Database Wizard panel will appear to guide you through adding the new database.

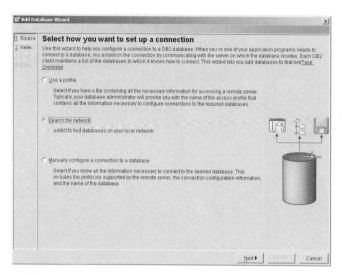

Fig. 3–5 *Select how you want to set up a connection*

Select the **Search the network** radio button. Click on the **Next** button.

If the system is located, then it is displayed under Known Systems, together with all its instances and databases:

Fig. 3–6 *Select a database from the network search result*

You can check if the database server is already known to the client by double click-ing on the folder next to Known Systems in Fig. 3–6. If it is not, then click on the **Add System** button. If it is already known, then expand the system until you see the desired database, as in Fig. 3–8.

Fig. 3–7 *Select a database from the network search result - Expanded*

Select the database **SAMPLE**, then click on the **Next** button.

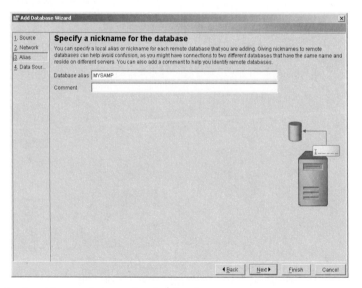

Fig. 3–8 *Specify a nickname for the database*

Choose an alias for the database and optionally add a comment. Click **Next**.

Fig. 3–9 *Register this database as a data source*

You can register the database as an ODBC data source by checking the "Register this database for ODBC" check box. You can choose an application from the "Optimize for Application" selection box to optimize the ODBC settings for that application. Click **Finish** when done. You are now able to use the database you added.

Fig. 3–10 *Configuration Assistant - Test Connection*

You can test the connection that has been added by selecting the database alias and clicking on **Test Connection**.

Fig. 3–11 *Test connection*

You can select multiple ways to test the connection (i.e. CLI and ODBC), enter the user ID and password to be used when connecting to the remote database. On this panel you can also change the password for the user ID defined at the database server machine. If the connection is successful, you will see a pop-up message similar to this:

Fig. 3–12 *Test connection successful*

Search Discovery Using the Configuration Assistant (CA)

Instead of entering the machine identifier (known discovery), you can use the CA to find databases on your local network (search discovery).

Start the Configuration Assistant (CA) and select **Add Database Using Wizard**.

Select the **Search the network** radio button. Click on the **Next** button.

Fig. 3–13 *Select a database from the network search result - Other Systems*

As in the previous example using known discovery, you should first check in the Known Systems to make sure that the database server is not already known to the client.

If the system that contains the database you require is not listed, double click on the folder beside the "Other Systems (Search the network)" icon to search the network for additional systems. When the search is over, the list of discovered systems is displayed. Click on the **[+]** sign beside the system you require to get a list of the instances and databases defined there (Fig. 3–13). Select the database that you want to add and proceed as shown in the known discovery example.

If the system you want is not listed, it can be added to the list of systems by clicking on the **Add Systems** push button.

 Note: Discovery only supports the TCP/IP protocol.

Using search discovery may appear to be simpler than known discovery. However, in larger networks, routers and bridges can filter the messages search discovery uses to find DB2 servers on the network. This may result in an incomplete or even empty list. In these cases, use known discovery.

Automated Configuration Using Access Profiles

Access profiles are another automated method to configure a DB2 client to access remote DB2 servers and their databases. An access profile contains the information that a client needs to catalog databases on a DB2 server.

As with discovery, when using access profiles, you do not need to provide any detailed communications information to enable the DB2 client to contact the DB2 server.

Two types of access profiles exist:

- *Client access profiles* are used for duplicating the cataloged databases and/or the client settings (dbm cfg, CLI/ODBC) from one client to another.

- *Server access profiles* are created from DB2 servers and contain information about all the instances and databases the DB2 server has cataloged.

Both types of profiles can be exported and then imported to another DB2 system using the Configuration Assistant. Use of access profiles is typical for configuring a large number of clients.

If you have a large number of clients to configure, you should also consider making use of LDAP (Lightweight Directory Access Protocol). This allows you to store catalog information in one centralized location. Each client just needs to know the centralized location to be able to connect to any database that has been made available in the network. See the *DB2 UDB V8.1 Administration Guide* for more details about LDAP.

 Note: In the Windows environment, DB2 supports Windows Active Directory as the LDAP Server and single sign-on using Kerberos security.

DB2 for OS/390 and DB2 for OS/400 do not support a searched discovery-based configuration. However, if you have a DB2 Connect server already configured with connections to either of these host servers, DB2 Discovery will search for your DB2 Connect server. You can then choose to connect through the DB2 Connect server or use its information to configure a direct connection to the host (if you have the appropriate DB2 Connect software installed on your local client machine).

Using Access Profiles

Access profiles are another automated method to configure a DB2 client to access remote DB2 servers and their databases. An access profile contains the information that a client needs to catalog databases on a DB2 server.

The generation of an access profile requires that the DISCOVER configuration parameter of the DAS service be set to either SEARCH or KNOWN. When the profile is generated, it includes all the instances that have ENABLE in the DISCOVER_INST database manager configuration parameter and all the databases that have the DISCOVER_DB database configuration parameter set to ENABLE. See "Configuring DB2 Discovery" on page 93 for more details about these settings.

The second part of the process is to import the server access profile to one or many client machines. To do this, the profile file must be made available to the DB2 client machine and then be imported using the Configuration Assistant.

The generated file is a text file and can be viewed but should not be changed.

Using the Configuration Assistant to Export a client profile

A client profile can be created by either the Configuration Assistant (CA) or by using the DB2CFEXP command. During the export process, the information necessary to create a connection between the client and server is created. The information in the client profile can then be imported to configure other clients.

Getting Connected

Fig. 3–14 *Configuration Assistant - Export Profile*

Fig. 3–14 shows the Configuration Assistant, by clicking on Export Profile, the following options are given:

- All - this will create a profile that contains all the databases cataloged on the system
- Database connection information - this will create a profile that contains all of the databases cataloged on the system without any of the configuration information for this client
- Customize - will allow you to select specific databases that are cataloged on the system

For this example, select **Customize**

Fig. 3–15 *Customize Export Profile*

Enter the name of the file where the information will be exported to, you can select specific parameters to be exported. If you click on **DBM configuration parameters** and then **Customize**, you will see the following screen:

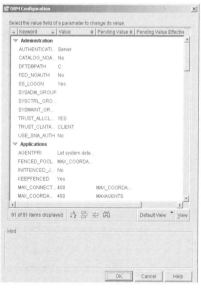

Fig. 3–16 *DBM Configuration*

The DBM Configuration panel allows the user to select a number of configuration parameters and change its value. Click **OK** to return and then click **Export**

Fig. 3–17 *Export Results*

This final panel shows the results of the Export command. The generated file is a text file and can be viewed but should not be changed.

Using the Configuration Assistant to Import a client profile

A client access profile can be used to configure a client by using the import function of the Configuration Assistant (CA) or by using the DB2CFIMP command. Clients can import all or a subset of the configuration information from a given profile.

Start the Configuration Assistant, and click on Import.

Fig. 3–18 *Import Profile*

By clicking on **Import Profile**, you are given the following options:

- All - this will import all information from a given profile
- Customize - this will allow you to select which parameters you want imported to your system.

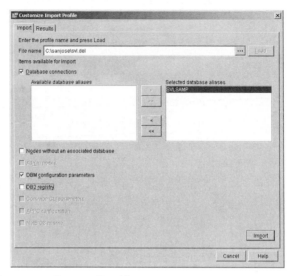

Fig. 3–19 *Customize Import Profile*

In this panel, select a file that contains the client information to import to this system and click **Load**. This will present you with the parameters found in the import file. You can choose which configuration parameters to import. Click **Import**.

Fig. 3–20 *Import Results*

The status of the configuration parameters selected by Import are displayed.

Using the Configuration Assistant to Import a server profile

A server access profile is a file that contains information about all the instances on the DB2 server and all the databases within each instance.

Start the Configuration Assistant and select **Add Database Using Wizard**.

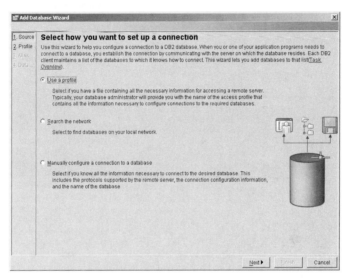

Fig. 3–21 *Select how you want to set up a connection*

Select the **Use a profile** radio button and click **Next**.

Fig. 3–22 *Select a database from a profile*

Select a server profile to load, click on **Load**, then select a database and click on **Next**.

Fig. 3–23 *Specify a nickname for the database*

Enter a unique name for the database alias for the system. Click on Next.

Fig. 3–24 *Register this database as a data source*

If the system will be using ODBC, register this database as an ODBC data source. Click Finish to exit.

Manual Configuration

It is also possible to manually configure a database connection. To manually configure the connection, you must know the following:

- One of the protocols supported by the server instance containing the database
- The protocol connection information required to configure the connection to the server instance
- The server name
- The name of the database on the remote server

There are two ways to manually configure connections:

- Using the Manual option in the Configuration Assistant - in this case, you are prompted via a GUI interface for all the values to enter.
- Using the CATALOG NODE/DB commands - in this case, you must know the syntax of the commands and enter the commands from a command line interface. The advantage of using the CATALOG NODE/DB commands is that the configuration steps can be put into scripts so that the configuration can be redone if

necessary.

In either case, manual configuration must be used to exploit some advanced options that are not available using automated methods; for example, choosing the location where authentication should take place.

Manual configuration using the CA will now be reviewed. With the information listed above, the Add Database Wizard can be used to guide you through the steps necessary to add the database connection.

Manual Configuration Using the Configuration Assistant

Start the Configuration Assistant (CA) and click on **Add** in the CA's main panel to start the Add Database Wizard. Select **Manually configure a connection to a DB2 database** and click on **Next**.

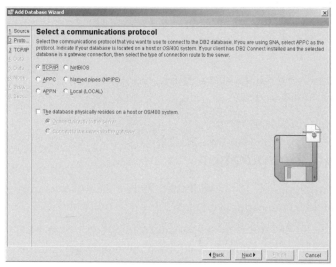

Fig. 3–25 *Select a communications protocol*

Select the protocol that you will use to connect to the database.

All of the protocols that DB2 supports are listed here, including APPC. If you have chosen APPC, your operating system choices are LAN-based, OS/390 or z/OS, OS/400, VM, or VSE. If you choose TCP/IP, your choices are LAN-based, OS/390, OS/400, or VM.

Click on **Next**.

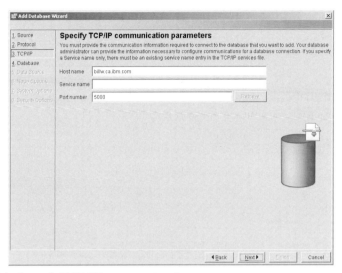

Fig. 3–26 *Specify TCP/IP communication parameters*

Enter the required protocol parameters. These parameters differ according to the protocol selected. These are the supported protocols together with their associated parameters:

- TCP/IP - Server hostname/IP address, port number
- NetBIOS - Server workstation name, adapter number
- Named Pipe - Server computer name, instance
- APPC - Server symbolic destination name

You should check that the machine is properly configured on the network before clicking on **OK**. For example, if using TCP/IP, ping the hostname to check if it is available.

Click on the **Next** button.

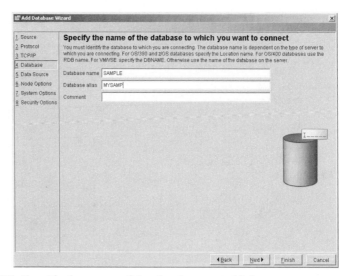

Fig. 3–27 *Specify the name of the database to which you want to connect*

Enter the name of the database (as known at the server) in the Database Name field.

You can accept the same name as the local alias for the database or change the alias to a name of your choice. You can also enter a description.

Fig. 3–28 *Register this database as a data source*

On this panel (Figure 3–28) you can enter the ODBC settings.

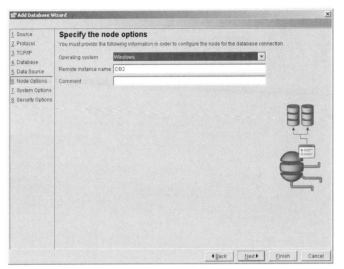

Fig. 3–29 *Specify the node options*

This panel allows you to enter options relating to the remote node. You should fill in these values as they affect the behavior of the Control Center. The system and instance names are given by the values of DB2SYSTEM and DB2INSTANCE at the server. You should also select the operating system of the remote system.

Fig. 3–30 *Specify the system options*

Enter system options relating to the database server, including system name, host name, and the operating system.

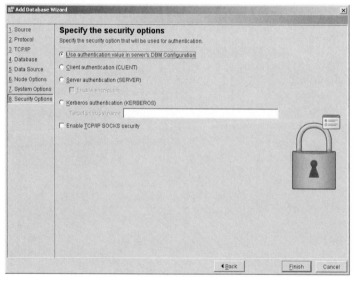

Fig. 3–31 *CA manual configuration - Enter security options*

In the final panel, there are many options relating to security that may be specified.

You can specify whether authentication of the user takes place as specified in the server's database manager configuration file (the default), at the client, at the server, or by Kerberos. These options are explained in more detail in "Controlling Data Access" on page 135. You can also choose to use SOCKS security for TCP/IP connections, which allows you to access a remote database outside your firewall.

Getting Connected

Manually cataloging the DB2 Directories

Access to both local and remote databases uses entries in the DB2 directories. The directories hide the requirement for the user to know where a database actually resides. Users are able to connect to local databases and remote databases (including DRDA databases) by specifying a database name. The directories that make this possible are:

- System database directory
- Local database directory
- Node directory
- DCS directory
- Administration node directory

System Database Directory

The *system database directory* resides in the SQLDBDIR subdirectory in the instance directory. This directory is used to catalog both local and remote data-bases. The directory contains the database name, alias, type, and node where the database resides. If the database is local, a pointer to the local database directory is located in the system database directory. If the database is remote, there is a pointer to the node directory.

Local Database Directory

The *local database directory* resides in every drive/path that contains a database. It is used to access local databases in that subdirectory. Each entry in the directory contains the database name, alias, type, and location information about the data-base.

Node Directory

Each database client maintains a *node directory*. The node directory contains entries for all instances that the client will access. The node directory contains communication information about the network connection to the instance. If multi-ple instances exist on a remote machine, then each instance must be cataloged as a separate node before you are able to access any information contained within the instance.

DCS Directory

The connection information for DRDA host databases is different from the infor-mation for LAN-connected databases. A separate directory maintains this host information. This directory is the *DCS directory*. It only exists if the DB2 Connect product is installed on your system. The DCS directory stores information used by the database manager to access databases on a DRDA Application Server.

Administration Node Directory

The *administration node directory* contains one definition for each remote system that is known to a DB2 client. Most of the entries for this directory are made during product installation, by the Control Center, or by the CA.

Examining DB2 Directories

Consider a scenario with two systems, a database server and a remote client. From the database server, issue the LIST DB DIRECTORY command to list the contents of the system database directory. The output is as follows:

```
System Database Directory

Number of entries in the directory = 4

Database 1 entry:

   Database alias                 = DB2CERT
   Database name                  = DB2CERT
   Local database directory       = /home/db2
   Database release level         = 9.00
   Comment                        = DB2 Certification DB
   Directory entry type           = Indirect
   Catalog node number            = 0

Database 2 entry:

   Database alias                 = MYDB
   ...
```

The results show that there are four databases cataloged on the server. The first database is the DB2CERT database.

The local database directory is set to /home/db2. If more detail is desired, the local database directory can be examined by using the command: LIST DB DIRECTORY ON /home/db2. This provides more detailed information regarding the location of some of the database files.

Next, examine the contents of two directories on the client workstation: the system database directory and the node directory. A client does not have a local database directory since it does not usually contain local databases. The command to examine the system database directory is LIST DB DIRECTORY. Here is the output:

```
System Database Directory

Number of entries in the directory = 2

Database 1 entry:

  Database alias                    = MYCERT
  Database name                     = DB2CERT
  Node name                         = DB2AIX
  Database release level            = 9.00
  Comment                           = DB2 Certification DB
  Directory entry type              = Remote
  Catalog node number               = 0

Database 2 entry:

  Database alias                    = OTHERDB
  ...
```

The database alias of the database on the client is MYCERT. This name corresponds to the actual database name on the server (DB2CERT). Note that the directory entry type is *indirect* on the server for the DB2CERT database and *remote* on the client.

 Note: When a database is created, an entry is automatically placed in the system database directory and the local database directory on the server.

When cataloging the remote database on the client, the database name on the client must match the database alias on the server. The database alias specified on the client workstation is used in the CONNECT statement. Therefore, the name used to CONNECT to the DB2CERT database is MYCERT.

There is always an associated *node name* with a client system database directory entry. The node name (in this example DB2AIX) defines the location of the DB2 server on the network.

To discover more information about the location of the database server, examine the DB2AIX node entry in the node directory using the LIST NODE DIRECTORY command. The output is as follows:

```
Node Directory

Number of entries in the directory = 1

Node 1 entry:

Node name                        = DB2AIX
Comment                          =
Protocol                         = TCPIP
Hostname                         = db2aix
Service name                     = db2tcp1
```

The DB2AIX node name corresponds to a TCP/IP connection. The TCP/IP host name for the DB2 server is DB2AIX and the service name is DB2TCP1. The TCP/IP information in the client's node directory must match the information in the server's DBM configuration file.

There are other options available when cataloging a database and node, such as where authentication takes place. These options are explained in detail in "Controlling Data Access" on page 135.

Using the CATALOG Commands

You can also use the CATALOG NODE and CATALOG DB commands from the DB2 Command Center or the DB2 Command Line Processor (CLP) to add a remote database.

Before cataloging a remote database, you should check that the client machine can communicate with the remote DB2 server. The client must then catalog the remote node and the remote database.

The format of the CATALOG NODE command depends on the protocol that you use. The TCP/IP, NetBIOS, Named Pipe, and APPC protocols are supported.

Other cataloguing for APPN, LDAP, and APPCLU nodes are not described in this book. For details on these cataloguing options, please refer to the DB2 Command Reference.

Cataloging a TCP/IP Node

When cataloging a TCP/IP node to communicate with a DB2 database server, you must specify a node name after CATALOG TCPIP NODE. This node name will be used in the CATALOG DB command and must be unique in the client node directory.

Getting Connected

```
catalog tcpip node mynode
remote billw.ca.ibm.com
server 5000
```

To specify the remote machine, you can use the host name or IP address as the value for the REMOTE parameter.

The SERVER parameter specifies either the service name or the port number used by the database server. These values are located in the /etc/services file (e.g., on AIX) at the server. This identifies which instance to use at the DB2 server instance.

Once the node has been cataloged, the remote database can be cataloged.

```
catalog db sample
as mysamp
at node mynode
```

 Note: In this chapter, the basic CATALOG command options are presented. There are many more options you can use - for details on these options, please refer to the *DB2 UDB V8.1 Command Reference*.

The database name you use after CATALOG DB must match the name of the database alias at the server. You can specify an alias for the remote database by specifying a different name for the value of the AS parameter. You will then use this alias to connect to the remote database. The node name you use for the AT NODE parameter must match the node name you used in the CATALOG TCPIP NODE command (in this example, MYNODE).

Once the remote database has been cataloged, you can test the connection using the CONNECT statement. For example:

```
connect to mysamp user db2admin using db2admin
```

Cataloging a NetBIOS Node

When cataloging a NetBIOS node to communicate with a DB2 database server, you must specify a node name after CATALOG NETBIOS NODE. This node name will be used in the CATALOG DB command and must be unique in the client node directory.

```
catalog netbios node billw
remote N01FCBE3
adapter 0
```

To specify the remote machine, you can use the server workstation name as the value for the REMOTE parameter. You should check that the machine is available on the network.The ADAPTER parameter specifies the outgoing local logical LAN adapter number.

The workstation name of the client (NNAME) must be defined in the client's DBM configuration file. This is usually done during the installation.

Once the node has been cataloged, the remote database can be cataloged (as shown for the TCP/IP node example).

Cataloging a Named Pipe Node

When cataloging a Named Pipe node to communicate with a DB2 database server, you must specify a node name after CATALOG NPIPE NODE. This node name will be used in the CATALOG DB command and must be unique in the client node directory.

```
catalog npipe node mynode
remote billw
instance db2
```

To specify the remote machine, you use the Computer Name of the database server as the value for the REMOTE parameter. This is specified in the Identification Tab of the Network folder in Windows. You should check that the machine is available on the network.

The INSTANCE parameter specifies the instance on the server where the database resides.

Once the node has been cataloged, the remote database can be cataloged (as shown for the TCP/IP node example).

Getting Connected

Cataloging an APPC Node

When cataloging an APPC node to communicate with a DB2 database server, you must specify a node name after CATALOG APPC NODE. This node name will be used in the CATALOG DB command and must be unique in the client node directory.

```
catalog appc node mynode
remote db2cpic00
security same
```

To specify the remote machine, you use the symbolic destination name used in the CPI-C Side Information profile as the value for the REMOTE parameter. You should check that the machine is available on the network.

The level of security can be specified as SAME, SECURITY, or PROGRAM. For details of these security types, please refer to the *DB2 UDB V8.1 Command Reference.*

Once the node has been cataloged, the remote database can be cataloged (as shown for the TCP/IP node example).

Summary of Configuring Connections

Choosing a client configuration method will depend on the number of database clients, the number of different configurations needed and the network complexity. The following table gives general recommendations on when to use each configuration method.

Table 3–1 *Choosing a Configuration Method*

Environment Considerations	Configuration Method
Large number of clients to configure Clients may have access to different databases	Server Access Profile
Large number of clients to configure Clients will have access to the same databases	Client Access Profile
Large network with many routers and bridges	Known discovery
Simple network Many clients Dynamic environment, new servers added frequently	Search discovery
Using APPC protocol Need advanced options	Manually from CA
Need to be able to redo the setup using scripts	CATALOG NODE/DB

Note: In an LDAP-enabled environment, the directory information about DB2 servers and databases is stored in the LDAP directory. When a new database is created, the database is automatically registered in the LDAP directory. It is not necessary to run the Configuration Assistant to configure LDAP protocol information. However, the one may want to use the CA in the LDAP environment to:

- Manually catalog a database in the LDAP directory.
- Register a database as an ODBC data source.
- Configure CLI/ODBC information.
- Remove a database cataloged in the LDAP directory.

Getting Connected

Binding Utilities

When a remote client wants access to a database server, the database utilities must be bound on the server for the client to use. The database utilities that a remote client must bind to the DB2 server include:

- CLI/ODBC support
- DB2 Command Line Processor
- Data import/export utilities
- REXX Support - If you want to use the REXX SQL interface

If you create a new database on the server, packages for the database utilities must also be created in the system catalog tables. All of the client utility packages are contained in a file called DB2UBIND.LST. Call Level Interface and ODBC packages are grouped together in the DB2CLI.LST file. These packages can be created by executing the BIND command from the client workstation after a connection has been made to the server database.

The BIND command must be run separately for each database that you wish to access. Once a package has been successfully bound to the database, all DB2 clients can access it. If you have different types or versions of clients on your network, you must bind the utilities from each type and version of client.

 Note: Bind files can be different for each client platform and each version of DB2. You have to bind them for each platform you want to use. Every time you install an update to the DB2 product that comes with new bind files, you also have to bind the new files.

Here is an example binding from a Windows client to the DB2CERT database that is on an AIX server. Issue the following commands:

```
connect to db2cert
bind @db2ubind.lst blocking all grant public
```

The output from the BIND command can be sent to a file using the MESSAGES parameter. By default, the information is displayed to the screen.

> **Note:** The symbol @ is used to specify that DB2UBIND.LST is a list of bind files and is not a bind file itself.

When a bind is performed, you should ensure that there are no errors. If errors are encountered, the package will not be created in the database. Common errors include nonexistent database objects used in static SQL.

Note that, the GRANT PUBLIC option of the BIND command was used. This option provides EXECUTE and BIND privileges to all users that can access the database. Also note that there are different BIND command options for DRDA (host) databases, such as DB2 for OS/390. (See the *DB2 UDB V8.1 Command Reference* for details.) The output of a successful BIND command should be similar to this excerpt:

```
LINE    MESSAGES FOR db2ubind.lst
------  ----------------------------------------------------------
        SQL0061W The binder is in progress.

LINE    MESSAGES FOR db2clpnc.bnd
------  ----------------------------------------------------------
        SQL0595W Isolation level "NC" has been escalated to "UR".
                 SQLSTATE=01526

LINE    MESSAGES FOR db2arxnc.bnd
------  ----------------------------------------------------------
        SQL0595W Isolation level "NC" has been escalated to "UR".
                 SQLSTATE=01526

LINE    MESSAGES FOR db2ubind.lst
------  ----------------------------------------------------------
        SQL0091N Binding was ended with "0" errors and "2"
                 warnings.
```

The utilities that are bound include IMPORT, EXPORT, LOAD, CLP, BACKUP, RESTORE, and REORG. The DB2UBIND.LST file contains the list of bind (.BND) files that are required to create the packages for these utilities.

> **Note:** Remember you must have BINDADD authority to create a new package in a database. If the package exists, then BIND privilege for the package is the only requirement needed to update the package.

Getting Connected

Binding Utilities Using the Configuration Assistant

Binding utilities can also be done with the Configuration Assistant. In this example, binding the utilities to a DB2 for OS/390 database will be demonstrated.

To do this, the user performing the bind operations must have SYSCTRL or SYSADM authority or be granted the BINDADD authority or CREATE IN COLLECTION NULLID privileges.

Note: While the Configuration Assistant is convenient to use, it gives you only a subset of the BIND options available from the command line

Start the CA. Select the DB2 for OS/390 database that has been catalogued. Click on the **Bind** button and the Bind Database dialog will pop up.

Fig. 3–32 *Configuration Assistant - Bind option*

Select **Bind**.

Note: Using this interface, you can also bind user application bind files, not just the DB2 utilities.

Fig. 3–33 *Bind Utilities - Connect to DB2 Database*

Select one or more utilities or files from the list:

- CLI/ODBC Support - If you want to use ODBC or CLI applications
- Command Line Processor - If you want to use interactive SQL from the DB2 command line interface
- Data Import/Export Utilities - If you want to import or export data on the DB2 database to or from the client
- REXX Support - If you want to use the REXX SQL interface

To change or review the bind options, click on the **Add** button.

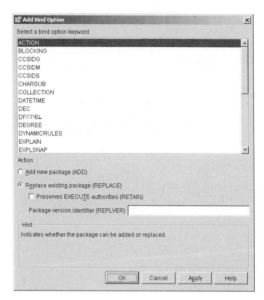

Fig. 3–34 *Add Bind Option*

Click on **OK** to return to the Bind Utilities dialog. Click on **OK** on the Bind Utilities dialog to start the bind process. Details about the bind progress as well as warnings and errors will be displayed in the Bind Results dialog.

Complete the **Enter connect information** panel by filling in a valid user ID and password, then click on **Bind**. The Bind Results panel is displayed.

Summary

This chapter presented an overview of manual and automated configuration methods that can be used to set up a remote database connection using the Configuration Assistant. This tool provides the ability to:

- Configure both local and remote servers.
- Import and export access profiles to exchange configuration information with other systems.
- View and update applicable database manager configuration parameters and DB2 registry variables.

For automated configurations, the discovery service is integrated with the Configuration Assistant and the DB2 Administration Server. To configure a connection to a remote machine, a user would logon to the client machine and run the Configuration Assistant. The Configuration Assistant sends a broadcast signal to all the machines on the network. Any machine that has a DAS installed and configured for discovery will respond to the broadcast signal from the CA by sending back a package that contains all the instance and database information on that machine. The CA then uses the information in this package to configure the client connectivity. Using the discovery method, catalog information for a remote server can be automatically generated in the local database and node directory.

Known Discovery allows you to discover instances and databases on systems that are known to the client machine, and add new systems so that their instances and databases can be discovered. Search Discovery provides all of the facilities of Known Discovery and adds the option to allow your local network to be searched for other DB2 servers. For environments where a large number of clients exists, an alternative is to use a directory service such as LDAP.

The concept of directories within DB2 was discussed as well as how the information contained in the directories is used to access databases, both locally and remotely.

Finally, how to bind the utilities to the server database when the client and server are on different systems was reviewed.

Getting Connected

Controlling Data Access

- ◆ AUTHENTICATING USERS
- ◆ ASSIGNING AUTHORITIES
- ◆ ASSIGNING PRIVILEGES
- ◆ USERS AND GROUPS
- ◆ WINDOWS NT/2000/XP CONSIDERATIONS
- ◆ AUDIT FACILITY

Security is an important consideration whenever data is stored in a relational database management system. In this chapter, we discuss controlling data access using many different methods. Access to data within DB2 is controlled at many levels including instance, database, database object, and application package. The topics of user authentication and authorization are discussed. We configure groups of typical database users such as database administrators, system administrators, transactional processing personnel, and decision support users. Each of these database user types may require different access privileges. We will also discuss the Audit facility. It allows you to monitor security-related events.

Note: DB2 UDB Version 8.1 introduces support for the Windows XP and Windows 2003 operating system. Throughout this chapter, references to Windows Server refers to Windows NT, Windows 2000, Windows XP, and Windows 2003 unless specifically stated.

Security

Access to a Relational Database Management System (RDBMS) needs to be controlled. There are three factors to consider when controlling access to an RDBMS:

- Who will access it? Users may need to be known at the database server.
- What will be accessed? Various objects can be accessed by users and administrators, such as instances, databases, tables, and views.
- How will it be accessed? Which actions is a user permitted to perform on objects, such as creating, updating, or deleting them.

Overview of Security

There are three levels of security that control access to a DB2 system. The first level controls the access to the instance. The second level controls the access to the database. The last level relates to the access of data or data-associated objects within the database.

All access to the instance is managed by a security facility external to DB2. The security facility can be part of the operating system or a separate product. It allows the system to make sure that the user really is who he or she claims to be and may also control access to other objects such as files and programs. Users and groups to which they may belong are normally used by these security facilities.

Access to a database and its objects is controlled at the database level by the database manager. Here, administrative authorities and user privileges are used to control access.

The database administrator must ensure that sensitive information is not accessed by those without a *need to know*. A security plan for DB2 should be developed by defining your objectives and implementing them using the appropriate privileges and authorities.

Authentication

The first step in managing security is to verify the user's identity. This is called *authentication*. Authentication is the operation of verifying whether a user is who he or she claims to be. This is typically accomplished by forcing the user to provide a valid user ID and password. Every time a user tries to connect to a local or remote database, he or she is authenticated. DB2 passes all user IDs and passwords to the operating system or external security facility to be verified.

When configuring the connection between DB2 clients and servers, you can specify where authentication should take place, either at the client or at the server. You can also specify which clients are allowed to authenticate users at the client and which ones at the server. DB2 groups clients into three groups:

Untrusted Clients

These clients run on operating systems that do not have integrated security facilities. They include Windows 95, Windows 98, and Windows Millennium Edition.

 Note: Microsoft has dropped support for Windows 95, so DB2 no longer supports this Operating System as a client or with DB2 Personal Edition.

Trusted Clients

These clients run on operating systems that have integrated security facilities. Trusted clients include Windows NT, Windows 2000, Windows XP, all the supported UNIX operating systems, MVS, OS/390, VM, VSE, and AS/400.

Host Clients

This group is a subset of the trusted client group. They run on one of the following operating systems: MVS, OS/390, VM, VSE, or AS/400.

Supplying a User ID and a Password for Authentication

A user can establish a connection between the client and an instance or between a client and a database. DB2 has two commands that can be used to establish these connections. For an instance connection, the ATTACH command is used. For a database connection, the CONNECT statement is used. With both, the user may or may not supply a user ID and password. If it is not supplied and the authentication type is CLIENT (the authentication type is discussed later), DB2 may use the user ID and password with which the user is logged on at the client for authentication. It may also prompt the user to supply a user ID and password. If the user ID and password is supplied with either ATTACH or CONNECT, DB2 will use them to authenticate the user. The user ID and password specified may differ from those used to log on to the client.

In addition, the user can also request a password change by supplying the user ID, password, new password, and confirmation of the new password. DB2 will authenticate the user first before requesting the password change from the security facility. Connecting to a database in an embedded SQL program does not require a user to supply the confirmation of the new password.

Example 1

A user wants to connect to the database named SAMPLE using his user ID PETE and his password MYPASS. The statement he would use would look like this:

```
CONNECT TO SAMPLE USER PETE USING MYPASS
```

Example 2

The same user as in Example 1 wants to connect to a database named SAMPLE, but he wants to change his password from MYPASS to NEWPWD. The statement he would use is:

```
CONNECT TO SAMPLE USER PETE USING MYPASS
     NEW NEWPWD CONFIRM NEWPWD
```

Example 3

The user specified by the host variable USERID wants to connect to the database named SAMPLE in an embedded SQL program, and he wants to change his password from the one specified by the host variable OLDPWD to NEWPWD. The SQL statement he would use is:

```
EXEC SQL CONNECT TO SAMPLE USER:USERID USING:OLDPWD
     NEW:NEWPWD
```

Controlling Where Authentication Takes Place

The *authentication type* defines where and how authentication will take place, for example, at the client or at the server. It can be specified at each machine taking part in establishing the connection. Authentication types are available depending on the environment. We will be looking at two environments commonly used to describe the authentication types available and what they will achieve.

Environment 1: Client Connected Directly to DB2 UDB Server

This environment consists of only two types of machines: servers and clients. The location where the authentication takes place is determined by the value of authentication parameter in the database manager configuration file at the DB2 server. You can, optionally, specify the authentication type at the DB2 client when cataloging a database; however, it must match the value of authentication parameter at the DB2 server. The exception is when KRB_SERVER_ENCRYPT is specified at the DB2 server. This is explained later.

Authentication types at the DB2 UDB server

At the server, the authentication type is defined in the database manager configuration file. This file is used to configure the instance with which it is associated. Its definition is shared among all the databases in the instance; therefore, if an authentication type is chosen for the instance, all the databases in that instance will use that authentication type, and all users connecting to a database in this instance are authenticated based on this authentication type. The authentication types available at the server are:

- **SERVER**

  This forces all authentication to take place at the server; therefore, a user ID and a password must be supplied when attaching to an instance or connecting to a database. The DB2 software at the client will not encrypt the password before it is sent to the server.

- **SERVER_ENCRYPT**

  This is the same as authentication SERVER in the sense that all authentication will take place at the server. However, all passwords are encrypted by DB2 at the client before they are sent to the server. At the server, it is decrypted and authenticated. It is important to note that if a password change is requested, the new password will not be encrypted before it is sent to the server.

- **CLIENT**

  Using this authentication type gives permission to the client to authenticate users on behalf of the server. It does not guarantee that authentication will take place at the client exclusively. We will discuss this setting in detail in a later section.

- **KERBEROS**

  This authentication type is used when both the DB2 client and server are on operating systems that support the Kerberos security protocol. The Kerberos security protocol performs authentication as a third-party authentication service by using conventional cryptography to create a shared secret key. This key becomes a user's credential and is used to verify the identity of users during all occasions when local or network services are requested. The key eliminates the need to pass the user name and password across the network as clear text. Using the Kerberos security protocol enables the use of a single sign-on to a remote DB2 server.

Controlling Data Access

- **KRB_SERVER_ENCRYPT**

  It specifies that the server accepts KERBEROS authentication or encrypted SERVER authentication schemes. If the client authentication is KERBEROS, the client is authenticated using the Kerberos security system. If the client authentication is not KERBEROS, then the system authentication type is equivalent to SERVER_ENCRYPT.

Notes:

1. The DCE and DCE_SERVER_ENCRYPT options are no longer available in DB2 Version 8.1. Support for DCE security has been removed in DB2 UDB Version 8 as the industry moves towards Kerberos as the mechanism for secure network authentication and single sign-on. Windows 2000 users should consider moving to Kerberos as a replacement for DCE Security prior to migrating to DB2 UDB Version 8.

2. KERBEROS and KRB_SERVER_ENCRYPT were introduced in DB2 UDB Version 7.1. In Version 8, Kerberos authentication types are only supported on clients and servers running Windows 2000/XP/2003.

3. In a future delivery of DB2 UDB Version 8, Kerberos support will be extended to other UNIX and Linux servers and clients.

Authentication types at the client

When cataloging a database for remote access, the authentication type may be specified in the database directory entry. For databases accessed using DB2 Connect: If a value is not specified, SERVER authentication is assumed.

The authentication type is not required. If it is not specified, the client will default to SERVER_ENCRYPT. However, if the server does not support SERVER_ENCRYPT, the client attempts to retry using a value supported by the server. If the server supports multiple authentication types, the client will not choose among them but instead return an error. This is done to ensure that the correct authentication type is used. In this case, the client must catalog the database using a supported authentication type. If an authentication type is specified, then authentication can begin immediately provided that the value specified matches that at the server. If a mismatch is detected, then DB2 attempts to recover. Recovery may result in more communication flows to reconcile the difference or in an error if DB2 cannot recover. In the case of a mismatch, the value at the server is assumed to be correct.

The authentication at the client is specified in the system database directory using the CATALOG DATABASE command; however, you can omit specifying an authentication type at the client. If you specify an authentication type at the client, you must keep it the same as the server. Not doing so may cause the connection to fail. The meanings of these authentication types are the same as the ones used at the server.

At the client the following authentication types are available:

- SERVER
- SERVER_ENCRYPT
- CLIENT
- KERBEROS
- DCE

If CLIENT is used, two other parameters in the database manager configuration file are evaluated to determine where the authentication will take place: at the client or at the server. These parameters are TRUST_ALLCLNTS and TRUST_CLNTAUTH. For more information on these parameters, please read the sections covering these parameters in more detail later in this chapter.

Example 1

In this example, we will show where authentication will take place when the authentication type is specified at the client and the server. We decided that all authentication should take place at the server, so we chose authentication type SERVER at the server and the client. This will allow all user IDs and passwords to be sent to the database server for authentication. All passwords will be sent to the server unencrypted. Fig. 4–1 shows the authentication type setting in the database manager configuration file of the server and the authentication type in the system database directory of the client.

Fig. 4–1 *Example 1 - Authentication SERVER*

Environment 2: Client Connecting to a Host Database via DB2 Connect

In this environment, there are three types of machines taking part in establishing the connection: clients, a DB2 Connect server, and a host database server. DB2 Connect Server will have to be installed on the DB2 Connect server machine. The client connects to the DB2 Connect server using a standard DB2 supported protocol, and then a connection is made from the DB2 Connect server to the host server using a DRDA protocol. In this environment, where authentication takes place is determined by the AUTHENTICATION parameter specified in the CATALOG DATABASE command executed at the DB2 Connect server.

Authentication types at the DB2 Connect server (V7)

We can configure the client and DB2 Connect server so authentication can take place at the client or at the host server. Valid authentication types on the DB2 Connect server include:

- **SERVER**

  Authentication takes place at the host database server.

- **SERVER_ENCRYPT**

  Authentication takes place at the host database server and the password is encrypted.

- **DCE**

  This allows an external security facility to do the authentication on behalf of the host database server. It is currently supported only on hosts running DB2 for MVS version 5.1 and higher.

- **CLIENT**

  This allows a client to authenticate the user on behalf of the host database server.

Notes:

1. Authentication is no longer performed at the DB2 Connect Server in Version 8.1. Authentication can only be done at the client (using CLIENT authentication) or at the server (using SERVER or SERVER_ENCRYPT). The authentication types listed in this section are only for DB2 Connect V7 users.

2. The DCS and DCS_ENCRYPT options are no longer available in DB2 Version 8.1. The SERVER and SERVER_ENCRYPT options need to be used instead. For more details on how applications may be affected, see the DB2 UDB Version 8 Application Development Guide.

Authentication types at the client

On the client, valid authentication types include:

Controlling Data Access

- **SERVER**
- **SERVER_ENCRYPT**
- **KERBEROS**
- **CLIENT**
- **DCE**

Table 4–1 shows where authentication will take place given combinations of the client's and server's authentication type, and also it shows whether the password is encrypted across the network. In this table, N/A means that the password does not flow across the network.

Table 4–1 *Authentication Options Between Client and Host using DB2 Connect*

Client Authentication Type	DB2 Connect Server Authentication Type	Authenticated at	Client to DB2 Connect Server Encryption	DB2 Connect Server to Host Encryption
SERVER	SERVER_ENCRYPT	DB2 Connect Server	No	N/A
SERVER_ENCRYPT	SERVER_ENCRYPT	DB2 Connect Server	Yes	N/A
SERVER_ENCRYPT	SERVER	DB2 Connect Server	Yes	N/A
SERVER	SERVER	DB2 Connect Server	No	N/A
DCE	DCE	DCE Server	Yes	Yes
CLIENT	CLIENT	Client	N/A	N/A

Example 2

In this example, we configured a client to a DB2 Connect server to DB2 OS/390 connection using TCP/IP as the communication protocol between the client and the DB2 Connect server and APPC between the DB2 Connect server and DB2 OS/390. Since APPC encrypts the passwords for us, there is no need to use the SERVER_ENCRYPT option on the DB2 Connect server. We will, however, use the SERVER_ENCRYPT authentication type on the client. This will allow the password to be encrypted at the client before it is passed to the DB2 Connect server. It will be decrypted at the DB2 Connect server and passed securely to the host using APPC as the communications protocol.

Fig. 4–2 *Example 2 - Authentication SERVER_ENCRYPT*

 Note: The encrypted authentication types may not be supported on all DB2 platforms. Please refer to your particular platform to find out if it will support encryption authentication as a client or server.

Table 4–2 shows the valid options for each of the four locations where authentication can be explicitly defined.

Table 4–2 *Authentication Setup and Options*

Specified at	Available Options	How to Specify
Specified at	Available Options	How to Specify
Client	CLIENT SERVER SERVER_ENCRYPT DCE	CATALOG DATABASE *dbname* AT NODE *nodename* AUTHENTICATION xxx

Table 4–2   *Authentication Setup and Options*

Specified at	Available Options	How to Specify
Server	CLIENT SERVER SERVER_ENCRYPT	UPDATE DBM CFG USING AUTHENTICATION xxx
Client (connection to host)	SERVER SERVER_ENCRYPT DCE *(DB2 for OS/390 V5.1 +)*	CATALOG DATABASE *dbname* AT NODE *nodename* AUTHENTICATION xxx
DB2 Connect server	SERVER SERVER_ENCRYPT DCE *(DB2 for OS/390 V5.1+)*	CATALOG DATABASE *dbname* AT NODE *nodename* AUTHENTICATION xxx

TRUST_ALLCLNTS and TRUST_CLNTAUTH Parameters

If an instance is set to authentication type CLIENT, two other database manager configuration parameters determine where the final authentication will actually take place: TRUST_ALLCLNTS and TRUST_CLNTAUTH.

TRUST_ALLCLNTS

DB2 allows the administrator to decide whether to trust all clients. In other words, the administrator can specify whether all clients can authenticate users. If there are clients that do not have a reliable security facility, you probably do not want them to authenticate users. You can configure this by changing the TRUST_ALLCLNTS parameter in the database manager configuration file of the database server. This is an instance level configuration file; so, all databases in the instance will use the same setting.

The TRUST_ALLCLNTS parameter can be set to one of three values:

- **YES**

  Setting the parameter to YES forces all clients, whether or not they are trusted, to authenticate at the client. As Fig. 4–3 shows, all clients will be allowed to authenticate on behalf of the database server if the authentication type is set to CLIENT.

Fig. 4–3 *TRUST_ALLCLNTS set to YES*

• **NO**

If NO is set, all untrusted clients will be authenticated at the server, meaning that a user ID and a password must be provided, and all trusted clients will be authenticated at the client machine. See Fig. 4–4.

Fig. 4–4 *TRUST_ALLCLNTS set to NO*

- **DRDAONLY**

  If DRDAONLY is used, only MVS, OS/390, VM, VSE, and OS/400 clients are allowed to authenticate users on behalf of the database server. Remember, using DRDAONLY does not imply a Windows client or an AIX client even if DRDA is used. See Fig. 4–5.

Fig. 4–5 *TRUST_ALLCLNTS set to DRDAONLY*

TRUST_CLNTAUTH

This is a parameter of the database manager configuration file on a DB2 server. This parameter allows you to specify where the authentication will take place when a user ID and a password are supplied with a CONNECT statement or an ATTACH command. This parameter is only used if the authentication type is CLIENT and affects clients that can authenticate users on behalf of a server; in other words, it affects all clients if TRUST_ALLCLNTS is set to YES, trusted clients and host clients if TRUST_ALLCLNTS is set to NO, and only host clients if TRUST_ALLCLNTS is set to DRDAONLY. Valid values for this parameter are:

- **CLIENT** (default)

The authentication is done at the client; a user ID and a password are not required. If user ID and password are not supplied, the authentication will take place on the client with the user ID and password that the user used to log on to the client.

- **SERVER**

If SERVER is specified, the authentication is done at the server.

Fig. 4–6 shows portions of a trusted client connection configuration with a DB2 server. In this example, the authentication type is CLIENT. TRUST_ALLCLNTS is set to NO. This will allow only trusted clients to authenticate users on behalf of the DB2 server. The TRUST_CI NTAUTH is set to SERVER. Therefore, if a uscr ID and a password are supplied with a CONNECT statement, they will be sent to the server for authentication. If user ID and password are not supplied, the authentication will take place on the client based on the user ID and password that the user used to log on to the client.

Fig. 4–6 *Trust_clntauth set to SERVER*

Cataloging Databases

DB2 has multiple directories that are used to access databases. These directories allow DB2 to find databases known to it whether they are on the local system or a remote system. The system database directory contains a list and pointer to where all the known databases can be found. The node directory contains information relating to how and where remote systems or instances can be found. To put an entry into any of these directories, the CATALOG command is used. To remove an entry, the UNCATALOG command is used.

When setting up the database server, you can choose who should be able to catalog and uncatalog databases. This can be done in the database manager configuration file by setting the CATALOG_NOAUTH parameter. The two available values are YES and NO. NO is the default value for a DB2 server with local and remote clients and prevents users without SYSADM or SYSCTRL authority from using the CATALOG or UNCATALOG commands. Setting it to YES allows other users to use these commands. YES is the default value for a DB2 client, a Satellite database server with local clients, and a DB2 server with local clients.

Setting the Authentication Type

The authentication type is specified in the database manager configuration file that is shared among all the databases contained in the instance. Therefore, all the databases in an instance will have the same authentication type. You can check the authentication type associated with the current instance with the following command:

```
GET DATABASE MANAGER CONFIGURATION
```

The current authentication type will be seen next to the AUTHENTICATION parameter in the database manager configuration file. The default setting for AUTHENTICATION is SERVER. To change it, issue the following command:

```
UPDATE DBM CFG USING AUTHENTICATION CLIENT
```

Notice that we have used a shorthand method of the command within the CLP. Database Manager can be abbreviated to DBM, and CONFIGURATION can be abbreviated to CFG.

 Note: The changes to the instance will take effect when the instance is stopped and restarted.

You must be a member of the SYSADM group for the instance (discussed later) to make changes to the parameters in the database manager configuration file.

Controlling Data Access

The client authentication type of a connection is stored in the system database directory. This is a list of all the databases known to the system. To look at it, use the following command:

```
LIST DATABASE DIRECTORY
```

All the remotely cataloged databases will show the authentication type with which the client will attempt to connect to the server. To change the authentication type for a connection, the database needs to be uncataloged from the database directory and recataloged with the new authentication type. Here is a sample of the catalog command; it catalogs a remote database named SAMPLE at a node named MYNODE using authentication SERVER.

```
CATALOG DATABASE sample AT NODE mynode AUTHENTICATION
SERVER
```

Authorities and Privileges

After successful authentication, access to database objects is controlled by DB2 itself. Access to these objects is controlled by associating *privileges* or *authorities* to users. Authorities are normally required for maintaining databases and instances. They are a high level set of user's rights that allow users to do things such as backup or create databases. Privileges are granted to users to work with objects in the database, such as tables. For example, a user may have SELECT and UPDATE privileges on a table.

Authorities

As mentioned above, authorities are used to control access to objects within an instance or for administrative tasks.

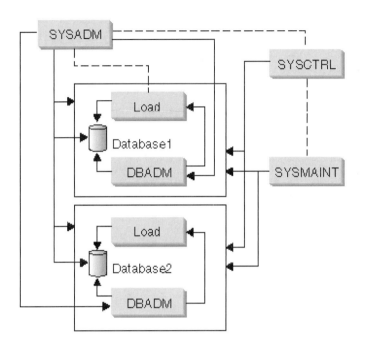

Fig. 4–7 *Authorities*

There are five authorities in DB2:

- SYSADM - System Administration Authority
- SYSCTRL - System Control Authority
- SYSMAINT - System Maintenance Authority
- LOAD - Load Table Authority
- DBADM - Database Administration Authority

Authorities in DB2 provide a hierarchy for administration capabilities as shown in Fig. 4–7. Authorities are assigned to a group of users. Exceptions to this rule include the DBADM and LOAD authority since they can be granted to a user or a group. If a certain authority is given to a group, each member of that group has the same DB2 authority unless they have had that authority explicitly revoked.

 Note: The LOAD authority enable users to load data into DB2 without requiring them to have DBA capabilities.

Controlling Data Access

SYSADM Authority

At the top of this hierarchy is the DB2 System Administrator or SYSADM authority. Any member of the SYSADM group is able to perform any of the DB2 administration operations as well as to access all database objects. SYSADM group members are the only users that are allowed to configure the DB2 instance.

On UNIX systems, the SYSADM group is set to the primary group of the instance owner by default.

On a Windows system, a member of the local administrator group has to install DB2 at which time the default instance named DB2 will be created. The default SYSADM authority will be granted to all the local administrators on the machine where DB2 is installed.

To give a group SYSADM authority, change the SYSADM_GROUP parameter in the database manager configuration file to include the name of the group.

SYSCTRL Authority

System control (SYSCTRL) authority provides the ability to perform most administration tasks. A member of the SYSCTRL user group does not have authority to access database objects or modify the instance configuration file (DBM configuration). SYSCTRL offers almost complete control of database objects defined in the DB2 instance but cannot access user data directly unless explicitly granted the privilege to do so. A user with this authority or higher can perform the following functions and all the functions of SYSMAINT authority:

- Create or drop a database
- Force applications
- Restore to a new database
- Create, drop, or alter a table space

SYSMAINT Authority

SYSMAINT, or System Maintenance authority, allows the execution of maintenance activities but does not allow access to user data. Only users with this level of authority or higher (SYSADM or SYSCTRL) can perform the following tasks:

- Update database configuration files
- Back up databases and table spaces
- Restore to an existing database
- Perform roll forward recovery
- Restore table spaces
- Start and stop the DB2 instance
- Run the database monitor
- Start and stop traces
- Query the state of a table space
- Update log history files
- Quiesce a table space
- Reorganize a table
- Execute the RUNSTATS utility

LOAD Authority

Users granted LOAD authority can run the LOAD utility without the need for SYSADM or DBADM authority. This allows users to perform more DB2 functions and gives database administrators more granular control over the administration of their databases. Users with LOAD authority can perform the following tasks:

- If they have INSERT privilege on a table, they can use the LOAD command or the AutoLoader utility to load data into a table.
- If they have INSERT privilege on a table, they can LOAD RESTART or LOAD TERMINATE if the previous load operation is a load to insert data.
- If the previous load operation was a LOAD REPLACE, the DELETE privilege must also have been granted to that user before the user can LOAD RESTART or LOAD TERMINATE.
- If exception tables are used as part of a LOAD, the user must have INSERT privilege on the exception tables.
- The user with LOAD authority can perform QUIESCE TABLESPACES FOR TABLE, RUNSTATS, and LIST TABLESPACES commands.

DBADM Authority

At the database level, there is the DBADM authority. A DBADM can do any administrative task on the database, such as loading data, creating objects within the database, and monitoring database activity. DBADM has complete authority over the database and may query, drop, or create any table and set privileges for users within the database. The creator of a database will automatically have DBADM authority for the new database. Other users may be granted DBADM authority by a SYSADM user with the GRANT statement. It is possible to hold DBADM authority for multiple databases.

Controlling Data Access

Table 4–3 shows some of the valid tasks for the various DB2 privilege levels. The DBADM column has * beside entries that are related to LOAD authority.

Table 4–3 *Database Authorities and Valid Tasks*

Function	SYSADM	SYSCTRL	SYSMAINT	DBADM
UPDATE DBM CFG	YES			
GRANT/REVOKE DBADM	YES			
ESTABLISH/CHANGE SYSCTRL	YES			
ESTABLISH/CHANGE SYSMAINT	YES			
FORCE USERS	YES	YES		
CREATE/DROP DATABASE	YES	YES		
RESTORE TO NEW DATABASE	YES	YES		
UPDATE DB CFG	YES	YES	YES	
BACKUP DATABASE/TABLE SPACE	YES	YES	YES	
RESTORE TO EXISTING DATABASE	YES	YES	YES	
PERFORM ROLL FORWARD RECOVERY	YES	YES	YES	
START/STOP INSTANCE	YES	YES	YES	
RESTORE TABLE SPACE	YES	YES	YES	
RUN TRACE	YES	YES	YES .	
OBTAIN MONITOR SNAPSHOTS	YES	YES	YES	
QUERY TABLE SPACE STATE	YES	YES	YES	YES*
PRUNE LOG HISTORY FILES	YES	YES	YES	YES
QUIESCE TABLE SPACE	YES	YES	YES	YES*
LOAD TABLES	YES			YES*
SET/UNSET CHECK PENDING STATUS	YES			YES
CREATE/DROP EVENT MONITORS	YES			YES

Security Considerations

The SYSADM, SYSCTRL, and SYSMAINT authorities are associated with groups and are specified at the instance level. As such, they must be set or changed in the database manager configuration file. The parameters are SYSADM_GROUP, SYSCTRL_GROUP, and SYSMAINT_GROUP. There are no default values for them.

A member of the system administration group (SYSADM) can either set or modify these authorities for the instance. For example, to change the SYSCTRL group to DB2CNTRL, the following commands would be issued.

```
UPDATE DATABASE MANAGER CONFIGURATION USING
SYSCTRL_GROUP db2cntrl
db2stop
db2start
```

The UPDATE DATABASE MANAGER CONFIGURATION command (or UPDATE DBM CFG) requires the USING option with the parameter to be updated followed by the new value. For any changes to take effect, the instance must be stopped and restarted. For the instance to be successfully stopped, all database connections must be released and attachments terminated. The new values in the DBM configuration file are as follows:

```
SYSADM group name      (SYSADM_GROUP)   =
SYSCTRL group name     (SYSCTRL_GROUP)  = db2cntrl
SYSMAINT group name    (SYSMAINT_GROUP) =
```

The user group DB2CNTRL should match an existing operating system group. DB2 does not verify that the operating system group exists during the modification of the DBM configuration file. Therefore, the database administrator must ensure that the operating system user IDs and groups are set properly.

The group authorities are also related to the security mechanisms of the operating system. For example, a UNIX user who is placed in the DB2CNTRL group has SYSCTRL authority over DB2. But, the same user can also have special access to UNIX resources that are unrelated to DB2.

Note: The creation of users and group assignments should be strictly controlled on any DB2 server.

Privileges

A privilege is the right to create or access a database object. DB2 authorities and privileges on database objects are hierarchical in nature. Fig. 4–8 shows the hierarchy of authorities and privileges within DB2.

Privileges are stored in the catalog. There are three types of privileges: *Ownership*, *Individual*, and *Implicit*.

1. Ownership or CONTROL privileges - For most objects, the user who creates an object has full access to that object. CONTROL privilege is automatically granted to the creator of an object. There are some database objects, such as views, that are exceptions to this rule.

    Having CONTROL privilege is like having ownership of the object. You have the right to access an object, give access to others, and give others permission to grant privileges on the object. Privileges are controlled by users with ownership or administrative authority. These users can grant or revoke privileges using GRANT or REVOKE SQL statements.

2. Individual privileges - These are privileges that allow you to perform a specific function, sometimes on a specific object. These privileges include SELECT, DELETE, INSERT, and UPDATE.

3. Implicit privileges - An implicit privilege is one that is granted to a user automatically when that user is explicitly granted certain higher level privileges. These privileges are not revoked when the higher level privileges are explicitly revoked.

    In addition, an implicit privilege can also be associated with a package. As an example, when a user executes a package that involves other privileges, they obtain those privileges while executing the package. The do not necessarily require explicit privilege on the data objects accessed within the package. These privileges can also be called *indirect* privileges.

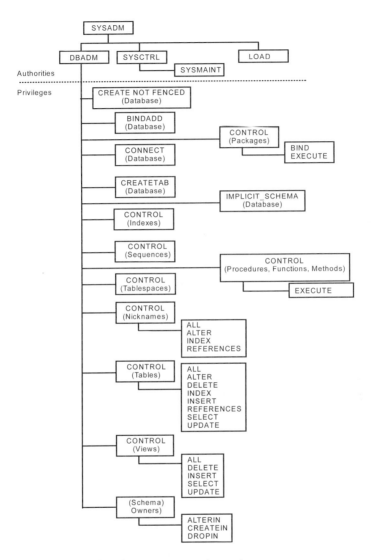

Fig. 4–8 *Hierarchy of authorizations and privileges*

Database Privileges

Database privileges involve actions on a database as a whole and only users with SYSADM or DBADM authority can grant and revoke these privileges to and from other users:

- CONNECT allows a user to access the database
- BINDADD allows a user to create new packages in the database
- CREATETAB allows a user to create new tables in the database
- CREATE_NOT_FENCED allows a user to create a user-defined function (UDF) or procedure that is "not fenced". UDFs or procedures that are "not fenced" must be extremely well tested because the database manager does not protect its storage or control blocks from these UDFs or procedures. As a result, a poorly written and tested UDF or procedure that is allowed to run "not fenced" can cause serious problems for your system!
- IMPLICIT_SCHEMA allows any user to create a schema implicitly by creating an object using a CREATE statement with a schema name that does not already exist. SYSIBM becomes the owner of the implicitly created schema and PUBLIC is given the privilege to create objects in this schema.
- LOAD allows a user to load data into a table.
- QUIESCE_CONNECT allows a user to access the database while it is quiesced.
- CREATE_EXTERNAL_ROUTINE allows a user to create a procedure for use by applications and other users of the database.

Notes:

1. The QUIESCE_CONNECT and CREATE_EXTERNAL_ROUTINE options are new to DB2 Version 8.1. QUIESCE_CONNECT gives the user the ability to connect to a database that is in a quiesced state. A database may be placed into a quiesced state to allow for stand-alone maintenance, or to allow an individual user or group of users to have exclusive use of the database.

2. The CREATE_EXTERNAL_ROUTINE privilege allows a user to create UDFs that run within the address space of the database. Creating UDFs that run in this mode can result in much faster performance due to reduced calling overhead between the database and the routine. However, care must be taken in developing these types of UDFs since any incorrect memory allocations could affect the operation of the database.

Database Object Privileges

For each DB2 object, a specific authority or privilege is required to create it, and a specific authority or privilege is needed to have control over it. The following list describes the privileges on various objects within the database.

- **Database authorities** - These include the ability to create and access a database.

Any creator of a database automatically receives DBADM authority. The DBADM can issue any SQL statement against the database. The DBADM can grant connect privilege, the ability to create tables or new packages in the database, the ability to create a schema implicitly, and the ability to create unfenced stored procedures or user-defined functions.

The IMPLICIT_SCHEMA privilege allows the user to create an object without specifying the schema name. The object will be assigned a schema that is the authorization ID of the user. This *implicitly created* schema is owned by SYSIBM. The group PUBLIC (anyone who can connect to the database) is given the privilege to create objects in the schema.

> **Note:** When a database is created, certain privileges are automatically granted to the group PUBLIC. If you want to control who can do what on the database, a DBADM or SYSADM user must revoke these privileges from PUBLIC (these include CREATETAB and BINDADD).

- **Schema privileges** - These include the permissions to create, alter, or drop objects within schemas. The owner of the schema has all these permissions and the ability to grant them to others. The objects that belong to schemas include tables, views, indexes, packages, user-defined data types, user-defined functions, triggers, stored procedures, and aliases.

- **Table privileges** - CONTROL privilege on a table or view can only be granted by a user who has SYSADM or DBADM authority. (However, the creator of the table implicitly gets CONTROL privilege on that table.) Having CONTROL privilege on a table allows you to add columns, create a primary key, delete, retrieve, update, or insert rows, create indexes, create referential constraints, grant these privileges to others, use the EXPORT utility, and perform maintenance such as reorganizing tables or updating statistics on the table.

  The UPDATE *on column* privilege allows users to modify only the specified columns of the table or view. In a similar way, the REFERENCE *on column* privilege allows the creation of foreign keys only on the stated columns.

- **View privileges** - To create a view, you must be able to issue the SQL SELECT statement or have CONTROL privilege on every table or view that is referenced. You need to have CONTROL privilege on the view to grant delete, insert, select, and update privileges on the view unless the view is defined as a read-only view. The privileges required must be explicitly held by the user or be granted to PUBLIC. (Alternately, holding the WITH GRANT OPTION for each additional privilege will also suffice.)

Controlling Data Access

- **Index privileges** - The user that creates the index receives CONTROL privileges on the index. This means that the user can drop the index. The table-level index privilege allows a user to create a new index on the table.

- **Procedures, Functions, and Methods privileges** - Execute privileges involve actions on all types of routines such as functions, procedures, and methods within a database. Once having execute privilege, a user can then invoke that routine, create a function that is sourced from that routine (applies to functions only), and to reference the routine in any DDL statement such as CREATE VIEW, CREATE TRIGGER; or, when defining a constraint.

  The user who defines the externally stored procedure, function, or method receives EXECUTE WITH GRANT privilege.

- **Sequence privileges** - The creator of a sequence automatically receives the USAGE privilege. The USAGE privilege is needed to use NEXTVAL and PREVVAL expressions for the sequence. To allow other users to use the NEXTVAL and PREVVAL expressions, sequence privileges must be granted to PUBLIC. This allows all users to use the expressions with the specified sequence.

- **Nickname privileges** - Nicknames refer to tables in a federated DB2 system. A DB2 federated system is a special type of distributed database management system (DBMS). The power of a DB2 federated system is in its ability to:

  1. Join data from local tables and remote data sources, as if all the data is local.

  2. Take advantage of the data source processing strengths, by sending distributed requests to the data sources for processing.

  3. Compensate for SQL limitations at the data source by processing parts of a distributed request at the federated server.

  With a federated system you can send distributed requests to multiple data sources within a single SQL statement. For example, you can join data that is located in a DB2 Universal Database table, an Oracle table, and a Sybase view in a single SQL statement.

  To define the data sources (tables) available to a federated application, the tables must first be defined using Nicknames. For more information on Federated Databases, see the *DB2 UDB V8.1 Administration Guide* and the *DB2 Universal Database Federated Systems Guide*.

- **Package privileges** - The creator of a package automatically receives CONTROL privilege on the package. That user can grant other users the ability to rebind or execute the package. However, the person that rebinds a package must have the necessary privileges to access the objects referenced in the embedded static SQL statements. The required privileges must be obtained before doing the rebind.

CONTROL privilege on a package also allows you to drop the package. Any user who has EXECUTE privilege on the package can execute the package without possessing the required privileges.

> **Note:** To bind a new package to the database, you must have BINDADD database authority or you must be in the SYSADM group or be a DBADM.

Two SQL statements used to administer privileges:

- The GRANT statement grants privileges.
- The REVOKE statement revokes privileges.

For example, suppose you want user Andrew to be able to drop the CANDIDATE table in the DB2CERT database. The statement would be as follows:

```
GRANT CONTROL ON TABLE candidate TO Andrew
```

Unless Andrew is a SYSADM or DBADM, he cannot grant another user the CONTROL privilege on the CANDIDATE table. The privileges and authorities combine to control the access to the database objects.

To grant privileges on a database object, a user must have SYSADM authority, DBADM authority, CONTROL privilege, or a privilege WITH GRANT OPTION on that object. A user can grant privileges only on existing database objects. A user must have SYSADM or DBADM authority to grant CONTROL privilege. To grant DBADM authority, a user must have SYSADM authority. Table 4–4 summarizes some of the privileges required for database objects within DB2 to perform the following:

- Create a resource (database, schema, table, view, index, or package)
- Control a resource

Controlling Data Access

Table 4–4 *Privileges and Authorities Related to Database Objects*

Object	Authority/Privilege Needed to Create	Authority/Privilege Needed to Control	Other Privileges on Object
DATABASE	SYSADM SYSCTRL	DBADM	CONNECT BINDADD CREATETAB CREATE_NOT_FEN CED IMPLICIT_SCHEMA CONNECT
SCHEMA	DBADM or IMPLICIT_SCHEMA	Ownership or IMPLICIT_SCHEMA	CREATEIN ALTERIN DROPIN
NICKNAME	SYSADM DBADM IMPLICIT_SCHEMA	CONTROL	NONE
PACKAGE	BINDADD	CONTROL	BIND EXECUTE
TABLE or VIEW	CREATETAB (Table) CONTROL or SELECT (View)	CONTROL	SELECT (Table/ View) INSERT (Table/ View) DELETE (Table/ View) UPDATE (Table/ View) ALTER (Table) INDEX (Table) REFERENCES (Table)
INDEX	INDEX	CONTROL	NONE
ALIAS	If the schema differs from current authid, requires DBADM or IMPLICIT_SCHEMA. If schema is the same as an existing schema, may need CREATEIN privilege.	CONTROL	NONE
DISTINCT TYPE (UDT)	If the schema differs from current authid, requires DBADM or IMPLICIT_SCHEMA. If the schema is the same as an existing schema, may need CREATEIN privilege.	CONTROL	NONE

Table 4–4 *Privileges and Authorities Related to Database Objects (Continued)*

Object	Authority/Privilege Needed to Create	Authority/Privilege Needed to Control	Other Privileges on Object
USER DEFINED FUNCTION (UDF)	If the schema differs from current authid, requires DBADM or IMPLICIT_SCHEMA. If the schema is the same as an existing schema, may require CREATIN privilege.	CONTROL	NONE
SEQUENCE	DBADM, SYSADM or CREATEIN privilege for the implicitly or explicitly specified schema.	DBADM, SYSADM, Ownership or IMPLICIT_SCHEMA	NONE

Application Development Privileges

There are certain privileges that apply only to application developers. Each step of the development process requires certain privileges on database objects. Let us examine the application development steps and the required privileges.

Table 4–5 summarizes the authorities and privileges needed for various tasks.

Table 4–5 *Privileges Required for Application Development*

Action	Privileges Required
Precompile to bindfile	CONNECT on database
Create a new package	CONNECT on database BINDADD on database Privileges needed to execute each static SQL statement explicitly or to PUBLIC
Modify an existing package	CONNECT on database BIND on package Privileges needed to execute each static SQL statement explicitly or to PUBLIC
Re-create an existing package	CONNECT on database BIND on package
Execute a package	CONNECT on database EXECUTE on package
Drop a package	CONNECT on database CONTROL on package or creator of package

Controlling Data Access

An embedded SQL program must have the SQL statements prepared and bound as a package in the DB2 database. The preparation step for a program with static embedded SQL does not require any privileges for the database objects. When the required privileges on objects are not held or objects do not exist, warning messages are generated. The objects must exist during the bind phase as the existence and privileges of the objects are verified.

If the program contains dynamic embedded SQL statements, the statements are prepared and executed at run time.

To create a new package for any embedded SQL application, you need CONNECT privilege and BINDADD authority on the database. You need BIND privilege on the package to update its contents. To execute a package, you need EXECUTE privilege on the package.

Let us look at a sample scenario where all the privileges granted to PUBLIC, except CONNECT, were removed and determine the necessary authorities and privileges on the database objects, according to the function that a user will be performing. In our scenario, we have a database where one of the applications, APP1, is used to manipulate names and addresses.

User George wants to execute a program called app1. He also wants to be able to have his own table called George.personal to store other data. Therefore, we grant George EXECUTE privilege for the app1 package. We also grant George the CONTROL privilege for the George.personal table. We could have given him CREATETAB authority for the database and let him create the table, but this would allow him the ability to create many tables. Remember, the app1 package must exist in the database before we can grant George EXECUTE privilege.

Katrina is the application developer who is writing the app1 program. She needs to have SELECT, INSERT, UPDATE, and DELETE access to the various tables in the database. We need to GRANT the required privileges to Katrina. She needs to be able to add the new package in the database and execute the application to test it; therefore, we will grant her BINDADD authority.

Bill needs to be able to load data using the LOAD utility into various tables, but he will never execute the application. He needs DBADM authority. He could also be given SYSADM authority, but, for security reasons, we have only one user with SYSADM authority.

Another option for Bill is to grant him LOAD authority on the database, rather than DBADM authority. In DB2, we can use the LOAD authority to allow him to run the LOAD utility against this table.

LOAD authority enables Bill to use the LOAD utility in this database. SYSADM and DBADM also have this authority by default. However, if a user only has LOAD authority (not SYSADM or DBADM), the user is also required to have table-level privileges.

Shirley needs to be able to create a database to store personal information. Shirley is granted SYSADM authority for the DB2 instance. Therefore, Shirley can create the database and modify the DBM configuration file for the instance.

 Note: SYSADM, SYSCTRL, and SYSMAINT are not granted in the same way as DBADM. They must be specified in the database manager configuration file.

Fig. 4–9 to depicts the authorities and privileges for the scenario we have just discussed.

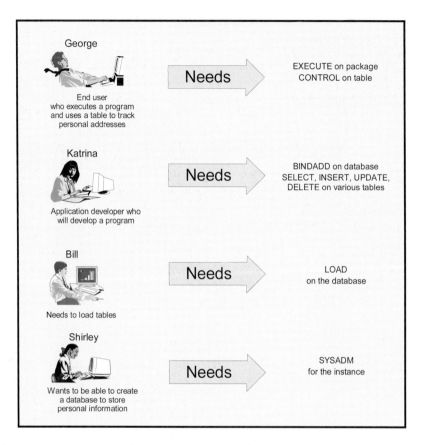

Fig. 4–9 *Authority and privilege scenario*

Privileges of Groups

In addition to granting privileges to users of the database, one could grant privileges to groups. These group definitions are not done in DB2 but in the operating system or external security facility (using DCE). A group consists of one or more users as defined in the security system. Every member of the group will have the same access privileges and authorities as were granted to the group they belong to unless they have been granted higher privileges individually or have had privileges individually revoked.

In addition to those groups, DB2 also has one special group definition: the PUBLIC group. This group consists of all users, and CONNECT privilege is granted automatically to the PUBLIC group. Granting a privilege to PUBLIC provides all users with the privilege. There are certain privileges granted to PUBLIC by default. For example, all have SELECT privilege on the catalog tables. You may decide to remove the SELECT privilege using the REVOKE statement after creating the database.

Explicit and Implicit Privileges and Authorities

Privileges and authorities within DB2 can be obtained either implicitly or explicitly. As a database administrator, you should be aware of the ways that users can obtain access to objects in your databases. This section examines the various ways that privileges and authorities can be obtained or revoked.

If a user who has SYSADM or SYSCTRL authority creates a database, the user is implicitly granted DBADM authority on that database. If that user has SYSADM or SYSCTRL authority removed, they maintain their DBADM authority on each database they created. Removing DBADM authority must be done explicitly for each database using the REVOKE statement.

When a user is granted DBADM authority on a database, the user is also implicitly granted CONNECT, CREATETAB, BINDADD, IMPLICIT_SCHEMA, and CREATE_NOT_FENCED privileges. If DBADM authority is later revoked, the implicitly granted privileges remain unless they are explicitly revoked.

When a user is granted CONTROL privilege on a table, the user is implicitly granted all of the other table privileges with the capability to allow others access to it. If the CONTROL privilege is removed, the implicitly granted privileges remain unless they are explicitly revoked. All remaining privileges for the table can be explicitly removed using the REVOKE ALL statement.

```
REVOKE ALL ON tablename FROM username/groupname
```

SYSADM or DBADM authority or CONTROL privilege on the table or view is required to revoke a privilege that was granted through the use of the WITH GRANT option. Note that, if Bill is granted privileges and the WITH GRANT option is specified, Bill can, subsequently, grant privileges to other users. If Bill has privileges revoked, the privileges granted by Bill are unaffected. In other words, there is no cascade effect when using the WITH GRANT option.

Determining Privileges and Authorities on a Database

Information about authorities and privileges is maintained in the following catalog views:

Controlling Data Access

- `SYSCAT.DBAUTH` - database authorities
- `SYSCAT.TABAUTH` - table and view privileges
- `SYSCAT.PACKAGEAUTH` - package privileges
- `SYSCAT.INDEXAUTH` - index privileges
- `SYSCAT.SCHEMAAUTH` - schema privileges

To examine the groups specified for `SYSADM`, `SYSCTRL`, and `SYSMAINT`, view the database manager (DBM) configuration file. For all other authorities and privileges, examine the catalog views listed in this section to determine the users and groups that have access rights. You may also use the DB2 Control Center to easily view and change the privileges and authorities granted to users and groups.

Group and User Support (UNIX)

Some operating systems allow the same name for a user and a group. This can cause confusion for authorization and privilege checking within DB2.

Note: Windows/NT/2000/XP/2003 do not permit a group and a user to have the same name.

Let us look at how DB2 handles the different scenarios regarding groups and users. Suppose we have a user named `AUSTIN`. We want to enable this user the ability to perform a `SELECT` on the `CANDIDATE` table:

```
GRANT SELECT ON candidate TO austin
GRANT SELECT ON candidate TO USER austin
```

Both of these statements grant `SELECT` privilege on the `CANDIDATE` table to the user named `AUSTIN`. Suppose we have a group named `AUSTIN`:

```
GRANT SELECT ON candidate TO austin
GRANT SELECT ON candidate TO GROUP austin
```

If there is no user named `AUSTIN` defined in the operating system, the members of the group named `AUSTIN` will be given the `SELECT` privilege. It is best to specify if the name is an individual user or a group. Therefore, the following statements specify that both the group and the user should be given `SELECT` privilege:

```
GRANT SELECT ON candidate TO USER austin
GRANT SELECT ON candidate TO GROUP austin
```

This will grant both user AUSTIN and group AUSTIN the SELECT privilege on the CANDIDATE table. The GRANT and REVOKE statements can include either the USER or GROUP keyword to indicate the level of privilege that should be provided or removed.

Windows NT/2000/XP/2003 Considerations

Windows implements user and group management in a slightly different manner than other operating systems. For example, a Windows user can belong to a group, which, in turn, belongs to another group. DB2 for Windows has added functionality to exploit and use this unique implementation of user and group management in Windows Servers. In this section, we will briefly discuss the basic concepts of user management as implemented by DB2 for Windows and how DB2 exploits it.

When using Windows, one can group users and resources in two ways: workgroups and domains.

Workgroups

A *workgroup* is a collection of Windows workstations. It can contain computers running various operating systems. A workgroup is identified by a unique name shared among all the workstations in the workgroup. Each workstation manages and maintains its own set of users and/or resources. Resources, such as shared disks and printers, can be made available to all workstations in the workgroup. A user remotely accessing such a resource will be authenticated on the resource server; that is, the user will have to have a user ID on the resource server and the right to work with the resource being accessed. The definition of the user and the rights is local to the resource server and is not shared among the workstations in the workgroup.

Domains

A Windows *domain* (hereafter referred to as a domain) is a collection of client workstations and server computers identified by a unique name that share a single security permissions (domain) database.

In every Windows domain, there must be one Primary Domain Controller (PDC). The PDC is a server running Windows Server. It holds the Security Access Manager (SAM) database (not a DB2 database) used to store information about all the users in the domain, their passwords, groups, and logon scripts.

Each Windows domain may also have one or more Backup Domain Controllers (BDCs). These BDCs store an copy of the SAM database located on the PDC. All changes to the PDCs SAM database are broadcast to the BDCs at configurable time intervals, thus keeping all the domain controllers synchronized.

Finally, the domain may also consist of multiple workstations running an assortment of operating systems, such as Windows 98/Me, Window NT Server, Windows NT Workstation, Windows 2000 (all versions) and Windows XP (all versions).

Users

Users can be defined as part of the domain (domain users) or as a local user on a workstation or server in the domain. If a domain user logs on to the domain, the user ID and password will be verified by any one of the domain controllers, PDC, or BDCs.

Local users on workstations in the domain do not have access to resources within the domain.

Local users on the domain controller have access to all the resources in the domain. Their user IDs are not valid outside the bounds of the domain. These should not be confused with users defined locally to workstations within the domain.

Domain users are defined on the domain controller. These users have access to all the resources in the domain as do local users defined on domain controllers. The difference lies in that domain users might have access to resources outside the bounds of the domain. This is true when a trust relationship is defined between two domains.

Groups

A group is a collection of users and can give access to resources. If a user belongs to a group and the group has been given access to a resource, the user will also have access to that resource. There are two types of groups to which users can belong: *local groups* and *global groups*.

Global groups are defined on the domain controller. These groups can be granted access to resources in their domain as well as resources at trusting domains. Only domain users may belong to a global group.

Local groups are defined on domain controllers or on workstations, and like local users defined on domain controllers, have access to the resources within the domain. They cannot be granted access to resources outside their domain. The following can be made part of a local group:

1. Local users
2. Domain users
3. Global groups from the domain
4. Any domain users belonging to a trusted domain
5. Any global groups belonging to a trusted domain

Local groups not defined on domain controllers can only be granted access to resources on the machine they are defined on. They may include any of the following:

1. Local users
2. Domain users
3. Global groups
4. Any domain user belonging to a trusted domain
5. Any global group belonging to a trusted domain

Trusted and Trusting Domains

In a large environment, users from multiple domains may need access to common data. *Trust relationships* are defined to allow users to log on to one domain yet be able to access resources in various trusting domains.

To be able to access these resources, a trust relationship needs to be set up between the two domains. If a user defined in domain A needs to have access to a resource in domain B, domain B needs to trust domain A to authenticate the user. Once this relationship is set up, domain A is referred to as the trusted domain, and domain B is referred to as the trusting domain. See Fig. 4–10.

Fig. 4–10 *Windows Server trusted domain*

If there is a user in domain B that wants to access a resource in domain A, a second relationship needs to be set up in which domain A trusts domain B.

Trusts relationships are not transitive. For example, if domain C trusts domain B and domain B trusts domain A, domain C does *NOT* implicitly trust domain A. If there is a requirement for domain C to trust domain A, an explicit trust relationship needs to be defined.

Models of Domain Trust

Trust relationships between domains lend themselves to very complex domain architectures. The following are some commonly used domain architectures:

The single domain model

In the *single domain model*, there is only one domain; all servers and workstations belong to this domain as shown in Fig. 4–11.

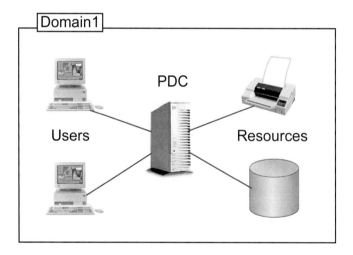

Fig. 4–11 *Single domain model*

The master domain model

The *master domain model* centralizes all the users in one domain, whereas most of the resources belong to various other domains. This model lends itself to centralized user management, where the resources are managed within their particular domains. See Fig. 4–12.

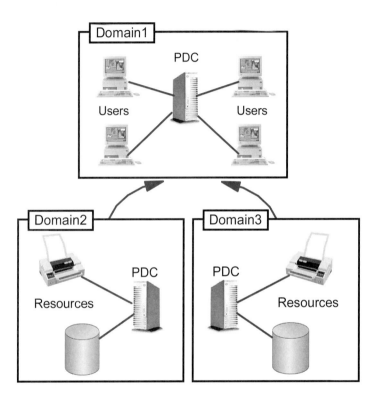

Fig. 4–12 *Master domain model*

The multiple master domain model

In the *multiple master domain model*, users are spread across multiple domains and resources are spread across multiple domains. Trust relationships are established between all user domains in both directions and between each resource domain and each master domain (one way). See Fig. 4–13.

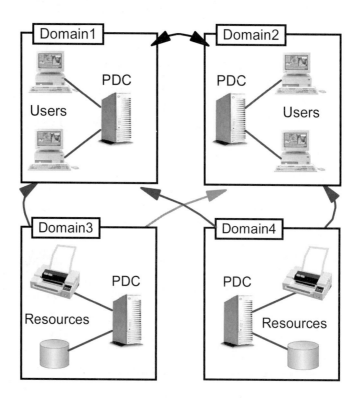

Fig. 4–13 *Multiple master domain model*

The complete trust model

If all the domains in the environment have both users and resources, a two-way trust relationship is set up between each and every domain. This model is called the *complete trust model*. See Fig. 4–14.

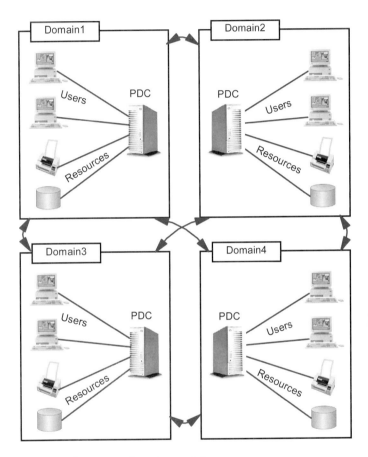

Fig. 4–14 *Complete trust domain model*

DB2 UDB for Windows Authentication and Security

As mentioned before, DB2 for Windows exploits the native Windows security system to assist in the management of the RDBMS security. In this section, we will be discussing how this is done.

When a user attempts to connect to a DB2 database on Windows (assume authentication type is server), DB2 passes the user ID and password to Windows for authentication. DB2 uses Windows to attempt to authenticate the user in the following order of user information:

1. Local SAM
2. Domain controller
3. Trusted domain controllers

Local SAM, in this case, refers to the SAM of a client, a server, or a gateway depending on which authentication type is specified.

If the authentication type is SERVER, the DB2 server attempts to authenticate the user at the server machine. If the user is not defined in the server machine's SAM, the authentication will be attempted on the domain controller of the domain that the DB2 server belongs to. If the user is not defined there either, the authentication will be attempted at the domain controllers of the trusted domains. If the user is not defined there, the authentication will fail.

If userA is defined on the local server and userA is also defined on the domain controller, authentication will take place at the local server. Notice that these two user accounts are independent and may have different passwords. Therefore, using the user ID userA and the password defined at the domain controller results in an error.

The order in which the trusted domains are checked is random; therefore, make sure the user ID of a trusted domain is unique among all the trusted domains.

Once authentication is done, the group list is enumerated at the machine where the user is defined.

Granting Privileges and Authorities

In the DB2 for Windows environment, administrators are allowed to grant privileges and authorities to the following:

- Locally defined user
- Local user defined on the domain controller
- Domain user
- Trusted domain user
- Local group to which the user directly belongs
- Global group to which the user directly belongs
- Local group that contains a global group to which the user belongs

DB2_GRP_LOOKUP

In a Windows domain environment, a group list for the authenticated user is enumerated at the machine where the authentication is done; so, if the user is defined at a domain controller of the trusted domain and the database administrator does not have the administrative authority for the domain, managing membership of the group the user belongs to is not possible. The DB2_GRP_LOOKUP registry variable allows DB2 administrators to specify where the list of groups a user belongs to should be enumerated.

If it is set to LOCAL at the DB2 server, the list of groups is enumerated using the local SAM at the DB2 server. By setting this value, the database administrator does not need to have the administrative authority for Windows domains. What he or she needs to be is the local administrator.

If this registry variable is set to DOMAIN, you are telling DB2 to always enumerate groups and validate user accounts on the user account's Windows domain.

If you do not set this registry variable, the list of groups a user belongs to will be enumerated as follows: The local SAM will be queried first, followed by the domain controller of the domain the DB2 server belongs to. Then, all the PDCs of the trusted domains will be queried. DB2 is told where the user account was validated and will use that location to enumerate groups.

Auditing

The DB2 *audit facility* is associated with an instance. It records auditable events associated with the instance and databases within it. It can be active even though the instance it is monitoring is not active. Only users with SYSADM authority can use the audit facility. The audit facility uses a binary configuration file located in the /sqllib/<instance_name>/security directory.

For each operation a user executes on a DB2 system, such as a SELECT statement, one or more audit records may be generated. These audit records are categorized into the following groups:

- AUDIT   All records logged associated with the audit facility.
- CHECKING   Events logged due to authorization checking when accessing DB2 objects.
- OBJMAINT   Records logged caused by dropping or creating objects.
- SECMAINT   Records logged due to changing SYSADM_GROUP, SYSCTRL_GROUP, SYSMAINT_GROUP, grant/revoke DBADM, or any privileges on any database objects.
- SYSADMIN   Records logged for operations that required SYSADM, SYSCTRL, and SYSMAINT authority.
- VALIDATE   Records are generated when authenticating users or retrieving system security information.
- CONTEXT   This type of audit record shows detailed information about an operation. This operation may have caused multiple records to be logged in the audit log. Such records can be associated with the CONTEXT record using the event correlator field.

The audit facility may generate multiple audit records for a single operation, each of which may belong to a different record category.

Buffering Audit Log Writes

When configuring the audit facility, a SYSADM user can specify whether the audit facility should write audit records directly to disk in a synchronous mode or buffer the records in an audit buffer for asynchronous writing. This buffer size can be specified using the AUDIT_BUFF_SZ parameter of the database manager configuration file. If the AUDIT_BUFF_SZ is set to 0, all audit record writing will be done synchronously; any number larger than zero indicates the buffer size as a multiple of 4KB.

If a buffer size is specified, the buffer will be written out to disk if the buffer is full or at regular intervals. The SYSADM can also force the buffer to be flushed to disk.

Handling Audit Facility Errors

SYSADM can also specify how an error occurring in the audit facility should be handled by setting the ERRORTYPE when the audit facility is configured. By setting it to AUDIT, any error occurring in the audit facility will return the SQLCODE of the error to the application for which the audit record was logged during the failure. It will also cause the operation attempted by the application to fail. If the ERRORTYPE is set to NORMAL, none of the applications executing will be affected if an attempt to generate an audit record fails.

Configuring the Audit Facility

Before starting the audit facility, you need to configure it. Use the DB2AUDIT CONFIGURE command to configure it. The syntax for the command is as follows:

```
db2audit CONFIGURE SCOPE scope STATUS status
    ERRORTYPE errortype
```

The SCOPE refers to which set of audit record categories should be logged. If ALL is specified as the category, it includes all the categories except the CONTEXT category.

The STATUS refers to whether an event should be logged if it returned successfully, failed, or both. The available values are SUCCESS, FAILURE, or BOTH.

The ERRORTYPE is as discussed above.

Looking at the Current Configuration

To see how the audit facility configuration looks, use the following command:

```
db2audit DESCRIBE
```

Starting the Audit Facility

Once the audit facility is configured, it can be started independently of whether the instance is started. Use the following command:

```
db2audit START
```

Flushing the Audit Buffer

Before extracting an audit log, SYSADM may want to make sure the audit buffer is flushed to disk. Use the following command:

```
db2audit FLUSH
```

Extracting the Audit Log

When the audit facility is started, it starts generating a binary audit log. This binary audit log can be extracted by SYSADM to one of two formats. One of the formats is a text file containing the audit records. The other format (DELASC) generates an ASCII-delimited file for each audit record category monitored. The file names correspond to the category names (listed on page 180). When choosing this output type, the users can also override the default delimiter *0xFF* by specifying the delimiter to use. These files can then be used to populate tables in a database by using the LOAD or IMPORT utilities.

For example, SYSADM wants to extract all the records in the validate and checking categories for the database SAMPLE to ASCII-delimited files using the "!" character as the delimiter. The command would be:

```
db2audit EXTRACT delasc DELIMITER ! CATEGORY validate,
    checking DATABASE sample
```

The output of this command will be two files named VALIDATE.DEL and CHECK-ING.DEL. The default delimiter *0xFF* was overridden by the DELIMITER option. Note that the file is placed in the /sqllib/<instance name>/security directory.

If SYSADM wants to extract all the validation records to a text file, the command would look like this:

```
db2audit EXTRACT file myfile.txt CATEGORY validate
    DATABASE sample
```

In this case, the output will be in a file named MYFILE.TXT. If the file existed prior to executing the command, the command will fail. Fig. 4–15 shows a sample of the output. It seems that a user named BAKLARZ connected to the SAMPLE database using the DB2DEMO.EXE program.

```
timestamp=2002-09-08-17.05.02.198000;category=VALIDATE;
   audit event=CHECK_GROUP_MEMBERSHIP;
   event correlator=1;event status=-1092;
   database=SAMPLE;userid=baklarz;authid=BAKLARZ;execution id=BAKLARZ;
   origin node=0;coordinator node=0;
   application id=*LOCAL.DB2.008988210456;application name=db2demo.exe;
   auth type=SERVER;
timestamp=2002-09-08-17.05.02.248000;category=VALIDATE;
   audit event=CHECK_GROUP_MEMBERSHIP;
   event correlator=1;event status=-1092;
   database=SAMPLE;userid=baklarz;authid=BAKLARZ;execution id=BAKLARZ;
   origin node=0;coordinator node=0;
   application id=*LOCAL.DB2.008988210456;application name=db2demo.exe;
   auth type=SERVER;
```

Fig. 4–15 *The audit log*

Pruning the Audit Log

To delete all the audit records from the audit log, use the following command:

```
db2audit PRUNE all
```

If the audit facility is set up to record events categorized as AUDIT events, an entry will be made in the audit log after the log has been cleared.

Another way to prune is to specify the date/time before which all entries should be cleared out of the audit log.

```
db2audit PRUNE DATE yyyymmddhh PATHNAME pathname
```

Adding the optional pathname allows SYSADM to prune the audit log if the drive or file system on which it is logged becomes full.

Stopping the Audit Facility

To stop the audit facility, use the following command:

```
db2audit STOP
```

One possible flow of the audit facility is shown in Fig. 4–16. First, the audit facility is configured and checked, then it is started. If SYSADM wants to look at the audit log, the audit buffer must be flushed and the audit log extracted either as a text file

Controlling Data Access

or as delimited files that the user can use to populate audit tables. At some point, the user can stop the audit facility and, if desired, clear the audit log of all or some of the records. It is important to note that SYSADM could have stopped the audit facility and extracted the audit log.

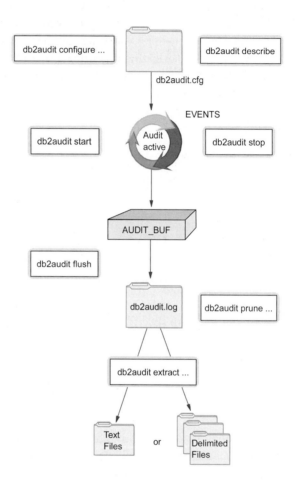

Fig. 4–16 *The audit facility*

Summary

This chapter discussed a number of topics relating to controlling data access. We discussed security, first to the database and then within DB2. We talked about authentication. There are three different methods of authentication: SERVER, CLI-ENT, and SERVER_ENCRYPT. To encrypt passwords passed to a server, you can specify SERVER_ENCRYPT. The other value that can be specified at the DB2 server is KRB_SERVER_ENCRYPT. By setting this value, you can have the SERVER authentication, SERVER_ENCRYPT authentication, and KERBEROS authentication dependent on the value specified at the DB2 client. Depending on the DB2 products installed, authentication tells where the user is to be validated. The authentication type can be set in the database manager configuration. All databases within the instance will have the same authentication type.

We talked about several of the authorization levels within DB2: SYSADM, SYSCTRL, SYSMAINT, DBADM, and LOAD. SYSADM has system administrative authority over the instance and is able to perform any administration operations as well as access any information from any database that exists within that instance. SYSCTRL does not have the authority to access the database (unless explicitly granted), nor can SYSC-TRL modify the database manager configuration. SYSMAINT also cannot access user data. SYSMAINT allows you to perform functions, such as backup or restore databases and table spaces, start and stop the instance, and use the database monitor. At the database level, DBADM has complete authority over the database objects. This authority includes creating or dropping tables, performing a query, and setting privileges for other users of the database. Finally, the LOAD authority allows individuals to insert information into tables using the LOAD command. We also examined the granting and revoking of authorities and privileges using the GRANT and REVOKE statements.

We also talked about the considerations when the DB2 server belongs to a Windows domain. DB2 attempts to authenticate users using the SAM of the local machine, the domain controller of the current domain, and the domain controllers of the trusted domains. The group list of the authenticated user is enumerated at the machine at which the user is defined.

Finally, we talked about the DB2 audit facility. It allows you to monitor security-related events and possible system abuse.

Controlling Data Access

P A R T 2

Using SQL

CHAPTER 5

Database Objects

- ◆ CREATING DATABASE OBJECTS
- ◆ DATA TYPES
- ◆ TABLES
- ◆ CONSTRAINTS
- ◆ VIEWS
- ◆ INDEXES

*T*he standard language of relational database access is SQL (Structured Query Language). SQL is not a conventional programming language. It was designed for the purpose of accessing tabular data. Every Relational Database Management System (RDBMS) implements a slightly different version of SQL.

In this chapter we examine the DB2 implementation of the SQL language. If you are familiar with other RDBMS products, you will already understand many aspects of the DB2 implementation of SQL thanks to the industry acceptance of the ISO/ANSI SQL standard.

We first examine the DB2 database objects that can be referenced in an SQL statement; then, we examine the SQL language elements. A database object, for the purpose of this book, is any component of a DB2 database, such as table spaces, tables, views, indexes, packages, logs, and locks. It is important to note that some of these database objects cannot be directly referenced using the SQL language.

SQL is divided into three major categories:

- DDL (Data Definition Language) - Used to create, modify, or drop database objects
- DML (Data Manipulation Language) - Used to select, insert, update, or delete database data (records)
- DCL (Data Control Language) - Used to provide data object access control

As SQL has evolved, many new statements have been added to provide a more complete set of data management methods. We explore some of these features, including constraints, triggers, outer joins, large object data access, and common table expressions.

Later in this chapter, the use of DDL (Data Definition Language) to create database objects is discussed.

DCL is discussed in "Controlling Data Access" on page 135.

Understanding Database Objects

A database is an organized collection of objects. Each database has its own system catalog, log files, security, and tuning parameters.

SQL is used throughout the database industry as a common method of issuing database queries. SQL is a language, composed of statements, functions, and data types. Before we examine the SQL language, we need to understand some DB2 terminology. We will be referring to the basic components or objects that are defined for each DB2 database. These objects include:

- Tables
- Schemas
- Table spaces
- Views
- Indexes
- Packages
- Buffer pools
- Transactions
- Locks
- Triggers
- Stored procedures
- Log files

Data Types

Each column in a DB2 table must be associated with a *data type*. The data type indicates the kind of data that is valid for the column. There are two major categories of data types in DB2.

- Built-in data types
- User-defined data types

Built-in data types are defined by DB2. DB2 supports a number of built-in data types that are described later in this chapter. DB2 also provides support for *user-defined data types*. User-defined types are classified into the following three types:

- User-defined distinct type
- User-defined structured type
- User-defined reference type

User-defined distinct types (UDT) enable you to create a new data type that has its own semantics based on existing built-in data types. *User-defined structured types* enable you to create a structure that contains a sequence of named attributes each of which has a data type. This is one of the extensions of DB2 Object Relational functions. A *user-defined reference type* is a companion type to a user-defined structured type. Similar to a user-defined distinct type, a user-defined reference type is a scalar type that shares a common representation with one of the built-in data types. A user-defined reference type may be used to reference rows in another table that uses a user-defined structured type. User-defined distinct types (UDTs) will be discussed in this chapter; user-defined structured types and user-defined reference types will be discussed in "Advanced SQL" on page 343.

Note: User-defined structured types allow a user to create structures in DB2 and use them as columns within a table. This is one way that DB2 extends the relational model to be more object-oriented.

Tables

A *table* is an unordered set of rows. Rows consist of columns. Each column is based on a data type. Tables, once created and populated with data, are referenced in the FROM and INTO clauses of the DML statements. There are three types of tables:

- Permanent (base) tables
- Temporary (declared) tables
- Temporary (derived) tables

We only discuss permanent tables in this chapter. These tables are created using the CREATE TABLE statement and each is a logical representation of the way the data is physically stored on disk. We discuss the temporary tables in "Advanced SQL" on page 343.

Note: Temporary declared tables were introduced in DB2 Version 7. This feauture allows the application developer or user to create temporary tables that exist only for the duration of the program.

Schemas

Schemas are database objects used in DB2 to logically group other database objects. Most database objects are named using a two-part naming convention (SCHEMA_NAME.OBJECT_NAME). The first part of the name is referred to as the schema (otherwise known as a qualifier for the database object). The second part is the *object name*.

When you create an object and do not specify a schema, the object will be associated with an *implicit schema* using your *authorization ID*. When an object is referenced in an SQL statement, it is also implicitly qualified with the authorization ID of the issuer (dynamic SQL) if no schema name is specified in the SQL statement.

The CURRENT SCHEMA special register contains the default qualifier to be used for unqualified objects referenced for dynamic SQL statements issued from within a specific DB2 connection. This value can be modified by the user with the SET CURRENT SCHEMA statement. Static SQL statements are qualified with the authorization ID of the person binding the application (by default). For example, if user KATRINA connected to the database and created a table called TASKS, the complete name of the table as stored in the database would be: KATRINA.TASKS. You can use the QUALIFIER option of the BIND command to define the default qualifier at bind time.

One additional schema qualifier is the SESSION keyword. This keyword is used for temporary tables that are created and used during a connection. The SESSION qualifier is discussed later in the section on "The DECLARE Statement" on page 200

Note: When a program or user declares a temporary table, the only way to reference it in the SQL is through the use of the SESSION qualifier. If the SESSION qualifier is not used, DB2 will attempt to find the table using the current schema.

Table Spaces

Table spaces are the logical layers between the database and the tables stored in that database. Table spaces are created within a database, and tables are created within table spaces. DB2 supports two kinds of table spaces:

- System Managed Space (SMS) - The operating system's file system manager allocates and manages the space where the table space is to be stored. SMS is the default table space type.
- Database Managed Space (DMS) - The database manager controls the storage space. This is, essentially, an implementation of a special purpose file system designed to best meet the needs of the database manager.

When a table is defined using the CREATE TABLE statement, you can explicitly state in which table space the table will reside. By default, all tables will be created in the USERSPACE1 table space. Table spaces provide the database administrator with the ability to control the location of tables, indexes, and large objects. You can define any number of table spaces within a single database and any number of tables within a tablespace.

Views

Views are virtual tables that are derived from one or more tables or views and can be used interchangeably with tables when retrieving data. When changes are made to the data through a view, the data is changed in the underlying table itself. Views do not contain real data. Only the definition exists in the database. Views can be created to limit access to sensitive data while allowing more general access to other data. Views can be deletable, updatable, insertable, and read-only. The classification indicates the kind of SQL operations allowed against the view.

Indexes

Indexes are physical objects that are associated with individual tables. Any permanent table or declared temporary table, can have indexes defined on it. You cannot define an index on a view. You can define multiple indexes for a single table. Indexes are used for two primary reasons:

- Ensure uniqueness of data values
- Improve SQL query performance

Indexes can be used to access data in a sorted order more quickly and avoid the time-consuming task of sorting the data using temporary storage. Indexes can also be created on computed columns so that the optimizer can save computation time by using the index instead of doing the calculations. Indexes are maintained automatically by DB2 as data is inserted, updated, and deleted.

Notes:

1. Another important feature in index creation is the ability to add additional values to the index, which can be used by the optimizer to get nonkey data. This can also result in much faster performance for queries, which can get their answer sets from the index rather than from the data pages.

2. The maintenance overhead of indexes can negatively impact the performance of INSERT, UPDATE, and DELETE statements.

Indexes can be defined in ascending or descending order. They can be defined as unique or nonunique, and they can be defined on a single column or multiple columns. They can also be defined to support both forward and reverse scans. The Visual Explain utility provides index usage information for every explainable SQL statement (if the explain data is gathered).

Database Objects

Note: DB2 UDB Version 8 introduces a new index structure in the database. These new indexes are referred to as "Type-2" indexes and help to eliminate a phenomena called "next-key locking". Transactions in prior releases could lock an adjacent record during processing. This could result in unnecessary delays in completing transactions that depended on this record. Any new indexes created in Version 8 will use this new index structure, while existing indexes will be replaced only when the user drops and recreates them, or reorganizes the indexes and specifies that they should be converted.

In addition, DB2 UDB Version 8 also allows indexes to be created on temporary tables. Prior to this, any query against a temporary table object would result in a complete scan of the table.

Packages

Packages are database objects that contain executable forms of SQL statements. These packages contain statements that are referenced from a DB2 application. A package corresponds to a program source module.

Note: Only the corresponding program source module can invoke the contents of a package.

Packages are stored in the catalog. Packages contain access plans selected by DB2 during the BIND or PREP process. This type of BIND is known as static binding since it is performed prior to the execution of the SQL statement. Packages cannot be directly referenced in DML statements.

Most applications that access a DB2 database will have a package or group of packages in the catalog.

Note: Packages can now exist with different version numbers. This option allows multiple versions of the same package name (package name and creator name) to coexist. This allows you to make changes to an existing application and not invalidate the existing package that users are running.

Buffer Pools

Buffer pools are database objects used to cache data pages in memory. Once a data page is placed in a buffer pool, physical I/O access to disk can be avoided. Buffer pools can be assigned to cache only a particular table space.

Every DB2 database must have a buffer pool. For each new database, DB2 defines the IBMDEFAULTBP default buffer pool for the database.

The CREATE BUFFERPOOL statement is used to define buffer pools other than the default IBMDEFAULTBP buffer pool. Once a buffer pool is created, table spaces can be assigned to it using the CREATE TABLESPACE statement or the ALTER TABLESPACE statements.

The SYSCAT.BUFFERPOOLS catalog view accesses the information for the buffer pools defined in the database.

Transactions

A *transaction* is a sequence of SQL statements that execute as a single operation. The term *unit of work* is synonymous with the term *transaction*.

A transaction either succeeds or fails. A transaction starts implicitly with the first executable SQL statement in a program. The transaction ends when either an explicit or implicit COMMIT or ROLLBACK statement is encountered. An implicit COMMIT or ROLLBACK can occur when a DB2 application terminates.

DB2 also allows supports SAVEPOINTs within a transaction. This allows a selective rollback without undoing work prior to the savepoint. More details on COMMIT, ROLLBACK, and SAVEPOINTS can be found in "Development SQL" on page 805.

Notes:

1. Application savepoints provide control over the work performed by a subset of SQL statements in a transaction or unit of work. Within your application you can set a savepoint, and later either release the savepoint or roll back the work performed since you set the savepoint.

2. It is best to explicitly COMMIT or ROLLBACK outstanding SQL transactions prior to terminating a DB2 application. Whether DB2 implicitly performs a COMMIT or ROLLBACK depends on the operating environment.

Locks

DB2 is a multiuser database product. As users request data, the DB2 locking mechanism attempts to avoid resource conflicts yet still provide full data integrity. As SQL statements are processed, the transactions may obtain locks. The locks are released when the resource is no longer required at the end of the transaction. The locks are stored in memory on the database server (in a structure known as the *locklist*). DB2 supports two types of locks, table locks and row locks.

The locking strategy used by DB2 during transaction processing is specified using an *isolation level* as defined when binding the application.

Note: Locking levels can be dynamically set in DB2. As part of the SQL statement, developers can assign the type of locking level they wish to have during the duration of that statement. This allows the developer more flexibility in the types of locks that are held at the statement level, rather than using one type of locking for the entire application.

Log Files

A number of *log files* are associated with each DB2 database. As transactions are processed, they are tracked within the log files. DB2 will track all of the SQL statements that are issued for a database within its database log files.

DB2 uses *write-ahead logging*. The changes are first written to the log files and, at a later time, applied to the physical database tables.

Note: Log files can now be 256GB in size in Version 8! This should allow long-running transactions to finish without filling up one log file. In the event that a transaction does exceed this limit, DB2 will now "chain" log files together so that theoretically a user should never run out of log space. However, applications should commit their work at regular intervals so that this type of log chaining does not occur!

Creating a DB2 Database

A DB2 database must exist before any of the database objects can be created in it. The database must be given a name. (There is no schema associated with the database.) Once the database has been created, the next logical step is to create the table spaces that will be used to store the user tables.

> **Note:** The CREATE DATABASE command is not an SQL statement but is a DB2 CLP command. The database name can be 1 - 8 characters long.

When you create a database without any table space options, three SMS table spaces are created by default:

- SYSCATSPACE - Contains the system catalog tables
- TEMPSPACE1 - Contains temporary tables used by DB2
- USERSPACE1 - Contains the user tables unless other user table spaces are created

These table spaces can be specified as DMS table spaces in the CREATE DATABASE command. In addition, a fourth tablespace type, USER temporary tablespace, needs to be defined if temporary tables are used.

Please refer to "Data Storage Management" on page 449 for more information about databases and table spaces.

> **Note:** Temporary tables that are DECLARED in a transaction require the use of a USER temporary tablespace. This needs to be created and access granted to users before temporary tables are used.

Managing Database Objects

To create, modify, or delete objects in a database, SQL Data Definition Language (DDL) is used.

Using SQL Data Definition Language (DDL)

DDL has four basic SQL statements:

- CREATE
- ALTER
- DROP
- DECLARE

Note: The DECLARE statement was introduced in DB2 Version 7 and is used for temporary tables used in an application. This can only be used for temporary tables and requires the use of USER temporary tablespaces.

The CREATE Statement

```
CREATE <database object>....
```

The CREATE statement is used to create database objects. The list of database objects that can be created are:

- Table
- Index
- Schema
- View
- User-defined function
- User-defined data type
- Buffer pool
- Table space
- Stored procedures
- Trigger
- Alias
- Method
- Transform
- Nickname
- Sequence

- Server
- Wrapper

The creation of any database object updates the catalog tables. Specific authorities and privileges are required to create database objects.

The DECLARE Statement

```
DECLARE <database object>....
```

The DECLARE statement is very similar to the CREATE statement, except that it is used to create temporary tables that are used only during a session. The only object that can be DECLARED is a table, and it must be placed into an existing USER temporary tablespace.

The creation of a temporary table does not update the catalog, so locking, logging, and other forms of contention are avoided with this object.

DECLARED tables can be DROPPED and ALTERED, but no other database objects (such as views or triggers) can be created to act against them. Temporary tables do allow for the specification of a partitioning key and the creation of indexes for improved performance.

Once a table is declared, it can be referenced like any other table. The following example shows a temporary table being declared and then used in a subsequent SQL statement.

```
DECLARE GLOBAL TEMPORARY TABLE T1
   LIKE TRANSACTIONS
   ON COMMIT PRESERVE ROWS NOT LOGGED IN SESSIONTEMP;

INSERT INTO SESSION.T1
  SELECT * FROM TRANSACTIONS WHERE SALES < 3000;

SELECT * FROM SESSION.T1;
```

 Note: The DECLARE statement is used to create temporary tables that are used only during the duration of session. The table does not cause any logging or contention against the catalog and is very useful for working with intermediate results.

Note: In DB2 Version 8, users can create indexes on temporary tables. This can dramatically improve the performance of queries against these objects since prior releases of DB2 only allowed for indexes against permanent tables. In addition, transactions against temporary tables can now be logged so that the user has the ability to undo transactions against these tables.

The DROP Statement

```
DROP <database object>....
```

The DROP statement is used to delete objects from the database. Since database objects can be dependent on other database objects, the act of dropping an object can result in a related object being rendered invalid. You can drop any object created with the CREATE <database object> and the DECLARE <table> statements.

The ALTER Statement

```
ALTER <database object>....
```

The ALTER statement allows you to change some characteristics of existing database objects. The types of database objects that can be altered are:

- Table
- Table space
- Database partition
- Server
- Procedure
- Function
- Nickname
- Sequence
- Type
- Wrapper
- View
- Method
- User mapping
- Buffer pool

Note: You cannot alter an index. You must drop and create a new index.

Every time you issue a DDL statement (except for the DECLARE statement), the catalog is updated. The update includes a creation or modification timestamp and the authorization ID of the user issuing the statement.

Let's look in detail at some of the objects that can be created in a database. We will cover data types, tables, views, and indexes.

 Notes:

1. It is useful to store all of the DDL statements for the database in a script file to allow for easier creation of the database objects. This script can either be used from the DB2 CLP or the DB2 Command Center.

2. It is possible to extract the DDL for objects using the DB2LOOK utility.

Data Types

Every column in a table must be assigned a data type. Before discussing tables, we have to understand the various data types supplied by DB2 or defined by users.

First let us look at the built-in data types supplied by DB2.

DB2 Built-in Data Types

Every DB2-supplied data type belongs to one of these three major categories (DATALINK is not included in this categorization list but is represented in the figure below):

- Numeric
- String (Binary, Single Byte, Double Byte)
- Datetime

The built-in DB2 data types are shown in Fig. 5–1.

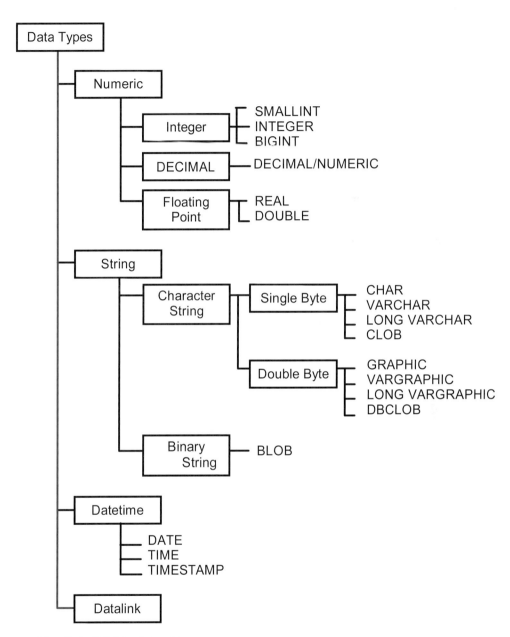

Fig. 5–1 *DB2 built-in data types*

Numeric Data Types

The six DB2 data types that can be used to store numeric data are:

- SMALLINT
- INTEGER
- BIGINT
- DECIMAL/NUMERIC
- REAL
- DOUBLE

These data types are used to store different numeric types and precisions. The precision of a number is the number of digits used to represent its value. The data is stored in the DB2 database using a fixed amount of storage for all numeric data types. The amount of storage required increases as the precision of the number goes up.

You must also be aware of the range limits of the data types and the corresponding application programming language when you are manipulating these numeric fields.

Some data values are of the integer type by nature, such as the number of test candidates. It would be impossible to have a number representing a number of people that contains fractional data (numbers to the right of the decimal). On the other hand, some values require decimal places to accurately reflect their value, such as test scores. These two examples should use different DB2 data types to store their values (SMALLINT and DECIMAL, respectively).

Numeric values should not be enclosed in quotation marks. If they are, the value is treated as a character string. Even if a field contains numbers in its representation, a DB2 numeric data type should be used to represent the data only if arithmetic operations should be allowed.

Small integer (SMALLINT)

A small integer uses the least amount of storage in the database for each value. An integer does not allow any digits to the right of the decimal.

The data value range for a SMALLINT is -32768 to 32767. The precision for a SMALLINT is 5 digits (to the left of the decimal). Two bytes of database storage are used for each SMALLINT column value.

Integer (INTEGER)

An INTEGER takes twice as much storage as a SMALLINT but has a greater range of possible values.

The range value for an INTEGER data type is -2,147,483,648 to 2,147,483,647. The precision for an INTEGER is 10 digits to the left of the decimal. Four bytes of database storage are used for each INTEGER column value.

Big integer (BIGINT)

The BIGINT data type is available for supporting 64-bit integers. The range for BIGINT is -9,223,372,036,854,775,808 to +9,223,372,036,854,775,807. As platforms include native support for 64 bit integers, the processing of large numbers with BIGINT is more efficient than processing with DECIMAL and more precise than DOUBLE or REAL. Eight bytes of database storage are used for each BIGINT column value.

Decimal (DECIMAL/NUMERIC)

A DECIMAL or NUMERIC data type is used for numbers with fractional and whole parts. The DECIMAL data is stored in a packed format.

The precision and scale must be provided when a decimal data type is used. The precision is the total number of digits (range from 1 to 31), and the scale is the number of digits in the fractional part of the number. For example, a decimal data type to store currency values of up to $1 million would require a definition of DECIMAL(9,2). The terms NUMERIC, NUM, DECIMAL, and DEC can all be used to declare a decimal/numeric column. If a decimal data type is to be used in a C program, the host variable must be declared as a double. A DECIMAL number takes up p/2 + 1 bytes of storage, where p is the precision used. For example, DEC(8,2) would take up 5 bytes of storage (8/2 + 1), whereas DEC(7,2) would take up only 4 bytes (truncate the division of p/2).

Note: If the precision and scale values are not supplied for a DECIMAL column definition, a default value (5,0) is used. This column would take up 3 bytes of space in the row.

Single-precision floating-point (REAL/FLOAT)

A REAL data type is an approximation of a number. The approximation requires 32 bits or 4 bytes of storage. To specify a single-precision number using the REAL data type, its length must be defined between 1 and 24 (especially if the FLOAT data type is used, as it can represent both single- and double-precision and is determined by the integer value specified).

Double-precision floating-point (DOUBLE/FLOAT)

A DOUBLE or FLOAT data type is an approximation of a number. The approximation requires 64 bits or 8 bytes of storage. To specify a double-precision number using the FLOAT data type, its length must be defined between 25 and 53.

 Note: Exponential notation is used to represent REAL, DOUBLE, and FLOAT data values.

String Data Types

This section discusses the string data types that include CHAR, VARCHAR, and LONG VARCHAR.

Fixed-length character string (CHAR)

Fixed-length character strings are stored in the database using the entire defined amount of storage. If the data being stored always has the same length, a CHAR data type should be used. In Fig. 5–2, the Candidate ID field is defined as a fixed-length character string of 8 characters.

Candidate ID
(8 characters)

DB2
Database

Character Data (Fixed length - up to 254 bytes/column)

Fig. 5–2 *Fixed-length character strings (CHARs)*

Using fixed-length character fields can potentially waste disk space within the database if the data is not using the defined amount of storage. However, there is overhead involved in storing varying-length character strings. The term CHARACTER can be used as a synonym for CHAR.

The length of a fixed-length string must be between 1 and 254 characters. If you do not supply a value for the length, a value of 1 is assumed.

Note: Character strings are stored in the database without a termination character. Depending on the development environment, a null-terminator may or may not be appended to the end of a character string when the data is stored or retrieved.

Varying-length character string (VARCHAR)

Varying-length character strings are stored in the database using only the amount of space required to store the data. The individual names, in our example, are stored as varying-length strings (VARCHAR) because each persons name has a different length (up to a maximum length of 30 characters). The term CHAR VARYING or CHARACTER VARYING can be used as a synonym for VARCHAR.

If a varying-length character string is updated and the resulting value is larger than the original, the record will be moved to another page in the table. These rows are known as *tombstone* records or pointer records. Too many of these records can cause significant performance degradation since multiple pages are required to return a single row. The maximum length of a VARCHAR column is 32,672 bytes.

Varying-length long character strings (LONG VARCHAR)

This data type is used to store character data with a varying length. In the past it was used when the VARCHAR was not large enough; however, with the increase of the VARCHAR column to 32,672, the LONG VARCHAR data type may not be used as often.

A VARCHAR column has the restriction that it must fit on one database page. This means that a 4K page would allow a VARCHAR of approximately 4000 characters long, an 8K page would be 8000 and so on up to a 32K page. This means that you must create a tablespace for this table that can accommodate the larger page size, and you must have sufficient space in the row to accommodate this string. A LONG VARCHAR only takes up 24 bytes of space in the row, no matter what the length is. The LONG VARCHAR format will result in the strings being stored in a separate database page, and this will result in longer processing time for these strings since the database will always need to make an extra hop to get to this data.

The maximum length of a LONG VARCHAR column is 32,700.

Notes:

1. LONG VARCHAR data types are similar to CLOB data types. (Both types have usage restrictions.)

2. The FOR BIT DATA clause can be used following a character string column definition. During data exchange, code page conversions are not performed. Rather data is treated and compared as binary (bit) data.

Character large object (CLOB)

Character large objects are varying-length SBCS (single-byte character set) or MBCS (multibyte character set) character strings that are stored in the database. There is a code page associated with each CLOB. For more details regarding a DB2 code page, please see "Code Page Considerations" on page 222 CLOB columns are used to store greater than 32KB of text. The maximum size for each CLOB column is 2GB (gigabytes). Since this data type is of varying length, the amount of disk space allocated is determined by the amount of data in each record. Therefore, you should create the column specifying the length of the longest string.

Text   Text

Fig. 5–3 *CLOB character strings*

Double-byte character strings (GRAPHIC)

The GRAPHIC data types represent a single character using 2 bytes of storage. The GRAPHIC data types include:

- GRAPHIC (fixed length - maximum 127 characters)
- VARGRAPHIC (varying length - maximum 16336 characters)
- LONG VARGRAPHIC (varying length - maximum 16350 characters).

Double-byte character large objects (DBCLOB)

Double-byte character large objects are varying-length character strings that are stored in the database using 2 bytes to represent each character. There is a code page associated with each column. DBCLOB columns are used for large amounts (>32KB) of double-byte text data such as Japanese text.

The maximum length should be specified during the column definition because each row will be variable in length.

Binary large object (BLOB)

Binary large objects are variable-length binary strings. The data is stored in a binary format in the database. There are restrictions when using this data type including the inability to sort using this type of column. The BLOB data type is useful for storing nontraditional relational database information as shown in Fig. 5–4.

The maximum size of each BLOB column is 2GB (gigabytes). Since this data type is of varying length, the amount of disk space allocated is determined by the amount of data in each record, not by the defined maximum size of the column in the table definition.

Fig. 5–4 *Binary large objects (BLOBs)*

Large Object Considerations

Traditionally, large unstructured data was stored somewhere outside the database. Therefore, the data could not be accessed using SQL. Besides the traditional database data types, DB2 implements data types that will store large amounts of unstructured data. These data types are known as Large Objects (LOBs). Multiple LOB columns can be defined for a single table.

DB2 provides special considerations for handling these large objects. You can choose not to log the LOB values to avoid exhausting the transaction log files.

There is a NOT LOGGED option that can be specified during the CREATE TABLE state-ment for each LOB column that you want to avoid logging any modifications. If you would like to define a LOB column greater than 1GB, you must specify the NOT LOGGED option.

There is also a COMPACT option that can be specified during the CREATE TABLE state-ment. This option is used to avoid allocating extra disk space when storing these large data objects, not for the compression of these objects!

In a database, you may choose to use BLOBs for the storage of pictures, images, or audio or video objects, along with large documents. BLOB columns will accept any binary string without regard to the contents.

If you would like to manipulate textual data that is greater than 32 KB in length, you would use CLOB or a character large object data type. For example, if each test candidate were required to submit their resume, the resume could be stored in a CLOB column along with the rest of the candidate's information. There are many SQL functions that can be used to manipulate large character data columns.

Date and Time Data Types

There are three DB2 data types specifically used to represent dates and times:

- DATE - This data type is stored internally as a (packed) string of 4 bytes. Exter-nally, the string has a length of 10 bytes (MM-DD-YYYY - this representation can vary and is dependent on the country code).
- TIME - This data type is stored internally as a (packed) string of 3 bytes. Exter-nally, the string has a length of 8 bytes (HH-MM-SS - this representation may vary).
- TIMESTAMP - This data type is stored internally as a (packed) string of 10 bytes. Externally, the string has a length of 26 bytes (YYYY-MM-DD-HH-MM-SS-NNNNNN).

From the user perspective, these data types can be treated as character or string data types. Every time you need to use a datetime attribute, you will need to enclose it in quotation marks. However, datetime data types are not stored in the database as fixed-length character strings.

DB2 provides special functions that allow you to manipulate these data types. These functions allow you to extract the month, hour, or year of a datetime column.

The date and time formats correspond to the country code of the database or a spec-ified format (since the representation of dates and times varies in different coun-tries). Therefore, the string that represents a date value will change depending on the country code (or format specified). In some countries, the date format is DD/MM/YYYY, whereas in other countries, it is YYYY-MM-DD. You should be aware of the country code/format used by your application to use the correct date string format. If an incorrect date format is used, an SQL error will be reported.

As a general recommendation, if you are interested in a single element of a date string, say month or year, always use the SQL functions provided by DB2 to interpret the column value. By using the SQL functions, your application will be more portable.

 Note: TIMESTAMP fields use the most storage, but they contain the most accurate time since they include microseconds.

We stated that all datetime data types have an internal and external format. The external format is always a character string. Let us examine the various datetime data type formats available in DB2.

Date string (DATE)

There are a number of valid methods of representing a DATE as a string.

Table 5–1 *Valid Date Formats*

Format Name	Abbreviation	Date Format
International Organization for Standardization	ISO	YYYY-MM-DD
IBM USA Standard	USA	MM/DD/YYYY
IBM European Standard	EUR	DD.MM.YYYY
Japanese Industrial Standard	JIS	YYYY-MM-DD
Site Defined	LOC	Depends on database country code

Any of the string formats shown in Table 5–1 can be used to store dates in a DB2 database. When the data is retrieved (using a SELECT statement), the output string will be in one of these formats. There is an option of the BIND command called DATETIME, which allows you to define the external format of the date and time values. The abbreviation column in Table 5–1 contains some possible values for the DATETIME option of the BIND command.

Time string (TIME)

There are a number of valid methods for representing a TIME as a string. Any of the string formats in Table 5–2 can be used to store times in a DB2 database. When data is retrieved, the external format of the time will be one of the formats shown in Table 5–2.

Table 5–2 *Valid Time Formats*

Format Name	Abbreviation	Date Format
International Organization for Standardization	ISO	HH.MM.SS
IBM USA Standard	USA	HH:MM AM or PM
IBM European Standard	EUR	HH.MM.SS
Japanese Industrial Standard	JIS	HH:MM:SS
Site Defined	LOC	Depends on the database country code

There is a BIND option, called DATETIME, which allows you to define the external format of the date and time values. The abbreviation column in Table 5–2 contains some possible values for the DATETIME BIND option.

Note: Regardless of the date and time format of the applications, TIME data types have the same internal representation. Their external representation can be changed with the BIND option.

Timestamp string (TIMESTAMP)

The timestamp data type has a single external format. Therefore, the DATETIME BIND option does not affect the external format of timestamps. Timestamps have an external representation as YYYY-MM-DD-HH.MM.SS.NNNNNN (Year-Month-Day-Hour-Minute-Seconds-Microseconds).

External File Data Types (DATALINK)

A DATALINK value is an encapsulated value that contains a logical reference from the database to a file stored in a Data Links Manager Server, which is outside the database (See "DB2 Data Links Manager" on page 27). The attributes of this encapsulated value are as follows:

- Link type - The currently supported type of link is a URL (Uniform Resource

Locator).

- Scheme - For URLs, this is a value like HTTP or FILE. The value, no matter what case it is entered in, is stored in the database in uppercase characters. If a value is not specified, FILE is included in the DATALINK value.

- File server name - The complete address of the file server. The value, no matter what case it is entered in, is stored in the database in uppercase characters. If a value is not specified, the file server name of the database server is selected and included in the DATALINK value.

- File path - The identity of the file within the server. The value is case-sensitive and, therefore, it is not converted to uppercase characters when stored in the database.

- Access control token - When appropriate, the access token is embedded within the file path. It is generated dynamically when a DATALINK value is extracted, and it is not necessary to provide it when a DATALINK value is inserted. In other words, it is not a permanent part of the DATALINK value that is stored in the database.

- Comment - Up to 254 bytes of descriptive information. This is intended for application specific uses such as further or alternative identification of the location of the data.

Insert and extract DATALINK values

When you are inserting rows into a table that has DATALINK columns, you should use a built-in scalar function, DLVALUE, to provide each attribute of the DATALINK value.

To extract encapsulated attributes of the DATALINK value, DB2 provides several built-in scalar functions, such as DLLINKTYPE, DLURLSCHEME, DLURLSERVER, DLURLCOMPLETE, DLURLPATH, DLURLPATHONLY, and DLCOMMENT.

Refer to the *DB2 UDB V8.1 SQL Reference* for more detailed information about these built-in scalar functions.

User-Defined Data Types

User-defined types (UDTs) allow a user to extend the data-types that DB2 understands. There are three kinds of UDTs:

- User-defined distinct type - User-defined data types (UDTs) can be created on an existing data type. UDTs are used to define further types of data being represented in the database. If columns are defined using different UDTs based on the same base data type, these UDTs cannot be directly compared. This is known as *strong typing*. DB2 provides this strong data typing to avoid end-user mistakes during the assignment or comparison of different types of real-world data.

- User-defined reference type - A UDT can also be a user-defined reference type used to reference rows in another table that uses a user-defined structured type. A structured type can be a subtype of another structured type (called supertype) defining a type hierarchy. User-defined structured types (for type hierarchy) will be discussed in "Advanced SQL" on page 343.
- User-defined structured data type - Structured type support has been extended to provide the ability to create tables with structured type columns. Additionally, structured types can be nested within a structured type. This means that the attributes of structured type are no longer restricted to the base SQL types, they can now be of another structured type. User-defined structured type as discussed in "Advanced SQL" on page 343.

Note: The user-defined structured data type allows the DBA or developer to create columns that are actually made up of a structure. This is part of the object-relational support found within DB2.

The SYSCAT.DATATYPES catalog view allows you to see the UDTs that have been defined in your database.

Creating User-Defined Distinct Types (UDTs)

Let us say we have a table that will be used to store different measures of weight such as pounds and kilograms. We should use a numeric data type for these columns since arithmetic operations are appropriate. We will use the INTEGER data type as the base DB2 data type for the UDTs, KILOGRAM and POUND. The values represent different units and, therefore, should not be directly compared.

Note: User-defined data types (UDTs) can only be based on existing DB2 data types.

Here we define two new data types: KILOGRAM and POUND. These data types will be based on the integer (INTEGER) data type. Once the KILOGRAM and POUND UDTs have been defined, they can be referenced in the CREATE TABLE statement.

When the UDTs are defined, system-generated SQL functions are created. These functions are known as *casting functions*. The casting functions allow comparison between the UDT and its base type. In the real world, you cannot directly compare pounds and kilograms without converting one of the values. In DB2, a user-defined function is required.

Let us create the user-defined data types for POUND and KILOGRAM.

```
CREATE DISTINCT TYPE pound
      AS INTEGER WITH COMPARISONS
CREATE DISTINCT TYPE kilogram
      AS INTEGER WITH COMPARISONS
```

In the example above, we are creating the new data types known as POUND and KILOGRAM.

The keyword DISTINCT is mandatory for all user-defined data types. The WITH COMPARISONS clause is also a mandatory clause (except for LOB, LONG, and DATALINK data types). The following table uses the pound and kilogram data types.

```
CREATE TABLE health
   (f_name VARCHAR(30),
   weight_p POUND,
   weight_k KILOGRAM)
```

The new data types are used in the table definition just like the DB2 built-in data types. DB2 will not allow you to compare or perform arithmetic operations on the POUND and KILOGRAM typed columns directly. A casting function would need to be used to perform arithmetic operations using the columns defined with these types. In other words, you could not use built-in functions, such as the average function (AVG), for a column defined as POUND or KILOGRAM, unless you use the appropriate casting functions or create a new user-defined function that can use those UDTs as an input parameter.

The following SQL will result in an error. The data type for the constant value of 30 is of type INTEGER, and the INTEGER data type cannot be directly compared with the POUND data type.

```
SELECT f_name, weight_p
   FROM health
WHERE weight_p > 30
```

To resolve the error, a cast of the constant value of 30 is required. By casting, the value of 30 is treated as an POUND data type. In the following example, the POUND(INTEGER) casting function is being used to convert the value of 30 to the POUND data type.

```
SELECT f_name, weight_p
  FROM health
WHERE weight_p > POUND(30)
```

Let us look at a simple example of a UDT involving telephone numbers. This example is here for the purpose of describing the use of user-defined types. Be aware that this example would not restrict the phone number to be numeric. You always compare phone numbers with other phone numbers; you do not compare them with street numbers or department numbers. This means that a column representing telephone numbers would be an ideal candidate to be defined using a distinct type or UDT.

Should telephone numbers be stored as numeric or string data? Does it make sense to perform arithmetic operations on a telephone number? No, a telephone number has no significant mathematical properties (e.g., adding one to your telephone number is not a useful operation). Therefore, we should base the new data type on a CHARACTER or CHAR type. A varying-length character string or VARCHAR is not required because the length of a telephone number is consistent.

We start by creating a user-defined data type for the telephone numbers. This will ensure that all the columns containing telephone numbers share the same data type.

Note: The valid data values for a user-defined data type cannot be specified. Therefore, any valid value for the base data type is allowed. Additional constraints can be placed on the column within the table.

The SQL statement to create the distinct type PHONENO is shown.

```
CREATE DISTINCT TYPE phoneno
              AS CHAR(10) WITH COMPARISONS
```

The creation of this user-defined data type will result in the creation of the following casting functions:

- CHAR(PHONENO), which translates data values from the PHONENO data type to the base data type CHAR
- PHONENO(CHAR), which translates data values from the base data type CHAR to the PHONENO data type

In fact, DB2 will create two PHONENO casting functions: one that converts fixed CHAR strings and another that works with VARCHAR columns. The number of casting functions created will vary according to the base data type being used. In addition, a casting function VARCHAR(PHONENO) is also created.

Let us say that we have two columns that represent phone numbers: HPHONE (home phone number) and WPHONE (work phone number). Both of these columns should be defined using the same data type PHONENO.

Here are some examples of using these columns in expressions:

- An expression involving the same data type (PHONENO) -
  PHONENO = HPHONE or HPHONE <> WPHONE
- An expression using the casting function PHONENO(CHAR) -
  HPHONE = PHONENO('5555551234')
- A similar expression using the casting function CHAR(PHONENO) -
  CHAR(hphone) = '5555551234'

Removing a User-Defined Distinct Type

User-defined distinct types (UDTs) are defined at the database level. They can only be created and dropped from a database by someone with database administrator (or higher) authority. If tables have been defined using a UDT, you will not be allowed to drop the UDT. The table would need to be dropped before the UDT could be dropped.

Assuming there is no table defined using the pound data type, you could remove the definition of the POUND data type using the following statement.

```
DROP DISTINCT TYPE pound
```

The DROP DISTINCT TYPE statement will drop the POUND data type and all of its related casting functions.

 Note: Remember that if you do not qualify a DB2 object, the current authorization ID will be used as the schema name. For example, if you are connected to the database as user geoffrey, the DROP statement in the previous example would attempt to drop the data type GEOFFREY.POUND.

Null Considerations

A null represents an unknown state. Therefore, when columns containing null values are used in calculations, the result is unknown. All of the data types discussed in the previous section support the presence of nulls. During table definition, you can specify that a value must be provided. This is accomplished by adding a phrase to the column definition. The CREATE TABLE statement can contain the phrase NOT NULL as part of the definition of each column. This will ensure that the column contains a value, i.e., is not null.

Special considerations are required to properly handle nulls when coding a DB2 application. DB2 treats nulls differently than it treats values.

 Note: Relational databases allow nulls. It is important to remember that they can be appropriate for your database design.

To define a column not to accept nulls, add the phrase NOT NULL to the end of the column definition, for example:

```
CREATE TABLE t1 (c1 CHAR(3) NOT NULL)
```

From the example above, DB2 will not allow any nulls to be stored in the c1 column. In general, avoid using nullable columns unless they are required to implement the database design. There is also overhead storage you must consider. An extra byte per nullable column is necessary if nulls are allowed.

Null with Default

When you insert a row into a table and omit the value of one or more columns, these columns may either be null (if the column is defined as nullable) or given a default value. If the column is defined as not nullable, the insert will fail unless a value has been provided for the column. DB2 has a defined default value for each of the DB2 data types, but you can explicitly provide a default value for any column. The default value is specified in the CREATE TABLE statement. By defining your own default value, you can ensure that the column has been populated with a desired value.

 Note: The DB2 default values may not be what you want! Explicity define the default values in your CREATE TABLE statement.

Database Objects

In Fig. 5–5, we can see how the default values can be specified in a CREATE TABLE statement.

```
CREATE TABLE Staff (
    ID      SMALLINT NOT NULL,
    NAME    VARCHAR(9),
    DEPT    SMALLINT NOT NULL WITH DEFAULT 10,
    JOB     CHAR(5),
    YEARS   SMALLINT,
    SALARY  DECIMAL(7,2),
    COMM    DECIMAL(7,2) WITH DEFAULT 15);
```

Fig. 5–5 *Defining user-specified default values for columns*

Now, all the INSERT statements that omit the DEPT column will populate the column with the default value of 10. The COMM column is defined as WITH DEFAULT, but allows NULLs. In this case, you can choose at insert time between NULL or the default value of 15.

To ensure that the default value is being used during an INSERT operation, the keyword DEFAULT should be specified in the VALUES portion of the INSERT statement. Fig. 5–6 shows two examples of inserting a record with user-defined default values. In this case, both cause the same result.

```
INSERT INTO STAFF
  values(360,'Chihoko',DEFAULT,'SE',8,20000,DEFAULT);

INSERT INTO STAFF (ID,NAME,JOB,YEARS,SALARY)
  values(360,'Chihoko','SE',8,20000,);

The result is
```

ID	NAME	DEPT	JOB	YEARS	SALARY	COMM
360	Chihoko	10	SE	8	20000.00	15.00

```
1 record(s) selected.
```

Fig. 5–6 *Inserting a row with a default value*

Note: Columns can also contain generated values, including a new sequence number value.

Identity Column

The previous section discussed how columns can be populated with values if no value was supplied by the user. It is also possible to have DB2 generate sequence numbers or other values during record insertion.

Often, a single column within a table represents a unique identifier for that row. Often this identifier is a number that gets sequentially updated as new records are added.

DB2 can automatically generate sequential values. Fig. 5–7 shows a table definition with the EMP_NO column automatically being generated.

```
CREATE TABLE EMPLOYEE (
  EMPNO  INT GENERATED ALWAYS AS IDENTITY,
  NAME CHAR(10));

INSERT INTO EMPLOYEE(NAME) VALUES 'George','Bill';

SELECT * FROM EMPLOYEE;

EMPNO           NAME
-----------  ----------
          1 George
          2 Bill
```

Fig. 5–7 *Inserting rows with generated values*

If the column is defined with GENERATED ALWAYS, then the INSERT statement cannot specify a value for the EMPNO field. By default, the numbering will start at 1 and increment by 1. The range and increment can be specified as part of the column definition:

 Note: Sequences do not guarantee unique values in the column. The user must specify either a unique index, or a primary key on this column to insure that values are not duplicated.

```
CREATE TABLE EMPLOYEE (
  EMPNO   INT GENERATED ALWAYS AS
     IDENTITY(START WITH 100, INCREMENT BY 10)),
  NAME CHAR(10));

INSERT INTO EMPLOYEE(NAME) VALUES 'George','Bill';

SELECT * FROM EMPLOYEE;

EMPNO          NAME
-----------    -----------
        100 George
        110 Bill
```

Fig. 5–8 *Inserting records with generated values*

In addition, the default value can be GENERATED BY DEFAULT, which means that the user has the option of supplying a value for the field. If no value is supplied (indicated by the DEFAULT keyword), DB2 will generate the next number in sequence.

One additional keyword is available as part of IDENTITY columns. As a DBA, you can decide how many numbers should be "pregenerated" by DB2. This can help reduce catalog contention since DB2 will cache that many numbers in memory rather than go back to the catalog tables to determine which number to generate next.

Identity columns are restricted to numeric values (integer or decimal) and can only be used in one column in the table. The GENERATE keyword can be used for other columns, but they cannot be IDENTITY columns.

The GENERATE keyword can be applied to other columns to generate values automatically. For instance, the EMPLOYEE table could include two columns that are components of the individuals pay.

```
CREATE TABLE EMPLOYEE (
   EMPNO   INT GENERATED ALWAYS AS IDENTITY,
   NAME    CHAR(10),
   SALARY INT,
   BONUS   INT,
   PAY     INT GENERATED ALWAYS AS (SALARY+BONUS)
   );

INSERT INTO EMPLOYEE(NAME, SALARY, BONUS) VALUES
   ('George',20000,2000),
   ('Bill',30000,5000);

SELECT * FROM EMPLOYEE;

EMPNO        NAME         SALARY       BONUS        PAY
-----------  -----------  -----------  -----------  -----------
         1 George              20000         2000        22000
         2 Bill                30000         5000        35000
```

Fig. 5–9 *Inserting records with a generated column*

EMPNO is generated as an IDENTITY column, and PAY is calculated automatically by DB2. If SALARY or BONUS are modified at a later time, DB2 will recalculate the PAY. A GENERATED column has the same options as an IDENTITY column. The value can be either calculated ALWAYS or generated by DEFAULT.

For more information on this powerful feature, please refer to the *DB2 UDB V8.1 SQL Reference* manual.

 Notes: DB2 also has a SEQUENCE object which can be used in place of a generated column. See "Advanced SQL" on page 343 for more information.

Code Page Considerations

A character *code page* is associated with all DB2 character data types (CHAR, VARCHAR, CLOB, DBCLOB). This code page is set at the database level during the CREATE DATABASE command.

A code page is a mapping between an alphanumeric "code" and its binary "encoding" (representation) in the database. A DB2 database can only use a single code page. The code page is established during the CREATE DATABASE command using the options CODESET and TERRITORY. The code page can use a single byte to represent an alphanumeric (a single byte can represent 256 unique elements) or multiple bytes.

Languages such as English contain relatively few unique characters; therefore, a single-byte code page is sufficient to store data. Languages like Japanese require more than 256 elements to represent all unique characters; therefore, a multi-byte code page (usually a double-byte code page) is required.

A code point is the location of a character within the code page. DB2 will attempt to perform *code page conversion* if the application and the database have not been defined using the same code page.

	0	1	2	3	4	5	6	7	8	9	A	B	C	D	E	F
0				0	@	P	`	p								
1			!	1	A	Q	a	q								
2			"	2	B	R	b	r								
3			#	3	C	S	c	s								
4			$	4	D	T	d	t								
5			%	5	E	U	e	u								
6			&	6	F	V	f	v								
7			"	7	G	W	g	w								
8			(	8	H	X	h	x								
9			)	9	I	Y	i	y								
A			*	:	J	Z	j	z								
B			+	;	K	[	k	{								
C			,	<	L	\	l	|								
D			-	=	M	]	m	}								
E			.	>	N	^	n	~								
F			/	?	O		o									

Fig. 5–10 *Code page*

In Fig. 5–10, an example code page is shown. This example represents a portion of the ASCII character set (e.g., hexadecimal code point 41 represents the character A).

Note: Binary data, such as columns specified with FOR BIT DATA and BLOB columns, do not require alphanumeric translation and are not associated with the database code page.

When a DB2 application is bound to a DB2 database, the application and database code page are compared. If the code pages are not the same, code page conversion will be attempted for each SQL statement. If you are using a code page other than that of the database you are accessing, it is important to ensure that the code pages are compatible and conversion can be accomplished.

By default, the collating sequence of a database is defined according to the code set used in the CREATE DATABASE command. If you specify the option COLLATE USING SYSTEM, the data values are compared based on the TERRITORY specified for the database. If the option COLLATE USING IDENTITY is used, all values are compared using their binary representation in a byte-to-byte manner.

When you need to store data in its native (binary) format, avoid using data types associated with code pages. It is generally advantageous to have the application and the database code page the same to avoid the code page conversion process.

Note: DB2 UDB Version 8 includes support for three new code pages:
- Arabic code page 425
- Latin-1 HOST code page 1047
- Unicode V3.1

Many code pages and code page conversion tables have also been enhanced to provide support for the euro currency symbol.

Unicode Support in DB2

The *Unicode* character encoding standard is a fixed-length, character-encoding scheme that includes characters from almost all the living languages of the world. Unicode characters are usually shown as U+xxxx, where xxxx is the hexadecimal code of the character. Each character is 16 bits (2 bytes) wide regardless of the language. While the resulting 65,536 code elements are sufficient for encoding most of the characters of the major languages of the world, the Unicode standard also provides an extension mechanism that allows for encoding as many as a million more characters. This extension reserves a range of code values (U+D800 to U+D8FF, known as *surrogates*) for encoding some 32-bit characters as two successive code elements.

DB2 supports ISO/IEC 10646 standard UCS-2, that is, Unicode without surrogates. UCS-2 is implemented with UTF-8 (UCS Transformation Format 8) algorithmic transformation. DB2 supported code page/CCSIDs are shown in Table 5–3.

Table 5–3 *Supported Code Pages/CCSIDs*

CP/CCSID	Single-Byte (SBCS) Space	Double-Byte (DBCS) Space
1200	N/A	U+0020
13488	N/A	U+0030

Database Objects

These are handled the same way except for the value of their DBCS space. Regarding the conversion table, since code page 1200 is a super set of CCSID 13488, the exact same tables are used for both.

UTF-8 has been registered as CCSID 1208, which is used as the multibyte (MBCS) code page number for the UCS-2/UTF-8 support of DB2. This is the database code page number and the code page of character string data within the database.The double-byte code page number (for UCS-2) is 1200, which is the code page of graphic string data within the database.

When a database is created in UCS-2/UTF-8, CHAR, VARCHAR, LONG VARCHAR, and CLOB data are stored in UTF-8, and GRAPHIC, VARGRAPHIC, LONG VARGRAPHIC, and DBCLOB data are stored in UCS-2. We will simply refer to this as a UCS-2 database.

If you are working with character string data in UTF-8, you should be aware that ASCII characters are encoded into 1-byte lengths; however, non-ASCII characters are encoded into 2- or 3-byte lengths in a multiple-byte character code set (MBCS). Therefore, if you define an n-byte length character column, you can store strings anywhere from n/3 to n characters depending on the ratio of ASCII to non-ASCII characters.

Following is the example to create a UCS-2 database named UCS2DB with the territory code for United States.

```
CREATE DATABASE UCS2DB USING CODESET UTF-8 TERRITORY US
```

 Note: Code set should be specified in uppercase characters.

For further DB2-supported code set or territory information, please refer to the *National Language Support (NLS) section in the DB2 UDB V8.1 Administration Guide.*

Selecting the Correct Data Type

Knowledge of the possible data values and their usage is required to be able to select the correct data type. Specifying an inappropriate data type when defining the tables can result in:

- Wasted disk space
- Improper expression evaluation
- Performance considerations

A small checklist for data type selection is shown in Table 5–4.

Table 5–4 *Data Type Checklist*

Question	Data Type
Is the data variable in length?	VARCHAR
If the data is variable in length, what is the maximum length?	VARCHAR
Do you need to sort (order) the data?	CHAR, VARCHAR, NUMERIC
Is the data going to be used in arithmetic operations?	DECIMAL, NUMERIC, REAL, DOUBLE, BIGINT, INTEGER, SMALLINT
Does the data element contain decimals?	DECIMAL, NUMERIC, REAL, DOUBLE
Is the data fixed in length?	CHAR
Does the data have a specific meaning (beyond DB2 base data types)?	USER DEFINED TYPE
Is the data larger than what a character string can store, or do you need to store non-traditional data?	CLOB, BLOB, DBCLOB

When using character data types, the choice between CHAR and VARCHAR is determined by the range of lengths of the columns. For example, if the range of column length is relatively small, use a fixed char with the maximum length. This will reduce the storage requirements and could improve performance.

Note: Remember that you need to create page sizes that are large enough to contain the length of a row in a table. This is particularly important for tables with large character columns. See "User Tables" on page 238

Tables

Tables are composed of rows; rows are composed of columns. Tables can have constraints to guarantee the uniqueness of rows maintaining relationships between tables. A constraint is a rule that the database manager enforces. There are three types of constraints:

- Unique constraint - Ensures the unique values of a key in a table. Any changes to the columns that comprise the unique key are checked for uniqueness.
- Referential integrity - Enforces referential constraints on insert, update, and delete operations. It is the state of a database in which all values of all foreign keys are valid.
- Table check constraint - Verifies that changed data does not violate conditions specified when a table was created or altered.

Unique Constraints

A *unique constraint* is the rule that the values of a key are valid only if they are unique within the table. Each column making up the key in a unique constraint must be defined as NOT NULL. Unique constraints are defined in the CREATE TABLE statement or the ALTER TABLE statement using the PRIMARY KEY clause or the UNIQUE clause.

A table can have any number of unique constraints; however, a table cannot have more than one unique constraint on the same set of columns.

 Note: The UNIQUERULE column of the SYSCAT.INDEXES view indicates the characteristic of the index. If the value of this column is P, the index is a primary key, and if it is U, the index is an unique index (but not a primary key).

When a unique constraint is defined, the database manager creates (if needed) a unique index and designates it as either a primary or unique system-required index. The enforcement of the constraint is through the unique index. Once a unique constraint has been established on a column, the check for uniqueness during multiple row updates is deferred until the end of the update (deferred unique constraint).

A unique constraint can also be used as the parent key in a referential constraint.

Referential Integrity

Referential integrity allows you to define required relationships between and within tables. The database manager maintains these relationships, which are expressed as referential constraints and requires that all values of a given attribute or table column also exist in some other table column. Fig. 5–11 shows an example of the referential integrity between two tables. This constraint requires that every employee in the EMPLOYEE table must be in a department that exists in the DEPARTMENT table. No employee can be in a department that does not exist.

DEPARTMENT table (Parent table)

DEPTNO (Primary key)	DEPTNAME	MGRNO

EMPLOYEE table (Dependent table)

EMPNO (Primary key)	FIRSTNAME	LASTNAME	WORKDEPT (Foreign key)	PHONENO

Fig. 5–11 *Referential integrity between two tables*

A *unique key* is a set of columns in which no two values are duplicated in any other row. Only one unique key can be defined as a primary key for each table. The unique key may also be known as the *parent key* when referenced by a foreign key.

A *primary key* is a special case of a unique key. Each table can only have one primary key. In this example, DEPTNO and EMPNO are the primary keys of the DEPARTMENT and EMPLOYEE tables.

A *foreign key* is a column or set of columns in a table that refer to a unique key or primary key of the same or another table. A foreign key is used to establish a relationship with a unique key or primary key and enforces referential integrity among tables. The column WORKDEPT in the EMPLOYEE table is a foreign key because it refers to the primary key, column DEPTNO, in the DEPARTMENT table.

A parent key is a primary key or unique key of a referential constraint.

A *parent table* is a table containing a parent key that is related to at least one foreign key in the same or another table. A table can be a parent in an arbitrary number of relationships. In this example, the DEPARTMENT table, which has a primary key of DEPTNO, is a parent of the EMPLOYEE table, which contains the foreign key WORKDEPT.

A dependent table is a table containing one or more foreign keys. A dependent table can also be a parent table. A table can be a dependent in an arbitrary number of relationships. For example, the EMPLOYEE table contains the foreign key WORKDEPT, which is dependent on the DEPARTMENT table that has a primary key.

A referential constraint is an assertion that non-null values of a designated foreign key are valid only if they also appear as values of a unique key of a designated parent table. The purpose of referential constraints is to guarantee that database relationships are maintained and data entry rules are followed.

Enforcement of referential constraints has special implications for some SQL operations that depend on whether the table is a parent or a dependent. The database manager enforces referential constraints across systems based on the referential integrity rules. The rules are

- INSERT rule
- DELETE rule
- UPDATE rule

INSERT Rules

The INSERT rule is implicit when a foreign key is specified.

You can insert a row at any time into a parent table without any action being taken in the dependent table.

You cannot insert a row into a dependent table unless there is a row in the parent table with a parent key value equal to the foreign key value of the row that is being inserted unless the foreign key value is null.

If an INSERT operation fails for one row during an attempt to insert more than one row, all rows inserted by the statement are removed from the database.

DELETE Rules

When you delete a row from a parent table, the database manager checks if there are any dependent rows in the dependent table with matching foreign key values. If any dependent rows are found, several actions can be taken. You determine which action will be taken by specifying a delete rule when you create the dependent table.

- RESTRICT - This rule prevents any row in the parent table from being deleted if any dependent rows are found. If you need to remove both parent and dependent rows, delete dependent rows first.
- NO ACTION - This rule enforces the presence of a parent row for every child after all the referential constraints are applied. This is the default. The difference between NO ACTION and RESTRICT is based on when the constraint is enforced. See the *DB2 UDB V8.1 SQL Reference* for further details.

- CASCADE DELETE - This rule implies that deleting a row in the parent table automatically deletes any related rows in the dependent table.
- SET NULL - This rule ensures that deletion of a row in the parent table sets the values of the foreign key in any dependent row to null (if nullable). Other parts of the row are unchanged.

UPDATE Rules

The database manager prevents the update of a unique key of a parent row. When you update a foreign key in a dependent table and the foreign key is defined with NOT NULL option, it must match some value of the parent key of the parent table. Two options exist:

- RESTRICT - The update for the parent key will be rejected if a row in the dependent table matches the original values of the key.
- NO ACTION - The update operation for the parent key will be rejected if any row in the dependent table does not have a corresponding parent key when the update statement is completed (excluding after triggers). This is the default.

Check Constraints

Table-check constraints will enforce data integrity at the table level. Once a table-check constraint has been defined for a table, every UPDATE and INSERT statement will involve checking the restriction or constraint. If the constraint is violated, the row will not be inserted or updated, and an SQL error will be returned.

A table-check constraint can be defined at table creation time or later using the ALTER TABLE statement.

The table-check constraints can help implement specific rules for the data values contained in the table by specifying the values allowed in one or more columns in every row of a table. This can save time for the application developer since the validation of each data value can be performed by the database and not by each of the applications accessing the database.

The check constraint's definition is stored in the system catalog tables, specifically the SYSIBM.SYSCHECKS table. In addition you can use the SYSCAT.CHECKS system catalog view to view the check constraint definitions.

Adding Check Constraints

When you add a check constraint to a table that contains data, one of two things can happen:

- All the rows meet the check constraint.
- Some or all the rows do not meet the check constraint.

In the first case, when all the rows meet the check constraint, the check constraint will be created successfully. Future attempts to insert or update data that does not meet the constraint business rule will be rejected.

When there are some rows that do not meet the check constraint, the check constraint will not be created (i.e., the ALTER TABLE statement will fail). The ALTER TABLE statement, which adds a new constraint to the EMPLOYEE table, is shown below. The check constraint is named CHECK_JOB. DB2 will use this name to inform us which constraint was violated if an INSERT or UPDATE statement fails. The CHECK clause is used to define a table-check constraint.

```
ALTER TABLE EMPLOYEE
  ADD CONSTRAINT check_job
  CHECK (JOB IN ('Engineer','Sales','Manager'));
```

An ALTER TABLE statement was used because the table had already been defined. If there are values in the EMPLOYEE table that conflict with the constraint being defined, the ALTER TABLE statement will not be completed successfully.

It is possible to turn off constraint checking to let you add a new constraint. The SET INTEGRITY statement enables you to turn off check constraint and referential constraint checking for one or more tables. When you turn off the constraint checking for a table, it will be put in a CHECK PENDING state, and only limited access to the table will be allowed. For example, once a table is in a check-pending state, use of SELECT, INSERT, UPDATE, and DELETE is disallowed on a table. See the *DB2 UDB V8.1 SQL Reference* for the complete syntax of the SET INTEGRITY statement.

Notes:

1. The SET CONSTRAINTS statement is replaced by the SET INTEGRITY statement in DB2 Universal Database V6.1. The SET CONSTRAINTS statement is still supported for backward compatibility.

2. It is a good idea to label every constraint (triggers, table-check, or referential integrity). This is particularly important for diagnosing errors that might occur.

Modifying Check Constraints

As check constraints are used to implement business rules, you may need to change them from time to time. This could happen when the business rules change in your organization.

There is no special command used to change a check constraint. Whenever a check constraint needs to be changed, you must drop it and create a new one. Check constraints can be dropped at any time, and this action will not affect your table or the data within it.

When you drop a check constraint, you must be aware that data validation performed by the constraint will no longer be in effect. The statement used to drop a constraint is the ALTER TABLE statement.

The following example shows how to modify the existing constraint. After dropping the constraint, you have to create it with the new definition.

```
ALTER TABLE EMPLOYEE DROP CONSTRAINT check_job;
```

```
ALTER TABLE EMPLOYEE
  ADD CONSTRAINT check_job
  CHECK (JOB IN ('OPERATOR','CLERK'));
```

Informational Constraints

All of the constraints that have been defined up to this point in time are enforced by DB2 when records are inserted or updated. This can lead to high amounts of system overhead, especially when loading large quantities of records that have referential integrity constraints.

If an application has already verified information before inserting a record into DB2, it may be more efficient to use informational constraints, rather than normal constraints. These constraints tell DB2 what format the data should be in, but are not enforced during insert or update processing. However, this information can be used by the DB2 optimizer and may result in better performance of SQL queries.

The following table will illustrate the use of information constraints and how they work. This simple table contains information on some employee salaries and gender (Figure 5–12):

```
CREATE TABLE EMPDATA
  (
  EMPNO   INT NOT NULL,
  SEX     CHAR(1) NOT NULL
          CONSTRAINT SEXOK
              CHECK (SEX IN ('M','F'))
              NOT ENFORCFD
              ENABLE QUERY OPTIMIZATION,
  SALARY INT NOT NULL,
          CONSTRAINT SALARYOK
              CHECK (SALARY BETWEEN 0 AND 100000)
              NOT ENFORCED
              ENABLE QUERY OPTIMIZATION
  );
```

Fig. 5–12 *Employee table with informational constraints*

This example contains two statements that change the behavior of the column constraints. The first option is NOT ENFORCED which instructs DB2 not to enforce the checking of this column when data is inserted or updated.

The second option is ENABLE QUERY OPTIMIZATION which is used by DB2 when SELECT statements are run against this table. When this value is specified, DB2 will use the information in the constraint when optimizing the SQL.

If the table contains the NOT ENFORCED option, the behavior of insert statements may appear odd. The following SQL will not result in any errors when run against the EMPDATA table (Figure 5–13):

```
INSERT INTO EMPDATA VALUES
  (1, 'M', 54200),
  (2, 'F', 28000),
  (3, 'M', 21240),
  (4, 'F', 89222),
  (5, 'Q', 34444),
  (6, 'K',132333);
```

Fig. 5–13 *Inserting into the Empdata table*

Employee number five has a questionable gender (Q) and employee number six has both an unusual gender and a salary that exceeds the limits of the salary column. In both cases DB2 will allow the insert to occur since the constraints are NOT ENFORCED. What probably will cause more confusion is the result of a select statement against this table (Figure 5–14):

```
SELECT * FROM EMPDATA
  WHERE SEX = 'Q';

EMPNO        SEX SALARY
----------- --- ----------

  0 record(s) selected.
```

Fig. 5–14 *Selecting from the Empdata table*

So DB2 instantly returned the incorrect answer to our query! We know that the value 'Q' is found within the table, but the constraint on this column tells DB2 that the only valid values are either 'M' or 'F'. The ENABLE QUERY OPTIMIZATION keyword also allowed DB2 to use this constraint information when optimizing the SQL statement. If this is not the behavior that the user wants, then the constraint needs to be changed through the use of the ALTER command (Figure 5–15):

```
ALTER TABLE EMPDATA
  ALTER CHECK SEXOK DISABLE QUERY OPTIMIZATION
```

Fig. 5–15 *Alter query optimization*

If the query is reissued, DB2 will return the following results (Figure 5–16):

```
SELECT * FROM EMPDATA
  WHERE SEX = 'Q';

EMPNO        SEX SALARY
----------- --- ----------
          5 Q           34444

  1 record(s) selected.
```

Fig. 5–16 *Selecting from the Empdata table without optimization*

This result takes longer to retrieve than the last one, but at least it is correct! So when should informational constraints be used in DB2? The best scenario for using informational constraints occurs when the user can guarantee that the application program is the only application inserting and updating the data. If the application already checks all of the information beforehand (like sex) then using informational constraints can result in faster performance and no duplication of effort.

The other possible use of information constraints is in the design of data warehouses. Many customers use a star schema (see "STAR Schemas" on page 363) in the design of their data warehouse. The following points are characteristic of a STAR schema design:

- There is a large *fact* table that contains data relating to *dimension* tables.
- The fact table contains the raw data or transactions that have been generated by an application.
- There are a number of small dimension tables that hold descriptive information about entities found in the fact table.
- The primary keys of the dimension tables involved in the STAR schema supply foreign key entries in the fact table. The concatenation of foreign keys from the dimension tables usually forms a small subset of the fact table.

The primary/foreign key constraints within the fact and dimension tables will cause significant amounts of overhead during load times (using INSERT commands) or during a validation step after loading the data. This validation can take more time than the load step itself due to the large number of checks that must take place.

If the application has already generated correct foreign/primary key values in the tables, then it may appropriate to define the referential integrity constraints as information constraints and avoid the large overhead of checking these values. These referential integrity constraints should not be removed from the table definition since DB2 can use them to optimize access to the fact table through the known relationships with the dimension tables. For this reason, the referential constraints should be kept as informational, and query optimization enabled so that DB2 can use this during SELECT optimization.

As with any optimization techniques, DBAs should prototype the changes on a smaller scale to ensure that the changes have the desired effects!

 Note: DB2 UDB Version 8 introduced support for Informational Constraints. These types of constraints allow DB2 to continue to optimize SELECT statements based on these constraints, but not have the overhead associated with enforcing these rules. For more information see "Informational Constraints" on page 232.

Physical DB2 Tables

In DB2, there are two types of permanent tables. One type is the system catalog tables and the other is the user tables.

System Catalog Tables

There are special tables used by DB2 that contain information about all objects within the database and are created for you when the database is created (for instance using the CREATE DATABASE command). These tables are called system catalog tables and they are examined by DB2 during query processing. Some of the information contained in the system catalog tables includes:

- Table/Index definitions
- Column data types
- Defined constraints
- Object dependencies
- Object privileges

When SQL Data Definition Language (DDL) statements are issued, the system catalog tables may in fact be updated for you. There are a number of base system tables and views in a DB2 database, and they always reside in a special table space called SYSCATSPACE.

 Note: To display the names of the system catalog tables and views along with their creation time enter the command LIST TABLES FOR SYSTEM or LIST TABLES FOR SCHEMA schemaname (SYSIBM, SYSCAT, or SYSSTAT).

The system catalog table data cannot be modified using an INSERT or DELETE SQL statement. However, some of the table data can be modified. For example, the COMMENT ON statement and ALTER statement will update information stored in the system catalog tables. For more details on the use of the ALTER statement, please refer to "The ALTER Statement" on page 201 and to the *DB2 UDB V8.1 SQL Reference*.

The system tables also contain statistical information about the tables in the database. For example, the number of physical pages allocated for each table is stored in the system catalog tables. The statistical information is calculated and updated by the RUNSTATS command.

Database object privileges, such as INSERT, SELECT, and CONTROL, are also maintained within the system catalog tables. The privileges are established using special SQL statements known as Data Control Language (DCL) statements. The primary DCL statements are GRANT and REVOKE. These statements were discussed in "Controlling Data Access" on page 135.

The system catalog tables are primarily for read-only purposes since they are maintained by DB2. However, there is a special set of system catalog views that are

Database Objects

updatable. This is a special set of views defined on the system catalog tables that are used to update database statistics. These views are defined in the SYSSTAT schema. For example, these views can be used to force the DB2 optimizer to change the access path when executing a query relating to a certain table.

 Note: Use the RUNSTATS command to update the database statistics. Update the SYSSTAT schema views to perform *what if* analysis of performance statistics.

There is also a set of read-only views defined for the system catalog base tables. To determine information about a DB2 database, the most common method is to issue SELECT statements against the system catalog tables. There are views defined for this purpose and they have the schema name SYSCAT.

The system catalog base tables are defined under the SYSIBM schema. However, you should query the SYSCAT views instead.

In general, there is at least one system catalog table for each of the database object types. Table 5–5 lists some of the system catalog views.

Table 5–5 *System Catalog Tables and Views*

Database Object	SYSCAT System Catalog Views	SYSSTAT Updatable Views
Table space	TABLESPACES	-
Table	TABLES	TABLES
Schema	SCHEMATA	
View	VIEWS	-
Column	COLUMNS	COLUMNS
Index	INDEXES	INDEXES
Package	PACKAGES	-
Trigger	TRIGGERS	-
Data Type	DATA TYPES	-
Stored Procedures	PROCEDURES	-
Constraint	CHECKS	-
Referential Integrity	REFERENCES	-

Table 5–5 *System Catalog Tables and Views*

Database Object	SYSCAT System Catalog Views	SYSSTAT Updatable Views
Function	FUNCTIONS	FUNCTIONS
Buffer Pool	BUFFERPOOLS	

The number of views defined within the SYSCAT schema or defined within the SYSSTAT schema can differ based on the version of DB2. Remember, the SYSSTAT schema views are used for updating statistical information for the database. An attempt to update any nonstatistical value is rejected by DB2.

User Tables

The CREATE TABLE statement allows users to define tables. The definition must include its name and the attributes of its columns. The definition may include other attributes of the table such as its primary key or check constraints.

Once the table is defined, column names and data types cannot be modified. Exceptions to this include increasing the length of a varchar column or modifying a reference type column to add a scope. However, new columns can be added to the table (be careful when adding new columns since default data values will be used for existing records). In addition, after a table is created you can change table options such as PCTFREE, the DATA CAPTURE option, LOCK SIZE, LOGGING, or APPEND MODE.

The RENAME TABLE statement can change the name of an existing table.

 Note: The longest unqualified table name is 128 bytes and the longest unqualified column name is 30 bytes.

The maximum number of columns that a table can have is 1012. This will vary depending on the data page size. DB2 supports 4K, 8K, 16K, and 32K data page sizes. Table 5–6 shows the maximum number of columns in a table and maximum length of a row by page size.

Table 5–6 *Table Limits*

	4k Page Size	8k Page Size	16k Page Size	32k Page Size
Maximum columns	500	1012	1012	1012
Maximum row length (bytes)	4005	8101	16293	32677

Database Objects

Table 5–6 *Table Limits*

	4k Page Size	8k Page Size	16k Page Size	32k Page Size
Maximum table size (per partition) (GB)	64	128	256	512

By default, user tables are stored in the USERSPACE1 table space. Users can specify the table space name in which the table will be stored. Tables and indexes can be placed separately into different table spaces (using DMS table spaces). LOB columns can also be placed into another table space in which the table is created (using DMS table spaces). If the table space name is not specified explicitly when creating a table, a table space for the table is determined as follows:

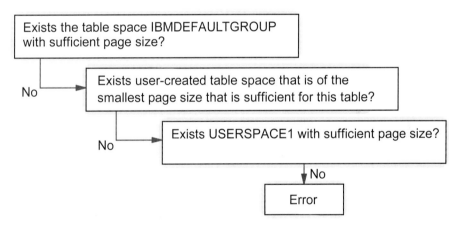

Fig. 5–17 *How DB2 chooses a table space for a table*

For detailed information about table spaces, please refer to "Data Storage Management" on page 449.

After creating a table, data can be stored in the table using one of these methods:

- INSERT statement
- IMPORT command
- LOAD command

Note: The terms *utility* and *command* are used interchangeably throughout the book. All of the DB2 utilities are documented in the *DB2 UDB V8.1 Command Reference*, but they can also be issued from an application using an API defined in the *DB2 UDB V8.1 API Reference.*

Not logged table

The NOT LOGGED INITIALLY option of the CREATE TABLE statement avoids the overhead of logging data. Any changes made to the table by an INSERT, DELETE, UPDATE, CREATE INDEX, DROP INDEX, or ALTER TABLE operation in the same transaction in which the table is created are not logged.

For a table created with the NOT LOGGED INITIALLY option, you can reactivate the not logged mode using the ALTER TABLE statement with the ACTIVATE NOT LOGGED INITIALLY option. Any changes made to the table by an INSERT, DELETE, UPDATE, CREATE INDEX, DROP INDEX, or ALTER TABLE operation in the same transaction in which the table is initially altered are not logged either. This option is useful for situations where a large amount of data needs to be inserted or updated and recovery of the table is not necessary.

Notes:

1. If you really need a temporary table that is only used during the duration of a program, use the DECLARE statement instead. This will result in no catalog contention, no logging, and no lock contention.

2. When the transaction is committed, all changes that were made to the table during it are flushed to disk.

3. When you run the ROLLFORWARD utility and it encounters a log record that indicates that a table in the database was created with the NOT LOGGED INITIALLY option, the table will be marked as unavailable. After the database is recovered, an error will be issued if any attempt is made to access the table (SQL1477N Table "" cannot be accessed. SQLSTATE=55019). The only operation permitted is to drop the table.

Sample Table Create Statements

Fig. 5–18 shows sample CREATE TABLE statements. This sample creates two tables. The definitions include unique constraints, check constraints, referential integrity, and NOT LOGGED INITIALLY attributes. In this example,

- The DEPARTMENT table has a primary key that consists of column DEPTNUMB.
- The EMPLOYEE table has a check constraint that says JOB should be Sales, Mgr, or Clerk.
- The default value is defined for the column HIREDATE in the EMPLOYEE table.
- EMPLOYEE table has a primary key that consists of column ID
- A Referential constraint is defined between the DEPARTMENT table and the EMPLOYEE table.
- The EMPLOYEE table is created in the table space HUMRES, and its index is created in the table space HUMRES_IDX.
- Any changes made to the table by an INSERT, DELETE, UPDATE, CREATE INDEX, DROP INDEX, or ALTER TABLE operation in the same transaction in which the EMPLOYEE table is created are not logged for the EMPLOYEE table.

```
CREATE TABLE Department
(Deptnumb   SMALLINT NOT NULL,
 Deptname   VARCHAR(20),
 Mgrno      SMALLINT,
 PRIMARY KEY(Deptnumb)
);

CREATE TABLE Employee
(Id         SMALLINT      NOT NULL,
 Name       VARCHAR(9)    NOT NULL,
 Dept       SMALLINT,
 Job        CHAR(5) CHECK (Job IN ('Sales','Mgr','Clerk')),
 Hiredate   DATE WITH DEFAULT CURRENT DATE,
 Salary     DECIMAL(7,2),
 Comm       DECIMAL(7,2),
 CONSTRAINT UNIQUEID PRIMARY KEY(Id),
 FOREIGN KEY(Dept) references DEPARTMENT(Deptnumb)
                         ON DELETE RESTRICT)
IN HUMRES
INDEX IN HUMRES_IDX
NOT LOGGED INITIALLY;
```

Fig. 5–18 *Create Table statement examples*

Compressed Tables

When creating a table the user has the option of using a form of data compression. This can be useful in environments where much of the data in a table consists of null or zero values.

DB2 allows two additional clauses on the CREATE TABLE statement to specify compression:

```
CREATE TABLE Products
(ProdNo       INT           NOT NULL,
 Description  VARCHAR(40),
 Quantity     NUMERIC(31,0) NOT NULL COMPRESS SYSTEM DEFAULT,
 Location     CHAR(10)
 )
VALUE COMPRESSION;
```

In order to take advantage of compression at the table level, the VALUE COMPRESSION clause must be used as part of the CREATE TABLE command. This parameter indicates to DB2 that it can use a different row format to store the information in the row.

The normal row format in DB2 contains information on each column value, including whether or not it can contain a null value. For fixed-length fields, like numbers, the entire object is still stored in the row whether or not the field contains null or zero. This can result in a large amount of wasted space, especially in data warehousing applications where much of the data may not contain a value.

The new DB2 row format will add an extra two bytes of storage to each variable length data type (i.e. BLOB, CLOB, DBCLOB, LONG VARCHAR, and LONG VARGRAPHIC) in the table when the VALUE COMPRESSION clause is used. This can result in a new row being longer than the original one if all of the fields are filled. However, if only a few of the fields have default or null values then the space savings can be significant.

In addition, other datatypes like SMALLINT, INTEGER, BIGINT, NUMERIC, FLOAT, DOUBLE, and REAL can be compressed if the COMPRESS SYSTEM DEFAULT clause is added to the column definition. These values will only be compressed out if the field is NULL or contains the system default value of zero. If the field contains anything other than the system default value, it cannot be compressed, even if it contains a user-defined default value. A future release of DB2 may include this capability.

All of these datatypes, regardless of length or precision, will be compressed to three bytes per column. The savings in space are dependent on the datatype. SMALLINT fields only occupy two bytes, so compressing them to three bytes is not really any savings! However, large numeric columns like NUMERIC(31,0) can be compressed from 16 bytes of storage to only three.

The TIME, TIMESTAMP, and DATE datatypes are not supported for compression. The system default value for these fields are continually changing, so there is no way for the system to know what the default value should be.

The space saving achieved from using compression comes at the cost of higher maintenance time in the database. Although retrieval of values will be extremely efficient, updating a value from a default of zero to something else will require that the row be expanded to accommodate the new column size. This additional work will impact total response time. In systems where update transactions are minimal, compressing the table may result in considerable space savings.

> **Note:** DB2 UDB Version 8 includes support for compressing data found in tables. DBAs should examine the potential space savings against the increased processing time when doing updates against the data. Data warehousing applications are good candidates for compression and should be considered first.

Modifying a Table

After creating a table, the ALTER TABLE statement enables you to modify existing tables. The ALTER TABLE statement modifies existing tables by:

- Adding one or more columns to a table
- Adding or dropping a primary key
- Adding or dropping one or more unique or referential constraints
- Adding or dropping one or more check constraint definitions
- Altering the length of a VARCHAR column
- Altering a reference type column to add a scope
- Altering or dropping a partitioning key
- Changing table attributes such as the DATA CAPTURE, PCTFREE, LOCKSIZE, or APPEND mode option
- Activating the not logged initially attribute of the table

In this chapter, not all of these operations are discussed. Refer to the *DB2 UDB V8.1 SQL Reference* for each option of the ALTER TABLE statement.

Some of the attributes of a table can be changed only after the table is created. For example, if users want to change the default lock level or enable insert by append mode for a table, the ALTER TABLE statement should be issued for a table. Fig. 5–19 shows us the ALTER TABLE statement with these options used.

```
ALTER TABLE Employee
  ACTIVATE NOT LOGGED INITIALLY
  LOCKSIZE TABLE
  APPEND ON
  VOLATILE;
```

Fig. 5–19 *Alter Table statement*

The LOCKSIZE option indicates the granularity of locks used when the table is accessed; in this case, the use of a table lock. By default, row-level locks are used when tables are accessed. This option of the ALTER TABLE statement allows locking to be pushed up to the table level. Using table-level locks may improve the performance of queries by reducing the number of locks that need to be obtained and released. However, concurrency may be reduced since all locks are held over the complete table.

The APPEND ON option indicates whether data is appended to the end of a table or inserted where free space is available. Specifying APPEND ON can improve performance by allowing for faster inserts and eliminating the maintenance of free space information. Note that the table must not have a clustered index when specifying this option.

If you want to activate the NOT LOGGED attribute of the table for the current transaction, the ACTIVATE NOT LOGGED INITIALLY option enables you to do this. However, notice that if you want to specify this option, the table must have been originally created with the NOT LOGGED INITIALLY attribute, and the create table transaction committed.

The VOLATILE parameter indicates to the optimizer that the cardinality of the table can vary significantly at run time, from empty to quite large. To access the table, the optimizer will use an index scan rather than a table scan, regardless of the statistics, if that access is index only (all columns referenced are in the index) or that access is able to apply a predicate in the index scan. An optional key word, CARDINALITY, is used to indicate that it is the number of rows in the table that is volatile and not the table itself.

Removing a Table

When you want to remove a table, issue this statement:

```
DROP TABLE EMPLOYEE;
```

Note that any objects that are directly or indirectly dependent on this table are deleted or made inoperative, for example, indexes, triggers, and views. Whenever a table is deleted, its description is deleted from the catalog and any packages that reference the object are invalidated.

> **Note:** To delete all of the rows from a table, without actually dropping it, you can use the ALTER TABLE statement:
>
> ALTER TABLE name ACTIVATE NOT LOGGED INITIALLY WITH EMPTY TABLE
>
> The advantage of using this format over a DROP table is that all of the security definitions, indexes, and other database objects are preserved.

Multidimensional Clustering

Multidimensional clustering (MDC) provides an elegant method for flexible, continuous, and automatic clustering of data along multiple dimensions. This results in significant improvement in the performance of queries, as well as a reduction in the overhead of data maintenance operations, such as reorganization, and index maintenance operations during insert, update, and delete operations. Multidimensional clustering is primarily intended for data warehousing and large database environments, but it can also be used in online transaction processing (OLTP) environments.

MDC enables a table to be physically clustered on more than one dimension simultaneously, rather than only one with a clustering index. In particular, an MDC table ensures that rows are organized on disk in blocks of consecutive pages, such that all rows within any block have the same dimension values. All blocks contain the same number of pages and multiple blocks can have the same dimension values.

> **Note:** DB2 UDB Version 8 introduced support for Multidimensional Clustering (MDC) in tables. These MDC tables store rows into extents based on dimension values, resulting in faster performance for range queries as well as eliminating the need for table reorganization.

When a clustering index is defined for a table, DB2 attempts to organize the rows on pages according to these index values (Figure 5–20).

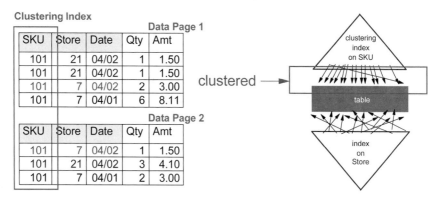

Fig. 5–20 *Clustering index*

In this example, the DBA has chosen the SKU column (product number) as the clustering index, so DB2 will attempt to place product records with the same SKU close to one another on the pages. From a query perspective, any range queries like SKU BETWEEN 101 AND 102 will result in very efficient retrieval of the records since they will all be close to one another on disk.

Any other indexes that might be created on this table will not be clustered. For instance, an index on the store number will not have the data on the pages ordered by store number. DB2 can still use this index for optimizing retrieval from the disk, but the record retrieval will be in a much more random fashion rather than sequentially if it was a clustering index.

With an MDC table, the data is clustered according to the dimensions you have defined for the table. The following diagram illustrates how DB2 would manage a table of two dimensions that have been specified for the table (Figure 5–21):

Fig. 5–21 *MDC table*

Each block in an MDC table corresponds to an extent in a DB2 tablespace. This can be as little as two physical pages (which can be 4, 8, 16, or 32K in size) up to whatever amount the DBA thinks is reasonable. Each one of these blocks will only contain records that have the same dimension values. The intersection of unique dimension values is called a cell and a cell is placed into its own extent. An MDC table can have up to 16 dimensions, but most tables will only have a small number of significant dimensions. In the previous diagram, one cell contains only records for store 7 and product number 101.

As records are added to the system, MDC will maintain these blocks automatically. The following table describes the actions that DB2 would take when inserts, deletes, and updates take place against an MDC table (Table 5–7).

Table 5–7 *MDC SQL Processing*

SQL statement	MDC Processing
INSERT - new dimensions	When a record with new dimension values (dimensions that are not already represented in the table) is inserted into an MDC table, DB2 will allocate a new extent for this record and place that record into this extent.

Table 5–7 *MDC SQL Processing*

SQL statement	MDC Processing
INSERT - existing dimension	If the record being inserted already has dimensions that exist in the table, DB2 will place the record into the same set of extents that contain records with the same dimensions. If the extent is full, DB2 will allocate another extent and place this record into it.
UPDATE - maintaining dimensions	Records will be updated in place if none of the dimension columns are changed. If the size of the row expands beyond the space available on a page, DB2 will attempt to place it elsewhere in the extents that are allocated for this dimension. If space cannot be found, a new extent will be allocated and this record moved to the new extent.
UPDATE - changing dimension	If any of the dimensions in a row are changed, DB2 will physically delete the record from the current dimension block that the record is in, and then place it into the new dimension block. If the dimension does not exist, DB2 will allocate a new extent for it.
DELETE - individual rows	A delete of individual row will remove it from the page it is on. If that delete request empties an extent of data, DB2 will return that extent to the tablespace for use in future inserts or updates.
DELETE - entire dimension	A delete of all values in a dimension will result in the extents being returned to the tablespace for future use in inserts and updates.

Block Indexes

In order to track the blocks which comprise a slice, or which blocks contain all records having a particular dimension key value, a dimension block index is automatically created for each dimension when an MDC table is created. The following SQL illustrates how a table is created with two dimensions (Figure 5–22):

```
CREATE TABLE SALES
   (
   STORE    INT  NOT NULL,
   SKU      INT  NOT NULL,
   DIVISION INT  NOT NULL,
   QUANTITY INT  NOT NULL,
   TXDATE   DATE NOT NULL,
   )
ORGANIZE BY DIMENSIONS(STORE,SKU);
```

Fig. 5–22 *MDC table creation*

The ORGANIZE BY option tells DB2 that you want to create an MDC table with two dimensions. In this case, the STORE and SKU columns will be the dimensions that DB2 will keep track of. With two dimensions, DB2 will create three block indexes:

- One block index for the unique STORE values
- One block index for the unique SKU values
- One composite block index for STORE/SKU pairs

The composite index is used by DB2 to find a block to insert a new record into as well as find the blocks for select processing. This index will contain all STORE/SKU pairs that have been inserted into the table (as opposed to all possible combinations). This is sometimes referred to as a sparse index since not every possible value in the cartesian join of department and division values is represented in the index.

The individual dimension blocks are used for quickly locating blocks of records in that particular dimension. The block indexes for the store example are illustrated in the following diagram (Figure 5–23):

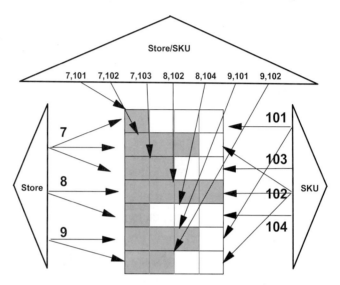

Fig. 5–23 *Block indexes*

These block indexes are typically very small since they only contain entries for the dimensions values and not for every possible record. Since these indexes are relatively small, they can be quickly traversed to find which block a record needs to be placed into, rather than using complicated clustering logic. This short search time can help OLTP workloads, especially if most dimension values have already been insert into the table. In the event that a particular dimension does not exist, DB2 will need to acquire another extent to insert this record into, and that will increase the transaction for this particular case. However, this can also occur with tables that are not defined as MDC.

Block Map

In addition to the new block indexes that are created for an MDC table, DB2 will also create a new structure which stores the status of each block of the table. This block map is stored as a separate BMP file in an SMS table space and as a new object in the object table in a DMS table space.

This file comprises an array containing an entry for each block of the table, where each entry is a set of status bits for a block. These status bits indicate:

- In-use: Currently contains data and block is assigned to a cell
- Load: Recently loaded; not yet visible by scans
- Constraint: Recently loaded; constraint checking still to be done
- Refresh: Recently loaded; ASTs still need to be refreshed

Normally a DBA would not be concerned with these internal objects that DB2 is generating. However, they will see his object being generated in file systems so they should be aware that it exists.

Candidate Dimensions

Choosing dimensions for a table may require some trial and error. In many cases the dimensions that are chosen should match the typical query patterns that users submit to the database. One should also take care to chose columns that have the following characteristics:

- A column that is used in typical queries including:
  - columns in equality or range queries
  - columns with coarse granularity
  - foreign key columns in fact tables
  - any generated column should be monotonically (continually) increasing or decreasing
- A column that has a low cardinality, or unique number of values

Choosing a column with a high cardinality may result in a lot of wasted space. For instance, a salary field is probably not a suitable candidate for a dimension since there is very low probability that any two salaries will be the same.

If the skew of the data is such that some cells will be sparsely populated while others will be full, you may wish to have a smaller block size, so that the sparse cells will not take up as much wasted space. For this reason, a DBA may want to create the table with a smaller extent size (2) to avoid wasting space in each extent. It is important to remember that each unique cell (combination of all dimensions) will occupy a minimum of one extent as opposed to a page.

If some of the dimensions do not have sufficient values, then it is possible to combine them with another column to create a composite dimension. In the sales table, the DBA may determine that store and division are always used together in a query. Since there may only be a handful of divisions, creating a dimension just on division may not be useful. The table creation command would be changed to that in figure 5–24:

```
CREATE TABLE SALES
   (
   STORE    INT  NOT NULL,
   SKU      INT  NOT NULL,
   DIVISION INT  NOT NULL,
   QUANTITY INT  NOT NULL,
   TXDATE   DATE NOT NULL,
   )
ORGANIZE BY DIMENSIONS((STORE,DIVISION),SKU);
```

Fig. 5–24 *MDC table with composite dimensions*

Note how STORE and DIVISION are combined as one dimension. This design still gives the user access to store and division ranges, but can also be used for store lookups as well.

Dimensions that have too many values can be modified through functions to lower their cardinality. A typical example would be salaries where it would not be practical to use this column as one of the dimensions, but the integer portion of salary/1000 might result in a reasonable number of values. To implement this type of dimension, the user must create a column in the table that contains this value. The easiest way to implement this is through the use of a generated column. If the use of the sales table indicates that the quantity field is used in many queries, a generated column on this field may be useful (figure 5–25):

```
CREATE TABLE SALES
   (
   STORE    INT  NOT NULL,
   SKU      INT  NOT NULL,
   DIVISION INT  NOT NULL,
   QUANTITY INT  NOT NULL,
   QTY_1K   INT  NOT NULL
      GENERATED ALWAYS AS (QUANTITY/1000),
   TXDATE   DATE NOT NULL,
   )
ORGANIZE BY DIMENSIONS(SKU, QTY_1k);
```

Fig. 5–25 *MDC table with a generated column*

One important caveat of using generated columns concerns the monotonicity of the function that is used. Generally the value generated by the function should be going up if the base value goes up and it should go down when the base value goes down.

In algebraic terms where A and B are values and f(A) and f(B) are functions against A and B:

$$A \geq B \rightarrow f(A) \geq f(B)$$
$$A \leq B \rightarrow f(A) \leq f(B)$$

If the values in the generated column holds to these rules, DB2 will be able to do range queries across the dimensions. SQL statements which include BETWEEN predicates are ideal candidates for this. The QTY_1K field in the SALES table follows this rule since the calculation for this field will increase as the quantity of sales increases.

A calculation that would not be a good candidate for generated column is the MONTH function. Over the course of a year, the function MONTH(DATE) would increase in value. As we go into the next year, the MONTH function will return a value of one for January, which would be less than December. However, from a date perspective, it should be greater than December. This function fails the monotonicity test and should not be used as one of the dimensions. While there is nothing that restricts you from using this type of generated column, DB2 will only be able to use the dimensions that are generated to search for exact matches and will not be able to do efficient range searching.

As an alternative to using the MONTH function, the INTEGER function has been extended to work with date fields. When the INTEGER function is used against a date, it returns a numeric representation of that date. For instance, INTEGER('2002-09-14') will return an integer value of 20020914. To generate an equivalent MONTH function using this new INTEGER function, the result can be divided by 100 to create a year and month value. This will always increase in value and so any dimension that is generated with this function will be eligible for range queries.

Alternative Index Considerations

An MDC table creates additional indexes that are used to track blocks within the table. These indexes are not under user control and are created automatically when you create the table.

Even though these indexes exist, there is no limitation on the type of indexes you can create on this table. A primary key, partitioning key, or any other type of key can work in conjunction with the MDC indexes.

MDC indexes can also be used to AND/OR with other indexes if they exist. This means that MDC indexes can be used to reduce the answer set before needing to use one of the other indexes. Using an MDC table may also reduce the need for many of the additional indexes that are in place.

Loading and Delete processing

An MDC table can be loaded using the high-speed LOAD command that is shipped with DB2. The loader is aware of the structure of an MDC table and so will generate the appropriate blocks of information. It will also take advantage of free extents that may be created during delete activity.

One important aspect of MDC tables is the reclamation of existing space after a delete. When an extent is cleared of records due to a delete operation, DB2 will release this extent back to the tablespace for future use. With standard SQL tables, space will not be reclaimed until a reorganization command is issued. In the case of MDC, the free space is instantly available to the user, thus eliminating the need for reorganizing the table. It may still be possible that pages within the extent become fragmented over a long period of time (row overflows) so the DBA may want to run a reorganization command against an MDC table. In most cases this will be a very infrequent activity.

MDC Performance

Preliminary tests have shown that MDC can speed up certain queries by over 50%. Much of this improvement comes from shortening the search and access time to blocks of records. Selecting individual records will still need traditional indexes to ensure good performance, but MDC will significantly improve access to groups of records. This benefit can be gained for both transactional (OLTP) and business intelligence (BI) workloads.

For OLTP workloads, MDC tables should improve insert time since the records are placed into existing extents based on dimensions, so the overhead of free space checking is reduced. For block deletes or updates, DB2 can go directly to the cell containing the appropriate records and modify all of the values in that extent. Contrast this to having to traverse an index and looking for individual rows that meet the update or delete criteria.

When creating a database for BI workloads, MDC tables will offer superior performance for any queries that access ranges of data. In these situations, DB2 can go directly to the cells that contain the required dimensions and read the values in the extent. This is much faster than using a traditional index to find the records. In addition, block indexes can be used with traditional indexes by using index ANDing or ORing to reduce the scope of searches within the table.

MDC tables offer an alternative to traditional clustering indexes for maintaining data order in tables. DBAs should access their table designs to see whether or not they can take advantage of this key technology that is found in DB2. In many cases a significant benefit in performance and a reduction of maintenance can be achieved.

Views

Views are virtual tables that are created using the CREATE VIEW statement. Once a view is defined, it may be accessed using DML statements, such as SELECT, INSERT, UPDATE, and DELETE, as if it were a table. A view is a temporary result and available only during query processing. We will talk about the *typed view* in "Advanced SQL" on page 343.

With a view, you can make a subset of table data available to an application program and validate data that is to be inserted or updated. A view can have column names that are different from the names of corresponding columns in the original tables. The use of views provides flexibility in the way the application programs and end-user queries look at the table data.

A sample CREATE VIEW statement is shown below. The underlying table, EMPLOYEE, has columns named SALARY and COMM. For security reasons, this view is created from the ID, NAME, DEPT, JOB, and HIREDATE columns. In addition, we are restricting access on the column DEPT. This definition will only show the information of employees who belong to the department whose DEPTNO is 10.

```
CREATE VIEW EMP_VIEW1
(EMPID,EMPNAME,DEPTNO,JOBTITLE,HIREDATE)
AS SELECT ID,NAME,DEPT,JOB,HIREDATE FROM EMPLOYEE
    WHERE DEPT=10;
```

After the view has been defined, the access privileges can be specified. This provides data security since a restricted view of the base table is accessible. As we have seen above, a view can contain a WHERE clause to restrict access to certain rows or can contain a subset of the columns to restrict access to certain columns of data.

The column names in the view do not have to match the column names of the base table. The table name has an associated schema as does the view name.

Once the view has been defined, it can be used in DML statements such as SELECT, INSERT, UPDATE, and DELETE (with restrictions). The database administrator can decide to provide a group of users with a higher level privilege on the view than the base table.

Views with Check Option

If the view definition includes conditions (such as a WHERE clause) and the intent is to ensure that any INSERT or UPDATE statement referencing the view will have the WHERE clause applied, the view must be defined using WITH CHECK OPTION. This option can ensure the integrity of the data being modified in the database. An SQL error will be returned if the condition is violated during an INSERT or UPDATE operation.

Fig. 5–26 is an example of a view definition using the WITH CHECK OPTION. The WITH CHECK OPTION is required to ensure that the condition is always checked. You want to ensure that the DEPT is always 10. This will restrict the input values for the DEPT column. When a view is used to insert a new value, the WITH CHECK OPTION is always enforced.

```
CREATE VIEW EMP_VIEW2
(EMPNO,EMPNAME,DEPTNO,JOBTITLE,HIREDATE)
AS SELECT ID,NAME,DEPT,JOB,HIREDATE FROM EMPLOYEE
    WHERE DEPT=10
WITH CHECK OPTION;
```

Fig. 5–26 *View definition using* WITH CHECK OPTION

If the view in Fig. 5–26 is used in an INSERT statement, the row will be rejected if the DEPTNO column is not the value 10. It is important to remember that there is no data validation during modification if the WITH CHECK OPTION is not specified.

If the view in Fig. 5–26 is used in a SELECT statement, the conditional (WHERE clause) would be invoked and the resulting table would only contain the matching rows of data. In other words, the WITH CHECK OPTION does not affect the result of a SELECT statement.

The WITH CHECK OPTION must not be specified for the following views:

• Views defined with the READ ONLY option (a read only view)
• Views that reference the NODENUMBER or PARTITION function, a nondeterministic function (e.g., RAND), or a function with external action
• Typed views (refer to "Advanced SQL" on page 343 for detailed information about typed views)

Nested View Definitions

If a view is based on another view, the number of predicates that must be evaluated is based on the WITH CHECK OPTION specification.

If a view is defined without WITH CHECK OPTION, the definition of the view is not used in the data validity checking of any insert or update operations. However, if the view directly or indirectly depends on another view defined with the WITH CHECK OPTION, the definition of that super view is used in the checking of any insert or update operation.

If a view is defined with the WITH CASCADED CHECK OPTION or just the WITH CHECK OPTION (CASCADED is the default value of the WITH CHECK OPTION), the definition of the view is used in the checking of any insert or update operations. In addition, the view inherits the search conditions from any updatable views on which the view depends. These conditions are inherited even if those views do not include the WITH CHECK OPTION. Then, the inherited conditions are multiplied together to conform to a constraint that is applied for any insert or update operations for the view or any views depending on the view.

As an example, if a view V2 is based on a view V1, and the check option for V2 is defined with the WITH CASCADED CHECK OPTION, the predicates for both views are evaluated when INSERT and UPDATE statements are performed against the view V2. Fig. 5–27 shows a CREATE VIEW statement using the WITH CASCADED CHECK OPTION. The view EMP_VIEW3 is created based on a view EMP_VIEW2, which has been created with the WITH CHECK OPTION (Fig. 5–26). If you want to insert or update a record to EMP_VIEW3, the record should have the values DEPTNO=10 and EMPNO>20.

Note: Notice that the condition DEPTNO=10 is enforced for inserting or updating operations to EMP_VIEW3 even if EMP_VIEW2 does not include the WITH CHECK OPTION.

```
CREATE VIEW EMP_VIEW3 AS
  SELECT EMPNO,EMPNAME,DEPTNO FROM EMP_VIEW2
    WHERE EMPNO >20
WITH CASCADED CHECK OPTION;
```

Fig. 5–27 *View definition using the* WITH CASCADED CHECK OPTION

We can also specify the WITH LOCAL CHECK OPTION when creating a view. If a view is defined with the WITH LOCAL CHECK OPTION, the definition of the view is used in the checking of any insert or update operations. However, the view does not inherit the search conditions from any updatable views on which it depends.

As an example, refer to the nested view example shown in Fig. 5–28.

```
CREATE TABLE T1
    (C1 INT, C2 INT, C3 INT, C4 INT, C5 INT);
CREATE VIEW V1 AS
    SELECT * FROM T1 WHERE C1=1;
CREATE VIEW V2 AS
    SELECT * FROM V1 WHERE C2=1 WITH LOCAL CHECK OPTION;
CREATE VIEW V3 AS
    SELECT * FROM V2 WHERE C3=1;
CREATE VIEW V4 AS
    SELECT * FROM V3 WHERE C4=1 WITH CASCADED CHECK OPTION;
CREATE VIEW V5 AS
    SELECT * FROM V4 WHERE C5=1;
```

Fig. 5–28 *Nested view table and view creation statements*

We created one table and five views. V2 depends on V1, V3 on V2, V4 on V3, and V5 on V4. V2 includes WITH LOCAL CHECK OPTION and V4 includes WITH CASCADED CHECK OPTION.

Let us test some insert statements against these views.

1. This insert statement succeeds because the view V1 does not include the WITH CHECK OPTION.

```
INSERT INTO V1 VALUES (2,1,1,1,1);
```

2. The next insert statement will cause an error because V2 includes the WITH LOCAL CHECK OPTION, and the value does not conform to the definition of V2.

```
INSERT INTO V2 VALUES (1,2,1,1,1);
```

3. The following insert statement succeeds because V2 includes the WITH LOCAL CHECK OPTION, which means the definition of V2 is used for the checking but the one of V1 is not. Therefore, it succeeds regardless of the value of the column C1.

```
INSERT INTO V2 VALUES (2,1,1,1,1);
```

4. The next insert returns an error even though V3 does not include the WITH CHECK OPTION, because V3 inherits search conditions from the views on which V3 depends directly or indirectly if those views have the WITH CHECK OPTION. Therefore, the search condition of V2, which is C2=1, is inherited and used for the checking of this insert.

```
INSERT INTO V3 VALUES (1,2,1,1,1);
```

5. The next insert succeeds because V3 does not inherit the definition of V1.

```
INSERT INTO V3 VALUES (2,1,1,1,1);
```

6. The next insert should return an error because V4 includes the WITH CASCADED CHECK OPTION, but the value does not conform to the definition of V4.

```
INSERT INTO V4 VALUES (1,1,1,2,1);
```

7. These insert statements return errors because V4 inherits all search conditions of V4, V3, V2, and V1. Each of these statements does not conform to the definition of V3 or V1.

```
INSERT INTO V4 VALUES (1,1,2,1,1);
INSERT INTO V4 VALUES (2,1,1,1,1);
```

8. This one succeeds because V5 does not include WITH CHECK OPTION, which means the condition C5=1 is not used.

```
INSERT INTO V5 VALUES (1,1,1,1,2);
```

9. This insert statement returns an error for the same reason as does the fourth example: V5 inherits the definition of V4, that is C4=4. This insert does not conform to this condition.

```
INSERT INTO V5 VALUES (1,1,1,2,1);
```

10. This last example returns an error because the inserting row is checked using
V4 and V4 inherits the definition of V3.

```
INSERT INTO V5 VALUES (1,1,2,1,1);
```

The inserting of rows into V5 must conform to the search conditions of V1, V2, V3,
and V4. If the WITH LOCAL CHECK OPTION is specified for V4, the search conditions
of V2 and V4 must be met. If the WITH CHECK OPTION is not specified for V4, the
search condition of V2 must be met.

Modifying a View

Views are virtual table definitions. The view definition is stored in the catalog.
Therefore, if a backup of the database is performed, the view definition is contained in the backup image. The data contained in the view is only available when
the view is being referenced in an SQL statement.

Unlike some other DB2 objects, a view definition cannot be altered using the
ALTER statement. If a view definition needs to be changed in any way, the original
view must be dropped and re-created with the desired configuration. (Note that in
DB2 there is the option to use the ALTER VIEW statement to alter a reference type
column to alter the scope; however, this is the only action on a view definition that
can be done.)

A view can become inoperative if any of the referenced database objects are
dropped from the database. These view dependencies are stored in the system catalog view called SYSCAT.VIEWDEP.

The system catalog view SYSCAT.VIEWS and the system catalog table
SYSIBM.SYSVIEWS contain a column called VALID that contains the character X if
the view has become inoperative. If the base table EMPLOYEE is dropped, the views
EMP_VIEW1 and EMP_VIEW2 would become inoperative as shown in Fig. 5–29.

```
SELECT VIEWNAME,VIEWCHECK,READONLY,VALID
FROM SYSCAT.VIEWS
WHERE VIEWSCHEMA ='DB2ADMIN'


VIEWNAME            VIEWCHECK READONLY VALID
------------------- --------- -------- -----
EMP_VIEW1           N         N        X
EMP_VIEW2           C         N        X

  2 record(s) selected.
```

Fig. 5–29 *Inoperative views*

Two inoperative views are shown in Fig. 5–29 since the valid column contains the value X (a value of Y means that the view is valid). The query in Fig. 5–29 does not show the contents of the TEXT column. This column contains the original CREATE VIEW statement text. The column VIEWCHECK corresponds to the WITH CHECK OPTION in the CREATE VIEW statement. A value of N means that no check option was specified, L means that the WITH LOCAL CHECK OPTION was specified, and C means that the WITH CASCADED CHECK OPTION was specified.

Note: A view will always enforce the base table constraints. These constraints could include a primary key, foreign key, table-check, or not-null constraint.

Removing a View

When you want to remove a view, issue the statement:

```
DROP VIEW EMP_VIEW1;
```

Note that when the specified view is deleted, the definition of any view or trigger that is directly or indirectly dependent on that view is marked inoperative, and any packages dependent on a view that is dropped or marked inoperative will be invalidated.

View Classifications

Views can be classified by the operations they allow. Views can be deletable, updatable, insertable, and read only. Essentially a view type is established according to its update capabilities, and the classification of the view indicates the kind of SQL operation that can be performed using the view.

Referential and check constraints are not taken into account when determining the classification of the view.

The rules determining the classification of a view are numerous and are not listed here. For details on DB2 V8.1 on the classification of views, please refer to the CREATE VIEW statement description in the *DB2 UDB V8.1 SQL Reference*.

Note: DB2 UDB Version 8 now allows Views with UNION ALL statements to be used in INSERT, UPDATE, DELETE, and SELECT commands. The only requirement is that an appropriate CHECK CONSTRAINT has been applied to each underlying table so that DB2 can determine which table is affected by the SQL statement. If the view is too complex for DB2 to determine which table gets modified, a new INSTEAD OF TRIGGER has been introduced to allow for user-defined handling of view operations.

Nicknames

A DB2 federated system is a special type of distributed database management system (DBMS). With a federated system you can send distributed requests to multiple data sources within a single SQL statement. For example, you can join data that is located in a DB2 Universal Database table, an Oracle table, and a Sybase view in a single SQL statement.

The base DB2 product contains support for federating SQL requests between all DB2 family members and Informix. Support for other database platforms are also available, but these require an optional product.

The basic steps to set up the federated server are:

1. Install and configure the client configuration software.

2. Install the DB2 server software on the server that will act as the federated server. This includes:

    *   Creating a DB2 instance on the federated server.
    *   Specifying the user authorities information for the instance.

3. Install and configure any additional required software on the federated server. This might include DB2 Connect.

4. Check the server setup. This includes:

- Confirming the link between the client libraries and DB2.
- Ensuring the proper permissions are on the wrapper library files.
- Checking the data source environment variables.
- Verifying the FEDERATED parameter is set to YES.

5. Create a DB2 database on the federated server instance that will act as the federated database.

Once a federated server and nicknames have been established, these tables can be used in an SQL statement along with other tables. From a user perspective, these tables are no different from tables that are found in a local database. Most of the DML that is described in this book can be used against federated objects.

The first step in setting up a federated system is to enable federated support in the database engine. This can be done either through the control center, or via a CLP command (Figure 5–30):

```
UPDATE DATABASE MANAGER CONFIGURATION USING FEDERATED YES
```

Fig. 5–30 *Enable federated support*

For each data source that you intend to select from you will need an appropriate wrapper. For DB2 sources this will be the DRDA wrapper and it needs to be created before you can catalog any remote data sources.

```
CREATE WRAPPER DRDA;
```

Fig. 5–31 *Create DB2 wrapper*

Once the wrapper is defined, the servers for the remote databases must be defined. These server definitions will then be used for the nickname definitions. For instance, the following server definition redefines the SAMPLE database as a remote server (Figure 5–32):

```
CREATE SERVER V8SAMPLE
  TYPE DB2/UDB VERSION '8.1'
  WRAPPER "DRDA"
  AUTHID "BAKLARZ"
  PASSWORD "******"
  OPTIONS ( DBNAME 'SAMPLE' );
```

Fig. 5–32 *Create server definition*

The CREATE SERVER command must specify a userid and password that can connect to the remote source with SYSADM or DBADM privileges. This statement tells DB2 that the local server name V8SAMPLE maps to the real database called SAMPLE. For all subsequent commands, V8SAMPLE will be the name of the database we refer to.

Now that the server definition is complete, a user mapping needs to be created so that the user issuing the SQL can be authenticated on the remote site (Figure 5–33).

```
CREATE USER MAPPING FOR USER
  SERVER V8SAMPLE
  OPTIONS( REMOTE_AUTHID 'BAKLARZ',
           REMOTE_PASSWORD '********');
```

Fig. 5–33 *Create user mapping*

Now all of the pieces are in place so that a nickname can be created for the remote tables that a user wants to access. The nickname command is used to create a local definition of a table that is found on a remote site. The following example illustrates how a remote table is defined (Figure 5–34):

```
CREATE NICKNAME R_DEPT FOR V8SAMPLE.BAKLARZ.DEPARTMENT;
```

Fig. 5–34 *Table nickname*

This simple example creates a nickname on the DEPARTMENT table that is found in the V8SAMPLE database (which is really the SAMPLE database). This means that the R_DEPT table is exactly the same as the DEPARTMENT table, but DB2 still considers them to be two different objects. Now that the nickname has been created, this table can be used in the same way as another local table. For instance, the following select statement would access this remote table, but this fact is hidden from the user (Figure 5–35):

```
SELECT * FROM R_DEPT;
```

Fig. 5–35 *Select against federated table*

Much more sophisticated SQL can be issued against a federated table. For instance, joins between local and federated tables are allowed, along with the creation of summary tables based on nicknames. The EXPLAIN facility included with DB2 will also describe access to remote objects as shown in the following diagram (Figure 5–36):

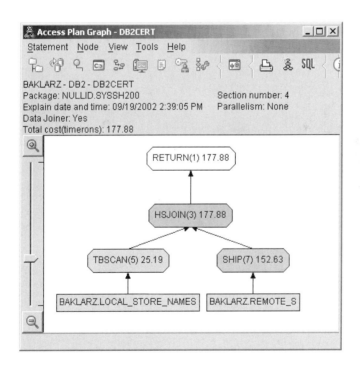

Fig. 5–36 *Visual Explain of federated join*

For more information on federated databases and tables, refer to the *DB2 Universal Database Federated Systems Guide*.

Indexes

An *index* is a list of the locations of rows sorted by the contents of one or more specified columns. Indexes are typically used to improve query performance. However, they can also serve a logical data design purpose. For example, a primary key does not allow the entry of duplicate values in columns, thereby guaranteeing that no rows of a table are the same. Indexes can be created to specify ascending or descending order by the values in a column. The indexes contain a pointer, known as a *record id (RID)*, to the physical location of the rows in the table.

These are two main purposes for creating indexes:

- To ensure uniqueness of values
- To improve query performance

More than one index can be defined on a particular table, which can have a beneficial effect on the performance of queries. However, the more indexes there are, the more the database manager must work to keep the indexes current during update, delete, and insert operations. Creating a large number of indexes for a table that receives many updates can slow down processing.

Unique Index and Non-unique Index

A *unique index* guarantees the uniqueness of the data values in one or more columns. The unique index can be used during query processing to perform faster retrieval of data. The uniqueness is enforced at the end of the SQL statement that updates rows or inserts new rows. The uniqueness is also checked during the execution of the CREATE INDEX statement. If the table already contains rows with duplicate key values, the index is not created.

A *nonunique index* can also improve query performance by maintaining a sorted order for the data.

Depending on how many columns are used to define a key, you can have one of the following types:

- An *scalar key* is a single column key.
- A *composite key* is composed of two or more columns.

The following are types of keys used to implement constraints:

- A *unique key* is used to implement unique constraints. A unique constraint does not allow two different rows to have the same values on the key columns.
- A *primary key* is used to implement entity integrity constraints. A primary key is a special type of unique key. There can be only one primary key per table. The primary key column must be defined with the NOT NULL attribute.
- A *foreign key* is used to implement referential integrity constraints. Referential

constraints can only reference a primary key or unique constraint. The values of a foreign key can only have values defined in the primary key or unique constraint they are referencing or NULL values. (A foreign key is not an index.)

Referential Integrity and Indexes

We have discussed how defining a primary key will ensure the uniqueness of rows and that the primary key is maintained using an index. The index supporting a primary key is known as the primary index of the table. If a constraint name is not provided, DB2-generated indexes are given the name SYSIBM.SQL<timestamp>.

Indexes supporting primary or unique key constraints cannot be dropped explicitly. To remove primary or unique key constraints indexes, you need to use the ALTER TABLE statement. Primary key indexes are dropped with the DROP PRIMARY KEY option. Unique key indexes are dropped using the DROP UNIQUE (CONSTRAINT NAME) option.

Note: DB2 uses unique indexes and the NOT NULL option to maintain primary and unique key constraints.

Null Values and Indexes

It is important to understand the difference between a primary or unique key constraint and a unique index. DB2 uses two elements to implement the relational database concept of primary and unique keys: unique indexes and the NOT NULL constraint. Therefore, unique indexes do not enforce the primary key constraint by themselves since they can allow nulls. Nulls, when it comes to indexing, are treated as equal to all other nulls. You cannot insert a null twice if the column is a key of a unique-index because it violates the uniqueness rule for the index.

General Indexing Guidelines

Indexes consume disk space. The amount of disk space will vary depending on the length of the key columns and the number of rows being indexed. The size of the index will increase as more data is inserted into the table. Therefore, consider the disk space required for indexes when planning the size of the database. Some of the indexing considerations include:

- Primary and unique key constraints will always create a system-generated unique index.
- It is usually beneficial to create indexes on foreign key constraint columns.

You can estimate the disk space consumed by an index using the Control Center. If you are creating an index using the Control Center, you can see the **Estimate Size** button. Clicking this button brings up the Estimate Size panel. You can supply the total number of rows and so forth from this panel and get the estimated size.

 Note: The maximum columns for an index key is 16 and the maximum indexes allowed on a table is 32767. The longest index key (including all overhead) is 1024 bytes.

Index Only Access (Unique Index Include)

The INCLUDE clause specifies additional columns to be appended to the set of index key columns. Any columns included with this clause are not used to enforce uniqueness. These included columns may improve the performance of some queries through index only access. This option may:

* Eliminate the need to access data pages for more queries
* Eliminate redundant indexes
* Maintain the uniqueness of an index

See the following example. If SELECT EMPNO,FIRSTNME,JOB FROM EMPNO is issued to the table on which this index resides, all of the required data can be retrieved from the index without reading data pages. It may improve performance.

```
CREATE UNIQUE INDEX EMP_IX
  ON EMPLOYEE(EMPNO)
  INCLUDE(FIRSTNME,JOB)
```

Bi-Directional Index

The ALLOW REVERSE SCANS clause enables both forward and reverse index scans, that is, in the order defined at index creation time and in the opposite (or reverse) order. This option allows you to:

* Facilitate MIN and MAX functions
* Fetch previous keys
* Eliminate the need for DB2 to create a temporary table for the reverse scan
* Eliminate redundant reverse order indexes

If the index is ordered in ascending order from left to right across its leaf pages, a bidirectional index contains leaf pointers pointing in both directions, that is, to left and right neighboring leaf pages. Therefore, a bidirectional index can be scanned or leaf-traversed from left to right (ascending) or right to left (descending). For example:

```
CREATE UNIQUE INDEX EMP_IX
 ON EMPLOYEE(EMPNO)
 INCLUDE(FIRSTNME,JOB)
 ALLOW REVERSE SCANS;
```

If a user issued the following select statement:

```
SELECT * FROM EMPLOYEE
ORDER BY EMPNO DESC
```

DB2 would not need to sort the results since the index already has the data in the proper sequence.

Modifying an Index

Index attributes cannot be changed without recreating the index definition. For example, you cannot add a column to the list of key columns without dropping the previous definition and creating a new index. You can add a comment to describe the purpose of the index using the COMMENT ON statement.

If you want to modify your index, you have to drop the index first and then create the index again. There is no ALTER INDEX statement.

Removing an Index

When you want to remove an index, issue the following statement:

```
DROP INDEX EMP_IX;
```

Note that packages having a dependency on a dropped index are invalidated.

Index Advisor

The DB2 V8.1 Index Advisor is a utility for automatically recommending indexes for the user to create. The Index Advisor helps you to:

- Find the best indexes for a problem query
- Find the best indexes for a set of queries (a workload), subject to resource limits that are optionally applied
- Test an index on a workload without having to create the index

The Index Advisor can be invoked using either:

- The Control Center
- The command DB2ADVIS

For more information on the Index Advisor, refer to the *DB2 UDB V8.1 Administration Guide: Performance.*

Database Design and Implementation

The best way to understand data type selection is to design a database and implement the design using DB2. We will create a database that can be used to schedule and track the results of a certification program. This database will be used to illustrate many aspects of the SQL language and features of DB2.

This database will be used to schedule test candidates' exams and, following the completion of the test, it will contain the candidates' test scores.

The database and its application will need to support the following tasks:

1. Insert/update/delete testing center information

2. Insert/update/delete test information

3. Insert/update/delete test candidate information

4. Guarantee a uniquely identified test name, regardless of the test number

5. Schedule a candidate to take a test

6. Update candidate test scores once exams have been completed

7. Determine which candidates qualify for certification

8. Generate various reports on the candidates and tests

The database will be named DB2CERT. The data to be stored in the DB2CERT database can easily be grouped into three reference tables and a fourth table used to relate the other tables. The primary relationship can be defined as *a test candidate takes a specific test at a test center.*

Fig. 5–37 *Tables for the DB2CERT database*

Fig. 5–37 shows the relationships within the problem domain. The rectangles represent the tables: CANDIDATE, TEST_CENTER, and TEST. The fourth table is a relationship table called TEST_TAKEN.

DB2CERT Database Table Descriptions

The following is the list of tables in the DB2CERT database:

- The CANDIDATE table stores information about each test candidate for the DB2 Certification Program. Data such as candidate name, address, ID, and phone number will be stored in this table. A row represents a single test candidate (person).

- The TEST_CENTER table stores information about the test centers where a candidate can take a DB2 Certification exam. Data such as the test-center name, address, number of seats, ID, and phone number will be stored in this table. A row represents a single test-center location.

- The TEST table stores information about each of the DB2 Certification exams. Data such as the test name, type, test ID, cut score (passing percentage) and length will be stored in this table. A row represents a single test. For our example, there are three tests in the DB2 Certification Program; therefore, there are only three rows in this table.

- The TEST_TAKEN table associates the rows from the other three tables. It serves the dual purpose of scheduling tests and tracking each test result. Data such as the candidates' test scores, date_taken, start time, and seat numbers will be stored in this table. This will be the most active of the four tables since multiple exams must be taken by each candidate to become certified, and each test taken will have a corresponding row in this table.

Once you have defined the tables and their relationships, the following should be defined:

1. User-defined data types

2. Columns

3. (Optional) primary keys (PK)

4. (Optional) unique keys

5. (Optional) foreign keys (referential constraints)

6. (Optional) table check constraints

7. (Optional) triggers

In Fig. 5–38, the database design is shown. The rectangles represent entities (tables). The ellipses represent attributes (columns). Note that some of the columns are derived (virtual) columns. A derived column is a column that represents a con-

Database Objects

cept and not a physical attribute of an object. The derived columns are included in the model since their values will be populated by the database using a constraint mechanism.

We must map the attributes shown in Fig. 5–38 to DB2 built-in or user-defined data types. To demonstrate some of the powerful features of DB2, we have decided to create distinct types for many of the attributes.

It is beneficial to have a primary key defined for each of the tables since this will ensure uniqueness of the rows. The attributes that are <u>underlined</u> will be used as primary keys. We will also create unique keys to illustrate their use. Unique key attributes are <u>double underlined</u>.

In the previous section, we mentioned that there are four tables in the DB2CERT database. However, the design shown in Fig. 5–38 has only three tables defined. There is an implied table defined in the relationship *candidate takes a test*. A table is required to store each occurrence of a candidate taking a certification test.

We will impose a restriction on the candidates: They can take the test only once on any given day. A candidate can take different tests on the same day, but not the same test. With this restriction in place, we will define a primary key for the *test_taken* table as a composite key including NUMBER (test ID), CID (candidate ID) and DATE_TAKEN (the date of the test). Defining the primary key as a combination of these three values, facilitates enforcing this constraint.

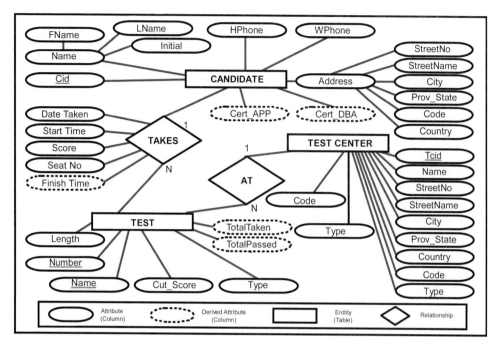

Fig. 5–38 *DB2 Certification database Entity - Relationship diagram*

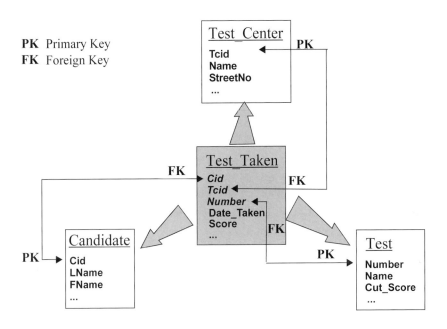

PK Primary Key
FK Foreign Key

Fig. 5–39 *DB2 Certification database - Referential integrity*

The diamond shapes are used to describe the relationships between the tables, including parent-child relationships. For example, there is a one-to-many relationship between the CANDIDATE and the TEST_TAKEN table because a single candidate can take many tests. This relationship is shown by denoting the values of 1 and N (many) on the appropriate side of the diamond.

The database design shown in Fig. 5–38 is just one type of diagramming technique. A logical database design can be represented in a number of ways, but it should not dictate the physical implementation of the database. We have included it here because it will be used in many of the SQL statements throughout the rest of the book.

Define User-Defined Data Types

If you wish to utilize user-defined data types, they must defined before they can be referenced in a CREATE TABLE statement.

We have decided to create a number of user-defined data types as shown in Fig. 5–40. The CANDIDATE_ID, TEST_ID, CENTER_ID, and PHONE data types are all fixed-length strings based on the CHAR data type. These attributes were chosen to be user defined because they have meaning in their structure, and they should not be used in expressions with other character data types. For example, a telephone number data type could be defined and then a user-defined function could be created to extract the area code. The function would only be used for phone data types.

```
CREATE DISTINCT TYPE candidate_id AS CHAR(8)
    WITH COMPARISONS
CREATE DISTINCT TYPE test_id AS CHAR(6)
    WITH COMPARISONS
CREATE DISTINCT TYPE center_id AS CHAR(4)
    WITH COMPARISONS
CREATE DISTINCT TYPE phone AS CHAR(10)
    WITH COMPARISONS
CREATE DISTINCT TYPE score AS DECIMAL(6,2)
    WITH COMPARISONS
CREATE DISTINCT TYPE minutes AS SMALLINT
    WITH COMPARISONS
```

Fig. 5–40 *Defining the user-defined data types*

We also decided to create some numeric user-defined data types, including SCORE and MINUTES.

Defining Columns

Designing a database involves many considerations. We will only examine some of these considerations in this book. If we use the database design in Fig. 5–38 as a starting point, we can start defining database objects.

The first step in creating a database is to issue the CREATE DATABASE command. This command is not an SQL statement since each database product has a different syntax for the creation of a database.

Once the database has been created, we can start defining objects. Let us start creating tables. The E-R diagram had a number of attributes shown. Each of these attributes will be a column in a table.

Every DB2 table contains one or more columns. Tables and their columns are given names. In previous sections, we discussed all of the data types that can be used for column definitions.

Data is stored in a DB2 table using the SQL statement INSERT or UPDATE. (The LOAD and IMPORT utilities are other options.) Usually, it is desirable for each column to have a value. Sometimes, no value is provided for a column in an INSERT statement. If the column is defined as NOT NULL, the INSERT statement will fail. If a default value is defined, it will be used.

The table in Fig. 5–41 is called DB2CERT.CANDIDATE and contains 15 columns.

Each column must have a name and a data type. There are three user-defined data types used in the DB2CERT.CANDIDATE table. These data types are CANDIDATE_ID, PHONE, and BITMAP. There are also constraints defined for some of the columns. For example, the NOT NULL constraint is specified for all of the columns except HPHONE, WPHONE, INITIAL, and PHOTO.

```
CREATE TABLE db2cert.candidate (
    Cid          candidate_id NOT NULL,
    LName        VARCHAR(30)  NOT NULL,
    FName        VARCHAR(30)  NOT NULL,
    Initial      CHAR(1),
    HPhone       phone,
    wPhone       phone,
    StreetNo     VARCHAR(8)   NOT NULL,
    StreetName   VARCHAR(20)  NOT NULL,
    City         VARCHAR(30)  NOT NULL,
    Prov_State   VARCHAR(30)  NOT NULL,
    Code         CHAR(6)      NOT NULL,
    Country      VARCHAR(20)  NOT NULL,
    Cert_DBA     CHAR(1)      NOT NULL WITH DEFAULT 'N',
    Cert_APP     CHAR(1)      NOT NULL WITH DEFAULT 'N',
    CONSTRAINT Unique_Candidate PRIMARY KEY (Cid));
```

Fig. 5–41 *Creating the* CANDIDATE *table*

Keys

Keys are sets of columns. They can be used to uniquely identify a row. Keys can be classified either by the columns they are composed of or by the database constraint they support.

Defining Primary Keys

It is usually beneficial to define a primary key for each table since this guarantees the uniqueness of the rows. In Fig. 5–41, the primary key for the table CANDIDATE is defined as the column CID (candidate ID). By specifying this column as a primary key, DB2 will create a system-unique index if one does not already exist.

Let us look at the other tables representing the tests and the test centers. In Fig. 5–42, the TEST and TEST_CENTER tables are shown. These tables each have a primary key defined.

In our example, the primary key constraint was given a name (unique_test and unique_center) for referencing purposes. If a name is not provided, DB2 will assign a system-generated name to the constraint.

```
CREATE TABLE db2cert.test (
   Number       test_id      NOT NULL,
   Name         VARCHAR(50)  NOT NULL,
   Type         CHAR(1)      NOT NULL,
   Cut_Score    score        NOT NULL,
   Length       minutes      NOT NULL,
   TotalTaken   SMALLINT     NOT NULL,
   TotalPassed  SMALLINT     NOT NULL,
   CONSTRAINT   Unique_Test    PRIMARY KEY(Number),
   CONSTRAINT   Unique_Test_Name UNIQUE (Name),
   CONSTRAINT   Test_Type CHECK (Type IN ('P','B')))

CREATE TABLE db2cert.test_center (
   Tcid         center_id    NOT NULL,
   Name         VARCHAR(40)  NOT NULL,
   StreetNo     VARCHAR(8)   NOT NULL,
   StreetName   VARCHAR(20)  NOT NULL,
   City         VARCHAR(30)  NOT NULL,
   Prov_State   VARCHAR(30)  NOT NULL,
   Country      VARCHAR(20)  NOT NULL,
   Code         CHAR(6)      NOT NULL,
   Type         CHAR(1)      NOT NULL,
   Phone        phone        NOT NULL,
   No_Seats     SMALLINT     NOT NULL,
   CONSTRAINT   Unique_Center PRIMARY KEY (Tcid))
```

Fig. 5–42 *Defining the test and test_center tables*

Defining Unique Keys

Unique keys can be used to enforce uniqueness on a set of columns. A table can have more than one unique key defined. The TEST table definition in Fig. 5–42 uses a unique constraint (UNIQUE_TEST_NAME) on column NAME to ensure that a test name is not used twice. There is also a primary key constraint on the column Number to avoid duplicate test numbers.

Having unique constraints on more than one set of columns of a table is different than defining a composite unique key that includes the whole set of columns. For example, if we define a composite primary key on the columns NUMBER and NAME, there is still a chance that a test name will be duplicated using a different test number.

Note: A unique index is always created for primary (if one does not already exist) or unique key constraints. If you define a constraint name, it will be used to name the index; otherwise, a system-generated name will be used for the index.

Defining Foreign Keys

A foreign key is a reference to the data values in another table. There are different types of foreign key constraints. Let us look at the remaining table in the DB2 Certification database and, in particular, its foreign key constraints. In Fig. 5–43, there is one composite primary key defined and three foreign key constraints.

The primary key is defined as the columns CID, TCID, and NUMBER. The foreign key constraints will perform the following:

- If a record in the candidate table is deleted, all matching records in the test_taken table will be deleted (DELETE CASCADE).
- If a test center in the test_center table is deleted, all of the matching records in the test_taken table will be deleted (DELETE CASCADE).
- If a test in the test table is deleted and there are matching records in the test_taken table, the DELETE statement will result in an error (DELETE RESTRICT).
- If a test in the test table is updated and there are matching records in the test_taken table, the UPDATE statement will result in an error (UPDATE RESTRICT).

Note: A foreign key constraint always relates to the primary or unique constraint of the table in the references clause.

```
CREATE TABLE db2cert.test_taken (
   Cid candidate_id NOT NULL,
   Tcid center_id NOT NULL,
   Number test_id NOT NULL,
   Date_Taken date NOT NULL WITH DEFAULT,
   Start_Time TIME NOT NULL,
   Finish_Time TIME NOT NULL,
   Score score,
   Seat_No CHAR(2) NOT NULL,
   CONSTRAINT number_const
PRIMARY KEY (Cid,Tcid,Number),
FOREIGN KEY (Cid)
   REFERENCES db2cert.candidate ON DELETE CASCADE,
FOREIGN KEY (Tcid)
   REFERENCES db2cert.test_center ON DELETE CASCADE,
FOREIGN KEY (Number)
   REFERENCES db2cert.test ON DELETE RESTRICT
                             ON UPDATE RESTRICT)
```

Fig. 5–43 *Defining the test_taken table*

Defining parent-child relationships between tables is known as declarative referential integrity because the child table refers to the parent table. These constraints are defined during table creation or by using the ALTER TABLE statement. DB2 will enforce referential constraints for all INSERT, UPDATE, and DELETE activity.

The relationship between all of these tables was previously illustrated in Fig. 5–39 on page 275.

Summary

In this chapter, we concentrated on the SQL Data Definition Language (DDL). DDL is used to create, modify, and remove database objects. There are three main statements in DDL: CREATE, ALTER, and DROP. If you want to use a DB2 database, you may learn DDL first to create some database objects. There are many kinds of objects in a DB2 database. Some of them are created by a DB2 command, but most of them are created by DDL statements.

Here we focused on data types, tables, views, and indexes among the database objects created by DDL. A data type must be specified for every column in a table. DB2 has two kinds of data types: built-in data types and user-defined data types. The built-in type is a DB2-supplied data type and falls into four main categories: Numeric, String (including large object [LOB]), Datetime, and DATALINK. Character data types (part of the String category) are associated with a character code page. We also discussed that DB2 supports Unicode. The user-defined data type enables you to create your application-oriented data type based on the built-in data type.

Tables are composed of rows; rows are composed of columns. Each column has a data type. A table itself can have some rules called CONSTRAINTS to guarantee the uniqueness of records or maintain the relationship between tables. A view may also reduce some application development workload. A logical table is created and is based on tables or other views. An index is one of the most important objects for performance. It can also be used to guarantee the uniqueness of each record. We also introduced some new options in the CREATE and ALTER statements.

Database Objects

Manipulating Database Objects

- ◆ DATA MANIPULATION LANGUAGE
- ◆ RETRIEVING DATA
- ◆ INSERTING DATA
- ◆ UPDATING DATA
- ◆ DELETING DATA
- ◆ VIEW CLASSIFICATION

In the previous chapter, we discussed the definition of various database objects using the Data Definition Language (DDL). In this chapter, we start manipulating database objects using the part of SQL known as Data Manipulation Language (DML). We will be populating (inserting) data into the database and retrieving the data using many powerful methods. The majority of the SQL statements within a DB2 application involve DML statements. Therefore, application developers must understand the various methods of inserting, updating, and retrieving data from the database. We will start with simple retrieval statements and gradually introduce more complex methods of data manipulation. The DB2 Certification database will be used for most of the examples. There are four main DML SQL statements we consider: SELECT, INSERT, UPDATE, and DELETE.

Data Retrieval

SQL is a set-oriented language and many of its language elements are directly related to relational algebraic terms, such as *PROJECTION, RESTRICTION, JOIN* and *UNION*.

Data is represented in a DB2 database as tables and is stored in tables without regard to order. To retrieve data in a particular order, an ORDER BY clause must be added to a SELECT. Similarly, if the data is to be grouped, then a GROUP BY clause must be added to the statement.

Now, let's review the DB2CERT database design defined in the previous chapter and manipulate data using various SQL statements. There are three main tables: CANDIDATE, TEST, and TEST_CENTER. Each of these tables is a set of rows that correspond to test candidates (persons), tests, and test centers (locations). There is an associative table, known as the TEST_TAKEN table, that is used to reflect the relationships among the three main tables. The TEST_TAKEN table is used to schedule the test candidates and also to maintain their test scores.

Notes:

1. An SQL statement can be up to 65,535 bytes long. Normally this wouldn't be a problem for most queries that developers or users may generate, but it does become a concern with large SQL PL statements or procedures. Customers who are converting from other database products will occasionally come across this problem.

2. Remember that to execute any SQL operation, one must have the necessary privileges.

Retrieving the Entire Table

The most basic of all retrieval commands involves the SELECT statement with no clauses other than FROM, that specifies the name of the table. The following SELECT retrieves all of the candidates who have taken a DB2 Certification exam. The information requested is contained in the table TEST_TAKEN.

```
SELECT * FROM db2cert.test_taken
```

SQL is a data access language that consists of language statements. There are many optional clauses that can be used to modify the statement. The SELECT is referred to as a *query* and the results are known as a *result set* or *result table*. The results from the previous SELECT are shown next.

```
CID TCID NUMBER DATE_TAKEN START_TIME FINISH_TIME SCORE PASS_FAIL SEAT_NO
--- ---- ------ ---------- ---------- ----------- ----- --------- -------
111 TX01 500    01/01/2000 11:30:00   12:30:00       65 Y               1
111 TX01 501    02/02/2000 10:30:00   11:45:00       73 Y               1
111 TX01 502    03/03/2000 12:30:00   13:30:00       67 Y               1
222 TR01 500    01/01/2000 14:00:00   15:30:00       55 N               2
222 TR01 502    01/02/2000 09:00:00   10:15:00       53 N               2
222 TR01 502    02/18/2000 10:00:00   11:30:00       75 Y               2
333 TX01 500    03/01/2000 11:30:00   13:00:00       82 Y               2
333 TX01 501    12/29/2000 14:00:00   -              - -                1
333 TX01 502    03/02/2000 14:00:00   14:30:00       92 Y               1

  9 record(s) selected.
```

Fig. 6–1 *Result from a simple SELECT*

In SQL, the asterisk (*) is used to indicate that all columns of a table are being referenced. In this example, the SELECT refers to all of the columns in the DB2CERT.TEST_TAKEN table.

If the table is altered and a new column is added, the result set would contain the new column.

Note: Adding a new column to an existing table will result in default values being populated for the existing rows. If default values are not specified, the alter will fail.

Since the results of a SELECT using the asterisk (*) varies according to the table definition, it is recommended that you explicitly specify all of the column names you want to see in any SELECT.

We could have obtained the same result as in Fig. 6–1 with the following SQL.

```
SELECT cid, tcid, number,date_taken,start_time,
       finish_time,score,seat_no
FROM db2cert.test_taken;
```

This SQL will provide the same result table even if new columns are added to the table.

Note: The asterisk (*) is used to refer to all of the columns in a table. In this case, the order of the columns in the result table is the same order as specified in the CREATE TABLE or CREATE VIEW statement.

The FROM clause is required in every SELECT since it describes the source of the data. Our example references a single table called DB2CERT.TEST_TAKEN. The list of columns following the SELECT keyword is referred to as the *select list*.

Projecting Columns from a Table

Projection is a relational operation that allows you to retrieve a subset of the columns from a table. The next example limits the output from the SELECT so that only the candidate ID, test center, and test number columns from the TEST_TAKEN table are shown (Fig. 6–2).

```
SELECT cid,tcid,number FROM db2cert.test_taken
```

The result of this SELECT is shown in Fig. 6–2. The order of the columns in the result table will always match the order in the select list. The order of the columns as they were defined in the CREATE TABLE or CREATE VIEW statement is ignored when a select list is provided.

```
CID TCID NUMBER
--- ---- ------
111 TX01 500
111 TX01 501
111 TX01 502
222 TR01 500
222 TR01 502
222 TR01 502
333 TX01 500
333 TX01 501
333 TX01 502

  9 record(s) selected.
```

Fig. 6–2 *Result table of a projection*

Changing the Order of the Columns

Permutation is the relational operation that allows you to change the order of the columns in your result table. Permutation is used every time you select columns in an order different than their order in the CREATE TABLE statement. For example, to display the test center ID prior to the candidate IDs and the test number you could execute the following:

```
SELECT tcid,cid,number FROM db2cert.test_taken
```

This SELECT retrieves the columns in a different order than defined in the table is shown in Fig. 6–3.

```
TCID CID NUMBER
---- --- ------
TX01 111 500
TX01 111 501
TX01 111 502
TR01 222 500
TR01 222 502
TR01 222 502
TX01 333 500
TX01 333 501
TX01 333 502

  9 record(s) selected.
```

Fig. 6–3 *Result table of a permutation*

 Note: We refer to the result of a SELECT as a *result table* because the results of all SELECTs are tables, but are not stored permanently in the database.

Restricting Rows from a Table

Restriction is a relational operation that filters the resulting rows of a table. Restriction is accomplished through the use of *predicates* specified in an SQL WHERE clause.

 Note: A predicate is a condition placed on the data. The value of condition can be TRUE, FALSE, or UNKNOWN.

To restrict the result set, we need to add a WHERE. The WHERE clause specifies conditions (predicates) that must be evaluated by DB2 before the result table is returned. There are many types of predicates. In the following example, the equality (=)

predicate is used to restrict the rows to only those candidates who have taken a
DB2 Certification test at the test center TR01.

```
SELECT tcid,cid FROM db2cert.test_taken
  WHERE tcid ='TR01'
```

Other comparison operators, such as greater than (>), less than (<), greater than or
equal to (>=), less than or equal to (<=), and not equal to (<>) can be used in a
WHERE clause. This statement is an example of a *basic predicate*. A basic predicate
compares two values.

Note: Trying to execute this example SELECT will result in a data type
compatibility error, because the column tcid is defined with a user-
defined distinct data type (UDT).

Limiting Result Table Size

DB2 does not limit the amount of rows returned from a SELECT. Occasionally a
user may only require the first 100 rows instead of the entire list. To indicate that
the SELECT is to return only a subset of rows, the FETCH FIRST ... ROWS must be
appended to the end of the SQL:

```
SELECT * FROM db2cert.test_taken
  FETCH FIRST 5 ROWS ONLY
```

The result table from this SQL statement is found in Figure 6–4:

```
CID TCID NUMBER DATE_TAKEN START_TIME FINISH_TIME SCORE PASS_FAIL SEAT_NO
--- ---- ------ ---------- ---------- ----------- ----- --------- -------
111 TX01 500    01/01/2000 11:30:00   12:30:00       65 Y                1
111 TX01 501    02/02/2000 10:30:00   11:45:00       73 Y                1
111 TX01 502    03/03/2000 12:30:00   13:30:00       67 Y                1
222 TR01 500    01/01/2000 14:00:00   15:30:00       55 N                2
222 TR01 502    01/02/2000 09:00:00   10:15:00       53 N                2

  5 record(s) selected.
```

Fig. 6–4 *Result table from a SELECT limited to 5 rows*

Predicate Evaluation for UDTs

The column TCID was defined as a *user-defined distinct data type* (UDT). To make the comparison in the WHERE clause valid, a casting function needs to be used. This technique is shown below:

```
SELECT tcid, cid FROM db2cert.test_taken
    WHERE tcid=CAST('TR01' AS db2cert.center_id)
```

Predicate evaluation requires that the data types be compatible (same data type or a convertible data type).

We can accomplish the data type conversion (cast) using one of two methods:

- Use the CAST expression
- Use a casting function

In the example above, we used the CAST expression to perform a comparison using compatible data types.

The CAST expression requires that you specify the input data value and the output data type. In our example, the input data value is TR01 and the output data type is DB2CERT.CENTER_ID (the full two-part name of the UDT).

The other method of converting UDTs involves the use of a system-generated SQL function known as a *casting function*. When we created the user-defined data type called DB2CERT.center_id, functions to cast between the distinct type (DB2CERT.CENTER_ID) and its source type (CHAR) and six comparison operators (=, <>, <, <=, >, and >=) were also generated.

The following example uses the casting function:

```
SELECT tcid,cid FROM db2cert.test_taken
    WHERE tcid=db2cert.center_id('TR01')
```

The casting function used in this example is called DB2CERT.CENTER_ID. It is easy to remember the name of the casting function, since it is the same as the UDT itself. It is also possible to cast the left-side argument using the CHAR casting function as follows:

```
SELECT tcid,cid FROM db2cert.test_taken
  WHERE CHAR(tcid)='TR01'
```

Restricting Rows Using Multiple Conditions

It is possible to combine multiple conditions (predicates) in a single WHERE clause. The predicates can be combined using boolean operators, such as the AND operator. These operators allow you to combine conditions. The order in which the predicates are specified does not affect the result table. The DB2 optimizer decides the order in which the conditions are applied to maximize query performance based on statistical information and other factors.

The next example retrieves the rows for the test candidates who took a test at test center TR01 and achieved a score greater than 65. The rows that satisfy the predicates are known as the *qualifying rows*. The following example is an SQL statement using multiple predicates:

```
SELECT tcid,cid,score FROM db2cert.test_taken
  WHERE tcid=db2cert.center_id('TR01')
       AND score > db2cert.score(65)
```

Note: In addition to user-defined datatypes, structured types can also be used within table definitions. User-defined types and structured types allow for greater control of data comparisons within a database as well as giving the relational model a more object-oriented feel. However, UDTs require the use of casting functions that require more knowledge by end-users and developers.

Selecting Columns from Multiple Tables

There are basically two operations that retrieve columns from multiple tables in a single SELECT. These operations are:

- Cartesian product
- Join

Cartesian Product

A *cartesian product* is a relational operation that will merge all the rows from one table with all the rows from another table. This operation is primarily of theoretical interest. In theory, any multitable access can be performed by constructing the Cartesian product and then removing extraneous rows and columns. In practice, this is almost always the most expensive way to do things.

The number of rows in the result table is always equal to the product of the number of rows in the qualifying rows for each of the tables being accessed.

The following example retrieves all test numbers and test names from the TEST table.

```
SELECT number,name FROM db2cert.test

NUMBER NAME
------ ---------------------------------------------------------
500    DB2 Fundamentals
501    DB2 Administration
502    DB2 Application Development

 3 record(s) selected.
```

Fig. 6–5 *Simple query (1)*

The following example retrieves all candidate and test center IDs from the TEST_TAKEN table.

```
SELECT cid,tcid FROM db2cert.test_taken

CID TCID
--- ----
222 TR01
222 TR01
222 TR01
111 TX01
111 TX01
111 TX01
333 TX01
333 TX01
333 TX01

 9 record(s) selected.
```

Fig. 6–6 *Simple query (2)*

An example of a cartesian product is shown in Fig. 6–7.

```
SELECT db2cert.test_taken.number,cid,tcid
  FROM db2cert.test_taken,db2cert.test

NUMBER CID TCID
------ --- ----
500    111 TX01
501    111 TX01
502    111 TX01
500    222 TR01
502    222 TR01
502    222 TR01
500    333 TX01
501    333 TX01
502    333 TX01
500    111 TX01
501    111 TX01
502    111 TX01
500    222 TR01
502    222 TR01
502    222 TR01
500    333 TX01
501    333 TX01
502    333 TX01
500    111 TX01
501    111 TX01
502    111 TX01
500    222 TR01
502    222 TR01
502    222 TR01
500    333 TX01
501    333 TX01
502    333 TX01

 27 record(s) selected.
```

Fig. 6–7 *Cartesian product query*

There are two tables referenced in the FROM clause in this SELECT. The tables are separated by commas. There is no predicate limiting the rows to be retrieved. This type of SELECT results in a cartesian product.

The result table is a representation of all possible combinations of the input tables. The TEST table has three rows and the TEST_TAKEN table has nine rows. Therefore, the SELECT shown in Fig. 6–7 returns 27 rows. Note the first column name in Fig. 6–7. It is necessary to fully qualify the column name with the schema and table name because the column exists in both the TEST and TEST_TAKEN tables. In this case, we needed to specify that the NUMBER column is to be retrieved from the DB2CERT.TEST_TAKEN table and not the DB2CERT.TEST table.

By adding a predicate to a the original statement, the result table can represent a more useful representation of the data. In Fig. 6–8, the query represents all of the tests that were taken by the candidate whose ID is 111.

```
SELECT db2cert.test_taken.number,cid,tcid
   FROM db2cert.test_taken,db2cert.test
      WHERE cid=db2cert.candidate_id('111')

NUMBER CID TCID
------ --- ----
500    111 TX01
500    111 TX01
500    111 TX01
501    111 TX01
501    111 TX01
501    111 TX01
502    111 TX01
502    111 TX01
502    111 TX01

 9 record(s) selected.
```

Fig. 6–8 *Adding additional predicates to the SELECT*

Adding a WHERE clause to your query does not always provide the desired result. In the example shown in Fig. 6–8, you want to know all of the tests that were taken by the candidate whose ID is 111 and the query returns nine rows. However, as the result in Fig. 6–9 shows, the candidate took only three tests. The query in Fig. 6–8 uses a WHERE clause to filter out the candidates whose ID is 111 from the TEST_TAKEN table, but there was no filter on the TEST_CENTER table. Therefore, the result of the query would always be a multiple of the number of testing centers. Usually, when multiple tables are referenced, you should include a cross-table relationship using a table join as shown in Fig. 6–9. We will examine table join methods in the next section.

```
SELECT db2cert.test_taken.number,cid,tcid
   FROM db2cert.test_taken,db2cert.test
      WHERE cid=db2cert.candidate_id('111')
         AND db2cert.test_taken.number=db2cert.test.number

NUMBER CID TCID
------ --- ----
500    111 TX01
501    111 TX01
502    111 TX01

 3 record(s) selected.
```

Fig. 6–9 *Join tables example*

Join

To avoid data redundancy it is recommended that the database tables be *normalized*. Following a normalization process, a number of related tables will exist. To satisfy some of the required queries, the tables must be reconstructed. The tables are reconstructed temporarily using a table join strategy to produce a single-result table.

The result tables in the previous examples usually provided candidate ID numbers and not the complete name of the test candidates. The candidate IDs are stored in the TEST_TAKEN table, and the full names are stored in the CANDIDATE table. To obtain the name of a candidate, the data must be retrieved from the CANDIDATE table using a relationship or join strategy.

Consider an example that will list the name and phone numbers of candidates who were registered to take a DB2 Certification test in 2000. To accomplish this, we need to select data from two different tables:

- DB2CERT.CANDIDATE
- DB2CERT.TEST_TAKEN

Let's retrieve a list of candidate names, phone numbers, and IDs from the CANDIDATE table. The candidate names were stored in multiple columns to allow for easy retrieval by last name.

```
SELECT fname,initial,lname,hphone,cid
  FROM db2cert.candidate
```

The results of this example follows. Pay special attention to the values in the CID column. It will be used as the *join column* in the next example.

```
FNAME     INITIAL LNAME       HPHONE      CID
--------  ------- ----------  ----------  ---
Bill      W       Wong        1115551234  111
George            Baklarz     2226543455  222
Susan     M       Visser      4442314244  333
Glen      R       Sheffield   5552143244  444
Jim       G       Stittle     6662341234  555
Kevin     W       Street      7773142134  666
Bert      F       Nicol       8886534534  777
Paul      C       Zikopoulos  9992112212  888

  8 record(s) selected..
```

Fig. 6–10 *A sample query result*

Now, let's retrieve the ID numbers of those candidates who were registered to take the test in 2000.

```
SELECT distinct cid FROM db2cert.test_taken
  WHERE YEAR(date_taken) = 2000
```

```
CID
---
222
111
333

 3 record(s) selected.
```

Fig. 6–11 *Retrieving the candidate IDs*

The candidate IDs in the TEST_TAKEN table must correspond to a candidate ID in the CANDIDATE table because of the declarative referential integrity constraints. The parent table in the relationship is the CANDIDATE table and the child table (dependent table) is the TEST_TAKEN table.

The result table from the second query in Fig. 6–11 does not include the test candidate 444 since that candidate did not have a test scheduled for 2000. We need to join the two result tables based on the candidate ID values. This column is known as the *join column*.

 Note: Query performance can significantly improve if the join columns are appropriately indexed.

The following single query will satisfy the end-user requirement.

```
SELECT distinct fname,initial,lname,hphone
  FROM db2cert.test_taken,db2cert.candidate
  WHERE YEAR(date_taken) = 2000
       AND db2cert.test_taken.cid=db2cert.candidate.cid
```

A table join requires a predicate that includes an expression based on columns from the tables referenced in the FROM clause. This is known as a *join predicate*. The FROM clause has not changed from the cartesian product examples. The only difference is in the join predicate (TEST_TAKEN.CID = CANDIDATE.CID).

 Note: This kind of join operation is also known as INNER JOIN. An inner join displays only the rows that are present in both of the joined tables.

The table names needed to be explicitly stated because there is a column named CID in both of the referenced tables. When multiple tables are being accessed in a single query, you have to qualify the column names with the table name.

Note: An error will occur if the columns being referenced are ambiguous (not properly qualified).

There is no defined limit, except in storage, to the number of tables that can be referenced in a single SQL statement. However, there is a 1012 column limit in the SELECT list of a query. (If the page size is 4K, the maximum number of columns in a select list is 500.)

Using Correlation Names

If each of the columns needed to be fully qualified with the table name, such as tableschema.tablename.columnname, queries would very large and cumbersome to work with. Fortunately, there is an easier way to disambiguate columns in multi-table SELECTs.

Columns can be qualified using *correlation names*. A correlation name is an alias for a table in an SQL statement. We can rewrite the previous query using correlation names as follows:

```
SELECT distinct fname,initial,lname,hphone
  FROM db2cert.test_taken tt, db2cert.candidate c
  WHERE YEAR(date_taken) = 2000
       AND tt.cid = c.cid
```

The correlation name immediately follows the name of the table in the FROM clause. In this example, the correlation name for the TEST_TAKEN table is TT and the correlation name for the CANDIDATE table is C.

Correlation names are accessible within the SQL statement only. Following the execution of the SQL statement, the correlation name is no longer defined. Once a correlation name has been defined, it can be referenced in the rest of the query in place of the table name.

Note: Use simple, easy-to-remember correlation names. Table initials are good candidates for correlation names.

Sorting Your Output

The order of the rows in the result table has not been specified in any of the SQL so far. Data is retrieved in an undetermined order if there is no ORDER BY clause in the SQL.

The following example produces a list of the test candidates in alphabetical order by last name for the candidates who have taken a DB2 Certification test at the TR01 test center.

```
SELECT lname,initial,fname
    FROM db2cert.candidate c,db2cert.test_taken tt
    WHERE c.cid=tt.cid
        AND tcid=db2cert.center_id('TR01')
    ORDER BY lname
```

This example contains a new clause, ORDER BY. After the ORDER BY clause, you list the columns that specify the sort order and the direction of the of sort.

The SQL above can be modified to descending order by last name and first name in ascending order.

```
SELECT lname,fname,hphone
    FROM db2cert.candidate c,db2cert.test_taken tt
    WHERE c.cid=tt.cid
        AND tcid=db2cert.center_id('TR01')
    ORDER BY lname DESC, fname
```

In this example, the DESC keyword that follows the LNAME column indicates that the result table should be in descending order based on the last name. More than one record can have the same last name. This situation is quite common. There is a second column specified in the ORDER BY clause, FNAME. There is no keyword specifying the sort sequence based on the FNAME column. Therefore, ascending sequence is used.

The next example contains three columns: LNAME, FNAME, and HPHONE. You can reference the column that should be used to sort the data using the column name or by specifying its position in the select list. Using the column position is very useful when the column in the select list is made up of derived columns (calculated columns) that have no explicit name.

Manipulating
Database Objects

```
SELECT lname,fname,hphone
  FROM db2cert.candidate c,db2cert.test_taken tt
  WHERE c.cid=tt.cid
        AND tcid=db2cert.center_id('TR01')
  ORDER BY 1 DESC, 2
```

In this example, the sort order is specified using the column position. Yet, the query result is exactly the same as the previous example.

You can also rename a column using an *alias*. The alias can then be referenced in the ORDER BY clause.

Note: The ORDER BY clause, if used, must be the last clause in your SQL statement.

Limiting Sort Results

The result set from a SELECT can be limited through the use of the FETCH FIRST ...
ROWS clause. This same clause can be applied to an ORDER BY clause to reduce the
size of the sorted result table. A good example would be a query that retrieves the
top five marks in an exam.

To limit the number of rows sorted in a SELECT, the FETCH FIRST ... ROWS must be
added to the end of the ORDER BY:

```
SELECT * FROM db2cert.test_taken
    ORDER BY CID DESC FETCH FIRST 5 ROWS ONLY
```

The result table from this SQL statement is found in Figure 6–12:

```
CID TCID  NUMBER DATE_TAKEN  START_TIME FINISH_TIME SCORE        PASS_FAIL SEAT_NO
--- ----  ------ ----------  ---------- ----------- -----------  --------- -------
333 TX01  500    03/01/2000  11:30:00   13:00:00    82 P           2
333 TX01  501    12/29/2000  14:00:00   -           - -            1
333 TX01  502    03/02/2000  14:00:00   14:30:00    92 P           1
222 TR01  500    01/01/2000  14:00:00   15:30:00    55 F           2
222 TR01  502    02/18/2000  10:00:00   11:30:00    75 P           2

  5 record(s) selected.
```

Fig. 6–12 *Result table from an ORDER BY limited to 5 rows*

Derived Columns

There are some cases when you will need to perform calculations on the data. The
SQL language has some basic mathematical and string functions built in. Mathematical operations include standard addition, subtraction, multiplication, and division.

The calculation can be defined in the WHERE clause of the SQL statement or in the
select list. Suppose that you need to calculate a passing rate for a DB2 test.
The passing rate is defined as the percentage of candidates that pass the test (totalpassed*100/totaltaken). The following SQL will accomplish this for us for test
number 500:

```
SELECT number, totalpassed*100/totaltaken
    FROM test
    WHERE number=test_id('500')
```

In this example, the second column of the results is a calculated column. Remember that you must use the column position if you want to use this calculated column in an ORDER BY clause unless you name it (as we now discuss).

> **Note:** Occasionally, the values of a derived column may not display as expected. The example using totalpassed*100/totaltaken will result in a value of 66 being retrieved. Since both the totalpassed and totaltaken columns are integers, the final result is also an integer and the fractional part is discarded. If this is not your desired result, you should use other functions (like DECIMAL) to change the way the calculation is done or displayed.

Naming Derived Columns

You can specify a column name for any calculation. By providing the derived (calculated) column with a name, the ORDER BY clause can reference the name to allow for more readable SQL.

The following SQL calculates the percentage of people that have passed the DB2 Certification exams and orders the result in descending order by the passing rate.

```
SELECT number,totalpassed*100/totaltaken AS PASSEDRATE
   FROM test
   ORDER BY PASSEDRATE DESC
```

The AS clause is used to override the default name of a column in the select list. In this example, we are giving the name PASSEDRATE to the result of the division of columns TOTALPASSED by TOTALTAKEN. The named column is used in the query to specify the column that should be used for the sorting of the output.

DB2 Functions

In DB2, there are different types of functions provided. For example, two types of functions provided by DB2 are scalar and column functions (a third type of function called a *table function* is not discussed here - for details on this function please refer to the *DB2 UDB V8.1 SQL Reference*):

- *Scalar functions* (also known as row functions) provide a result for each row of the result table. A scalar function can be used any place an expression is allowed.
- *Column functions* (also known as vector functions). They work on a group of rows to provide a result. The group is specified using a fullselect and optionally

grouped using the GROUP BY clause.

In this section, we introduce you to some of the SQL functions provided with DB2. SQL functions are categorized by their implementation type. Either the functions are built-in or they are extensions of DB2 and are known as user-defined functions (UDFs).

- *Built-in functions* are provided by DB2. These can be either scalar, column or table functions.
- *User-defined functions (UDFs)* are extensions of the current SQL language. These functions can be developed by a DB2 administrator or application developer. Once the UDFs have been created, they can be invoked by any user with the proper privileges. Some of the new functions provided in DB2 are scalar UDFs. The functions with the schema name of SYSFUN are provided by DB2.

 Note: For detailed information about UDFs, refer to "Advanced SQL" on page 343.

Scalar Functions

Scalar functions are applied to each row of data, and there is a per-row result provided. If we wanted to retrieve only the first three digits of telephone numbers for each candidate, we could use a scalar function. The function that will be used is called SUBSTR. The arguments for this function include a string data type column, a beginning offset, and length. The output data type are dependent on the definition of the function.

The following example extracts the telephone area code from the column WPHONE.

```
SELECT lname, SUBSTR(CHAR(wphone),1,3)
  FROM db2cert.candidate
```

The SUBSTR function is a scalar function. In this example, SUBSTR returns a character string of three characters.

The result string corresponds to the first three characters of the WPHONE column. This function is known as a string function because it works with any string data type. If we wanted to provide the output column with a meaningful name, we could provide an alias, as was done for calculated columns.

In the example above, the substring starts from the beginning of the string because we indicate one (1) as the second parameter of the function. The length of the result string is indicated by the third argument. In our example, the length is three. Note that the data type of the WPHONE column is PHONE, so a casting function is used to convert the PHONE data type to the CHAR data type.

The following query will provide the month when the exam was taken. The input for this function is a DATE and the output is a character string.

```
SELECT fname, MONTHNAME(date_taken)
  FROM candidate c, test_taken tt
  WHERE c.cid=tt.cid
```

Column Functions

Column functions provide a single result for a group of qualifying rows for a specified table or view. Many common queries can be satisfied using column functions, such as finding the smallest value, the largest value, or the average value for a group of rows.

Let's obtain the maximum length of time of any of the DB2 Certification exams:

```
SELECT MAX(smallint(length)) FROM test
```

Because the column LENGTH is specified as the MINUTES data type, a casting function is required to convert the MINUTES data type to the SMALLINT data type in this example.

If we added a WHERE clause to this example, the maximum would represent the maximum length for the qualifying rows.

This next example calculates the average of the number of seats for all of the test centers. Notice the column function AVG is used in this example:

```
SELECT AVG(noseats) FROM test_center
```

DB2 does provide many more built-in functions. If you are interested in calculating statistical information, you can use Business Intelligence-related functions, such as CORRELATION, COVARIANCE, and some regression functions. See the *DB2 UDB V8.1 SQL Reference* for more detailed information.

Grouping Values

Many queries require some level of aggregated data. This is accomplished in SQL through the use of the GROUP BY clause.

The following SQL obtains the average number of seats for each country:

```
SELECT country, AVG(noseats) FROM test_center
  GROUP BY country
```

This SELECT obtains the average number of seats per country. The GROUP BY clause tells DB2 to group together the rows that have the same values in the columns indicated in the group by list. In our example, we are grouping countries into subsets. As the subsets are created, DB2 calculates the average of each of those groups or subsets, in this case, by each country.

When you combine vector functions and other elements, such as column names, scalar functions, or calculated columns, you must use the GROUP BY clause. In this case, you must include every element that is not a column function in the group by list. The only elements that can be omitted in the GROUP BY list are constant values.

The next SELECT retrieves data that includes the average cut score and minimum test length for the DB2 Certification exams. We group this list data by the type of exam as follows:

```
SELECT type, AVG(integer(cut_score)), MIN(smallint(length))
  FROM test
  GROUP BY type
```

It is possible to sort the output of the previous example using an ORDER BY clause. Note that the ORDER BY clause should always be the last clause in an SQL statement.

On-line analytical processing (OLAP) applications use different levels of grouping within the same data. DB2 supports OLAP requirements implementing *super group* or aggregation features. OLAP-oriented grouping functions will be discussed in "Advanced SQL" on page 343.

Manipulating Database Objects

Restricting the Use of Sets of Data

Up to now, we have discussed how to restrict rows based on row conditions. With SQL, it is also possible to restrict rows using vector functions and the GROUP BY clause.

Suppose you want a list of all the test centers that have administered more than five DB2 Certification exams.

To make it easier to understand, let's first get the number of tests that have been taken in each test center.

```
SELECT tcid, count(*) FROM test_taken GROUP BY tcid
```

We use the COUNT vector function to get the total number of tests that have been taken in each test center. When you use an asterisk (*) with the COUNT function, you are indicating that you want the number of rows in a table that meet the selection or aggregation criteria in the WHERE or GROUP BY clauses. In this example, we are grouping by TCID because we have a number of occurrences for all the test centers in the TEST_TAKEN table. The TEST_TAKEN table has an entry for every DB2 Certification exam that has been taken.

Finally, the result is restricted to only those test centers that have administered more than four exams.

```
SELECT tcid FROM test_taken
  GROUP BY tcid HAVING COUNT(*) > 4
```

This example introduces the HAVING clause. The HAVING clause for groups, is analogous to the WHERE clause for tables. The HAVING clause will restrict the result to only the groups of rows that meet the condition specified in it.

In our example, only the test centers that have administered more than four DB2 Certification exams will be displayed.

Note: If you have an extremely large table (>2 147 483 647 rows), it is possible that the COUNT function cannot return the proper result. In this case you should use the COUNT_BIG function which will return a DECIMAL(31,0) result instead of an integer value.

Eliminating Duplicates

When you execute a query, you might get duplicate rows in the results. The SQL language provides a special keyword to remove the duplicate rows from your output.

The following SQL generates a list of names and phone numbers for all the candidates who have taken a test. In the following example, we eliminate the duplicate rows from our output list using the DISTINCT keyword.

```
SELECT DISTINCT fname,wphone,hphone
   FROM candidate c,test_taken tt
   WHERE c.cid=tt.cid
```

The DISTINCT keyword can also be used with the COUNT function. When you use DISTINCT inside a COUNT function, it will not count the duplicate entries for a particular column.

Let's say that you want to count how many different test centers have candidates registered.

```
SELECT COUNT(DISTINCT char(tcid)) FROM test_taken
```

This example provides the number of test centers that are registered in the test taken table. Remember that all the candidates who have registered for DB2 Certification exams are stored in this table.

Make sure that you understand the difference between COUNT(*) and COUNT(DISTINCT colname). They are very similar in syntax but differ in function.

Searching for String Patterns

SQL has a powerful predicate that allows you to search for patterns in character strings columns. This is the LIKE predicate.

Suppose you want to generate a list of the candidates whose first name starts with the letter G.

```
SELECT fname,lname,wphone,hphone FROM candidate
   WHERE fname LIKE 'G%' ORDER BY lname, fname
```

In this query, we are using a *wildcard character* with the LIKE predicate.

In SQL, the percent character (%) represents zero or more characters. The search string (G%) can be matched with names like George, Geoffrey, Ginger, and so on (since the percent character can match zero or more characters, the search string can also match a single letter G).

The percent character can be used any place in the search string. It also can be used as many times as you need it. The percent sign is not case sensitive, so it can take the place of uppercase or lowercase letters. However, the constant characters included in your search string are case sensitive.

Another wildcard character used with the LIKE predicate is the underline character (_). This character represents one and only one character. The underline character can take the place of any character. However, the underline character does not represent and cannot match an empty character.

The previous SQL can be modified to include all candidates' names and the telephone numbers for those candidates whose name has a lowercase letter "a" as its second letter.

```
SELECT fname,lname,wphone,hphone FROM candidate
  WHERE fname LIKE '_a%' ORDER BY lname,fname
```

This example uses two wildcard characters that work with the LIKE predicate. The search string, in this example, can include names, such as Paul, Gabriel, or Natalie. (The first character may be any character, the lowercase letter "a" is the second character in the string, and the string ends with any number of characters.)

Searching for Data in Ranges

SQL also offers us a range operator. This operator is used to restrict rows that are in a particular range of values.

Consider the requirement to list those candidates whose scores in the DB2 Certification exam are between 60 and 75.

```
SELECT DISTINCT fname,lname,wphone,hphone
  FROM candidate c, test_taken tt
  WHERE c.cid=tt.cid
        AND integer (score) BETWEEN 60 AND 75
```

The BETWEEN predicate includes the values that you specify for searching your data. An important fact about the BETWEEN predicate is that it can work with character ranges as well.

In addition to the score requirement, this example modifies the SQL to include only those candidates whose last name begins with a letter between B and G.

```
SELECT DISTINCT fname,lname,wphone,hphone
  FROM candidate c, test_taken tt
  WHERE c.cid=tt.cid
        AND integer(score) BETWEEN 60 AND 75
        AND lname BETWEEN 'B' AND 'GZ'
```

In this example, the second BETWEEN predicate contains character values. We need to specify the GZ value to include all the possible names that start with the letter G. This was done assuming that the letter Z is the last possible value in the alphabet.

Searching for Null Values

NULL values represent an unknown value for a particular occurrence of an entity. We can use a NULL value in the cases where we don't know a particular value of a column.

Let's say that we want a list of all those candidates whose score is not yet input. This condition is represented with a NULL value.

```
SELECT fname,lname,wphone,hphone
  FROM candidate c, test_taken tt
  WHERE c.cid=tt.cid AND score IS NULL
```

The IS predicate is used to search for the NULL value in this example. Remember that the NULL value means "unknown." Because it has no particular value, it can't be compared with other values. You can't use relational operators, such as equal (=), with null values.

Searching for Negative Conditions

The BETWEEN, IS, and LIKE predicates always look for the values that meet a particular condition. These predicates can also be used to look for values that don't meet a particular criterion.

Manipulating Database Objects

The NOT predicate can be used to look for the opposite condition, combined with the LIKE, BETWEEN, and IS predicate, to accomplish negative searches as shown in the following example.

This example has a LIKE predicate combined with the NOT predicate. We want a list of those candidates whose last names do not start with the letter S.

```
SELECT DISTINCT fname,lname,wphone,hphone FROM candidate
     WHERE lname NOT LIKE 'S%'
ORDER BY lname,fname
```

The next example has a BETWEEN predicate combined with the NOT predicate. We want the list of those candidates whose score, in any test, is not in the range 60 to 75.

```
SELECT DISTINCT fname,lname,wphone,hphone
  FROM candidate c, test_taken tt
  WHERE c.cid=tt.cid
        AND integer(score) NOT BETWEEN 60 and 75
```

In this example, the NOT predicate will exclude all the values that are in the range 60 to 75.

Negation can also be applied to the NULL value. This SQL produces a report that searches for those candidates that have a seat number assigned. This is expressed with a NOT NULL value.

```
SELECT DISTINCT fname,lname,wphone,hphone
  FROM candidate c, test_taken tt
  WHERE c.cid=tt.cid AND seat_no IS NOT NULL
```

Searching for a Set of Values

In SQL, it is possible to select rows based on a set of values. Suppose that you need the test centers that have candidates registered for the DB2 Fundamentals test and for the DB2 Application Development test. This can be queried with the following statement:

```
SELECT DISTINCT name,phone
   FROM test_center tc, test_taken tt
   WHERE tc.tcid=tt.tcid
   AND char(number) IN ('500','502')
```

The IN clause is used to denote a set of values. In this example, we are using a constant set of values. In this particular case, the SQL statement could also be written using the OR operator to restrict the test numbers.

You can also use the NOT predicate with the IN clause. In this case, the condition will be true when a value is not present in the set of values provided to the IN clause.

You can use as many values as you wish in the IN clause. However, there will be cases when the list of values is very long, and it would be better to retrieve them using another SQL statement.

The IN predicate can also be used to define a set based on conditions. In this case, the IN predicate also accepts an SQL statement that defines the set of values. When you define the set of values using an SQL statement, the SQL statement that defines that set is called a subquery.

Subqueries

Subqueries can be used in the IN clause to specify the search arguments for an SQL statement.

Consider the difficulty of producing a report on the number of DB2 Certification exams if the name and number of the exams is unknown. The following SQL produces a report that includes all the test centers that have candidates registered for the DB2 Certification exams.

In the example, we'll use the word DB2 as the search string to find the numbers of the DB2 Certification program exams:

```
SELECT DISTINCT name,phone
   FROM test_center tc, test_taken tt
   WHERE tc.tcid=tt.tcid
         AND number IN
             (SELECT number FROM test
                 WHERE name LIKE 'DB2%')
```

Fig. 6–13 *Using a subquery*

In this example, the subquery appears as part of the IN clause. In the subquery, we are retrieving all the numbers for those tests that have the word DB2 in their name.

As you can see in the last example, the subquery looks like a standard SQL statement. The only difference here is that the subquery is used as a selection criterion. You will never see its results. We are only using the subquery to create a list of values that will be used later by the outer SELECT.

The subquery used in this example is known as an uncorrelated subquery. An uncorrelated subquery is one where the values retrieved by the subquery are not directly related to the rows processed by the outer SELECT. A correlated subquery is a query in which the subquery references values of the outer SELECT.

In the next example, you want to count how many candidates are registered in each test center. This time you want to display the name of the center near the number of candidates. We use a correlated subquery to accomplish this.

```
SELECT tc.name, count(*)
   FROM test_center tc,test t
   WHERE tc.tcid IN
         (SELECT tcid FROM test_taken tt
             WHERE tt.number=t.number)
   GROUP BY tc.name
```

Fig. 6–14 *Correlated subquery*

Observe the WHERE clause in the subquery in this example. It references a table in the outer FROM clause.

If you write this query as a uncorrelated subquery, you will have different results. In this example, you need to use a correlated subquery to be sure that all the rows of the TEST_TAKEN table are counted. When you use an uncorrelated subquery, you will only count one occurrence of the test number for each test center.

Note: You should understand the difference between subselects and subqueries. Subselects are queries that do not include an ORDER BY clause, an UPDATE clause, or UNION operators. Subqueries are to be used with the IN clause to specify the search arguments for an SQL statement as already described.

Quantified Predicates

A quantified predicate is used to compare a value or values with a collection of values. In Fig. 6–15, the partial syntax diagram for a quantified predicate is shown (please refer to the *DB2 UDB V8.1 SQL Reference* for the complete discussion). The right side of the expression is a fullselect.

A *fullselect* is a subselect, a VALUES clause, or a number of both that are combined by set operators.

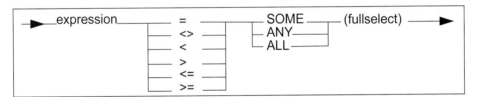

Fig. 6–15 *Quantified predicates*

Let's examine the use of a quantified predicate in a SELECT. First we look at the original queries:

```
SELECT cid, lname, fname FROM db2cert.candidate
```

```
CID LNAME      FNAME
--- ---------- --------
111 Wong       Bill
222 Baklarz    George
333 Visser     Susan
444 Sheffield  Glen
555 Stittle    Jim
666 Street     Kevin
777 Nicol      Bert
888 Zikopoulos Paul

 8 record(s) selected.
```

Fig. 6–16 *A simple query (1)*

```
SELECT cid FROM db2cert.test_taken
```

```
CID
---
222
222
222
111
111
111
333
333
333

 9 record(s) selected.
```

Fig. 6–17 *A simple query (2)*

```
SELECT c.cid, lname, fname FROM db2cert.candidate c
   WHERE cid = SOME
       (SELECT tt.cid FROM db2cert.test_taken tt
          WHERE c.cid = tt.cid)
```

```
CID LNAME       FNAME
--- ----------  --------
111 Wong        Bill
222 Baklarz     George
333 Visser      Susan

 3 record(s) selected.
```

Fig. 6–18 *Using a quantified predicate in a SELECT*

A *quantified predicate* is used in Fig. 6–18 to find the test candidates who have taken or are scheduled to take a test. When SOME or ANY is specified for the fullselect statement, the predicate is true if the relationship is true for at least one value returned by the fullselect. The clause ALL would result in all of the test candidate names being returned because the specified relationship is true for every value returned by the fullselect. The relationship CID = fullselect is true for all values returned by the fullselect because of the referential integrity constraints between our defined tables. It is impossible to have a cid value in the TEST_TAKEN table that does not have a corresponding value in the CANDIDATE table.

Note that if you use an equality predicate in with a subselect, the subselect must only return one row, or else an error message will be returned. If the previous example was rewritten without the SOME operator, an error would occur:

```
SQL0811N The result of a scalar fullselect, SELECT INTO
statement, or VALUES INTO statement is more than one
row.  SQLSTATE=21000
```

This is due to the SQL restriction that only one value can be compared with the equal sign. To avoid this problem, you can use the FETCH FIRST ROW ONLY clause to force only one row to be returned:

```
SELECT c.cid, lname, fname FROM db2cert.candidate c
  WHERE cid =
        (SELECT tt.cid FROM db2cert.test_taken tt
          WHERE c.cid = tt.cid FETCH FIRST ROW ONLY)
```

Manipulating Database Objects

Case Expressions

You can add some logic to your SQL using CASE expressions. Consider the generation of a list of those candidates who have passed the DB2 Fundamentals exam.

In the report, you want to print the score of the tests, but instead of printing the numeric score, you want to print a message. If the score is below the cut_score, you want to print Not Passed. If it is between the cut_score and 90, you want to print Passed, and if the score is above 90, you want to print "Excellent". The following SQL statement using a CASE expression accomplishes this:

```
SELECT fname,lname,
       CASE
         WHEN  integer(SCORE) < 65 THEN 'Not Passed'
         WHEN  integer(SCORE) <=90 THEN 'Passed'
         ELSE 'Excellent'
       END
  FROM candidate c, test_taken tt
 WHERE c.cid=tt.cid
       AND char(number)='500'
```

Fig. 6–19 *CASE expressions*

The SQL presented in Fig. 6–19 provides string messages based on the conditions of the CASE expression. In this example, the SCORE column features a numeric value, but we are using it to produce a character string.

The order of the conditions for the CASE expression is very important. DB2 will process the first condition first, then the second, and so on. If you do not pay attention to the order in which the conditions are processed, you might retrieve the same result for every row in your table. For example, if you coded the "<=90" option before the "<65", all the data that is lower than 91, even 64 or 30, will display the message "Passed".

Note: You must use the END keyword to finish a CASE expression.

CASE expressions can also be used in places other than select lists. CASE expressions can be used inside functions and in a group list. Samples of these features will be presented in "Advanced SQL" on page 343.

Nested Table Expressions

A nested table expression is a special kind of subquery. This subquery is used in the FROM clause to create local temporary tables that are only known in the SQL that defines them.

Consider the problem of obtaining the maximum average score for the DB2 Certification program exams. To gather this result, you must first obtain the averages and then you must select the maximum value from that list.

Let's use a nested table expression to accomplish this request:

```
SELECT MAX(avg_score)
  FROM (
    SELECT number,
    avg(integer(score)) as avg_score
    FROM test_taken
    GROUP BY number
) AS averages
```

Fig. 6–20 *Using table expressions*

In this example, Fig. 6–20, the nested sub-select will create a temporary table that will be used by the outer SELECT to obtain the maximum average score. This temporary table is called AVERAGES.

The NUMBER column is included in the subquery to be able to gather the average for each one of the exams. After the subquery is completed, the outer SELECT will be able to obtain the maximum value of the averages calculated in the nested table expression.

An advantage of using nested table expressions over views is that nested table expressions exist only during the execution of the query, so you don't have to worry about their maintenance. They reduce contention over the system catalog tables, and since they are created at execution time, they can be defined using host variables.

 Note: The TABLE clause can also be used to denote that the subquery following it will create a temporary table. This keyword is also used to denote TABLE user-defined functions. Refer to "Advanced SQL" on page 343 for information about UDFs.

Scalar Fullselect

A scalar fullselect is a SELECT that returns only one value. This type of SELECT can be used in different parts of an SQL statement. It can be used in the select list or in the WHERE clause.

Scalar fullselects can be used to combine grouped information, such as averages or sums, with detailed information in a single query.

Occasionally, you may need to include row data in the report that includes information based on the entire table. For instance, you may want a report that shows the candidate's ID, score, the average score, and the maximum score for the DB2 Certification exams. This information cannot be gathered without the help of temporary tables or views. Let's see how the scalar fullselect can be used to assist in the retrieval of this data.

```
SELECT cid,number,score,
   (SELECT AVG(integer(score))
      FROM test_taken) AS AVG_Score,
   (SELECT MAX(integer(score))
      FROM test_taken) AS MAX_Score
  FROM test_taken
```

Fig. 6–21 *Combining detailed and aggregated information*

In the example shown in Fig. 6–21, we are using two scalar fullselects to retrieve the information about the aggregated data.

The first scalar fullselect calculates the average SCORE and the second one calculates the maximum SCORE for the DB2 Certification exams.

Observe how the SQL statements that produce the average and the maximum values are scalar fullselects. Now, let's extend this SQL to calculate the average and maximum scores for each one of the DB2 Certification exams.

To accomplish this request you need to use a correlated sub-select. This is because you must ensure that the SELECT returns only one value at a time.

The correlated sub-select will let you generate the average and maximum scores for each one of the DB2 Certification exams:

```
SELECT cid,number,score,
   (SELECT AVG(integer(score))
      FROM test_taken tt1
      WHERE tt1.number=tt.number
) AS AVG_Score,
   (SELECT MAX(integer(score))
      FROM test_taken tt2
      WHERE tt2.number=tt.number
) AS MAX_Score
FROM test_taken tt
```

Fig. 6–22 *Using a correlated scalar fullselect*

Examine the WHERE clauses in the Fig. 6–22 example. They both make reference to the table of the outer SELECT. The WHERE clauses are used to obtain a separate average and maximum value for each one of the test numbers in the TEST_TAKEN table.

Now, let's use a scalar fullselect to create a list of those candidates who have a higher SCORE than the average for the DB2 Fundamentals exam.

```
SELECT fname,lname,score
  FROM candidate c, test_taken tt
  WHERE c.cid=tt.cid
  AND integer(tt.score) > (SELECT AVG(integer(score))
                             FROM test_taken
                             WHERE number=test_id('500'))
```

Fig. 6–23 *Using a scalar fullselect in the WHERE clause*

In Fig. 6–23, the scalar fullselect is used in the WHERE clause. This scalar fullselect calculates the average score for the DB2 Fundamentals exam.

The value returned from the scalar fullselect is compared with the score of the candidate. In this way we retrieve those candidates whose SCORE is higher than the average.

Common Table Expressions

A common table is a local temporary table that can be referenced many times in an SQL statement. However, this temporary table only exists for the duration of the SQL statement in which it is used. A common table expression defines a common table and provides many of the advantages of nested table expressions discussed earlier.

Every time that you reference a common table expression, the result will be the same. This means that the SELECT statement that generates it will not be reexecuted each time the common table expression is referenced.

Consider a report that lists the candidates who have earned the highest score for each of the DB2 Certification program exams.

This can be accomplished using three common table expressions. Each of them corresponds to one of the DB2 Certification program exams. The common table expressions will be called MAX500, MAX501, and MAX502. They will contain the maximum score value for each one of the DB2 Certification program exams.

After calculating the maximum score for each one of the tests, we use those values to search for the candidates whose score is equal to the maximum score for a particular test. This will be accomplished by joining the score of each candidate with the maximum score of each one of the exams.

After specifying a common table expression, you can refer to the common table like any other table. An example is shown in Fig. 6–24.

```
WITH MAX500 AS
  (SELECT MAX(integer(score)) AS M500 FROM test_taken
  WHERE number=test_id('500')),
MAX501 AS
  (SELECT MAX(integer(score)) AS M501 FROM test_taken
  WHERE number=test_id('501')),
MAX502 AS
  (SELECT MAX(integer(score)) AS M502 FROM test_taken
  WHERE number=test_id('502'))

SELECT fname, lname, wphone
   FROM max500,max501,max502,candidate c, test_taken tt
   WHERE c.cid=tt.cid
   AND ((integer(score)=M500 and number=test_id('500'))
   OR (integer(score)=M501 and number=test_id('501'))
   OR (integer(score)=M502 and number=test_id('502')));
```

Fig. 6–24 *Using common table expressions*

The WITH clause is used to specify a common table expression. The example shown in Fig. 6–24 specifies three different common table expressions: MAX500, MAX501, and MAX502. Observe the commas that are used to separate each one of the common table expressions.

You can refer to a common as many times as you wish. You can specify a common table expression based on a previously defined common table. However, you can only use common tables in the SQL statement that defines them.

Set Operators

SQL offers a group of operators that are used to implement the relational algebra operations union (UNION operator), intersection (INTERSECT operator), and difference (EXCEPT operator).

Union

The UNION operator lets you combine the results of two or more different SELECTs into one result table. You can combine up to 16 different result tables using the UNION operator; the only restriction is that every table or SQL statement must be *UNION compatible*, i.e., have the same type, number, and order of columns.

Suppose you wanted to combine the minimum and maximum score for each of the DB2 Certification program exams and add a string constant that indicates which values are the maximum and minimum.

```
SELECT number,'Minimum:', MIN(integer(score))
  FROM test_taken
  GROUP BY number
UNION
SELECT number,'Maximum:', MAX(integer(score))
  FROM test_taken
  GROUP BY number
ORDER BY number,2
```

Fig. 6–25 *UNION operator*

The UNION operator combines the results of two or more separate queries into a single result. In our example, the first query calculates the minimum score of the TEST_TAKEN table. The the second query calculates the maximum score value. Both select lists have the same type, order, and number of columns.

In Fig. 6–25, the two queries are very similar. However, you can combine very different queries using the UNION operator. Just remember the results must be UNION compatible.

The UNION operator removes duplicate rows from the result table. However, there will be times when you'll need to list all the rows processed by your SQL statements.

SQL provides you with a way keep all the rows involved in a UNION operation. This is the ALL keyword. Let's create a list of all the first names and last names in our CANDIDATE table. In this example, shown in Fig. 6–26, we want all the first names that start with a letter G and all the last names for the candidates who have taken the DB2 Administration exam.

```
SELECT fname FROM candidate
  WHERE fname like'G%'
UNION ALL
SELECT lname FROM candidate c,test_taken tt
  WHERE c.cid=tt.cid
        AND   char(number) = '501'
```

Fig. 6–26 *An example of UNION ALL*

 Note: Only code a UNION when duplicates are not desired. The UNION ALL offers better performance since it avoids sorting to eliminate duplicates. However, you can't always substitute a UNION for a UNION ALL.

The UNION ALL operator provides us with a powerful mechanism, but unions are usually no longer needed, superseded by the far more powerful outer join operators. However as we will see when we discuss advanced SQL, it is required when writing recursive SQL.

Intersection (Intersect Operator)

The intersection operation is implemented in DB2 using the INTERSECT operator. Using INTERSECT, we can find the rows that belong to two different result tables.

For example, we want a list of all the candidate IDs that are present in the TEST_TAKEN table and in the CANDIDATE table. This requirement can be seen as the intersection of the set *candidate IDs* and the set *candidates IDs present in TEST_TAKEN.*

```
SELECT cid FROM candidate
  INTERSECT
SELECT cid FROM test_taken
```

Like the UNION operator, there is an INTERSECT ALL operator. If you use the INTERSECT ALL operator, the result table can contain duplicate rows, which is sometimes desirable.

Difference (Except Operator)

The difference operation is the complement of the intersection operation. It is implemented in DB2 using the EXCEPT operator. Using EXCEPT, we can find out which rows of one result table are not present in another result table.

This time, we want to know which candidate IDs are not present in the TEST_TAKEN table. This is effectively saying, "Show me all the candidate IDs except those candidate IDs present in the TEST_TAKEN table."

The query using the EXCEPT operator is shown in the following example:

```
SELECT cid FROM candidate
  EXCEPT
SELECT cid FROM test_taken
```

The first part of the example retrieves all the candidate IDs. The second section of the query retrieves the candidate IDs present in the TEST_TAKEN table. Finally, the EXCEPT operator performs the difference operation that selects only those candidate IDs not present in the TEST_TAKEN table. Without the EXCEPT operator, the query would have been more complicated. As with the other relational algebra operators, there is also an EXCEPT ALL operator that does not eliminate duplicates from the result.

Note: The select lists of the operands of UNION, INTERSECT, and EXCEPT, must be "compatible".

Manipulating Database Objects

Data Modification

Up to now, we have discussed retrieval queries. The SELECT statement allows you to retrieve data from your database and assumes the data has been previously loaded into tables. Now we will concentrate on getting data into the database using SQL. There are three main statements that can be used to add and change data stored in a DB2 database table. They are the INSERT, DELETE, and UPDATE statements.

To perform these operations, you must have the required privileges on the tables being accessed. These privileges must be granted with caution since they can allow the end-user to modify rows.

Inserting Rows

To initially populate a DB2 table with data, the INSERT statement can be used to store one row or many data records at a time. The statement can be targeted to insert data directly into a table, or a view, if updatable, can be used instead. If a view is being used as the target, remember that it is a table where the data actually is stored.

Every row that is populated using the INSERT statement must adhere to table-check constraints, data type validation, dynamic (trigger) constraints, and referential integrity constraints. An SQL error will occur if any of these conditions are violated during the processing of the INSERT statement.

Note: Remember that you must have the necessary privileges to perform an INSERT statement.

The first example is a simple INSERT statement. This statement will insert the data for the DB2 Data Propagation (#508) exam into the test table.

```
INSERT INTO db2cert.test
(number,name,type,cut_score,length,totaltaken,totalpassed)
VALUES
('508','DB2 Data Propagation','P',NULL,90,0,0);
```

In this example, we specify all the column names and their corresponding values for this row. Following the VALUES clause, we include values for each column.

In the VALUES clause, the number and order of the inserted elements must match the number and order of the column names specified in the INSERT column list. However, the order of the columns doesn't have to match the order in which they are defined in the table. For those columns that don't require a value, you can indicate null or default values. In this example, we are using the NULL value for the CUT_SCORE column.

> **Note:** The number of values in the VALUES clause must match the number of names in the insert column list.

Depending on your column definition, the DEFAULT value can cause to be inserted a system-defined default, a user-defined default, or NULL. Be aware that if the column doesn't accept nulls (NOT NULL) and wasn't defined as WITH DEFAULT, you will receive an error message when using the DEFAULT value. This error is because the default value for those columns not using the WITH DEFAULT option is the NULL value.

When you want to insert values into all the columns of a table, you do not have to provide a column list in the INSERT statement. This example is shown next.

```
INSERT INTO db2cert.test VALUES
('508','DB2 Data Propagation','P',DEFAULT,90,79,11)
```

This method will only work if you specify a value for all the columns in a table. If you miss one of the columns of the table, DB2 will not allow you to insert the row into the table. The DEFAULT keyword used in this example will insert the default value for the CUT_SCORE column.

> **Note:** Remember, depending on the column definition, the default value could be a user-defined default value, a system-defined default value, or NULL.

Inserting Data into Specific Columns

There are times when you need to insert data only for specific columns. Every column that is not included in the INSERT statement will receive its default value.

This operation can be accomplished only if the omitted columns accept nulls or have a default value definition. This means that you must specify a value for the columns defined as NOT NULL. This restriction excludes columns defined as NOT NULL WITH DEFAULT.

Let's insert a row into the TEST_TAKEN table. In the following example, we will only insert data for the columns CID, TCID, NUMBER, and SEAT_NO.

```
INSERT INTO db2cert.test_taken
  (CID,TCID,NUMBER,SEAT_NO)
    VALUES('888','TR01','508','1')
```

Remember that columns defined using WITH DEFAULT that are not listed in the INSERT statement will receive the NULL value or a default value.

 Note: The TEST_TAKEN table has referential constraints with three other tables. If you want to insert a record into the TEST_TAKEN table, the appropriate values should be inserted into the other three tables in advance.

Inserting Multiple Rows

You can insert multiple rows into a table using a single INSERT statement. For instance, you may want to schedule a candidate for the DB2 Certification exams. This candidate will take all the exams on three different days:

```
INSERT INTO db2cert.test_taken
  (CID,TCID,NUMBER,DATE_TAKEN,SEAT_NO)
VALUES
  ('888','TR01','500','2000-06-04','1'),
  ('888','TR01','501','2000-07-11','2')
  ('888','TR01','502','2000-11-08','1')
```

Fig. 6–27 *Multiple row INSERT statement*

In Fig. 6–27, we enclose the values for each row in parentheses and separate each value list with a comma. When inserting multiple rows with a single statement, you have to consider that all the rows must have the same number, type, and order of columns. This means, for example, that you cannot insert values into one column in the first row and into five columns in the last row.

Inserting a Set of Values

Using INSERT, you can insert the result of a subselect into the same or a different table. The subselect must follow these rules:

- The number of columns must equal the number of columns in the INSERT column list.
- The data type of each of the columns must match the data type of the corresponding columns in the INSERT list.
- The INSERT column list can be omitted only if values are inserted into all the columns in the table.
- Only columns defined to allow NULL or defined as NOT NULL WITH DEFAULT can be omitted from the INSERT column list.

In some situations, it might be useful to create tables that are duplicates of others so that you can do multiple calculations against them. The next example uses a table called TEST_PASSED, which is a copy of the TEST_TAKEN table. This new table will be used to extract the information about those candidates who have passed any of the DB2 Certification exams.

```
INSERT INTO db2cert.test_passed
  (cid,tcid,number,
  date_taken,start_time,finish_time,
  pass_fail,score,seat_no)

(SELECT cid,tcid,number,
        date_taken,start_time,finish_time,
        pass_fail,score,seat_no
 FROM db2cert.test_taken
   WHERE pass_fail='P')
```

Fig. 6–28 *Using a subselect to insert values*

The select list used in the subselect in Fig. 6–28 can also be replaced by an asterisk (*). This is possible because the TEST_PASSED table has the same column structure as does the TEST_TAKEN table. However, to keep this query independent of future table modifications, it is recommended that you use the explicit select list instead of an asterisk.

When you use a subselect to insert data into a table, you must enclose it in parentheses. You can also use a common table expression to insert values into a table or view using the INSERT clause.

Inserting Large Amounts of Data

It is recommended that you do not load large amounts of data into a table using the INSERT statement as the transaction logging overhead can be unmanageable.

DB2 provides you with two utilities that are designed to load large amounts of data into a table. These utilities are IMPORT and LOAD and are described in "Maintaining Data" on page 493.

> **Note:** The NOT LOGGED INITIALLY option on table creation can improve your performance on high-volume inserts. This option tells DB2 not to log changes to the table during the current unit of work. Subsequent changes to the table will be logged. If future loads require that logging be turned off, the table can be placed back into a no-logging status with the command: ALTER TABLE ... ACTIVATE NOT LOGGED INITIALLY.
> Before taking advantage of this feature, make sure you understand the recovery implications of logging being turned off during loads.

Updating Rows

So far we have looked at the INSERT statement as a method of loading data into your DB2 table. You may wish to update only a column with values for a group of rows. There is an SQL UPDATE statement that can be used to specify the column and its new values. A table or a view can be referenced as the target for the UPDATE statement.

> **Note:** Remember that you must have the correct privileges in order to execute the UPDATE statement.

The UPDATE statement can be used in two forms:

- *Searched update.* This type of UPDATE statement is used to update one or more rows in a table. It requires a WHERE clause to select which rows are to be updated.
- *Positioned update.* This kind of UPDATE statement is always embedded in a program. It uses *cursors* to update rows where the cursor is positioned. As the cursor is repositioned using the FETCH statement, the target row for the UPDATE statement changes.

We focus on searched updates in this chapter.

Similar to INSERT, all relevant constraints are enforced during an UPDATE. Update constraints can be different from insert constraints.

For example, the following is a transaction that updates candidate ID 888's exam date for the DB2 Fundamentals certification exam.

```
UPDATE db2cert.test_taken
  SET date_taken=date_taken + 3 days
  WHERE char(cid) ='888'
        AND number=test_id('500')
```

In this example, we are using an operation known as a *labeled duration* to add three days to the original date. DB2 labeled durations for data types include: YEARS, MONTHS, DAYS, HOURS, MINUTES, SECONDS, and MICROSECONDS.

It is very important that you provide the proper WHERE clause to avoid updating unintended rows. In this example, we needed to specify the predicate number=test_id('500') to avoid changing the date for any of the other tests that the candidate can be scheduled for.

The UPDATE statement can also be used with scalar fullselects. In this case, the fullselect must return a row with exactly the same number of columns and column data types of the row that will be updated. Observe that this scalar fullselect must return only one row.

Let's update a row using a scalar fullselect to set the new value. Candidate ID 888 decides to take the DB2 Fundamentals test today in the test center located in Toronto, Canada.

```
UPDATE db2cert.test_taken
  SET (date_taken,tcid)=
      (SELECT current date,tcid FROM db2cert.test_center
          WHERE substr(city,1,7)='Toronto'
          AND country='Canada')
  WHERE CHAR(cid)= '888' AND number=test_id('500');
```

Fig. 6–29 *Using a scalar fullselect to update data*

In Fig. 6–29, we are updating two different columns. These columns are listed in the parentheses following the SET clause.

After indicating which columns are going to be updated, we use a scalar fullselect to retrieve the current date (today) and the test center ID for the test center located in Toronto, Canada. Notice the last WHERE clause in the statement will restrict the rows that will be updated.

 Note: If you forget the WHERE clause in an UPDATE, all of the rows in your table will be updated.

The SQL statement that will update the DATE_TAKEN and TCID columns is known as a scalar fullselect. This name is given because it returns only one row. Observe that the scalar fullselect can be considered a special case of a row fullselect.

 Note: CURRENT DATE is a DB2 special register that gives the system date. Others include: CURRENT TIME, CURRENT TIMESTAMP, and USER (the authid).

Updating Large Amounts of Data

There are times when you need to update a large number of rows of a particular table. This can be accomplished by issuing a searched update. However, this also could allocate a large amount of transactional log space. You can accomplish updates using positioned updates, where you can easily control the commit frequency. The other option is to create tables with the NOT LOGGED INITIALLY attribute and turn logging off during large update operations.

Removing Data

There are many methods available to remove data from a DB2 database. To remove all of the data within a database, perform the DROP DATABASE command. This may remove more data than you intended because the entire database, including its configuration, will be physically removed.

It is also possible to remove data using the DROP TABLESPACE or DROP TABLE statements. These statements are usually only issued by the SYSADM or DBADM, since they will remove large amounts of data. If you wish to remove all of the rows from a table, it is easier and quicker to perform the DROP TABLE statement. If the table is dropped, it must be re-created before any data can be populated again in the table.

The DELETE statement removes rows from tables. The syntax of the DELETE statement is different from the SELECT or INSERT statements because columns cannot be selected, only rows can be deleted.

The DELETE statement can also be used with views. However, there are restrictions on the type of views that can be used within a DELETE statement. Views must be considered deletable in order to allow deletes to be performed against them.

 Note: Remember that you must have the necessary privileges over a table to execute the DELETE statement.

In general, there are two kinds of DELETE statements:

- *Searched delete* - This DELETE statement is used to delete one or multiple rows from a table. It uses a WHERE clause to select the rows to be deleted.
- *Positioned delete* - This kind of DELETE operation is always embedded into a program. It uses *cursors* to delete the row where the cursor is positioned.

In this section we will focus on the searched delete.

The following DELETE statement deletes candidates who don't have telephone numbers. We use a searched delete to accomplish this.

```
DELETE FROM db2cert.candidate
   WHERE hphone IS NULL
         AND wphone IS NULL
```

This example uses a WHERE clause to delete the data that meets a specific criterion.

To verify the result of the DELETE statement, you can issue a SELECT with the same WHERE clause. If the DELETE was successful, the SELECT will return an empty result table.

A delete can also become more sophisticated by using subselects. The next SQL statement deletes all the candidates who took the DB2 Certification exams in February of any given year.

```
DELETE FROM db2cert.candidate
   WHERE cid IN (SELECT cid FROM db2cert.test_taken
                 WHERE MONTH(date_taken)=2)
```

In this example, we are using a subselect to retrieve the CID values of the candidates who took a DB2 Certification exam in the month of February. This list will be used to search for the candidates we want to delete.

Deleting All the Rows in a Table

You will delete all the rows in a table if you don't specify a search condition in your DELETE statement. You must be aware of the implications of this type of statement. However, this is not the only way to delete all the rows in a table. You will also delete all the rows in a table if all the rows meet the search condition.

Deleting all the rows in a table by using a DELETE statement may not be the most efficient method. This kind of statement can consume a lot of log space when your tables are big.

Note: If a table has been created with the NOT LOGGED INITIALLY option, there is a way to delete all of the contents of the table without physically dropping it. Use the following command to tell DB2 to drop the contents of the rows (without logging): ALTER TABLE ... ACTIVATE NOT LOGGED INITIALLY WITH EMPTY TABLE. The advantage of deleting rows with this technique is that definitions relying on this table do not get dropped.

View Classification

Now that we have examined various SQL DML statements, let's take a closer look at views. We have already discussed creating views. Now we'll examine the different types of views.

Views are classified by the operations they allow. They can be:

- Deletable
- Updatable
- Insertable
- Read-only

The view type is established according to its update capabilities. The classification indicates the kind of SQL operation that is allowed against the view.

Referential and check constraints are treated independently. They do not affect the view classification.

For example, you may not be able to insert a value into a table because of a referential constraint. If you create a view using that table, you also can't insert that value using the view. However, if the view satisfies all the rules for an insertable view, it will still be considered an insertable view. This is because the insert restriction is on the base table, not on the view definition.

Deletable Views

Depending on how a view is defined, the view can be deletable. A deletable view is a view against which you can successfully issue a DELETE statement. There are a few rules that need to be followed for a view to be considered deletable:

- Each FROM clause of the outer fullselect identifies only one base table (with no OUTER clause), deletable view (with no OUTER clause), deletable nested table expression, or deletable common table expression.
- The outer fullselect doesn't use the VALUES clause.
- The outer fullselect doesn't use the GROUP BY or HAVING clauses.
- The outer fullselect doesn't include column functions in its select list.
- The outer fullselect doesn't use set operations (UNION, EXCEPT, or INTERSECT) with the exception of UNION ALL.
- The base tables in the operands of a UNION ALL must not be the same table, and each operand must be deletable.
- The select list of the outer fullselect does not include DISTINCT.

A view must meet all the rules listed above to be considered a deletable view.

```
CREATE VIEW deletable_view
 (tcid,cid,number,date_taken,start_time,seat_no,score)
AS
 SELECT tcid,cid,number,date_taken,
         start_time,seat_no,score
 FROM db2cert.test_taken
 WHERE tcid=center_id('TR01')
```

Fig. 6–30 *Example of a deletable view*

The view shown in Fig. 6–30 is deletable. It follows all the rules for a deletable view.

Updatable Views

An updatable view is a special case of a deletable view. A deletable view becomes an updatable view when at least one of its columns is updatable.

A column of a view is updatable when all of the following rules are true:

- The view is deletable.
- The column resolves to a column of a table (not using a dereference operation) and the READ ONLY option is not specified.
- All the corresponding columns of the operands of a UNION ALL have exactly matching data types (including length or precision and scale) and matching default values if the fullselect of the view includes a UNION ALL.

```
CREATE VIEW updatable_view
 (tcid,cid,number,current_date,current_time,seat_no,score)
AS
 SELECT tcid,cid,number,CURRENT DATE,
                 CURRENT TIME,seat_no,score
 FROM db2cert.test_taken
 WHERE char(tcid)='TX01'
```

Fig. 6–31 *Example of an updatable view*

The view definition in Fig. 6–31 uses constant values that cannot be updated. However, the view is a deletable view and at least you can update one of its columns. Therefore, it is an updatable view.

Insertable Views

Insertable views allow you to insert rows using the view definition. A view is insertable when:

- All of its columns are updatable.

```
CREATE VIEW insertable_view
    (test_number,test_name,total_taken)
AS
SELECT number,name,totaltaken FROM db2cert.test
```

Fig. 6–32 *Example of an insertable view*

The view shown in Fig. 6–32 is an insertable view. However, an attempt to insert the view will fail. This is because there are columns in the table that don't accept null values. Some of these columns are not present in the view definition. When you try to insert a value using the view, DB2 will try to insert a NULL into a NOT NULL column. This action is not permitted.

Note: Remember, the constraints defined on the table are independent of the operations that can be performed using a view based on that table.

Read-Only Views

A read-only view is a nondeletable view. A view can be read-only if it is a view that doesn't comply with at least one of the rules for deletable views.

The READONLY column in the SYSCAT.VIEWS catalog view indicates a view is read-only (R).

Let's examine a read-only view:

Manipulating Database Objects

```
CREATE VIEW read_only_view
   (name,work_phone,home_phone)
AS
SELECT DISTINCT fname,wphone,hphone
   FROM db2cert.candidate c, db2cert.test_taken tt
   WHERE c.cid=tt.cid
```

Fig. 6–33 *Example of a read-only view*

The view shown in Fig. 6–33 is not a deletable view as it uses the DISTINCT clause and the SQL statement involves more than one table.

Note: Even if a view is considered Read-only, a DBA can create INSTEAD OF triggers to handle the INSERT, UPDATE, and DELETE processing against the view. For more information on triggers, see "Triggers" on page 344.

Views with UNION ALL

Views with tables connected through the use of UNION ALL have been supported for a number of releases. SELECT, DELETE, and UPDATE operators have been allowed as long as DB2 could determine which table the corresponding command was to be applied to.

In DB2 Version 8, support for the INSERT operator has been extended to views with UNION ALL, as long as the following conditions hold:

1. The expressions have the same datatypes

2. A constraint exists on at least one column that can be used to uniquely identify where a row should be inserted and the constraint ranges are non-overlapping.

Views defined in this fashion will also support UPDATE operations as long as the column being changed does not violate the constraint for that column. In this case, the user must first DELETE and then INSERT the record.

A few examples will clarify how this will work.

Consider four tables that have been created to represent the sales for each quarter of the year. The tables all have the same definition as shown in Figure 6–34.

```
CREATE TABLE Q1SALES
  (
  store    int    not null,
  tx_date  date   not null,
  item     int    not null,
  quantity int    not null
  );
CREATE TABLE Q2SALES LIKE Q1SALES;
CREATE TABLE Q3SALES LIKE Q1SALES;
CREATE TABLE Q4SALES LIKE Q1SALES;
```

Fig. 6–34 *Multiple tables representing a year of sales*

These tables could be UNIONed together to create a single view of the entire year as shown in Figure 6–35.

```
CREATE VIEW ALLQ AS
  (
  SELECT * FROM Q1SALES
  UNION ALL
  SELECT * FROM Q2SALES
  UNION ALL
  SELECT * FROM Q3SALES
  UNION ALL
  SELECT * FROM Q4SALES
  )
```

Fig. 6–35 *View of entire year's sales*

Although DB2 could use this view for SELECT, UPDATE, and DELETE commands, it would not be handled in the most efficient way. For instance, consider the SELECT in Figure 6–36.

```
SELECT * FROM ALLQ WHERE
  item = 142 AND
  tx_date between '2002-05-14' AND '2002-07-21'
```

Fig. 6–36 *SELECT against view ALLQ*

When DB2 optimizes this statement, it has no information about where the data might reside in the four tables. A Visual Explain of this SELECT shows the work that DB2 must do in order to satisfy this request (Figure 6–37).

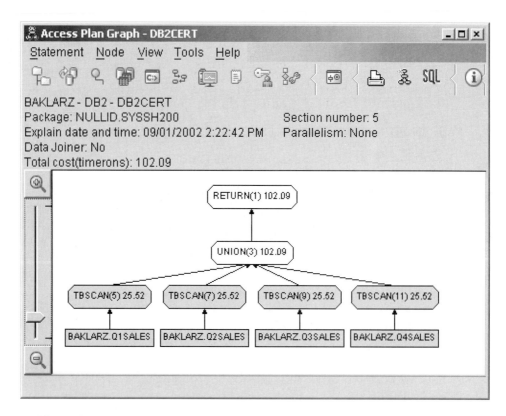

Fig. 6–37 *EXPLAIN statement of SELECT across UNION ALL*

In order to give DB2 better information on how to handle these rows, a check constraint needs to be added to the original table definition. This can be accomplished at either table creation time, or through the use of the ALTER TABLE command. For the existing tables defined above, the ALTER TABLE command would be similar to that found in Figure 6–38.

```
ALTER TABLE Q1SALES
   ADD CONTRAINT Q1_DATES
   CHECK (tx_date BETWEEN '2002-01-01' AND '2002-03-31');
```

Fig. 6–38 *Adding constraints to the table definitions*

Each table would have its own range of dates in the TX_DATE field. With this additional constraint added, the query will now be executed using the following explain plan (Figure 6–39):

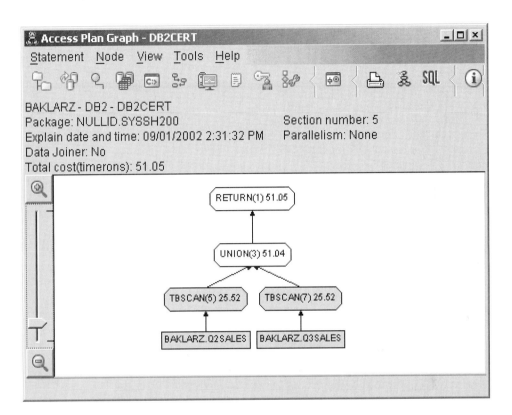

Fig. 6–39 *Explain plan after addition of check constraints*

Note how DB2 is able to eliminate two tables (Q1SALES and Q4SALES) from the access logic since the constraints tell DB2 that only Q2SALES and Q3SALES have the ranges of dates that we are interested in.

When a user issues an INSERT, DELETE, UPDATE, or SELECT against the ALLQ view, DB2 can use this new constraint information to direct the transaction to the proper table. This is especially important in the case of queries where tables that are not appropriate to the query can be eliminated from the search. Note that for proper handling of this view, the check constraints (range) must not overlap. In addition, modification to the column defined in the check constraint must not be updated outside the range. For instance, consider the UPDATE statements found in Figure 6–40.

```
UPDATE ALLQ
  SET   STORE = 4
  WHERE STORE = 1;

UPDATE ALLQ
  SET   TX_DATE = '2002-02-26'
  WHERE TX_DATE = '2002-02-27';

UPDATE ALLQ
  SET   TX_DATE = '2002-04-01'
  WHERE TX_DATE = '2002-03-30';
```

Fig. 6–40 *Update commands against a UNION ALL View*

The first update does not change any value in the check constraint so it will run successfully. Note that since we don't define a date range, all tables will have store number 4 changed to store number 1.

The second update runs successfully since we have changed a date from the 27th to the 26th and the date is still within the check constraint ('2002-01-01' to '2002-03-31').

The last update will not complete successfully due to the updated value being outside the check constraint range. In order to update this record, the user must first delete the record and then insert it. It is anticipated that this restriction will be removed from DB2 in some future release.

Note: Inserting into views with UNION ALL operators is new to DB2 UDB Version 8. Note that views could be defined with UNION ALL in prior releases, but only SELECT, UPDATE and DELETE statements were supported.

Using Tables Spaces with UNION ALL

A UNION ALL in a view can be used to circumvent some restrictions in DB2 and allow for more flexible maintenance in time-series data.

Tables in DB2 can only occupy 64GB of storage if a 4K data page is specified. Increasing the page size to 8K, 16K, or 32K can result in larger table sizes, but the restriction of 255 rows per page may still limit the amount of data that you can store.

A user could get around this space limitation by breaking up a table into smaller units and placing each one of these units into a separate table space. Consider the quarterly sales data tables found in Figure 6–34 where each table was placed into the default table space. This designed limited all tables to a limit of 64GB of data. Instead of using the default table space for these tables, the user could create a separate table space for each individual table (Figure 6–41).

```
CREATE REGULAR TABLESPACE Q1_2002
   PAGESIZE 4 K MANAGED BY SYSTEM
   USING('Q1_2002') EXTENTSIZE 2;
CREATE REGULAR TABLESPACE Q2_2002
   PAGESIZE 4 K MANAGED BY SYSTEM
   USING('Q2_2002') EXTENTSIZE 2;
CREATE REGULAR TABLESPACE Q3_2002
   PAGESIZE 4 K MANAGED BY SYSTEM
   USING('Q3_2002') EXTENTSIZE 2;
CREATE REGULAR TABLESPACE Q4_2002
   PAGESIZE 4 K MANAGED BY SYSTEM
   USING('Q4_2002') EXTENTSIZE 2;
```

Fig. 6–41 *Creation of table spaces*

Once these table spaces have been created, each table can be placed into its own table space. Only one table definition is show in Figure 6–42.

```
CREATE TABLE Q1SALES
   (
   store    int     not null,
   tx_date  date    not null,
   item     int     not null,
   quantity int     not null
   ) in Q1_2002;
```

Fig. 6–42 *Creation of Q1SALES table in a separate table space*

At this point, each quarterly sales table can take up to 64GB of space using a 4K page size. All transactions against this view, including INSERTs, will be directed to the appropriate table. Applications could still be written that directed their transactions to the appropriate quarterly sales table, but the view makes the handling of queries much easier. In addition, by designing the view as a UNION ALL of four separate tables, it is possible for the user to load new data into the system without impacting current workloads and then making the new data "live" with a minimum of administration.

If data is continually being refreshed on a monthly or quarterly basis, a user could create a separate table and table space and load the information into that table first. When the load is complete, then only a few commands need to be issued to make this data "live" to all users. In the case of the quarterly data, assume that a new set of data comes in for the first quarter of 2003 and you want to be able to make that part of the four quarters of information rather than the first quarter of 2002. A new table for the first quarter of 2003 has to be created that mimics the same table design as the prior four quarters of information (Figure 6–43).

```
CREATE REGULAR TABLESPACE Q1_2003
   PAGESIZE 4 K MANAGED BY SYSTEM
   USING('Q1_2003') EXTENTSIZE 2;

CREATE TABLE Q1SALES_2003
   (
   store      int     not null,
   tx_date    date    not null,
   item       int     not null,
   quantity int       not null
   ) in Q1_2003;
```

Fig. 6–43 *New quarter of sales information*

We need to change the name of the table since Q1SALES already exists in our data-base. Once the table is loaded with data from quarter 1, the existing Q1SALES table needs to be dropped and the view recreated to include the new Q1SALES_2003 table (Figure 6–44).

When a DROP statement is issued against a table space, typically no logging occurs. This means that a user can eliminate these rows from the database without the over-head associated with logging row deletes. An added benefit of separating the tables is the ability to manage LOADs and other activities on this new quarterly informa-tion without affecting production data.

There are some maintenance aspects that a user must be aware of when separating tables into different table spaces. Although SELECT processing can be relatively efficient, INSERT statements running against these tables will require some addi-tional overhead to determine which base table the transaction needs to be directed to. This may only amount to a few milliseconds of additional optimization time, but may make a difference on a heavily-loaded system. Finally, DB2 does not recog-nize the relationship between the tables that make up the view from a recovery per-spective. Normal logging and transaction rollbacks are handled the same as any other SQL statement. However, the table spaces that make up the various tables need to be backed up at the same time (if doing individual table space backups) so that they are recovered as one complete unit. If the table spaces are not recovered based on the same unit, it may be possible that transactions across the tables are not synchronized.

```
DROP TABLESPACE Q1_2002;
CREATE VIEW ALLQ AS
  (
  SELECT * FROM Q1SALES_2003
  UNION ALL
  SELECT * FROM Q2SALES
  UNION ALL
  SELECT * FROM Q3SALES
  UNION ALL
  SELECT * FROM Q4SALES
  )
```

Fig. 6–44 *New quarter of sales information*

Inoperative Views

A inoperative view is a view that is no longer available for SQL statements. A view becomes inoperative if:

- A privilege on which the view definition is dependent is revoked.
- An object, such as a table, alias, or function, on which the view definition is dependent is dropped.
- A view on which the view definition is dependent becomes inoperative.
- A view that is the superview of the view definition (the subview) becomes inoperative.

Summary

In this chapter, we have discussed SQL's Data Manipulation Language (DML). DML has four primary statements: SELECT, UPDATE, INSERT, and DELETE. These statements enable all database object data manipulation.

The SELECT statement has a rich set of features that allow a user to specify what rows should be retrieved and how they should be formatted. The columns to be retrieved from a table are specified in the select list. These columns can also contain calculations and functions that aggregate rows over ranges of values. The rows that are retrieved from tables must match the criteria in the WHERE clause. Result sets are returned to the user, optionally sorted by column values.

Multiple tables can be joined together in SELECT statements. Result sets can be further manipulated using UNION, INTERSECT, and EXCEPT operators. These operators add additional flexibility to the SELECT statement. Temporary result sets can be created using the WITH operator and subsequently used in the SELECT statement it was defined in.

The INSERT, UPDATE, and DELETE statements modify the contents of a table. These statements allow for the use of SELECT logic to limit the number of rows that are affected by the data modification.

Views are virtual tables. Views do not exist until a query is executed that requires the contents. Views can be classified deletable, updatable, insertable and read-only. The classification is important when designing applications or queries that need to access these views.

DB2 supports many more powerful SQL features, and these will be discussed in the next chapter.

Advanced SQL

- ◆ TRIGGERS
- ◆ RECURSIVE SQL
- ◆ OUTER JOIN
- ◆ OLAP
- ◆ CASE EXPRESSIONS
- ◆ TYPED TABLES
- ◆ SUMMARY TABLES
- ◆ SEQUENCES
- ◆ ADVANCED FUNCTIONS

*T*his chapter will cover some very powerful features found in DB2's SQL. Features, such as triggers, recursion, outer join, OLAP features, and uses of the case expression, will be discussed. In addition, we will discuss structured types, typed tables, user-defined functions, summary tables, sequences and some advanced functions.

Triggers

A *trigger* is a set of actions that will be executed when a defined event occurs. The triggering events can be the following SQL statements:

- `INSERT`
- `UPDATE`
- `DELETE`

Triggers are defined for a specific table and once defined, a trigger is automatically active. A table can have multiple triggers defined for it, and if multiple triggers are defined for a given table, the order of trigger activation is based on the trigger creation timestamp (the order in which the triggers were created). Trigger definitions are stored in the system catalog tables. You can see them through these catalog views:

- `SYSCAT.TRIGGERS` - contains the trigger definition information; one row for each trigger defined

- `SYSCAT.TRIGDEP` - contains one row for every dependency of a trigger on some other object

Triggers can also be defined on views. These types of triggers would be created when you need to manage how `INSERTS`, `DELETES`, or `UPDATES` need to be handled against the base tables. There are situations where DB2 cannot determine which table in a view needs to modified, so `INSTEAD OF` triggers can be used to direct the update to the proper tables.

Trigger Usage

Some of the uses of a trigger include:

- Data Validation - ensures that a new data value is within the proper range. This is similar to table-check constraints, but it is a more flexible data validation mechanism.
- Data Conditioning - implemented using triggers that fire before data record modification. This allows the new data value to be modified or conditioned to a predefined value.
- Data Integrity - can be used to ensure that cross-table dependencies are maintained. The triggered action could involve updating data records in related tables. This is similar to referential integrity, but it is a more flexible alternative.

Trigger Activation

A trigger can be defined to fire (be activated) in one of two ways:

- A *before trigger* will fire for each row in the set of affected rows before the triggering SQL statement executes. Therefore, the trigger body is seeing the new data values prior to their being inserted or updated into the table.

- An *after trigger* will fire for each row in the set of affected rows or after the statement has successfully completed (depending on the defined granularity). Therefore, the trigger body is seeing the table as being in a consistent state. (All transactions have been completed.)

Another important feature about triggers is that they can fire other triggers (or the same trigger) or other constraints. These are known as *cascading triggers*.

During the execution of a trigger, the new and old data values can be accessible to the trigger depending on the nature of the trigger (before or after).

By using triggers you can:

- Reduce the amount of application development and make development faster. Since triggers are stored in DB2 itself and are processed by DB2, you do not need to code the triggers or their actions into your applications.
- Provide a global environment for your business rules. Since the triggers only have to be defined once and then are stored in the database, they are available to all applications executing against the database.
- Reduce the maintenance of your applications. Again, since the trigger is handled by DB2 and is stored in the database itself, any changes to the trigger due to changes in your environment only have to occur in one not multiple applications.

The best method of understanding the usage of triggers is to see some in action. The DB2CERT database contains many relationships that can be maintained using triggers.

Trigger Example (After Trigger)

In Fig. 7–1, a trigger is defined to set the value of the PASS_FAIL column for each of the tests taken by a candidate. (Note that we add this column for this scenario.) The trigger has been given the name PASSFAIL (no relationship with the column called PASS_FAIL). Once the trigger has been created, it is active.

The PASSFAIL trigger is an AFTER, INSERT, and FOR EACH ROW trigger. Every time there is a row inserted into the TEST_TAKEN table, this trigger will fire. The trigger body section will perform an UPDATE statement to set the value of the PASS_FAIL column for the newly inserted row. The column is populated with either the value P (representing a passing grade) or the value F (representing a failing grade).

Note: Remember that a trigger defined against one table can modify other tables in the trigger body.

```
CREATE TRIGGER PassFail AFTER INSERT ON
db2cert.test_taken
     REFERENCING NEW AS n
     FOR EACH ROW MODE DB2SQL
UPDATE db2cert.test_taken
SET PASS_FAIL =
          CASE
          WHEN n.score >=
              (SELECT cut_score FROM db2cert.test
               WHERE number = n.number)
              THEN'P'
          WHEN n.score <
              (SELECT cut_score FROM db2cert.test
               WHERE number = n.number)
              THEN'F'
          END
WHERE n.cid        = cid
 AND n.tcid        = tcid
 AND n.number      = number
 AND n.date_taken = date_taken
```

Fig. 7–1 *Creating an AFTER trigger*

Trigger Example (Before Trigger)

A before trigger will be activated before the trigger operation has completed. The triggering operation can be an INSERT, UPDATE, or DELETE statement. This type of trigger is very useful for three purposes: to condition data, to provide default values, or to enforce data value constraints dynamically.

There are three before trigger examples shown in Fig. 7–2 through Fig. 7–4 that are used in the DB2 Certification application.

All three of these triggers have been implemented to avoid seat conflicts for test candidates. The triggers will fire during an insert of each new candidate for a test.

```
CREATE TRIGGER pre9 NO CASCADE BEFORE
    INSERT ON db2cert.test_taken
        REFERENCING NEW AS n
        FOR EACH ROW MODE DB2SQL
        WHEN (n.start_time <'09:00:00')
    SIGNAL SQLSTATE '70003'
    ('Cannot assign seat before 09:00:00!')
```

Fig. 7–2 *Before trigger example (1)*

```
CREATE TRIGGER aft5 NO CASCADE BEFORE
    INSERT ON db2cert.test_taken
        REFERENCING NEW AS n
        FOR EACH ROW MODE DB2SQL
        WHEN (n.start_time +
                (SELECT SMALLINT(length) FROM db2cert.test
                    WHERE number = n.number) MINUTES
                                        > '17:00:00')
    SIGNAL SQLSTATE '70004'
    ('Cannot assign seat after 17:00:00!')
```

Fig. 7–3 *Before trigger example (2)*

```
CREATE TRIGGER start NO CASCADE BEFORE
    INSERT ON db2cert.test_taken
        REFERENCING NEW AS n
        FOR EACH ROW MODE DB2SQL
        WHEN (
        EXISTS (SELECT cid FROM db2cert.test_taken
                    WHERE seat_no    = n.seat_no    AND
                          tcid       = n.tcid       AND
                          date_taken = n.date_taken AND
                          n.start_time BETWEEN
                              start_time AND finish_time))
    SIGNAL SQLSTATE '70001'
    ('Start Time Conflict!')
```

Fig. 7–4 *Before trigger example (3)*

If the conditions are encountered, an SQL error will be flagged using the SQL function called SIGNAL. A different SQLSTATE value will be provided when the triggered conditions are encountered.

The PRE9 trigger, shown in Fig. 7–2, is used to ensure that a test candidate is not scheduled to take a test before 9:00 a.m. The AFT5 trigger is used to ensure that a test candidate is not scheduled to take a test after 5:00 p.m. The START trigger is used to avoid conflicts during a testing day.

Instead Of Triggers

In many installations, views are used as a way of limiting access to base tables. With a view, a DBA can restrict both the columns and sets of rows that a user can access. However, the use of views causes some difficulties when data modification commands need to be applied to rows in the base table. For instance, a user may have created a customer reference table with the following definition (Figure 7–5):

```
CREATE TABLE CUSTOMERS
    (
    CUSTNO        INT           NOT NULL,
    CUSTNAME      VARCHAR(20)   NOT NULL,
    PHONE         CHAR(12)      NOT NULL,
    CREDIT_CARD   VARCHAR(20)   FOR BIT DATA NOT NULL,
    YTD_SALES     DECIMAL(15,2) NOT NULL
    )
```

Fig. 7–5 *Customer reference table*

This table needs to be made available to a variety of people in the company including the sales people, order desk, customer service, and accounts receivable. However, some of this information is not relevant to all users and from a security perspective you may not want all users to see everything in the table. A possible solution is to create a view for each group of users. The customer service staff may have the following view defined for them (see Figure 7–6):

```
CREATE VIEW CUSTOMER_SERVICE AS
    (
    SELECT CUSTNO, CUSTNAME, PHONE, CREDIT_CARD
        FROM CUSTOMERS
    )
```

Fig. 7–6 *Customer reference table*

Now the customer service staff can select from this table and get all of the contact information from the customer table without seeing the yearly sales numbers. Although this fixes the security problem, it raises new issues when the service staff have to add new records. Based on their knowledge of the view that they have access to (`CUSTOMER_SERVICE`), adding a new customer to their table would look like this (Figure 7–7):

```
INSERT INTO CUSTOMER_SERVICE VALUES
  (1234, 'WONGS DONUTS','887-555-1212','3922 1111 2222');
```

Fig. 7–7 *Insert into the Customer_Service table*

Unfortunately, DB2 will issue an error message (Figure 7–8) since this insert violates a constraint on the base table. In this case, the `YTD_SALES` column is not included as part of the `INSERT` statement and it must be supplied according to the original table definition (`NOT NULL`).

```
SQL0407N  Assignment of a NULL value to a NOT NULL column
"TBSPACEID=5, TABLEID=61, COLNO=4" is not allowed.
SQLSTATE=23502
```

Fig. 7–8 *Error on insert*

In order to get around this problem the DBA can do one of the following steps:

- Create a better database design to avoid this error
- Allow `NULL` values in the `YTD_SALES` field or set the `DEFAULT` to zero
- Create an `INSTEAD OF` trigger

One could argue that the system should be redesigned not have to this problem, but if we are stuck with the current table definitions an `INSTEAD OF` trigger will help solve the problem.

An `INSTEAD OF` trigger is used only on `VIEWS`, not base tables. It has similar characteristics to a normal trigger except for the following restrictions:

- Only allowed on views
- Always `FOR EACH ROW`
- `DEFAULT` values get passed as `NULL`
- Cannot use positioned `UPDATE/DELETE` on cursor over view with `INSTEAD OF` `UPDATE/DELETE` trigger

Advanced SQL

For the CUSTOMER_SERVICE view, we can create an INSTEAD OF trigger that will handle the missing field during an insert operation (Figure 7–9):

```
CREATE TRIGGER I_CUSTOMER_SERVICE
  INSTEAD OF INSERT ON CUSTOMER_SERVICE
  REFERENCING NEW AS CUST
  FOR EACH ROW MODE DB2SQL
BEGIN ATOMIC
  INSERT INTO CUSTOMERS VALUES (
      cust.custno,
      cust.custname,
      cust.phone,
      cust.credit_card,
      0);
END
```

Fig. 7–9 *Instead of trigger on insert*

When an INSERT is executed against this view, DB2 will now invoke this INSTEAD OF trigger and the record will be successfully inserted into the table. Although this is a trivial example, the INSTEAD OF trigger can be used for variety of purposes, including encrypting and decrypting fields in the table. For instance, the CREDIT_CARD information in this table could be encrypted for security reasons. If we decide to use a fixed password for the encryption and decryption, we can create the following view to select the records with the values decrypted (Figure 7–10):

```
CREATE VIEW CUSTOMER_SERVICE AS
  (
  SELECT CUSTNO, CUSTNAME, PHONE,
    DECRYPT_CHAR(CREDIT_CARD,'SECRET') AS CREDIT_CARD
    FROM CUSTOMERS
  )
```

Fig. 7–10 *View with decryption*

The INSTEAD OF trigger also needs to modified to encrypt the values as well as insert the zero sales for the year (Figure 7–11):

```
CREATE TRIGGER I_CUSTOMER_SERVICE
  INSTEAD OF INSERT ON CUSTOMER_SERVICE
  REFERENCING NEW AS CUST
  DEFAULTS NULL
  FOR EACH ROW MODE DB2SQL
BEGIN ATOMIC
  INSERT INTO CUSTOMERS VALUES (
    cust.custno,
    cust.custname,
    cust.phone,
    encrypt(cust.credit_card,'SECRET'),
    0);
END
```

Fig. 7–11 *Instead of trigger with encryption*

When a user does a select from the CUSTOMER_SERVICE table, they would see the following results (Figure 7–12):

```
CUSTNO CUSTNAME        PHONE         CREDIT_CARD
------ --------------- ------------- ---------------
  1234 WONGS DONUTS    887-555-1212  3922 1111 2222
```

Fig. 7–12 *Select from Customer_Service table*

Note what happens if another user selected from the base table instead (Figure 7–13):

```
CUSTNO CUSTNAME        PHONE         CREDIT_CARD
------ --------------- ------------- ---------------
  1234 WONGS DONUTS    887-555-1212  x'00B749FFE...
```

Fig. 7–13 *Select from Customers table*

Since the decryption is not occurring on the base table, any other user accessing this field will not see the results.

In summary, the INSTEAD OF trigger can give you greater flexibility in the use of views, and allow you to handle situations with INSERTs, UPDATEs, and DELETEs that DB2 cannot figure out on its own.

Note: The `INSTEAD OF` trigger was introduced in DB2 Version 8.1. This trigger can only be used with views and will fail if used against base tables.

Recursive SQL

A *recursive SQL* statement is one where an SQL statement repeatedly uses the resulting set to determine further results. This kind of SQL statement is built using a common table expression that make references to itself (i.e., it uses its own definition).

Such statements are useful to solve queries, such as hierarchical trees, routing airline flights, or bill-of-material types of queries.

Let's say that we have a table that indicates the distance between two cities. For this example, we are using the `FLIGHTS` table. It contains information about the origin, destination, and distance between cities.

The table is shown in Fig. 7–14.

```
ORIGIN       DESTINATION DISTANCE
----------   ----------- -----------
Germany      New York         8000
Germany      Chicago          8700
Chicago      Austin           1300
New York     Houston          2100
Houston      Austin            300
New York     Chicago           950
Italy        New York        10000
Italy        Chicago         11000
Ireland      Chicago         10700
Chicago      Toronto           400
New York     Toronto           350
Mexico       Houston           770
```

Fig. 7–14 *Recursive SQL: Content of the flights table*

Our goal is to obtain a list with the distance and number of stops of all the destinations you can reach departing from Germany. We will create a recursive SQL statement to retrieve this information.

Let's first explain why this kind of query is resolved using recursive SQL. The table contains information about destinations and origins. After reaching one specific destination, this destination can be treated as an origin. This is where the recursion appears: The destination becomes an origin, and the next destination can become a new origin, and so on.

The way to resolve this query is by writing an SQL statement that, given an origin, will retrieve its destinations, then treat them as origins, obtain the new destinations, and so on.

```
WITH path (origin,destination,distance,stops)
AS(
    SELECT f.origin, f.destination, f.distance,0   1
FROM flights f
 WHERE origin='Germany'
 UNION ALL
    SELECT p.origin,f.destination,                 2
           p.distance+f.distance, p.stops+1
    FROM flights f, path p
    WHERE p.destination=f.origin)
                                                   3
SELECT origin, destination, distance, stops FROM path
```

Fig. 7–15 *Recursive SQL: Obtaining all the destinations from Germany*

As we have said before, recursion is built on common table expressions. In the recursive SQL example shown in Fig. 7–15, the common table expression is called PATH.

In **1**, we are obtaining the destinations that can be reached directly from Germany. In this case, the stops column is set to 0, because the flights are nonstop.

Then, in **2**, we are referencing the recently created common table expression path. In this part, we join the common table expression with the base table to create the recursion. This is where the destination becomes a new origin. We are also incrementing the distance and the number of stops. Observe that a UNION ALL clause is needed in the definition of a recursive query.

Finally, in **3**, we are retrieving all the possible routes accessible from Germany, the distance, and the number of stops.

The output of the recursive SQL statement is show in Fig. 7–16.

```
ORIGIN      DESTINATION DISTANCE  STOPS
----------- ----------- --------- -----
SQL0347W The recursive common table expression "DB2.PATH"
may contain an infinite loop. SQLSTATE=01605

Germany     New York         8000     0
Germany     Chicago          8700     0
Germany     Houston         10100     1
Germany     Chicago          8950     1
Germany     Toronto          8350     1
Germany     Austin          10000     1
Germany     Toronto          9100     1
Germany     Austin          10400     2
Germany     Austin          10250     2
Germany     Toronto          9350     2
```

Fig. 7–16 *Recursive SQL: Destinations reached from Germany*

The SQL statement shown in Fig. 7–15 can run forever if there is a loop found in the flights table. When you are coding this kind of SQL statement, you must be aware of the possibility of infinite loops. To avoid an infinite loop, you can restrict the query using the number of stops.

Let's say that you are only interested in the routes that make less than five stops. You need to add the following restriction to the last SQL statement:

```
WHERE stops < 5
```

This condition can be used to avoid an infinite loop.

Now, let's create a more complex example based on the same idea. We want to obtain a list of the possible flights from Germany to Austin. This time, we want to obtain the flight route, the distance, and the number of stops.

As we can see from the output in Fig. 7–16, there are three different paths to reach Austin from Germany. Let's create the SQL statement that can tell us the complete path for each case.

```
WITH detail_path (origin,destination,route,distance,stops)
AS(
   SELECT f.origin, f.destination,
      VARCHAR(SUBSTR(f.origin,1,2),35),f.distance,0     1
      FROM flights f
      WHERE origin='Germany'
   UNION ALL
   SELECT p.origin,f.destination,
         route ||'>' || SUBSTR(p.destination,1,2),     2
         p.distance+f.distance, p.stops+1
      FROM flights f,detail_path p
      WHERE p.destination=f.origin
   )
                                                        3
SELECT route ||'>' || SUBSTR(destination,1,2),
      distance, stops
   FROM detail_path WHERE destination='Austin'
   ORDER BY distance
```

Fig. 7–17 *Recursive SQL: Obtaining routes from Germany to Austin*

The basics of the SQL statement in Fig. 7–17 are the same as the previous example. The difference is that now we are creating the route column. This column is created by extracting the first two characters of each visited airport on the way from Germany to Austin. The || (concatenation) operator is used to link each one of the cities visited to another.

In **1**, we are using the VARCHAR function to create a varchar column that will store all the cities visited in a specific path. This step will also add the origin city.

Then, in **2**, we are linking the route with each one of the intermediary cities visited.

Finally, in **3**, we link the final destination to the path. Also in this step, we specify the desired destination.

Advanced SQL

```
1                          DISTANCE    STOPS
-------------------------  ----------  ----------
SQL0347W The recursive common table expression
"DB2.DETAIL_PATH" may contain an infinite loop.
SQLSTATE=01605

Ge>Ch>Au                      10000         1
Ge>Ne>Ch>Au                   10250         2
Ge>Ne>Ho>Au                   10400         2
```

Fig. 7–18 *Detailed path from Germany to Austin*

Outer Join

The join operation used most often is the one we have been using in the book exercises, which is known as an INNER JOIN. Now, we will talk about a different kind of join operation.

The result set of an inner join consists only of those matched rows that are present in both joined tables. What happens when we need to include those values that are present in one or another joined table, but not in both of them? This is the case when we need to use an OUTER JOIN operation. Outer joins are designed to generate an answer set that includes those values that are present in joined tables and those that are not. There are different kinds of outer joins as we will see.

Before getting into the details of the outer join, we will examine the explicit syntax used to code joins between tables. Let's start with an inner join coded with this syntax. The following join example produces an answer set containing the first name, the phone number, and the highest score for each candidate in the TEST_TAKEN table.

```
SELECT fname, wphone, MAX(INTEGER(score))
  FROM db2cert.candidate c
      INNER JOIN db2cert.test_taken tt ON c.cid=tt.cid
GROUP BY fname, wphone
```

In this syntax, you indicate the tables that will be joined, along with the join operation, and the join columns that are required.

Observe the INNER JOIN operator in the example above. It belongs to the FROM clause of the statement. The INNER JOIN operator specifies that an inner join operation will be used for the statement. The keyword ON is used to specify the join conditions for the tables being joined. In our example, the join condition is based on the join columns, CID of the CANDIDATE table, and CID of the TEST_TAKEN table.

The explicit join syntax also allows you to specify an outer join as we will see in the next sections.

Left Outer Join

A LEFT OUTER JOIN operation, also known as left join, produces an answer set that includes the matching values of both joined tables and those values only present in the left joined table. The left joined table is the one used in the left part of the LEFT OUTER JOIN operator when coding the join operation.

Note: You can also use LEFT JOIN to indicate a left outer join operation.

We have been requested to generate a report that includes the first name, the phone number, and the highest score for all the candidates present in the CANDIDATE table. If an inner join is used, as is shown in the last example, the report will only include data of those candidates present in the TEST_TAKEN table.

The request could be solved using some SQL statements already discussed; however, the construction will be complex. We will use the left outer join to satisfy the request as the following example shows.

```
SELECT fname, wphone, MAX(INTEGER(score))
  FROM db2cert.candidate c
      LEFT OUTER JOIN db2cert.test_taken tt ON c.cid=tt.cid
  GROUP BY fname, wphone
```

Observe the syntax used to indicate a left outer join. The LEFT OUTER JOIN operator is used to indicate the left outer join operation. In this example, the answer set includes those candidates not present in the test_taken table. The MAX(INTEGER(score)) column will show nulls for those candidates.

Right Outer Join

A RIGHT OUTER JOIN operation, also known as right join, produces an answer set that includes the matching values of both joined tables and those values only present in the right joined table. The right joined table is the one used in the right part of the RIGHT OUTER JOIN operator when coding the join operation.

The example using a right outer join is shown below:

```
SELECT name, count(DISTINCT char(tt.cid))
    FROM db2cert.test_taken tt
      RIGHT OUTER JOIN db2cert.test t
      ON tt.number = t.number
    GROUP BY name
```

In this example, all test names present in the TEST table and the number of candidates who scheduled or took each test are requested. Notice there may be some tests for which no candidate was scheduled. You cannot report such tests using a inner join statement; however, you can do it using right outer join.

Full Outer Join

The FULL OUTER JOIN operation produces an answer set that includes the matching values of both joined tables and those values not present in one or the other of the tables.

To show a full outer join operation, we will create two sample tables: city and country. They show the relationship between a city and a country (CITY table) and a country and a continent (COUNTRY table). The city table is designed to have countries that are not in the country table. The country table is also designed to have countries that are not in the city table. The contents of both tables are shown in Fig. 7–19 and Fig. 7–20.

```
CITY_NAME            COUNTRY_NAME
----------------     ---------------
Sidney               Australia
London               England
Dublin               Ireland
Firenze              Italy
Milano               Italy
Mexico               Mexico
Lima                 Peru
Toronto              Canada
Vienna               Austria
Hannover             Germany
```

Fig. 7–19 *City table used in outer join*

```
COUNTRY_NAME         CONTINENT
----------------     ----------------------------
Australia            Australian Continent
England              European Continent
Ireland              European Continent
Italy                European Continent
Mexico               American Continent
Austria              European Continent
South Africa         African Continent
Spain                European Continent
```

Fig. 7–20 *Country table used in outer join*

We want to show all the countries, cities, and the continents that are in the tables. Therefore, we are using a full outer join as the following example shows:

```
SELECT ctry.continent, ctry.country_name,
       cty.country_name, cty.city_name
    FROM country ctry
         FULL OUTER JOIN
         city cty
         ON cty.country_name=ctry.country_name
    ORDER BY ctry.continent,
             cty.country_name,
             cty.city_name
```

Fig. 7–21 *Full outer join*

The result of the query is as follows:

```
CONTINENT                COUNTRY_NAME   COUNTRY_NAME   CITY_NAME
----------------------   ------------   ------------   ----------
African Continent        South Africa   -              -
American Continent       Mexico         Mexico         Mexico
Australian Continent     Australia      Australia      Sidney
European Continent       Austria        Austria        Vienna
European Continent       England        England        London
European Continent       Ireland        Ireland        Dublin
European Continent       Italy          Italy          Firenze
European Continent       Italy          Italy          Milano
European Continent       Spain          -              -
-                        -              Canada         Toronto
-                        -              Germany        Hannover
-                        -              Peru           Lima
```

Fig. 7–22 *Output of the full outer join*

As shown in Fig. 7–22, the rows that have a null value were added by the outer join operation. The COUNTRY_NAME column is shown twice to see those countries present in the country table that are not present in the city table and vice versa.

Combining Outer Joins

Up to now we have discussed each outer join operation separately. Now, we will show a more complex example combining two outer joins in one single query. Let's display all the candidates and all the tests with their respective scores.

To create this query, we need two outer joins. The first outer join will obtain all candidates and their scores including candidates who did not schedule or take any tests. The second outer join will retrieve all the tests present in the test table even if no candidate scheduled or took those tests.

```
SELECT c.cid, t.name, score
       FROM (db2cert.candidate c
             LEFT OUTER JOIN db2cert.test_taken tt 1
                   ON tt.cid=c.cid)
             FULL OUTER JOIN db2cert.test t        2
                   ON tt.number = t.number
       ORDER BY c.cid
```

Fig. 7–23 *Two outer joins in one SQL statement*

The first outer join **1** is enclosed in parentheses. The parentheses are used for readability and to denote that the left outer join will be resolved first. This left outer join gathers all the candidate IDs. We only need a left outer join here. Because of referential integrity constraints, table TEST_TAKEN can only have candidates present in the CANDIDATE table.

The second part is a full outer join **2**. With this outer join, we take all the tests taken by the candidates, the result of the left outer join, and join them with all the tests in the TEST table. We need a full outer join this time even though the TEST_TAKEN table can only have test numbers that are present in the TEST table, because the left table of this outer join, which is the result of the first join, may include NULL values as a test number. The TEST table does not have null values, so we need to use a full outer join.

The output of the SQL statement is shown in Fig. 7–24.

Advanced SQL

```
CID NAME                                SCORE
--- ----------------------------------- -----------
111 DB2 Fundamentals                       65
111 DB2 Administration                     73
111 DB2 Application Development             67
222 DB2 Fundamentals                       55
222 DB2 Application Development             53
222 DB2 Application Development             75
333 DB2 Fundamentals                       82
333 DB2 Administration                      -
333 DB2 Application Development             92
444 -                                       -
555 -                                       -
666 -                                       -
777 -                                       -
888 -                                       -

  14 record(s) selected.
```

Fig. 7–24 *Result of two outer joins combined*

OLAP Features

Databases normally hold large amounts of data that can be updated, deleted, queried, and inserted on a daily basis. Databases in which data is constantly updated, deleted, and inserted are known as *Online Transaction Processing (OLTP)* systems. Databases that hold large amounts of data and do not have a heavy transaction work load but do have a large number of concurrent queries executing all the time, are known as *Decision Support Systems (DSS)*. Certain decision support systems have fewer queries, but each query can be very complex. These allow users to examine the data from different perspectives by performing *Online Analytical Processing (OLAP)*.

The functionality of the database is required to provide multidimensional views of relational data, without a significant performance effect. DB2 provides this capability, using a number of joining methods, SQL statements, and other database features. The next few sections explain the database technology found in DB2 that enhances the performance of OLAP queries.

STAR Schemas

The concept of a *STAR schema* is illustrated in Fig. 7–25. A business view of a highly normalized database often requires a number of attributes associated with one primary object. Each of these attributes is contained in separate tables.

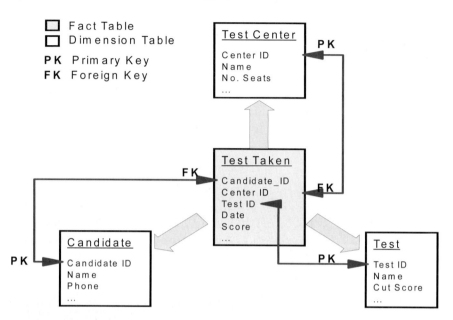

Fig. 7–25 *STAR schema in the DB2CERT database*

The following points are characteristic of a STAR schema design:

- There is a large Fact table that contains data relating to the Dimension tables. In Fig. 7–25, the Fact table is the test_taken table. It contains detailed information on each test taken, including exactly which test was taken, in which center the test was taken, and who took the test.
- There are a number of small Dimension tables that typically hold descriptive information about an entity that has a small number of rows. In Fig. 7–25, the Dimension tables are test, candidate, and test_center.
- The primary keys of the Dimension tables involved in the STAR schema supply foreign key entries in the Fact table. The concatenation of foreign keys from the Dimension tables usually forms a small subset of the Fact table. In Fig. 7–25, the foreign keys are Candidate ID, Center ID, and Test ID.

This approach allows as few attributes as possible to be stored in the Fact table. The benefit of this is that the Fact table is usually very large and therefore any data duplication in this table would be very costly in terms of storage and access times. If the DB2CERT database were used to store information on a university's entrance examinations, for example, the test_taken table could grow enormously.

OLAP schemas, such as the STAR schemas, are frequently used for large databases. These schemas make it very important to access the data in these databases in the optimal manner. Otherwise, the joins involved in the schemas may result in poor performance.

OLAP Indexes

A typical STAR schema includes a large number of indexes. This is due to the adhoc nature of queries in an OLAP environment. Such an environment is typically not subjected to constant insert or update activity and, therefore, does not have to suffer from significant performance degradation as a result of index maintenance.

The prime consideration of indexes in an OLAP environment is to facilitate the joining of tables and the ordering of output. This is particularly important for the fact table where multiple indexes are defined, especially on foreign key columns relating to the dimension tables. The benefit of multiple indexes in this environment is improved query performance against the fact table. The indexes defined on the tables could either be single-column or multicolumn indexes.

There are also certain issues to be considered when using multiple indexes in the OLAP environment. The first is that multiple indexes will require a certain amount of space, depending on the number of columns in each index and the size of the tables. The second is that there will be a significant one-time cost when building indexes, perhaps during a bulk load.

STAR Joins

A typical query against databases designed with the STAR schema would consist of multiple local predicates referencing values in the dimension tables and contain join predicates connecting the dimension tables to the fact table as shown in Fig. 7–26. These types of queries are called *STAR joins*.

In this example, we wish to find the average score of DB2 tests taken by Canadian citizens in the small test centers year by year. A STAR join query is difficult to execute efficiently, because no single join predicate reduces the cardinality of the fact rows significantly, although the combination of join predicates results in a small answer set. The more dimension tables involved in the join result, the more potential there is to plan an inefficient access path. To execute STAR join queries efficiently, multiple index access can be performed by the optimizer.

Advanced SQL

```
SELECT t.name, YEAR(tt.date_taken) AS year,
       AVG(integer(tt.score)) AS avgsc
FROM test t, test_taken tt, test_center tc,
     candidate c
WHERE c.cid = tt.cid          AND
      tc.tcid = tt.tcid       AND
      t.number = tt.number    AND
      t.name LIKE 'DB2%'      AND
      c.country='Canada'      AND
      tc.noseats < 10
GROUP BY t.name, YEAR(tt.date_taken);
```

Fig. 7–26 *STAR join*

Super Grouping

We will now discuss OLAP features known as *super grouping* functions. These functions are used to analyze data in multiple dimensions. The dimensions can be seen as different levels of aggregation over a set of tables. The term super grouping is used to describe OLAP features, because they allow the retrieval of multiple aggregation levels in one single pass of data.

Multiple Groups (Grouping Sets)

The GROUPING SETS specification in the GROUP BY clause is used to generate multiple aggregation groups in a single SQL statement. This feature is used to generate aggregated data based on different grouping criteria. Using GROUPING SETS, it is possible to calculate aggregations that would otherwise require a set operation, such as UNION, to put together the different aggregated answer sets.

Let's suppose we want to know the following:

- How may tests have been taken at the test centers?
- How many tests of each type have been taken in each test center?

To gather this information, we first need to count the tests taken grouped by test center and then count the tests taken in each test center. This requirement needs two different grouping sets, one grouped by test center and another grouped by test name and test center. See the following example and the result:

```
SELECT tt.tcid,t.name,count(*)
    FROM db2cert.test_taken tt, db2cert.test t
    WHERE tt.number=t.number
    GROUP BY
        GROUPING SETS (tt.tcid,(tt.tcid,t.name))
```

Fig. 7–27 *Grouping sets used in an SQL statement*

```
TCID NAME                                              3
---- ----------------------------------------- -----------
TR01 -                                                 3
TX01 -                                                 6
TR01 DB2 Application Development                       2
TR01 DB2 Fundamentals                                 1
TX01 DB2 Administration                               2
TX01 DB2 Application Development                       2
TX01 DB2 Fundamentals                                 2

  7 record(s) selected.
```

Fig. 7–28 *Result of grouping sets*

The GROUPING SETS specification calculates the first requirement, which is the number of tests taken at each test center, by listing the TCID column of the TEST_TAKEN table. Then the second requirement, which is the number of tests by test center and test name, is calculated by listing TCID column of the TEST_TAKEN table and NAME column of the TEST table. This second grouping is the same as if you coded a regular GROUP BY by using GROUP BY TT.TCID,T.NAME.

As seen in the result set shown in Fig. 7–28, the grouping sets can be formed by one or more columns.

Adding a Grand Total

Using the GROUPING SETS specification, you can add a grand total to your query. The example shown in Fig. 7–27 doesn't display the total of all tests taken at all test centers. This can be calculated by adding the grand total group to the grouping sets list.

As groups are created, null values are added to those columns that don't have a value in a particular group. In this way, the grand total row will show null values in all columns except for the grand total itself.

Let's see the next example. This one is similar to the example shown in Fig. 7–27. This time we are including a grand total group and converting the null-generated values to character strings using the VALUE SQL function. In this example, if the first argument of the VALUE function is null, the character string supplied as the second argument will be the result of the VALUE function.

```
SELECT value(char(tt.tcid),'All'),
       value(t.name,'All Tests'),
       count(*)
  FROM test_taken tt, test t
 WHERE tt.number=t.number
 GROUP BY
    GROUPING SETS
        (char(tt.tcid),(char(tt.tcid),t.name),())
```

Fig. 7–29 *Grouping sets with a grand total*

```
1    2                                        3
---- ------------------------------------ -----------
All  All Tests                                  9
TR01 All Tests                                  3
TX01 All Tests                                  6
TR01 DB2 Application Development                 2
TR01 DB2 Fundamentals                           1
TX01 DB2 Administration                         2
TX01 DB2 Application Development                 2
TX01 DB2 Fundamentals                           2

8 record(s) selected.
```

Fig. 7–30 *Result of grouping sets with a grand total*

The grand total group is specified with a pair of empty parentheses () in the grouping set list.

Recognizing Group Added Null Values

There will be cases when the data used in a grouping function contains null values. In this case, is important to be able to distinguish between a null value and a group-generated null value.

DB2 provides the GROUPING function that identifies those null-generated values by giving them a value of 1.

Note: The GROUPING function returns only the values of 1 or 0. One (1) means that the null value was generated by DB2, and 0 means that the value was not generated by DB2.

Now, let's use the GROUPING function inside a CASE expression to differentiate between those groups with added null values and regular null values. To keep the query small, the example will only use the CASE expression for the TT.TCID column.

```
SELECT
    CASE                                           1
      WHEN GROUPING(tt.tcid)=1
            THEN 'All'
      WHEN GROUPING(tt.tcid)=0
            THEN char(tt.tcid)
      END,
      VALUE(t.name,'All Tests'),
      GROUPING(tt.tcid) AS grouped_tcid,          2
      GROUPING(t.name) AS grouped_name,
      COUNT(*)
  FROM db2cert.test_taken tt, db2cert.test t
  WHERE tt.number=t.number
  GROUP BY
        GROUPING SETS (tt.tcid,(t.name,tt.tcid),())
```

Fig. 7–31 *Using the grouping function to identify group added null*

```
 1    2                                 GROUPED_TCID   GROUPED_NAME 5
 ---- -----------------------------     ------------   ------------ ------
 All  All Tests                              1              1          9
 TR01 All Tests                              0              1          3
 TX01 All Tests                              0              1          6
 TR01 DB2 Application Development            0              0          2
 TR01 DB2 Fundamentals                       0              0          1
 TX01 DB2 Administration                      0              0          2
 TX01 DB2 Application Development            0              0          2
 TX01 DB2 Fundamentals                       0              0          2

 8 record(s) selected.
```

Fig. 7–32 *The Result of the grouping function*

The case expression **1**, uses the GROUPING function over the TCID column. If a value of 1 is returned, then ALL will be printed. In our example, ALL indicates that the row contains a group-added null value. A null-generated value represents all the tests centers. If the GROUPING function returns a 0, it means that the value of the TCID column for that row was not generated by DB2.

The GROUPING functions shown in will display a value of 1 or 0 depending on the value of the columns TT.TCID and T.NAME for a particular row. A value of 1 in GROUPING(TT.TCID) means that the row is a total grouped on the TCID column.

ROLLUP

The GROUPING SETS specification shown in the previous section allows you to create different levels of aggregation in one single pass of data. However, you need to specify each of the groups you want. There are cases when you need to create a report in which you require a total for each column you are grouping. Here is when a super group feature such as ROLLUP is required.

The ROLLUP grouping can generate various groups in one single pass. This will allow you to review different levels of aggregation as if you created a control break report.

Let's say that you need a report showing the following:

- How many tests have been taken by country?
- How many tests have been taken by country and test center?
- How many tests have been taken by country, test center, and test name?
- What is the total number of tests taken?

To solve this requirement, we will use the ROLLUP grouping, which will generate the aggregations requested. The SQL statement is shown in Fig. 7–33.

```
SELECT
  c.country,
  tt.tcid,
  substr(t.name,1,27) as test_name,
  count(*) as tests_taken
FROM db2cert.test_taken tt,db2cert.test t,db2cert.candidate c
WHERE tt.number=t.number AND tt.cid=c.cid
GROUP BY ROLLUP (c.country,tt.tcid,t.name)
ORDER BY c.country,tt.tcid,t.name
```

Fig. 7–33 *Using the ROLLUP operator*

The report generated allows you to roll up your information and drill down into your information. You can analyze the report from a grand-total level down to the country, test center, and test name.

```
COUNTRY        TCID TEST_NAME                        TESTS_TAKEN
-------------- ---- -------------------------------- -------------
Canada         TX01 DB2 Administration                         2
Canada         TX01 DB2 Application Development                2
Canada         TX01 DB2 Fundamentals                           2
Canada         TX01 -                                          6
Canada         -    -                                          6
Germany        TR01 DB2 Application Development                2
Germany        TR01 DB2 Fundamentals                           1
Germany        TR01 -                                          3
Germany        -    -                                          3
-              -    -                                          9

 10 record(s) selected.
```

Fig. 7–34 *The result of the ROLLUP operator*

Note: The ROLLUP operation is not commutative; the order in which you specify your groups is important. The resulting set of ROLLUP(COUNTRY, TCID, NAME) is different from ROLLUP(TCID, COUNTRY, NAME).

Super-group operations such as ROLLUP are built over the GROUPING SETS operation. The ROLLUP shown in Fig. 7–33 is equivalent to GROUPING SETS ((COUNTRY,TCID,NAME),(COUNTRY,TCID),COUNTRY,()). This is why they are considered super-groups operations.

CUBE

From the answer set obtained by the ROLLUP operation shown in Fig. 7–33, there are some groups not present that can be useful. These groups include the number of tests taken only by test center or by test number.

The CUBE operation obtains all combinations of groups that can be formed in a grouping list. The groups, listed in the grouping list of a CUBE operation, will be permuted to calculate all the groups possible in that list. This creates all the aggregations needed to construct a cube of data.

The resulting cube can be sliced and diced in multiple dimensions to allow the users multidimensional analysis of data stored in DB2.

Now use the CUBE operation to generate the following groups:

- Tests taken by country
- Tests taken by test center
- Tests taken by test number
- All intermediate groups

You can write a statement as shown in Fig. 7–35.

Advanced SQL

```
SELECT c.country,tt.tcid,
        SUBSTR(t.name,1,27) AS test_name,
        COUNT(*) AS tests_taken
     FROM db2cert.test_taken tt,
         db2cert.test t,
         db2cert.candidate c
          WHERE tt.number=t.number
          AND   tt.cid=c.cid
           GROUP BY
              CUBE (c.country,tt.tcid,t.name)
           ORDER BY c.country,tt.tcid,t.name
```

Fig. 7–35 *Using the CUBE operator*

COUNTRY	TCID	TEST_NAME	TESTS_TAKEN
Canada	TX01	DB2 Administration	2
Canada	TX01	DB2 Application Development	2
Canada	TX01	DB2 Fundamentals	2
Canada	TX01	-	6
Canada	-	DB2 Administration	2
Canada	-	DB2 Application Development	2
Canada	-	DB2 Fundamentals	2
Canada	-	-	6
Germany	TR01	DB2 Application Development	2
Germany	TR01	DB2 Fundamentals	1
Germany	TR01	-	3
Germany	-	DB2 Application Development	2
Germany	-	DB2 Fundamentals	1
Germany	-	-	3
-	TR01	DB2 Application Development	2
-	TR01	DB2 Fundamentals	1
-	TR01	-	3
-	TX01	DB2 Administration	2
-	TX01	DB2 Application Development	2
-	TX01	DB2 Fundamentals	2
-	TX01	-	6
-	-	DB2 Administration	2
-	-	DB2 Application Development	4
-	-	DB2 Fundamentals	3
-	-	-	9

```
25 record(s) selected.
```

Fig. 7–36 *The result of the CUBE operator*

The CUBE operation shown in Fig. 7–35 generates eight different groups, including a grand total group. The number of groups generated by a CUBE operation is the result of the number of permutations that can be generated by the number of different groups listed in the grouping list.

The number of rows that super-group operations generate depends on the number of groups generated and the number of distinct values in each group.

The SQL statement shown in Fig. 7–35 can be written using the following GROUPING SETS:

```
GROUPING SETS ((COUNTRY,TCID,NAME),
               (COUNTRY,TCID),
               (COUNTRY,NAME),
               (TCID,NAME),
               (COUNTRY),
               (TCID),
               (NAME),
               ()
)
```

Fig. 7–37 *Grouping Sets generated by CUBE (COUNTRY, TCID, NAME)*

Moving Functions

DB2 contains a number of built-in functions that can help in the analysis of data. One type of calculation that is difficult to do in the relational model is one that is based on a "window" of data. For instance, you may want to know what the average of three sales is over a point in time. Column functions within DB2 (along with CUBE and ROLLUP) deal only with complete sets, not partial values.

Moving functions help to overcome this limitation with column functions. Along with the definition of a column function, a user can now supply a "window" specification to DB2 that defines how much data should be included as part of the calculation. For instance, Figure 7–38 shows a table with 10 values in it. These values could represent the sales of a store over 10 days. An AVG function applied to this data would give the average sales across all 10 days.

```
CREATE TABLE SALES (DAY INT, SALES INT);
INSERT INTO SALES VALUES (1,10),(2,14),(3,13),(4,15),
  (5,20),(6,14),(7,16),(8,17),(9,18),(10,9);

SELECT AVG(SALES) FROM SALES;

1
-----------
         14
```

Fig. 7–38 *Simple average calculation*

This AVG function could be modified to use a moving window. This is accomplished through the use of the OVER specification. Figure 7–39 shows the use of this function to calculate the moving 3-day average sales (1 day before and 1 day after).

```
SELECT DAY, AVG(SALES) OVER
  (ORDER BY DAY ROWS BETWEEN 1 PRECEDING AND 1 FOLLOWING)
  AS SMOOTH_VALUE FROM SALES;

DAY             SMOOTH_VALUE
-----------     ------------
          1          12
          2          12
          3          14
          4          16
          5          16
          6          16
          7          15
          8          17
          9          14
         10          13
```

Fig. 7–39 *Moving average calculation*

The moving average function gives a completely different picture from just doing an average against the column!

Advanced CASE Expressions

Up to now, we have been using the CASE expression in the select list of select statements. CASE expressions can also be used in other SQL statements, such as grouping lists, WHERE predicates, functions, and so on. We will review some of these uses in this section.

Using CASE Expressions to Group Values

As stated earlier, CASE expressions may be part of a grouping list. Being part of the grouping list can be used to rank data.

Suppose we want to know how many candidates have not passed the exams, how many have passed, and how many of them have an excellent score along with an average score for each classification. To solve this request, we will use a case expression in the select list and another one in the grouping list. The CASE expression used in the select list is used to rank the candidates. The CASE expression in the grouping list is used to create the groups based on the ranking defined in it.

```
SELECT number,
       CASE
          WHEN integer(SCORE) < 65 THEN 'Not Passed'
          WHEN integer(SCORE) < 90   THEN 'Passed'
          ELSE
            'Excellent'
       END as GROUPBY_CASE,
       COUNT(*) AS COUNT,
       AVG(integer(SCORE)) AS AVERAGE
       FROM candidate c, test_taken tt
       WHERE c.cid=tt.cid
       GROUP BY
         number,
         CASE
          WHEN integer(SCORE) < 65 THEN 'Not Passed'
          WHEN integer(SCORE) < 90 THEN 'Passed'
          ELSE
             'Excellent'
         END;
```

Fig. 7–40 *Grouping with CASE expressions*

Whenever you group using a CASE expression, the CASE expression in the grouping list must be exactly the same as the one used in the select list. What can be different is the use of the AS clause, because it is not permitted in the grouping list.

Using CASE Expressions in Functions

CASE expressions can be embedded as functions parameters. This allows you to pass different parameters to the function in a single pass of the data. Suppose that the TEST_TAKEN table is very large and we have the following requirements:

- The number of tests taken with a score higher than 90
- The number of tests taken with a score of 90
- The number of tests taken with a score lower than 70
- The number of DB2 Fundamentals exams taken

Without the use of case expressions, this will require four different queries that will read the entire table. We want to do this in one single pass of the data, because the table is very large.

The query will use four count functions, each one evaluating different criteria using a CASE expression.

```
SELECT COUNT (CASE WHEN integer (score) > 90 then 1
                   ELSE null
             END) AS moregb90,
       COUNT (CASE WHEN integer (score) = 90 then 1
                   ELSE null
             END) AS equalgb90,
       COUNT (CASE WHEN integer (score) < 70 then 1
                   ELSE null
             END) AS minorgb70,
       COUNT (CASE WHEN number=test_id('500') then 1
                   ELSE null
             END) AS equalgb500
FROM db2cert.test_taken;
```

Fig. 7–41 *Using CASE expressions in functions*

This type of query may be useful when performing data inspection analysis. Notice that the four different requirements are solved in a single pass of the data.

The query was created using a different column function for each one of the conditions presented as a requirement. The conditions are evaluated in the case expression inside each function. When the condition evaluates true, it will return a value of 1 and the row will be counted. When the condition evaluates false, the case expression will return a null value and the row will not be counted.

Structured Types and Typed Tables

As mentioned in "Database Objects" on page 189, *user-defined structured types* are one of the data types in DB2 that allow you to create a structure that contains a sequence of named attributes, each of which has a data type. This structured type can be used as the type of a table or a view.

A table defined using a structured type is called a *typed table*, whereas a view defined using a structured type is called a *typed view*. A structured type can be a *sub-type* of another structured type, called a *super-type*. A sub-type inherits all attributes from its super-type and can be added to other attributes. A sub-type can be a super-type for other structured types. Therefore, you can create a hierarchy of structured types using this relationship between sub-type and super-type. Also, a hierarchy of typed tables can be created based on the structured type hierarchy. Structured types and typed tables enable you to configure a better model of business entities and relationships in the real world.

A structured type can be created by using the CREATE TYPE SQL statement. As discussed in "Database Objects" on page 189, a user-defined distinct type can also be created by a CREATE TYPE statement, and it represents a column type of a table. For a user-defined structured type, you can call it a row type of a table. See Fig. 7–42 for an example.

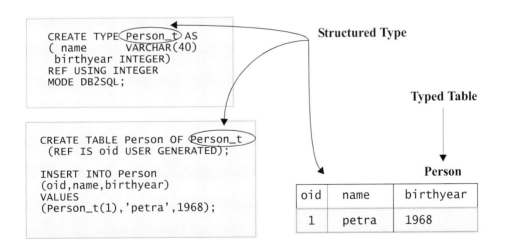

Fig. 7–42 *User-defined structured type*

In this example, a structured type PERSON_T is defined with two attributes, NAME and BIRTHYEAR, and then a table PERSON is defined using the structured type.

Notice the table PERSON has NAME and BIRTHYEAR columns that are defined by the PERSON_T type. The other column is called the *object identifier* (OID). Every typed table must have the OID column as its first column and the value of the OID column must be unique in the whole table hierarchy. The data type of the OID column is REFERENCE. Notice that the casting function PERSON_T is used to provide a value for the OID column in our example. The OID column will be talked about in greater detail later.

Creating Structured Types

A structured type supports a hierarchical structure. Therefore, a structured type can be created as a sub-type of another structured type (thereby inheriting the attributes of that type). Fig. 7–43 shows a simple structured type hierarchy. PERSON_T is defined as a Root type (not depending on other types) with two attributes, NAME and BIRTHYEAR. EMP_T and STUDENT_T are defined as sub-types of PERSON_T. Thus, EMP_T and STUDENT_T inherit all attributes of PERSON_T. In addition, the structured type EMP_T and STUDENT_T have several additional attributes that are specific to their particular types.

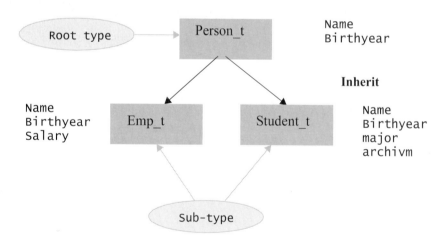

Fig. 7–43 *Hierarchy of structured types*

Let's see how we can define this structured type hierarchy. Look at the example shown in Fig. 7–44.

```
CREATE TYPE Person_t AS
  (Name VARCHAR(20),Birthyear SMALLINT)
    REF USING INTEGER
    MODE DB2SQL;

CREATE TYPE Emp_t UNDER Person_t
  AS (Salary INT)
  MODE DB2SQL;

CREATE TYPE Student_t UNDER Person_t
  AS (Major VARCHAR(10),
      Archivm DECIMAL(5,2))
  MODE DB2SQL;
```

Fig. 7–44 *Creating structured types and structured type hierarchies*

The AS clause provides the attribute definitions associated with the type. The UNDER clause specifies that the structured type is being defined as a sub-type of the specified super-type. In our example, the EMP_T type has SALARY as its attribute. The STUDENT_T type has Major and Archivm as its attributes. In addition, both have attributes NAME and BIRTHYEAR, which are inherited from the PERSON_T type.

The REF USING clause is used when defining a root-type and specifies the built in data type used as the representation for the REFERENCE type of this structured type and all its sub-types. As seen in Fig. 7–42, a typed table must have the OID column, and a casting function is used when supplying a value for the OID column. This casting function casts the data type specified by the REF USING clause of the root type definition into the REFERENCE type. You can specify the following for the REFERENCE type: INTEGER, SMALLINT, BIGINT, DECIMAL, CHAR, VARCHAR, GRAPHIC, or VARGRAPHIC. The default type is VARCHAR(16) FOR BIT DATA.

Note: Successful execution of the CREATE TYPE statement also generates functions to cast between the REFERENCE type and its representation type (the built-in type specified by REF USING clause) and generates support for the comparison operators (=, <>, <, <=, >, and >=) for users with the REFERENCE type.

The MODE clause is used to specify the mode of the type. DB2SQL is the only value for MODE currently supported.

Altering Structured Types

The ALTER TYPE statement enables you to add or drop an attribute of an existing structured type. The following example shows the ALTER TYPE statements adding an attribute TEL to the PERSON_T type and dropping the attribute.

```
ALTER TYPE Person_t ADD ATTRIBUTE Tel CHAR(12);
ALTER TYPE Person_t DROP ATTRIBUTE Tel;
```

 Note: The ALTER TYPE statement cannot be executed against a type if it, or one of its sub-types, is the type of an existing table.

Creating Typed Tables

A typed table is a table defined with a structured data type (refer to Fig. 7–42). Typed tables can have a hierarchy of structured types. A sub-table inherits all attributes of its super-table. All tables in an inherit relationship form a table hierarchy. A table that does not have a super-table in a hierarchy is called a *root-table*. In other words, a root-table is a table defined with the root-type of a type hierarchy.

A simple hierarchy of a typed table is shown in Fig. 7–45. You can see the two columns of the PERSON table are inherited by the STUDENT table and the EMP table.

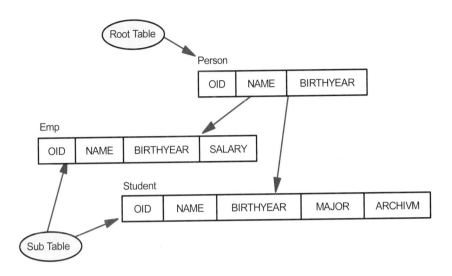

Fig. 7–45 *Hierarchy of typed tables*

Fig. 7–46 shows sample statements to create these typed tables. Typed tables are created using the CREATE TABLE statement.

```
CREATE TABLE Person OF Person_t
   (REF IS OID USER GENERATED);

CREATE TABLE Emp OF Emp_t UNDER Person
   INHERIT SELECT PRIVILEGES;

CREATE TABLE Student OF Student_t UNDER Person
   INHERIT SELECT PRIVILEGES;
```

Fig. 7–46 *Create typed tables*

In our example, the PERSON table is the root-table, and the EMP table and the STUDENT table are sub-tables. The PERSON table is defined to be of the structured type PERSON_T. This means that it has a column corresponding to each attribute of the structured type PERSON_T. The EMP table and the STUDENT table inherit all attributes of the PERSON table.

As explained before, every typed table must have an OID column. The OID is defined at the root-table of a table hierarchy, and all sub-tables inherit the OID. The column name of the OID column is defined at the root-table of a table hierarchy using the REF IS clause. In our example, it is OID. Each row must have a unique

Advanced SQL

value of OID in the whole hierarchy. The data type of the OID column is a system type REFERENCE.

The USER GENERATED clause indicates that the initial value for the OID column of each newly inserted row will be provided by the user when inserting a row. Once a row is inserted, the OID column cannot be updated.

The INHERIT SELECT PRIVILEGES clause means that any user or group holding SELECT privilege on the super table will be granted an equivalent privilege on the newly created sub-table. The definer of a sub-table is considered to be the grantor of this privilege.

Note: Within a typed table hierarchy, only one sub-table may exist of a particular sub-type.

Dropping Typed Tables

You can use a DROP TABLE statement to drop a typed table as well as a regular table. When you drop a typed table, you must make sure it does not have any sub-tables. If the typed table being dropped has sub-tables, the DROP TABLE statement will return an error.

Dropping a sub-table has the effect of deleting all the rows of the sub-table from the super-tables. Therefore, this may result in the activation of triggers or referential integrity constraints defined on the super-tables.

If you want to drop a whole table hierarchy, you can use the DROP TABLE HIERARCHY statement. Unlike dropping a single sub-table, dropping the table hierarchy does not result in the activation of triggers nor in referential integrity constraints of any tables in the hierarchy. The following example shows dropping the whole table hierarchy. You should specify the root table name of the table hierarchy.

```
DROP TABLE HIERARCHY Person
```

Note: You can use the DROP VIEW HIERARCHY statement to drop a total view hierarchy. The view hierarchy is explained later.

Inserting Rows into a Typed Table

Rows can be inserted into a typed table using an INSERT SQL statement. Examples of this are shown in Fig. 7–47.

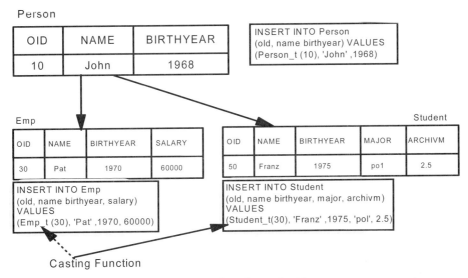

Fig. 7–47 *Inserting into a hierarchy of typed tables*

Notice that each INSERT statement uses a casting function for the value of the OID column. All OID values (of type REFERENCE) must be cast into the REFERENCE type of the table to which the value is being inserted. When you create a structured type, the casting function is created implicitly. The argument of the casing function should be of the built-in data type specified with the REF USING clause of the root type definition. The name of the casting function is the same as the underlying structured type, but optionally, you can specify another casting function name in the CREATE TYPE statement. See the *DB2 UDB V8.1 SQL Reference* manual for further details.

Selecting a Row from a Typed Table

When you issue a select statement for a typed table, the rows are returned from the target table and all of its sub-tables in the table hierarchy. Fig. 7–48 shows the SELECT statements against some typed tables. Each SELECT statement retrieves all columns and all rows from each table. Notice the select statement for the PERSON table returns not only the rows of the PERSON table but also the rows of the EMP table and STUDENT table.

```
SELECT * FROM Person;

OID  NAME    BIRTHYEAR
----  ------  -----------
  10 John          1968
  30 Pat           1970
  50 Franz         1975

SELECT * FROM Emp;

OID  NAME    BIRTHYEAR    SALARY
----  ------  -----------  ----------
  30 Pat           1970     60000

SELECT * FROM Student;

OID  NAME    BIRTHYEAR  MAJOR  ARCHIVM
----  ------  -----------  ------  -------
  50  Franz         1975 POL        2.5
```

Fig. 7–48 *Issuing a SELECT statement against typed tables*

If you want to retrieve only rows of the PERSON table, you can use the ONLY clause for a select statement as follows:

```
SELECT * FROM ONLY(Person)
```

If you want to retrieve columns from not only the specified table but also its subtables, you can use the OUTER clause for a select statement as follows.

```
SELECT * FROM OUTER(Person)
```

The result is shown in Fig. 7–49 on page 385.

```
OID  NAME  BIRTHYEAR   SALARY   MAJOR   ARCHIVM
----  -----  -----------  --------  ------  ---------
  10  John       1968       -  -                    -
  30  Pat        1970   60000  -                    -
  50  Franz      1975       -  Pol              2.5
```

Fig. 7–49 *Using the OUTER clause against a typed table*

Updating and Deleting Rows from Typed Tables

As in a regular table, you can use UPDATE and DELETE statements to update or delete rows of a typed table. Be aware that update and delete statements affect the target table and its sub-tables in a manner like a select statement. Let's take a look at some examples.

The first example changes the birthyear of a person whose OID is 10 to 1969. This statement will affect PERSON and its sub-tables (EMP and STUDENT). Notice that a casting function, EMP_T, is used to cast the type INTEGER into the REFERENCE type.

```
UPDATE Person SET birthyear=1969 WHERE oid=Emp_t(10)
```

The next example deletes all rows from the PERSON table and its sub-tables (EMP and STUDENT).

```
DELETE FROM Person
```

If you want to update or delete rows of a particular typed table only (and not its sub-tables), you can use the ONLY clause for an update or a delete statement, as the following example shows:

```
DELETE FROM ONLY(Person)
```

Physical Implementation of Typed Tables

The physical implementation of a typed table hierarchy is one table that holds all attributes of the tables in the table hierarchy. This table is called a *Hierarchy table* (H-Table). When a root-table is created, an H-Table is automatically created. Each time a sub-table having other columns different than its root table is created, the H-Table is altered and new columns are added. You can specify the name of the H-Table using the HIERARCHY option of the create table statement, but the default name is the root-table name followed by the suffix _HIERARCHY. This physical implementation has an advantage in performance and you can regard typed tables as if they are views defined for an H-Table. Fig. 7–50 shows a logical view of the typed table hierarchy and H-Table.

 Note: The H-Table cannot be manipulated with SQL statements.

Hierarchy Table

Person_Hierarchy

TYPE_ID	OID	NAME	BIRTHYEAR	SALARY	MAJOR	ARCHIVM
1035	10	John	1968	–	–	–
1037	30	Pat	1970	60000	–	–
1039	50	Franz	1975	–	pol	2.5

Fig. 7–50 *Logical view of a Hierarchy table (H-Table)*

The first column of an H-Table is the TYPE_ID column. Each value of this column specifies the structured type of the typed table to which this row was inserted.

Once a structured type and a typed table are defined, the DB2 system catalog tables hold their information. Let's peek into the system catalog tables through some system catalog views.

You can see the ROWTYPESCHEMA and the ROWTYPENAME column from the SYSCAT.TABLES view. These columns have the information to maintain typed tables. You can see each structured type through the SYSCAT.DATATYPES view as shown in Fig. 7–51. The values of the SOURCENAME column of the SYSCAT.DATATYPES catalog view is the name of the built-in type which was specified with the REF USING clause when creating the root type. You can see that EMP_T and STUDENT_T inherit the attributes from their root-type, PERSON_T.

```
SELECT TYPENAME,SOURCENAME,METATYPE FROM SYSCAT.DATATYPES
```

```
TYPENAME              SOURCENAME          METATYPE
------------------    ----------------    --------
PERSON_T              INTEGER             R
EMP_T                 INTEGER             R
STUDENT_T             INTEGER             R
```

Fig. 7–51 *System catalog view information for typed tables*

In this example, only rows for structured types are extracted. The SOURCENAME column would be NULL, and the METATYPE column would have an S for built in data types. For user-defined distinct types, the METATYPE column would be T.

The SYSCAT.HIERARCHIES system catalog view contains the relationship between a sub-table and its immediate super-table, and between a sub-type and its immediate super-type. Fig. 7–52 shows some information from SYSCAT.HIERARCHIES.

```
SELECT METATYPE,SUB_NAME,SUPER_NAME, ROOT_NAME FROM
SYSCAT.HIERARCHIES;
```

```
METATYPE SUB_NAME     SUPER_NAME    ROOT_NAME
-------- -----------  ------------  -----------
R        EMP_T        PERSON_T      PERSON_T
R        STUDENT_T    PERSON_T      PERSON_T
U        EMP          PERSON        PERSON
U        STUDENT      PERSON        PERSON
```

Fig. 7–52 *System catalog view information for hierarchy relationships*

The METATYPE column of the SYSCAT.HIERARCHIES catalog view encodes the relationship type of the object as follows:

R - Between structured types

U - Between typed tables

W- Between typed views

Typed views are described later in this chapter.

Advanced SQL

Reference Columns

In a typed table definition, you can define columns as *reference columns* to another typed table. This referenced typed table is called a *target table*. A reference column holds values that correspond to OID values of the target table and clearly identify rows in the target tables. The data type of a reference column is REFERENCE, the same type as OID in the target table. The reference column is similar to a foreign key; however, the evaluation, like a foreign key, is not performed for operations such as insert, update, or delete.

Look at Fig. 7–53. This shows you a typed table, EMP, which has a reference column referring another typed table DEPT. This relationship is defined when the CREATE TABLE statement is executed and is called a *scope*.

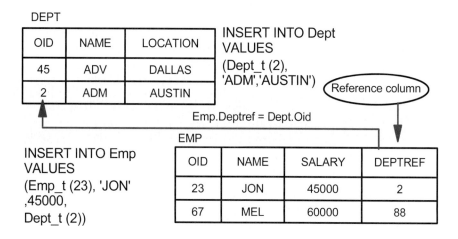

Fig. 7–53 *Reference column relationship*

As shown in Fig. 7–53, a reference column can have a value that the target table does not have. Notice the casting function DEPT_T is used to provide a value for the reference column.

The reference column is defined through the CREATE TYPE and CREATE TABLE statements. Fig. 7–54 shows CREATE TYPE statements to set up a reference column, assuming the root type PERSON_T is already defined, as shown in Fig. 7–44 on page 379.

```
CREATE TYPE Dept_t AS (name CHAR(40),location CHAR(20))
  REF USING INTEGER MODE DB2SQL;

CREATE TYPE Emp_t UNDER Person_t
  AS (Salary INTEGER, Deptref REF(Dept_t)) MODE DB2SQL;
```

Fig. 7–54 *Create Type statement to define a reference column*

In our example, DEPT_T is a root type of a different table hierarchy from the one to which EMP_T and PERSON_T belong. The definition of EMP_T supplies two attributes: one is SALARY, which is of the INTEGER type, and the other is DEPTREF, which is of the REFERENCE type. Deptref REF(Dept_t) means that this attribute DEPTREF of EMP_T type is the reference type and the target of the reference is a row of the table whose row type is DEPT_T or its sub-type.

You then need to create typed tables based on the structured types defined in Fig. 7–54. Fig. 7–55 shows the sample CREATE TABLE statements to define a reference column (define a scope). The second CREATE TABLE statement in this example creates a table with a reference column.

```
CREATE TABLE Dept OF Dept_t (REF IS Oid USER GENERATED);

CREATE TABLE Emp OF Emp_t UNDER Person
  INHERIT SELECT PRIVILEGES
  (Deptref WITH OPTIONS SCOPE Dept);
```

Fig. 7–55 *Create Table with a reference column*

In the CREATE TABLE statement, DEPTREF WITH OPTIONS SCOPE DEPT means that the values in the column DEPTREF are pointing to rows in the table DEPT or values in any sub-tables of the DEPT table.

Dereference Operator

The *dereference operator* (->) returns the named column value of the target table or its sub-table from the row with the matching OID column. The following example shows a SELECT statement using the dereference operator.

```
SELECT E.name from emp E
    WHERE E.Deptref->location ='AUSTIN';
```

In this example, each DEPTREF column value is interrogated and checked. We check to see if the target table (DEPT table) or its sub-table has a row whose OID value is the same. If such a row is found, the value of the LOCATION column is taken from that row and returned. That is how DEPTREF->LOCATION works. This predicate is true if the returned value is AUSTIN.

The SELECT statement above using the dereference operator (->) can be rewritten using a JOIN operation. The next example shows the equivalent SQL statement using a JOIN operation.

```
SELECT E.name from emp E, dept D
    WHERE E.deptref = D.oid
        AND D.location ='AUSTIN'
```

View Hierarchies

Typed views are views whose definition is based on structured types. You can create a view hierarchy with typed views as you would create a table hierarchy with typed tables. Fig. 7–56 shows the CREATE VIEW statements to define typed views. In our example, two typed views PERSON_V and EMP_V are created using the PERSON_T type and the EMP_T type. The PERSON_V view is defined as a root view of the view hierarchy and references all columns and rows of the PERSON table. The EMP_V view is defined as a sub-view of the PERSON_V view and references all columns and rows of the EMP table.

Notice that the PERSON_V definition uses the ONLY clause so that rows are selected from only the PERSON table. This is necessary because the PERSON_V view has a sub-view (EMP_V), and the PERSON_V view should not have rows that are assigned to the EMP_V view. Remember, it is not allowed to have duplicated OID values in the same view hierarchy.

The first CREATE VIEW statement will succeed even if FROM PERSON is used instead of FROM ONLY(PERSON); however, you will get an error when creating the EMP_V view since all rows that conform to the full select of the EMP_V definition are referred to by the PERSON_V view. You do not need to use the ONLY clause for the EMP_V view because the EMP_V view does not have any sub-views.

```
CREATE VIEW Person_v OF Person_t MODE DB2SQL
  (REF IS Void USER GENERATED)
  AS SELECT Person_t(INTEGER(Oid)),Name,Birthyear
      FROM ONLY(Person);

CREATE VIEW Emp_v OF Emp_t MODE DB2SQL UNDER Person_v
  INHERIT SELECT PRIVILEGES
  AS SELECT Emp_t(INTEGER(Oid)),Name,Birthyear,Salary
      FROM Emp;
```

Fig. 7–56 *Create typed views*

SQL Functions for Typed Tables and Typed Views

You can use the following SQL functions for typed tables or typed views:

- DEREF (function)
- TYPE_ID (expression)
- TYPE_NAME (expression)
- TYPE_SCHEMA (expression)

The DEREF function returns the structured type of the argument. The argument can be the OID column or a reference column. The value that the DEREF function returns is also called a *dynamic data type*. This function can only be used on the left side of the TYPE predicate (explained later) or in the argument of the TYPE_ID, TYPE_NAME, or TYPE_SCHEMA functions. Let's look at each of the functions.

The TYPE_ID function returns the internal type identifier of the dynamic data type. The argument must be a structured type. The data type of the result of this function is an INTEGER. The following example shows an SQL statement using the TYPE_ID function. It retrieves the type identifier of each row and the person's name from the PERSON table.

```
SELECT TYPE_ID(DEREF(Oid)),name FROM Person
```

Note: The values returned by the TYPE_ID function are not portable across databases. The type identifier may be different in each database even if the type schema and type name are the same.

The TYPE_NAME function returns the unqualified name of the dynamic data type. The argument must be a structured type. The data type of the result of the function is a VARCHAR(18). The next example shows an SQL statement using the TYPE_NAME function. It retrieves the type name of each row (represented by OID values), NAME, BIRTHYEAR, and the SALARY from the table EMP.

```
SELECT TYPE_NAME(DEREF(Oid)),Name,Birthyear,Salary
     FROM Emp
```

The TYPE_SCHEMA function returns the schema name of the dynamic data type. The argument must be a structured type. The data type of the result of the function is a VARCHAR(128). The next example shows an SQL statement using the TYPE_SCHEMA function. It retrieves the schema name of the dynamic type of each row (represented by OID values) and the NAME from the table PERSON.

```
SELECT TYPE_SCHEMA(DEREF(Oid)),name FROM Person
```

TYPE Predicate

The TYPE predicate compares the type of an expression with one or more user-defined structured types. The DEREF function should be used whenever a TYPE predicate has an expression involving a reference type value. It evaluates whether the value that the DEREF function returns matches one or more candidates in the list. If there is a match, the result of the predicate is true. The next example shows an SQL statement using the TYPE predicate. It returns all attributes and rows whose OID type is PERSON_T and not a sub-type of PERSON_T.

```
SELECT * FROM Person
     WHERE DEREF(Oid) IS OF DYNAMIC TYPE (only Person_t);
```

You can leave out the keywords DYNAMIC TYPE and rewrite this example as follows:

```
SELECT * FROM Person
     WHERE DEREF(Oid) IS OF (only Person_t);
```

Considerations When Using Typed Tables and Views

Some considerations when using typed tables and views are:

- A primary key cannot be created on a sub-table (the primary key (OID) is inherited from the super table).
- An unique index cannot be created on a sub-table.
- A check constraint defined on a table automatically applies to all sub-tables of that table.
- The LOAD command is not supported.
- Replication is not supported.
- RUNSTATS, REORG, and REORGCHK can only be executed on a root-table.

Examples of a Typed Table Hierarchy

Now let's look at more examples of the user-defined structured type and typed table.

Assume you are building a data model of the people in a university. Each person has two base attributes, name and birth year. A person who works for the university is an employee. An employee belongs to a department and gets a salary. Therefore, salary and department are the attributes for an employee. A person who studies at the university is a student. A student majors in a subject and has an achievement record. Major and achievement are particular attributes for a student. A professor is working for the university, so he or she is an employee, but has a speciality. On the other hand, there are a lot of departments in an university. Each department has a manager, and the manager is working for the university as an employee.

The model of this example represents these relationships. Fig. 7–57 shows these relationships using structured types and a typed table hierarchy. There is a hierarchy whose root-type is PERSON_T. EMP_T and STUDENT_T are the sub-types of PERSON_T, and PROF_T is a sub-type of EMP_T. There are two reference attributes, MGR in DEPT_T that points to EMP_T and DEPT in EMP_T that points to DEPT_T.

Advanced SQL

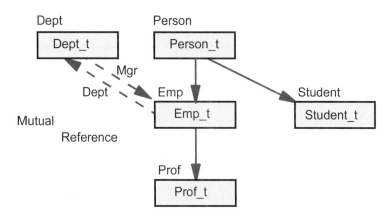

Fig. 7–57 *Example: Hierarchy of structured types and typed tables*

DEPT_T and EMP_T reference each other. When you define two structured types referencing each other (mutual definition), you must create one of them first without the reference definition, and then add a reference attribute with the ALTER TYPE statement after the other type is created. This is because the referenced type should be defined in advance when a structured type is created with a reference.

In our example, the EMP_T type is created without a reference attribute first, and then the DEPT_T type is created with the reference attribute MGR, which refers the EMP_T type. Finally, the reference attribute DEPT is added to the EMP_T type using an ALTER TYPE statement. See the SQL statements shown in Fig. 7–58.

```
CREATE TYPE Person_t AS
 (Name VARCHAR(20), Birthyear SMALLINT)
 REF USING INTEGER MODE DB2SQL;

CREATE TYPE Emp_t UNDER Person_t
 AS (Salary INT) MODE DB2SQL;

CREATE TYPE Student_t UNDER Person_t
 AS (Major CHAR(20), Archivm DECIMAL(5,2))
 MODE DB2SQL;

CREATE TYPE Dept_t AS
 (Name VARCHAR(20), Budget INT, Mgr REF(Emp_t))
 REF USING INTEGER MODE DB2SQL;

ALTER TYPE Emp_t ADD ATTRIBUTE Dept REF(Dept_t);

CREATE TYPE Prof_t UNDER Emp_t
 AS (Speciality VARCHAR(20)) MODE DB2SQL;
```

Fig. 7–58 *Example: Creating structured types*

Now let's create the table hierarchy. The table PERSON, which is created based on the PERSON_T type, is a root-table and has two sub-tables, EMP and STUDENT. PROF is a sub-table of EMP. The table DEPT has a scope of the reference column MGR, which points to rows in the table EMP. The table EMP has a scope of the reference column DEPT, which points to rows in the table DEPT. Therefore, you should create the EMP table without a reference column, and then add a reference column after the DEPT table is created. See the SQL statements shown Fig. 7–59.

Advanced SQL

```
CREATE TABLE Person OF Person_t
  (REF IS Oid USER GENERATED);

CREATE TABLE Emp OF Emp_t UNDER Person
  INHERIT SELECT PRIVILEGES;

CREATE TABLE Student OF Student_t UNDER Person
  INHERIT SELECT PRIVILEGES;

CREATE TABLE Dept OF Dept_t
  (REF IS Oid USER GENERATED, Mgr with options scope Emp);

ALTER TABLE Emp ALTER COLUMN Dept ADD SCOPE Dept;

CREATE TABLE Prof OF Prof_t UNDER Emp
        INHERIT SELECT PRIVILEGES;
```

Fig. 7–59 *Example: Creating typed tables*

The content of all the tables are shown in Fig. 7–60 (assuming these rows are previously inserted).

```
   Person                                    Dept

 OID     NAME    BIRTHYEAR              OID     NAME    BUDGET        MGR
------  -------  ----------            ------  --------  -----------  ----
    10  John         1968                  10  math         300000    80
    20  Paul         1961                  20  oec          500000    70
                                           30  headq       5000000    90
                                           40  itso        1000000    60

   Emp

 OID     NAME    BIRTHYEAR   SALARY   DEPT
------  -------  ----------  -------- ------
    30  Pat          1970      60000     10
    40  Hitomi       1977      65000     20
    90  Lou            -          -       -
    50  Sam          1968      60000     40
    60  Uta          1961      95000     30

   Student

 OID     NAME    BIRTHYEAR   MAJOR   ARCHIVM
------  -------  ----------  ------- -------
   100  Franzis      1975 pol         2.50
   110  Herb         1980 math        1.70

   Prof

 OID     NAME    BIRTHYEAR   SALARY   DEPT   SPECIALITY
------  -------  ----------  -------- ------ ----------
    70  Rich         1941      90000     30 oec
    80  Herb         1962     120000     30 math
```

Fig. 7–60 *Example: Records that each typed table contains*

As already described, one hierarchy table (H-Table) is created for a table hierarchy. All columns and all rows of typed tables in a table hierarchy are stored in one hierarchy table. Let's look at the PERSON_HIERARCHY table, which is the hierarchy table of our example, and see how a SELECT statement against typed tables is processed. Note that a hierarchy table cannot be directly manipulated by an SQL statement. See the following three examples. Each of them is a simple query from a typed table.

```
SELECT * FROM Person;

SELECT * FROM Emp;

SELECT * FROM OUTER(Emp);
```

The answer set is shown in Fig. 7–61. This figure shows the hierarchy table of our example and the answer set of the previous queries.

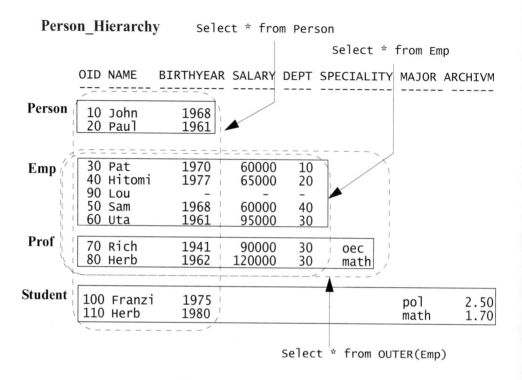

Fig. 7–61 *Example: Logical view of hierarchy tables (H-table)*

Note: Remember you cannot select rows directly from the hierarchy table.

Now let's look at other examples.

This example inserts an employee TETSU with the OID 200, born in 1968, earning a $65,000 salary, and working in the ITSO department.

```
INSERT INTO Emp (Oid, Name, Birthyear, Salary, Dept)
 VALUES(Emp_t(200),'Tetsu',1968,65000,
        (SELECT Oid FROM Dept WHERE Name='itso'));
```

The next example selects all attributes of all employees born after 1970 who earn more than $50,000 a year.

```
SELECT * FROM emp WHERE birthyear > 1970 AND
   salary > 50000
```

The rows are retrieved from the EMP and PROF tables. The result is:

```
OID     NAME        BIRTHYEAR    SALARY    DEPT
------  ----------  -----------  --------  ------
    40  Hitomi            1977     65000      20
```

The next example selects all persons who were born before 1965 who are either students or persons (excluding employees and professors).

```
SELECT * FROM Person WHERE Birthyear < 1965 AND
   DEREF(Oid) IS OF DYNAMIC TYPE (Student_t,ONLY Person_t)
```

This example uses the TYPE predicate, which compares a dynamic data type with a list of types. As already explained, the predicate is true if the dynamic type is specified in the list. In our example, STUDENT_T and PERSON_T (with the keyword ONLY) are specified. Therefore, only rows whose data type is STUDENT_T, its sub-types (although STUDENT_T does not have any sub-types), or PERSON_T type are returned. The result is:

```
OID          NAME                   BIRTHYEAR
-----------  ---------------------  -----------
    20  Paul                          1961
```

Let's look at some reference column examples. Remember the DEPT table and EMP table have a mutual reference relationship as shown in Fig. 7–62.

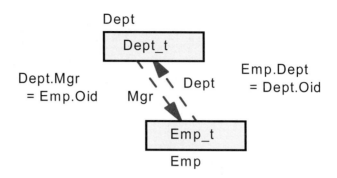

Fig. 7–62 *Reference column*

The next example finds the employee's name, salary, department name, and budget. It selects only the employees whose department's budget is greater than $500,000.

```
SELECT Name, Salary, Dept->Name, Dept->Budget FROM Emp
                WHERE Dept->Budget > 500000;
```

Notice the department's name and the department's budget are retrieved from the DEPT table, which is referenced by the reference column DEPT of the EMP table and its sub-table, the PROF table. The result is as follows:

```
NAME       SALARY      NAME        BUDGET
-------    ---------   ---------   ----------
Sam         60000 itso             1000000
Uta         95000 headq            5000000
Rich        90000 headq            5000000
Herb       120000 headq            5000000
Tetsu       65000 itso             5000000
```

Summary Tables

A *summary table* is a table whose definition is based on the result of a query. As such, the summary table typically contains precomputed results based on the data existing in the table, or tables, on which its definition is based. If the DB2 optimizer determines that a dynamic query will run more efficiently against a summary table than the base table, the query executes against the summary table, and you obtain the result faster than you otherwise would.

 Note: DB2 Version 8 introduces the term materialized query table. A materialized query table is a table whose definition is based on the result of a query, and whose data is in the form of precomputed results that are taken from one or more tables on which the materialized query table definition is based. A materialized query table whose fullselect contains a GROUP BY clause is summarizing data from the tables that are referenced in the fullselect. Such a materialized query table is also known as a summary table. A summary table is a specialized type of materialized query table.

The query rewrite function of the optimizer will access a summary table if it determines that the query can be answered by using the data in the summary table instead of accessing the base tables.

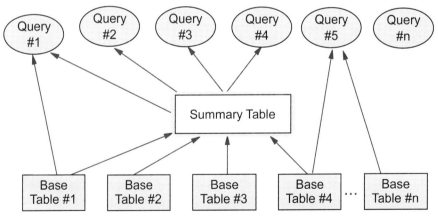

Fig. 7–63 *Summary table concept*

 Note: Summary tables are only accessed for dynamic SQL.

Creating a Summary Table

A summary table can be created by a CREATE TABLE statement. Fig. 7–64 shows the CREATE TABLE statement to create a summary table.

```
CREATE SUMMARY TABLE Dept_group
  AS (SELECT Workdept,
             SUM(Salary) AS Salary,
             SUM(Bonus) AS Bonus
      FROM Employee GROUP BY Workdept)
   DATA INITIALLY DEFERRED
   REFRESH DEFERRED;
```

Fig. 7–64 *Create a summary table*

In this example, the keyword SUMMARY is used to indicate that this is a summary table; however, you can omit this keyword if you so choose. The keyword AS followed by a fullselect means that this is a summary table. The column attributes of the summary table are defined by this fullselect.

There are two options to update the data in the summary table, deferred refresh and immediate refresh. This is specified in the CREATE TABLE statement using REFRESH DEFERRED or REFRESH IMMEDIATE. The last example uses REFRESH DEFERRED, which means that the data in the table is refreshed when a REFRESH TABLE statement is executed. The data in the summary table reflects the result of the query at the time the REFRESH TABLE statement is executed. REFRESH IMMEDIATE means that the changes made to the underlying tables as part of a DELETE, INSERT, or UPDATE statement are cascaded to the summary table immediately.

The DATA INITIALLY DEFERRED clause indicates that data is not inserted into the table as part of the CREATE TABLE statement, and the REFRESH TABLE statement is the only way to populate the table.

 Note: After creating a summary table, the table is in check-pending state. The REFRESH TABLE statement or SET INTEGRITY statement with the IMMEDIATE CHECKED option enables you to get out of this check-pending state.

Fig. 7–65 shows a CREATE TABLE statement to create a summary table with the REFRESH IMMEDIATE option.

```
CREATE SUMMARY TABLE dept_group2
  AS (SELECT workdept,
             count(*) as reccount,
             SUM(salary) AS salary,
             SUM(bonus) AS bonus
      FROM employee GROUP BY workdept)
    DATA INITIALLY DEFERRED
    REFRESH IMMEDIATE;
```

Fig. 7–65 *Create a Summary table with the REFRESH IMMEDIATE option*

Note: The summary table cannot be directly modified by the INSERT, UPDATE, or DELETE statements.

CURRENT REFRESH AGE Special Register

The CURRENT REFRESH AGE special register specifies a timestamp duration value with a data type of DECIMAL(20,6). This duration is the maximum duration, since a REFRESH TABLE statement has been processed on a deferred refresh summary table. It determines if a summary table can be used to optimize the processing of a query. The SET CURRENT REFRESH AGE statement enables you to change the value of the CURRENT REFRESH AGE special register. The value must be 0 or 99999999999999 (9999 years, 99 months, 99 days, 99 hours, 99 minutes, and 99 seconds).

- Zero (0) means that only summary tables defined with REFRESH IMMEDIATE may be used to optimize the processing of a query.
- 99999999999999 means that any summary tables defined with REFRESH DEFERRED or REFRESH IMMEDIATE may be used to optimize the processing of a query.

Note: The keyword ANY is shorthand for 99999999999999.

The initial value of CURRENT REFRESH AGE is 0. If you want the DB2 optimizer to consider using the deferred refresh summary tables, you must set the CURRENT REFRESH AGE special register to ANY or 99999999999999 as follows:

```
SET CURRENT REFRESH AGE ANY
```

Considerations of Using Summary Tables

There are some considerations when you create a summary table. The fullselect of the summary table definition must not have following:

- References to a view (see *DB2 UDB V8.1 SQL Reference SQL Reference* for details), summary table, or typed table in any FROM clause
- Expressions that are a reference type or DATALINK type (or a distinct type based on these types)
- Functions that have an external action
- Functions that depend on physical characteristics (e.g., NODENUMBER, PARTITION)
- Table or view references to system objects (explain tables also should not be specified)

Other considerations you should be aware of include:

- The summary table does not support IMPORT or LOAD.
- A unique index cannot be created on a summary table.
- If the summary table is specified in the ALTER TABLE statement, the ALTER is limited to activating not logged initially, changing pctfree, locksize, append, or volatile.

Additionally, if you create a summary table with the REFRESH IMMEDIATE option, the following considerations exist:

- The fullselect in the summary table definition must be a sub-select and cannot include:
    - Functions that are not deterministic
    - Scalar full selects
    - Predicates with full selects
    - Special registers
- A GROUP BY clause must be included in the sub-select.
- The select list must have a COUNT(*) function (or COUNT_BIG(*)) and no DISTINCT.
- Only SUM (of not nullable columns), COUNT, or COUNT_BIG column functions are allowed in the select list (without DISTINCT) and other select list items must be included in the GROUP BY clause.
- All GROUP BY items must be included in the select list.
- No grouping sets are allowed (including CUBE and ROLLUP) or grouping on constants.
- A HAVING clause is not allowed.

System Catalog Information for Summary Tables

The system catalog tables maintain the information about summary tables as well as the usual tables. Here is the output of the LIST TABLES command. The value s in the type column indicates that this table is a summary table.

Table/View	Schema	Type	Creation time
DEPT_GROUP	AUSRES33	S	1999-04-19-16.21.48.826001
DEPT_GROUP2	AUSRES33	S	1999-04-19-16.21.48.756001

Fig. 7–66 *Output of LIST TABLES command showing summary tables*

User-maintained Summary Tables

There may be circumstances where a user is already generating summarization data. For example, a nightly batch job may be run that calculates sales by store, region, and country before loading the raw data into the database tables. In this case, it might be to their advantage to take this summarization data and place it into a user-defined summary table.

A user-maintained summary table is no different than a system summary table other than the creation and loading of the summary table is under user control. Since the data is generated by the user, DB2 does not refresh this information, so the user must update the table on a periodic basis. In addition, DB2 will assume that information within the summary table is correct and may produce incorrect results if the user has not loaded valid information into the table.

To create a user-maintained summary table, the CREATE SUMMARY TABLE command must have the MAINTAINED BY USER option added to the end. The example found in figure 7–64 is changed to a user-maintained summary table in the following example (Figure 7–67):

Advanced SQL

```
CREATE SUMMARY TABLE UMST_EMPLOYEE AS
  (
  SELECT
    WORKDEPT,
    COUNT(*) AS EMPCOUNT,
    SUM(SALARY) AS TOTSALARY,
    SUM(BONUS) AS TOTBONUS
  FROM EMPLOYEE GROUP BY WORKDEPT
  )
  DATA INITIALLY DEFERRED REFRESH DEFERRED
  MAINTAINED BY USER;
```

Fig. 7–67 *Create a Summary table that is user-defined*

Once the table is created, the user can load data into this table from their application and then have DB2 optimize queries based on this information. Before loading the data, the summary table must be taken out of the check pending state (Figure 7–68):

```
SET INTEGRITY FOR UMST_EMPLOYEE ALL IMMEDIATE UNCHECKED;
```

Fig. 7–68 *Reset of check pending condition*

After the CHECK INTEGRITY command has been issued, the user can use insert statements to load this table. For instance, the following SQL can be used to load this summary table with current information from the EMPLOYEE table ():

```
INSERT INTO UMST_EMPLOYEE
  SELECT * FROM
    (
    SELECT WORKDEPT, COUNT(*), SUM(SALARY), SUM(BONUS)
      FROM EMPLOYEE
    GROUP BY WORKDEPT
    ) AS T;
```

Fig. 7–69 *Loading the summary table*

The user may also have to set the special optimization register to prevent other summary tables to be used when loading this table. Prior to running this insert statement, the user should issue the following command (Figure 7–70):

```
SET CURRENT MAINTAINED TABLE TYPES FOR OPTIMIZATION = NONE;
```

Fig. 7–70 *Optimization setting*

Setting the register to NONE will prevent any summary tables from being used during SQL processing. However, this value should be set back on if you want ot take advantage of the summary tables that have been created. Note that this special register can contain one of four values:

- ALL

  Specifies that all possible types of maintained tables controlled by this special register, now and in the future, are to be considered when optimizing the processing of dynamic SQL queries.

- NONE

  Specifies that none of the object types that are controlled by this special register are to be considered when optimizing the processing of dynamic SQL queries.

- SYSTEM

  Specifies that system-maintained refresh-deferred materialized query tables can be considered to optimize the processing of dynamic SQL queries. (Immediate materialized query tables are always available.)

- USER

  Specifies that user-maintained refresh-deferred materialized query tables can be considered to optimize the processing of dynamic SQL queries.

In addition to this optimization register, the user will also have to set the CURRENT REFERESH AGE register to ensure DB2 will use these user-maintained summary tables (Figure 7–71). If this value is set to zero, DB2 will only consider summary tables that are automatically maintain by the system.

```
SET CURRENT REFRESH AGE ANY
```

Fig. 7–71 *Current refresh age*

Materialized Query Table

A materialized query table is a table whose definition is based on the result of a query, and whose data is in the form of precomputed results that are taken from one or more tables on which the materialized query table definition is based. The definition of a materialized query table contains joins, functions, and other SQL elements that are not allowed in automatic summary tables.

The following two SQL statements highlight the difference between an automatic summary table and a material query table. The first example (Figure 7–72) is a typical summary table that contains summarization using a GROUP BY clause. The second example (Figure 7–73) contains a join between two tables and does not have any summarization or grouping associated with it. Both tables need to be refreshed before they can be used in queries.

```
CREATE SUMMARY TABLE Dept_group
  AS (SELECT Workdept,
             SUM(Salary) AS Salary,
             SUM(Bonus) AS Bonus
       FROM Employee GROUP BY Workdept)
   DATA INITIALLY DEFERRED
   REFRESH DEFERRED;
```

Fig. 7–72 *Automatic summary table*

```
CREATE SUMMARY TABLE EPLUSD
  AS (SELECT EMPNO, LASTNAME, DEPT, DEPTNAME
       FROM EMPLOYEE E, DEPARTMENT D
       WHERE E.DEPT = D.DEPTNO)
   DATA INITIALLY DEFERRED
   REFRESH DEFERRED;
```

Fig. 7–73 *Materialized query table*

The materialized query table could be used to pre-join tables together. This allows the optimizer to bypass joining tables together if the materialized table contains the columns and rows that it needs.

Sequences

Many applications that are written require the use of sequence numbers to track invoice numbers, customer numbers, and other objects which get incremented by one whenever a new item is required. DB2 can autoincrement values in a table through the use of identity columns (See "Identity Column" on page 220.) Although this technique works well for individual tables, it may not be the most convenient way of generating unique values that need to be used across multiple tables.

The SEQUENCE object in DB2 lets the DBA or developer create a value that gets incremented under programmer control and can be used across many different tables. Figure 7–74 shows a sample sequence number being created for customer numbers using a datatype of integer:

```
CREATE SEQUENCE CUSTOMER_NO AS INTEGER
```

Fig. 7–74 *Customer_no sequence*

By default this sequence number starts at one and increments by one at a time and is of an INTEGER datatype. The application needs to get the next value in the sequence by using the NEXTVAL function. This function generates the next value for the sequence which can then be used for subsequent SQL statements (Figure 7–75):

```
VALUES NEXTVAL FOR CUSTOMER_NO
```

Fig. 7–75 *Customer_no sequence*

Instead of generating the next number with the VALUES function, the programmer could have used this function within an INSERT statement. For instance, if the first column of the customer table contained the customer number, an INSERT statement could be written as follows (Figure 7–76)

```
INSERT INTO CUSTOMERS VALUE
   (NEXTVAL FOR CUSTOMER_NO, 'Berts House of Moving', ...)
```

Fig. 7–76 *Insert with a sequence number*

If the sequence number needs to be used for inserts into other tables, the PREVVAL function can be used to retrieve the previously generated value. For instance, if the customer number we just created need to be used for a subsequent invoice record, the SQL would include the PREVVAL function (Figure 7–77):

```
INSERT INTO INVOICES
   (34,PREVVAL FOR CUSTOMER_NO, 234.44, ...)
```

Fig. 7–77 *Subsequent insert with PREVVAL*

The PREVVAL function can be used multiple times within the application and it will only return the last value generated by that application. It may be possible that subsequent transactions have already incremented the sequence to another value, but the user will always see the last number that they generated.

In addition to being simple to set up and create, the SEQUENCE object has a variety of additional options that allows the user more flexibility in generating the values:

- use a different datatype (SMALLINT, INTEGER, BIGINT, DECIMAL)
- change starting values (START WITH)
- change the sequence increment, including specifying increasing or decreasing values (INCREMENT BY)
- set minimum and maximum values where the sequence would stop (MAXVALUE/ MINVALUE)
- allow wrapping of values so that sequences can start over again (CYCLE/NO CYCLE)
- allow caching of sequences to minimize catalog contention (CACHE/NO CACHE)

Even after the sequence has been generated, many of these values can be ALTERED by the user. For instance, the DBA may want to set a different starting value depending on the day of the week.

The one option that a DBA should be aware of is the caching value. This value tells DB2 how many sequence values should be generated by the system before going back to the DB2 catalog to generate another set of sequences. The CACHE value is set to a value of 20 if the user does not specify it at creation time. DB2 will automatically generate 20 sequential values in memory (1, 2,..., 19) when it first starts up the database. Whenever a new sequence number is required, this memory cache of values is used to return the next value to the user. Once this cache of values is used up, DB2 will generate the next twenty values (20, 21,..., 39).

By implementing caching of sequence numbers in this manner, DB2 does not have to continually go to the catalog tables to get the next value. This will reduce the overhead associated with retrieving sequence numbers, but it also leads to possible gaps in the sequences if a system failure occurs, or if the system is shut down at the end of the day. For instance, if the DBA decided to set the sequence cache to 100, DB2 will cache 100 values of these numbers and also set the system catalog to show that the next sequence of values should begin at 200. In the event that the database is shut down, the next set of sequence numbers will begin at 200. The numbers that were generated from 100 to 199 will be lost from the set of sequences if they were not used. If gaps in generated values cannot be tolerated in the application, the DBA will need to set the caching value to NO CACHE at the expense of higher system overhead.

Advanced Functions

DB2 contains a large number of built-in column and scalar functions that can add flexibility to the type of calculations the user can perform against the data. These functions can be broken down into the following categories:

- Trigonometric Functions (COS, SIN, TAN, COT, TANH, COSH, SINH, ATAH, ATAN2.)
- Math Functions (INTEGER, FLOOR, CEILING, TRUNC, SQRT, LN, EXP)
- String Functions (RTRIM, LTRIM, INSTR, TRANSLATE, REPEAT, REPLACE, CONCAT, SUBSTR, LENGTH, LOWER, UPPER)
- Statistical Functions (CORRELATION, STDDEV, VARIANCE)
- Date Functions (DATE, TIME, TO_CHAR, TO_DATE, DAYNAME, DAYOFWEEK)
- Logic Functions (COALESCE, NULLIF)
- Speciality Functions (MQPUBLISH, MQREAD, ENCRYPT, REC2XML)

There are many more functions available within DB2 that a user can take advantage of. For a complete listing of available functions, refer to the *DB2 UDB V8.1 SQL Reference*. Some specific functions that have been introduced over the last few release of DB2 are described below.

MULTIPLY_ALT

The rules of decimal multiplication can cause problems when dealing with extremely large values. This is primarily due to the multiplication precision rules that have been developed over the years. The following SQL calculation highlights the problem with decimal math (Figure 7–78):

```
VALUES 1234567890.0000000 * 1234567890.0000000
SQL0802N  Arithmetic overflow or other arithmetic excep-
tion occurred. SQLSTATE=22003
```

Fig. 7–78 *Large number multiplication*

If the decimal values had not been included in the calculation, DB2 would have returned a valid result (Figure 7–79):

```
VALUES 1234567890.0 * 1234567890.0

1
-------------------------
  1524157875019052100.00
```

Fig. 7–79 *Successful multiplication*

This bizarre behavior is due to the rules of decimal math. A calculation using decimal math uses the following rule to determine the number of significant digits and decimal places, where p is the precision of the number and s is the scale:

- Precision = $\min(31, p^1+p^2)$
- Scale = $\min(31, s^1+s^2)$

In our first example, the precision of both numbers was 17.7 (seventeen digits of precision with 7 decimal places). The rule would tell us that the final result should contain the minimum of $(31, 17+17) = 31$ digits of precision and at least $(31, 7+7) = 14$ digits in the scale (numbers after the decimal place). If we set aside 14 digits for the scale, this will only leave 17 digits for the significant part. The answer (Figure 7–79) contains 19 significant digits, so the number could not be placed into a normal numeric field. The only way to get around this limitation was to cast the values into floating point numbers, but this could result in a loss of precision.

The alternative way of doing decimal multiplication was introduced in DB2 UDB Version 7.2. Instead of using the standard multiplication operator, the MULTIPLY_ALT function could be used instead to maintain the significant digit precision and limit the number of digits in the fractional portion. The original calculation in figure 7–78 can now be done using this new function (Figure 7–80):

```
VALUES MULTIPLY_ALT(1234567890.0000000,1234567890.0000000)

1
---------------------------------
  1524157875019052100.00000000000
```

Fig. 7–80 *Successful multiplication using Multiply_Alt*

The decimal portion of the number is truncated, with the scale being reduced to accommodate the more significant digits. This function should be considered for any decimal multiplication where the scale may force arithmetic overflow situations.

SNAPSHOT Table Functions

DB2 has a number of table functions that return data on internal objects that are normally only accessible via an API call. The advantage of using SQL to retrieve this information is that scripts can be written to extract this information rather than writing C++ programs to do the same thing. In addition, Java developers can also take advantage of these SQL calls rather than having to link C routines into their applications.

These snapshot functions return information on a variety of objects within DB2 (Table 7–1):

Table 7–1 *Snapshot Functions*

Function	Purpose
SNAPSHOT_AGENT	The SNAPSHOT_AGENT function returns information about agents from an application snapshot.
SNAPSHOT_APPL	The SNAPSHOT_APPL function returns general information from an application snapshot.
SNAPSHOT_APPL_INFO	The SNAPSHOT_APPL_INFO function returns general information from an application snapshot.
SNAPSHOT_BP	The SNAPSHOT_BP function returns information from a buffer pool snapshot.
SNAPSHOT_CONTAINER	The SNAPSHOT_CONTAINER function returns container configuration information from a tablespace snapshot.
SNAPSHOT_DATABASE	The SNAPSHOT_DATABASE function returns information from a database snapshot.

Table 7–1 *Snapshot Functions*

Function	Purpose
SNAPSHOT_DBM	The SNAPSHOT_DBM function returns information from a snapshot of the DB2 database manager.
SNAPSHOT_DYN_SQL	The SNAPSHOT_DYN_SQL function returns information from a dynamic SQL snapshot. It replaces the SQLCACHE_SNAPSHOT function, which is still available for compatibility reasons.
SNAPSHOT_FCM	The SNAPSHOT_FCM function returns database manager level information regarding the fast communication manager (FCM).
SNAPSHOT_FCMPARTITION	The SNAPSHOT_FCMPARTITION function returns information from a snapshot of the fast communication manager in the database manager.
SNAPSHOT_LOCK	The SNAPSHOT_LOCK function returns information from a lock snapshot.
SNAPSHOT_LOCKWAIT	The SNAPSHOT_LOCKWAIT function returns lock waits information from an application snapshot.
SNAPSHOT_QUIESCERS	The SNAPSHOT_QUIESCERS function returns information about agents that are trying to quiesce the database.
SNAPSHOT_RANGES	The SNAPSHOT_RANGES function returns information from a range snapshot.
SNAPSHOT_STATEMENT	The SNAPSHOT_STATEMENT function returns information about statements from an application snapshot.
SNAPSHOT_SUBSECT	The SNAPSHOT_SUBSECT function returns information about subsections of access plans from an application snapshot.
SNAPSHOT_SWITCHES	The SNAPSHOT_SWITCHES function returns information about the database snapshot switch state.
SNAPSHOT_TABLE	The SNAPSHOT_TABLE function returns activity information from a table snapshot.
SNAPSHOT_TBS	The SNAPSHOT_TBS function returns activity information from a table space snapshot.
SNAPSHOT_TBS_CFG	The SNAPSHOT_TBS_CFG function returns configuration information from a table space snapshot.
SQLCACHE_SNAPSHOT	The SQLCACHE_SNAPSHOT function returns the results of a snapshot of the DB2 dynamic SQL statement cache.

The general form of a snapshot function is:

```
SELECT *
  FROM TABLE(SNAPSHOT_FUNCTION(database, partition)) AS S;
```

Fig. 7–81 *General Snapshot function*

The SNAPSHOT_FUNCTION is replaced with the appropriate snapshot command, and the DATABASE field contains the name of the database you want the snapshot to be taken against. The partition should be set to -1 to return information for the current partition and -2 for all partitions. If this field is not included or set to null, the command will only work against the current partition.

A DBA may want to use these commands to monitor the status of various objects within DB2 from within a script. For instance, the following SQL will retrieve information on all tablespaces in the SAMPLE database (Figure 7–82).

```
SELECT TABLESPACE_ID, TABLESPACE_NAME, TOTAL_PAGES
  FROM TABLE(SNAPSHOT_CONTAINER('SAMPLE',-2)) AS S;

TABLESPACE_ID TABLESPACE_NAME                      TOTAL_PAGES
------------- ----------------------------------- -----------
            0 SYSCATSPACE                                 3644
            1 TEMPSPACE1                                     1
            2 USERSPACE1                                  4150
            3 DB2DEMO                                        1
            4 TEMPSESSION                                    1
            5 MDC                                          458
            6 ORVRTS                                       108
            8 Q2_2001                                       22
            9 Q3_2001                                       23
           10 Q1_2002                                        2
           11 Q4_2001                                       22

 11 record(s) selected.
```

Fig. 7–82 *Output from snapshot function*

Note: The SNAPSHOT functions were introduced in DB2 Version 8.1. The SQL reference manuals lists these functions, but more details on the use of snapshots and monitoring can be found in the *DB2 Universal Database System Monitor Guide and Reference.*

MQSeries Functions

DB2 provides a set of MQSeries functions and a MQ-Assist wizard. The MQ-Assist wizard helps you to create a table function that reads from an MQSeries queue using the MQSeries user-defined functions. The wizard treats each MQ message as a delimited string, parses the string according to user specifications, and returns the result as a row of the table function. It also allows you to create a view on top of the table function.

A set of MQSeries functions are provided with DB2 UDB to allow SQL statements to include messaging operations. This means that this support is available to applications written in any supported language, for example, C, Java, or SQL, using any of the database interfaces. This SQL may be used from other programming languages in all the standard ways.

The MQSeries Functions can be used in a wide variety of scenarios, including basic messaging, application connectivity, and data publication. These functions are described in the following table (Table 7–2).

Table 7–2 *MQSeries Functions*

Function	Purpose
MQPUBLISH	The MQPUBLISH function publishes data to MQSeries. This function requires the installation of either MQSeries Publish/Subscribe or MQSeries Integrator.
MQREAD	The MQREAD function returns a message from the MQSeries service. The message does not get removed from the queue using this function. The maximum length of the message is 4000 bytes.
MQREADCLOB	The MQREADCLOB function returns a message from the MQSeries service. The message does not get removed from the queue using this function. The maximum length of the message is 1M bytes.
MQREADALL MQREADALLCLOB	The MQREADALL function returns a table of all messages returned from the MQSeries service.
MQRECEIVE	The MQRECEIVE function returns a message from the MQSeries service. The receive function does remove the message from the queue. The maximum length of the message is 4000 bytes.
MQRECEIVECLOB	The MQRECEIVECLOB function returns a message from the MQSeries service. The receive function does remove the message from the queue. The maximum length of the message is 1M bytes.
MQRECEIVEALL MQRECEIVEALLCLOB	The MQRECEIVEALL function returns a table of all messages returned from the MQSeries service and removes all of the messages from the queue.
MQSEND	The MQSEND function sends the data to an MQSeries service.
MQSUBSCRIBE	The MQSUBSCRIBE function is used to register interest in MQSeries messages.
MQUNSUBSCRIBE	The MQUNSUBSCRIBE function is used to unregister an existing message subscription.

Advanced SQL

XML Functions

DB2 has had support for XML structures for a number of releases. These functions allow a developer to store and retrieve XML information from a DB2 database.

Within the SQL language, a number of XML functions are supported that allow for formatting of the data in an XML format. These functions are described in table (Table 7–3):

Table 7–3 *XML Functions*

Function	Purpose
XML2CLOB	The XML2CLOB function returns the argument as a CLOB value. The argument must be an expression of data type XML. The result has the CLOB data type.
XMLAGG	The XMLAGG function returns the concatenation of a set of XML data. If the XMLAGG function is applied to an empty set, the result is a null value. Otherwise, the result is the concatenation of the values in the set.
XMLELEMENT	Constructs an XML element from the arguments. This function takes an element name, an optional collection of attributes, and zero or more arguments that will make up the element's content. The result data type is XML.
XMLATTRIBUTES	XMLATTRIBUTES constructs an XML element from the arguments. This function takes an element name, an optional collection of attributes, and zero or more arguments that will make up the element's content. The result data type is XML.
REC2XML	The REC2XML function returns a string formatted with XML tags and containing column names and column data.
COLATTVAL COLATTVAL_XML	This is a format value for the REC2XML function which formats return a string with columns as attribute values.

Note: The REC2XML function was introduced in DB2 UDB V8.1. This simplifies the creation of XML strings within an SQL statement.

In addition to these built-in functions, there is an XML extender available that can extend DB2's ability to deal with XML objects. For more information on the XML extender, see the *DB2 Universal Database XML Extender Administration and Programming Reference*. These XML functions are also described in detail in the *DB2 UDB V8.1 SQL Reference*.

The following example shows how the REC2XML function can be used to return data in an XML format for either browsing on the web or for sending to another application that can interpret this information. The first figure (Figure 7–83) shows the standard output that would be retrieved by using a SELECT statement.

```
SELECT * FROM NAMES;

EMP_NO        NAME    LASTNAME  DEPT_NO
----------- ------- --------- -------
      10001 George  Baklarz   307
      10002 Bill    Wong      204
      10003 Beverly Crusher   305
```

Fig. 7–83 *Select of information from Name table*

To format this information in an XML format, the REC2XML (or XML2CLOB) functions could be used to extract information. The following SQL is used to generate an XML record for each row in the table (Figure 7–84):

```
SELECT REC2XML (1.0,'COLATTVAL','EMPLOYEE',
                    EMP_NO,NAME,LASTNAME,DEPT_NO)
FROM NAMES;

<EMPLOYEE>
  <column name="EMP_NO">10001</column>
  <column name="NAME">George </column>
  <column name="LASTNAME">Baklarz</column>
  <column name="DEPT_NO">307</column>
</EMPLOYEE>
<EMPLOYEE>
  <column name="EMP_NO">10002</column>
  <column name="NAME">Bill    </column>
  <column name="LASTNAME">Wong    </column>
  <column name="DEPT_NO">204</column></EMPLOYEE>
<EMPLOYEE>
  <column name="EMP_NO">10003</column>
  <column name="NAME">Beverly</column>
  <column name="LASTNAME">Crusher</column><column
name="DEPT_NO">305</column>
</EMPLOYEE>
```

Fig. 7–84 *Select of information in XML format*

This is an extremely simple example, but it shows some of the power of using XML functions within DB2. The other XML functions give the user more control over the formatting and output of the records. The REC2XML simplifies the creation of XML output, but doesn't have as much flexibility as the other XML commands. Note that the XML functions are considered part of the SELECT command and are not shown as scalar or column functions.

Summary

In this chapter we have talked about very powerful SQL features, such as triggers, recursive SQL, outer joins, the OLAP functions, case expressions, and a number of advanced external functions. These SQL features that DB2 provides can reduce the amount of application development time and maintenance.

We have also discussed user-defined structured types. This is one of the capabilities that DB2 provides to manage the Object Relational Model. As explained in "Database Objects" on page 189, DB2 has implemented some Object Relational functions, Large Object (LOB) support, user-defined distinct types, user-defined functions, and so on. The concept of structured types and tables is very similar to object-oriented programming.

We have also introduced the summary table. The summary table is a physical table that contains precomputed results based on the data existing in the table, or tables, on which its definition is based. Many customers execute complex SQL to summarize the operational data for reporting or analysis purposes. These types of SQL often take a long time to provide the result. The summary table can be helpful in improving query performance.

In addition to many of the advanced SQL features, DB2 also provides support for MQSERIES integration, XML documents manipulation, and table functions for querying the operational status of DB2.

Advanced SQL

CHAPTER **8**

Concurrency

- ◆ CONCURRENCY
- ◆ ISOLATION LEVELS
- ◆ LOCKS
- ◆ LOCK CONVERSION
- ◆ LOCK ESCALATION
- ◆ LOCK WAIT

A database server acts as a central source of data access for users. The number of users can vary from one to thousands. When more than one user accesses the same data source at the same time, some rules must be established for the reading, inserting, deleting, and updating of the data to guarantee data integrity.

The rules for data access are set by each application connected to a DB2 database and are established using two methods:

- Explicit control - Locking resources using an SQL statement or using a DB2 command
- Implicit control - Locking resources by specifying an *isolation level*

Some of the DB2 database resources, databases, table spaces, and tables can be explicitly controlled (for concurrency purposes). DB2 implicitly locks database resources at the row level. This can provide good concurrency and avoid resource conflicts. Record locking behavior is specified by isolation levels. We will examine the supported isolation levels and their locking semantics.

We will also examine the locks in DB2 and their behavior in an application environment. DB2 must also handle concurrency conflicts, including deadlocks, lock timeout, and resource contention. Some of the database configuration parameters affect the amount and type of locks acquired and the maximum length of time they are held by DB2 applications.

We will also examine concurrency problems that can occur in a multiuser environment. The concurrency examples are based on the DB2CERT certification testing application.

Concurrency

Data integrity is the primary concern in any database environment. The database server must guarantee the integrity of the data as it is modified. Every executable SQL statement that is issued is considered to be part of a *transaction*.

A transaction will contain at least one SQL statement. Multiple SQL statements can be grouped together and executed as a single transaction. Any data that has been accessed or modified by SQL statements will be tracked by DB2 and either permanently changed (committed), or returned to their original state (rolled back). This all-or-nothing behavior is known as *atomicity*. A transaction does not only guarantee atomicity, it also guarantees *persistency*. Persistency is provided through transactional logging. The log files are used to ensure that all committed transactions are physically applied to the database.

A transaction is started implicitly during the processing of the first SQL statement. The transaction is completed when a COMMIT or ROLLBACK statement has been issued, either explicitly or implicitly.

Note: The term *unit of work* is the same as *transaction*.

When the data has been permanently changed using the COMMIT or ROLLBACK statement, a point of consistency is established. A point of consistency is important because it is used during database crash recovery and roll forward recovery.

In a previous chapter, we discussed data access control. The GRANT and REVOKE statements can be used by users to provide and take away the ability to access tables, views, and packages. Once access control has been established, resource control must be considered. Concurrency problems can occur if resource control is not properly managed.

DB2 provides mechanisms to manage resource control. We discuss these mechanisms and strategies. The accuracy of the data is based on the correctness of the input and the extent to which data modification is controlled. The correctness of the input data needs to be monitored by the database administrator. DB2 provides some mechanisms to avoid incorrect data entry, including triggers, check constraints, and referential constraints.

We will discuss the control of data modification using transactions, examine some of the possible concurrency problems and the strategies that can be used to avoid them and examine some concurrency issues that need to be addressed by the DB2CERT application.

Concurrency Considerations

Database resource control requires the use of data modification rules. There are concurrency anomalies that we will consider when using the DB2CERT database application. They include:

- Lost update
- Uncommitted read
- Nonrepeatable read
- Phantom read

Lost Update Problem

A *lost update* problem occurs when the same data is retrieved by two test coordinators, both of whom change and save the data. The last successful change to the data will be kept, and the first change will be overwritten.

Here is an example. Suppose Shirley is a DB2 Universal Database Certification test candidate, and she wants to take the first DB2 exam. Shirley calls the testing center in Toronto. The test coordinator, Linda, gets the call. She looks at the availability of seats at the Toronto testing center for the date that Shirley wants. Linda's application screen is shown in Fig. 8–1. Linda notes that seat number 4 is available.

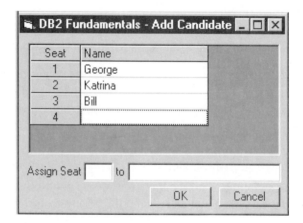

Fig. 8–1 *Available seats at Toronto testing center*

Shirley is not sure if she wants to take the test that day. Linda maintains her list of seats on the screen until Shirley decides if she will take the test on that day.

Meanwhile, Mike calls the testing center. Andrea, another test coordinator, takes Mike's call. Mike wants to take the same DB2 exam on the same day that Shirley has requested. Andrea checks the seat availability and obtains the same list as Linda. Andrea's screen is same as Linda's that is shown in Fig. 8–1.

The other test candidate, Shirley, decides to take the test and Linda assigns seat 4 to Shirley by clicking the OK button, as shown in Fig. 8–2.

Fig. 8–2 *Linda assigns a seat to Shirley*

Andrea does not see that Linda has assigned seat 4 to Shirley, so she assigns the same seat to Mike. Remember, Andrea sees seat 4 as unassigned. The commit operation was successful for Andrea because no resource conflict was encountered.

Fig. 8–3 *Andrea assigns a seat to Mike*

If the list of seats is refreshed (retrieved again), we see that seat 4 was assigned to Mike and the update made by Linda was overwritten. Fig. 8–4 shows the refreshed screen. On the day of the test, Shirley and Mike arrive at the testing center, and the database shows that Mike has a proper seat assignment. Shirley walks away unhappy and has to reschedule to take the exam another day.

Fig. 8–4 *A refresh of the seat assignments*

What was the problem? To maintain the accuracy of the data, control mechanisms needed to be enforced. The goal of the database manager (DB2) is to avoid lost updates and guarantee the integrity of the data.

If table-level locking was used, then Linda's application would have restricted any update to the table. However, if Linda's application had update control for the table, then other test centers would not be able to assign seats since all test centers access the same table. Should only one test center coordinator be allowed to update data records for a given day? For some applications, this can be appropriate, but this does not provide a sufficient degree of concurrency for others.

The integrity of the database is not guaranteed in this example. An application has to lock the updated data to make it impossible for another application to overwrite the data. Record-level locking usually involves cursor processing.

 Note: DB2 has built-in mechanisms to protect against lost updates.

Lost Update Solution

To avoid lost updates, control of each data record must be maintained by DB2. The control mechanism involves obtaining update control of all of the matching records or possible matching records for the query. This is known as *repeatable read*. See "Repeatable Read" on page 435 for more details on establishing a repeatable read concurrency strategy.

The only explicit SQL control mechanism provided by DB2 is the LOCK TABLE statement. According to the design of the DB2CERT database, there is a table that represents all of the tests taken at all of the tests centers, the DB2CERT.TEST_TAKEN table. If the application explicitly locked the table for update (known as EXCLUSIVE mode), other test centers would not be allowed to update or even read any of the committed data in the table. If the application explicitly locked the table not for update (SHARE mode) other test centers would be allowed to read but not update the data.

Linda's application could have obtained a share lock on the TEST_TAKEN table. The share lock would have prevented Andrea from successfully performing an UPDATE of the table (assignment of seat four to Mike). The table lock would remain in effect until Linda's application released the lock using the COMMIT or ROLLBACK statement.

An alternative method involves record or row-level locking. If Linda's application acquired record locks for seat 4, Andrea's update would have failed. You cannot explicitly acquire row-level locks using an SQL statement. See "Cursor Stability" on page 434 for more details on row-level locking.

Uncommitted Read

Linda's application locks the rows of unassigned seats and makes a temporary update to assign seat 4 to Shirley. Until Linda has committed or rolled back this update, no one else can update the record for seat 4. Fig. 8–5 shows the list retrieved by George. George has permission to read uncommitted changes, so he can see Shirley assigned to seat 4 instead of Mike.

Concurrency

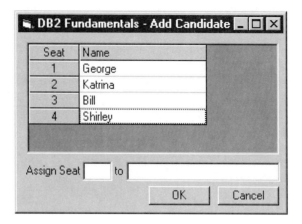

Fig. 8–5 *George retrieves uncommitted data*

If George were to reissue his query after Andrea assigned seat 4 to Mike, he would obtain a different result. This is known as an *uncommitted read* (dirty read).

Let's look at another example. The test center secretary runs a report to determine how many people will be tested in February. The following query is issued.

```
SELECT COUNT(*) FROM db2cert.test_taken
WHERE date_taken
BETWEEN ('2000-02-01') AND ('2000-02-28')
```

The result will include the temporary assigned seat. To avoid this behavior, the application should not be able to read uncommitted changes.

Nonrepeatable Read

A nonrepeatable read scenario can obtain a different result set within the same transaction. Uncommitted read applications do not guarantee a repeatable read.

Let's look at an example of a nonrepeatable read scenario. Suppose Shirley is going to take the certification exam. She asks Linda to check where (Toronto or Rockwood) he can take the exam. Linda sends a request to the database and retrieves the list of available seats in Toronto and Rockwood, as shown in Fig. 8–6.

Fig. 8–6 *List of available seats (first query)*

In the meantime, Andrea has assigned and committed the last available seat in Rockwood to Mike. Shirley would like to take the test in Rockwood, so Linda attempts to assign the seat. The update fails, and when Linda refreshes her screen, the seat in Rockwood is no longer available. Linda's refreshed screen is shown in Fig. 8–7.

Fig. 8–7 *Linda's refreshed screen*

The application was coded to only lock the rows of data being updated. In this case, an exclusive lock was obtained by Andrea when she assigned the seat to Mike. This did not conflict with the locks held by Linda because she did not have that row locked. We are assuming that the row is only locked when it is chosen for update by the administrator.

To avoid this type of nonrepeatable read scenario, all of the retrieved data needs to be locked. If you want to guarantee that none of the selected data is modified, locking these rows is sufficient. This is known as read stability in DB2. If you would like to guarantee that the rows you have selected in getting this result will never change within the transaction, use repeatable read. This may require additional locking.

Phantom Read Problem

The *phantom read* phenomenon occurs if an application executes the same query twice; the second time the query is issued additional rows are returned. For many applications, this is an acceptable scenario. For example, if the query involved finding all of the available seats at a concert, then reissuing the query and obtaining a better seat selection is a desirable feature.

Let's take a look at our application again. Shirley wants to take the exam in Toronto or Rockwood. Linda requests the list of available seats for these locations, as shown in Fig. 8–8.

Fig. 8–8 *Available seats in Toronto and Rockwood (first query)*

Another test coordinator adds an additional seat to the Rockwood testing site. Now it is possible to test five candidates in Rockwood at the same time. If the query is issued again, Linda retrieves a different result set that includes five available seats. Although the application locked the previously retrieved rows, the application was able to add a new row to the result set, as shown in Fig. 8–9.

Fig. 8–9 *Linda's query (second query)*

Phantom Read Solution

Depending on the situation, a phantom read may be desirable. If you wish to avoid this behavior, the application has to lock all of the possible qualifying rows. This ensures that no other application can update, delete, or insert a row that would affect the result table. This is an important concept to understand.

 Note: If DB2 needs to acquire locks for every row in the table to provide the required level of isolation, a table-level lock may be obtained instead of multiple row-level locks.

Isolation Levels

In the previous examples, we have seen some of the possible concurrency problems. DB2 Universal Database provides different levels of protection to isolate the data from each of the database applications while it is being accessed.

These levels of protection are known as isolation levels or locking strategies. The isolation levels supported by DB2 include:

- Uncommitted read
- Cursor stability
- Read stability
- Repeatable read

The isolation level is defined for embedded SQL statements during the binding of a package to a database using the ISOLATION option of the PREP or the BIND command. If no isolation level is specified, the default level of cursor stability is used.

If you are using the command line processor, you may change the isolation level using the CHANGE ISOLATION LEVEL command.

For DB2 Call Level Interface (DB2 CLI), you may change the isolation level as part of the DB2 CLI configuration (DB2CLI.INI) file.

Uncommitted Read

The Uncommitted Read (UR) isolation level, also known as dirty read, is the lowest level of isolation supported by DB2. It can be used to access uncommitted data changes of other applications. For example, an application using the uncommitted read isolation level will return all of the matching rows for a query, even if that data is in the process of being modified, and may not be committed to the database.

If you decide to use this isolation level, your application might access incorrect data. There will be very few locks held by uncommitted read transactions. Nonrepeatable read and phantom read phenomena are possible when this isolation level is being used.

Cursor Stability

The Cursor Stability (CS) isolation level locks any row on which the cursor is positioned during a transaction. The lock on the row is held until the next row is fetched or the transaction is terminated. If a row has been updated, the lock is held until the transaction is terminated. A transaction is terminated when either a COMMIT or ROLLBACK statement is executed.

An application using cursor stability cannot read uncommitted data. In addition, the application locks the row that has been currently fetched, and no other application can modify the contents of the current row.

If you decide to use this isolation level, your application will always read consistent data, but nonrepeatable read or phantom read situations are still possible.

Read Stability

The Read Stability (RS) isolation level locks those rows that are part of a result table. If you have a table containing 10,000 rows and the query returns 10 rows, then only 10 rows are locked.

An application using read stability cannot read uncommitted data. Instead of locking a single row, it locks all rows that are part of the result table. No other application can change or modify these rows.

If you decide to use this isolation level, your application will always get the same result if the query is executed more than once in a transaction, though you may get additional phantom rows.

Repeatable Read

The Repeatable Read (RR) isolation level is the highest isolation level available in DB2. It locks all rows and application references within a transaction. Locks are held on all rows processed to build the result set, no matter how large the result set. A table lock may be obtained instead depending on a number of factors.

An application using repeatable read cannot read uncommitted data of a concurrent application. If you decide to use this isolation level, none of the previous discussed situations (lost update, phantom read, unrepeatable read, or uncommitted read) can occur in your application.

Choosing an Isolation Level

Choosing the proper isolation level is very important, because the isolation level influences not only the concurrency, but also the performance of the application. The more protection you have, the less concurrency is available.

Decide which concurrency problems are unacceptable for your application and then choose the isolation level that prevents these problems:

- Use the Uncommitted Read isolation level only if you use queries on read-only tables, or if you are using only SELECT statements and do not care whether you get uncommitted data from concurrent applications.

Concurrency

- Use the Cursor Stability isolation level when you want the maximum concurrency while seeing only committed data from concurrent applications.
- Use the Read Stability isolation level when your application operates in a concurrent environment. This means that qualified rows have to remain stable for the duration of the transaction.
- Use the Repeatable Read isolation level if changes to your result set are unacceptable.

Locking

DB2 provides isolation levels to control concurrency. In most cases, you do not need to take direct action to establish locks. In general, locks are acquired implicitly by DB2 according to the semantics defined by the isolation level.

Lock Attributes

The resource being locked is called an object. The only objects you can explicitly lock are tables and table spaces. Implicit locks on other types of objects, such as rows, index keys, and sometimes tables, are acquired by DB2 according to the isolation level and processing situations. The object being locked represents the granularity of the lock.

Note: The database itself can be locked if the CONNECT statement contains the clause IN EXCLUSIVE MODE. This will acquire an exclusive lock on the database and prevent any other users applications from connecting.

The length of time a lock is held is called the duration and is affected by the isolation level.

The access and rules that pertain to a lock are defined by the lock mode. Some lock modes are only used for locking table objects, while other lock modes are used for row objects. DB2 uses the following hierarchy of lockable database objects:

- Table spaces
- Tables
- Rows

The different modes of *table locks* are listed below in order of increasing control:

- IN (Intent None) - The owner of the lock can read any data, committed or noncommitted, in the table. Other applications can read or update the table.
- IS (Intent Share) - The owner of the lock can read any data in the table and obtains an S or NS lock on each row read. Other applications can read or update rows in the table.
- S (Share) - The owner of the lock can read any data in the table and will not obtain row locks. Other applications can read the table data.
- IX (Intent Exclusive) - The owner of the lock can read any data in the table if a U, S, NS, or X lock can be obtained on rows and also can change any data in the

Concurrency

table if an X lock can be obtained on rows. Other applications can both read and update table rows.

- SIX (Share with Intent Exclusive) -The owner of the lock can read any data in the table and change rows if it can obtain an X lock on the target row(s). Other applications can only read the table data.
- U (Update) - The owner of the lock can read any data in the table and can change data if an X lock on the table can be obtained prior to the update. Other applications can only read the table data.
- X (Exclusive) - The owner of the lock can read or update any data in the table. No row locks are obtained.Only other applications using the Uncommitted Read isolation level can read rows of the table.
- Z (Super exclusive) - No other application can access the table.

The different modes of *row locking* are listed below in order of increasing control over resources:

- NS (Next Key Share) -The row is being read by one application and can be read by concurrent applications. Held by applications using RS or CS isolation levels. It is compatible with the NX lock.
- S (Share) - The row is being read by one application and is available for *read-only* by concurrent applications.
- U (Update) - The row is being read by one application, which intends to update the data in this row. It is available for read-only by concurrent applications. Only one application can possess a U lock on a row. The lock owner will acquire X locks on the rows prior to update.
- NX (Next Key Exclusive) - This lock is acquired on the next row when a row is deleted from an index or inserted into an index in a table. The lock owner can read but not change the locked row. For type 2 indexes, this occurs only if the next row is currently locked by an RR scan.
- NW (Next Key Weak Exclusive) - This lock is acquired on the next row when a row is inserted into the index of a noncatalog table. The lock owner can read, but not change, the locked row. Only individual rows can be locked in NW mode. This is similar to X and NX locks except that it is compatible with the W and NS locks. For type 2 indexes, this lock occurs only if the next row is currently locked by an RR scan.
- X (Exclusive) - The row is being changed by one application and is not available for concurrent applications, except for those with uncommitted read isolation level. The lock owner can read and change data in the locked object.
- W (Weak Exclusive) - This lock is acquired on the row when a row is inserted into a noncatalog table. The lock owner can change the locked row. This lock is similar to a X lock except that it is compatible with the NW lock. Only uncommitted read applications can access the locked row.

The following table illustrates how all the lock modes work together (called *lock compatibility*). The table demonstrates whether one lock is compatible with another; "no" means the requesting application must wait for the lock to be released and "yes" means the lock can be granted.

Table 8–1 *Lock Type Compatibility*

State being Requested	State of Held Resource												
	none	IN	IS	NS	S	IX	SIX	U	NX	X	Z	NW	W
none	yes	yes	yes	yes	yes	yes	yes	yes	yes	yes	yes	yes	yes
IN	yes	yes	yes	yes	yes	yes	yes	yes	yes	yes	no	yes	yes
IS	yes	yes	yes	yes	yes	yes	yes	yes	no	no	no	no	no
NS	yes	yes	yes	yes	yes	no	no	yes	yes	no	no	yes	no
S	yes	yes	yes	yes	yes	no	no	yes	no	no	no	no	no
IX	yes	yes	yes	no	no	yes	no	no	no	no	no	no	no
SIX	yes	yes	yes	no	no	no	no	no	no	no	no	no	no
U	yes	yes	yes	yes	yes	no	no	no	no	no	no	no	no
NX	yes	yes	no	yes	no	no	no	no	no	no	no	no	no
X	yes	yes	no	no	no	no	no	no	no	no	no	no	no
Z	yes	no	no	no	no	no	no	no	no	no	no	no	no
NW	yes	yes	no	yes	no	no	no	no	no	no	no	no	yes
W	yes	yes	no	no	no	no	no	no	no	no	no	yes	no

Note: DB2 UDB Version 8 introduces a new index structure in the database. These new indexes are referred to as "Type-2" indexes and help to eliminate a phenomena called "next-key locking". Transactions in prior releases could lock an adjacent record during processing. This could result in unnecessary delays in completing transactions that depended on this record. Any new indexes created in Version 8 will use this new index structure, while existing indexes will be replaced only when the user reorganizes them or drops and recreates them.

Concurrency

Lock Conversion

If an application holds a lock on a data object, and the mode of access requires a more restrictive lock, the lock is converted to the more-restrictive lock. This process is known as *lock conversion*. During the lock conversion process, the more-restrictive lock may or may not be granted.

Let's look at an example of lock conversion. Assume that the application fetches a row from the test_taken table with the intent to update this row. The intent to update tells DB2 to acquire an update lock on the currently positioned row during the query processing.

The database manager holds an IX lock on the table and a U lock on the specified row. The SQL statements shown in Fig. 8–10 assign all test candidates currently scheduled to take the test at seat_no 1 to take the test at seat_no to 2.

When the update statement of our example is issued, the database manager holds an IX lock on the test_taken table and an X lock on the changed row.

```
SELECT * FROM db2cert.test_taken
WHERE seat_no = '1' AND date_taken = CURRENT DATE
FOR UPDATE OF seat_no;

UPDATE db2cert.test_taken
SET seat_no = '2'
WHERE seat_no = '1' AND date_taken = CURRENT DATE
```

Fig. 8–10 *Update a row - Lock conversion*

All the locks are released when your application terminates the transaction with either a COMMIT or ROLLBACK.

The cursor stability isolation level was used in this example.

 Note: When rows are being modified, an X lock is always required.

Lock Escalation

If your application changes many rows in one table, it may be better to have one lock on the entire table rather than many locks on each of the rows. DB2 requires memory for each lock; therefore, if a number of row locks can be replaced with a single table lock, the locking storage area can be used by other applications.

When DB2 converts the row locks to a table lock on your behalf, this is called *lock escalation*. DB2 will perform lock escalation to avoid resource problems by too many resources being held for the individual locks.

 Note: Each DB2 lock consumes the same amount of memory.

Two database configuration parameters have a direct effect on lock escalation. They are:

- LOCKLIST - Defines the amount of memory allocated for the locks.
- MAXLOCKS - Defines the percentage of the total locklist permitted to be allocated to a single application.

There are two different situations for lock escalation:

- One application exceeds the percentage of the locklist as defined by the MAXLOCKS configuration parameter. The database manager will attempt to free memory by obtaining a table lock and releasing row locks for this application.
- Many applications connected to the database fill the locklist by acquiring a large number of locks. DB2 will attempt to free memory by obtaining a table lock and releasing row locks.

Also note that the isolation level used by the application has an effect on lock escalation:

- Cursor stability will acquire row level locks initially. If required, table level locks can be obtained. Usually, a very small number of locks are acquired by each cursor stability application since they only have to guarantee the integrity of the data in the current row.
- Read stability locks all rows in the original result set.
- Repeatable read may or may not obtain row locks on all rows read to determine the result set. If it does not, then a table lock will be obtain instead.

Lock Wait Behavior

What happens if one application requests to update a row that is already locked with an exclusive (X) lock? The application requesting the update will simply wait until the exclusive lock is released by the other application.

To ensure that the waiting application can continue without needed to wait indefinitely, the LOCKTIMEOUT configuration parameter can be set to define the length of the timeout period. The value is specified in seconds. By default, the lock timeout

Concurrency

is disabled (set to a value of -1). This means the waiting application will not receive a timeout and will wait indefinitely.

Deadlock Behavior

In DB2, contention for locks by processes using the database can result in a deadlock situation.

A deadlock may occur in the following manner:

- Jon locks record 1.
- Finn locks record 5.
- Jon attempts to lock record 5, but waits since Finn already holds a lock on this record.
- Finn then tries to lock record 1, but waits since Jon already holds a lock on this record.

In this situation, both Jon and Finn will wait indefinitely for each other's locks until an external event causes one or both of them to ROLLBACK.

DB2 uses a background process, called the deadlock detector, to check for deadlocks. The process is activated periodically as determined by the DLCHKTIME parameter in the database configuration file. When activated it checks the lock system for deadlocks.

When the deadlock detector finds a deadlock situation, one of the deadlocked applications will receive an error code and the current transaction for that application will be rolled back automatically by DB2. When the rollback is complete, the locks held by this chosen application are released, thereby allowing other applications to continue.

Lock Table Statement

You can use the LOCK TABLE statement to override the rules for acquiring initial lock modes. It locks the specified table until the transaction is committed or rolled back. A table can be locked either in SHARE MODE or in EXCLUSIVE MODE.

When using the LOCK TABLE statement in SHARE MODE, no other application can update, delete, or insert data in the locked table. If you need a snapshot of a table that is frequently changed by concurrent applications, you can use this statement to lock the table for changes without using the repeatable read isolation level for your application.

The EXCLUSIVE MODE is more restrictive than SHARE MODE. It prevents concurrent applications from accessing the table for read, update, delete, and insert. If you want to update a large part of the table, you can use the LOCK TABLE statement in EXCLUSIVE MODE rather than locking each row.

LOCKSIZE parameter of ALTER TABLE statement

The default locking method for tables in DB2 is row locking. DB2 now provides you with the ability to override this default for a table by using the ALTER TABLE statement and the LOCKSIZE parameter.

The LOCKSIZE parameter allows you to specify the granularity of locking you wish DB2 to do for a particular table, either row or table level locking. For example, to change the default locking method for the TEST_TAKEN table from row locking to table locking you would issue the following SQL statement:

```
ALTER TABLE db2cert.test_taken LOCKSIZE TABLE
```

Whenever an application requires a lock to access data in the table, an appropriate table level lock will be issued. It is important to realize that since all locks on the table are on the table level and not on the row level, it reduces the concurrency of applications accessing this table.

Changing the Locking Level in SQL

When a new application is developed, the default locking behavior is usually defined for all of the SQL within that application. For instance, a program using call-level interface SQL calls may have the default locking level set to cursor stability. This may not be the behavior that the developer wants, especially if some of the SQL statements are only for quick table lookups and shouldn't be holding any locks. In this case, the developer should be using the WITH clause that is available on the SELECT, INSERT, DELETE, and UPDATE statements.

The WITH statement is placed at the end of any of the SELECT or data modification statements, followed by the locking level that you want for that statement:

- RR - Repeatable Read
- RS - Read Stability
- CS - Cursor Stability
- UR - Uncommitted Read

The following example shows how a SELECT statement can be changed to hold no locks during the duration of the request (Figure 8–11):

Concurrency

```
SELECT * FROM db2cert.test_taken
  WHERE seat_no = '1' AND date_taken = CURRENT DATE
  WITH UR
```

Fig. 8–11 *Select with no locking*

Summary

In this chapter, we have discussed some of the possible concurrency problems that can occur in a multiuser database environment. To protect the data as it is being modified, rules are established and the changes are grouped together in transactions.

The data updated by a transaction is either made permanent by the COMMIT statement or removed using the ROLLBACK statement. Each transaction is made up of one or more SQL statements. The rules of concurrent data access are determined by the isolation level, which are set for static and dynamic SQL application modules.

DB2 will implement the isolation level semantics of data access by implicitly acquiring locks on behalf of the applications. Applications can decide to lock a resource for EXCLUSIVE or SHARE mode. The only resource that can be directly locked using an SQL statement is a table. All row-level locks are acquired, according to the isolation level, by DB2.

If a requested lock is more restrictive, and another application already has the resource locked, a wait on the release of the lock will occur. The amount of time an application will wait is determined by a database configuration parameter known as LOCKTIMEOUT. The default amount of lock wait time is indefinite.

If multiple applications require access to data that is held by other applications, a deadlock scenario can occur. DB2 will detect the occurrence of any deadlocks and force one of the transactions to ROLLBACK. Every lock requested requires memory on the DB2 server. The amount of lock storage is configurable using the LOCKLIST and MAXLOCKS parameters.

Concurrency

P A R T **3**

DB2 UDB Administration

CHAPTER 9

Data Storage Management

- ◆ PROCESSOR, MEMORY, DISK CONSIDERATIONS
- ◆ DB2 STORAGE MODEL
- ◆ TABLE SPACE DESIGN
- ◆ IMPLEMENTATION EXAMPLES
- ◆ MAINTENANCE

Being able to efficiently store and quickly retrieve large amounts of data is one of the main functions of any relational database management system. The physical placement of the data can directly affect the query performance. It is the responsibility of the database administrator to understand the concepts of data placement and to create an appropriate physical database design.

Processor, Memory, and Disk Resources

Before looking at specific DB2 objects, you should consider the hardware that will be used to implement your DB2 system. Besides the minimum amount of processor, disk, and memory required to install the various DB2 components, how much of each component do you need to support your databases? Like most questions of this nature, the answer is: *it depends*.

Without adequate hardware resources, you will need to limit your performance expectations. No amount of tuning inside DB2 and/or the operating system can compensate for a hardware configuration that is lacking in processing power, hard disk capacity, or the amount of real memory.

On the other hand, if not enough attention is paid to configuring DB2 when there is enough hardware resource, your system may underperform.

Processors

DB2 can operate in the following hardware environments:

- Single partition on a single processor (uniprocessor).
- Single partition with multiple processors.
- Multiple partition configurations. These configurations are supported on a single machine or across multiple servers. For these scenarios, refer to the *Advanced DBA Certification Guide and Reference for DB2 UDB V8 for Linux, Unix and Windows* for a discussion of these products.

Single Partition on a Single Processor

The database in this environment serves the needs of a department or small office. A single processor system is restricted by the amount of disk-related processing the processor can handle. As workload increases, a single processor may become insufficient in processing user requests any faster, regardless of other additional components such as disk and memory that you may add to the system.

Single Partition with Multiple Processors

This environment is typically made up of several equally powerful processors within the same machine and is called a symmetric multiprocessor (SMP) system. Resources such as disk space and memory are shared. More disks and memory are found in this machine compared to the single-partition database, single processor environment.

This environment is easier to manage than multiple machines are since all components are physically contained in one machine. With multiple processors available, different database operations can be completed more quickly than with database operations assigned to only a single processor. DB2 can also divide the work of a single query among available processors to improve processing speed. Other database operations such as the LOAD, BACKUP, and RESTORE utilities, and the CREATE INDEX statement can take advantage of the multiple processors.

Parallel I/O operations are much more likely to occur in this environment, especially if data is spread out over multiple containers over multiple disk drives.

Memory

As previously mentioned, buffer pools are a very important tuning area in DB2 performance tuning. The way that you configure the system's real and virtual memory, DB2's internal memory usage, and the DB2 buffer pools will greatly influence the performance of the system.

Generally speaking, the more real memory, the better the overall performance. Balance this against the number of processors in the system. Not enough real memory will cause excessive paging in the operating system, which affects all applications, including DB2. The situation can arise where even though a page of DB2 data is sitting in the buffer pool, because the operating system does not have enough memory to keep that page in its real memory, it has to write it out to disk temporarily. This situation can have a severe performance effect on DB2.

Try to make the database server a dedicated machine. If DB2 has to share the machine with other applications, be aware of their memory requirements and factor that into how much memory is acquired for the machine.

Memory requirements are influenced by the number of concurrent users you will have. For example, in a Windows environment, it is recommended that you start with a minimum of 256 MB of memory and additional memory may be required as the number of users are increased. Refer to the *DB2 UDB V8.1 Quick Beginnings* manual for the relevant operating system for further exact details for your release level.

Disk

The amount of disk required will ultimately depend on the amount of data that is required to be stored in your databases. Factors to be aware of in planning your hard disk configuration include:

- The capacity of the disks used. Sometimes it is better to use multiple disks of lower capacity so that greater degrees of parallel I/O operations can take place. The tradeoff to this approach is that additional hardware is required.
- The speed of disks used. Hard disk attributes such as latency and seek time affect the I/O performance. DB2's optimizer can make use of disk attributes in

its calculation for the best access path.

- Compressed file systems can be used to hold DB2 table space containers when disk space is at a premium and/or when the performance requirements allow for the extra overhead incurred.
- If availability is a high priority issue you may want to mirror disks. If so this will double your disk requirements.

Performance and availability can be influenced by the hard disk controllers you use and how many disks are attached to the controller. By placing disks on separate controllers you can reduce the traffic going through the controllers, thereby reducing the contention for the disks.

DB2 Storage Model

The following data objects will be discussed:

- Buffer pool - allocates memory to DB2.
- Table space - logical layer between physical tables with data and the database.
- Table - represented by rows and columns. Several tables can reside in one table space.
- Container - allocates storage to a table space.

The DB2 storage model illustrates the relationship between tables, table spaces, databases, and a DB2 instance (Figure 9–1).

Fig. 9–1 *DB2 storage model*

Buffer Pool

A *buffer pool* is an area of main memory allocated to the database manager to cache table and index data pages as they are read from disk or modified. The purpose of a buffer pool is to improve database system performance. The database manager decides when to bring data from disk into a buffer pool and when old data in a buffer pool is unlikely to be used in the short term and can be written back out to disk. Data can be accessed much faster from memory than from disk; therefore, the fewer times the database manager needs to read from or write to a disk, the better the performance. Multiple buffer pools can be created. The configuration of buffer pools is a very important tuning area, since you can reduce the delay caused by excessive physical I/O.

Note: On UNIX platforms, the creation of a DB2 database will create a default buffer pool called `IBMDEFAULTBP` of 1000 four-kilobyte pages. For other platforms, the buffer pool size is 250 four-kilobyte pages.

Table Spaces

One of the first tasks in setting up a relational database is mapping the logical database design to physical storage on your system. The object used to specify the physical location of data is known as a *table space*. A table space is used as a layer between the database and the container objects that hold the actual table data. A table space can contain more than one table.

As all DB2 tables reside in table spaces, this means you can control where table data is physically stored. This gives you the ability to create a physical database design to fit your particular environment. For example, you can choose slower disks to store less frequently accessed data.

Backup and recovery can be performed at the table space level. This will give you more granularity and control since you can back up or restore each table space individually.

There are two types of table spaces: System Managed Space and Database Managed Space.

SMS Table Spaces

In a *System Managed Space* (SMS) table space, the operating system's file system manager allocates and manages the space where the table is to be stored. This storage model typically consists of many files representing table objects, stored in the file system space. The user decides on the location of the files, DB2 controls their names, and the file system is responsible for managing them. Each container is a directory in the file space of the operating system.

DMS Table Spaces

In a *Database Managed Space* (DMS) table space, the database manager controls the storage space. The storage model consists of a limited number of devices, whose space is managed by DB2. The Database Administrator decides which devices to use, and DB2 manages the space on the devices. This type of table space is essentially an implementation of a special purpose file system designed to best meet the needs of the database manager. The table space definition includes a list of the devices or files belonging to the table space in which data can be stored. Each container is either a fixed size preallocated file or a physical device such as a disk.

Containers

A container is a physical storage device. It can be identified by a directory name, a device name, or a file name.

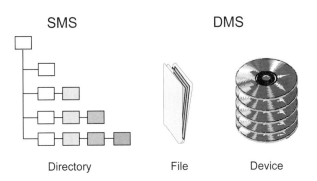

SMS	DMS	
Directory	File	Device

Fig. 9–2 *Containers in DB2*

A container is assigned to a table space. All database and table data is assigned to table spaces. A table space's definitions and attributes are recorded in the database system catalog. Once a table space is created, you can then create tables within this table space. Details about containers can obtained by using the LIST TABLESPACE CONTAINERS command. A single table space can span many containers, but each container can belong to only one table space. Figure Fig. 9–3 shows an example of the relationship between tables and a table space within a database and the associated containers and disks.

Containers must reside on disks that are local; therefore resources such as LAN-redirected drives or NFS-mounted file systems cannot be used for table spaces.

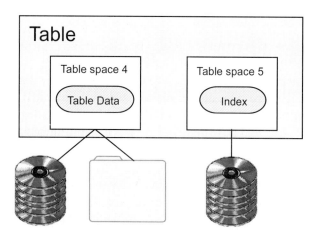

Fig. 9–3 *Table spaces and containers*

Directory Containers

Containers that are directory names are the only types of containers that can be used in SMS table spaces. An SMS table space can be defined with more than one container, each one of which could be mapped to a different physical disk to balance the I/O workload. DB2 will balance the amount data written to the multiple containers. It is very important to identify all the containers you want to use, since you cannot add or delete containers to an SMS table space after it has been created using the ALTER TABLESPACE statement.

The name for a directory container identifies an absolute or relative directory name. The directory named must not contain any files or subdirectories. The relative directory name is relative to the database directory. Refer to the CREATE TABLESPACE statement in the *DB2 UDB V8.1 SQL Reference* for more details.

 Note: A table space container layout can be redefined during a restore of the table space. This is known as a *redirected restore*.

Device Containers

The device that the container is created on cannot be used in another table space. So when specifying the size of the container, make sure that all the space on the device is used because any unused space will be wasted. The amount space required can be specified in pages, kilobytes, megabytes, or gigabytes.

File Containers

File containers are files of preallocated size used by DMS table spaces. No operational differences exist between a file and a device. When defining the container name, you can use an absolute or relative file name. If any component of the directory name does not exist, it will be created by DB2. Similarly, if the file does not exist, it will be created and initialized to the specific size by DB2. The amount of space specified must exist when the table space is created. The amount space required can be specified in pages, kilobytes, megabytes, or gigabytes.

Note: A container can only be added to a DMS table space. Containers cannot be added to an SMS table space with the ALTER TABLESPACE statement. You can add a container to an SMS table space during a *redirected restore* operation.

Table Space Design

In addition to defining whether a table space is SMS or DMS managed, there are several other parameters that may be specified during the CREATE TABLESPACE command.

Here is the syntax of the CREATE TABLESPACE statement:

Some of the key parameters to the CREATE TABLESPACE statement include (see the DB2 SQL Reference for further detail):

- REGULAR | TEMPORARY | LONG TABLESPACE - specifies the type of table space to be created; REGULAR will be selected if nothing is specified.
- MANAGED BY SYSTEM | DATABASE USING - specifies SMS (SYSTEM) or DMS (DATABASE) table space; the containers are defined with the USING clause. For SMS table spaces, the container is a directory name. For DMS table spaces, a FILE or DEVICE container is specified and its size in PAGESIZE pages.
- PAGESIZE - allowable values for the page size of the table space: 4, 8, 16, or 32
- EXTENTSIZE - number of PAGESIZE pages that are written to a container before

moving to the next container.

- PREFETCHSIZE - number of PAGESIZE pages read if prefetch is performed.
- BUFFERPOOL - name of buffer pool to be used for tables in this table space.
- OVERHEAD - number of milliseconds for the I/O controller to read a page (disk seek and latency time, default = 24.1).
- TRANSFERRATE - number of milliseconds to read one page into memory; this value is used by the optimizer in calculating I/O costs (default = 0.9).
- DROPPED TABLE RECOVERY ON | OFF - specifies if dropped tables in the table space can be recovered using the RECOVER TABLE ON option of the ROLLFORWARD command.
- DATABASE PARTITION GROUP - used to specify which database partition group a table space will belong to in a clustered environment; the default assumes a non-clustered environment.

Some of the major table space parameters will now be reviewed in more detail.

Regular Table Space

Tables containing user data exist in one or many *regular* table spaces. By default, a table space called USERSPACE1 is created when the CREATE DATABASE command is executed. Indexes are also stored in regular table spaces. The system catalog tables exist in a regular table space as well. The default system catalog table space is called SYSCATSPACE. By default, both USERSPACE1 and SYSCATSPACE are created as SMSs, but can be defined as DMSs in the CREATE DATABASE command. While it is optional to use the USERSPACE1 table space (it is always created but may be dropped), it is mandatory to use SYSCATSPACE as the name of the table space holding the system catalog tables. The maximum size of a regular table space (including index data) depends on the page size used by the table space. For example, the maximum is 64 GB for 4 KB pages and 128 GB for 8 KB pages.

Large Table Space

Tables containing long field data or long object data, such as multimedia objects, exist in one or many *long* table spaces. Their use is optional, as long data can also reside in regular table spaces. Long table spaces must be DMSs. The maximum size of a long table space is 2 TB.

 Note: Long table space have been renamed to large table spaces.

System Temporary Table Space

Temporary table spaces are used by the database manager during SQL operations for holding transient data such as immediate tables during sort operations, reorganizing tables, creating indexes, and joining tables. A database must have at least one temporary table space. By default, an SMS table space called TEMPSPACE1 is created when the database is created. It can be dropped after another temporary table space is created (one must always be in existence), and it can be called any legal table space name. The name TEMPSPACE1 does not have to be used. Temporary table spaces can be either SMSs or DMSs. The maximum size of a temporary table space is 2 TB.

> **Note:** DB2 supports system temporary table spaces and user temporary table spaces. A system temporary table space must exist for DB2 to operate properly. User temporary table spaces can be used to place temporary tables.

Extentsize

An *extent* is a unit of space within a container of a table space. Database objects are stored in pages within DB2 (except for LOBs and long varchars). These pages are grouped into allocation units called extents. The extent size is defined at the table space level. Once the extent size is established for the table space, it cannot be altered. A database configuration parameter DFT_EXTENT_SZ specifies the default extent size for all table spaces in the database. The range this value can take is from 2 to 256 pages; for example, 8 - 1024 KB for 4 KB pages or 16 - 2048 KB for 8 KB pages. This figure can be overridden by using the EXTENTSIZE parameter in the CREATE TABLESPACE statement. Although this parameter can be also specified in kilobytes or megabytes, DB2 ensures that the extent size is always a whole number of pages by taking the floor of the number of bytes divided by the page size.

Data Storage Management

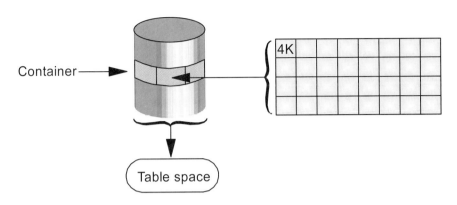

Container ───►

(Table space)

Fig. 9–4 *Extents and containers*

 Note: In addition to using extents for storing user data, extents are also used for space management within the table space.

Pagesize

Rows of DB2 table data are organized into blocks called *pages*. Pages can be four sizes: 4, 8, 16, and 32 KB. Table data pages do not contain the data for columns defined with LONG VARCHAR, LONG VARGRAPHIC, BLOB, CLOB, or DBCLOB data types.

In a page of table data, 76 bytes are reserved for DB2. The other 4020 bytes (8040 bytes for 8 KB pages) are available for user data, although no individual row can exceed 4005 bytes (8101 bytes for 8 KB pages) in length. The maximum number of columns in a table defined using a table space that uses 4 KB pages is 500; for 8, 16, and 32 KB pages, it is 1012 columns.

 Note: LOB and long field data can reside in table spaces of any page size.

Performance Considerations

The type and design of your table space determines the efficiency of the I/O performed against that table space. The following concepts are important in understanding how DB2 performs I/O operations:

Big-Block Reads

If several pages (usually an extent) are retrieved in a single request, then *big-block reads* have occurred. If rows that are in pages within the extent retrieved are used, another physical I/O will not be required, resulting in optimum performance.

Sequential Prefetching

Sequential prefetching is the ability of the database manager to read pages in advance of those pages being referenced by a query, in anticipation of being required by the query. This asynchronous retrieval can reduce execution times significantly.

You can control how aggressively the prefetching is performed by changing the PREFETCHSIZE parameter on the CREATE TABLESPACE or ALTER TABLESPACE statement. By default, this value is set to the DFT_PREFETCH_SZ database configuration parameter. This value represents how many pages will be read at a time when a prefetch request is triggered by DB2. By setting this value to a multiple of the extent size, multiple extents can be read in parallel. This function is even more effective when the containers for the table space are on separate hard disks.

 Note: On Linux and UNIX platforms, prefetching will create separate I/O processes. On Windows, prefetching is accomplished using threads.

To enable prefetching, DB2 starts separate threads of control, known as *I/O servers*, to perform page reading. These I/O servers wait for requests for pages from database agents that manage the processing of all SQL requests. The first available I/O server will read the prefetch request from a queue and read the data into the buffer pool. Depending on the number of prefetch requests in the queue and the number of I/O servers configured by the NUM_IOSERVERS database configuration parameter, multiple I/O servers can be fetching data at the same time.

DB2 can monitor I/O activity in the system. If sequential page reading is occurring, DB2 will initiate prefetching requests. The function is called *sequential detection* and is implemented via the SEQDETECT database configuration parameter. By default, this parameter is set to YES. If set to NO, DB2 will only initiate sequential prefetching in a predetermined manner during query optimization for activities such as table sorts and scans where sets of contiguous pages of data are required during query processing.

Another form of prefetching that can occur regardless of the SEQDETECT parameter is *list prefetching*. This is when DB2 builds up a list of internal row identifiers that are required, usually after scanning an index, then sorts them into physical address sequence and starts scanning the table for the rows. Because DB2 knows beforehand which pages are required, it can retrieve them ahead of when the application needs them; thus, the time to retrieve the data is shortened significantly due to the asynchronous processing.

Page Cleaning

As pages are read and modified, they accumulate in the buffer pool. Whenever a page is read in, there must be a buffer pool page to read it into. If the buffer pool is full of modified pages, one of these modified pages must be written out to the disk before the new page can be read in. To prevent the buffer pool from becoming full, *page cleaner* tasks write out modified pages to guarantee the availability of buffer pool pages for use by read requests. This feature is implemented via the NUM_IOCLEANERS database configuration parameter.

The CHNGPGS_THRESH database configuration parameter specifies the level (percentage) of changed pages at which the page cleaner tasks will start. When started, they will build a list of the pages to write to disk. Once they have completed writing the pages to disk, they will become inactive again and wait for the next trigger to start. The default value for this parameter is 60%.

In addition to I/O considerations, there are also considerations relating to the use of the table space containers. These are detailed as follows.

Number of Extents Required

Five is the minimum number of extents required in a DMS table space:

- Three extents for overhead and control information
- Two extents for each table object (always assume one object)

Number of Pages Required

In a DMS table space, one page in every container is reserved for overhead, and the remaining pages will be used one extent at a time. Only full extents are used in the container, so for optimum space management, you can use the following formula to help determine the appropriate size to use when allocating a container size:

```
(extent size in pages * n) + 1
```

where `extent size` is the size of each extent for the table space and n is the number of extents you want to store in the container. Recall above that you need a minimum of five extents for a DMS table space.

Recall that with SMS table spaces, space is allocated by the operating system file system as required.

Striping

Given that a table space can span multiple containers, DB2 writes to each container in a *round robin* fashion, where an extent as it is filled with data is written to each container in turn. This is known as striping.

In an SMS table space, if any container becomes full, then the entire table space is considered full, and no more data can be added.

In a DMS table space, if a container becomes full, DB2 will continue to use space available in other containers.

In both cases, it is preferable that containers be designed so that they are of equal size on different physical drives to optimize space usage and DB2 parallel operations.

Using RAID Devices

If you plan to use RAID devices, here are some guidelines. For further information and details, please refer to the DB2 Administration Guide:

- Define a single container for the table space (using the RAID device).
- Make the extent size equal to, or a multiple of the RAID stripe size.
- Ensure the prefetch size of the table space is the RAID stripe size multiplied by the number of RAID parallel devices (or a whole multiple of this product) and a multiple of the extent size.
- Use the DB2 registry variable `DB2_STRIPED_CONTAINERS` to align extents to the RAID stripe size.
- Use the DB2 registry variable `DB2_PARALLEL_IO` to enable parallel disk I/O.

Device Containers Versus File Containers

For DMS table spaces, files can be less efficient than devices due to the runtime overhead of the filesystem. Files are useful when:

- A device is not available.
- Maximum performance is not required. By bypassing the file system layer, DB2 manages device containers directly, improving performance, whereas for files, DB2 interacts with the file system.
- You do not want the extra administrative overhead associated with setting up and maintaining devices.

Some operating systems allow you to have physical devices greater than 2 GB in size. You should consider partitioning the physical device into multiple logical devices so that no container is bigger than the size allowed by the operating system.

Here are some considerations specific to the different supported operating systems:

- In Windows, a DMS table space can use devices. If you want to use an entire physical drive as a container, specify \\.\N, where N is the physical drive number. If you want to use a logical drive as a container, specify \\.\X:, where X is the logical drive letter. The drive must not be formatted. Other applications must not use these container locations.
- In AIX, create a volume group over the physical disks you are going to use for DB2 containers.
- On UNIX platforms, the creator of the logical volume must have write access to the character portion of the device container being used.

Multipage File Allocation

In an SMS table space, the associated file is extended one page at a time as the object grows. When inserting a large number of rows, some delay may result from waiting for the system to allocate another page. If you need improved insert performance, you can enable *multipage file allocation*. This allows the system to allocate or extend the file by more than one extent at a time. It will allocate empty pages to fill up the last extent in all SMS table space containers (see the *DB2 UDB V8.1 Command Reference* for more information).

This facility is implemented by running the DB2EMPFA utility and is indicated by the MULTIPAGE_ALLOC database configuration parameter.

Comparison of SMS and DMS Table Spaces

The following table compares the key features of SMS and DMS table spaces.

Table 9–1 *Characteristics of SMS and DMS User Table Spaces*

Characteristics	SMS	DMS
Can dynamically increase number of containers in table spaces	No	Yes

Table 9–1 *Characteristics of SMS and DMS User Table Spaces*

Characteristics	SMS	DMS
Can store index data for a table in a separate table space	No	Yes
Can store long data for a table in a separate table space	No	Yes
One table can span several table spaces	No	Yes
Space allocated only when needed	Yes	No
Table space can be placed on different disks	Yes	Yes
Extent size can be changed after creation	No	No

Note: Administrators can drop a container from a table space and reduce the size of existing containers without the need to perform a redirected restore.

The Catalog Table Space

The DB2 system catalog is where DB2 keeps all its metadata about all the DB2 objects in the database. Previously we had mentioned that catalog table space is called SYSCATSPACE and that its definition occurs in the CREATE DATABASE command. The following are considerations when planning for the system catalog:

- The system catalog consists of many tables of varying sizes. In using a DMS table space, a minimum of two extents are allocated for each table object. Depending on the extent size chosen, a significant amount of allocated and unused space may result. If using a DMS table space, a small extent size (2 - 4 pages) should be chosen; otherwise, an SMS table space should be used.
- The catalog tables use large object data type columns. These columns are not kept in the buffer pool and are read from disk each time they are needed. By using an SMS table space or DMS table space with file containers, you can take advantage of the file system cache for LOB data types.
- As more DB2 objects are created, the size of the catalog will increase. If you use an SMS table space, you cannot add more containers. All you can do is use operating system functionality to increase the underlying file system size. If you use a DMS table space, you can add more containers.

Temporary Table Spaces

Temporary table spaces are important as they are DB2's work areas for placing intermediate tables as it determines the final result set of data in satisfying SQL queries. Therefore, a significant amount of activity takes place in temporary table spaces. Another important use is for intermediate storage during the REORG TABLE utility. Its use here is optional, as by default, DB2 will place the copy of the table in the same table space where the original table resides. Refer to the *DB2 UDB V8.1 Administration Guide* for more considerations about the REORG TABLE utility and temporary table spaces.

If a database has more than one temporary table space defined, temporary objects are allocated among the temporary table spaces in a round robin fashion. Each temporary table space must be large enough to accommodate the largest possible temporary table. An application may encounter a temporary table space full condition even though there is unused space in other temporary table spaces. It is recommended that just one temporary table space be defined for a database and that multiple containers on separate disks be used to improve performance.

Some guidelines for temporary table spaces are:

- Create one SMS temporary table space for every page size.
- Define the containers for these table spaces so that they share the same file system(s). This maximizes disk sharing and minimizes the total disk requirement. As each temporary table is created and deleted by DB2, the disk space used will be reclaimed.
- If you require the highest level of performance and can afford the dedicated disk space, consider using DMS for temporary table spaces. Although you will lose the benefits of flexibility that you have with SMS, you may benefit from the performance advantages of using DMS.

 Note: There must be at least one temporary table space for use by the database at all times. In most cases, SMS is the preferred choice for TEMP table spaces.

Choosing an Extent Size

The extent size for a table space indicates the number of pages of table data that will be written to a container before data will be written to the next container. When selecting an extent size, you should consider the size and type of tables in the table space.

Space in DMS table spaces is allocated to a table an extent at a time. As the table is populated and an extent becomes full, a new extent is allocated. A table is made up of the following separate table objects:

- A DATA object - This is where the regular column data is stored.

- An INDEX object - All indexes defined on the table are stored here.
- A LONG FIELD object - If your table has one or more LONG columns, they are all stored here.
- Two LOB objects - If your table has one or more LOB columns, they are stored in these two table objects: one table object for the LOB data and a second table object for metadata describing the LOB data.

Each table object is stored separately, and each allocates new extents as needed. Each table object is also paired up with a metadata object called an *extent map*, which describes all the extents in the table space that belong to the table object. Space for extent maps is also allocated an extent at a time.

The initial allocation of space for a table is two extents for each table object. If you have many small tables in a table space, you may have a large amount of space allocated to store a relatively small amount of data. In such a case, you should specify a small extent size or use an SMS table space that allocates pages one at a time.

If, on the other hand, you have a very large table that has a high growth rate, and you are using a DMS table space with a small extent size, you could have unnecessary overhead related to the frequent allocation of additional extents.

In addition, the type of access to the tables should also be considered. Sequential scanning of tables, such as the type of SQL queries used in a data warehousing environment, will need to access a large percentage of rows in a table. In this type of workload, a larger extent size may be preferred to reduce the number of I/O operations DB2 has to perform. In addition, prefetching of data can also take place to reduce the time the application has to wait for DB2 to return data to it.

In contrast, an online transaction processing (OLTP) workload involves queries that access tables usually in a random manner, retrieving data by key values. In this case, a large extent would bring many data pages into the buffer pool that are not required by the application. In this case, a smaller extent size may be justified.

Long Field Data

For the data types of LONG VARCHAR and LONG VARGRAPHIC, 20 bytes are used for the descriptor that is kept in the table data row. For further information about how long field data is stored, see the *DB2 UDB V8.1 Administration Guide*.

Large Object Data

If a table has BLOB, CLOB, or DBCLOB data, in addition to the byte count (between 72 and 312 bytes) for the descriptor (in the table row), the data itself must be stored. This data is stored in two separate table objects that are structured differently than other data types.

LOB Data Objects

Data is stored in 64 MB areas that are broken up into segments whose sizes are a power of two times 1 KB. Hence these segments can be 1024 bytes, 2048 bytes, 4096 bytes, and so on, up to 64 MB.

To reduce the amount of disk space used by the LOB data, you can use the COMPACT parameter in the lob-options-clause on the CREATE TABLE and ALTER TABLE statements. The COMPACT option minimizes the amount of disk space required by allowing the LOB data to be split into smaller segments so that it will use the smallest amount of space possible. This does not involve data compression but is simply using the minimum amount of space to the nearest 1 KB boundary. Without the COMPACT option, there is no attempt to reduce the space used to the nearest 1 KB boundary. Appending to LOB values stored using the COMPACT option may result in slower performance compared with appending LOB values for which the COMPACT option is not specified. The amount of free space contained in LOB data objects will be influenced by the amount of update and delete activity as well as the size of the LOB values being inserted.

LOB Allocation Objects

Allocation and free space information is stored in 4 KB allocation pages separated from the actual data. The number of these 4 KB pages is dependent on the amount of data, including unused space, allocated for the large object data. The overhead is calculated as follows: one 4 KB page for every 64 GB plus one 4 KB page for every 8 MB.

If character data is less than 4 KB in length, and it fits in the record with the rest of the data, the CHAR, GRAPHIC, VARCHAR, or VARGRAPHIC data types should be used instead of the large object data types.

Mapping Tables to Table Spaces

When determining how to map tables to table spaces in your design, consider the following:

- The *amount* of data. If your design involves tables with a small amount of data, consider using SMS table spaces for them. The effort in administering many small tables, each in their own DMS table space, would not be proportional to the benefit gained.

  It would be more prudent to concentrate on larger, more frequently accessed tables. Here you could justify placing each table in its own DMS table space.

- The *type* of data in the table. Historical data that is used infrequently and does not have a critical response time requirement can be placed on slower, less-expensive devices.

Conversely, the tables with fastest response time requirements should be assigned to the fastest devices available. In extreme cases, these table spaces could be given their own buffer pool.

Another approach is to group related tables together in table spaces. They may be related via referential integrity, triggers, or structured data types. Since the BACKUP and RESTORE utilities can work at the table space level, the related data between the tables can be relied on stay consistent and recoverable.

- Separating out index and long data components. By assigning the indexes for a table into a separate table space, the containers for this table space can be placed on different disks, thus reducing contention on the disks containing the actual table data. Indexes can then be given their own buffer pool to reduce index physical I/O.

Similarly, contention is also reduced by separating the long data from the other components. In addition, if long data is included with the regular data, it will take longer because of the extra I/O required to sequentially scan the table.

Implementation Examples

Now that we understand the characteristics of the DB2 storage objects we can implement them via the commands and SQL statements that create and delete them. For a detailed description of all the options available on the following commands and SQL statements, see the *DB2 UDB V8.1 Administration Guide*, the *DB2 UDB V8.1 SQL Reference* and the *DB2 UDB V8.1 Command Reference*.

Creating a Database

This is the simplest form of the CREATE DATABASE command. Note that this is a command and not an SQL statement.

```
CREATE DATABASE DB2CERT
```

The LIST TABLESPACES SHOW DETAIL command output below shows us the result of the above CREATE DATABASE command. Note that for this example, these commands are being executed in a Windows environment.

```
Tablespaces for Current Database

Tablespace ID                     = 0
Name                              = SYSCATSPACE
Type                              = System managed space
Contents                          = Any data
State                             = 0x0000
 Detailed explanation:
    Normal
Total pages                       = 975
Useable pages                     = 975
Used pages                        = 975
Free pages                        = Not applicable
High water mark (pages)           = Not applicable
Page size (bytes)                 = 4096
Extent size (pages)               = 32
Prefetch size (pages)             = 16
Number of containers              = 1

Tablespace ID                     = 1
Name                              = TEMPSPACE1
Type                              = System managed space
Contents                          = Temporary data
State                             = 0x0000
 Detailed explanation:
    Normal
Total pages                       = 1
Useable pages                     = 1
Used pages                        = 1
Free pages                        = Not applicable
High water mark (pages)           = Not applicable
Page size (bytes)                 = 4096
Extent size (pages)               = 32
Prefetch size (pages)             = 16
Number of containers              = 1

Tablespace ID                     = 2
Name                              = USERSPACE1
Type                              = System managed space
Contents                          = Any data
State                             = 0x0000
 Detailed explanation:
```

```
           Normal
 Total pages                               = 1
 Useable pages                             = 1
 Used pages                                = 1
 Free pages                                = Not applicable
 High water mark (pages)                   = Not applicable
 Page size (bytes)                         = 4096
 Extent size (pages)                       = 32
 Prefetch size (pages)                     = 16
 Number of containers                      = 1
```

Note how the default values have been applied. The three table spaces SYSCATSPACE, TEMPSPACE1, and USERSPACE1 have been created as SMS table spaces with an extent size of 32. The total page count for SYSCATSPACE is 975 at a page size of 4 KB, which means the catalog by default occupies 3.9 MB. This will grow as objects are created in the database. The other two table spaces have only one page in them.

Let's look at a more complex example:

```
CREATE DATABASE DB2CERT
       DFT_EXTENT_SZ 4
       CATALOG TABLESPACE
             MANAGED BY DATABASE USING
                       (FILE 'C:\CAT\CATALOG.DAT' 2000
                       ,FILE 'D:\CAT\CATALOG.DAT' 2000)
             EXTENTSIZE 8
             PREFETCHSIZE 16
       TEMPORARY TABLESPACE
             MANAGED BY SYSTEM USING
                       ('C:\TEMPTS','D:\TEMPTS')
       USER TABLESPACE
             MANAGED BY DATABASE USING
                       (FILE 'C:\TS\USERTS.DAT' 121)
             EXTENTSIZE 24
             PREFETCHSIZE 48
```

Here we are asking DB2 to create a database with:

- A default extent size of four pages
- The system catalog table space as a DMS table space with two file containers, each with 2000 pages, 8-page extents, and prefetch size of 16 pages
- The temporary table space TEMPSPACE1 as an SMS table space with two containers
- The user table space USERSPACE1 as a DMS table space of one container, with 121 pages, 24-page extents, and prefetch size of 48 pages

The output from LIST TABLESPACES SHOW DETAIL in this case is as follows:

```
        Tablespaces for Current Database

Tablespace ID                    = 0
Name                             = SYSCATSPACE
Type                             = Database managed space
Contents                         = Any data
State                            = 0x0000
 Detailed explanation:
     Normal
Total pages                      = 4000
Useable pages                    = 3984
Used pages                       = 2440
Free pages                       = 1544
High water mark (pages)          = 2440
Page size (bytes)                = 4096
Extent size (pages)              = 8
Prefetch size (pages)            = 16
Number of containers             = 2

Tablespace ID                    = 1
Name                             = TEMPSPACE1
Type                             = System managed space
Contents                         = Temporary data
State                            = 0x0000
 Detailed explanation:
     Normal
Total pages                      = 2
Useable pages                    = 2
Used pages                       = 2
Free pages                       = Not applicable
High water mark (pages)          = Not applicable
Page size (bytes)                = 4096
Extent size (pages)              = 4
Prefetch size (pages)            = 16
Number of containers             = 2

Tablespace ID                    = 2
Name                             = USERSPACE1
Type                             = Database managed space
Contents                         = Any data
State                            = 0x0000
 Detailed explanation:
     Normal
Total pages                      = 121
Useable pages                    = 120
Used pages                       = 72
Free pages                       = 48
High water mark (pages)          = 72
Page size (bytes)                = 4096
Extent size (pages)              = 24
Prefetch size (pages)            = 48
Number of containers             = 1
```

Note how the number of usable pages in SYSCATSPACE is 3984. Because one page per container is required for overhead, this leaves 1999 pages available for use by extents.

Since the extent size is 8, this leaves a spare seven pages unable to be used for extents in each container because only full extents are used. Add to this the one mandatory page for overhead and you have a total of eight pages per container unusable. Therefore, 16 pages out of 4000 for the entire table space are unusable.

In the USERSPACE1 table space, note that the container size is 121. One page is used for overhead, leaving 120 pages usable. Three extents are also used for overhead, accounting for the used page count of 72. This leaves 48 pages (two extents) available free for user data. Given the extent size, this is minimum number of pages the container can be defined with.

The LIST TABLESPACE CONTAINERS FOR 2 SHOW DETAIL command produces the following output. Note that the table space ID that the command requires is for the table space USERSPACE1.

```
                Tablespace Containers for Tablespace 2

     Container ID                              = 0
     Name                                      = C:\TS\USERTS.DAT
     Type                                      = File
     Total pages                               = 121
     Useable pages                             = 120
     Accessible                                = Yes
```

Creating Buffer Pools

This statement creates a buffer pool of 2000 four-kilobyte pages (8 MB):

```
CREATE BUFFERPOOL BPCERT4K
       SIZE 2000
       PAGESIZE 4096
```

This statement creates a buffer pool of 1000 eight-kilobyte pages (8 MB):

```
CREATE BUFFERPOOL BPCERT8K
       SIZE 1000
       PAGESIZE 8192
```

A buffer pool with the same page size must exist before a table space with a non-4 KB page size can be created.

Creating Table Spaces

This is an example of how to define a table space that has a raw device container under Windows. In this case, we are using an unformatted logical drive.

```
CREATE TABLESPACE RAWTS
       PAGESIZE 4096
       MANAGED BY DATABASE USING
                (DEVICE '\\.\E:' 8001)
       EXTENTSIZE 8
       PREFETCHSIZE 16
       BUFFERPOOL BPCERT4K
```

This example uses the buffer pool created previously. The reports on the table space and container are:

```
Tablespace ID                    = 3
Name                             = RAWTS
Type                             = Database managed space
Contents                         = Any data
State                            = 0x0000
 Detailed explanation:
     Normal
Total pages                      = 8001
Useable pages                    = 8000
Used pages                       = 24
Free pages                       = 7976
High water mark (pages)          = 24
Page size (bytes)                = 4096
Extent size (pages)              = 8
Prefetch size (pages)            = 16
Number of containers             = 1

          Tablespace Containers for Tablespace 3

Container ID                     = 0
Name                             = \\.\E:
Type                             = Disk
Total pages                      = 8001
Useable pages                    = 8000
Accessible                       = Yes
```

Creating Tables

This example shows how a table and its indexes can be separated into separate table spaces. Both table spaces must be defined as DMS.

```
CREATE TABLE CERTTAB
       (COL1    CHAR(7) NOT NULL
        COL2    INTEGER NOT NULL)
       IN RAWTS INDEX IN USERSPACE1
```

Dropping Table Spaces

This example shows how to drop table spaces. More than one can be dropped at the same time. All objects defined in the table spaces will be implicitly dropped or invalidated. Containers that were created by DB2 are deleted.

```
DROP TABLESPACE RAWTS,USERSPACE1
```

Dropping Buffer Pools

This example shows how to drop buffer pools. Note that the default buffer pool IBMDEFAULTBP cannot be dropped. This command will fail if table spaces that use the buffer pool are still defined. Once dropped, the memory that the buffer pool used will not be released until the database is stopped.

```
DROP BUFFERPOOL BPCERT4K
```

Dropping a Database

A DB2 command (not an SQL statement) is used to drop a database. This completely deletes all objects in the database. All users must be disconnected from the database before this command can succeed.

```
DROP DATABASE DB2CERT
```

Creating Table Spaces Using the Control Center

Besides being able to execute the above statements via the command line processor or DB2 Command Center, you can also use the Control Center to create DB2 objects. Here is an example of creating the table space RAWTS, using the table space wizard.

Fig. 9–5 *Control Center - Create Table Space Wizard*

From the Control Center, right click on the Table Space icon to start the Create
Table Space Wizard dialog.

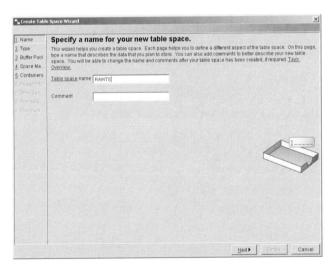

Fig. 9–6 *Specify a name for your new table space*

Enter the name of the table space and click **Next**.

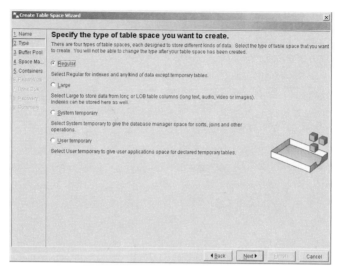

Fig. 9–7 *Specify the type of table space you want to create*

Select whether the table space will be a regular, long, or system temporary table space. Click **Next**.

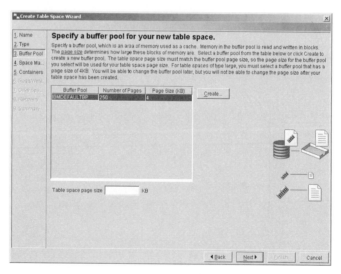

Fig. 9–8 *Specify a buffer pool for you new table space*

Select which buffer pool you want the table space to be associated with. Note, that you have the option of creating a new buffer pool, rather than accepting the default buffer pool. Click **Next**.

Fig. 9–9 *Select the space management system that you want to use*

Select whether the table space will be a SMS or DMS. Click **Next**.

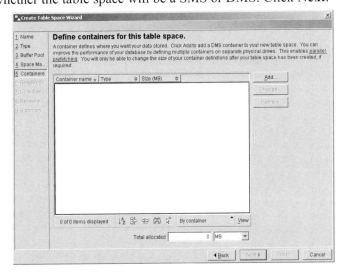

Fig. 9–10 *Defining a container for this table space*

In this example, a file will be the container. Click **Add**.

Fig. 9–11 *Define Container*

Select a file name that will be used. Click **OK**.

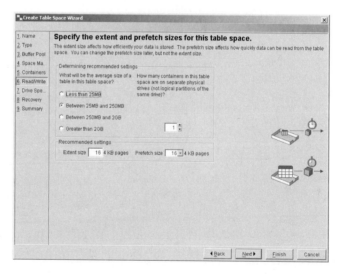

Fig. 9–12 *Specify the extent and prefetch sizes for this table space*

Select extent and prefetch size.Click **Next**.

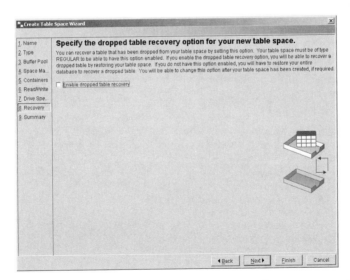

Fig. 9–13 *Describe hard disk specifications*

Select disk specifications that the optimizer will consider for optimizing data access. Click **Next**.

Fig. 9–14 *Specify the dropped table recovery option for your new table space*

This panel allows you the option of recovering a dropped table with a table space recovery (Regular table space only). Click **Next**.

Fig. 9–15 *Review the actions that will take place when you click Finish*

This final panel summarizes the options specified for creating this table space.

Fig. 9–16 *Show SQL*

One additional option is to select Show SQL, which gives the further option of saving the results to a script. As a DBA becomes more familiar with creating table spaces, the technique of submitting scripts will likely be less time consuming.

Table Space Maintenance

We have covered the creation of the DB2 storage objects to hold the database data. There are some additional commands and concepts to be aware of for maintaining them and monitoring changes in their size.

Database Files

The physical files that DB2 creates to support the database need to be protected from any direct access from outside of DB2.

* Do not make any direct changes to these files. They can only be accessed indirectly using the documented application programming interfaces (APIs) and by tools that implement those APIs.
* Do not remove or move these files.
* Using the security functions of the operating system, make sure all DB2 files and directories are secured. No one other than DB2 itself requires direct access to DB2 files and directories.
* The only supported means of backing up a database or table space is through the BACKUP API, including implementations of that API, such as those provided by the command line processor and Control Center.

Listing Table Spaces

To list basic or detailed information about table spaces, use the LIST TABLESPACES command. The syntax for this command is:

```
LIST TABLESPACES [SHOW DETAIL]
```

The basic information displayed by using this command is:

* Table space ID, the internal ID that DB2 uses for the table space
* Table space name
* Storage type (DMS or SMS)
* Table space type, which can be Regular (any data), Long, or Temporary
* State, a hexadecimal value indicating the current table space state

If the SHOW DETAIL option is used, the following additional details are normally shown:

- Total number of pages
- Number of usable pages
- Number of used pages
- Number of free pages
- High water mark (in pages)
- Page size (in bytes)
- Extent size (in bytes)
- Prefetch size (in pages)
- Extent size (in pages)
- Prefetch size (in pages)
- Number of containers

This information is important for informing you of how full the table spaces are and whether some action is required, such as adding new containers and running backups.

For examples of the output from this command, see the CREATE DATABASE command and the CREATE TABLESPACE statement in "Implementation Examples" on page 471.

Listing Table Space Containers

To list basic or detailed information about the table space containers for a specific table space, use the LIST TABLESPACE CONTAINERS command. The syntax for this command is:

```
LIST TABLESPACE CONTAINERS FOR tablespace_id [SHOW DETAIL]
```

The basic information displayed by using this command is:

- Container ID
- Container name
- Container type

When the SHOW DETAIL option is used the additional information shown is:

- Total number of pages
- Number of usable pages
- Accessible (yes or no)

Data Storage Management

Table Space States

DB2 maintains information about the states of table spaces and will not allow access using SQL (DML) statements if the table space is not in a *normal* state. Table space states are expressed in hexadecimal numbers. Sometimes, a table space can have more than one state associated with it. This will result in a combined hexadecimal number. There is a description of the state provided with the LIST TABLESPACES SHOW DETAIL command.

To view the table space state, issue the LIST TABLESPACES command and note the detailed explanation of the state. A table space is placed in a nonnormal state during load, backup, and recovery operations, or if placed in a quiesced condition via the QUIESCE TABLESPACE command. This command is not used very often by itself but is used by various DB2 utilities.

The LOAD command will place the table space in a LOAD PENDING state and leave the table space in this pending state until it has completed successfully. The RESTORE command will place the table space in ROLLFORWARD PENDING following a successful restore of the database. The table space will remain in this state until a successful ROLLFORWARD DATABASE command has been issued. The table space states are important to understand because if a table space is in any nonnormal state (not 0x0000) no SELECT, INSERT, UPDATE, or DELETE statements can be issued for any of the related table objects.

A list of some of the possible table space states follows:

- 0x0000 - Access to the table space is allowed (normal)
- 0x0001 - Quiesced share
- 0x0002 - Quiesced update
- 0x0004 - Quiesced exclusive
- 0x0008 - Load pending
- 0x0010 - Delete pending
- 0x0020 - Backup pending
- 0x0100 - Restore pending

For the further information about table space states, see the LIST TABLESPACES command in the *DB2 UDB V8.1 Command Reference*.

Note: If a container is not accessible, DB2 will place the associated table space in an OFFLINE state. Once the problem is resolved the ALTER TABLESPACE statement can be used with the SWITCH ONLINE option to make the table space available again.

System Catalog Information About Table Spaces

Table space information is kept in the SYSCAT.TABLESPACES catalog view. You are able to query this information using SQL. The layout of the view follows:

Table 9–2 *SYSCAT.TABLESPACES*

Column Name	Data Type	Nulls?	Description
TBSPACE	VARCHAR(18)		Name of table space
DEFINER	VARCHAR(128)		Authorization ID of table space definer
CREATE_TIME	TIMESTAMP		Creation time of table space
TBSPACEID	INTEGER		Internal table space identifier
TBSPACETYPE	CHAR(1)		The type of the table space: S = System managed space D = Database managed space
DATATYPE	CHAR(1)		Type of data that can be stored: A = All types of permanent data L = Long data only T = Temporary tables only
EXTENTSIZE	INTEGER		Size of extent, in pages of size PAGESIZE
PREFETCHSIZE	INTEGER		Number of pages of size PAGESIZE to be read when prefetch is performed
OVERHEAD	DOUBLE		Controller overhead and disk seek and latency time in milliseconds
TRANSFERRATE	DOUBLE		Time to read one page of size PAGESIZE into the buffer
PAGESIZE	INTEGER		Size (in bytes) of pages in the table space
NGNAME	VARCHAR(18)		Name of the database partition group for the table space
BUFFERPOOLID	INTEGER		ID of buffer pool used by this table space (1 indicates default buffer pool)
DROP_RECOVERY	CHAR(1)		N = table is not recoverable after a DROP TABLE statement Y = table is recoverable after a DROP TABLE statement
REMARKS	VARCHAR(254)	Yes	User-provided comment

The following columns are of interest for table spaces from the SYSCAT.TABLES catalog view.

Table 9–3 *SYSCAT.TABLES*

Column Name	Data Type	Nulls?	Description
TBSPACEID	SMALLINT		Internal identifier of the primary table space of the table
TBSPACE	VARCHAR(18)	Yes	Name of primary table space for the table
INDEX_TBSPACE	VARCHAR(18)	Yes	Name of the table space that holds all indexes for the table
LONG_TBSPACE	VARCHAR(18)	Yes	Name of the table space that holds all long data for the table

Adding Containers to DMS Table Spaces

You can add a container to an existing table space to increase its storage capacity with the ALTER TABLESPACE statement. The contents of the table space are then rebalanced across all containers. Access to the table space is not restricted during the rebalancing. If you need to add more than one container, you should add them at the same time either in one ALTER TABLESPACE statement or within the same transaction to prevent DB2 from rebalancing the containers more than once.

You should check how full the containers are by using the LIST TABLESPACES and LIST TABLESPACE CONTAINERS commands. Adding new containers should be done before the existing containers are almost or completely full. The new space across all the containers is not available until the rebalance is complete.

Adding a container that is smaller than existing containers results in a uneven distribution of data. This can cause parallel I/O operations, such as prefetching data, to perform less efficiently than they otherwise could on containers of equal size.

Adding a New Container Using the CLP

This is an example of how to add another container, in this case, a file container to the table space that was created in an earlier example.

```
ALTER TABLESPACE RAWTS
      ADD (FILE 'C:\TS\FILECON1.DAT' 8001)
      PREFETCHSIZE 32
      BUFFERPOOL IBMDEFAULTBP
```

Note how the ALTER TABLESPACE statement can be used to change the prefetch quantity and the buffer pool for the table space.

Note: Prior to V8, when a new container was added, existing data would be automatically redistributed or rebalanced across all available devices. The new BEGIN STRIPE option of the ALTER command allows the addition of new containers to a table space such that a rebalance does not occur.

Adding a New Container Using the Control Center

Alternatively, you can also use the Control Center to add a container. In the list of table spaces, right-click on the table space you wish to alter.

Fig. 9–17 *Control Center - Choosing a table space to alter*

The Alter Table Space panel is displayed:

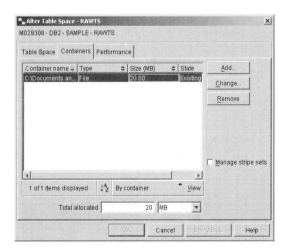

Fig. 9–18 *Alter table space*

Then click on the Containers tab and then **Add**. You can then enter the details of the new container. Options that cannot be changed have been grayed out.

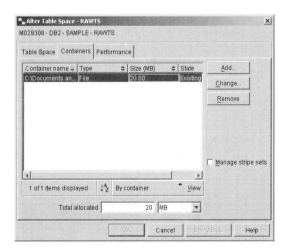

Fig. 9–19 *Define Container*

After defining the additional containers, the Alter Table Space panel displays the following:

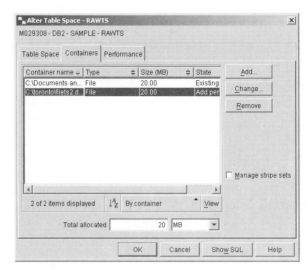

Fig. 9–20 *Alter table space (2)*

Select **OK** to add the container and DB2 will automatically rebalance the data across the containers.

Summary

This chapter discussed the physical placement of objects in DB2 databases. The types of objects discussed included:

- *Buffer pools* - Areas of main memory allocated to cache table and index data pages as they are being read or written to the hard disk.
- *Table spaces* - DB2 objects that isolate the logical definition of the table from the details of the physical storage. The storage types available are SMS (System Managed Space) and DMS (Database Managed Space). SMS is a storage model where space is acquired when needed. Its main benefit is its flexibility. DMS is preallocated storage space. Its main benefit is that it generally performs better than SMS. Regular table spaces can store any DB2 data. Optionally, indexes and long data can be placed in their own table spaces.
- *Containers* - Physical storage objects. They can be directories, files, or devices. Containers can be only assigned to one table space. Table spaces can consist of multiple containers.
- *Extents* - Units of space within a container. DB2 can use these units to transfer data between disk and buffer pools. Extents range in size from 2 to 256 pages. Once defined, the extent size for a table space cannot be changed.
- *Pages* - Blocks of storage that hold the rows of data. They can be either 4, 8, 16, or 32 KB in size. Buffer pool storage is divided into pages.
- *Large Object* (LOB) data is stored differently than other data types in DB2. LOB data objects are stored in 64 MB areas, broken up into segments. LOB allocation objects maintain allocation and free space information about large objects.

We discussed planning and design considerations for the DB2 physical environment:

- SMP systems have the capability of performing query and I/O operations in parallel.
- DB2 can operate in a single partition, single or multiple processor (SMP) environment. Multiple partition environments are also possible on SMP machines and across a cluster of SMP machines.
- The way DB2 is configured to use the available memory resources is critical to its performance characteristics.
- Placing containers on separate disks gives DB2 the opportunity to perform parallel I/O operations by using sequential prefetching of pages.
- When a database is created, the system catalog table space SYSCATSPACE is created along with the temporary table space TEMPSPACE1 and user table space USERSPACE1.

- The choice of an extent size for a table space depends on factors such as the size and type of tables in the table space and the type of access to the tables.
- The mapping of tables to table spaces depends on factors such as the amount of data and the type of data in the table.

We then looked at how to implement, monitor, and change the objects via DB2 commands, SQL statements, and the Control Center.

CHAPTER **10**

Maintaining Data

- ◆ EXPORTING DATA
- ◆ IMPORTING DATA
- ◆ LOADING DATA
- ◆ ANALYZING DATA PLACEMENT
- ◆ REORGANIZING DATA
- ◆ GATHERING STATISTICS

*I*n this chapter, the techniques of how to populate and extract DB2 data using the LOAD, IMPORT, and EXPORT utilities will be examined. The differences between these utilities will be examined along with the scenarios that would favor using one over another.

Additional maintenance topics will include examining the physical data placement and gathering statistics. Some of the utilities examined will include REORGCHK, REORG, RUNSTATS, and REBIND.

Moving Data

Whenever data is extracted or inserted into the database, particular care must be taken to check the format of the data. Sometimes a DBA may spend more time correcting the data format than actually inserting or extracting the data. To assist the DBA in this regard, DB2 supports various data formats for extraction and insertion. The formats include:

- DEL - delimited ASCII files
- ASC - fixed-length ASCII files
- IXF - Integrated Exchange Format files
- WSF - Worksheet Format files

Delimited ASCII Files

This file type, used extensively in Relational Database Management Systems (RDBMS) and other software packages, makes use of delimiters. A delimiter is a character that is used to identify the beginning or end of a data element. Some of the most important delimiters used in delimited ASCII (DEL) files include:

- *Character* delimiter - As the name suggests, this is used to mark the beginning and end of a character field. By default, DB2 uses the double quote (") character as a character delimiter. The DBA can optionally override this default and cause DB2 to make use of another character as the character delimiter.
- *Column* delimiter - This delimiter is used to mark the end of a field. The default column delimiter used is the comma (,) character, but the DBA may choose another character to use.
- *Row* delimiter - Used to mark the end of a record or row. DB2 assumes the new line character X'0A' (commonly used on UNIX operating systems to mark a new line) to be the row delimiter. On Windows, the carriage return/linefeed characters X'0D0A' are used by DB2 as the row delimiter.

In DEL files, the rows are streamed into the file one after the other. They are separated with the *row delimiter*. The fields in the row are separated from one another by a *column delimiter*.

Character fields are encapsulated by two character delimiters.

Numeric fields are represented by their ASCII equivalent. A period (.) character is used to indicate the decimal point, if required. Float values are represented with the E notation, negative values with a leading minus (-) character, and positive values with a plus (+) sign.

To illustrate, a table named NAMES contains the following data:

Table 10–1 *Names Table*

EMP_NO	NAME	LASTNAME	DEPT_NO
10001	George	Baklarz	307
10002	Bill	Wong	204
10003	Beverly	Crusher	305

Assume the EMP_NO column is of type INTEGER and all the other columns are of a CHARACTER type. If the column delimiter is the comma (,), the row delimeter is the linefeed character and the character delimiter is the double quote (") character, a DEL file containing the data would consist of a datastream that looks like this:

```
10001,"George","Baklarz","307"
10002,"Bill","Wong","204"
10003,"Beverly","Crusher","305"
```

When choosing the column delimiter and the row delimiter of a DEL file, be careful not to use characters that are used in the datastream.

Non-Delimited ASCII Files

Non-delimited ASCII (ASC) files are sometimes referred to as fixed-length ASCII files. This file consists of a stream of ASCII characters of data values organized by row and column. Rows in the data stream are separated by a carriage return/line feed or new line character, and all column values are of fixed length (if a record length is specified, there is no need for the row delimiter). All variable-length character types are padded with blanks and represented using their maximum length. There are no column or character delimiters. Using the same example as above, an ASC file representing the data in the NAMES table would look like this:

```
10001George Baklarz307
10002Bill   Wong   204
10003BeverlyCrusher305
```

 Note: The columns are aligned in non-delimited ASCII files.

IXF Files

Integrated Exchange Format (IXF) files are used to move data among DB2 databases. For example, you can export a data file from a host database and use it as input to populate a table in a database on a DB2 server. In general, an IXF file consists of an unbroken sequence of variable-length records. Numeric values are stored as packed decimal or binary values, depending on the data type. Character values are stored in their ASCII representation, and only the used part of variable-length character types are stored. An IXF file also has the table definition stored within it along with the data.

Note: If the host table contains packed fields, you will have to convert these fields before transferring the file to a DB2 database. To perform this conversion, create a view in the host database for all the columns that you require. A view automatically forms character fields out of the packed fields. From the view, you can export the required data as an IXF file.

IXF files cannot be edited by using a normal text editor.

An advantage of using this type of format is that the table definition is included in the file, so a table and its indexes can be recreated and populated with this file format.

Worksheet Format Files

Lotus 1-2-3 and Symphony products use this type of file format to extract or import data. Although different releases have new added functions in their release-specific file types, the Worksheet Format (WSF) only uses a subset of this functionality accepted by most versions of these products. This format is not used to move data from one DB2 table to another.

Data Movement Utilities

A set of utilities is provided with DB2 to populate tables or to extract data from tables. These utilities enable you to easily move large amounts of data into or out of DB2 databases. The speed of these operations is very important. When working with large databases and tables, extracting or inserting new data may take a long time.

In this section, three DB2 utilities will be examined. The various options for each utility will be reviewed to explore their function and performance benefit. These utilities are:

- EXPORT
- IMPORT
- LOAD

The Export Utility

The EXPORT utility is used to extract data from a table into a file. Data can be extracted into several different file formats, which can be used by either the IMPORT or LOAD utilities to populate tables. These files can also be used by other software products such as spreadsheets, word processors, and other RDBMSs to populate tables or generate reports.

You must already be connected to the database from which data is to be exported, and you must have SYSADM or DBADM authority, or CONTROL or SELECT privilege on the tables or views you access during the export.

Here is the syntax of the EXPORT utility:

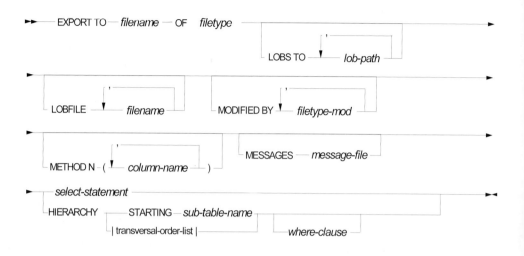

Using the EXPORT Command

To export all the data from a table NAMES into a file NAMES.DEL of type DEL using all the default options, one would use the command:

```
EXPORT TO names.del OF DEL SELECT * FROM NAMES
```

Names	
First_Name	**Last_Name**
George	Baklarz
Bill	Wong
Beverly	Crusher

export to names.del
of del
select * from names

names.del

"George","Baklarz"
"Bill","Wong"
"Beverly","Crusher"

Fig. 10–1 *Simple export*

Some of the key parameters to the EXPORT command include (see the *DB2 UDB V8.1 Command Reference* for further detail):

- TO filename - specifies the name of the file to which data is to be exported.
- OF filetype - specifies the format of the data in the output file: DEL, WSF,

IXF.

- METHOD N column-name - specifies one or more column names to be used in the output file, valid only for WSF and IXF files.
- select-statement - specifies the SELECT statement that will return the data to be exported.
- MESSAGES message-file - specifies the file where warning and error messages will be written, otherwise the messages are written to standard output.

Supported File Formats

The export utility allows the user to export data into one of three supported file types: IXF, DEL, or WSF.

To specify the file type, use the OF FILETYPE clause. For example, data from the PRODUCT table can be exported to a file PRODUCT.IXF of type IXF by using the command options (note that other options can also be specified):

```
EXPORT TO product.ixf OF IXF... SELECT... FROM product...
```

Although the ASC file type is not supported with the EXPORT command, the user can still generate a data file of type ASC by modifying the SELECT statement. For example, if two columns named FIRST_NAME defined as CHAR(10) and EMP_NO as CHAR(5) are to be exported to a file of type ASC, the user can specify the DEL file type and modify the select statement to:

```
EXPORT.. OF DEL.. SELECT first_name CONCAT emp_no FROM...
```

The output of the command is shown below:

```
"George     10001"
"Bill       10002"
"Beverly    10003"
```

When importing the data into a table, the column start position of the first column should be given as 2, thus ignoring the double quote (") character in the first position. Numeric values can be cast to a character type and then concatenated to the other columns.

Date Format Modification

For DEL and WSF files, the default format used for date values is *yyyymmdd*. The user has the option of changing the format to the ISO standard representation *yyyy-mm-dd* by specifying the DATESISO file type modifier with the EXPORT command:

```
EXPORT... MODIFIED BY DATESISO...
```

Delimiters Used with DEL Files

The default character delimiter is the double quote (") character. To override this, specify the CHARDEL file type modifier. For example, to use the asterisk (*) character as the character delimiter:

```
EXPORT... MODIFIED BY CHARDEL*
```

 Note: The same character cannot be used for more than one delimiter in the file.

Handling Decimal Columns

When exporting to DEL files, decimal data types are exported with a decimal point (.) character. Leading and trailing zeros and a plus (+) or minus (-) sign are inserted before (or after) the value. For example, a value of 22.5 in a column named AMOUNT defined as DECIMAL(8,2) will be exported as:

```
+000022.50
```

To change the decimal point delimiter, specify the DECPT file type modifier:

```
EXPORT... MODIFIED BY DECPT^
```

The user can also change the way that positive decimal values are exported. By default, a plus (+) character is added in front of the value to identify it as a positive, value. By using the DECPLUSBLANK filetype modifier, no plus (+) will be added to positive values. Negative values are unaffected.

```
EXPORT... MODIFIED BY DECPLUSBLANK
```

Derived Column Names When Exporting

In some cases, the user may want to export data derived from one or more columns into a single column in the output file. For example, the SELECT statement may include a derived column defined as "Salary minus Deductions." In this case, a number will be generated and used as the name of the derived column. There are two ways to force the column to be renamed. You can do this for IXF and WSF formats only.

First, you can use the AS clause in the SELECT statement. In our example, "Salary minus Deductions" can be written as SALARY - DEDUCTIONS AS PAY. The name of the derived column will now be PAY.

```
EXPORT... SELECT SALARY - DEDUCTION AS PAY... FROM...
```

Alternatively, you can specify the METHOD N option followed by the names to be used for the columns, in the order in which they are selected. In our example, if the first column is the "Salary minus Deductions" column, the first name specified after the METHOD N option would be PAY:

```
EXPORT... METHOD N ('PAY',...)...
        SELECT salary - deduction,... FROM...
```

An IXF data file can be used to create a table in another database by using the table definition stored in the IXF file itself. By changing the names of the columns when exporting to the IXF file, the subsequent table can be created with the desired column names when the file is imported into the target database.

Capturing Error and Warning Messages

Use the MESSAGES option to specify a file that should be used to record all error and warning messages:

```
EXPORT... MESSAGES X:\Error_logs\Exports\Exp1.txt...
```

Exporting Large Object Data

When exporting tables that contain LOB data types, the user has two options of how the LOB values can be exported. The first 32 KB of LOB data can be included in the target file with the regular table data, or the LOB can be stored separately, in a file. If the user decides on the first option, there are no extra parameters that need to be specified with the EXPORT command. However, only LOBs of 32 KB or less should be exported in this way. If a LOB value exceeds 32 KB in size, it will be truncated, and only the first 32 KB will be exported into the file.

For the export utility to export each LOB value to a seperate file, the user must specify where the files are to be put and what names are to be used. This is done by specifing three parameters:

- LOBSINFILE - A file type modifier, which when specified, informs the EXPORT utility that all LOB values are to be exported into separate files (DB2 can concatenate multiple LOBs in a file). If it is not specified, the export utility will ignore all other parameters related to exporting LOBs into separate files.
- LOBS TO lob-path specifies the path or paths where the LOB values will be exported as individual files. If the first path specified becomes full, the second will be used, and so on. When specifying the path name, make sure it ends with a "\" character for Windows or "/" for UNIX.
- LOBFILE filename tells the EXPORT utility what file name to use for the files. A three-digit number will be generated and added to the filename as an extension to ensure uniqueness.

In exporting LOB data from a table named EMP_PHOTO to a file named EMP_PHOTO.DEL and its LOB values to the directories D:\LOBDIR1 and D:\LOBDIR2 and the LOB file name to be used is EMP_PHOTO_LOB, the EXPORT command would be written as follows:

```
EXPORT TO Emp_photo.del OF DEL LOBS TO
    D:\lobdir1\,D:\lobdir2\
    LOBFILE Emp_photo_lob... MODIFIED BY LOBSINFILE
  SELECT * FROM Emp_photo
```

The first LOB files exported would be named as follows:

```
d:\lobdir1\emp_photo_lob.001
d:\lobdir1\emp_photo_lob.002
d:\lobdir1\emp_photo_lob.003
.....and so on........
```

If the D:\LOBDIR1 directory becomes full, the D:\LOBDIR2 directory will be used.

Exporting Typed Tables

There arc two ways in which data can be exported from typed tables. The first way is to treat the typed table as a normal table by using a SELECT statement.

For example, if a user wants to export rows from the EMPLOYEE table and no records from any subtables defined under it, then the ONLY option in the SELECT statement should be used:

```
EXPORT... SELECT... FROM ONLY(db2admin.Employee)...
```

If all the records in the EMPLOYEE table should be returned, including records from subtables under it, do not specify the ONLY option in the SELECT statement:

```
EXPORT... SELECT... FROM db2admin.Employee...
```

Another option is to export some or all tables in the hierarchy. The user needs to specify two things: which subtables to export and the order in which they are to be exported. This order is referred to as the *traversal order*. Figure 10–2 shows a table hierarchy.

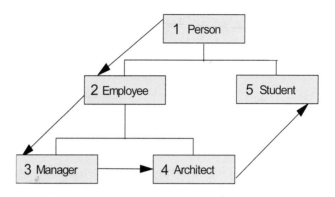

Fig. 10–2 *Exporting a table hierarchy - Traversal order*

The default traversal order starts from the highest table in the hierarchy – in our example, the PERSON table. The next table in the list can be either STUDENT or EMPLOYEE, depending on which of the two was created first. Assume that the EMPLOYEE table was created first. The next table in the list could be MANAGER or ARCHITECT; this is also dependent on which was created earlier. Assume the MANAGER table was created before the ARCHITECT table. There are no tables defined under MANAGER, so the ARCHITECT table will be the next table in the traversal order. Because the ARCHITECT table has no tables defined under it, the next in the list will be the STUDENT table.

It is important to realize that databases with the same table hierarchies may have two distinctly different default traversal orders. Make a note of the traversal order in which the tables in the hierarchy are exported because the same order must be used to import the tables.

To use the default traversal order, specify the subtable to start the export from after the STARTING option, in our case, the root table of the hierarchy, DB2ADMIN.PERSON:

```
EXPORT... HIERARCHY STARTING db2admin.Person
```

To specify another traversal order to use for the export, list the order of the tables instead of the STARTING table_name option. All subtables must be listed.

```
EXPORT... HIERARCHY (Person,Student,
   Employee,Architect,Manager)...
```

If rows are exported as part of a hierarchy, the first column in the output file will be a numeric value identifying the subtable to which the exported row belongs. The numeric value is derived from the position of the subtable in the traversal order list as defined with the EXPORT command, "1" being the first table in the list.

When exporting data as part of a hierarchy (or a result export for that matter), an optional WHERE clause also can be used to qualify the rows to export. For example, to export all data from the employees, managers, and architects working in the Sales Department, the following command could be used:

```
EXPORT... HIERARCHY STARTING Employee
   WHERE dept = 'Sales'
```

Using the Control Center to Export a Table

The Control Center provides an easy interface to the EXPORT utility. To invoke it, select the table that needs to be exported and right-click on it. Select the **Export** option as shown in Fig. 10–3.

Once invoked, the user may specify the different options as discussed above. The Control Center will also be used to demonstrate EXPORT by showing how a user can export a table named PRODUCT to a DEL file. The output file name and message file name are specified as: C:\TORONTO\PROJECT.DEL and D:\TORONTO\PROJECT.MSG.

Maintaining Data

Fig. 10–3 *Invoking the EXPORT utility from the Control Center*

The Export Table panel is displayed:

Fig. 10–4 *The EXPORT utility*

As indicated by the SELECT statement in Fig. 10–4, all rows and columns will be exported.

If the user chooses either DEL or WSF file types, modifiers specific to these file types may be specified by clicking on the **Options** button next to the file type. Fig. 10–5 shows the file type options that can be specified for DEL files.

Export Delimited Options

Code page (CODEPAGE)

☑ Prefix positive decimal values with a blank (DECPLUSBLANK)

☑ Use ISO date format (DATESISO)

☐ Suppress recognition of double character delimiters (NODOUBLEDEL)

Column delimiter (COLDEL)

Character string delimiter (CHARDEL)

Decimal point character (DECPT)

OK   Cancel   Help

Fig. 10–5 *Changing the DEL EXPORT options*

The Columns tab (see Fig. 10–4) can be used to specify the column names to use in the exported file (IXF or WSF only). If not specified, the column names in the SELECT statement will be used.

If LOBs are to be exported into separate files, use the Large Objects tab to specify the paths and filenames to use.

Once all the information is captured in the relevant panels, the user may opt to run the EXPORT command by clicking on the **OK** button. Alternatively, the user may choose to look at the command that will be executed. Fig. 10–7 shows the command generated to export the PROJECT table. The user may also choose to save the command to a script file to be executed at a later time.

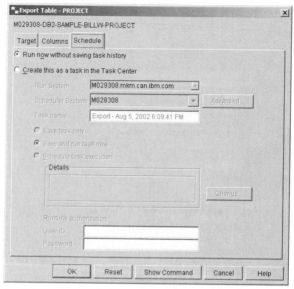

Fig. 10–6 *Schedule Tab*

If the tools catalog has been created, this panel will give you the option to schedule the this task, otherwise, you have the option to create the tools catalog from the panel that is displayed if the tools catalog has not been created. Type in a valid user id and password and click OK.

Invoking the EXPORT utility from the Control Center

Fig. 10–7 *The EXPORT command generated*

EXPORT Considerations

The following information is required when exporting data:

- A SELECT statement (or hierarchy selection clause for typed tables) specifying the data to be exported

- The path and name of the file that will store the exported data
- The format the data will be written in (IXF, DEL, or WSF)

 Note: An ASC format can be generated by translating and concatenating the columns in the SELECT statement.

The following information is optional when exporting data:

- A message file name
- New column names when exporting to IXF or WSF files
- A file type modifier to specify additional formatting when creating DEL and WSF files
- File names and paths for exported LOB columns

Performance of the EXPORT Utility

When using the EXPORT utility, a DBA should make sure that the utility extracts the data efficiently. The SELECT statement used with this utility has the greatest effect on performance. There are some tools (like Visual Explain) available in DB2 that can be used to evaluate the performance of a SELECT statement.

The IMPORT Utility

The IMPORT utility inserts data from an input file into a table or view. You can either replace data or append data to the table or view if it already contains data.

With the IMPORT utility, you can specify how to add or replace the data into the target table. You must be connected to the database to use the utility, and if you want to import data into a new table using the CREATE option, you must have SYSADM or DBADM authorities or CREATETAB privilege for the database. To replace data in a table or view, you must have SYSADM or DBADM authorities or CONTROL privilege for the table or view. If you want to add data to an existing table or view, you must have SELECT and INSERT privileges for the table or view.

 Note: If the existing table contains a primary key or unique constraint that is referenced by a foreign key in another table, data cannot be replaced, only appended.

Here is the syntax of the IMPORT utility:

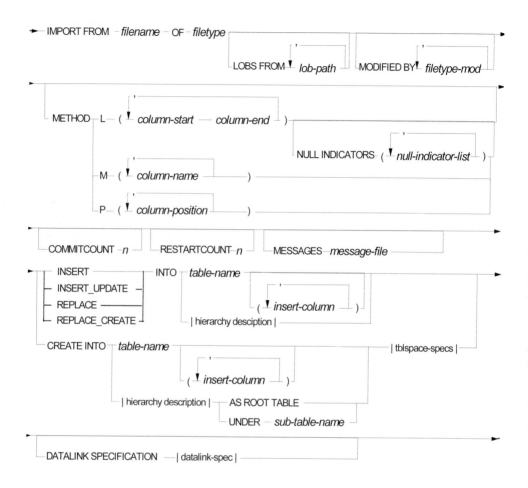

Using the IMPORT Command

To import data from a file named `Names.del` of type DEL into an empty table named `NAMES` using all the default options, use the following command:

```
IMPORT FROM Names.del OF DEL INSERT INTO Names
```

Fig. 10-8 *Simple import*

In this section, the use of the IMPORT command will be examined by looking at some of its most useful functions. Some of the options or parameters used with the IMPORT command are identical to the EXPORT command and will not be duplicated here. Some of the key parameters to the IMPORT command include (see the *DB2 UDB V8.1 Command Reference* for further details):

- INSERT - adds new rows to the data table without changing the current data.
- INSERT_UPDATE - adds new rows to the target table, or updates existing rows with matching primary keys.
- REPLACE - deletes all existing data from the table and inserts the imported data.
- REPLACE_CREATE - creates the table and index definitions and row contents if the table does not exist, otherwise, it deletes all existing data from the table and inserts the imported data without changing the table or index definitions.
- COMMITCOUNT n - specifies a COMMIT after every n records are imported.
- CREATE - creates the table definition and inserts new rows.
- IN tablespace-name - specifies the table space in which the table will be created.
- INDEX IN tablespace-name - specifies the table space in which any indexes on the table will be created, only for DMS table spaces.
- INTO table-name - specifies the table in which data is to be imported.
- METHOD L |N - L specifies the start and end column numbers from which to import data (numbering starts at 1, for ASC files only). N specifies the names of the columns being imported (IXF files only).

File Types Supported

The file types supported are IXF, DEL, WSF, and ASC. To specify the file type, use the OF FILE-TYPE clause. For example, a file named PRODUCT.IXF of type IXF can be imported by using the command:

```
IMPORT FROM Product.ixf OF IXF...
```

Insert Mode

If the data in the source file is to be added to the data in the target table, the INSERT option should be used. For example, if the order of the columns in the exported file is the same as the order of the columns in the target table, the following command will insert the new rows into the existing table named PRODUCT:

```
IMPORT... INSERT INTO Product
```

If the order of the columns in the source file is not the same as the order in which columns in the target table, then the order of the columns must be specified after the table name. For example, if the Product table has three columns named PROD_NO, PRICE, and DESCRIPTION in that order, and the source file contains the three columns in the order PRICE, PROD_NO, DESCRIPTION, the following command needs to be specified:

```
IMPORT... INSERT INTO Product(Price,Prod_no,Description)
```

Insert and Update Mode

Sometimes a DBA receives a file that contains updated data for a table. Some of the rows in the file do not exist in the target table, however, most do. Some of the existing data needs to be updated to reflect the new values. For example, the DBA receives a file named Product.del that contains the new prices for some of the existing products as well as for new products. He cannot *insert* all the new data because it contains values for some existing products nor can he *replace* all the data because some of the valid product values do not yet exist in the table. The only option is to use the INSERT_UPDATE option of the IMPORT command. This will *insert* all the new rows and *update* existing rows to reflect the new values.

The IMPORT utility uses the primary key and unique constraints defined on the table to determine if a row exists and whether it should be updated or inserted. In our example, the PRODUCT table has a primary key value defined as the product number (PROD_NO). In Fig. 10–9, four rows in the input file and three rows in the table before the import are shown.

Product.del

| 00001,15.00,"Book" |
| 00005,3.00,"Pen" |
| 00003,35.00,"Lamp - Green" |
| 00004,20.00,"Table" |

Products table (before)

Prod_no	Price	Description
00001	10.00	Book
00002	20.00	Table
00003	30.00	Lamp

IMPORT FROM Product.del of DEL...
INSERT_UPDATE INTO Product

Products table (after)

Prod_no	Price	Description
00001	15.00	Book
00002	20.00	Table
00003	30.00	Lamp - Green
00004	20.00	Table
00005	3.00	Pen

Fig. 10–9 *Using IMPORT with INSERT_UPDATE option*

The IMPORT command is invoked with the INSERT_UPDATE option. The first record in the input file will cause the first row in the table to be updated. The reason for this is that the PROD_NO value supplied in the file matches an existing row in the table. As shown in the PRODUCTS table after the import, the value associated with the PRICE column has been updated to show the new price.

The second record in the input file has a PROD_NO value that does not exist in the PRODUCT table before the import. It is therefore treated as a new row that needs to be inserted into the table.

The third record updates both the description and the price of an existing row.

The fourth record in the input file is inserted as a new row because the PROD_NO value does not match an existing row in the table, even though the PRICE and DESCRIPTION do match an existing row in the table.

Replace Mode

To replace existing data in the table, you can specify the REPLACE option. This option is not valid if the table for which data needs to be replaced has a primary key that is referenced by a foreign key in another table. This is to enforce referential integrity. Assume that the PRODUCT table did not have any referential dependencies and that it is desired to replace the existing data with data in a file named PROD-UCT.IXF. The following would be specified with the IMPORT command:

```
IMPORT FROM Product.ixf OF IXF... REPLACE INTO Product
```

Replace and Create Mode

When an IXF file is created using the EXPORT command, the table structure and definition is stored in it. The IMPORT utility can make use of the structure to recreate the table and its indexes. There are two ways to recreate the table. If the table already exists, it can be recreated by using the REPLACE_CREATE option. For example, if a table named Product exists and is to be recreated when importing new data, the IMPORT command can be invoked as follows. Note that this does not change the table definition – it only deletes all the data before doing the import. If the table does not exist and this option is used, the table will be created.

```
IMPORT FROM Product.ixf of IXF...
   REPLACE_CREATE INTO Product...
```

 Note: If the PRODUCT table has a primary key defined that is referenced by another table's foreign key, the REPLACE_CREATE option can not be used.

If the PRODUCT table does not exist prior to the import, the CREATE option can be used to create it. For example:

```
IMPORT FROM Product.ixf of IXF...
   CREATE INTO Product...
```

When creating a table in this way, a user can also specify the table space in which it should be created. Optionally, the index and long table spaces can also be specified. For example, assume the source table PRODUCT has two indexes and contains long data. This example has a new table named PRODUCT created in an existing table space named DMS1 of type DMS, its indexes in table space INDEXDMS1 of type

DMS, and its long data in table space LONG1 of type DMS. To accomplish this, the following command would be issued on the command line:

```
IMPORT FROM Product.ixf OF IXF...
   CREATE INTO Product IN Dms1
   INDEX IN Indexdms1 LONG IN Long1
```

Forcing Intermediate Commits

By default, the IMPORT utility will only issue a commit at the end of a successful import. If the utility fails during its execution, all the changes to the table will be rolled back, so that it will seem as if the import never took place. The user may also direct the IMPORT utility to issue commit statements after a certain number of rows are successfully imported. If an error occurs during the import, only the changes since the last commit will be rolled back.

To specify the frequency of such intermediate commit statements, use the COMMITCOUNT option followed by the number of rows to be imported before a COMMIT is issued. (For more details on using IMPORT and committing records, please refer to the *DB2 UDB V8.1 Command Reference*.) For example, if a COMMIT is to be issued after every 50 records processed from the input file, the following command would be issued:

```
IMPORT... COMMITCOUNT 50...
```

Before and after the commit is executed, a message is written to the message file (if defined) or to the screen. The number of records read and committed are recorded in the message file. In the event of a failure, the DBA can find out how many records have been processed and which how many have not been imported by looking at the message file.

All changes to data are logged in the transaction log files, and they have to stay active for as long as they contain records of uncommitted transactions. The amount of available active log file space can be limited; therefore, an import of a large file may fail if the COMMITCOUNT option is not used. In the case of a failure, all the changes may be rolled back or an automatic commit done based on the type of IMPORT being done (see the *DB2 UDB V8.1 Command Reference* for details). It is highly recommended that this option be used when importing data.

Maintaining Data

Restarting a Failed Import

If an IMPORT operation that did not specify COMMITCOUNT fails, it can be restarted after fixing the problem that caused it to fail. The type of IMPORT being done will dictate the recovery needed.

If the IMPORT operation is invoked with the COMMITCOUNT option and subsequently fails, it can be restarted by using the RESTARTCOUNT option. This is used to tell the IMPORT utility to skip a certain number of records at the beginning of the file but to import the remainder.

For example, a file named PRODUCT.DEL was imported into a table named Product by making use of the COMMITCOUNT 50 option. During the processing of the IMPORT command, the user accidently terminated the import session. This caused the import to fail half way through. The following extract is from the messages file:

```
SQL3109N The utility is beginning to load data from file
"Product.del".

SQL3221W...Begin COMMIT WORK. Input Record Count = "50".

SQL3222W...COMMIT of any database changes was successful.

SQL3221W...Begin COMMIT WORK. Input Record Count = "100".

SQL3222W...COMMIT of any database changes was successful.

SQL3005N Processing was interrupted.

SQL3110N The utility has completed processing. "100" rows were
read from the input file.
```

This shows that the first 100 records were committed. By restarting the IMPORT utility with the RESTARTCOUNT 100 option, the first 100 records found in the input file are skipped. Processing will continue starting with record 101 of the input file.

```
IMPORT FROM Product.del OF DEL...
    COMMITCOUNT 50 RESTARTCOUNT 100...
    INTO Product...
```

Importing ASC Files

When importing a file of type ASC, the IMPORT utility needs to be told where the column values start and end. The starting position and the ending position for all columns to be imported must be specified. This is done by making use of the

METHOD L modifier. In Fig. 10–10, an input file of type ASC is shown. It consists of three columns that match the type and length of the three columns of the PRODUCT table. The first is the PROD_NO column, which is of type CHAR(5); the second is the PRICE column of type DECIMAL(8,2); and the last is DESCRIPTION of type VARCHAR(10). All blanks will be represented with the character "~".

import from product.asc of asc
method L (1 5,6 14, 15 24)
insert into product

Fig. 10–10 *Import using METHOD L*

Selecting Columns to Import

Sometimes a data file contains more columns than required by the target table. If the file is of type IXF or DEL, column numbers can be used to import it by specifying the METHOD P option. For example, a DEL file contains data in four columns, PROD_NO, PRICE, SUPPLIER, and DESCRIPTION. The target table PRODUCT only requires the columns PROD_NO, PRICE, and DESCRIPTION (columns 1, 2, and 4 of the input file). To import the data into the PRODUCT table, the following command can be used:

```
IMPORT FROM Product.del OF DEL... METHOD P (1,2,4)...
INTO Product(Prod_no,Price,Description)...
```

Importing Large Objects

LOBs can be exported as part of the table data in the exported file or in separate files. If the LOB data is in the same file as the rest of the table data, it can be imported without any extra parameters being specified with the IMPORT utility.

If the LOB values are exported into separate files, the IMPORT utility needs two things: the directory or directories where the LOB files can be located and the file names of the LOB files.

Since the file names of the LOB files are stored in the exported file, the user does not need to specify them. To specify the source directory, use the LOBS FROM option followed by one or more directories that will serve as the source directories. Then specify the LOBSINFILE file-type modifier. If the LOBSINFILE modifier is not specified, the LOBS FROM option will be ignored.

For example, a table named EMP_PHOTO was exported to a file named EMP_PHOTO.DEL of type DEL, and its LOB files were exported with filenames EMP_PHOTO_LOB.XXX into two directories. The EMP_PHOTO.DEL file is copied to another database server. The EMP_PHOTO_LOB.XXX files in the first directory on the source database server are copied to the D:\LOBDIRA directory, and the EMP_PHOTO_LOB.XXX files in the second directory are copied to the D:\LOBDIRB directory. To import the data into the EMPLOYEE_PHOTO table in the target database, the following options should be specified with the IMPORT command.

```
IMPORT FROM emp_photo.del OF DEL
   LOBS FROM d:\lobdirA\,d:\lobdirB\
   MODIFIED BY LOBSINFILE... INTO employee_photo...
```

Note: When specifying the path, it must include the "\" character at the end for a Windows path or "/" when it is a UNIX path.

Importing Typed Tables

When importing data into a hierarchical structure, the user can specify the traversal order, which must match the order used when it was exported. It may be that the hierarchy structure at the destination differs from the one the data was exported from. For example, an extra table named TEMP_EMPLOYEES was created under the EMPLOYEE table as in our example. In this case, the default traversal order and the number and/or names of the tables are different than those in the original design. The user can compensate for these differences by specifying a list of subtables to import into.

For example, an exported file contains the data associated with the Employee and the Manager subtables only. The default traversal order can be used and imported with the command options:

```
IMPORT... (Employee,Manager)
   IN HIERARCHY STARTING Employee...
```

The traversal order could also be specified as:

```
IMPORT... (Employee,Manager)
    IN HIERARCHY (Employee,Manager)
```

If all the subtables named in the traversal order are to be imported, the ALL TABLES option could be used. In our example, this is only the EMPLOYEE and MANAGER tables:

```
IMPORT... ALL TABLES IN HIERARCHY (Employee,Manager)...
```

To import all tables including the EMPLOYEE table using the default traversal order, issue the command as follows:

```
IMPORT... ALL TABLES IN HIERARCHY STARTING Employee...
```

 Note: If one of the records in the compound group cannot be inserted, all will be rejected. Use this option only if you know the data to be correct.

Invoking Import Using the Control Center

The IMPORT utility can also be invoked from the Control Center. Select the target table and click the right mouse button, then select the **Import** option. Fig. 10–11 shows the File tab of the Import Notebook. This next example will demonstrate the use of the Import Notebook.

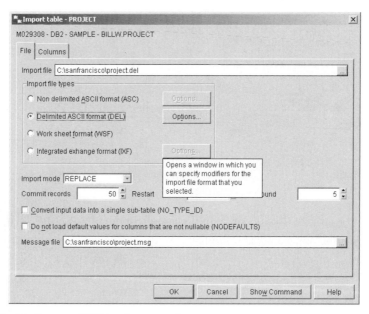

Fig. 10–11 *Import GUI in the control center*

The DBA is asked to import a file named C:\SANFRANCISCO\PROJECT.DEL into an existing table named PROJECT. The table is empty, so all the data in the DEL file has to be inserted. The DBA chooses the file C:\SANFRANCISCO\PROJECT.MSG as the import message file. Since a large number of records are to be imported, the DBA decides to use a COMMITCOUNT of 50 to make sure the log files do not fill up. He also decides to use the COMPOUND=5 file type modifier. This will cause five records to be grouped together when inserted. It will improve the performance of the import.

Fig. 10–12 *Delimited Options*

Fig. 10–12 shows the file-type-specific options for DEL files. The DATESISO option has been selected, since the file was produced with this option.

Fig. 10–13 *Columns Tab*

The Columns tab can be used to specify which columns are present in the source file. The user can also use it to specify the order of the columns and new names to use if the file is an IXF file and if the table is to be created with the CREATE or REPLACE_CREATE options.

If LOBs are to be imported from separate files, fill in the field at the bottom of this panel.

Once all the information is captured in the relevant panels, the user may opt to run the IMPORT command by clicking on the **OK** button. Alternatively, the user may choose to look at the command that is to be executed. Fig. 10–14 shows the command generated to import the file into the PROJECT table. The user may also choose to save the command to a script file to be executed at a later time.

Fig. 10–14 *The IMPORT command generated*

IMPORT Considerations

The following information is required when importing data into a table or view:

- The path and the input file name where the data to import is stored.
- The name or alias of the table or view where the data is to be imported.
- The format of the data in the input file. This format can be IXF, DEL, ASC, or WSF.
- Whether the data in the input file is to be inserted, updated into the table, or view, or if the existing data is to be replaced.

You may also provide the following:

- A message file
- The number of rows to insert before committing changes to the table
- The number of records in the file to skip before beginning the import
- The names of the columns within the table or view into which the data is inserted

Note: The IMPORT utility will issue a COMMIT or a ROLLBACK, depending on the success or failure of the import.

Examples of Using EXPORT and IMPORT

The first example shows how to export information from the PRODUCT table in the SALES database. Export to the file product.ixf with the output in IXF format:

```
EXPORT TO product.ixf OF IXF MESSAGES product.msg
   SELECT * FROM products
```

You must be connected to the database before you issue the command. To import the data into another database and create a table named PRODS in an existing table space named SMS1, the following command can be used:

```
IMPORT FROM product.ixf OF IXF
   COMMITCOUNT 50 MESSAGES product.msg
   CREATE INTO Prods IN SMS1
```

Note the use of the COMMITCOUNT option. This may prevent the log files from filling up.

In this second example, export all the data in a table hierarchy defined in the SALES database. The table hierarchy is defined as follows:

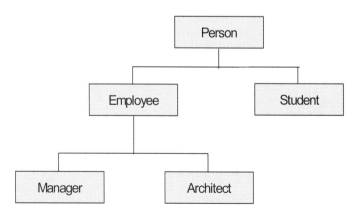

Fig. 10–15 *Table hierarchy of the Sales database*

Export the data to a DEL file named personh.del:

```
EXPORT TO personh.del OF DEL MESSAGES personh.msg
   HIERARCHY STARTING person
```

A portion of the output file looks like this:

```
2,"y","James        ","Kirk      ",35,"000054",90000,"b",,,,
2,"z","Leonard      ","McCoy       ",45,"000145",120000,"b",,,,
2,"A","Hikaru       ","Sulu       ",31,"000167",11000,"b",,,,
2,"B","Pavel        ","Chkalov   ",28,"000170",90000,"b",,,'
2,"C","Montgomery   ","Scott      ",42,"000301",100000,"b",,,,
```

Import the PERSONH.DEL file into the entire PERSON hierarchy. Assuming all the tables in the hierarchy are empty, use the INSERT command option. The command to issue is:

```
IMPORT FROM personh.del OF DEL
   COMMITCOUNT 50 MESSAGES personh.msg
   INSERT INTO ALL TABLES IN HIERARCHY STARTING person
```

Assume the import failed. The message file shows the following entries:

```
SQL3109N The utility is beginning to load data from file
"personh.del".
SQL3221W...Begin COMMIT WORK. Input Record Count = "50".
SQL3222W...COMMIT of any database changes was successful.
SQL3221W...Begin COMMIT WORK. Input Record Count = "100".
SQL3222W...COMMIT of any database changes was successful.
SQL3005N Processing was interrupted.
SQL3110N The utility has completed processing. "100" rows were
read from the input file.
```

The message file shows that 100 records were inserted into the table and committed. If one selected to restart the import, the first 100 rows need to be skipped. To do this the RESTARTCOUNT option is used. The following command will restart the import:

```
IMPORT FROM personh.del OF DEL
   COMMITCOUNT 50 RESTARTCOUNT 100
   MESSAGES personh.msg
   INSERT INTO ALL TABLES IN HIERARCHY STARTING person
```

The Load Utility

The LOAD utility, like the IMPORT utility, moves data supplied in an input file into a target table. Unlike the IMPORT utility, the target table *must* exist within the database prior to the start of the load process. The target table may be a new table that was created just before the load or an existing table in which data will be added to or replaced. Indexes on the table may or may not already exist. The load process does not create new indexes – it only maintains indexes that are already defined on the table.

To the DBA, the most important difference between the IMPORT and LOAD utilities relates to performance. The IMPORT utility inserts the data one row at a time. Each row inserted has to be checked for compliance with constraints (such as foreign key constraints or table check constraints). Changes are also logged in the log files.

The LOAD utility will insert data into a table much faster than will the IMPORT utility, because instead of inserting one row at a time, the LOAD utility will use the rows read from the input file to build pages which are then written directly into the database. Existing indexes (including primary keys or unique indexes) may be rebuilt after the data pages are inserted (rebuilt either totally or partially based on newly added data), and finally all the duplicate rows that do not comply with unique or primary key constraints are deleted from the table. During the load operation, individual records loaded are not logged in the log files.

Since the LOAD utility changes are not logged, it cannot be rolled forward by using the log files. However, the LOAD utility can use a copy of the source data (a load copy), so it can be reloaded if required.

Use of the LOAD utility requires either SYSADM, DBADM, or LOAD authority on the database with INSERT privilege on the table. The DELETE privilege on the table is also required when REPLACE mode is selected, TERMINATE mode (to terminate a previous load replace operation), or RESTART mode (to restart a previous load replace operation).

Before using the LOAD utility, the DBA must understand how it works, to exploit its performance benefits and to avoid any problems that may occur if it is used incorrectly.

Note: Load operations now take place at the table level. This means that the load utility no longer requires exclusive access to the entire table space, and concurrent access to other table objects in the same table space is possible during a load operation.

Fig. 10–16 *Phases of LOAD*

The phases of the LOAD utility as shown in Fig. 10–16 will now be examined.

1. *Load* phase - Two things happen during the load phase: Data is stored in the table, and index keys are collected and sorted.

    When running the LOAD utility the DBA can specify how often it should generate points of consistency. A consistency point serves as a checkpoint to the LOAD utility. If the LOAD is interrupted during its execution, it can be restarted and will continue from the last consistency point. As part of taking a consistency point, the LOAD utility will write a message to the message file stating how many records have been loaded. This can then be used by the DBA to monitor the progress of the LOAD utility.

2. *Build* phase - During the build phase, indexes are created based on the index keys collected in the load phase. If a failure occurs during the build phase and the LOAD utility is restarted (with the RESTART option), it will restart from the beginning of the build phase.

3. *Delete* Phase - During the delete phase, all rows that have violated a unique or primary key constraint are deleted and copied to an exception table (if it is specified when the LOAD utility is invoked). Only these two constraint types are checked. If a failure occurs during the delete phase and the LOAD utility is

restarted, it will do so from the beginning of the delete phase, however, if an online LOAD was invoked or COPY YES was specified, then restart will occur from the BUILD phase if a failure occurs here.

When input rows are rejected, messages are generated in the message file.

4. *Index Copy* Phase - If a system temporary table space was specified for index creation during a load operation and the READ ACCESS option selected, this index data will be copied from the system temporary table space to the original table space.

All phases of the load process are part of one operation that is complete only after all four phases complete successfully. The LOAD utility will generate messages during the progress of each phase. Should a failure occur during one of the phases, these messages can assist the DBA in problem analysis and resolution.

Here is the syntax of the LOAD utility:

Maintaining Data

Using the LOAD Command

Some of the key parameters to the LOAD utility are here (see the *DB2 UDB V8.1 Command Reference* for further details):

- CLIENT - specifies the data to be loaded resides on a remotely connected client.
- FROM - specifies the input data as: filename, pipename, device, cursorname (SQL statement that contains the data being loaded).
- OF filetype - specifies the format of the data: ASC, DEL, IXF, CURSOR (a cursor declared against a SELECT or VALUES statement).
- METHOD L | N | P - L specifies the start and end column numbers from which to load data (numbered from 1, for ASC files only). N specifies the names of the columns being loaded (IXF files only). P specifies the field numbers (numbered from 1) of the input data fields to be loaded (supports IXF, DEL, or CURSOR).
- ALLOW NO ACCESS - specifies that LOAD will lock the target table with an exclusive lock during the load, this is the default setting.
- ALLOW READ ACCESS - specifies that LOAD will lock the target table with a share lock, readers may access the non-delta portion of the data while the table is

being loaded.

 Note: The LOAD utility has the ability to query pre-existing data in a table while new data is being loaded. You can do this by specifying the READ ACCESS option of the LOAD command.

Insert Mode

By using the INSERT option with the LOAD command, all data in the input file will be inserted as new data into an existing table. For example, to load the table named PRODUCT by inserting the data contained in PRODUCT.IXF, the user would specify the following command:

```
LOAD FROM Product.ixf OF IXF... INSERT INTO Product...
```

Replace Mode

By using the REPLACE option, the LOAD utility will delete all the data in an existing table before loading the new data. It will not recreate the table. For example, if a file named PRODUCT.IXF contains data that should replace the data in an existing table named PRODUCT, the user would use the following command:

```
LOAD FROM Product.ixf OF IXF... REPLACE INTO Product...
```

Terminate Mode

Sometimes it is necessary to terminate a load process; for example, the user is loading the wrong file, or the LOAD utility was invoked with the wrong options. To terminate the interrupted load operation, the user has to invoke the LOAD utility again, using the exact options it was invoked with the first time, but replacing the INSERT or REPLACE option with the TERMINATE option. For example, if the LOAD utility was invoked with the following options and then interrupted:

```
LOAD FROM Product.del OF DEL SAVECOUNT 500
   INSERT INTO Product
```

The load operation can be terminated by replacing the INSERT option with
TERMINATE:

```
LOAD FROM Product.del OF DEL SAVECOUNT 500
    TERMINATE INTO Product
```

In the case of the original load being invoked with the INSERT option, all the new
records loaded into the table will be deleted, and the state of the table will be the
same as it was before the LOAD utility was invoked.

 Note: The LOCK WITH FORCE option has been introduced in this release. It
allows you to force applications to release the locks they have on a table,
allowing the load operation to proceed and to acquire the locks it needs.

If the original load was invoked with the REPLACE command option, all the records
in the table, old and new, will be deleted.

Restart Mode

If the load operation should fail, the DBA should look at the message file and error
logs to determine the reason for the failure. Once the problem has been identified
and fixed, the user can than reinvoke the LOAD utility with the RESTART command
option. Care should be taken to reinvoke it with the same options as the first invocation, replacing the INSERT or REPLACE command option with the RESTART command option.

If the load failed during the load phase and consistency points were generated, it
will restart the load phase from the last consistency point.

If the load failed in the build or delete phases, it will restart from the beginning of
the phase in question (with the exception of an online load or if COPY YES was
specified, restart will occur at the build phase even if failure occurs during the
delete phase).

Cursor file type

By specifying the CURSOR file type when using the LOAD command, you can load
the results of an SQL query directly into a target table without creating an intermediate exported file. By referencing a nickname within the SQL query, the LOAD utility can also load data from another database in a single step.

To execute a load from cursor operation from the CLP, a cursor must first be
declared against an SQL query. Once this is done, you can issue the LOAD command
using the declared cursor's name as the cursorname and CURSOR as the file type.

```
DECLARE mycurs CURSOR FOR SELECT ONE,TWO,THREE FROM
ABC.TABLE1
LOAD FROM mycurs OF CURSOR INSERT INTO ABC.TABLE2
```

In the above example, the column names of each table are the same, however, the source column types of the SQL query do not need to be identical to their target column types, although they do have to be compatible.

Generated Columns

The load utility can be used to load data into a table containing (non-identity) generated columns. The column values will be generated by this utility. This means that following a load operation, the target table will not be left in check pending state if the only constraints on the table are generated column constraints.

The GENERATEDMISSING modifier makes loading a table with generated columns more convenient if the input data file does not contain any values (not even nulls) for all generated columns present in the table

```
LOAD FROM Load.del MODIFIED BY GENERATEDMISSING
   REPLACE INTO Table1
```

The GENERATEDIGNORE modifier is in some ways the opposite of the GENERATED-MISSING modifier: it indicates to the load utility that even though the input data file contains data for all generated columns present in the target table, the data should be ignored, and the computed values should be loaded into each generated column.

Both modifiers simplify the syntax of the load operation especially if many columns are involved. The GENERATEDOVERRIDE modifier is used for loading user-supplied values into a table with generated columns. This can be quite useful when migrating data from another database system, or when loading a table from data that was recovered using the RECOVER DROPPED TABLE option of the ROLLFORWARD DATABASE command. When this modifier is used, any rows with no data (or null data) for non-nullable generated columns are rejected (SQL3116W).

Generating Consistency Points

The user may choose to generate consistency points during the load operation. During the generation of consistency points, all internal buffers are flushed to disk. A record is also written to the message file. These consistency points are used to monitor the progress of the LOAD utility and to restart a failed load.

Note: The generation of a consistency point has some performance overhead.

To specify the frequency with which the consistency points should be generated, use the SAVECOUNT command option followed by the number of rows to load between consistency points. For example, if roughly 500 rows should be loaded between consistency points, the following option should be used with the LOAD command:

```
LOAD FROM... SAVECOUNT 500...
```

Although the user specifies the number of rows with this option, it is converted internally to the number of pages on which that number of rows will fit. It is then rounded up to the nearest extent.

Limiting the Number of Rows To Load

Sometimes the DBA may want to load only part of the data file, for example, to test the load options without loading all the data. When invoking the LOAD utility, the ROWCOUNT command option can be used to specify the number of records to load from the beginning of the file.

Forcing the Load to Fail on Warnings

In some cases, all the rows in the input file *must* be loaded into the target table, for example, an account table at a bank. If even a single record is not loaded correctly, this could cause a problem. To specify that the load should fail if one or more warnings are generated, use the following option when invoking the LOAD utility:

```
LOAD FROM... WARNINGCOUNT 1...
```

If the load fails because of the WARNINGCOUNT option, it can be restarted by using the RESTART option.

Preventing Generation of Warning Messages

If the user is not interested in warning messages about rejected rows, he can suppress them by using the NOROWWARNINGS file type modifier to specify that they should not be recorded. This can enhance the performance of the LOAD utility if large amounts of row warning messages would otherwise be generated.

Specifying a File For Rejected Rows

Rows that are not formatted correctly may be rejected by the LOAD utility and not be loaded. For example, if a row has a character value where the load expects a numeric or date value, it will not be loaded. These rows can be placed separately, from the other records, in a file by specifying the DUMPFILE file type modifier. This option is only valid for DEL and ASC filetypes. For example:

```
LOAD FROM... OF DEL... MODIFIED BY DUMPFILE=C:\dump.del..
```

Using an Exception Table

A user-defined exception table can be used to store rows that do not comply with unique or primary key constraints. Using an exception table is an optional parameter of the LOAD command. However, if an exception table is not specified with the LOAD utility, any rows that violate unique constraints will be discarded without any chance of recovering or altering them.

The exception table definition is very similar to the target table definition. The first n columns match exactly the column names and data types of the target table. The $n + 1$ column is an optional column, which if defined must be of data type TIMESTAMP. The $n + 2$ column is also an optional column. It can only be created if the TIMESTAMP column $n + 1$ precedes it. It should be defined as type CLOB of 32 KB or larger. This is to be used as a message column. It stores information about the particular constraint that caused the rejection of the row (Fig. 10–17).

Note: The LOAD exception table is defined without any constraints or triggers.

Target Table

Name CHAR(20)	Age INT	Serial_num CHAR(3)	Salary INT	Department CHAR(25)
Bill	26	105	30000	Toy
Shirley	31	83	45000	Shoe
George	28	214	39000	Shoe
Katrina	35	251	55000	Toy
Dana	10	317	85000	Shoe

Valid exception table 1

Name CHAR(20)	Age INT	Serial_num CHAR(3)	Salary INT	Department CHAR(25)	Timestamp TIMESTAMP

Valid exception table 2

Name CHAR(20)	Age INT	Serial_num CHAR(3)	Salary INT	Department CHAR(25)	Timestamp TIMESTAMP	Description CLOB(32k)

Fig. 10–17 *Exception table definition*

Indexing Modes

During the build phase, the indexes that existed prior to the load can be rebuilt. The user can define the method to be used for the rebuild. There are four options available:

- *Rebuild* - This option will force all indexes to be recreated independent of the type of load, INSERT or REPLACE.
- *Incremental* - This will allow the LOAD utility to use the data in the existing indexes and add the new data to them when the load is invoked with the INSERT option. This is useful if the amount of data loaded into the table is small compared with the existing data.
- *Deferred* - This option will prevent the LOAD utility from rebuilding indexes; instead, the indexes will be flagged as needing a refresh. They will subsequently be rebuilt upon the first access to the table or when the database is restarted. The value specified for the INDEXREC parameter in the database configuration file is used to determine when the indexes are recreated. This option is not supported

for tables that have a primary key index or unique indexes defined, since they need to be used for checking for duplicates.

- *Autoselect* - Will allow the LOAD utility to choose between the REBUILD and INCREMENTAL options.

For example, if a table named Product has two indexes defined and no unique or primary key constraints, and the LOAD utility is used to replace all existing data, the following options specified with the LOAD command will allow the index build to be deferred:

```
LOAD FROM... INDEXING MODE DEFERRED...
    REPLACE INTO Product...
```

If the DBA needs to add some data to the PRODUCT table immediately after the load completes, the following options can be used to rebuild the indexes:

```
LOAD FROM... INDEXING MODE REBUILD...
    INSERT INTO Product...
```

When performing consecutive load operations on the same table, the index build should be deferred until the last LOAD is performed on the table.

Leaving Free Space

The LOAD utility provides the functionality to leave some free space on the pages created during the load for both index and data pages. It can also format some additional pages and leave them empty. This space can then be used for subsequent inserts into the table or indexes. The file type modifiers used to do this are:

- PAGEFREESPACE - Indicates the percentage free space to leave at the end of each data page
- INDEXFREESPACE - Indicates the percentage free space to leave at the end of each index page
- TOTALFREESPACE - Indicates the number of empty pages to be added to the table as a percentage of the total number of used pages

For example, if you want to load a table named PERSON by replacing all the existing data, leaving 20% of each data page empty, 20% of each index page empty, and ensuring that 15% of the total number of used pages are to be empty pages at the end of the table, use the following options:

```
LOAD FROM... MODIFIED BY PAGEFREESPACE 20
   INDEXFREESPACE 20 TOTALFREESPACE 15...
   INTO Person...
```

Generating Statistics

The LOAD utility can be used to generate statistics associated with the table and or indexes. These statistics are used by the optimizer to determine the most efficient way in which an SQL statement should be executed. The user can also specify how detailed the statistics should be for tables and/or indexes if they use the REPLACE load option. Table 10–2 shows the different combinations of statistics that can be generated for tables and indexes.

Table 10–2 *Load - Generating Statistics*

	Max Table Stats	Min Table Stats	No Table Stats
Max Index Stats	YES WITH DISTRIBUTION AND DETAILED INDEXES ALL	YES AND DETAILED INDEXES ALL	YES FOR DETAILED INDEXES ALL
Min Index Stats	YES WITH DISTRIBUTION AND INDEXES ALL	YES AND INDEXES ALL	YES FOR INDEXES ALL
No Index Stats	YES WITH DISTRIBUTION	YES	NO

For example, if you require the maximum statistics to be generated for both indexes and the associated table, use the following command:

```
LOAD FROM... STATISTICS YES WITH DISTRIBUTION AND
DETAILED INDEXES ALL...
```

If minimal statistics need to be generated for both indexes and the associated table, use the following options:

```
LOAD FROM... STATISTICS YES AND INDEXES ALL...
```

For maximum statistics on the table only:

Maintaining Data

```
LOAD FROM... STATISTICS YES WITH DISTRIBUTION...
```

If no statistics should be generated, use the following option:

```
LOAD FROM... STATISTICS NO...
```

Specifying a Temporary Directory

By default, the LOAD utility uses a subdirectory in the directory where the database is created to store temporary files. These files are deleted after successful completion of the LOAD utility. The user may specify a directory to use as the temporary directory. Specifying a directory on a separate device where the data is read from and written to may increase the performance of the LOAD utility.

```
LOAD FROM... TEMPFILES PATH E:\tempdir...
```

Note: Do not modify or tamper with these temporary files! It could cause the load to fail and put the database in jeopardy.

Loading Large Object Files

The same considerations that apply to the IMPORT utility apply to the LOAD utility. See "Importing Large Objects" on page 517. The parameter names and specification are also the same.

Performance Considerations

The LOAD utility has a number of performance-related options. Some of these are:

- COPY YES/NO
- NONRECOVERABLE
- FASTPARSE
- ANYORDER
- DATA BUFFER
- CPU_PARALLELISM
- DISK_PARALLELISM

These options are now examined in more detail.

Copy Yes/No and Nonrecoverable

During the load process, no logging of changes is done. This means that a user cannot perform roll-forward recovery for the load operation using the RESTORE and ROLLFORWARD commands. The user can choose to make the table recoverable but at the expense of performance.

> **Note:** When the COPY NO option is specified for a recoverable database, the table space will be placed in the backup pending table space state when the load operation begins.

The LOAD utility provides three ways in which the performance and recoverability can be balanced. The options are:

- *Nonrecoverable* - Specifies that the load operation is to be marked as non-recoverable and that it will not be possible to recover it by a subsequent roll forward action. The rollforward utility will skip the transaction and will mark the table into which data was being loaded as "invalid". The utility will also ignore any subsequent transactions against that table. After the roll forward operation is completed, such a table can only be dropped or restored from a backup (full or table space) taken after a commit point following the completion of the non-recoverable load operation. With this option, table spaces are not put in backup pending state following the load operation, and a copy of the loaded data does not have to be made during the load operation. A nonrecoverable load is useful when loading large read-only tables. You could also load multiple tables into a table space with the nonrecoverable option. Then, once the last table has been loaded, you can back up the database or the table spaces in which the table, its indexes, and long data reside.

- *Copy No* - (Default) If this option is specified and archival logging is enabled for the database, the table space in which the table resides will be placed in backup-pending state after the load. The table space will not be accessible for write operations until a database or table space backup is made. Since the LOAD utility's changes to the data are not logged, taking a backup of the table space or database is required to be able to recover it in the event of damage after the load operation has completed.

- *Copy Yes* - If YES is specified for the COPY option and archival logging is enabled for the database, a copy of the changes caused by the load process will be saved to tape, directory, or TSM server, and the table spaces will not be left in backup-pending state. This option does not apply to a database that uses circular logging and is thus nonrecoverable. If database damage occurs just after the load operation has completed, an existing backup can be restored and rolled forward (assuming archival logging is used).

Fastparse

This is a file type modifier that can be used to reduce the amount of data checking. It should only be used if the data is known to be correct. Since IXF files can only contain the data in the correct format, this parameter may not improve the performance of the LOAD when IXF file types are used. If DEL or ASC files are used, the LOAD utility may perform faster.

Anyorder

If the SAVECOUNT option is not used, this parameter will allow the LOAD utility to load the data into the table without having to respect the order in which the data appears in the input file. If the data in the input file is ordered according to a clustering index, then this option may not be a very good choice because it will affect the performance of a subsequent REORG operation. When used, this file type modifier may improve the performance of the LOAD utility, particularly in SMP systems (and the CPU_PARALLELISM option is > 1).

Data Buffer

Specifies the amount of memory in 4 KB pages allocated from the Utility Heap to be used as an internal load buffer. If not specified, a calculated default will be used that takes into consideration the size allocated in the Utility heap and the characteristics of the table being loaded. Specifying a large buffer size may improve the performance of the load.

CPU_parallelism

This option should be used on SMP machines to indicate how many processes or threads should be used to parse, convert, or format the data. If no value is specified, a default is calculated based on the number of CPUs on the machine. The data is loaded using the order that it appears in the input file. Choosing the correct value may considerably improve the performance of the LOAD utility if it runs on an SMP machine.

Disk_parallelism

This option specifies the number of processes or threads to use for writing data to disk. The default value is calculated based on the number of containers specified for all the table spaces in which objects for the table are stored and other table characteristics.

Other LOAD options and file type modifiers that may affect the performance include:

- *Norowwarnings* - If specified, this will usually improve the performance.
- *Savecount* - The larger amount of records loaded before a consistency point, the better for performance.
- *Statistics* - The less statistics generated, the better the performance. However, the combined runtime for the LOAD and the RUNSTATS utilities is very often longer than using the LOAD utility to generate the statistics.

Using the Load Utility from the Control Center

You run the LOAD utility in much the same way as the IMPORT and EXPORT utilities. Use the Control Center and select the target table to be loaded. Click the right mouse button and select the **Load** option.

Maintaining Data

Once invoked, the user can specify all the options available on the command line. The use of the Control Center approach will be demonstrated by an example.

Fig. 10–18 *Choose to replace or keep the original table data*

The DBA selects if the load is to append or replace data. Click **Next**

Fig. 10–19 *Specify input and output files*

The DBA wants to load a file named `sales.del` into a table named `SALES`, appending the data currently in the table. Click on **DEL Options** button.

Fig. 10–20 *Delimited Options*

Figure 10–20 shows the options that were selected. Click **OK**.

Fig. 10–21 *Load from Control Center - Columns tab*

The Columns tab as shown in Fig. 10–21 is used to specify whether and how you want the columns from the data files loaded into the table columns.

Fig. 10–22 *Specify performance and statistics collection options*

The DBA is given a number of parameters that can affect the performance of the LOAD operation. Click **Next**.

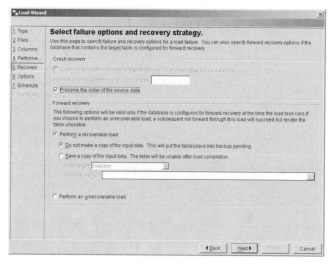

Fig. 10–23 *Select failure options and recovery strategy*

The DBA is given a number of options on what actions should take if the load should not complete normally. Click **Next**.

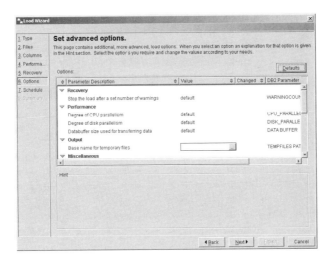

Fig. 10–24 *Set advanced options*

Additional options are provided here with respect to recovery, performance, and other miscellaneous parameters. Values can be updated from this panel. Click **Next**.

Fig. 10–25 *Scheduling task execution*

The DBA is given the option to execute the load now, or to schedule it at a later time with the use of the Task Center. Enter an authorized id and password, click **Next**.

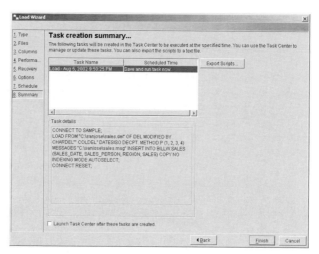

Fig. 10–26 *Task creation summary*

By clicking on the task, the task details appear in the window. The user can choose to save the command as a script to be invoked at a later time. Click **Finish** to save the task and optionally start the Task Center.

After Load Has Finished

The LOAD utility can put the table space in which the target table resides in one of two pending states or can set the table to a pending state. If this happens, users cannot access the tables in the table space or access the table itself.

To query the state of a table space, use the LIST TABLESPACES command as described in "Data Storage Management" on page 449. The states that the LOAD utility can put the table space into are as follows:

Backup Pending

If a table is loaded with the COPY NO command option and archival logging is switched on, the table spaces involved in the load operation will be put in a BACKUP PENDING state.

This state forces the user to take a backup of the database or table space the target table resides in. This is done to ensure that if needed, the table can be recovered.

If the LOAD utility was invoked with the NONRECOVERABLE or COPY YES command options, the table space will not be put in a backup-pending state. It is recommended that the DBA take a backup of the table space or database as soon as possible if NONRECOVERABLE is used. If not, the DBA will *not* be able to recover it by restoring a older backup and then rolling forward using the log files. If this is attempted, the table will be flagged as invalid. The only operation that can be performed is to drop the table.

Table in Check Pending

The load utility can also put the *table* in check-pending state. This state occurs if constraints other than primary key and unique constraints are defined on the target table. They include the following:

- Foreign key constraints - Used to enforce referential integrity.
- Check constraints - User-defined constraints. Normally used to check for valid data ranges on columns.
- Summary table involved in the scenario - if this table is used to refresh a summary table that has the REFRESH IMMEDIATE option set.

The state of a table is recorded in the SYSCAT.TABLES catalog view. To find the state associated with a table, issue the following select statement:

```
select tabschema,tabname,status, const_checked from
syscat.tables where
tabname='MYTAB' and tabschema='MYSCHEMA'
```

The status column is of type CHAR and indicates the state the table is in. Valid values for it are:

- C - Check pending
- N - Normal
- X - Inoperative view

The CONST_CHECKED column is of type CHAR(32). The first character denotes the status of the foreign key constraints, character two denotes the status of the check constraints, and character five denotes the status of the summary table refresh. Valid values for these states are:

- Y - Checked by the system.
- N - Not checked. This is a check-pending state.
- U - Checked by the user.
- W - Was in the state "U" before it was placed in this state. This is also a check-pending state.

The SELECT statement can be rewritten to eliminate all the unnecessary information returned by the previous one:

Maintaining Data

```
SELECT TABSCHEMA AS Schema,
       TABNAME AS Name,
       STATUS AS State,
       SUBSTR(CONST_CHECKED,1,1) AS Foreign_Keys,
       SUBSTR(CONST_CHECKED,2,1) AS Check_Constraints,
       SUBSTR(CONST_CHECKED,5,1) AS Summary_Tables
FROM SYSCAT.TABLES
WHERE TABNAME='MYTAB' AND TABSCHEMA='MYSCHEMA'
```

To remove the check-pending state on the table, the SET INTEGRITY statement can be used. The usage of this statement is discussed in "The SET INTEGRITY Statement" on page 553.

The DBA can check for records that could not be loaded because of formatting or null value violations by looking in the dump file (as specified with the MODIFIED BY DUMPFILE option). In addition, the exception table (if specified) can be queried to find records that were rejected because of duplicate values. The remote file can be queried by using the LOAD QUERY command. It contains information about the number of rows read, rejected, and loaded, as well as any error or warning messages generated by the LOAD utility. In the event of failure, an SQL error code with a short description will be returned. Also, the DB2DIAG.LOG file can be checked. It can give useful information about the sequence of events that preceded the failure.

Multi-Dimensional Clustering Considerations:

The following restrictions apply to multi-dimensional clustering (MDC) tables:

- The SAVECOUNT option of the LOAD utility is not supported.
- The TOTALFREESPACE file type modifier is not supported since these tables manage their own free space.

When using the LOAD utility with MDC, violations of unique constraints will be handled as follows:

- If the table included a unique key prior to the load operation and duplicate records are loaded into the table, the original record will remain and the new records will be deleted during the delete phase.
- If the table did not include a unique key prior to the load operation and both a unique key and duplicate records are loaded into the table, only one of the records with the unique key will be loaded and the others will be deleted during the delete phase.

Note, that there is no explicit technique for determining which record will be loaded and which will be deleted.

The LOAD QUERY Command

The LOAD QUERY command is used to interrogate a LOAD operation and generate a report on its progress. The user may direct it to summarize or to display the difference or delta since the last invocation.

Load Query Syntax

The syntax of the LOAD QUERY command is provided to add to the discussion of the command. Figure 10–27 shows the syntax diagram.

Fig. 10–27 *The LOAD QUERY command*

The key parameters are:

- `table-name` - The name of the table that is being loaded.
- `TO local-message-file` - The name of a file on the server (where the LOAD is executed). The load query report will be output to this file. This cannot be the same file as the message file specified in the LOAD command. If the file specified exists, all new output will be appended to it.
- NOSUMMARY - Indicates that no summary information should be generated.
- SUMMARYONLY - Will generate summary information about the number of records read, loaded, rejected, and so on.
- SHOWDELTA - Will cause only the new information since the last invocation of LOAD QUERY to be displayed.

Using LOAD QUERY and LOAD

Here is an example of using the LOAD QUERY command.

In this example, a load will be performed on a table named SALES from a file named SALES.DEL with the character delimiter (*) and the column delimiter (|). New data will be added to the table.

Note: The LOAD QUERY command now returns the table state of the target table into which data is being loaded as well as the status information it previously included on a load operation in progress. The command can be used to query table states whether or not a load operation is in progress on a particular table.

There are two summary tables defined on the SALES table. The first is a summary table on the sales per employee, and the second is defined to summarize the sales per product. The first, EMP_SALES, is defined with the option REFRESH DEFERRED, and the second, PROD_SALES, is defined with the option REFRESH IMMEDIATE.

The SALES table also has a foreign key constraint defined that references the PRODUCT table. It also has a check constraint defined on the AMOUNT column. This constraint ensures that any row inserted or updated in the table has an amount that is greater than zero. Figure 10–28 shows the relationships between these tables:

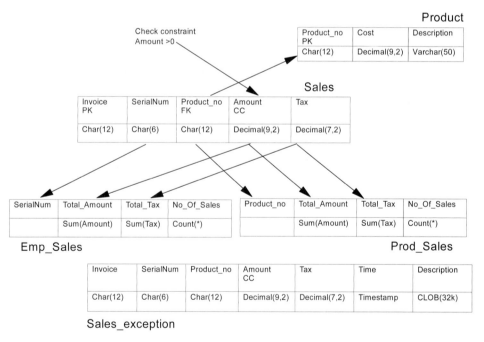

Fig. 10–28 *The SALES table dependencies*

After evaluating the information, the DBA decided to load the SALES table with the following options:

```
LOAD FROM Sales.del OF DEL
   MODIFIED BY COLDEL| CHARDEL*
   SAVECOUNT 100
   MESSAGES msgs.txt
   TEMPFILES PATH d:\temp
   INSERT INTO Sales FOR EXCEPTION Sales_exception
   STATISTICS YES AND INDEXES ALL
   COPY NO
   CPU_PARALLELISM 4
   DISK_PARALLELISM 3
   INDEXING MODE INCREMENTAL
```

The LOAD utility will move all the duplicate rows to the exception table
SALES_EXCEPTION during the delete phase.

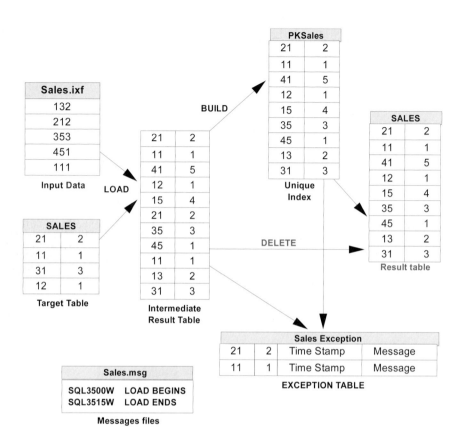

Fig. 10–29 *Loading the SALES table*

It will not make a copy of the data loaded during the load, but it will force the user to take a backup of the table space(s) involved.

During the load of the SALES table, the DBA decided to monitor the load progress using the following command. He would be able to query this file to determine the status of the LOAD at that time.

```
LOAD QUERY TABLE Sales TO D:\messages\load\Sales.msg
```

After loading the data into the SALES table, the DBA attempts to issue an INSERT statement on the SALES table. It fails with the following error message:

```
DB21034E The command was processed as an SQL statement because
it was not a valid Command Line Processor command. During SQL
processing it returned:
SQL0290N Table space access is not allowed. SQLSTATE=55039
```

This indicates that the table space is in a backup-pending state. The reason for this is the DBA specified the COPY NO option. After taking a backup of the table space, the DBA attempts to select data from the table. This time it fails with the following error message:

```
SQL0668N Operation not allowed when the underlying table (or a
dependent table) is in the Check Pending state. SQLSTATE=57016
```

This error occurs because the table is in check-pending state. To verify this, the DBA executes the following SQL statement:

```
SELECT TABNAME,STATUS FROM SYSCAT.TABLES
   WHERE TABNAME='SALES'
```

Resulting in:

```
TABNAME                        STATUS
-----------------------        ------
SALES                          C
```

Recovery from this state by using the SET INTEGRITY statement will be examined in the next section.

The SET INTEGRITY Statement

The integrity or validity of data in a database is of crucial importance. It is difficult to ensure the validity of data being inserted into a database; many RDBMS products, however, including DB2, provide the ability to define some rule-based constraints or checks that can be incorporated into the database. In DB2, the following checks can be used to minimize the risk of inserting incorrect data into a table:

- The fields in a row are checked to see if they conform to the data type and length of the columns with which they are associated. For example, the value "g553g" does not match a column data type of DECIMAL, and therefore the row will be rejected, thus ensuring the validity of the data in the database.
- If a *primary key* constraint has been defined on a table, then each row in the table must have a unique value in the column or columns that collectively form

the primary key. If a row is inserted with the same key as an existing one, the new row will be rejected.

- If a *unique* constraint has been defined on a table, each row in the table must comply with this constraint by having a unique value or combination of values that make up the unique key.

- If a *foreign key* constraint has been defined, each row in the table must have a value in the foreign key column or columns that matches a primary key of a row in the parent table. In some cases, a null value may be acceptable if the column or columns defined as part of the foreign key are also defined as nullable.

- If a *check* constraint has been defined on a column, each row must comply with the constraint. For example, a check constraint on a salary column of an employee table may prevent an application or user from inserting a new employee record or row for which the salary is less than zero. Any row inserted into the table that has a salary value of less than zero will be rejected, thus minimizing the risk of inserting incorrect data into the table.

In most cases, the enforcing of these rules or constraints is done automatically. For instance, whenever a row is inserted, updated, imported, or loaded, the following will always be checked:

- Validity of the data format and length
- Primary key values
- Unique constraints

Whenever a row is inserted, updated, or imported, the following checks will also be done:

- Compliance with foreign key constraints
- Compliance with check constraints
- Updating of summary tables defined with IMMEDIATE CHECKED option

The second list above is *not* checked or executed when data is *loaded* into a table. Because it is not checked, the validity of the data remains in doubt until such time as the data is checked and found to be consistent. For this reason, DB2 restricts access to the table by placing it in a check-pending state. This prevents the data in the table from being accessed and indicates that explicit checking of the data is required.

A table might also be placed into this state if a new constraint is defined on the table, and the checking of the constraint is not performed immediately. This is done because there is no guarantee that the existing rows in the table comply with the new constraint.

Here is the syntax of the SET INTEGRITY statement:

The validity of the existing data in a table can be checked by using one of these statements:

- SET INTEGRITY (also known as SET CONSTRAINTS)
- REFRESH TABLE

The SET INTEGRITY statement can be used to do the following:

- *Set* a table to check-pending state and mark one or more of the following as *not* checked: check constraints, foreign key constraints, and the refreshing of refresh immediate summary tables.

  By marking any one of the above as *not* checked, the table is set to check-pending state. Primary key and unique key constraint checking cannot be turned off and will still be enforced. Because the table is set to the check-pending state, access to the table data is restricted.

- *Reset* the check-pending state of a table by *checking* all or some of the following constraints: check constraints, foreign key constraints, and the refreshing of refresh immediate summary tables.

- *Reset* a check-pending state by *marking* any of the following constraints as checked: check constraints, foreign key constraints, and the refreshing of refresh immediate summary tables. The actual checking of the constraints will not be done. This is referred to as deferred checking.

The REFRESH TABLE statement can be used on summary tables only. It will update the data in the summary table by making use of the current data in the table that it is derived from.

Maintaining Data

Note: Prior to Version 8, following a load operation the target table remained in check pending state if it contained generated columns. The load utility will now generate column values, and you no longer need to issue the SET INTEGRITY statement after a load operation into a table that contains generated columns and has no other table constraints.

If existing data is to be checked, the user can specify that it should be done incrementally. This means that only the data that has been added to the table since checking has turned off has to be checked.

The following example is a continuation of the LOAD example in "Using LOAD QUERY and LOAD" on page 549. In the previous example, after the LOAD completed, the table space was in a backup-pending state. After a backup was made, a SELECT statement failed with the following error message:

```
SQL0668N Operation not allowed when the underlying table (or a
dependent table) is in the Check Pending state. SQLSTATE=57016
```

This message indicates that the table is in a check-pending state. As mentioned before, this pending state can occur on tables that have foreign key constraints or check constraints defined. Use the following statement to find the reason for the check-pending state on the SALES table.

```
SELECT TABSCHEMA AS Schema,
       TABNAME AS Name,
       STATUS AS State,
       SUBSTR(CONST_CHECKED,1,1) AS Foreign_Keys,
       SUBSTR(CONST_CHECKED,2,1) AS Check_Constraints,
       SUBSTR(CONST_CHECKED,5,1) AS Summary_Tables
FROM SYSCAT.TABLES
   WHERE TABNAME='SALES' AND TABSCHEMA='DB2ADMIN'
```

The result is shown below. The value "c" in the STATUS column indicates that the table is in a check-pending state.

SCHEMA	NAME	STATE	FOREIGN_KEYS	CHECK_CONSTRAINTS	SUMMARY_TABLES
DB2ADMIN	SALES	C	N	N	Y

The "N" shown in the output indicates the reason for the check-pending state. In our case it is because one or more constraints have not been checked. To remove the check-pending state on the table, use the SET INTEGRITY statement:

```
SET INTEGRITY FOR Sales IMMEDIATE CHECKED
    FOR EXCEPTION IN Sales USE Sales_Exception
```

The statement generates the following message:

```
SQL3602W Check data processing found constraint violations and
moved them into the exception table. SQLSTATE-01603
```

At this point, the table should now be accessible.

Using Set Integrity from the Control Center

The SET INTEGRITY statement can also be executed from the Control Center. To do so, right-click on the table in question and choose the **Set Integrity** option. Fig. 10–30 illustrates how you can choose the constraint checking options.

Fig. 10–30 *Set Integrity from the Control Center*

During the execution of the SET INTEGRITY statement, all the rows that do not comply with either of the two constraints defined on the SALES table will be copied to the SALES_EXCEPTION exception table. This exception table can also be used during the LOAD operation.

Fig. 10–31 shows how a foreign key constraint defined on the SALES table is evaluated. All the rows in the SALES table that refer to a nonexistent value in the PRODUCT table will be deleted from the SALES table and copied to the exception table. The same process will be used to delete the rows in the SALES table that do not comply with the check constraint defined on the table. Copies of these rows will also be placed in the SALES_EXCEPTION table.

After completion of the SET INTEGRITY operation, the user can query the message column (if defined) in the SALES_EXCEPTION table to determine the reason a given row was rejected. These rows can then be modified and reinserted into the SALES table at a later time.

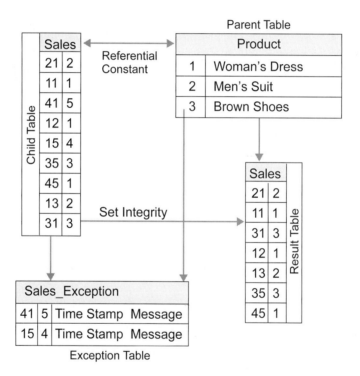

Fig. 10–31 *SET INTEGRITY and the use of the exception table*

The DB2MOVE Utility

The DB2MOVE utility can be used to move data between different DB2 databases that may reside on different servers. It is very useful when a large number of tables need to be copied from one database to another. The utility can run in one of three modes: EXPORT, IMPORT, or LOAD.

When running in the *export* mode, it will use the EXPORT utility to export data from the table or tables specified into data files of type IXF. It will also produce a file named DB2MOVE.LST that records all the names of the tables exported and the file names produced when they were exported. It will also produce various message files that record any errors or warning messages generated during the execution of the utility.

If the DB2MOVE utility is executed in *import* mode, the IMPORT utility will be used to import data files of type IXF into a given database. It will attempt to read the DB2MOVE.LST file to find the link between the file names of the data files and the table names into which the data must be imported.

In the *load* mode, the input files specified in the DB2MOVE.LST file will be loaded into the tables using the LOAD utility.

Here is the syntax of the DB2MOVE utility:

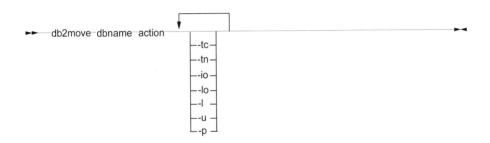

Key parameters include the following (see the *DB2 UDB V8.1 Command Reference* for more detail):

- dbname - The name of the database.
- action - Valid actions are IMPORT, EXPORT, or LOAD
- -tc - Followed by one or more creator IDs separated by a comma. The "*" may be used as a wildcard character. If this option is not used, the default behavior of this utility is to work with all the creator IDs.
- -tn - Flag only valid if used with the EXPORT action. If specified, it should be followed by one or more (maximum ten) table names separated by commas.
- -io - Flag used to specify the import action to take. If specified, it should be followed by any one of the following options: INSERT, INSERT_UPDATE, REPLACE, CREATE, or REPLACE_CREATE. If not specified when the IMPORT action is specified, the option REPLACE_CREATE will be used as the default.
- -lo - Flag used to specify the load option to use. Valid options are INSERT and REPLACE. If not specified when the LOAD action is specified, INSERT will be used

as the default load option.

- -l - Specify the absolute path names for the directories to be used when importing, exporting, or loading LOB values into or from separate files. If specified with the EXPORT action, the directories will be cleared before the LOBs are exported to files in the directory or directories.
- -u - Followed by a userid that is to be used to run the utility. If not specified, the userid of the logged-on user will be used to execute the utility.
- -p - Followed by the password to be used to authenticate the userid that is used when executing the utility.

Here is an example of using the DB2MOVE utility:

An existing database, DB2CERT, needs to be copied to a new database on another server. The new database name is NEWCERT. The user has not defined any tables in the new database and plans to do this using the DB2MOVE utility. To export all the tables in the DB2CERT database, the user uses the following command:

```
db2move db2cert export
```

This produces the following files:

- EXPORT.OUT - The results of the EXPORT action
- DB2MOVE.LST - A file containing a list of file names and the table names they originate from
- TABNNN.IXF - The IXF files containing the data from the tables
- TABNNN.MSG - The messages file associated with the export operation on each table

The user now wants to recreate the database structure in the NEWCERT database and populate it with the data in the IXF files. The following command can now be used:

```
db2move newcert import -io REPLACE_CREATE
```

The use of the -io option is not required in our case because the default option is REPLACE_CREATE.

The files used as input by the utility are:

- DB2MOVE.LST - The list file containing the table names and file names of the data files for the tables
- TABNNN.IXF - The actual data files of type IXF

The output files of this operation are:

- `IMPORT.OUT` - This file contains a summary of the results of the individual import operations.
- `TABNNN.MSG` - These files contains error and warning messages generated during the import of the various files.

Maintaining Data

Data Maintenance

The physical distribution of the data stored in tables has a significant effect on the performance of applications using those tables. The way the data is stored in a table is affected by the update, insert, and delete operations on the table. For example, a delete operation may leave empty pages of data that may not be reused later. Also, updates to variable-length columns may result in the new column value not fitting in the same data page. This can cause the row to be moved to a different page and so produce internal gaps or unused space in the table. As a consequence, DB2 may have to read more physical pages to retrieve the information required by the application.

These scenarios are almost unavoidable. However, as the database administrator, you can use the data maintenance commands provided in DB2 to optimize the physical distribution of the data stored in your tables.

There are three related utilities or commands that can help you organize the data in your tables. These are:

- REORGCHK
- REORG
- RUNSTATS

Analyzing Data's Physical Organization

It has been discussed that certain SQL operations may produce internal gaps in tables. So the question you may ask is how can you determine the physical organization of your tables or indexes? How can you know how much space is currently being used and how much is free?

Questions like these can be answered by using the REORGCHK utility. This utility is used to analyze the system catalog tables and gather information about the physical organization of your tables and indexes. The user has the option of using the current information in the catalog or to make the REORGCHK utility update the information before using it.

With the information collected from the system catalog tables, the REORGCHK utility displays the space allocation characteristics of the tables and indexes. The utility uses a number of formulas to help you decide if your tables and indexes require physical reorganization.

These formulas are general recommendations that show the relationship between the allocated space and the space that is being used for the data in your tables. Three formulas are used for tables, and three are used for indexes.

It is recommended that you establish a data maintenance policy to ensure that the data in your table is stored as efficiently as possible. If you don't, you may discover that your applications start to experience degradation in performance. This may be caused by the poor physical organization of your data, so before this happens, do preventive maintenance on your tables.

Here is the syntax of the REORGCHK utility:

Fig. 10–32 *REORGCHK command*

Some of the key parameters to the REORGCHK command include (see the *DB2 UDB V8.1 Command Reference* for further detail):

* UPDATE STATISTICS - updates table statistics, and uses the updated statistics to determine if a table reorganization is required.

* CURRENT STATISTICS - uses current table statistics to determine if a table reorganization is required.

To use the REORGCHK utility you must have one of the following authorities: SYSADM, DBADM or CONTROL privilege on the table. The following is an example of using the REORGCHK utility. This utility will be executed against the table DB2CERT.CANDIDATE.

```
REORGCHK UPDATE STATISTICS ON TABLE db2cert.candidate
```

The output of the REORGCHK utility is shown here:

```
Doing RUNSTATS....


Table statistics:

F1: 100 * OVERFLOW/CARD < 5
F2: 100 * Effective Space Utilization of Data Pages > 70
F3: 100 * (Required Pages / Total Pages) > 80

SCHEMA   NAME             CARD   OV   NP   FP    TSIZE  F1  F2 F3 REORG
----------------------------------------------------------------------
DB2CERT CANDIDATE           8    0    1    1       72   0  -  100 ---
```

```
-------------------------------------------------------------------------
Index statistics:

F4: CLUSTERRATIO or normalized CLUSTERFACTOR > 80
F5: 100 *( KEYS*(ISIZE+9)+(CARD-KEYS)*5) / ((NLEAF-NUM EMPTY LEAFS)*INDEXPAGESIZE) >
50
F6: (100-PCTFREE) * (INDEXPAGESIZE-96) / (ISIZE+12) ** (NLEVELS-2) * (INDEXPAGES
IZE-96) / (KEYS * (ISIZE+9) + (CARD-KEYS) * 5) < 100
F7: 100 * (NUMRIDS DELETED / (NUMRIDS DELETED + CARD)) < 20
F8: 100 * (NUM EMPTY LEAFS / NLEAF) < 20

SCHEMA   NAME             CARD LEAF LVLS ISIZE  KEYS   F4  F5  F6 F7 F8  REORG
-------------------------------------------------------------------------
Table: DB2CERT.CANDIDATE
SYSIBM  SQL970812225853720   8    1    1     9     8  100   -   -  -  -   ---
-------------------------------------------------------------------------
```

```
CLUSTERRATIO or normalized CLUSTERFACTOR (F4) will indicate REORG is necessary
for indexes that are not in the same sequence as the base table. When multiple
indexes are defined on a table, one or more indexes may be flagged as needing
REORG. Specify the most important index for REORG sequencing.
```

The output of REORGCHK is divided into two sections. The first section shows the table statistics and formulas. The second section displays information about the table's indexes and associated formulas.

Interpreting the Output from REORGCHK

The REORGCHK utility uses formulas that may help you decide whether a table requires reorganization. An explanation of the elements that are used to calculate these formulas are examined in this section:

```
Table statistics:

F1: 100 * OVERFLOW/CARD < 5
F2: 100 * Effective Space Utilization of Data Pages > 70
F3: 100 * (Required Pages / Total Pages) > 80

SCHEMA  NAME             CARD   OV    NP    FP    TSIZE  F1 F2 F3 REORG
-------------------------------------------------------------------------
DB2CERT CANDIDATE          8     0     1     1       72   0  -  100 ---
-------------------------------------------------------------------------
```

- SCHEMA - Column indicates the schema to which the table belongs. Remember that the authorization ID of the creator of an object is used as the default schema.
- NAME - Column indicates the name of the table for which the REORGCHK utility has been run. REORGCHK can check a set of tables at one time.
- CARD - Indicates the number of data rows in the base table.
- OV (OVERFLOW) - The overflow indicator. It indicates the number of overflow rows. An overflow may occur when a new column is added to a table or when a variable-length value increases its size.
- NP (NPAGES)- Indicates the total number of pages that contain data.
- FP (FPAGES) - Indicates the total number of pages allocated to the table.
- TSIZE - Indicates the table size in bytes. This value is calculated from the result

of multiplying the number of rows in the table times the average row length.

- TABLEPAGESIZE - Indicates the page size of the table space in which the table resides.
- REORG - Column has a separate indicator for each one of the first three formulas. A hyphen (-) indicates that reorganization is not recommended. An asterisk (*) indicates that reorganization is recommended.

The formulas F1, F2, and F3 provide guidelines for table reorganization. The formulas are shown in the REORGCHK output.

- *F1* works with the number of overflow rows. It recommends a table reorganization if 5% or more of the total number of rows are overflow rows.
- *F2* works with the free or unused space. It recommends a table reorganization if the table size (TSIZE) is less than or equal to 70% the size of the total space allocated to the table. In other words, it recommends to reorganize a table when more than 30% of the allocated space is unused.
- *F3* works with free pages. It recommends a table reorganization when more than 20% of the pages in a table are free. A page is considered free when it contains no rows.

Whenever the formulas find that table reorganization is needed an asterisk will be shown in the REORG column of the output.

For example, if the overflow rows of a table exceed the recommended value, the REORG column will look like this:

```
REORG
-----
*--
```

Remember, these values are only general guidelines. You may use your own thresholds. However, most of the time, you will find these values adequate for your environment.

Another part of REORGCHK involves interpreting the output gathered from indexes. To do this, some information about the structure of indexes is needed. Indexes in DB2 are created using a B+ tree structure. These data structures provide an efficient search method to locate the entry values of an index. The logical structure of a DB2 index is shown in Fig. 10–33:

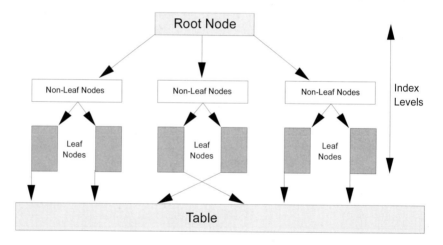

Fig. 10–33 *DB2 index structure*

An index can have several levels. The fewer levels an index has, the more quickly DB2 can access the table or data pages. The index shown in Fig. 10–33 has two levels. Here is a review of the REORGCHK index information.

```
F4: CLUSTERRATIO or normalized CLUSTERFACTOR > 80
F5: 100 *( KEYS*(ISIZE+9)+(CARD-KEYS)*5) / ((NLEAF-NUM EMPTY LEAFS)*INDEXPAGESIZE) >
50
F6: (100-PCTFREE) * (INDEXPAGESIZE-96) / (ISIZE+12) ** (NLEVELS-2) * (INDEXPAGES
IZE-96) / (KEYS * (ISIZE+9) + (CARD-KEYS) * 5) < 100
F7: 100 * (NUMRIDS DELETED / (NUMRIDS DELETED + CARD)) < 20
F8: 100 * (NUM EMPTY LEAFS / NLEAF) < 20
```

```
SCHEMA NAME                    CARD LEAF LVLS ISIZE  KEYS  F4   F5 F6 F7 F8 REORG
--------------------------------------------------------------------------------
Table: DB2CERT.CANDIDATE
SYSIBM  SQL970812225853720   8     1    1    9     8  100   -   -  -  -  ---
--------------------------------------------------------------------------------
```

- SCHEMA - Column indicates the schema to which the index belongs. Remember that the creator of an object is used as the default schema.
- NAME - Column indicates the name of the index. REORGCHK is only specified at the table level. It will show statistics about all the indexes of a table. The information is also collected for system-defined indexes, such as primary key indexes.
- CARD - Indicates the number of rows in the associated base table.
- LEAF - Indicates the number of leaf nodes of the index.
- LVLS (LEVELS) - Indicates the total number of levels of the index.
- ISIZE - Index size calculated from the average column length of the key columns.
- INDEXPAGESIZE - Page size of the table space in which the table indexes reside.
- KEYS - Indicates the number of unique index entries.
- PCTFREE - Percentage of each index page to leave as free space.
- REORG - Column has a separate indicator for each one of the index formulas. An asterisk indicates that reorganization is recommended, and a hyphen indicates that the reorganization is not recommended.

The formulas F4, F5, F6, F7, and F8 provides guidelines for index reorganization. The formulas are shown in the REORGCHK output.

- *F4* indicates the CLUSTERRATIO or normalized CLUSTERFACTOR. This ratio shows the percentage of data rows that are stored in same physical sequence as the index. The clustering ratio of an index should be greater than 80%.
- *F5* calculates space reserved for index entries. Less than 50% of the space allocated for the index should be empty.
- *F6* measures the usage of the index pages. The number of index pages should be more than 90% of the total entries that NLEVELS can handle.
- *F7* measures the number of pseudo-deleted RIDs on non-pseudo-empty pages and should be less than 20%.
- *F8* measures the number of pseudo-empty leaf pages and should be less than 20% of the total number of leaf pages.

Whenever the formulas find that an table reorganization is needed, an asterisk will be shown in the REORG column of the output.

For example, if the CLUSTERRATIO of an index is below the recommended level, the REORG column will appear as:

Maintaining Data

```
REORG
-----
*--
```

 Note: The REORGCHK utility is an analysis tool provided with DB2. To reorganize your tables, you must use the REORG utility.

REORGCHK Options

You can use the CURRENT STATISTICS option of the REORGCHK utility to use the statistics in the system catalog tables at that time. For example, to analyze the current statistics of table DB2CERT.TEST_TAKEN:

```
REORGCHK CURRENT STATISTICS ON TABLE db2cert.test_taken
```

To review the current statistics of all the tables in a database, including the system catalog and user tables:

```
REORGCHK CURRENT STATISTICS ON TABLE ALL
```

You can also verify the organization of the system catalog tables using the SYSTEM option. Alternatively, you can select all the tables under the current user schema name by specifying the USER keyword:

```
REORGCHK CURRENT STATISTICS ON TABLE SYSTEM
```

If you don't specify the CURRENT STATISTICS parameter, REORGCHK will call the RUNSTATS utility.

 Note: REORGCHK cannot be run from the Control Center. You can use the Command Center to run the REORGCHK command and to capture the output for analysis.

Table Reorganization

After using the REORGCHK utility, you may find the physical reorganization of a table necessary. This reorganization is done using the REORG command. To use the REORG utility you must have one of the following authorities: SYSADM, SYSCTRL, SYSMAINT, DBADM, or CONTROL privilege on the table.

 Note: To use the REORG command, you must have one of the following authorities: SYSADM, SYSCTRL, SYSMAINT, DBADM, or CONTROL privilege on the table.

The REORG utility will delete all the unused space and write the table and index data in contiguous pages. With the help of an index, it can also be used to place the data rows in the same physical sequence as the index. These actions can be used to increase the CLUSTERRATIO of the selected index.

Assume that, after running the REORGCHK utility, you find that it is necessary to reorganize the DB2CERT.TEST_TAKEN table.

Here is the syntax of the REORG utility:

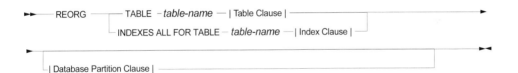

Some of the key parameters to the REORG command include (see the *DB2 UDB V8.1 Command Reference* for further details):

- ALLOW READ ACCESS - allows read access to the table during reorganization.
- ALLOW WRITE ACCESS - allows write access to the table during reorganization.
- RESUME - resumes a previously paused inplace table reorganization.

This command will reorganize the DB2CERT.TEST_TAKEN table and all of its indexes, but will *not* put the data in any specific order.

```
REORG TABLE db2cert.test_taken
```

Maintaining Data

Note: When using REORG, it is mandatory to use the fully qualified name of the table.

Note: DB2 has the ability to perform an online REORG and supports READ/WRITE operations for the entire table, except for the small portion of the table that is being REORGed. Also, the reorg can be performed 'in-place', so there is no requirement to allocate a large amount of temporary space during its operation. Only Type 2 indexes are supported for this operation.

Using an Index to Reorganize a Table

With the help of an index, REORG will put the table data in the same physical order as the selected index is. This operation can help improve the response time in the execution of your applications. This is because the data pages of the table will be placed in sequential order according to an index key. This will help DB2 find the data in contiguous space and in the desired order, reducing the seek time needed to read the data.

If DB2 finds an index with a very high cluster ratio, it may use it to avoid a sort, thus improving the performance of applications that require sort operations.

When your tables have only one index, it is recommended to reorganize the table using that index. If your table has more than one index defined on it, you should select the most frequently used index for that table.

Note: DB2 allows read and update operations on a table and its existing indexes during an index reorganization using the new REORG INDEXES command.

As an example, assume that the table DB2CERT.TEST_CENTER has an index called BY_COUNTRY and that most of the queries that use the table are grouped by country. Therefore, you might want to reorganize the DB2CERT.TEST_CENTER table using the BY_COUNTRY index.

The REORG command is as follows:

```
REORG TABLE db2cert.test_center INDEX BY_COUNTRY
```

The INDEX option tells the REORG utility to use the specified index to reorganize the table. After the REORG command has completed, the physical organization of the table should match the order of the selected index. In this way, the key columns will be found sequentially in the table.

In Fig. 10–34, the *high* cluster ratio index was used to REORG the table shown. The *low* cluster ratio index is shown to emphasize the difference between using and not using an index to perform the reorganization.

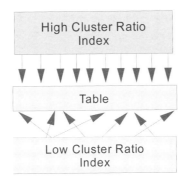

Fig. 10–34 *Cluster ratio*

The arrows in Fig. 10–34 illustrate the position of the index keys in the table. In high cluster ratio index, the keys will be in sequential order. In a low cluster ratio index, the keys will be distributed throughout the table.

A *clustering index* defined on the table may assist DB2 in keeping future data in a clustered index order by trying to insert new rows physically close to the rows for which the key values of the index are in the same range. You can only have one clustering index for a table.

After reorganizing a table using the index option, DB2 will not force the subsequent inserts or updates to match the physical organization of the table. You may wish to run the REORG utility on a regular basis.

Using a Temporary Table Space for Reorganization

While REORG is executing, it creates temporary files (or tables) in the table space where the table resides. You can specify a different table space for the REORG utility. If you want to have control over the location of these tables, you need to specify the USE option.

If the page size of the table space where the table being reorganized resides is 8 KB for instance and you want to use the USE option, the table space specified with this option must have the same page size of 8 KB.

In this example, the temporary tables created during the processing of the REORG utility will be placed in the temporary table space, TEMPSPACE1.

```
REORG TABLE db2cert.test_center INDEX BY_COUNTRY USE
tempspace1
```

Note: In the event of a failure, do *not* delete the temporary files created by REORG. DB2 will need them for recovery purposes.

In addition to using the REORG utility, an index may be created with the MINPCTUSED option to enable an online reorganization of only the index. This parameter indicates the minimum acceptable amount of space used on index pages. If the deletion of records leads to the deletion of index entries on a page in the index and the percentage space used on the index page is less than the MINPCTUSED value, then DB2 may merge two pages, marking one as completely empty. This will impove the performance of the index. The empty page will not be deleted, however; therefore, the size of the index file (SMS) or storage used by the index (DMS) will be unaffected. To delete the empty page and reduce the amount of storage space used, the user must explicitly reorganize the table.

Using the REORG Utility from the Control Center

You can also REORG a table from the Control Center by right-clicking on the table and selecting **Reorganize**. Fig. 10–35 gives an example of how a temporary table space and index to use for the REORG is specified.

Fig. 10–35 *Reorganize Table*

The user has the option to see the command that is generated and to save it or schedule it for later execution (Fig. 10–36):

Fig. 10–36 *REORG command generated*

Recommended Actions After Reorganizing a Table

Table reorganization may help to improve the performance of your applications. There are some additional steps that you should follow. These actions will allow your existing applications to benefit from the table reorganization:

1. Use the RUNSTATS command on the tables and their indexes. This will provide the optimizer with the updated information about the new physical organization of each table and its indexes.

2. Use the REBIND utility on the packages that access the reorganized table. This will allow your applications to take advantage of any changes selected by the optimizer to improve the access strategy of your SQL statements.

Generating Statistics

The system catalog tables contain information about columns, tables, and indexes. They contain such information as the number of rows in a table, the use of space by a table or index, and the number of different values in a column.

However, this information is not kept current. It has to be generated by a utility called RUNSTATS.

The statistics collected by the RUNSTATS utility can be used in two ways: to display the physical organization of the data and to provide information that the DB2 optimizer needs to select the best access path for executing SQL statements.

To have efficient access paths to data, current statistics must exist that reflect the actual state of your tables, columns, and indexes. Whenever a dynamic SQL statement is issued, the DB2 optimizer reads the system catalog tables to review the available indexes, the size of each table, the characteristics of a column, and other information to select the best access path for executing the query.

If the statistics do not reflect the current state of the tables, the DB2 optimizer will not have the correct information to make the best choice in selecting an access path to execute your query. This becomes more crucial as the complexity of the SQL statements increases. When only one table is accessed without indexes, there are fewer choices available to the optimizer. However, when the SQL statement involves several tables, each one with one or more indexes, the number of choices available to the optimizer increases dramatically. Choosing the correct access path can reduce the response time considerably. The next step in improving performance involves the use of the RUNSTATS utility.

It is recommended to you execute RUNSTATS on a frequent basis on tables that have a large number of updates, inserts, or deletes. For tables with a great deal of insert or delete activity, you may decide to run statistics after a fixed period of time or after the insert or delete activity.

 Note: It is recommended to use the RUNSTATS utility after a REORG of a table.

An important feature of DB2 is that it allows you to reorganize and use the RUNSTATS utility on the system catalog tables. This feature of DB2 can improve the access plans generated when querying the system catalog tables. DB2 may access these tables when you issue an SQL statement, even though you are referencing only user tables. Therefore, it is very important to have current statistics on the system catalog tables.

Using the RUNSTATS Utility

To use the RUNSTATS utility you must have one of the following authorities: SYSADM, SYSCTRL, SYSMAINT, DBADM CONTROL privilege on the table, or LOAD authority.

Here is the syntax of the RUNSTATS utility:

Some of the key parameters to the RUNSTATS command include (see the *DB2 UDB V8.1 Command Reference* for further detail):

- FOR INDEXES - collects and updates statistics for indexes only.
- AND INDEXES - collects and updates statistics for both the table and the indexes.
- DETAILED - calculates extended index statistics that are gathered for large indexes.
- SAMPLED - when used with the DETAILED option, a sampling technique is used to estimate the extended index statistics.
- ALLOW WRITE ACCESS - allows users to read and write to the table while statistics are calculated.
- ALLOW READ ACCESS - allows users read access to the table while statistics are calculated.

Maintaining Data

Note: The RUNSTATS command has enhanced the statistics it collects, including: statistics on column combinations, prefetching statistics on the table, index, and index-to-table relationship, able to aaccept a list of index names (previously available only with the API), accept a list of columns on which statistics are to be collected, aaccept distribution statistics limits: NUM_FREQVALUES and NUM_QUANTILES values at the table level (without having to change the configuration parameters, and then disconnect and reconnect all users). The utility also performs faster by taking a sample collection of DETAILED index statistics.

Suppose you are the database administrator and have noticed that every time your decision support system tries to resolve a user request, it takes a considerable amount of time before data is retrieved. You decide to investigate by using the RUNSTATS utility on some of the system catalog tables. This example will use the SYSIBM.SYSCOLUMNS table:

```
RUNSTATS ON TABLE SYSIBM.SYSCOLUMNS
```

The RUNSTATS utility does not produce an explicit result. You can only see its results by querying the system catalog tables.

Here is some of the data updated by RUNSTATS:

TABSCHEMA	TABNAME	CARD	NPAGES	FPAGES	OVERFLOW
SYSIBM	SYSCOLUMNS	927	32	32	1
SYSIBM	SYSTABLES	-1	-1	-1	-1

This output was obtained by selecting all the columns of the SYSSTAT.TABLES catalog view. The -1 (negative one) value indicates that there are no statistics available for that object. The columns of the SYSSTAT.TABLES view have the same meaning as those of the REORGCHK utility:

- CARD - Indicates the number of data rows in the table
- NPAGES - Indicates the total number of pages that contain data
- FPAGES - Indicates the total number of pages that have been allocated to the table
- OVERFLOW - Indicates the number of overflow rows

Identifying Updated Statistics

It is not difficult to identify the absence of available statistics for a specific object. The -1 (negative one) value in the statistical information columns indicates this state. However, it is also important to identify the time of the last update of the object's statistics.

When you perform RUNSTATS on an object, the utility records the timestamp of its execution in the system catalog tables. Depending on the type of object, you can find the timestamp information in SYSCAT.TABLES or SYSCAT.INDEXES. In both views, the information is stored in the STATS_TIME column.

Old statistics may also affect the access path selection. They can mislead the optimizer to choose a improper access plan for an SQL statement.

Having current statistics is the best way to help the optimizer choose the best access path for a particular SQL statement.

Collecting Statistics for Tables and Indexes

It is possible to perform RUNSTATS on a table and all of its indexes at the same time. This is shown in the following command:

```
RUNSTATS ON TABLE db2cert.test_taken AND INDEXES ALL
```

The REORGCHK utility executes the command shown above when it calls the RUNSTATS utility. The INDEXES ALL option indicates that statistics for all the indexes of a table are required. The AND option specifies that you want statistics for the table and the indexes.

Collecting Statistics for Indexes Only

After creating a new index on a table, you may find it useful to gather statistics only for the indexes of that table. If table statistics have never been generated, then this command will generate both table and index statistics; otherwise, only index statistics will be generated.

```
RUNSTATS ON TABLE db2cert.test_taken FOR INDEXES ALL
```

Collecting Distribution Statistics on Table Columns

There may be some columns in which the values are not distributed in a uniform manner or in which the values are concentrated in a particular range.

This kind of nonuniform distribution of data may mislead the optimizer when choosing the most appropriate access method. However, the RUNSTATS utility provides the ability to show this non-uniform distribution to the optimizer. This may improve the access plans for such tables.

In this example, suppose that 75% of the DB2 certification program exams are taken in one testing center and the other 25% are distributed in other testing centers. This nonuniform distribution of values is stored in the DB2CERT.TEST_TAKEN table.

The following command can be used to collect distribution statistics:

```
RUNSTATS ON TABLE db2cert.test_taken WITH DISTRIBUTION
```

The WITH DISTRIBUTION option is used to instruct DB2 to collect data about the distribution of values for the columns in a table. This option is related to three database configuration parameters: NUM_FREQVALUES, NUM_QUANTILES, and STAT_HEAP_SZ. These parameters will limit the action of the WITH DISTRIBUTION option.

- NUM_FREQVALUES - Indicates the number of most frequent values that DB2 will collect. For example, if it is set to 10, only information for the 10 most frequent values will be obtained.

- NUM_QUANTILES - Indicates the number of quantiles that DB2 will look for. This is the amount of information DB2 retains about the distribution of values for columns in the table.

- STAT_HEAP_SZ - Indicates how much memory DB2 uses for collecting these statistics.

This procedure is demanding, and it is not recommended for all your tables. Only tables presenting a high volume of nonuniform values are candidates for this option.

Collecting Detailed Information About Indexes

It is possible to collect data that will give more information about an index, in this example, information on the indexes of the table DB2CERT.TEST_TAKEN:

```
RUNSTATS ON TABLE db2cert.test_taken FOR DETAILED
INDEXES ALL
```

The DETAILED option is used to gather this information. The statistics collected are stored in the CLUSTERFACTOR and PAGE_FETCH_PATRS columns of the SYSIBM.SYSINDEXES system catalog table.

This option generates statistics similar to the CLUSTERRATIO. However, CLUSTERFACTOR and PAGE_FETCH_PAIRS provide a more accurate measurement of the relationship between the index and the data pages. These two values can give the optimizer a more detailed way to model the I/O operations and select a better access path for an SQL statement. The DETAILED option is also affected by the STAT_HEAP_SZ database parameter.

Access to Tables During RUNSTATS

The RUNSTATS utility allows applications different types of access to the table being analyzed:

- CHANGE - Other applications have read/write access to the table.
- REFERENCE - Other applications have read-only access to the table.

You specify this level of access (also known as the *share level*) using the SHRLEVEL option in the RUNSTATS command. For example, while executing RUNSTATS on the CANDIDATE table, you could prevent other applications from writing to the table by using the following command:

```
RUNSTATS ON TABLE db2cert.candidate SHRLEVEL REFERENCE
```

The default level of access allowed to other applications during a RUNSTATS is CHANGE.

Recommended Actions After RUNSTATS

Now that the system catalog tables have been updated, you should perform the following procedures. This will give your applications the benefit of the recently collected statistics about your tables.

- Do a REBIND on the packages that access the reorganized table. This will provide your applications with any changes selected by the DB2 optimizer to

Maintaining Data

improve the access strategy for your SQL statements.

- Dynamic SQL statements will experience immediate benefits from the execution of the RUNSTATS utility. Packages in this situation do not need to be rebound.

Collecting Statistics from the Control Center

By right-clicking on a table in the Control Center, you can click on **Runstats** and update the table's statistics through the graphical interface. You can specify what statistics you would like to collect for both the table and the indexes on that table. Fig. 10–37 shows a RUNSTATS against the SALES table. The Extended Index Statistics option is identical to the DETAILED INDEXES parameter in the RUNSTATS command.

Fig. 10–37 *RUNSTATS from the Control Center*

The user has the option to review the command generated and to save or schedule it to be executed at a later time. Fig. 10–38 shows the command generated:

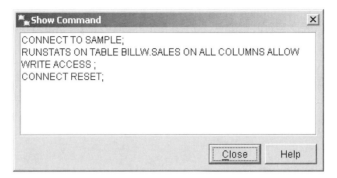

Fig. 10–38 *RUNSTATS command generated*

The Rebind Utility

The REBIND utility provides the ability to recreate a package with the information available in the system catalog tables. This may allow your embedded SQL applications to use a different access path selected by the optimizer.

The REBIND utility is recommended after doing REORG or RUNSTATS. The DB2 SQL optimizer will use the new organization and recently collected statistics to generate an access path. This access path may be better suited to the new physical organization of your data.

Here is the syntax of the REBIND utility:

Fig. 10–39 *REBIND command*

For example, suppose you have an application called db2cert that uses the table DB2CERT.TEST_TAKEN. You have just created a new index for the table, and you need to use REBIND so that the db2cert application can try to use the new index for data access.

```
REBIND db2cert
```

If you made significant changes to your database and updated all the statistics, you might want to recreate the packages for *all* applications that use the database. In this scenario, you might want to use the db2rbind tool. The db2rbind tool allows you to do an explicit rebind of all packages that are currently in the SYSCAT.PACKAGES catalog view. The following command rebinds all packages in the DB2CERT database, and logs the results to db2rbind.log.

```
db2rbind db2cert /l db2rbind.log
```

Data Maintenance Process

As shown in Fig. 10–40, the data mainenance process starts with the RUNSTATS and REORGCHK utilities. The REORGCHK utility can execute the RUNSTATS utility at the same time. However, it is recommended to call RUNSTATS separately, so you can control the utility's options and customize it for your environment.

After performing RUNSTATS, the REORGCHK utility reviews the statistics collected, applies six formulas, and then gives recommendations about whether a REORG is needed.

Fig. 10–40 *The data maintenance process*

If reorganization is recommended, use the REORG utility on the selected objects and then do RUNSTATS and REBIND. You must perform a REBIND on any packages affected by the above operations, so they can take advantage of the benefits of the new physical organization and updated statistics. After performing subsequent update, insert, and delete operations, as part of the data maintenance process, repeat by first executing the RUNSTATS utility.

Establish a routine for RUNSTATS and the REBIND processes. Updated statistics will give you precise information about your database state.

Modeling a Production Environment

You can use the SYSSTAT schema to update system catalog statistical information. You can enter values for statistics such as table cardinality, column distribution, or index cluster ratio. In doing so, you will be able to model different volumes of data on test databases.

This is useful when you want to be sure that the access paths your applications use in your production environment are the same as those in your development environment. The access paths selected by the optimizer in each environment may differ because of different data volumes.

By updating the SYSSTAT views, you will be able to provide the optimizer with the same environment found in different databases. The update procedure is performed using the SQL UPDATE statement.

There are five updatable views under the SYSSTAT schema. These views are:

- SYSSTAT.TABLES
- SYSSTAT.COLUMNS
- SYSSTAT.INDEXES
- SYSSTAT.COLDIST
- SYSSTAT.FUNCTIONS

These catalog views can be used to provide a "what-if" analysis for your database applications. For example, you can increase the cardinality of a table or the cluster ratio of an index.

You can use the REBIND utility to model the behavior of your static SQL applications in the "what-if" analysis process. You can create or drop an index and then use the REBIND utility to see how the access plan is affected.

As a general recommendation, only update the SYSSTAT schema view in a development environment.

The DB2LOOK Utility

The DB2LOOK utility can be used to do one of three tasks. It can generate a report of database statistics. This report file can be a postscript, LaTeX, or a normal text file. (LaTeX, like HTML, is a markup language used to represent documents.)

DB2LOOK can also be used extract statistics and/or the Data Definition Language (DDL) statements for the creation of tables, indexes, views, and so on that are needed to generate a Command Line Processor (CLP) script file used to recreate database objects and/or to update the statistics.

Why is it useful? If an application developer needs access to a database that is the same as the production database except for the data it contains, the DB2LOOK utility can be used to extract the DDL and statistics into a script. This script can then be used to create a "development" database and update the statistics without actually copying the production data to the development database. An application programer can now use the development database for testing code. In addition, performance evaluation can be undertaken using utilities like Visual Explain, which use the database statistics to report on how an SQL statement will be executed and give an indication of its likely performance.

Here is the syntax of the db2look utility:

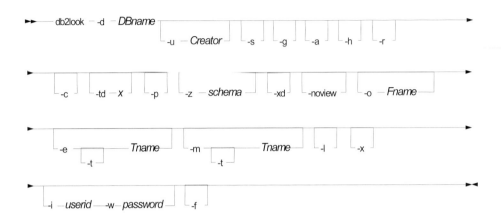

Some of the key parameters to the db2look command include (see the *DB2 UDB V8.1 Command Reference* for further detail):

- -d DBname - The name of the database must be specified. This is not optional.
- -u Creator - If specified, only information about objects created by the Creator will be extracted.
- -a - Option will allow information to be extracted for all objects in the database. If neither -u or -a is specified, the USER environment variable is used. When using Windows NT, no default value is specified for this environment variable, in which case a SET USER=XXXX statement can be used prior to the invocation of the utility to set the USER environment variable.
- -s - Flag will cause the utility to format the output to LaTeX file and then convert it to a postscript file. This requires LaTeX software to be installed.
- -g - Flag is similar to the -s option. The difference is a graph that will be created to show fetch page pairs for indices. This requires LaTeX and Gnuplot software to be installed.
- -p - If specified, this flag will cause the information extracted to be formatted as a plain text file.
- -o filename - Specifies the file name that is to be used for the output files. The extension need not be specified. If the output file is a LaTeX file, the tex extension will be used. If the output file is a postscript file, ps will be used, and if it is a text file, then txt will be used. If the utility is used to generate a CLP script file, no extension will be added to the file name.
- -e - Flag will inform the utility to extract the necessary DDL statements to rec-

reate some objects in the database, including tables, indexes, views, and triggers.

- -l - Option indicate that DDL statements for the creation of table spaces, buffer pools and database partition groups.
- -x - Should be used to extract various GRANT statements used to duplicate the authorization aspects of the database and the objects in it.
- -m - If this flag is specified, the utility will run in mimic mode. It will generate a text file that contains all the SQL statements required to update the statistics in the updatable catalog views of a target database to reflect that of the source database.
- -c - Flag indicates to the utility that no COMMIT, CONNECT, or CONNECT RESET statements should be generated in the output file. This flag is ignored if the -m flag is not specified.
- -r - Flag will cause the utility to not execute the RUNSTATS command prior to the extraction of statistics from the catalog.
- -i userid - Specifies the userid to use when running the DB2LOOK utility against a remote database.
- -w password - Specifies the password to use when running the DB2LOOK utility against a remote database.

Here is an example of using the DB2LOOK command:

A production database named DB2CERT exists on a server that is exclusively used for production. Application programmers that develop applications that use the DB2CERT database require access to a database that has the same structure as the one in production. The DBA decides to extract the DDL script from the DB2CERT database to use it to build a database named NEWCERT on the server that is to be used for development only. The command the DBA uses to extract the DDL is:

```
db2look -d db2cert -a -o db2cert.ddl -e -x -l
```

The DBA edits the DB2CERT.DDL file, replaces DB2CERT with NEWCERT in the CONNECT statement and executes the following command:

```
db2 -tvf db2cert.ddl
```

The Control Center allows a user-friendly method to invoke the DB2LOOK utility. Simply right-click the mouse on the required database object and select the **Generate DDL** option (Fig. 10–41).

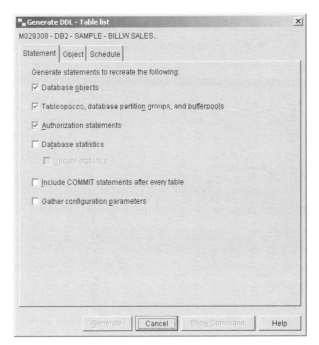

Fig. 10–41 *Generate DDL*

Executing DB2LOOK from the Control Center

The DB2LOOK utility can be invoked remotely, so the user does not specify the output file name in which the output will be stored. Instead, the user can look at the script file produced by invoking the Script Center to view and edit the script, as shown in Figure 10–42.

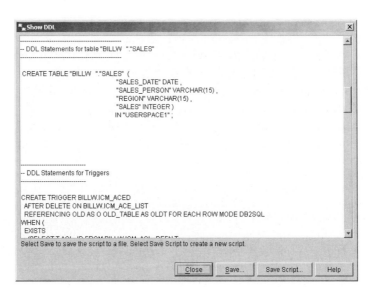

Fig. 10–42 *Task Center listing the DB2LOOK output script*

Summary

This chapter has dealt with the issues of data movement, organization, and placement in your database. Various utilities in DB2 Universal Database that move data into database tables and to extract data from tables have been reviewed. These included the EXPORT, IMPORT, and LOAD utilities. Included in this discussion was a summary of the various file types allowed by DB2. The numerous options provided with these commands give you flexibility in their use. These utilities can be invoked either graphically through the Control Center or by any of the command line tools.

The EXPORT utility exports data from a database to an operating system file, which can be in one of several external file formats. The following information is required when exporting data:

- A SELECT statement specifying the data to be exported
- The path and name of the operating system file that will store the exported data.
- The format of the data in the input file. This format can be IXF, WSF, or DEL.

The IMPORT utility inserts data from an input file into a table or updatable view. If the table or view receiving the imported data already contains data, you can either replace or append to the existing data. The IMPORT utility requires the following information:

- The path and the name of the input file.
- The name or alias of the target table or view.
- The format of the data in the input file. This format can be IXF, WSF, DEL, or ASC.
- Whether the input data is to be inserted into the table or view, or whether existing data in the table or view is to be updated or replaced by the input data.

The LOAD utility is capable of efficiently moving large quantities of data into newly created tables, or into tables that already contain data. The utility can handle most data types, including large objects (LOBs) and user-defined types (UDTs). The LOAD utility is faster than the IMPORT utility, because it writes formatted pages directly into the database, while the IMPORT utility performs INSERTs. The LOAD utility does not fire triggers, and does not perform referential or table constraints checking (other than validating the uniqueness of the indexes). The following information is required for loading data:

- The path and the name of the input file, named pipe, or device.
- The name or alias of the target table.
- The format of the input source. This format can be DEL, ASC, PC/IXF, or CURSOR.
- Whether the input data is to be appended to the table, or is to replace the existing data in the table.

Maintaining Data

Getting data into relational tables is just the first step. DB2 utilities and commands are provided to maintain the data. This includes the analysis of data in tables and indexes with the REORGCHK utility, physically changing the organization of the table and index data using the REORG command, and how to update the statistics of table and index data using the RUNSTATS command.

When an indexed table has been modified many times, the data in the indexes may become fragmented. If the table is clustered with respect to an index, the table and index can get out of cluster order. Both of these factors can adversely affect the performance of scans using the index, and can impact the effectiveness of index page prefetching. REORG INDEXES can be used to reorganize all of the indexes on a table, to remove any fragmentation and restore physical clustering to the leaf pages.

Tables that have been modified so many times that data is fragmented and access performance is noticeably slow are candidates for the REORG TABLE command. After reorganizing a table, use RUNSTATS to update the table statistics. After running RUNSTATS, a REBIND should be issued to ensure that the applications are aware of the updated statistics in your environment.

CHAPTER **11**

Database Recovery

- ◆ LOG FILES
- ◆ LOGGING
- ◆ BACKUP
- ◆ RESTORE
- ◆ ROLLFORWARD RECOVERY
- ◆ HIGH AVAILABILITY SCENARIOS

One of the fundamental functions of any database management system is the ability to recover from events that would lead to the integrity of the database being compromised. DB2 is no different in this regard and has a number of features and functions available to help you manage your environment and ensure that you can perform adequate recovery of your data.

In this chapter, the concept of logging in a relational database system as it relates to the recovery of a database will be discussed. In addition, the major utilities involved in the area of database recovery, BACKUP and RESTORE, will be reviewed.

Database Recovery Concepts

While DB2 has mechanisms to provide automatic recovery from situations that threaten the integrity of its databases, it cannot cater to all situations, especially unforeseen external events. While it is impossible to cover every possible scenario, careful planning can ensure that recovery is possible for the majority of situations with minimum loss of data.

Some situations you should consider are:

- System outage - The operating system fails due to a hardware or software problem. An interruption to the power supply also falls under this category.
- Transaction failure - A transaction fails before completion. What happens to changes made to the database before the point of failure?
- Media failure - A disk drive failure causes a partial or complete loss of data on the disk.
- Disaster - A wide range of nontrivial damage to more than just a single component of the system. The facility at which the system is located suffers damage that impacts the system's operation.

Unit of Work

To ensure consistency of the data in a database, it is often necessary for applications to apply a number of changes together as a unit. This is called a *unit of work*. A unit of work is a recoverable sequence of operations within an application process. It is the basic mechanism that an application uses to ensure database integrity. At any time, an application process has a single unit of work, but the life of an application process may involve many units of work.

Transaction

Units of work are also known as *transactions*. Any application that successfully connects to a database automatically starts a transaction. The application must end the transaction by issuing a COMMIT or a ROLLBACK statement. The COMMIT statement tells the database manager to apply all database changes (inserts, updates, deletes, creates, alters, grants, revokes) to the database at once. The ROLLBACK statement tells the database manager not to apply the changes but to return the affected rows back to their state before the beginning of the transaction.

Types of Recovery

Recovery can be one of the following: crash, version, or roll-forward. Each type will now be examined.

Crash Recovery

Crash recovery protects a database from being left in an inconsistent or unusable state. Units of work against the database can be interrupted unexpectedly. For example, should a power failure occur before all of the changes that are part of a unit of work are completed and committed, the database will be left in an inconsistent state.

The database is made consistent again by undoing the uncommitted transactions. The RESTART DATABASE command initiates this function. If the AUTORESTART database configuration parameter is set to ON (which is the default), the first connection to the database after a failure will initiate the RESTART DATABASE.

Version Recovery

Version recovery allows for the restoration of a previous version or image of the database that was made using the BACKUP command.

Restoration of the database will rebuild the entire database using a backup of the database made at some point in time earlier. A backup of the database allows you to restore a database to a state identical to the time when the backup was made. Every unit of work from the time of the backup to the end of the log files is lost. (These can be recovered using roll-forward recovery.)

The version recovery method requires a full database backup for each version you may want to restore in the future. DB2 supports version recovery by default.

Roll-Forward Recovery

This technique extends the version recovery by using full database backups in conjunction with log files to provide the capability of restoring a database or selected table spaces to a particular point in time.

By using a full database backup as a baseline, if all the log files are available covering the time period from the time of the backup to the current time, you can choose to have DB2 apply all the units of work for any or all table spaces in the database, up to any time within the time period covered by the logs.

Roll-forward recovery is specified at a database level in DB2 and has to be explicitly enabled.

Database Recovery

> **Note:** The catalog table space SYSCATSPACE, when used in table space roll-forward recovery, *must* be rolled forward to the end of the logs. It can be rolled forward to a point in time as part of database roll-forward recovery.

Recovery Strategies

Some of the factors to consider when formulating a recovery strategy include:

- Will the database be recoverable or nonrecoverable?
- How near to the time of failure will you need to recover the database (the point of recovery)?
- How much time can be spent recovering the database?
- How large a window do you have for all recovery activities?
- What storage resources are available for storing backups and log files?

In general, a database maintenance and recovery strategy should ensure that all information is available when it is required for database recovery. In addition, you should include elements that reduce the likelihood and impact of database failure.

Recoverable and Nonrecoverable Databases

Recoverable databases in DB2 are distinguished by the LOGRETAIN and/or USEREXIT database configuration parameters being enabled. This means that crash, version, *and* roll-forward recovery techniques are available for use.

Nonrecoverable databases *do not* support roll-forward recovery.

The decision whether a database should be recoverable depends on factors such as:

- If the database is query only, then there will be no units of work in the log, therefore the database may not need to be recoverable.
- If there is little volatility in the database (that is, few changes to the data) and the data can be recreated easily, then you may wish to consider not having your database recoverable.
- Databases that have data that is not easily recreated should be made recoverable.
- If there is a lot of update activity, a recoverable database should be considered.

Online and Offline Access

When performing the various database recovery activities, the database can be considered *offline* or *online*.

Online means that other applications can connect to the database during the operation being performed. Conversely, offline means that no other application can use the database while the operation is in progress.

Offline and online are not available for all recovery activities.

Use of Log Files

All DB2 databases have logs associated with them. These logs keep a record of all changes made to database objects and data. All the changes are first written to log buffers in memory before being flushed to the log files on disk at COMMIT time.

For example, in case of a mishap such as power failure, the log files would be used to bring the database back to a consistent state. All units of work would be re-applied using the log files, and then all uncommitted units of work would be rolled back.

Log files have a predefined, configurable size. Therefore, when one log file is filled, logging continues in another log file.

Fig. 11–1 shows how multiple log files are being used to manage concurrent transactions. The top part of the diagram represents the evolution of three user processes (1 - 3) accessing the same database. The boxes represent database changes such as inserts or updates. The life of every transaction is also depicted (A - F). The lower-middle section of the diagram shows how the database changes are synchronously recorded in the log files (x,y). The letter in each box indicates the transaction to which the database change belongs.

 Note: DB2 uses a write-ahead-logging scheme to ensure data integrity by having any updates, deletes, or inserts of data written first to the log files. At a later time, these changes are then written to the relational database.

When a COMMIT is issued, the log buffer containing the transaction is written to disk. This is represented by the arrows and the small wavy lines. Transaction E is never written to disk because it ends with a ROLLBACK statement. When log file x runs out of room to store the first database change of transaction D, the logging process switches to log file y. Log file x remains active until all transaction C changes are written to the database disk files. The period of time during which log file x remains active after logging is switched to log file y is represented by the hexagon.

Fig. 11–1 *Transaction log file use*

Log Buffers

Before being written to the log files, log records are first written into buffers. The size of these buffers range from 4 to 512 four-kilobyte pages, with the default setting of eight pages. The database configuration parameter that defines the size of the log buffer is called LOGBUFSZ. The memory is allocated from an area called the database heap, whose size is controlled by the database configuration parameter DBHEAP.

The log records are written to disk when one of the following occurs:

- A transaction commits or a group of transactions commit, as defined by the MINCOMMIT database configuration parameter.
- The log buffer is full.
- As a result of some other *internal* database manager event.

Buffering the log records will result in more efficient logging file I/O because the log records will be written to disk less frequently, and more log records will be written to the log files at each I/O. If there is considerable logging activity in the system, increase the size of the log buffers to improve performance.

Primary and Secondary Log Files

There are two types of log files: primary and secondary.

- *Primary* log files establish a fixed amount of storage allocated to the recovery log files. These files are preallocated during the first connection to the database. The database configuration parameter LOGPRIMARY determines the number of primary log files created of a size specified by the LOGFILSIZ database configuration parameter.

- *Secondary* log files are allocated one at a time as needed (up to the value of the database configuration parameter LOGSECOND) when the primary log files become full. The size of secondary log files is also specified by the LOGFILSIZ database configuration parameter.

  One recommendation is to use secondary log files for databases that have periodic needs for large amounts of log space. For example, an application that is run once a month may require log space beyond that provided by the primary log files.

 Note: The default value of LOGFILSIZ is 1000 pages for Linux and UNIX-based versions of DB2. For Windows, the value is 250 pages. The page size is always 4 KB.

Types of Logging

There are two types of logging that can occur in DB2: circular and archival.

- *Circular logging* supports nonrecoverable databases. This type of logging uses active log files only (see below for details). Primary and secondary log files are used as described above. When a log file has had all of its transactions committed or rolled back, then it can be reused. Roll-forward recovery is not possible with this logging method, whereas crash recovery and version recovery are available. This is the default logging method when a DB2 database is created.

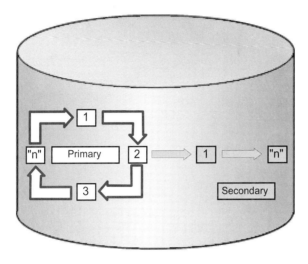

Fig. 11–2 *Circular logging*

The circular logging method is shown in Fig. 11–2.

- *Archival logging* is where log files are archived when they become inactive. Archival logging is not the default logging method. It is the only method that will allow you to support roll-forward recovery and implement recoverable databases. There are three types of log files associated with this method, shown in Fig. 11–3.

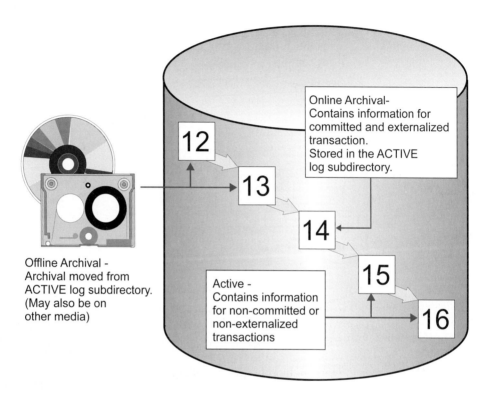

Fig. 11–3 *Archival logging*

Log files can be classified as follows:

- *Active* - Indicated by numbers 15 and 16. These files contain information related to units of work that have not yet been committed (or rolled back). They also contain information about transactions that have been committed but whose changes have not yet been written to the database files.

  Active log files are used by crash recovery to prevent a failure from leaving the database in an inconsistent state. The RESTART DATABASE situation (for crash recovery) and ROLLFORWARD command (for point-in-time recovery or recovery to the end of the logs) use the active logs to reapply or roll back units of work if necessary to bring the database to a point of consistency.

 Note: DB2 supports log mirroring at the database level. The DB2 configuration parameter, MIRRORLOGPATH, enables the database to write an identical copy of the log files to a different path.

- *Online Archived* - Indicated by number 14. When all changes in the active log are no longer needed for normal processing, the log is closed and becomes an archived log.

  These files contain information related to completed transactions no longer required for restart recovery. They are called *online* because they reside in the same subdirectory as the active log files.

- *Offline Archived* - Indicated by numbers 12 and 13. These log files have been moved from the active log file directory. The method of moving these files could be a manual or automated process such as that invoked by a user exit. Archived log files can be placed offline simply by moving them to another directory or storing them on tape or other medium. They can also be managed by an external storage manager such as IBM's TSM (Tivoli Storage Manager) products.

Two database configuration parameters, LOGRETAIN and USEREXIT, allow you to configure a database for archival logging.

When the LOGRETAIN database configuration parameter is enabled, log files are not deleted when they become inactive. When the USEREXIT database configuration parameter is enabled, DB2 will call the user exit program when a log file is ready for archiving. The database name, path of the log file, and several other parameters are passed to the program.

If the user exit option is enabled, you have the option of issuing the ARCHIVE LOG command to force a log archive.

> **Note:** The default setting for LOGRETAIN and USEREXIT is NO; thus circular logging is the default.

Roll-forward recovery can use online archived logs, offline archived logs, and active logs to rebuild a database or table space either at the end of the logs or at a specific point in time. The roll-forward function achieves this by reapplying committed units of work that are found in the archived and active logs to the restored database.

> **Note:** The current log file path is indicated by the database configuration parameter LOGPATH. When a database is created, the log files are placed under the default database directory. The NEWLOGPATH database configuration parameter is used to change the log file location.

Database Recovery

Log File Usage

There are some considerations to bear in mind in relation to the use of log files. These considerations are as follows.

Erasing Logs

If an active log is erased, the database becomes unusable and must be restored before it can be used again.

If an archive log is erased, you will only be able to roll-forward changes up to the first log erased.

It is critical that all log files be protected by the security subsystem of the operating system. Other than the process of moving archive logs out of the log path directory, no other user or application other than DB2 has any need to access the log files.

Using the Not Logged Initially Option

The NOT LOGGED INITIALLY option exists for the CREATE TABLE and ALTER TABLE statements. When this option is used, no loggable activity within the unit of work that creates or alters the table or activates this option at a later time is logged. This is an advantage when inserting or updating a large amount of data into a table for the first time. This option is also suitable for work tables where data can be easily recreated.

The advantage of this option is the improvement in performance due to the absence of logging overhead; the disadvantage is the lack of recoverability of the unit of work.

Logging Using Raw Devices

Normally, log files use the standard operating system file systems to support their implementation (e.g., NTFS for Windows, JFS for AIX).

In addition to the standard file systems, you can use raw devices for logging. By using raw devices, you can avoid the overhead of using the file system, and therefore logging performance should be improved. This support is available on the Windows, AIX, and Solaris operating systems.

This involves using an unformatted hard disk partition (Windows) or a raw logical volume (AIX). The database configuration parameter NEWLOGPATH is set to point to the raw device.

Some considerations for using raw devices for logging are:

- Primary log files (extents) are still used according to the LOGPRIMARY and LOGFILSIZ database configuration parameters. The amount of space in the raw device must be at least ($LOGPRIMARY * (LOGFILSIZ + 2)) + 1$) pages of 4 KB each.

- Secondary log files are not used. You may have to increase the number and/or size of primary log files to compensate for this.

Refer to the *DB2 UDB V8.1 Administration Guide* for more details about logging using raw devices.

Block Transactions When Log Directory is Full

The DBM configuration parameter BLK_LOG_DSK_FUL can be used to prevent "disk full" errors from being generated when DB2 cannot create a new log file in the active log path. DB2 attempts to create the log file every five minutes and writes a message to the db2diag.log file after each attempt. An analysis of the db2diag.log file can confirm if the application is hanging.

 Note: The maximum amount of log space has been increased from 32GB to 256GB. Infinite active logging is also new and allows an active unit of work to span the primary logs and archive logs, enabling a transaction to use an infinite number of log files.

Version Recovery Using Backup and Restore

Version recovery is implemented using the BACKUP and RESTORE commands. These two commands will now be examined in greater detail.

Backing Up a Database

The BACKUP command can be invoked from the Command Line Processor, Command Center, application programming interface, or Control Center.

Before taking a backup, consider the following:

- You must have SYSADM, SYSCTRL, or SYSMAINT authority to invoke BACKUP.
- The database may be local or remote. The backup itself remains on the database server.
- The BACKUP command can interface with an external storage manager such as TSM to directly manage the backup image.
- BACKUP can directly send its output to tape via the operating system.
- BACKUP can directly send its output to disk on all platforms.
- Multiple backup files may be created to contain the backed-up data from the database.

When you invoke the BACKUP command, you should be aware of the following:

- DB2 must be started.
- The database must be in a normal or backup-pending state.
- When using the BACKUP utility, refer to the database name by its alias. In most cases this will be the same name as the database.
- You can run the backup in online mode via the ONLINE parameter or in offline mode, which is the default. Online mode allows other applications to remain connected to the database and do active work while the backup is proceeding. Alternately, for an offline backup, only the backup job itself may be connected to the database.

  For online mode, the database must be recoverable; that is, archive logging must be enabled. When running in online mode, DB2 attempts to acquire S (share) locks on tables with LOBs (large objects). This might result in failures running the utility due to applications connected to the database holding incompatible locks.

In addition, consider the following to improve the backup performance:

- The value of the PARALLELISM parameter. Using this parameter can reduce the amount of time required to complete the backup. It defines the number of processes or threads that are started to read data from the database. Each process or thread is assigned to back up a specific table space. When it completes backing up the table space, it requests another. Increasing the value requires additional processor and memory resources. The default value is one.
- The backup buffer size and number of buffers. If you use multiple buffers and I/O channels, you should use at least twice as many buffers as channels to ensure that the channels do not have to wait for data. The size of the buffers should ideally be a multiple of the table space extent size. If you have differing extent sizes, choose a multiple of the largest extent size. If the buffer size if not specified the value is taken from the database manager configuration parameter BACKBUFSZ, which by default is 1024 (4 KB) pages.

Backup Images Created by Backup

Backup images are created at the target specified when the BACKUP utility is invoked:

- In the directory for disk backups
- At the device specified for tape backups
- At an external storage manager server

The *recovery history file* is updated automatically with summary information whenever you carry out a backup of a database. This information is useful when tracking the backup history of a database. Other utilities' activities are also recorded in this file.

In UNIX-based environments, the file name(s) created on disk will consist of a concatenation of the following information, separated by periods; on other platforms, a four-level subdirectory tree structure is used:

- *Database alias* - A one to eight character database alias name that was supplied when the backup command was invoked.
- *Type* - Type of backup taken, where: "0" is for full database, "3" is for table space.
- *Instance name* - A one to eight character name of the instance.
- *Node number* - The node number.
- *Catalog node number* - The node number of the database's catalog node.
- *Time stamp* - A 14-character representation of the date and time the backup was performed. The timestamp is in the format yyyymmddhhmmss, where:

    yyyy is the year (1995 to 9999), mm is the month (01 to 12),
    dd is the day of the month (01 to 31), hh is the hour (00 to 23),
    mm is the minutes (00 to 59), ss is the seconds (00 to 59).
- *Sequence number* - A three-digit sequence number used as a file extension.

In UNIX-based operating systems, the format would appear as:

```
DB_alias.Type.Inst.nodennnn.catnnnn.timestamp.seq_num
```

For example, a database named STAFF in the DB601 instance is backed up to disk as a file named:

```
STAFF.0.DB601.NODE0000.CATN0000.20000715120112.001
```

On Windows, the format appears as:

```
DB_alias.Type\Inst\nodennnn\catnnnn\yyyymmdd\hhmmss.seq_num
```

Database Recovery

For example, a database called DB2CERT in instance DB2 is backed up to disk as a file named:

```
D:\DB2CERT.0\DB2\NODE0000\CATN0000\20020715\122229.001
```

For tape-directed output, file names are not created; however, the above information is stored in the backup header for verification purposes.

Examples of Using Backup

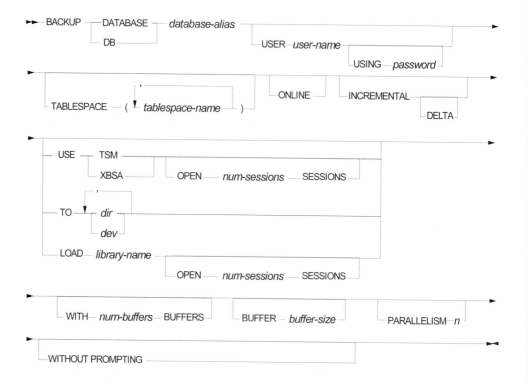

Some of the key parameters to the BACKUP command include (see the *DB2 UDB V8.1 Command Reference* for further details):

- ONLINE - specifies an online backup, offline is the default.
- INCREMENTAL - specifies a backup of all data since the last full backup.
- DELTA - specifies a backup of data since the most recent backup operation of any type.

You can run the BACKUP command from the DB2 Command Line Processor or DB2 Command Center. For example:

```
BACKUP DATABASE DB2CERT TO C:\DBBACKUP
```

This command backs up the database DB2CERT to the C:\DBBACKUP directory on a Windows system. The other parameters take their default values.

```
BACKUP DATABASE DB2CERT TO /dev/rmt0
        WITH 2 BUFFERS
        BUFFER 512
        PARALLELISM 2
```

This command backs up the database DB2CERT to a tape device on an AIX system. Two buffers of 512 (4 KB) pages each are allocated. Two parallel tasks are used to backup in parallel.

You can also use the Control Center to invoke a backup. After right-clicking on the database you wish to back up, select the Backup Database option, as shown in Fig. 11–4:

Database Recovery

Fig. 11–4 *Backing up a database from the Control Center*

The Backup Wizard panel is displayed:

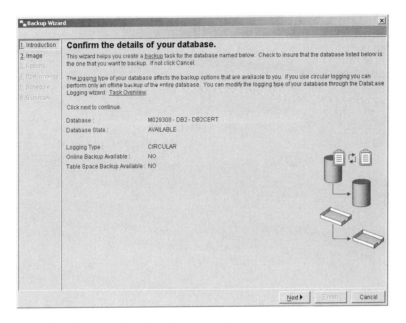

Fig. 11–5 *Confirm the details of your database*

This panel introduces the Backup Wizard. Click **Next**.

Fig. 11–6 *Specify where to store your backup image*

Here you can choose whether to perform the backup to a file system, tape, TSM, XBSA, or third-party. In this example, select File System, click on Add, and select the directory DBBACKUP and click OK to get back to this panel. Click Next.

Note: The DB2 backup can now interface with solutions from storage vendors that have implemented the XBSA (Backup Services APIs) industry standard interface.

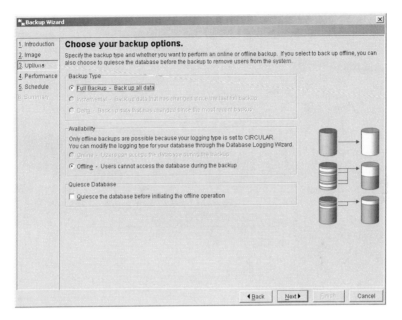

Fig. 11–7 *Choose your backup options*

If archive logging was enabled, this panel would offer the DBA the choice of performing the backup procedure online. Archive logging also enables the incremental backup to be performed. For this example, click **Next**.

Database Recovery

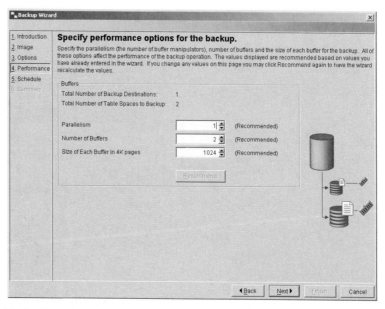

Fig. 11–8 *Specify performance options for the backup*

This panel lets you select options that affect the performance of the backup procedure. Click **Next**.

Note: After an online backup is complete, DB2 will close the current active log. This operational enhancement makes it easier to ensure that the online backup has the necessary archived logs for recovery.

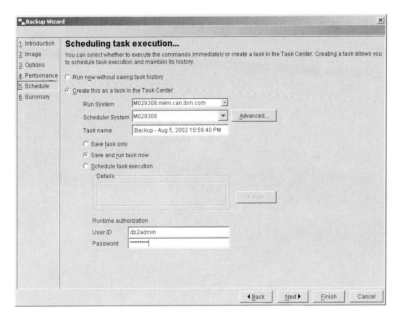

Fig. 11–9 *Scheduling task execution...*

You can perform the backup procedure to execute immediately or schedule it as a task for the Task Center. Select the radio button Save and run task now, enter a valid user ID and password, Click **Next**.

Fig. 11–10 *Task creation summary...*

Before launching the backup procedure, you have the option to save the script into a file. Click **Finish**.

In both cases, you can monitor and view the results of running the BACKUP command through the Journal, which can be invoked from the Control Center.

Incremental Backup

DB2 allows for two kinds of incremental backup, they are:

- Incremental - a copy of all of the data that has changed since the last full backup operation.
- Delta - a copy of all of the data that has changed since the last successful backup (full, incremental, or delta).

Combinations of database and table space incremental backups are allowed, and the operations can take place either offline or online.

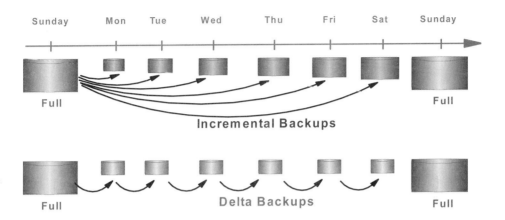

Fig. 11–11 *Incremental backup usage*

 Note: DB2 will now allow a database backup to restored to a system with a different code page.

Restoring a Database

The RESTORE command can be invoked from the Command Line Processor, Command Center, application programming interface, or Control Center.

Before performing a restore, consider the following:

- You must have SYSADM, SYSCTRL, or SYSMAINT authority to perform a RESTORE to an existing database and SYSADM or SYSCTRL if performing a RESTORE to an new database.
- You can only use this command if the database has been previously backed up with the BACKUP command.
- The RESTORE command can interface with an external storage manager such as TSM to directly use a backup image managed by the external storage manager.
- RESTORE requires an exclusive connection to the database; no applications can be running against the database when the utility is started. Once it starts, it prevents other applications from accessing the database until the restore is completed.
- The database may be local or remote.

When you invoke the RESTORE command, you should be aware of the following:

- DB2 must be started.
- You can restore to a new or an existing database.

- You can run the restore in online mode via the ONLINE parameter for table space restores only.
- The TAKEN AT parameter requires the timestamp for the backup. If there is more than one backup image in the same directory, this parameter is required. The timestamp can be exactly as it was displayed after the completion of a successful backup, that is, the format yyyymmddhhmmss. It can also be a partial timestamp as long as it is not ambiguous in identifying a backup image. If this parameter is not specified when using TSM, the latest the backup image is used for restoration.

In addition, consider the following to improve the performance of RESTORE:

- The value of the PARALLELISM parameter. Using this parameter can reduce the amount of time required to complete the restore. It defines the number of processes or threads that started for restore processing. The default value is one

Note: There is no affiliation between a thread/process with a table space during the recovery process.

- Increasing the restore buffer size and number of buffers. You can improve the performance of RESTORE by increasing the restore buffer size (BUFFER parameter) and number of buffers (WITH n BUFFERS parameter).

  The minimum value for the BUFFER parameter is 8 pages; the default value is 1024 pages. The restore buffer pool size must be a positive integer multiple of the backup buffer size specified during the backup operation.

  For example, if a backup buffer size of 1024 pages was specified and an attempt made to restore this backup with a buffer size of 16 pages, the actual restore buffer size would be 1024. If the specified restore buffer size were 2049, the actual restore buffer size would be 2048.

Note: If a failure occurs during a database restore, the database will not be usable until a successful restore is completed.

Examples of Using Restore

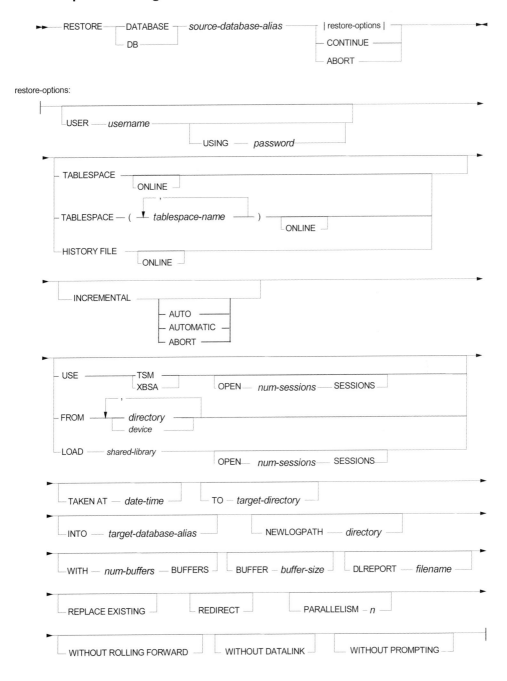

Some of the key parameters to the RESTORE command include (see the *DB2 UDB V8.1 Command Reference* for further detail):

- ONLINE - applicable only when performing a table space-level restore.
- HISTORY FILE - specifies to restore only the history file from the backup image.
- INCREMENTAL - without any additional parameters, this specifies a manual cumulative restore operation.
- INCREMENTAL AUTO/AUTOMATIC - specifies an automatic cumulative restore operation.
- REDIRECT - specifies a redirected restore operation. This command should be followed by one or more SET TABLESPACE CONTAINERS commands, and then by a RESTORE DATABASE command with the CONTINUE option.
- WITHOUT ROLLING FORWARD - specifies the database is not to be put in rollforward pending state after it has been successfully restored.

You can run the RESTORE command from the Command Line Processor or Command Center. For example:

```
RESTORE DATABASE DB2CERT FROM C:\DBBACKUP
```

This command restores the database DB2CERT from the C:\DBBACKUP directory on a Windows system. The other parameters use their default values. This may leave the database in a roll-forward pending state that requires the ROLLFORWARD command be executed before the database can be accessed.

```
RESTORE DATABASE DB2CERT FROM C:\DBBACKUP
        WITHOUT ROLLING FORWARD
        WITHOUT PROMPTING
```

The above RESTORE command eliminates the requirement for the ROLLFORWARD command to be executed. The ROLLFORWARD command is discussed in greater detail later in this chapter in "Rolling Forward Databases and Table Spaces" on page 633.

The WITHOUT PROMPTING option specifies that the restore will run unattended and any actions that normally require user intervention will instead return an error message.

```
RESTORE DATABASE DB2CERT FROM C:\DBBACKUP
        INTO NEWDB
        WITH 2 BUFFERS
        BUFFER 512
        WITHOUT ROLLING FORWARD
```

The above command restores the database into a new database called NEWDB and assigns two restore buffers of 512 pages each.

You can also use the Control Center to invoke a restore. After right-clicking on the database you wish to restore, select the Restore Database option, as shown in Fig. 11–12. The example below allows us to restore to an existing database.

Fig. 11–12 *Restoring a database using the Control Center*

The Restore Data Wizard panel is displayed:

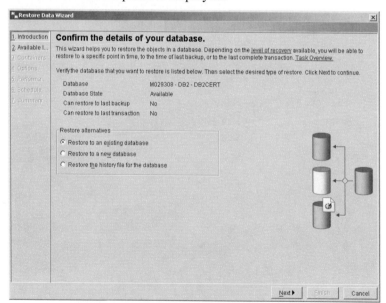

Fig. 11–13 *Confirm the details of your database*

The first panel of the restore wizard allows you the option to restore to an existing database, a new database (redirected restore), or restore the history file of the database. Select the Restore to an existing database option, click Next.

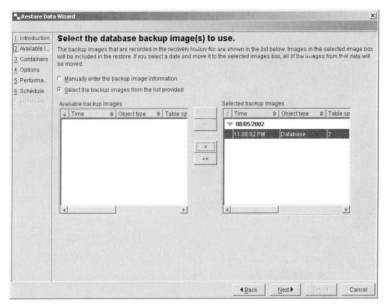

Fig. 11–14 *Select the database backup image(s) to use*

If a backup is on the system, it will be highlighted. Select the appropriate backup and move the selection to the Selected backup images window, by clicking on the arrow key.

Database Recovery

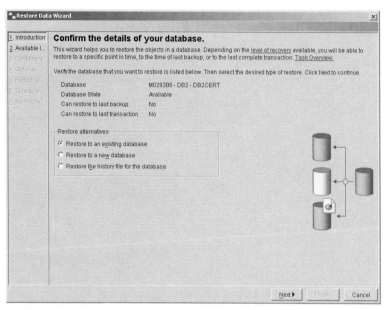

Fig. 11–15 *Set your containers for a redirected restore*

The Containers tab allows you to redefine the containers that a table space uses. You should only do this if you want to change the containers from those defined in the backup image. This is known as a *redirected restore*. Click **Next**.

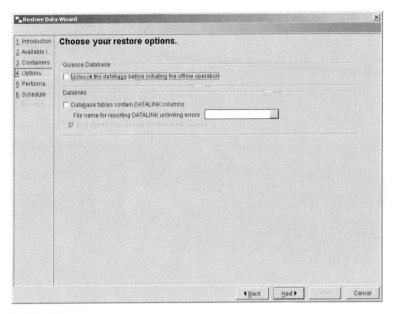

Fig. 11–16 *Choose your restore options*

The option of quiescing the database is given before initiating an offline restore. Click Next (you do not need select an option on this panel).

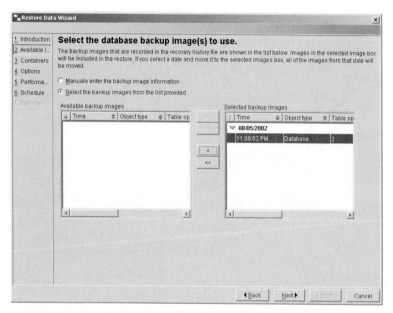

Fig. 11–17 *Select performance options for the restore*

These parameters affect he performance of restore, similar to backup. Change the values if desired, click **Next**.

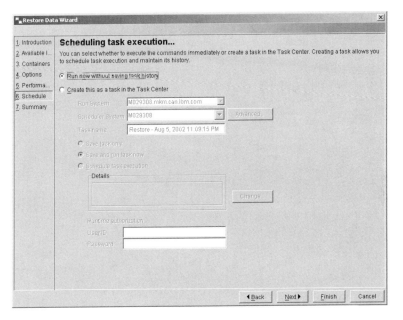

Fig. 11–18 *Scheduling task execution*

This panel gives you the option of executing the restore operation immediately or scheduling it through the Task Center, click **Next**.

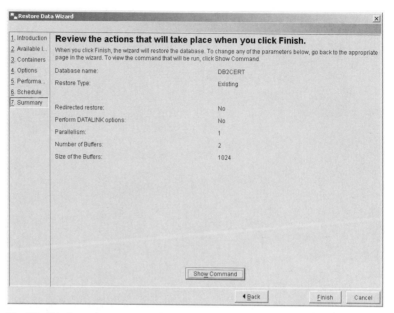

Fig. 11–19 *Review the actions that will take place when you click Finish*

As with the Backup command, you have the option of invoking the **Restore Database Using Wizard** panel from the Control Center.

Redefining Table Space Containers During Restore

During a backup of a database, a record is kept of all the table space containers in use by the table spaces being backed up. During a restore, all containers listed in the backup are checked to see if they currently exist and are accessible. If one or more of the containers is inaccessible for any other reason, the restore will fail. To allow a restore in such a case, the redirecting of table space containers is supported during the restore. This support includes the adding, changing, or removing of table space containers.

There are cases in which you want to restore, even though the containers listed in the backup do not exist on the system. An example of such a case is where you wish to recover from a disaster on a system other than that from which the backup was taken. The new system may not have the necessary containers defined.
To allow a restore in this case, the redirecting of table space containers at the time of the restore to alternate containers is supported.

In both cases, the process of restoring and redefining containers is called a *redirected restore*.

Note: A redirected restore can also be useful for backing up a production database at the primary site to a database at a designated backup site, which will typically be configured with less resources, such as the amount of disk available for containers.

As shown previously, you can use the restore dialog in the Control Center to perform a redirected restore or use the Command Center or Command Line Processor.

Here is an example of a redirected restore from a command line interface:

```
RESTORE DATABASE DB2CERT FROM C:\DBBACKUP
        INTO NEWDB
        REDIRECT
        WITHOUT ROLLING FORWARD
```

The above command requests that the DB2CERT database be restored into a new database called NEWDB. However, since DB2CERT has table spaces with specific SMS and DMS containers and containers cannot be shared by databases, new containers for the new database must be defined. The RESTORE utility returns the following messages:

```
SQL1277N Restore has detected that one or more table space
containers are inaccessible, or has set their state to
'storage must be defined'.
DB20000I The RESTORE DATABASE command completed
successfully.
```

Note: All commands associated with a single redirected restore operation must be invoked from the same window or CLP session.

To list the containers to be redefined, issue the LIST TABLESPACES command, which produces the following output. Note that from the previous RESTORE command, you are connected to the NEWDB database, with restricted functionality.

```
                    Tablespaces for Current Database
Tablespace ID                          = 0
Name                                   = SYSCATSPACE
Type                                   = Database managed space
Contents                               = Any data
State                                  = 0x2001100
   Detailed explanation:
      Restore pending
      Storage must be defined
      Storage may be defined

Tablespace ID                          = 1
Name                                   = TEMPSPACE1
Type                                   = System managed space
Contents                               = Temporary data
State                                  = 0x2001100
   Detailed explanation:
      Restore pending
      Storage must be defined
      Storage may be defined

Tablespace ID                          = 2
Name                                   = USERSPACE1
Type                                   = Database managed space
Contents                               = Any data
State                                  = 0x2001100
   Detailed explanation:
      Restore pending
      Storage must be defined
      Storage may be defined

Tablespace ID                          = 3
Name                                   = FILETS
Type                                   = Database managed space
Contents                               = Any data
State                                  = 0x2001100
   Detailed explanation:
      Restore pending
      Storage must be defined
      Storage may be defined
```

Note that all the table spaces are in the "Storage must be defined" state. To continue, define new containers for all the table spaces using the SET TABLESPACE CONTAINERS command as follows:

```
SET TABLESPACE CONTAINERS FOR 0
    USING (FILE "d:\newdb\cat.dat" 5000)

SET TABLESPACE CONTAINERS FOR 1
    USING (PATH "d:\newdb2")

SET TABLESPACE CONTAINERS FOR 2
    USING (FILE "d:\newdb\user.dat" 1000)

SET TABLESPACE CONTAINERS FOR 3
    USING (FILE "d:\newdb\newdb.dat" 1000)
```

Now that the containers are defined, continue the redirected restore with the following statement:

```
RESTORE DATABASE DB2CERT CONTINUE
```

This completes the redirected restore. Note that table spaces that were SMS and ones that were DMS must stay with their respective storage types during the redirection.

You should also be aware of the following considerations when using redirected restores:

- Directory and file containers are automatically created if they do not exist. No redirection is necessary unless the containers are inaccessible for some other reason. DB2 does not automatically create device containers.
- The ability to perform container redirection on any restore provides considerable flexibility in managing table space containers. For example, even though DB2 does not directly support adding containers to SMS table spaces, you could accomplish this by simply specifying an additional container on a redirected restore. Similarly, you could move a DMS table space from file containers to device containers.

Restoring to an Existing Database

DB2 uses *database seeds* to determine the database that a given database backup was created from. A database seed is an unique identifier of a database that remains constant for the life of the database. This seed is assigned by DB2 when the database is first created.

When restoring to an existing database, the following functions are performed:

- Delete table, index, long field, and large object contents for the existing database and replace them with the contents from the backup.
- Replace table space entries for each table space being restored.
- Retain the recovery history file unless the existing one is damaged, in which case it will be replaced with the one from the backup image.
- Retain the authentication for the existing database.
- Retain the database directories for the existing database that define where the database resides and how it is cataloged.

Certain functions depend on the database seed. When the database seeds are different:

Database Recovery

- Delete the logs associated with the existing database.
- Copy the database configuration file from the backup.
- Change the database configuration file to indicate that the default log file path should be used for logging.

When the database seeds are the same:

- Retain the current database configuration file, unless it is damaged.
- Delete the logs if the image is of a nonrecoverable database.
- The LOGPATH parameter from the database configuration file in the backup is used to set the log file directory path.

Restoring to a New Database

When restoring to a new database, the following functions are performed:

- Create a new database, using the database name and alias that was specified by the target database alias. If not specified, a database with the name and alias of the source database alias will be created.
- Restore the database configuration file from the backup.
- Modify the database configuration file to indicate that the default log file path should be used for logging.
- Restore the authentication type from the backup.
- Restore the recovery history file for the database.

Roll-Forward Recovery

Roll-forward recovery enables *recoverable* databases. When enabled, in addition to what can be performed for version recovery, the following can be performed:

- Recovery at an individual table space level
- Point in time recovery using the ROLLFORWARD command
- Online processing of BACKUP and RESTORE commands

As previously mentioned, roll-forward recovery is enabled by enabling either or both the LOGRETAIN or USEREXIT database configuration parameters. When roll-forward recovery is enabled, the database goes into backup-pending state, which requires that a full database backup be taken before the database can be used.

Backing Up a Database

The points made here are in addition to the considerations discussed in the version recovery section earlier in this chapter.

Before taking a backup, consider the following:

- By using the TABLESPACE option of the BACKUP command, you can back up individual table spaces. This can reduce the overall time it takes to back up the database by backing up only the more volatile table spaces. The PARALLELISM parameter can also used to back up multiple table spaces in parallel.
- A table space backup and a table space restore cannot be run at the same time, even if the backup and restore are working on different table spaces.
- If you have the index or large object components of a table in different table spaces, the set of table spaces encompassing the entire table should be backed up together to ensure a consistent point of recovery.

When you invoke the BACKUP command, you should be aware of the following point in addition to the points made in the version recovery discussion:

- The database or table spaces must be in a normal or backup-pending state for BACKUP to function.

Example of Backing Up at the Table Space Level

You can run the BACKUP command from the Command Line Processor or Command Center. The same function can also be done graphically from the Control Center. For example, using the Command Line Processor:

```
BACKUP DATABASE DB2CERT
        TABLESPACE (SYSCATSPACE,FILETS) TO C:\DBBACKUP
```

This command backs up the catalog table space SYSCATSPACE and user table space FILETS in the DB2CERT database to the C:\DBBACKUP directory on a Windows system. Default values are used for the other parameters.

Restoring a Database

The points made here are in addition to the considerations discussed under version recovery.

Before performing a restore, consider the following:

- You can restore a backup copy of a full database or table space backup to an existing database. The backup image may differ from the existing database in its alias name, database name, or its database seed.
- Database restores can be in offline mode only.
- Table spaces can be restored in offline or online mode. While in online mode, connections to the database can be made. This is advantageous in the case of table space restoration when other table spaces can still be used concurrently while the restore is executing.
- A database enabled for roll-forward recovery must be rolled forward after it is restored unless the WITHOUT ROLLING FORWARD option is used. However, this option cannot be used if the backup was taken with the ONLINE option or if the backup image is of table spaces only.
- Even though the restore and roll-forward are separate functions, your recovery strategy may have restore as the first phase of a complete roll-forward recovery of a database. After a successful restore, a database that was configured for roll-forward recovery at the time the backup was taken enters a roll-forward-pending state, being unusable until the ROLLFORWARD command has been run successfully.
- When the ROLLFORWARD command is issued, if the database is in roll-forward-pending status, the database is rolled forward. If the database is not in roll-forward-pending status, but the table spaces are, when you issue the ROLLFORWARD command and specify a list of table spaces, only those table spaces are rolled forward. If you do not specify a list, all table spaces that are in roll-forward-pending status are rolled forward.
- Another database RESTORE is not allowed when the roll-forward process is running.
- You can only restore a table space if the table space currently exists and is the *same* table space. This means it must have the same name and has not been dropped and recreated between taking the backup image and restoration.
- You cannot use a table space backup image to restore the table space to a different database.

- If you have the index or large object components of a table in different table spaces, the set of table spaces encompassing the entire table should be restored together to ensure a consistent point of recovery.
- You can restore selected table spaces from a full database backup image. All log files associated with the table space must exist from the time the backup was created.

Example of Restoring at the Table Space Level

You can run the RESTORE command from the Command Line Processor or Command Center. Of course, the same function can also be done from the Control Center. From the Command Line Processor, for example:

```
RESTORE DATABASE DB2CERT
        TABLESPACE (FILETS) ONLINE FROM C:\DBBACKUP
```

This command restores the table space FILETS in database DB2CERT from the C:\DBBACKUP directory in online mode on a Windows system. Connections can still be made to the database. Default values are used for the other parameters. This command will leave the table space in a roll-forward-pending state, which requires that the ROLLFORWARD command be executed before the table space can be accessed.

Rolling Forward Databases and Table Spaces

The ROLLFORWARD command can be invoked from the Command Line Processor, application programming interface (API), or Control Center.

Before performing a roll-forward, consider the following:

> **Note:** When using point-in-time (PIT) rollforward recovery, the local time can be specified rather than UTC time with the USING LOCAL TIME option of the ROLLFORWARD command.

- You must have SYSADM, SYSCTRL, or SYSMAINT authority to invoke ROLLFORWARD.
- The database may be local or remote.
- The database must be recoverable.
- A database must be restored successfully (using the RESTORE command) before it can be rolled forward.
- A table space, besides being restored, can also be put into roll-forward-pending

state from a media error or some other unexpected event.

- A database roll-forward runs in offline mode. The database is not available for use until the roll-forward completes. Online roll-forward for table spaces is available, except for the catalog table space SYSCATSPACE, which requires an offline roll-forward. Other table spaces are available for use during online roll-forward.
- You can use any backup image that you have as long as you have the necessary log files to cover the period you wish to roll-forward.
- Frequent backups reduce the execution time of ROLLFORWARD, as less log data has to be read between the time of the backup and the recovery point.

Generally, the sequence of commands when invoking ROLLFORWARD is as follows:

- Issue the ROLLFORWARD command without the STOP/COMPLETE option.
- Issue the ROLLFORWARD command with the QUERY STATUS option. The QUERY STATUS option can indicate that log file(s) may be missing if the point in time returned is earlier than expected for rolling forward to the end of the log.
- Issue the ROLLFORWARD command with the STOP/COMPLETE option. After this command is invoked, it is not possible to roll forward additional changes.

When you invoke the ROLLFORWARD command, you should be aware of the following:

- If you need to cancel a roll-forward operation, you can use ROLLFORWARD with the CANCEL option. This places the database into restore-pending state, whether or not a roll-forward is in progress against the database.
- If you issue ROLLFORWARD with the CANCEL option and specify a list of table spaces that are in roll-forward pending state, they are put in restore-pending state.
- You cannot use ROLLFORWARD with the CANCEL option to cancel a roll-forward operation that is running. You can only use it to cancel a roll-forward operation that completed but did not have a ROLLFORWARD STOP issued for it or for a roll-forward operation that failed before completing.
- A log uses a timestamp associated with the completion of a unit of work. The timestamp in the logs uses Coordinated Universal Time (UTC). The format is yyyy-mm-dd-hh.mm.ss.nnnnnn (year, month, day, hour, minutes, seconds, microseconds). When you want to roll-forward to a point in time, you have to specify the time using the local time or UTC time.
- If you are rolling forward one or many table spaces to a point in time, you must roll-forward at least to the minimum recovery time, which is the last update to the system catalogs for the table spaces. The minimum recovery time is shown

in the output of the `LIST TABLESPACES SHOW DETAIL` command.

Table Space States During Roll-Forward

Different states are associated with a table space to indicate its current status:

- A table space will be placed in *roll-forward-pending* state after restoration or following an I/O error. The table space must be rolled forward to remove the roll-forward-pending state. If the cause was an I/O error, this situation must be corrected before doing a roll-forward.
- A table space will be placed in *roll-forward-in-progress* state when a roll-forward operation is in progress on that table space. The state remains until roll-forward operations are completed successfully. If the `STOP/COMPLETE` option was not used on a point in time recovery, the table space will also stay in this state.
- A table space will be placed in the *restore-pending* state after a `ROLLFORWARD` with `CANCEL` option or an unrecoverable error occurs in the execution of `ROLLFORWARD`. The table space must be restored and rolled forward again.
- A table space will be placed in the *backup-pending* state after a `ROLLFORWARD` to a point in time or after a `LOAD NO COPY` operation. The table space must be

Database Recovery

backed up before it can be used.

Examples of Rolling Forward

Some of the key parameters to the ROLLFORWARD command include (see the *DB2 UDB V8.1 Command Reference* for further detail):

- isotime - the point in time where all committed transactions are to be rolled forward. This value is a timestamp, expressed in Coordinated Universal Time (UTC). The CURRENT TIMEZONE special register specifies the difference between UTC and local time at the database server.
- USING LOCAL TIME - allows the user to rollforward to a point in time that is t the user's local time, rather than the UTC time.
- COMPLETE/STOP - stops the rolling forward of log records, and completes the rollforward recovery process by rolling back any incomplete transactions and

turning off the rollforward pending state of the database.

- CANCEL - cancels the rollforward recovery operation and places the database or one or more table spaces in restore pending state.
- ONLINE - specifies a table space-level rollforward recovery operation to be performed online.
- NORETRIEVE - specifies the administrator controls which log files will be rolled forward on the standby machine, allowing the ability to disable the retrieval of archived logs.

You can run the ROLLFORWARD command from the Command Line Processor or Command Center. For example:

```
ROLLFORWARD DATABASE DB2CERT
           TO END OF LOGS
           OVERFLOW LOG PATH (C:\LOGS)
```

This command rolls forward the DB2CERT database that was in roll-forward-pending status from the RESTORE command. The roll-forward will be performed to the end of the logs, which means that it will reapply all units of work in the logs up to the last unit of work in all online archive log files. This does not mean that the roll-forward will process up to the current time. For example, if there is a problem with the availability of the most recent active log, the command will still succeed. Use the QUERY STATUS option to ensure that the latest unit of work is at the expected time and that the log files were processed as expected.

The directory where the log files are kept (as listed in the database configuration parameter LOGPATH) is used by ROLLFORWARD to find active and online archive logs. The OVERFLOW LOG PATH parameter specifies the directory where offline archive log files are kept so that ROLLFORWARD can use them for reapplying units of work.

```
ROLLFORWARD DATABASE DB2CERT
           TO END OF LOGS AND COMPLETE
           TABLESPACE (FILETS) ONLINE
```

This command rolls forward the FILETS table space that is in roll-forward-pending status from the RESTORE command. The ONLINE parameter allows concurrent access to other table spaces. The AND COMPLETE parameter instructs DB2 to complete the rolling forward, roll back any incomplete units of work, and to enable the database to become available for general use by turning off the roll-forward-pending state.

```
ROLLFORWARD DATABASE DB2CERT
            QUERY STATUS
```

This command lists the log files that DB2 has rolled forward, the next archive file required, and the timestamp (in UTC) of the last committed transaction since roll-forward processing began. The information returned contains the following:

- Rollforward status - The status may be database or table space roll-forward pending, database or table space roll-forward in progress, database or table space roll-forward processing stop, or no roll-forward pending.
- Next log file to be read - A string containing the name of the next required log file.
- Log files processed - A string containing the names of the processed log files that are no longer needed for recovery and that can be removed from the directory.
- Last committed transaction - A string containing a timestamp in ISO format (yyyy-mm-dd-hh.mm.ss). This timestamp marks the last transaction committed after the completion of roll-forward recovery. The timestamp applies to the database. For table space roll-forward, it is the timestamp of the last transaction committed to the database.

 Note: For the recovery of a table space, only the log files required to recover the database are processed; log files that not required are skipped.

Here is sample output of the QUERY STATUS option:

```
                Rollforward Status

Input database alias              = db2cert
Number of nodes returned status   = 1
Node number                       = 0
Rollforward status                = DB working
Next log file to be read          = S0000019.LOG
Log files processed               = S0000014.LOG - S0000018.LOG
Last committed transaction        = 2002-07-15-00.09.51.000000
```

Note the status is DB WORKING, meaning that this is a database roll-forward and that it is still in progress, as the STOP/COMPLETE option has not been specified.

```
ROLLFORWARD DATABASE DB2CERT
          COMPLETE
```

This command stops the rolling forward of log records and completes the roll-forward recovery process by rolling back any incomplete transactions and turning off the roll-forward-pending state of the database. This allows access to the database or table spaces that have been rolled forward. The keywords STOP and COMPLETE are equivalent. When rolling table spaces forward to a point in time, the table spaces are placed in backup-pending state.

Here is output of the QUERY STATUS option:

```
                  Rollforward Status

   Input database alias           = db2cert
   Number of nodes returned status = 1
   Node number                    = 0
   Rollforward status             = not pending
   Next log file to be read       =
   Log files processed            = S0000014.LOG - S0000018.LOG
   Last committed transaction     = 2002-07-15-00.09.51.000000
```

Note that the status has now changed to not pending.

```
ROLLFORWARD DATABASE DB2CERT
          TO 2002-07-24-00.00.00.000000
          TABLESPACE (FILETS) ONLINE
```

This command rolls forward the FILETS table space to a particular point in time. Note that the roll-forward time is UTC, regardless of the local time.

Here is the output of the QUERY STATUS option (which is produced by default as a function of the above command):

Database Recovery

Rollforward Status

```
Input database alias            = db2cert
Number of nodes returned status = 1
Node number                     = 0
Rollforward status              = TBS working
Next log file to be read        =
Log files processed             = -
Last committed transaction      = 2002-07-15-00.09.51.000000
```

Note that the status has now changed to TBS working, as this is a table space roll-forward. You can keep rolling forward past the nominated time, as there are still units of work that could be applied (note the "Last committed transaction" time is later than the requested point in time) or issue the ROLLFORWARD command with the COMPLETE option to roll back incomplete units of work and make the table space available for general use.

You can also use the Control Center to invoke a roll-forward. After right-clicking on the database you wish to roll-forward and selecting the **Roll-forward** option, the Roll-Forward Wizard panel is displayed (Fig. 11–20). You will not be able to enter this panel unless the database is in roll-forward-pending state.

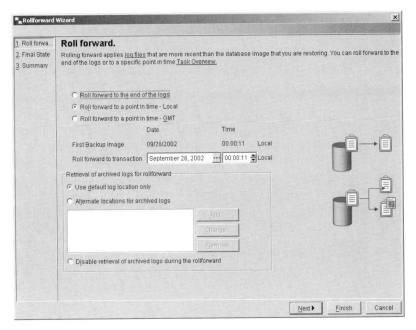

Fig. 11–20 *Rollforward Wizard*

In this panel, you can see options for end of log recovery, point in time recovery, and the options for using the archived logs. Click on **Next**.

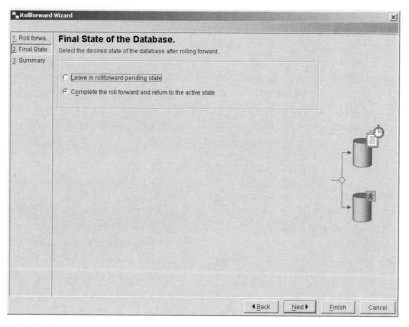

Fig. 11–21 *Rollforward Wizard - Final State of the Database*

This panel allows you to select the final state of the database, either in in roll-for-ward-pending state (equivalent to the STOP/COMPLETE option) or in an active state.

Fig. 11–22 *Rollforward Wizard - Review*

In the last panel of the Rollforward Wizard, you can press the **Show Command** button to see the command that will be issued by DB2.

Managing Log Files

In this section, aspects of log file management will be reviewed, such as how log files are named and how to avoid losing them.

Log File Naming Scheme

Log file names are of the format Snnnnnnn.LOG, where nnnnnnn is a seven-digit number ranging from 0000000 to 9999999. When a database is first created, logs starting from S0000000.LOG are created.

DB2 restarts the log file numbering sequence at S0000000.LOG under the following conditions:

- When the database configuration file is changed to enable archival logging
- When the database configuration file is changed to disable archival logging
- When the log file sequence wraps, that is after log S9999999.LOG is used

When the ROLLFORWARD command has been run and you have issued the STOP/COMPLETE option successfully, the last log used is truncated and logging begins with the next sequential log. Any log in the log path directory with a sequence number greater than the last log used by ROLLFORWARD is reused. You can make a copy of the old logs and place them in a different directory if you want to be able to reexecute the ROLLFORWARD command using the old logs.

 Note: DB2 allows the database administrator to force the archive of a log on demand. This allows greater flexibility in managing log files, especially in situations that support offsite recovery.

Log File Placement for Recovery

DB2 ensures that an incorrect log is not applied during roll-forward recovery, but it cannot detect the location of the required logs.

If you moved log files to a location other than specified by the LOGPATH database configuration parameter, use the OVERFLOW LOG PATH parameter of the ROLLFORWARD command to specify the path for DB2 to search.

If you are rolling forward changes in a database or table space and ROLLFORWARD cannot find the next log, then ROLLFORWARD stops and returns the next log name in the SQL Communications Area (SQLCA).

If you change the log path directory via the NEWLOGPATH database configuration parameter, any existing archive logs are unaffected and do not get moved to the new path. You must keep track of the location of these logs.

Losing Logs

Log files can be erased in the following ways:

- Dropping a database erases all logs in the current log path directory. You may need to back these logs up for any future restoration purposes.
- As noted previously, when recovering to a point in time, log files chronologically past the point in time are reused. If you need to restore again past the point in time used earlier, you cannot do so because the logs were reused. You must back up the original set of logs to a different location and copy them back for the restoration.
- If you change the log path directory and then remove the subdirectory or erase any logs in that subdirectory requested by DB2 in the log path, DB2 will look for logs in the default log path (SQLOGDIR) when the database is opened. If the logs are not found, the database will enter a backup-pending state.
- If you lose the log containing the point in time of the end of the online backup and you are rolling forward the corresponding restored image, the database will not be useable. To make the database usable, you must restore the database from a different backup and all its associated logs.

Prune Logfile Command

This command will delete all log files created prior to a specified log file. It will only do so from the active log path, so if any log files have been moved to another path they will not be considered by this command. For example:

```
PRUNE LOGFILE PRIOR TO S0000100.LOG
```

This command will delete all log files in the active log path up to and including S0000099.LOG.

Other Recovery Considerations

Additional considerations related to recovery will be covered here, such as the time taken to recover a database, the recovery history file, and how to recover dropped tables.

Recovery Time Required

The time required to recover a database is composed of:

- The time required to complete the restore of the backup.
- If the database is recoverable, the time it takes to roll-forward through the logs.

When formulating a recovery plan, you should plan a sufficient amount of time for your business operations to be affected while the database is being recovered.

Testing your overall recovery plan will assist you in determining whether the time required to recover the database is reasonable given your business requirements. Following each test, you may want to increase the frequency with which you take a backup. If roll-forward recovery is part of the strategy, this will reduce the number of logs that are archived between backups and reduce the time taken in rolling forward through the units of work.

Storage Considerations For Log Files

To prevent a media failure from destroying a database and your ability to rebuild it, you should keep the database backup, the database logs, and the database itself on other devices. Use the LOGPATH database configuration parameter to move the logs to a new device once the database is created.

Because the log files can occupy a large amount of disk space, if you plan on using roll-forward recovery, you have to plan how to manage the archive logs. You can:

- Dedicate enough space in the database log path directory to retain the logs
- Manually copy the archive logs to a storage device or directory other than the database log path directory
- Use a user exit program to copy the logs to another storage device

When using disk mirroring of the log files, you need to account for twice the amount of disk storage.

The Quiesce Command

You can issue the QUIESCE TABLESPACES FOR TABLE command to create a point of consistency that can be used for subsequent roll-forward recovery. When you quiesce table spaces for a table, the request will wait (through locking) for all running transactions that are accessing objects in the table spaces to complete, at the same time blocking new requests against the table spaces. When the quiesce request is granted, all outstanding transactions are already completed (committed or rolled back), and the table spaces are in a consistent state. You can look in the recovery history file to find quiesce points and check whether they are past the minimum recovery time to determine a desirable time to stop the roll-forward.

```
QUIESCE TABLESPACES FOR TABLE DB2CERT.EMPLOYEE SHARE
```

In the example above, when the quiesce share request is received, the transaction requests intent share locks for the table spaces and one for the table.
When the transaction obtains the locks, the state of the table spaces is changed to QUIESCED SHARE. The state is granted to the quiescer only if there is no conflicting state held by other users.

 Note: QUIESCE can now force all users off an instance or database and put it into a quiesced mode for database maintenance activities.

The table cannot be changed while the table spaces for the table are in QUIESCED SHARE state. Other share mode requests to the table and table spaces will be allowed. When the unit of work commits or rolls back, the locks are released, but the table spaces for the table remain in QUIESCED SHARE state until the state is explicitly reset by issuing the following command:

```
QUIESCE TABLESPACES FOR TABLE DB2CERT.EMPLOYEE RESET
```

The QUIESCE command can be invoked from the Command Line Processor, Command Center, or application programming interface.

The Recovery History File

A recovery history file is created with each database and is automatically updated whenever there is a:

Database Recovery

- Archive of a log
- BACKUP of a database or table space
- RESTORE of a database or table space
- ROLLFORWARD of a database or table space
- CREATE of a table space
- ALTER of a table space
- RENAME of a table space
- QUIESCE of a table space
- DROP of a table
- LOAD of a table
- REORG of a table

You can use the summarized backup information in this file to recover all or part of the database to a point in time. The information in the file includes:

- The part of the database that was copied and the copy procedure
- The time that the copy was made
- The location of the copy
- The last time a restore was done

Every backup operation includes a copy of the recovery history file. The file is linked to the database, so when a database is dropped, the file is deleted.

If the current database is unusable and the file is damaged or deleted, an option in the RESTORE command allows only the recovery history file to be restored.

The file is managed with the PRUNE HISTORY command. Entries in the file earlier than a specified date and time can be deleted with this command.

The LIST HISTORY command reports on information in the recovery history file. For example:

```
LIST HISTORY ALL FOR DB2CERT
```

This command produces this sample output:

```
                    List History File for db2cert
  Number of matching file entries = 45


  Op Obj Timestamp+Sequence Type Dev Earliest Log Current Log Backup ID
  -- --- ------------------ ---- --- ------------ ------------ ------------
   B  D   20020715120004001   F    D   S0000000.LOG S0000000.LOG
```

```
----------------------------------------------------------------------
Contains 3      tablespace(s):

00001 SYSCATSPACE
00002 USERSPACE1
00003 FILETS
----------------------------------------------------------------------
    Comment: DB2 BACKUP DB2CERT OFFLINE
Start Time: 20020715120004
  End Time: 20020715120034
----------------------------------------------------------------------
00001 Location: d:\temp\DB2CERT.0\DB2\NODE0000\CATN0000\20000715


Op Obj Timestamp+Sequence Type Dev Earliest Log Current Log  Backup ID
-- --- ----------------- ---- --- ------------ ------------ -----------
R   D   20020715120335001   F    D                          20020715120004
----------------------------------------------------------------------
Contains 3      tablespace(s):

00001 SYSCATSPACE
00002 USERSPACE1
00003 FILETS
----------------------------------------------------------------------
    Comment: DB2 RESTORE DB2CERT WITH RF
Start Time: 20020715120335
  End Time: 20020715120352
----------------------------------------------------------------------
00002 Location: d:\temp\DB2CERT.0\DB2\NODE0000\CATN0000\20020715
```

Here is a backup and restore event displayed. Note that the full name and path of the backup is shown.

For further details on the contents of the recovery history file, please refer to the *DB2 UDB V8.1 Command Reference* and the *DB2 UDB V8.1 Administration Guide*.

Tables Related to Other Tables

If you want to roll-forward a table space to a point in time and a table in the table space participates in a referential constraint with another table in another table space, you should roll-forward both table spaces to the same point in time; otherwise, both tables will be placed into check-pending state.

Similarly, for an underlying table for a summary table that is in another table space or vice versa, you should roll-forward both table spaces to the same point in time; otherwise, the summary table is placed into check pending state.

When tables affect other tables via triggers, you should consider backing up and recovering the related table spaces together as well keeping the same consistency points and therefore the integrity of the data. The updates to the database as a result of triggers *firing* will still occur during roll-forward processing.

Database Recovery

Dropped Table Recovery

Tables that have been accidentally dropped can be recovered using the following technique:

Prior to the table being accidentally dropped:

- Use the CREATE or ALTER TABLESPACE statement with the DROPPED TABLE RECOVERY ON option. DB2 will write additional log and recovery history file entries to support recovery of dropped tables.

When a table has been dropped and needs to be recovered, do the following:

- Extract the DDL from the recovery history file using the LIST HISTORY DROPPED TABLES command. This will provide you with not only the list of tables that have been dropped but also the statements needed to recreate them.
- Restore a database or table space from a backup image. Of course, this image must have coexisted before the table was dropped.
- Roll-forward the database or table space using the RECOVER DROPPED TABLE option. This option requires you to specify both a tableid and an export directory. The tableid is taken from the LIST HISTORY command, and the export directory is the directory where DB2 will place an export file of the data for the dropped table.
- Recreate the table with the extracted DDL from the history file.
- Import the recovered data.

This technique should only be used on regular table spaces.

Reorganization of Tables

If you reorganize a table, you should back up the affected table spaces after the operation completes. If you later issue the roll forward command and you did not back up, you will have to roll forward through the entire REORG operation.

Large Objects

If a table contains long field or large object (LOB) columns, you should consider placing this data into a separate table space. With the amount of time and disk space potentially required to back up LOB data, by putting it in a separate table space, you can decide to back it up at a lower frequency than the regular table spaces.

You can also choose not to log LOB columns when creating or altering tables, which will also save log file space. This is feasible if the LOB data is easily recreatable.

Offline and Online Table Space States

During database start-up/activation, DB2 checks to make sure that all of the table space containers are accessible.

If a container is not accessible, the table space will be placed into an *offline* state in addition to the other recovery states it may have, such as back-up-pending, restore-pending, roll-forward-pending, and so on. So a table space may have a state of, for example, BACKUP PENDING + OFFLINE.

To get a table space back into an *online* state after resolving the container problem:

*   Disconnect all applications and reconnect to or restart the database.
*   If the database still has applications connected to it, use the ALTER TABLESPACE statement with the SWITCH ONLINE option.

The table space can also be dropped while in an *offline* state.

If the container problem cannot be resolved, to restart the database cleanly so that there are no errors, use the RESTART DATABASE command with the DROP PENDING TABLESPACES option. This will instruct DB2 to start the database successfully, even though the list of supplied table spaces are in error. Once the database is started, the only operation that can be performed on those table spaces that cannot be recovered is to drop them.

High Availability

DB2 supports high availability functionality, where in the event that one machine running a DB2 instance fails, another machine automatically takes over the processing for the failed machine.

Database Recovery

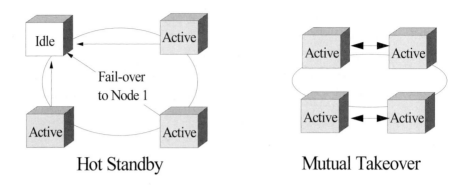

Fig. 11–23 *High availability scenarios*

For example, on AIX, this support uses and is enabled by the High Availability Cluster Multi-Processing (HACMP) product. HACMP provides increased availability through clusters of processors that share resources such as disks or network access. If one processor fails, another in the cluster can substitute for the failed one. Additional high-availability programs are available depending on the operating environment.

A brief description of the hot standby and mutual takeover modes follows.

- *Hot standby* - Active processors are being actively used to run the DB2 instance and a DB2 server is in standby mode ready to take over the instance if there is an operating system or hardware failure involving the first processor.

- *Mutual takeover* - The various processors are either used to run separate DB2 instances or used to run a DB2 instance while another processor is used to run DB2 applications. If there is an operating system or hardware failure on one of the processors, the other processor takes over the tasks of the failing processor. Once the failover is complete, the remaining processor is doing the work of both processors.

 Note: Other popular high availability software programs include: Microsoft Cluster Server (MSCS), Sun Cluster (SC), and Steeleye (for Linux environments), and Veritas Cluster Server.

SET WRITE Command

Advances in disk technology have increased database availability by providing the ability to create a duplicate or mirrored copy. By splitting a consistent copy of the data, the primary or production database can continue normal operations while the copy can be used either online or offline operations.

The SET WRITE command is used in high availability scenarios by enabling the disk storage systems to split a mirrored database. This command can be used to supsend I/O writes or to resume I/O writes for a given database.

You must have SYSADM, SYSCTRL, or SYSMAINT authority to issue this command.

Here is the syntax of the SET WRITE command:

The key parameters to the SET WRITE command include (see the *DB2 UDB V8.1 Command Reference* for further detail):

• SUSPEND - this will suspend I/O writes and put all tablespaces into a SUSPEND_WRITE state. Writes to the logs are also suspended by this command.

• RESUME - this will resume I/O writes and remove the SUSPEND_WRITE state from all of the tablespaces and make the tablespaces available for update activities.

 Note: You can use the DB2 LIST TABLESPACES command to view the state of the table space in SUSPEND_WRITE.

DB2INIDB Command

The DB2INIDB command is used to initialize a mirrored database in a split mirror envirnoment. The mirrored database can be initialized as a clone of the primary database, place in roll forward pending state, or used as a backup image to restore the primary database.

You must have SYSADM, SYSCTRL, or SYSMAINT authority to issue this command.

Here is the syntax of the DB2INIDB command:

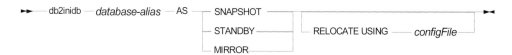

The key parameters to the DB2INIDB command include (see the *DB2 UDB V8.1 Command Reference* for further detail):

• SNAPSHOT - specifies that the mirrored database will be initialized as a clone of the primary database.

- STANDBY - specifies the database will be placed in roll forward pending state. Logs from the primary database can be applied to the standby database. The standby will be able to take place of the primary database if it goes down.
- MIRROR - specifies the mirrored database will be a backup image that can be used to restore the primary database.
- RELOCATE USING configfile - specifies the database files are to be relocated based on the information listed in the configuration file.

Using Split Mirror to Clone a Database

Creating a snapshot or clone of the primary database can be useful to run queries or reports, thereby offloading the workload off the primary database. The steps to create a clone database are:

1. Suspend I/O on the primary database:

   db2 set write suspend for database

2. Split the mirror

3. Resume I/O on the primary database:

   db2 set write resume for database

4. Attach the mirrored database to another instance.

5. Start the database instance:

   db2start

6. Initialize the mirrored database as a clone of the primary database:

   db2inidb database_alias as snapshot

 Note: The write resume command forces a restart for databases in SUSPEND_WRITE state. This command can only be applied to the primary database, not the mirrored databases.

Using Split Mirror as a Standby Database

A standby database is created to increase availability by decreasing the potential recovery time to assume operational workload. The standby database is constantly rolling forward through the log and continually fetching logs from the primary system. The steps to create a mirrored standby database are:

1. Suspend I/O on the primary database:

   db2 set write suspend for database

2. Split the mirror

3. Resume I/O on the primary database:

   ```
   db2 set write resume for database
   ```

4. Attach the mirrored database to another instance.

5. Place the mirrored database in rollforward pending state:

   ```
   db2inidb database_alias as standby
   ```

   Recommend taking a backup of the mirrored database at this time, before any records are written to the standby.

6. Set up a user exit program to retrieve the log files from the primary system.

7. Roll the database forward to the end of the logs or a point-in-time.

8. Continue retrieving log files, and rolling the database forward through the logs until the end of the logs or the point-in-time required has been reached for the standby database.

9. Bring the standby database online by issuing the ROLLFORWARD command with the STOP option specified. The DB2 clients are now ready to reconnect to the standby database.

   ```
   db2 rollforward database <db> to end of logs and stop
   ```

 Note: The WRITE RESUME command must be issued from the same window or CLP session as the WRITE SUSPEND command.

Using Split Mirror as a Backup Image

A backup image of the mirrored system can be restored on the primary system when the primary database needs recovery. The steps to create a backup image of the mirrored database are:

1. Suspend I/O on the primary database:

   ```
   db2 set write suspend for database
   ```

2. Split the mirror

3. Resume I/O on the primary database:

   ```
   db2 set write resume for database
   ```

4. A failure occurs on the primary system, requiring a restore from a backup image.

5. Stop the primary database instance:

   ```
   db2stop
   ```

6. Use operating system-level commands to copy the split-off data over to the primary system. Do not copy the split-off log files, because the primary logs will be required for rollforward recovery.

7. Start the primary database instance:

   ```
   db2start
   ```

8. Initialize the primary database:

   ```
   db2inidb database_alias as mirror
   ```

9. Bring the standby database online by issuing the ROLLFORWARD command with the STOP option specified. The DB2 clients are now ready to reconnect.

   ```
   db2 rollforward db <db> to end of logs and stop
   ```

Summary

This chapter discussed concepts and facilities of DB2 recovery. These included:

- *Unit of work* - A recoverable sequence of operations within an application process. This could involve one or many SQL statements depending upon the business logic required. Either all the SQL covering the unit of work gets applied or none of it. This is also known as a *transaction*.

There are three kinds of recovery to consider:

- *Crash recovery* - Protects the database from being left in an inconsistent or unusable state. Unexpected interruptions that leave incomplete units of work are handled by crash recovery, which rolls back the changes made by uncommitted transactions.
- *Version recovery* - Allows the restoration of a database from a backup image taken at an earlier point in time. Table spaces can also be version recovered.
- *Roll-forward recovery* - Extends version recovery by using full database backups in conjunction with log files to provide the capability of recovering to any point in time covered by the log files.

Recoverable databases support crash, version, and roll-forward recovery. DB2 supports recoverable databases by allowing the LOGRETAIN and/or USEREXIT database configuration parameters. Nonrecoverable databases support crash and version recovery. DB2 implements this type of database by not allowing the use of the above two parameters.

Offline access to the database means that access to the database is in exclusive mode; no one else can connect to the database. Online access means that other applications can concurrently connect to the database when the particular operation is being performed.

Primary log files establish a fixed, preallocated amount of storage to the recovery log files. Enough disk space for the primary log files must be allocated before the database is connected to. Secondary log files are used when the primary log files become full and are allocated one at a time when required.

There are two kinds of logging supported by DB2:

- *Circular logging* - Supports nonrecoverable databases, as primary log files are reused in a circular manner.
- *Archival logging* - Supports recoverable databases by archiving logs once they have been written to; that is, log files are not reused.

Log files can be characterized as one of the following:

Database Recovery

- *Active log files* - The log files written to by DB2 that support crash recovery.
- *Archive log files* - The log files that have been written to by DB2 and are no longer needed to support crash recovery. Online archive log files reside in the active log path directory. Offline archive log files do no reside in the active log path directory. They can be moved manually or by an external storage management product.

The following DB2 commands enable the recoverability of databases:

- The BACKUP command creates images of databases or table spaces that are used for restoration purposes, this operation can occur either online or offline. Incremental backup is also supported.
- The RESTORE command takes the backup images created by the BACKUP command and restores databases or table spaces.
- The ROLLFORWARD command supports roll-forward recovery by reapplying units of work captured in the log up to the nominated point in time that roll-forward recovery stops.
- The QUIESCE command establishes a point of consistency for related table spaces that can be used in roll-forward operations later on. It does this by taking locks on tables which ensures that no other application can update the tables being quiesced.

To improve the availability of DB2, you can use high availability products such as HACMP on AIX to implement hot standby and mutual takeover modes. This allows automatic switching of DB2 operations to a backup machine if the primary machine fails without interruption to operations. This can significantly improve the operational availability of DB2.

Several storage vendors have provided advanced disk mirroring capabilities. DB2 has provided commands to leverage this technology and can initialize a mirrored database as a:

- SNAPSHOT - a clone of the primary database.
- STANDBY - a database in roll forward pending state, ready to take place of the primary system if it goes down.
- MIRROR - a backup image that can be used to restore the primary database.

12

Monitoring and Tuning

- ◆ PLANNING
- ◆ DB2 ARCHITECTURE OVERVIEW
- ◆ DATABASE MONITORING
- ◆ SQL MONITORING
- ◆ TUNING CONFIGURATION PARAMETERS
- ◆ PROBLEM DETERMINATION

*U*nderstanding the performance of the DB2 database management system, its databases, and active applications in a dynamic environment requires monitoring. This means that a database administrator should gather information regarding the usage of the database. An application programmer may also require SQL statement execution information. Gathering database information using DB2's monitoring facilities and information regarding SQL statement processing will be discussed.

In this chapter, the various DB2 facilities for the monitoring and gathering of information that is input into the tuning process will be reviewed. The *Explain Facility*, *Snapshot Monitor*, and *Event Monitor* are the main tools used to monitor DB2 databases and SQL statements.

These tools may be used to perform the following tasks:

- Understand user and application activity within DB2
- Better understand how an SQL statement is processed
- Determine the sources and causes of problems
- Tune configuration parameters
- Improve database and application performance

Elements of Performance

Performance is the way a computer system behaves given a particular work load. Performance is measured through one or more of the system's response time, throughput, and availability. It is affected by:

- The resources available
- How well the resources are utilized

Performance tuning should be undertaken when you want to improve the cost-benefit ratio of your system. Specific situations include:

- You want to process a larger, more demanding work load without increasing processing costs that may include having to acquire additional hardware.
- Obtaining faster system response time, or higher throughput, without increasing processing costs.
- Reducing processing costs without negatively affecting service to the client(s).

Translating performance from technical terms to economic terms is difficult. Performance tuning costs money through labor and machine resources, so the cost of tuning must be weighed against the benefits tuning may or may not deliver.

Some of these benefits, including less resource usage and the ability to add more users to the system, are tangible, whereas other benefits, such as increased customer satisfaction, are less tangible from a monetary perspective.

Tuning Guidelines

The following guidelines should be considered in developing an overall approach to performance tuning:

Remember the Law of Diminishing Returns

Your greatest performance benefits usually come from your initial efforts. Further changes generally produce smaller and smaller benefits and require greater effort.

Do Not Tune Just for the Sake of Tuning

Tune to relieve identified constraints. If you tune resources that are not the primary cause of performance problems, this can have little or no effect on response time until you have relieved the major constraints, and it can actually make subsequent tuning work more difficult. If there is any significant improvement potential, it lies in improving the performance of the resources that are major factors in the response time.

Consider the Whole System

You can never tune one parameter or system in isolation. Before you make any adjustments, consider how it will affect the system as a whole.

Change One Parameter at a Time

Do not change more than one performance tuning parameter at a time. Even if you are sure that all the changes will be beneficial, you will have no way of evaluating how much each change has contributed. You also cannot effectively judge the trade-off you have made by changing more than one parameter at a time. Every time you adjust a parameter to improve one area, you almost always affect at least one other area that may not have been considered.

Measure and Reconfigure by Levels

For the same reasons that you should change only one parameter at a time, tune one level of your system at a time. You can use the following list of levels within a system as a guide:

- Hardware
- Operating system
- Application server and requester
- Database
- SQL statements
- Application programs

Check for Hardware and Software Problems

Some performance problems may be corrected by applying service to your hardware, your software, or to both. Do not spend excessive time monitoring and tuning your system when simply applying service may be the solution to the problem.

Understand the Problem Before Upgrading Hardware

Even if it seems that an additional storage or processor resource could immediately improve performance, take the time to understand where the bottlenecks are. You may spend money on additional disk storage only to find that you do not have the processor resource to exploit it.

Put Fall Back Procedures in Place Before You Start Tuning

Because changes are being made to an existing system, you must be prepared to back out those changes out if they do not have the desired effect or have a negative effect on the system.

Performance Improvement Process

Monitoring and tuning a database and its applications should be performed using the following basic process:

- Establish performance indicators.
- Define performance objectives.
- Develop a performance monitoring plan.
- Implement the plan.
- Analyze the measurements. Determine if the objectives have been met. If so, consider reducing the number of measurements to keep to a minimum the amount of resource consumed for monitoring.
- Determine the major constraints in the system.
- Decide where you can afford to make trade-offs and which resources can bear an additional load. Most tuning activities involve trade-offs among system resources and various elements of performance.
- Adjust the configuration of the system. If you think that it is feasible to change more than one tuning option, implement one at a time.
- Based on the results, start another iteration of the monitoring cycle.

You may want to follow the above process for periodic monitoring or when significant changes occur to the system and/or work load taken on by the system.

How Much Can a System Be Tuned?

There are limits to how much you can improve the efficiency of a system. Consider how much time and money you should spend on improving system performance and how much the spending of additional time and money will help the users of the system.

Your system may perform adequately without any tuning at all, but it probably will not perform to its potential. Each database is unique. As soon as you develop your own database and applications for it, investigate the tuning parameters available and learn how you can customize their settings to reflect your situation. In some circumstances, there will only be a small benefit from tuning a system. In most circumstances, however, the benefit may be significant.

There are wizards available from the DB2 Control Center that assist in tuning the database parameters. The performance Configuration Wizard can be found by clicking the right mouse button on the database you want to tune.

If your system encounters performance bottlenecks, it is likely that tuning will be effective. If you are close to the performance limits, and you increase the number of users on the system by about 10%, the response time may rise by much more

Monitoring and Tuning

than 10%. In this situation, you will need to determine how to counterbalance this degradation in performance by tuning your system. However, there is a point beyond which tuning cannot help. At that point, you should consider revising your goals and expectations within that environment. Or you should change your system environment by considering more disk storage, faster/additional processors, additional memory, or faster networking solutions.

A Less-Formal Approach

If you do not have enough time to set performance objectives and to monitor and tune in a comprehensive manner, you can address performance by listening to your users. Find out if they are having performance-related problems. You can usually locate the problem or determine where to start looking for the problem by asking a few simple questions. For example, you can ask your users:

- What do you mean by slow response? Is it 10% slower than you expect it to be or ten times slower?
- When did you notice the problem? Is it recent or has it always been there?
- Do you know of other users who are complaining of the same problem? Are those complaining one or two individuals or a whole group?
- Are the problems you are experiencing related to a specific transaction or application program?
- Do your problems appear during regular periods, such as at lunch hour, or are they continuous?

DB2 Architecture Overview

To understand performance and what can be monitored, a brief overview of DB2 from an architectural perspective will be presented. The architectural components that will be examined include:

- Process model
- DB2 memory usage
- SQL compiler/optimizer

Process Model

The process model or server architecture for DB2 is known as an *n-n process model*. The main feature of this architecture is its ability to ensure database integrity. It isolates all database applications from critical database resources. These resources include database control blocks and critical database files.

During the database connection process, a DB2 coordinating agent is assigned to each database application. Each DB2 agent works on behalf of the database application and handles all of the SQL requests. The application and database agents communicate using Inter-Process Communication (IPC) techniques (such as message queues, shared memory, and semaphores). DB2 coordinating agents work with DB2 subagents if intra-partition parallelism is enabled.

 Note: The DB2 agents are *threads* in Windows and *processes* in Linux and UNIX operating systems.

This architecture provides a firewall to protect the database resources from an errant application.

A many to one process model is made possible by the DB2 connection concentrator. The use of a concentrator can improve performance by allowing many more client connections to be processed and reducing memory use for each connection. The connection concentrator is enabled when the value of MAX_CONNECTIONS is greater than the value of MAX_COORDAGENTS.

Monitoring and Tuning

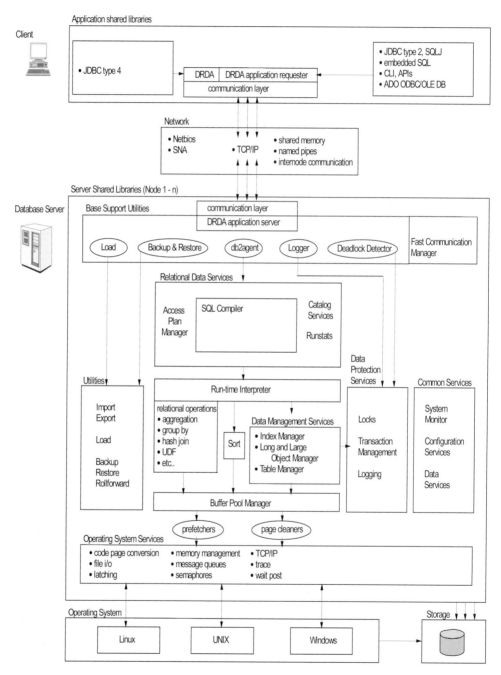

Fig. 12–1 *DB2 Architecture Overview*

Fenced/Not Fenced Resources

A database stored procedure is a dynamically loadable library (DLL) that can be invoked from a database application by using the CALL statement. The library is stored on the DB2 database server, and it can execute as a *fenced* resource or a *not fenced* resource. A fenced resource is one that executes in a separate process from the database agent. A not fenced resource will execute in the same process as the database agent.

A not fenced resource will have better performance than a fenced resource since there is less interprocess communication overhead. However, a not fenced resource can overwrite DB2 control blocks if it is not well tested.

 Note: User-defined functions (UDFs) can also be defined to execute as a fenced or unfenced (not fenced) resource.

Query Parallelism

In Chapter 1, the scalability options of how DB2 can grow from a small uniprocessor machine to a massively parallel system was briefly discussed. There are certain elements inside DB2 that take advantage of hardware parallelism in addition to the benefits of a multitasking operating system. The exploitation of parallelism has significant performance benefits for queries against DB2 as well as other administrative tasks.

There are two types of query parallelism: *inter-query* parallelism and *intra-query* parallelism.

- *Inter-query* parallelism refers to the ability of multiple applications to query a database at the same time. Each query will execute independently of the others, but DB2 will execute all of them at the same time. DB2 has always supported this type of parallelism.
- *Intra-query* parallelism refers to the processing of parts of a single query at the same time using either *intra-partition* parallelism or *inter-partition* parallelism or both. With intra-query parallelism, one single complex query can be taken by the DB2 optimizer and split into pieces that can be executed in parallel.

Intra-Partition Parallelism

Intra-partition parallelism refers to the ability to break up a query into multiple parts. This type of parallelism subdivides what is usually considered a single database operation such as index creation, database load, or SQL queries into multiple parts, many or all of which can be executed in parallel within a single database par-

Monitoring and Tuning

tition. Intra-partition parallelism is best suited to take advantage of the symmetric multiprocessor (SMP) system.

Fig. 12–2 *Intra-partition parallelism*

Fig. 12–2 shows a query broken into four pieces that can be executed in parallel, with the results returned more quickly than if the query were run in a serial fashion. To utilize intra-partition parallelism, you need to configure the database appropriately. You can choose the degree of parallelism or let the system do it for you. The degree of parallelism is the number of pieces of a query that execute in parallel. It will be discussed later in this section.

In a parallel environment, the DB2 optimizer considers access plans that do not run a complete query but break the query down into different parts (also called *query decomposition*). The DB2 optimizer considers different groupings of operators that can be sent to different processes or threads to be executed. The parts are called Subsection Pieces (SSPs) with one SQL statement consisting of one or many subsection pieces.

Note: The use of subsection pieces or SSPs will only be considered by the optimizer if intra-partition parallelism is enabled.

A subsection piece is a sequence of one or more database operators belonging to the same SQL query that, when executed, completes the processing part of that query. A subsection piece must be executed in one DB2 process or thread. A subsection piece may receive data from other DB2 subsection pieces or feed data to another subsection piece or return data to the user. Subsection pieces can be cloned or duplicated by the optimizer to speed up the processing.

DB2 provides the capability to change the *degree of parallelism*. The degree of parallelism limits the number of SSPs a query can be broken down into.

The optimizer handles all of this behind the scenes; therefore, users do not need to change anything in their applications to utilize SMP parallelism other than setting the intra-parallel database manager configuration parameter to yes and setting the degree of parallelism >1. Users can explicitly set the degree of parallelism for the DB2 instance, the application, or the statement. In addition, if a section is built by the optimizer with a specific degree of parallelism, it will be reduced if the instance default degree of parallelism is lower.

When breaking a query into multiple SSPs, the optimizer will also determine if the SSPs will work on the same data or if the data can be partitioned among the SSPs. In determining the optimal way to split the section into SSPs and to partition the data, the optimizer will be mainly influenced by the degree of parallelism and the cardinality of the data.

In an SMP environment, the SSPs will be duplicates or clones of each other. DB2 will then execute the SSPs in parallel and return the results faster than if the query were run on one processor. Each SSP copy will work on a subset of the data. As determined by the optimizer, this subset may be based on the data values or on equal divisions of the data based on the number of rows.

Note: If the degree of parallelism is set to a value >1, the number of SSPs created is equal to that value.

Inter-Partition Parallelism

Inter-partition parallelism refers to the ability to break up a query into multiple parts across multiple partitions of a partitioned database on one machine or multiple machines. The query is performed in parallel. Inter-partition parallelism is best suited to take advantage of clusters or massively parallel processing (MPP) systems.

Monitoring and Tuning

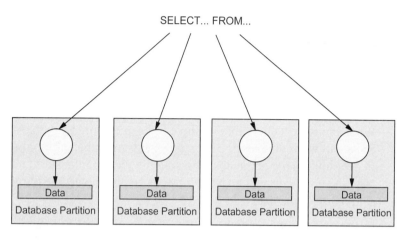

Fig. 12–3 *Inter-partition parallelism*

Fig. 12–3 shows a query broken into four pieces that can be executed in parallel, with the results returned more quickly than if the query were run in a serial fashion in a single partition. The degree of parallelism is largely determined by the number of partitions you create and how you define your nodegroups. DB2 Server Edition allows for inter-partition parallelism as well as combining intra-partition and inter-partition parallelism. This product is covered in detail in the *DB2 UDB V8.1 Administration Guide.*

DB2 Memory Usage

Database activity involves disk access (I/O) and memory access (CPU). Each of the DB2 configuration parameters affects either the memory or disk resources. Because disk access is much slower than memory access is, the key database performance tuning objective is to decrease the amount of disk activity. If you are able to eliminate I/O wait time, the database requests are CPU bound, and increasing performance would then require faster CPUs or multiple CPUs.

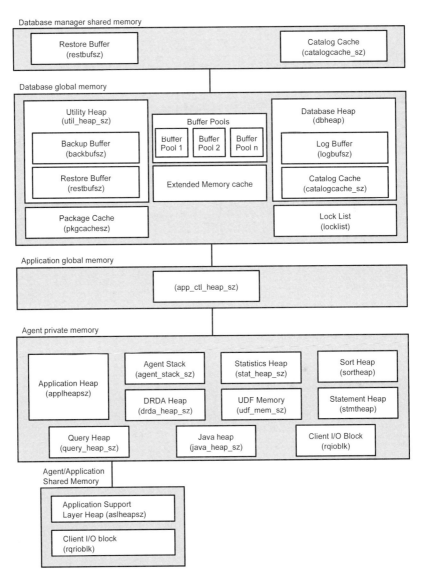

Fig. 12–4 *Memory used by DB2*

Fig. 12–4 shows the relationship of the various configurable memory parameters. Memory is allocated on the server or the client. The number of memory segments allocated for the Database Global Memory depends on the number of currently active databases.

Each DB2 application has an associated DB2 *coordinating agent*. The database agent accesses the database resources on behalf of the application. Therefore, there are tuning parameters that adjust resource usage of the database agent. The Agent Private Memory exists for each agent, and the size is determined by the values of the following parameters:

- Application heap size (APPLHEAPSZ)
- Sort heap size (SORTHEAP)
- Statement heap size (STMTHEAP)
- Statistics heap size (STAT_HEAP_SZ)
- Query heap size (QUERY_HEAP_SZ)
- DRDA heap size (DRDA_HEAP_SZ)
- UDF shared memory set size (UDF_MEM_SZ)
- Agent stack size (AGENT_STACK_SZ)

If intra-partition parallelism is enabled by setting the intra-parallel database manager configuration parameter to yes, which is the default value in an SMP environment, the coordinating agent distributes database requests to *subagents*, and these agents perform the requests for the application. Once the coordinating agent is created, it handles all database requests on behalf of its application by coordinating the subagents that perform requests on the database.

The application control heap is used as a global work area for all the agents (coordinating and subordinate) working for the application. The database parameter is APP_CTL_HEAP_SZ.

The memory area, known as application shared memory, is used to determine the amount of memory used to communicate between the application and its DB2 coordinating agent. Record blocking occurs within this memory area. The DBM parameter is ASLHEAPSZ.

Prefetching data into the buffer pool

As referenced in Chapter 9, prefetching pages means that one or more pages are retrieved from disk in the expectation that they will be required by an application. Prefetching index and data pages into the buffer pool can help improve performance by reducing the I/O wait time. In addition, parallel I/O enhances prefetching efficiency. The two types of prefetching are:

- Sequential prefetch - consecutive pages are read into the buffer pool before the pages are required by an application.
- List prefetch - also known as list sequential prefetch, prefetches a set of non-consecutive data pages.

The two methods of reading data are in addition to a normal read. A normal read is used when only one or a few consecutive pages are retrieved.

Prefetching is important to the performance of intra-partition parallelism, which uses multiple subagents when scanning an index or a table. Such parallel scans introduce larger data consumption rates, which require higher prefetch rates.

The cost of inadequate prefetching is higher for parallel scans than serial scans. If prefetching does not occur for a serial scan, the query runs more slowly because the agent always needs to wait for I/O. If prefetching does not occur for a parallel scan, all subagents might need to wait because one subagent is waiting for I/O.

Because of its importance, prefetching is performed more aggressively with intra-partition parallelism. The sequential detection mechanism tolerates larger gaps between adjacent pages so that the pages can be considered sequential. The width of these gaps increases with the number of subagents involved in the scan.

SQL Compiler Overview

The SQL compiler performs a number of tasks during the creation of the compiled form of the SQL statements. These phases are described below and are also shown in Fig. 12–5 on page 675. As you can see in this figure, the representation of the query is stored in an internal in-memory structure known as the *Query Graph Model*.

- Parse query - The first task of the SQL compiler is to analyze the SQL query to validate the syntax. If any syntax errors are detected, the SQL compiler stops processing, and the appropriate SQL error is returned to the application attempting to compile the SQL statement. When parsing is complete, an internal representation of the query is created.

- Check Semantics - The second task of the compiler is to further validate the SQL statement by checking to ensure that the parts of the statement make sense given the other parts, for example, ensuring that the data types of the columns input into scalar functions are correct for those functions.

  Also during this stage, the compiler adds the behavioral semantics to the query graph model, such as the effects of referential constraints, table check constraints, triggers, and views.

- Rewrite query - The SQL compiler uses global semantics provided in the query graph model to transform the query into a form that can be optimized more easily. For example, the compiler might move a predicate, altering the level at which it is applied, in an attempt to improve query performance. This particular process is called *general predicate pushdown*.

  Any changes made to the query are rewritten back to the query graph model.

- Optimize access plan - The SQL optimizer portion of the SQL compiler uses the query graph model as input and generates many alternative execution plans for satisfying the user's request. It estimates the execution cost of each alternative plan using the statistics for tables, indexes, columns, and functions, and chooses the plan with the smallest estimated execution cost.

The optimizer uses the query graph model to analyze the query semantics and to obtain information about a wide variety of factors, including indexes, base tables, derived tables, subqueries, correlation, and recursion.

The output from this step of the SQL compiler is an access plan. The access plan provides the basis for the information captured in the *explain tables*. The information used to generate the access plan can be captured with an *explain snapshot*.

- Generate executable code - The final step of the SQL compiler uses the access plan and the query graph model to create an executable access plan, or section, for the query. This code generation step uses information from the query graph model to avoid repetitive execution of expressions that only need to be computed once for a query. Examples for which this optimization is possible include code page conversions and the use of host variables.

Information about access plans for static SQL is stored in the system catalog tables. When the package is executed, DB2 will use the information stored in the system catalog tables to determine how to access the data and provide results for the query. It is this information that is used by the db2expln tool.

It is recommended that the RUNSTATS command be done periodically on tables used in queries where good performance is desired. The optimizer will then be better equipped with relevant statistical information on the nature of the data. If the RUNSTATS command is not run, or the optimizer determines that RUNSTATS was run on empty or near-empty tables, the optimizer may either use defaults or attempt to derive certain statistics based on the number of pages used to store the table on disk.

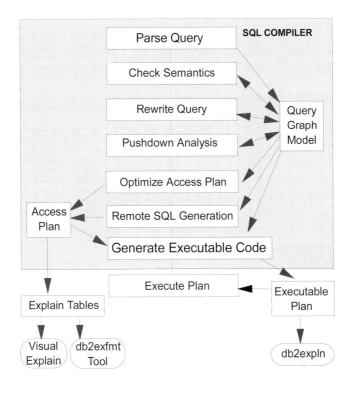

Fig. 12–5 *Steps performed by SQL compiler*

Explain information must be captured before you can review it using one of DB2's explain tools. You can decide to capture detailed information regarding the access plan. While the query is being compiled, the information can be captured into a file or special tables known as explain tables.

DB2 Sorting Methods

When an SQL query requires the data to be returned in a defined sequence or order, the result may or may not require sorting. DB2 will attempt to perform the ordering through index usage. If an index cannot be used, the sort will occur. A sort involves two steps:

1. A sort phase

2. Return of the results of the sort phase

How the sort is handled within these two steps results in different categories or types by which the sort can be described. When considering the sort phase, the sort can be categorized as *overflowed* or *nonoverflowed*. When considering the return of the results of the sort phase, the sort can be categorized as *piped* or *non-piped*.

Overflowed and Nonoverflowed

If the information being sorted cannot fit entirely into the sort heap (a block of memory that is allocated each time a sort is performed), it overflows into temporary database tables. Sorts that do not overflow always perform better than those that do.

Piped and Non-Piped

If sorted information can return directly without requiring a temporary table to store a final, sorted list of data, it is referred to as a piped sort. If the sorted information requires a temporary table to be returned, it is referred to as a non-piped sort. A piped sort always performs better than a non-piped sort.

The DB2 optimizer will determine if a nonoverflowed sort can be performed and if a piped sort can be performed by comparing the expected result set with the value of the SORTHEAP database configuration parameter, and so forth.

Note: To obtain an ordered result set, a sort is not always required. If an index scan is the access method used, then the data is already in the order of the index, and sorting is not required.

Monitoring the DB2 System

The first step in the database monitoring process is defining your objectives. Defining the objectives is very important in selecting the best facility to meet your requirements. An objective can be:

• Understanding how a given query will be optimized in a specific environment.

For example, there is a query used in an application that does not perform well.

- Understanding how applications use database manager resources at a specific point of time. For example, database concurrency is reduced if a specific application is started.

Understanding which database manager events have occurred when running applications. For example, you notice a degradation in overall performance when certain applications are run.

Once your monitoring objectives have been determined, decide on the process and tools to implement and maintain the overall health of the DB2 system.

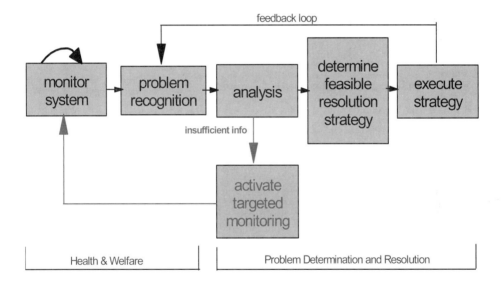

Fig. 12–6 *DB2 monitoring process*

DB2 Health Monitor

The Health Monitor is a server-side tool that constantly monitors the health of the instance, even without user interaction. If the Health Monitor finds that a defined threshold has been exceeded (for example, the available log space is not sufficient), or if it detects an abnormal state for an object (for example, an instance is down), the Health Monitor will raise an alert. When an alert is raised two things can occur:

- Alert notifications can be sent by e-mail or to a pager address, allowing you to contact whoever is responsible for a system.
- Preconfigured actions can be taken. For example, a script or a task (implemented from the Task Center) can be run.

A health indicator is a system characteristic that the Health Monitor checks. The Health Monitor comes with a set of predefined thresholds for these health indicators. The Health Monitor checks the state of your system against these health-indicator thresholds when determining whether to issue an alert. Using the Health Center, commands, or APIs, you can customize the threshold settings of the health indicators, and define who should be notified and what script or task should be run if an alert is issued. The following are the categories of health indicators:

- Application concurrency
- Database management system
- Database
- Logging
- Memory
- Package and catalog caches
- Sorting
- Table space storage

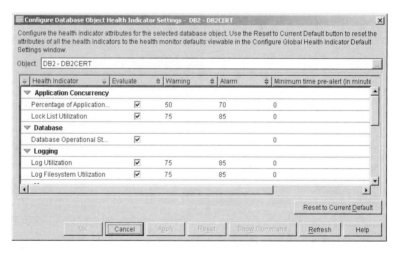

Fig. 12–7 *Health Indicator settings*

The Health Center provides the graphical interface to the Health Monitor. You use it to configure the Health Monitor, and to see the rolled up alert state of your instances and database objects. Using the Health Monitor's drill-down capability, you can access details about current alerts and obtain a list of recommended actions that describe how to resolve the alert. You can follow one of the recommended actions to address the alert. If the recommended action is to make a database or database manager configuration change, a new value will be recommended and you can implement the recommendation by clicking on a button. In other cases, the recommendation will be to investigate the problem further by launching a tool, such as the CLP or the Memory Visualizer.

Fig. 12–8 *Memory Visualizer*

Database Monitoring

There are various methods to obtain detailed monitoring information. These methods involve using the following DB2 facilities: *Snapshot Monitor, Event Monitor, and Explain Facility.* The following is a description of the information provided by the Explain Facility and the database monitors:

- Choose the Snapshot or Event Monitor if you want to gather data about DB2's operation, performance, and the applications using it. This data is maintained as DB2 runs and can provide important performance and trouble-shooting information.

- Choose the Explain Facility if you want to analyze the access plan for an SQL statement or a group of SQL statements.

This chapter will give you information to decide which of the existing facilities is the best for your needs. It shows how to capture data using the Explain Facility, the Snapshot Monitor, the Event Monitor, and how to interpret the collected information.

This chapter also gives you information on how to diagnose problems in DB2 applications, CLI/ODBC/JDBC applications.

Monitoring and Tuning

Database Monitors

Database monitors are used to collect detailed resource usage information. Monitoring activity may be performed from a DB2 client or a DB2 server. The monitor interface can be invoked using CLP commands, graphical monitors, or monitoring APIs. DB2 provides different kinds of monitoring, which differ in the way monitoring data is gathered. The two ways of monitoring are:

- *Snapshot Monitoring* - Provides information regarding database activity at a specific point in time. It is a picture of the current state of DB2 activity. The amount of data returned to the user when a snapshot is taken is determined using monitor switches. These switches can be set at the instance or application level.
- *Event Monitoring* - Records the occurrence of specific milestones of DB2 events. This can allow you to collect information about transient events, including deadlocks, connections, and SQL statements.

The system monitor provides multiple means of presenting monitor data to the administrator. For snapshot and event monitors, you have the option of storing monitor information in files, SQL tables, viewing it on the screen, or processing it with a client application.

The two monitoring options are discussed in the following pages.

 Note: Snapshots can now be taken using SELECT statements against a set of new user-defined table functions. Event monitors can now write data to SQL tables, as well as to files or pipes.

Snapshot Monitoring

Snapshots are useful for determining the status of a database system. Taken at regular intervals, they can be useful for observing trends and anticipating potential performance bottlenecks. The Snapshot Monitor provides cumulative information in the form of counters. These counters can be reset. The snapshot information is provided in special data structures that can be examined by the application issuing the snapshot.

The amount of data returned by the Snapshot Monitor is set according to switches. The monitor switches, along with the information they provide, are displayed in the following table.

Table 12–1 *Data Returned by the Snapshot Monitor*

Group	Information Provided	Monitor Switch	DBM Parameter
Sorts	Number of heaps used, overflows, sorts performance	SORT	DFT_MON_SORT
Locks	Number of locks held, number of deadlocks	LOCK	DFT_MON_LOCK
Tables	Measure activity (rows read, rows written)	TABLE	DFT_MON_TABLE
Bufferpools	Number of reads and writes, time taken	BUFFERPOOL	DFT_MON_BUFPOOL
Unit of work	Start times, end times, completion status	UOW	DFT_MON_UOW
SQL statements	Start time, stop time, statement identification	STATEMENT	DFT_MON_STMT
Timestamps	Monitors timestamp	TIMESTAMP	DFT_MON_TIMESTAMP

The monitor switches can be turned on and off at the instance (DBM configuration) level or at the application level (using the UPDATE MONITOR SWITCHES command). There is also base information provided by the Snapshot Monitor that is gathered regardless of the monitor switches settings.

Setting the instance configuration parameters for monitor switches will affect all databases within the instance. Every application connecting to a database will inherit the default switches set within the DBM configuration.

Note: DB2 Snapshot Monitors can only be used by users having SYSADM, SYSCTRL, or SYSMAINT authority. Event Monitors require SYSADM or DBADM authority.

For example, to capture detailed information about SQL statements executing in DB2, the appropriate monitor switches must be turned on. The commands are:

```
UPDATE DBM CONFIGURATION USING DFT_MON_STMT ON
```

You can alternatively use this command:

UPDATE MONITOR SWITCHES USING STATEMENT ON

The UPDATE DBM CONFIGURATION command will modify the database manager configuration. Therefore, SQL statement information will be captured for applications accessing all databases within the instance.

> **Note:** When you change the value of the database manager configuration parameters, you usually need to stop and start the instance to make those changes effective; however, the changes of the default monitor switches will be effective immediately. Therefore, you don't need to stop and start the instance.

On the other hand, the UPDATE MONITOR SWITCHES command will only capture SQL statements for the application that activated the switch. (In this example, the application is the command line processor.)

> **Note:** Even if none of the switches are turned on, there will be some basic information captured by the Snapshot Monitor.

Viewing Snapshot Monitor Data

When a monitor switch is turned on, the monitor data starts being collected. To view the monitor data, a *snapshot* must be taken.

> **Note:** There is a minor performance effect when the data is recorded. Issuing the snapshot incurs additional performance overhead.

A snapshot is requested using the DB2 command GET SNAPSHOT. This command can be executed in different ways. It can be executed within the Command Center GUI tool, embedded in an application using the appropriate API, executed from the Command Center or CLP.

Before the output of the Snapshot Monitor is examined, how the snapshot information is captured will be discussed. Use the Command Center interface to capture database monitor snapshots. While taking a snapshot, it is possible to define a particular area of interest.

There are different levels of monitoring used with the Snapshot Monitor. These levels allow you to focus your analysis in a particular area of interest.

The following Snapshot Monitor levels are available:

- *Database manager* - Captures information for an active instance
- *Database* - Captures database(s) information
- *Application* - Captures application(s) information
- *Bufferpools* - Captures buffer pool activity information
- *Table space* - Captures information for table spaces within a database
- *Table* - Captures information for tables within a database
- *Lock* - Captures information for locks held by applications against a database
- *Dynamic SQL cache* - Captures point-in-time statement information from the SQL statement cache for the database

Snapshot Monitor switches and levels are combined to provide different monitoring information when taking a snapshot. The two are very closely related. If the proper monitor switch is not turned on, the snapshot level used may not return any data.

As said before, the GET SNAPSHOT command is used to review the Snapshot Monitor data.

To gather lock information for the Certification database, execute the following DB2 command from the Command Center:

```
GET SNAPSHOT FOR LOCKS ON db2cert
```

The output of the snapshot is displayed in the Command Center Results window. It is a good idea to save the output to a file for analysis purposes.

The output of the SNAPSHOT FOR LOCKS command is shown in Fig. 12–9. If you want detailed information about locks, as shown in Fig. 12–9, you must turn on the Lock Monitor Switch.

Analyzing the snapshot, you can see that the first application (application ID *LOCAL.DB2.020613040452) is in Lock-Wait status. It is attempting to acquire a row lock on a row having an X lock held by the second application (application ID *LOCAL.DB2.020613145839). To release the lock, the application holding it must complete its transaction using a COMMIT or ROLLBACK statement.

Monitoring and Tuning

Note: The LOCKTIMEOUT database configuration parameter controls the maximum time that an application should wait in Lock-Wait status. Its default value is to wait until the locked resource is available.

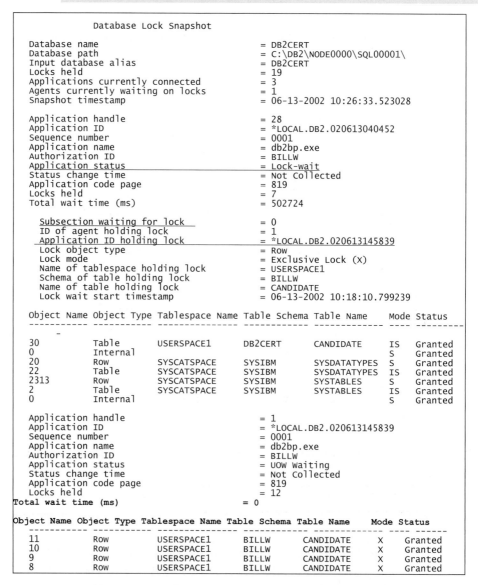

```
                    Database Lock Snapshot

Database name                           = DB2CERT
Database path                           = C:\DB2\NODE0000\SQL00001\
Input database alias                    = DB2CERT
Locks held                              = 19
Applications currently connected        = 3
Agents currently waiting on locks       = 1
Snapshot timestamp                      = 06-13-2002 10:26:33.523028

Application handle                      = 28
Application ID                          = *LOCAL.DB2.020613040452
Sequence number                         = 0001
Application name                        = db2bp.exe
Authorization ID                        = BILLW
Application status                      = Lock-wait
Status change time                      = Not Collected
Application code page                   = 819
Locks held                              = 7
Total wait time (ms)                    = 502724

    Subsection waiting for lock         = 0
    ID of agent holding lock            = 1
    Application ID holding lock         = *LOCAL.DB2.020613145839
    Lock object type                    = Row
    Lock mode                           = Exclusive Lock (X)
    Name of tablespace holding lock     = USERSPACE1
    Schema of table holding lock        = BILLW
    Name of table holding lock          = CANDIDATE
    Lock wait start timestamp           = 06-13-2002 10:18:10.799239
```

Object Name	Object Type	Tablespace Name	Table Schema	Table Name	Mode	Status
30	Table	USERSPACE1	DB2CERT	CANDIDATE	IS	Granted
0	Internal				S	Granted
20	Row	SYSCATSPACE	SYSIBM	SYSDATATYPES	S	Granted
22	Table	SYSCATSPACE	SYSIBM	SYSDATATYPES	IS	Granted
2313	Row	SYSCATSPACE	SYSIBM	SYSTABLES	S	Granted
2	Table	SYSCATSPACE	SYSIBM	SYSTABLES	IS	Granted
0	Internal				S	Granted

```
Application handle                      = 1
Application ID                          = *LOCAL.DB2.020613145839
Sequence number                         = 0001
Application name                        = db2bp.exe
Authorization ID                        = BILLW
Application status                      = UOW Waiting
Status change time                      = Not Collected
Application code page                   = 819
Locks held                              = 12
Total wait time (ms)                    = 0
```

Object Name	Object Type	Tablespace Name	Table Schema	Table Name	Mode	Status
11	Row	USERSPACE1	BILLW	CANDIDATE	X	Granted
10	Row	USERSPACE1	BILLW	CANDIDATE	X	Granted
9	Row	USERSPACE1	BILLW	CANDIDATE	X	Granted
8	Row	USERSPACE1	BILLW	CANDIDATE	X	Granted

Fig. 12–9 *Output of GET SNAPSHOT for locks on DB2CERT*

The information provided by the Snapshot Monitor is a valuable resource to solve many problems. At the time of the snapshot shown in Fig. 12–9, there was a concurrency problem in the database. Therefore, the LOCKS monitoring level was used to analyze the database activity.

The information from APPLICATIONS Snapshot Monitor level as shown in Fig. 12–10 was taken using the following command:

```
GET SNAPSHOT FOR APPLICATIONS ON db2cert
```

```
              Application Snapshot

Application handle                     = 1
Application status                     = Lock-wait
Status change time                     = Not Collected
Application code page                  = 819
Application country code               = 1
DUOW correlation token                 = *LOCAL.DB2.020613040432
Application name                       = db2bp.exe
Application ID                         = *LOCAL.DB2.020613040452
Sequence number                        = 0001
Connection request start timestamp     = 06-13-2002 23:04:52.725918
Connect request completion timestamp   = 06-13-2002 23:04:53.355324
Application idle time                  = Not Collected
Authorization ID                       = BILLW
Execution ID                           = BILLW
Configuration NNAME of client          =
Client database manager product ID     = SQL06010
Process ID of client application       = 24030
Platform of client application         = NT
Communication protocol of client       = Local Client
Database name                          = DB2CERT
Database path                          = C:\DB2\NODE0000\SQL00001\
Client database alias                  = db2cert
Input database alias                   = DB2CERT
Last reset timestamp                   =
Snapshot timestamp                     = 06-13-2002 13:52:55.373922
......
Locks held by application              = 8
Lock escalations                       = 0
Exclusive lock escalations             = 0
Number of Lock Timeouts since connected = 0
Total time UOW waited on locks (ms)    = Not Collected
......
Number of SQL requests since last commit = 38
Commit statements                      = 43
Rollback statements                    = 5
Dynamic SQL statements attempted       = 486
Static SQL statements attempted        = 48
Failed statement operations            = 6
Select SQL statements executed         = 38
Update/Insert/Delete statements executed = 2
DDL statements executed                = 6
.......
Internal rollbacks due to deadlock     = 0
Rows deleted                           = 0
Rows inserted                          = 18
Rows updated                           = 0
```

Fig. 12–10 *Partial output of Get Snapshot for applications command*

The snapshot provides detailed data about the activity of applications. In this example, only a portion of the output is shown. Using this snapshot, you can see application activity, such as how may rows have been read, updated, or deleted by an application. To obtain more information regarding database objects shown in an application snapshot, such as tables or locks, the appropriate monitor switches and monitoring levels should be used.

To review a table level snapshot, issue the following command:

```
GET SNAPSHOT FOR TABLES ON db2cert
```

The output from the table level snapshot is shown in Fig. 12–11. By using a table snapshot, further information can be obtained, such as which table has the most activity in the database.

```
              Table Snapshot
First database connect timestamp     = 06-13-2002 23:04:52.725918

Last reset timestamp                 =
Snapshot timestamp                   = 06-13-2002 14:21:13.529358
Database name                        = DB2CERT
Database path                        = C:\DB2\NODE0000/SQL00001/
Input database alias                 = DB2CERT
Number of accessed tables            = 6

Table Schema      Table Name      Table Type     Rows    Written    Rows Read  Overflows
---------------   -------------   -------------   ------  ---------  ---------  ---------
SYSIBM            SYSFUNCTIONS    Catalog             0          4          0          0
SYSIBM            SYSTABLES       Catalog             0          8          0          0
SYSIBM            SYSPLAN         Catalog             0          2          0          0
SYSIBM            SYSDBAUTH       Catalog             0          4          0          0
BILLW             CANDIDATE       User               24         48          0          0
SYSIBM            SYSDATATYPES    Catalog             0          8          0          0
```

Fig. 12–11 *GET SNAPSHOT for tables on the db2cert database*

Note: To collect the snapshot information shown in Fig. 12–11, the TABLE monitor switch must be set to ON.

The table snapshot output shows different tables being accessed. In our example, user and catalog tables were accessed. Catalog tables are used by DB2 for different activities, such as checking the authorizations granted to the user requesting an SQL statement, reviewing distinct types used, and so on.

The snapshots that have been presented show data related to DB2 logical objects, such as tables, locks, and applications. Snapshots can be used to provide information related to the physical database environment, such as disk activity and memory usage. This kind of information is gathered using a table space level snapshot using the command below. Partial output follows in Figure 12–12.

```
GET SNAPSHOT FOR TABLESPACES ON db2cert
```

```
                 Tablespace Snapshot

First database connect timestamp     = 06-13-2002 14:59:55.061853
Last reset timestamp                 =
Snapshot timestamp                   = 06-13-2002 15:04:20.450507
Database name                        = DB2CERT
Database path                        = C:\DB2\NODE0000\SQL00001\
Input database alias                 = DB2CERT
Number of accessed tablespaces       = 3

Tablespace name                      = SYSCATSPACE
  Data pages copied to extended storage     = 0
  Index pages copied to extended storage    = 0
  Data pages copied from extended storage   = 0
  Index pages copied from extended storage  = 0
  Buffer pool data logical reads            = 33
  Buffer pool data physical reads           = 9
  Asynchronous pool data page reads         = 0
  Buffer pool data writes                   = 0
  Asynchronous pool data page writes        = 0
  Buffer pool index logical reads           = 71
  Buffer pool index physical reads          = 23
  Asynchronous pool index page reads        = 0
  Buffer pool index writes                  = 0
  Asynchronous pool index page writes       = 0
  Total buffer pool read time (ms)          = 399
  Total buffer pool write time (ms)         = 0
  Total elapsed asynchronous read time      = 0
  Total elapsed asynchronous write time     = 0
  Asynchronous read requests                = 0

  Direct reads                              = 40
  Direct writes                             = 0
  Direct read requests                      = 8
  Direct write requests                     = 0
  Direct reads elapsed time (ms)            = 97
  Direct write elapsed time (ms)            = 0
  Number of files closed                    = 0
. . . . .
Tablespace name                      = USERSPACE1

  Data pages copied to extended storage     = 0
  Index pages copied to extended storage    = 0
  Data pages copied from extended storage   = 0
  Index pages copied from extended storage  = 0
  Buffer pool data logical reads            = 32
  Buffer pool data physical reads           = 4
  Asynchronous pool data page reads         = 0
  Buffer pool data writes                   = 0
  Asynchronous pool data page writes        = 0
  Buffer pool index logical reads           = 20
  Buffer pool index physical reads          = 10
  Asynchronous pool index page reads        = 0
  Buffer pool index writes                  = 0
  Asynchronous pool index page writes       = 0
  Total buffer pool read time (ms)          = 132
  Total buffer pool write time (ms)         = 0
  Total elapsed asynchronous read time      = 0
  Total elapsed asynchronous write time     = 0
  Asynchronous read requests                = 0

  Direct reads                              = 576
```

Fig. 12–12 *Partial output of GET SNAPSHOT for table spaces on DB2CERT*

The snapshot in Fig. 12–12 is organized according to the I/O and buffer pool activity for each table space. The data captured shows different counters representing time (expressed in milliseconds) or times that a different activity has occurred. Along with the table space information, this monitor level shows information about the buffer pool usage. Buffer pool information is only gathered if the BUFFER-POOL monitor switch is turned on.

Any I/O prefetching activity is shown as asynchronous reads, and any buffer pool asynchronous page cleaning is shown as asynchronous writes. The term direct read/write corresponds to the number of read operations that do not use the buffer pool.

Reviewing the Snapshot Monitor Switch Status

At any time, you can determine the current settings of database monitor switches by issuing the following command:

```
GET MONITOR SWITCHES
```

The switch states are shown in Fig. 12–13. The timestamps correspond to the last time the switches were reset or turned on.

```
                     Monitor Recording Switches

Switch list for db partition number 0
Buffer Pool Activity Information  (BUFFERPOOL) = OFF
Lock Information                        (LOCK) = ON  08-27-2002 15:01:22.624422
Sorting Information                     (SORT) = OFF
SQL Statement Information          (STATEMENT) = ON  08-27-2002 15:01:27.155032
Table Activity Information             (TABLE) = ON  08-27-2002 15:01:09.482143
Table Timestamp Information         (TIMESTAMP) = ON  08-27-2002 15:01:18.482143
Unit of Work Information                 (UOW) = ON  08-27-2002 15:01:15.340116
```

Fig. 12–13 *Monitor switch settings*

The monitor switch settings for an application are shown in Fig. 12–13. If you want to know the instance settings for the monitor switches, use the following command:

```
GET DBM MONITOR SWITCHES
```

Resetting the Snapshot Monitor Switches

As demonstrated, the data returned by a Snapshot Monitor is based primarily on counters. These counters are associated with a monitor switch.

Monitor switches are initialized or reset when one of the following occurs:

- Application level monitoring is used, and the application connects to the

database.
- Database level monitoring is used, and the first application connects.
- Table level monitoring is used, and the table is first accessed.
- Table space level monitoring is used, and the table space is first accessed.
- Issuing the `RESET MONITOR` command.
- Turning on a particular monitor switch.

Monitor switches can be reset at any time by issuing the command:

```
RESET MONITOR FOR DATABASE db2cert
```

Resetting the monitor switches effectively starts all of the counters at zero, and further snapshots are based on the new counter values.

To reset the monitor switches for all databases within an instance, the `RESET MONITOR ALL` command should be used.

> **Note:** Every application has its own copy of the snapshot monitor values. Resetting the monitor switches only affects the counters of the application that issues the reset.

Event Monitoring

While Snapshot Monitoring records the state of database activity when the snapshot is taken, an Event Monitor records the database activity when an *event* or *transition* occurs. Some database activities that need to be monitored cannot be easily captured using the Snapshot Monitor. These activities include deadlock scenarios. When a deadlock occurs, DB2 will resolve the deadlock by issuing a `ROLLBACK` for one of the transactions. Information regarding the deadlock event cannot be easily captured using the Snapshot Monitor because the deadlock was probably resolved before a snapshot could be taken.

Event Monitors are created using SQL Data Definition Language (DDL) like other database objects. Event Monitors can be turned on or off much like the Snapshot Monitor switches.

> **Note:** SYSADM or DBADM authority is required to create an Event Monitor.

When an Event Monitor is created, the type of event to be monitored must be stated. The Event Monitor can monitor the following events:

- *Database* - Records an event record when the last application disconnects from the database.
- *Tables* - Records an event record for each active table when the last application disconnects from the database. An active table is a table that has changed since the first connection to the database.
- *Deadlocks* - Records an event record for each deadlock event.
- *Tablespaces* - Records an event record for each active table space when the last application disconnects from the database.
- *Bufferpools* - Records an event record for buffer pools when the last application disconnects from the database.
- *Connections* - Records an event record for each database connection event when an application disconnects from a database.
- *Statements* - Records an event record for every SQL statement issued by an application (dynamic and static).
- *Transactions* - Records an event record for every transaction when it completes (COMMIT or ROLLBACK statement).

The output of an Event Monitor is stored in a SQL table, directory or in a named pipe. The existence of the pipe or the file will be verified when the Event Monitor is activated. If the target location for an Event Monitor is a named pipe, then it is the responsibility of the application to promptly read the data from the pipe. If the target for an Event Monitor is a directory, then the stream of data will be written to a series of files.

The following system catalog tables are used to store Event Monitor definitions:

- SYSCAT.EVENTMONITORS - Contains a record for each Event Monitor, including the current state of the Event Monitor, and identifies the target output as a SQL table, file, or pipe.
- SYSCAT.EVENTS - Contains a record for each event being monitored. A single Event Monitor can be defined to monitor multiple events (e.g., DEADLOCKS and STATEMENTS).
- SYSIBM.EVENTTABLES - Contains a row for every target table of an Event Monitor that writes to a SQL table.

Analyzing Event Monitor Output

These utilities are available to analyze Event Monitor data:

- *db2eva* - A GUI tool that can be invoked from a command line (used to read data written to SQL tables).
- *db2evmon* - A text-based tool that will read the event records and generate a report (used to read files).

A deadlock situation will now be created to demonstrate the Event Monitor. To do this, you need two DB2 Command Center windows with the AUTOCOMMIT feature turned off. Don't forget to make sure you have created an event monitor for DEADLOCKS and activate it. Here are the steps to create a deadlock situation:

- In the first window, issue: LOCK TABLE TEST_TAKEN IN SHARE MODE
- In the second window, issue: LOCK TABLE TEST IN SHARE MODE
- Back in the first window, issue: LOCK TABLE TEST IN EXCLUSIVE MODE
- Back in the second window, issue: LOCK TABLE TEST_TAKEN IN EXCLUSIVE MODE

These steps will generate a deadlock situation that will be resolved by DB2. The data captured by the Event Monitor will now be analyzed.

Event Analyzer/Monitor

The Event Analyzer displays the Event Monitor records that have been previously collected. To invoke the Event Analyzer, execute the DB2EVA command. If you are working on a Windows machine, you can select the **Event Analyzer** icon in the DB2 folder.

Monitoring and Tuning

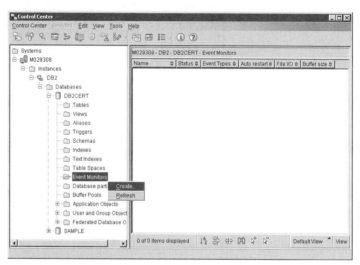

Fig. 12–14 *Invoking the Event Monitor from the Control Center*

An alternative to selecting the **Event Analyzer** icon is to right-click on the Event Monitor object in the Control Center as show Fig. 12–14.

Fig. 12–15 *Create Event Monitor*

In this example, the event monitor named **dlmon** will be created to monitor deadlocks. Note, that this monitor could also be used to monitor additional events as besides deadlock events.

Fig. 12–16 *SQL generated for Create Event Monitor*

The SQL generated can be saved as a script. Click Close and OK.

Fig. 12–17 *Deadlock Monitor activated*

After creating the monitor, it can be displayed from the Control Center.

Monitoring and Tuning

Fig. 12–18 *Monitored Periods View of an Event Monitor*

From the Monitored Periods View window, as shown in Fig. 12–18 you can analyze the event records for a specific time frame when the Event Monitor was active. Right-click on the desired time period to bring up a pop-up menu. From the pop-up menu, you should select the event to analyze. In this example, select the **DEADLOCKS** event. This is shown in Fig. 12–19.

Fig. 12–19 *Selecting the deadlock event for a particular period of time*

After selecting the deadlock Event Monitor, notice the information in the Dead-locks View window as shown in Fig. 12–20.

Fig. 12–20 *Deadlock event view*

The Deadlocks View window indicates that a deadlock was detected.

Fig. 12–20 displayed two connections that caused the deadlock. Drill down to **Deadlocked Connections**, the Deadlocked Connections window is shown in Fig. 12–21.

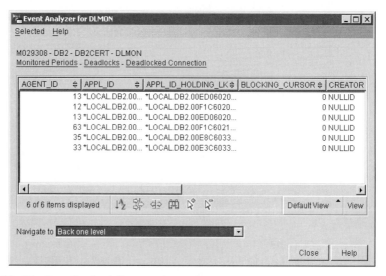

Fig. 12–21 *Deadlocked Connections view*

If you want additional information on the connection, drill down to the **Data Elements** option, Fig. 12–22 shows additional data available on the waiting connection of the deadlock.

Fig. 12–22 *Data Elements View*

The Event Analyzer will only display previously captured data. Therefore, there is no overhead in using the Event Analyzer as there is with the Snapshot Monitor. The Event Analyzer may not contain the desired information as it can only display the event records that have been previously captured. For example, if you select **Open as Statements** and no statement information was defined for the Event Monitor, the display will not contain SQL statement information.

Event Monitoring using file output

As mentioned, Event Monitors are database objects created using SQL DDL statements. In this example, a deadlock Event Monitor will be created to store its event records in the "/EVENTMONITORS/DEADLOCK/EVMON1" directory.

> **Note:** When using file output, the Event Monitor output directory will not be created by DB2. It must be created by the database administrator, and the instance owner must be able to write to the specified directory.

The following SQL statement creates an Event Monitor using file output. In our example, the Event Monitor is called EVMON1.

Monitoring and Tuning

```
CREATE EVENT MONITOR evmon1 FOR DEADLOCKS
WRITE TO FILE '/eventmonitors/deadlock/evmon1'
MAXFILES 3 MAXFILESIZE 1000
```

This Event Monitor is defined to allocate up to three files, each 4 MB in size, for a total monitor storage area of 12 MB. Other Event Monitor options include specifying the size of the write buffer, synchronous (BLOCKED) writes, asynchronous (UNBLOCKED) writes, APPEND the Event Monitor data to existing records, or REPLACE the Event Monitor data in the directory when the monitor is activated.

 Note: There is no limit in the number of defined Event Monitors, but a maximum of 32 Event Monitors can be active per DB2 instance at a time.

An Event Monitor must be active in order to collect the monitoring data. Once the Event Monitor has been defined using the CREATE EVENT MONITOR statement, it must be activated. The following statement is used to activate an Event Monitor.

```
SET EVENT MONITOR evmon1 STATE = 1
```

When the Event Monitor has been activated, Event Monitor records are written to the files contained in the defined directory or pipe (such as /EVENTMONITORS/DEADLOCKS/EVMON1 in our example).

An Event Monitor can be started automatically each time the database is started using the AUTOSTART option. This option is specified at creation time. To turn off an Event Monitor, the SET EVENT MONITOR STATE statement is once again used:

```
SET EVENT MONITOR evmon1 STATE = 0
```

Turning off an Event Monitor will also flush all of its contents.

Even when an Event Monitor has been turned off, it is still defined in the system catalog tables. However, it is not recording monitor information.

To determine if an Event Monitor is active or inactive, use the SQL function EVENT_MON_STATE or view the status in the Control Center. The EVENT_MON_STATE function returns a value of "1" if the Event Monitor is active and "0" if the monitor is not active.

A sample SQL statement using the EVENT_MON_STATE function to query the state of the EVMON1 Event Monitor is as follows:

```
SELECT evmonname, EVENT_MON_STATE(evmonname)
FROM SYSCAT.EVENTMONITORS WHERE evmonname = 'EVMON1'
```

Just like other database objects, Event Monitors can be dropped from the database. An example of removing the EVMON1 Event Monitor is as follows:

```
DROP EVENT MONITOR evmon1
```

Event Monitor files cannot be analyzed directly. An application must be used. There are a few alternatives provided by DB2 for analyzing Event Monitor data that will be discussed. First some of the Event Monitor records will be examined.

To ensure that all of the event records have been written to disk (some may be buffered), simply turn the Event Monitor off. You can also use the BUFFER option of FLUSH EVENT MONITOR command as follows:

```
FLUSH EVENT MONITOR evmon1 BUFFER
```

It forces the Event Monitor buffers to be written out. The FLUSH EVENT MONITOR command with the BUFFER option does not generate a partial record. Only the data already present in the Event Monitor buffers are written out.

If an Event Monitor is monitoring database, table space, or table events, it will write complete event records when the last application using the database disconnects. As already explained, you can use the FLUSH EVENT MONITOR command to record the partial event records.

To generate the Event Monitor report for the evmon1 monitor, issue the following command indicating where the event monitor files are located:

```
db2evmon -path /eventmonitors/deadlock/evmon1
```

Monitoring and Tuning

or

```
db2evmon -db db2cert -evm evmon1
```

The -PATH option of the DB2EVMON command is used to indicate the path where the Event Monitor files reside.

Note: It is a good idea to name the directories used for Event Monitor files using the type of Event Monitor (deadlock) and its name (evmon1).

The output of the DB2EVMON utility will be displayed on the screen by default. It is best to redirect the output to a file for analysis. A portion of the Event Monitor output for the evmon1 Event Monitor as shown in Fig. 12–23 will now be examined.

The files are sequentially numbered and have a file extension of "evt" (e.g., 00000000.EVT and 00000001.EVT). The maximum size and number of Event Monitor files is specified when the monitor is defined.

Note: An Event Monitor will turn itself off if the defined file space has been exceeded.

```
----------------------------------------------------------------
                       EVENT LOG HEADER
   Event Monitor name: EVMON1
   Server Product ID: SQL07010
   Version of event monitor data: 7
   Byte order: LITTLE ENDIAN
   Number of nodes in db2 instance: 1
   Codepage of database: 1252
   Country code of database: 1
   Server instance name: DB2
----------------------------------------------------------------


----------------------------------------------------------------
   Database Name: DB2CERT
   Database Path: C:\DB2\NODE0000\SQL00001\
   First connection timestamp: 07-17-2002 20:31:35.953271
   Event Monitor Start time:   07-17-2002 20:51:50.622910
----------------------------------------------------------------

8) Deadlock Event ...
   Number of applications deadlocked: 2
   Deadlock detection time: 07-17-2002 20:53:39.275268
   Rolled back Appl Id: : *LOCAL.DB2.020718012735
   Rolled back Appl seq number: : 0001

9) Deadlocked Connection ...
   Appl Id: *LOCAL.DB2.020718012735
   Appl Seq number: 0001
   Appl Id of connection holding the lock: *LOCAL.DB2.020718012741
   Seq. no. of connection holding the lock: 0001
   Lock wait start time: 07-17-2002 20:53:29.893465
   Requesting lock as part of escalation: FALSE
   Deadlock detection time: 07-17-2002 20:53:39.275268
   Table of lock waited on     : TEST_TAKEN
   Schema of lock waited on     : BILLW
   Tablespace of lock waited on : USERSPACE1
   Type of lock: Table
   Mode of lock: S
   Mode application requested on lock: X
   Node lock occured on: 0
   Lock object name: 5
   Application Handle: 11

10) Deadlocked Connection ...
   Appl Id: *LOCAL.DB2.020718012741
   Appl Seq number: 0001
   Appl Id of connection holding the lock: *LOCAL.DB2.020718012735
   Seq. no. of connection holding the lock: 0001
   Lock wait start time: 07-17-2002 20:53:23.737501
   Requesting lock as part of escalation: FALSE
   Deadlock detection time: 07-17-2002 20:53:39.275268
   Table of lock waited on     : TEST
   Schema of lock waited on     : BILLW
   Tablespace of lock waited on : USERSPACE1
   Type of lock: Table
   Mode of lock: S
   Mode application requested on lock: X
   Node lock occured on: 0
   Lock object name: 3
   Application Handle: 12
```

Fig. 12–23 *Deadlock event monitor records*

In Fig. 12–23, a deadlock event record and two deadlock connection event records are shown. The information identifies the two applications involved in the deadlock and the reason for the deadlock.

Monitoring and Tuning

In this example, the deadlock involves two shared locks: one on the `BILLW.TEST_TAKEN` table and the other on the `BILLW.TEST` table. The Event Monitor shows the ID of the application that was rolled back and the time when the deadlock occurred.

Additional Utilities

DB2 provides several additional tools that can be used to monitor and manage specific events. The following will be reviewed:

- DB2 Governor
- Inspect Command
- Audit Facility Administrator Tool
- Storage Management Tool
- Indoubt Transaction Manager
- Database Benchmarking Tool

DB2 Governor

When monitoring DB2, you can detect where bottlenecks are occurring in the system, where certain types of database activity are occurring, and if DB2 is using all the server's resources to their full extent. You can also analyze the behavior of database applications to see if certain applications are more resource intensive than others. However, if an application is resource intensive or is stopping other applications from obtaining resources, the DBA must first detect the application using monitoring techniques and then change the behavior of the application or explicitly force the application off the system.

The *DB2 Governor* is a server application that performs such checking automatically. The governor can also force an application that is deemed to be using too many resources on the server. (Please note that you can also use the FORCE APPLICATIONS command of DB2 to force an application or all applications off of the instance. Please refer to the *DB2 UDB V8.1 Command Reference* for further details on this command.)

The governor collects statistics about applications running against a database. It then checks these statistics against rules that have been specified for that database. Such rules might include:

- Increase the priority of application X so that it always completes quickly.
- Slow down a subset of applications, namely A, B, and C.
- Don't let any unit of work run for more than 15 minutes.

The governor then enforces these rules by changing the parameters for the specified applications or by forcing the application off the system. You start and stop the DB2 Governor the same way you might start and stop monitoring DB2. For example, using a governor configuration file (which contains the governor rules) called MYGOV.CFG, you can start the governor monitoring the DB2CERT database using the DB2GOV utility at the operating system command prompt.

```
db2gov START DB2CERT mygov.cfg gov.log
```

The file that was specified, GOV.LOG, is where the DB2 Governor will log any actions it takes. You can then stop the governor running against the DB2CERT database.

```
db2gov STOP DB2CERT
```

You can have multiple instances of the DB2 Governor running against multiple databases. The DB2 Governor does incur a performance impact when running against a DB2 database because it collects statistics and monitors the activity of database applications at regular intervals. You can examine the logs generated by the DB2 Governor using the DB2GOVLG tool.

Inspect Command

This command provides the ability to check the pages of the database for their architectural integrity. The command can select to check the structures of table objects and of table spaces.

Here is the syntax of the INSPECT command:

Monitoring and Tuning

Some of the key parameters to the INSPECT command include (see the *DB2 UDB V8.1 Command Reference* for further details):

- CHECK - specifies check processing.
- DATABASE - specifies whole database.
- CATALOG TO TABLESPACE CONSISTENCY - specifies to include checking for the consistency of physical tables in the table space to the tables listed in the catalog.
- LIMIT ERROR TO n - specifies number of pages in error for an object to limit reporting.
- LIMIT ERROR TO DEFAULT - specifies the default number of pages (extent size of the object) be used to limit reporting.
- KEEP - specifies to always keep the result output file.

Note that while the DB2DART command (Database Analysis and Reporting Tool) can also be used to check for architectural integrity, this tool runs offline, so no users can using the system while it is in operation.

Audit Facility Administrator Tool

DB2 provides an audit facility to assist in the detection of unknown or unantici-pated access to data. The DB2 audit facility generates and permits the maintenance of an audit trail for a series of predefined database events. The records generated from this facility are kept in an audit log file (db2audit.log). The analysis of these records can reveal usage patterns which would identify system misuse. Once identified, actions can be taken to reduce or eliminate such system misuse. The audit facility acts at an instance level, recording all instance level activities and database level activities. A brief overview of the tool's monitoring capabilities will be reviewed here, and a detailed analysis of its capabilities with respect to security was discussed in "Controlling Data Access" on page 135.

Authorized users of the audit facility can control the following actions within the audit facility, using *db2audit*:

- Start recording auditable events within the DB2 instance.
- Stop recording auditable events within the DB2 instance.
- Configure the behavior of the audit facility.
- Select the categories of the auditable events to be recorded.
- Request a description of the current audit configuration.
- Flush any pending audit records from the instance and write them to the audit log.
- Extract audit records by formatting and copying them from the audit log to a flat file or ASCII delimited files. Extraction is done for one of two reasons: In preparation for analysis of log records, or in preparation for pruning of log records.
- Prune audit records from the current audit log.

The categories of events available for auditing are:

- Audit (AUDIT). Generates records when audit settings are changed or when the audit log is accessed.
- Authorization Checking (CHECKING). Generates records during authorization checking of attempts to access or manipulate DB2 objects or functions.
- Object Maintenance (OBJMAINT). Generates records when creating or dropping data objects.
- Security Maintenance (SECMAINT). Generates records when granting or revoking: object or database privileges, or DBADM authority. Records are also generated when the database manager security configuration parameters SYSADM_GROUP, SYSCTRL_GROUP, or SYSMAINT_GROUP are modified.
- System Administration (SYSADMIN). Generates records when operations requiring SYSADM, SYSMAINT, or SYSCTRL authority are performed.
- User Validation (VALIDATE). Generates records when authenticating users or retrieving system security information.
- Operation Context (CONTEXT). Generates records to show the operation context when a database operation is performed. This category allows for better interpretation of the audit log file. When used with the log's event correlator field, a group of events can be associated back to a single database operation. For exam-

ple, an SQL statement for dynamic SQL, a package identifier for static SQL, or an indicator of the type of operation being performed, such as CONNECT, can provide needed context when analyzing audit results.

In most cases, you will configure the audit facility for a more restricted or focused view of the events you wish to audit. For example, you may want to only audit those events that fail. In this case, the audit facility could be configured as follows:

```
db2audit configure scope audit,
         checking,
         objmaint,
         secmaint,
         sysadmin,
         validate status failure
```

Storage Management Tool

A Storage Management tool is available through the Control Center, by right-clicking on a database icon in the Control Center window and select Manage Storage. From this tool you can access the Storage Management view that displays a snapshot of the storage for a particular database, database partition group, or table space.

Statistical information can be captured periodically and displayed depending on the object chosen:

- For table spaces, information is displayed from the system catalogs and database monitor for tables, indexes and containers defined under the scope of the given table space.
- For databases or database partition groups, information is displayed for all the table spaces defined in the given database or database partition group.
- For databases, information is also collected for all the database partition groups within the database.

You can use the information displayed in this view to monitor various aspects of your storage, such as space usage for table spaces, data skew (database distribution) for database partition groups, and capture cluster ratio of indexes for database partition groups and table spaces.

From the Storage Management view you can also set thresholds for data skew, space usage, and index cluster ratio. A warning or alarm flag will let you know if a target object exceeds a specified threshold.

Fig. 12–24 *Storage Management Tool*

Indoubt Transaction Manager

Invoking the Indoubt Transaction Manager will check the status of the current indoubt transactions for a given database. Usually, the transaction manager will attempt to resynchronize indoubt transactions. However, it is possible that an indoubt transaction may not be resolved automatically. For example, an indoubt transaction may involve more than just your DB2 system. If a third party tool involved in the transaction cannot be reached due to communication failure, or is unavailable, the indoubt transaction may not be resolved automatically. If something like this has happened, or if you cannot wait for the transaction manager to automatically resolve indoubt transactions, there are actions you can take to manually and heuristically resolve indoubt transactions and free up log space.

The Indoubt Transaction Manager is available from the command line by typing:

```
db2indbt
```

Database Benchmarking Tool

The DB2BATCH command is a useful tool to benchmark SQL statements. It can read SQL statements from either a flat file or standard input, dynamically preparing and describing the statements, and returning the answer set.

Here is the syntax of the DB2BATCH command:

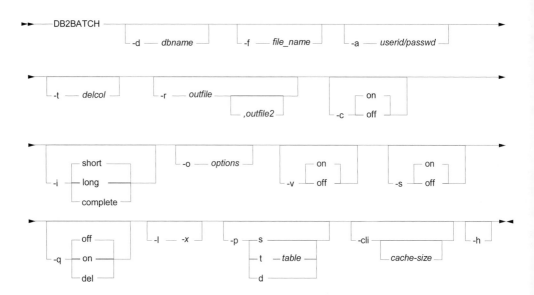

Some of the key parameters to the DB2BATCH command include (see the *DB2 UDB V8.1 Command Reference* for further details):

- -o options - specifies control options, valid options are:

  f rows_fetch (-1 to n) - specifies number of rows to be fetched (-1 indicates all rows to be fetched).

  r rows_out (-1 to n) - specifies the number of fetched rows to be sent to output.

  p perf_detail - specifies the level of performance information to be returned.

  0 - No timing is to be done.

  1 - Return elapsed time only.

  2 - Return elapsed time and CPU time.

  3 - Return a summary of monitoring information.

  4 - Return a snapshot for the database manager, database, application, and statement.

  5 - Return a snapshot for the database manager, database, application, statement, bufferpools, table spaces and FCM (if in a multi-partitioned environment).

  o query_optimization_class - specifies the query optimization class.

  e explain_mode - specifies the explain mode which DB2BATCH runs

0 - Run query only (default).

1 - Populate explain tables only.

2 - Populate explain tables and run query.

-1 x - specifies the termination character.

SQL Monitoring

If you want to know how a query will be executed by DB2, you must analyze its *access plan*, which is the method for retrieving data from a relational table. The explain facilities will provide information about how DB2 accesses the data to resolve the SQL statements.

Before describing the capabilities and features of the explain facilities, you should understand at a high level how SQL statements are processed by the DB2 database engine. Each SQL statement is analyzed by DB2, and then it is determined how to process the statement during a static bind or when executed dynamically. The method used to retrieve data from tables is called the *access plan*.

The component within DB2 that determines the access plan to be used is known as the optimizer. During the static preparation of an SQL statement, the SQL compiler is called on to generate an access plan. The access plan contains the data access strategy including index usage, sort methods, locking semantics, and join methods. The executable form of the SQL statement is stored in the system catalog tables when a BIND command is executed (assuming a deferred binding method). This is called a *package*.

> **Note:** The method for retrieving data from a specific table, such as whether indexes are used, is called the access path. The access plan involves a set of access paths.

Sometimes, the complete statement is not known at application development time. In this case, the compiler is invoked during program execution to generate an access plan for the query that can be used by the database manager to access the data. Such an SQL statement is called a dynamic SQL statement. The access plans for a dynamic SQL statement are not stored in the system catalogs. They are temporarily stored in memory (known as the global package cache). The compiler will not be invoked if the access plans for the dynamic SQL statements already exist in the package cache.

Explain Tables

DB2 uses explain tables to store access plan information so that users can see the decisions the optimizer has made. These tables are called:

- EXPLAIN_ARGUMENT - Represents the unique characteristics for each individual operator.

- EXPLAIN_INSTANCE - Main control table for all explain information. Each row of data in the explain tables is explicitly linked to one unique row in this table. Basic information about the source of the SQL statements being explained and environment information is kept in this table.
- EXPLAIN_OBJECT - Contains data objects required by the access plan generated to satisfy the SQL statement.
- EXPLAIN_OPERATOR - Contains all the operators needed to satisfy the SQL statement.
- EXPLAIN_PREDICATE - Identifies which predicates are applied by a specific operator.
- EXPLAIN_STATEMENT - Contains the text of the SQL statement in two forms. The original version entered by the user is stored in addition to the re-written version that is the result of the compilation process.
- EXPLAIN_STREAM - This table represents the input and output data streams between individual operators and data objects. The data objects themselves are represented in the EXPLAIN_OBJECT table. The operators involved in a data stream are represented in the EXPLAIN_OPERATOR table.

The explain tables have to be created before any explain information can be gathered. The CLP input file, called EXPLAIN.DDL, located in the misc directory of the SQLLIB directory, contains the definition of the explain tables. To create the explain tables, you can connect to the database and use the following command:

```
db2 -tvf EXPLAIN.DDL
```

 Note: Explain tables are created the first time you use Visual Explain.

Gathering Explain Data

There are different kinds of explain data that can be collected. They differ in the explain table columns that will be populated. The explain data options are:

- EXPLAIN - Captures detailed information of the access plan and stores the information in the explain tables. No snapshot information is stored.
- EXPLAIN SNAPSHOT - Captures the current internal representation of an SQL query and related information. The snapshot information is stored in the SNAPSHOT column of the EXPLAIN_STATEMENT table.

Monitoring and Tuning

Not all explain tools require the same kind of explain data. Some tools use the data captured using the EXPLAIN option and others, such as Visual Explain, require snapshot data.

After creating the explain tables, you can start capturing the explain data that will populate them. Not all SQL statements can be explained. The explainable SQL statements include: SELECT, SELECT INTO, UPDATE, INSERT, DELETE, VALUES, and VALUES INTO statements.

Depending on the number of SQL statements or kind of application you want to explain, you should use different methods. These methods include the following:

- EXPLAIN statement - Gathers explain data for an SQL statement
- CURRENT EXPLAIN MODE special register - Specifies the gathering of explain data for dynamic SQL statements
- CURRENT EXPLAIN SNAPSHOT special register - Specifies the gathering of explain snapshot data for dynamic SQL statements
- BIND options - Specify the gathering of explain data for static and/or dynamic embedded SQL statements in a package

Each of these methods will be examined in turn.

EXPLAIN Statement

The EXPLAIN statement is useful when you want to gather explain information for a single dynamic SQL statement. The EXPLAIN statement can be invoked either from the Command Line Processor, Command Center, or from within an application.

You can control the amount of explain information that the EXPLAIN statement will store in the explain tables. The default is to only capture regular explain table information and not the snapshot information. If you wish to modify this behavior, use the following EXPLAIN statement options:

- WITH SNAPSHOT- Captures explain and explain snapshot data into the explain tables.

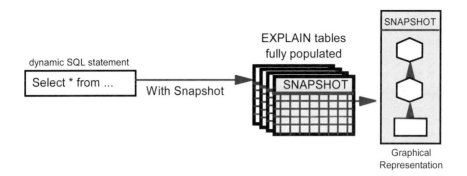

- `FOR SNAPSHOT` - Only captures the explain snapshot information. No other explain information is captured other than that normally found in the `EXPLAIN_INSTANCE` and `EXPLAIN_STATEMENT` tables.

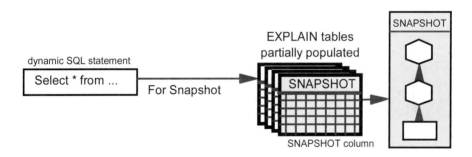

The default case is used when no other explain option is specified. In the default case, the `EXPLAIN` statement will only gather the explain data. No explain snapshot data is captured.

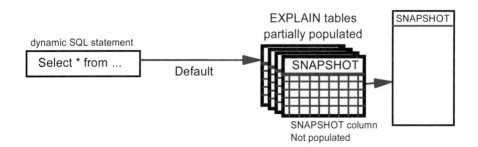

Monitoring and Tuning

To issue the EXPLAIN statement, the user must have INSERT privilege on the explain tables.

 Note: The SQL statement being explained using the EXPLAIN statement will not be executed; only the explain data is captured.

An example of gathering access plan information using the EXPLAIN statement will now be examined. The explain statement is shown below. This example collects all the available explain information for the explain tables.

```
EXPLAIN ALL WITH SNAPSHOT FOR "SELECT * FROM candidate"
```

 Note: Instead of the keyword ALL, used in our example, the keywords PLAN and PLAN SELECTION can be used. Your EXPLAIN statement must include one of them.

The EXPLAIN statement shown in the last example populates a number of explain tables including the SNAPSHOT column of the EXPLAIN_STATEMENT table.

The SNAPSHOT_TAKEN column in the EXPLAIN_INSTANCE table indicates the existence of a Visual Explain snapshot for each explained statement.

The EXPLAIN statement can also be embedded in an application that populates the explain tables. Once the explain tables are populated, they can be queried. Special operators can be examined to determine if the ideal access plan was used for the query.

Explain Special Register

Another way to collect explain information is to use the explain special registers. There are two special registers used by DB2 for gathering explain information for dynamic SQL statements. These registers can be set interactively, or they can be used in a dynamic embedded SQL program. The values of special registers are modified using the SET statement.

The special registers are:

• CURRENT EXPLAIN MODE - Used to populate only the explain data. No snapshot will be taken.

- CURRENT EXPLAIN SNAPSHOT - Used to capture only the explain snapshot data.

The following statements are used to set the value of the explain special registers:

```
SET CURRENT EXPLAIN MODE     option
SET CURRENT EXPLAIN SNAPSHOT option
```

The explain registers options are:

- NO - No explain information is captured for dynamic SQL statements.
- YES - Explain tables or snapshot information will be populated for dynamic SQL statements while executing the SQL statement, and the result is returned.
- EXPLAIN - Explain tables or snapshot information will be populated for dynamic SQL statements without executing the SQL statement. Use this state to obtain explain information without executing the SQL statement.

The following two options are for the CURRENT EXPLAIN MODE register only. They will be illustrated in the section that discusses the Index Advisor.

- RECOMMEND INDEXES
- EVALUATE INDEXES

Note: Once you have set a register to YES or EXPLAIN, any subsequent dynamic SQL statements will be explained until the register is reset to NO.

Explain BIND Options

The BIND command is discussed in "Development Considerations" on page 777. However, in this section, the bind options related to the explain information will be reviewed.

There are two explain BIND options that can be specified: EXPLAIN and EXPLSNAP. The EXPLSNAP option collects explain snapshot information. If you want to view the access plan using Visual Explain, you use the EXPLSNAP option. The EXPLAIN option only populates the explain information without including a snapshot.

Note: Explain snapshots cannot be performed for DRDA application-servers.

Fig. 12–25 shows options of the BIND command and the explain tables that are populated when the options are used.

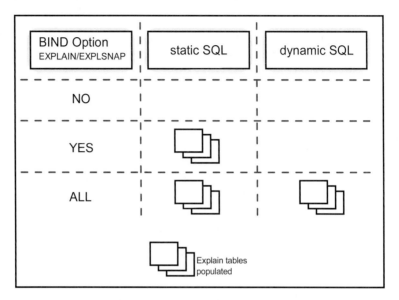

Fig. 12–25 *Using the EXPLAIN or EXPLSNAP option for BIND command*

Explain data using a bind option will now be captured.

```
BIND checkid.bnd EXPLSNAP ALL
```

In this example, the explain snapshot information will be populated for all of the static SQL statements defined in the CHECKID.BND package. Because the ALL option was specified, the dynamic SQL statements issued during package execution will also have explain snapshot information gathered at run time.

The method of obtaining explain information during binds is useful for an administrator to determine the access plans of static or dynamic statements executed from packages.

To examine the access plan data for individual dynamic SQL statements, the special register technique is an easier method to use.

Using the Explain Report Tools to Gather and Analyze Explain Data

There are alternative methods of gathering explain data that is stored in a report rather than in the explain tables. They are the *dynexpln* tool and the *db2expln* tool.

The db2expln tool describes the access plan selected for static SQL statements in the packages stored in the system catalog tables, and the dynexpln tool describes the access plan selected for dynamic SQL statements. It creates a static package for the statements and then uses the db2expln tool to describe them.

The explain output of both utility programs is stored in a readable report file. The explain report tools are useful as quick and easy methods for gathering access plan information.

Examining Explain Data

Once the explain data has been stored in the explain tables, it can be queried or displayed using Visual Explain or other explain tools. How to use Visual Explain and analyze access plan data will now be reviewed.

Visual Explain

Visual Explain is a Graphical User Interface (GUI) utility that gives the database administrator or application developer the ability to examine the access plan determined by the optimizer. Visual Explain can only be used with access plans explained using the snapshot option.

Visual Explain can be used to analyze previously generated explain snapshots or to gather explain data and explain dynamic SQL statements. If the explain tables have not been created when you start Visual Explain, it will create them for you. You can invoke Visual Explain from either the Command Center or Control Center.

From the Control Center interface, right-click the database icon, you will notice that there is an option called **Show Explained Statements History,** as shown in Fig. 12–26.

Fig. 12–26 *DB2 Control Center - Accessing Visual Explain*

The **Explain SQL...** option, also shown in Fig. 12–26, allows you to gather explain data and show the graphical representation of a dynamic SQL statement. This is the easiest way to explain a single SQL statement.

Once the Explained Statement History window has been opened, all of the explained statements will be listed as shown in Fig. 12–27. Because it can be customized to your environment, the displayed information may differ. In Fig. 12–27, the total costs and the SQL statements are shown.

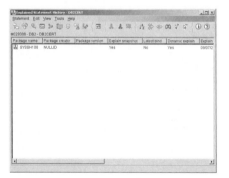

Fig. 12–27 *Customized display of Explained Statement History panel*

To examine an access plan in detail, simply double-click the explained statement or highlight the entry of interest and use the panel menu to select **Statement → Show access plan** on the Explained Statement History window.

All of the explain statements will be displayed in the Explained Statement History list, but only the explained statements with EXPLAIN SNAPSHOT information can be examined using Visual Explain.

 Note: The Explain SQL option on the Control Center or the Command Center are useful to explain a single dynamic SQL statement.

You can add comments to the explain snapshots listed in the Explained Statement History window. To add a comment describing a query, highlight the entry and then select **Statement → Change**. This option can be used to provide a query tag, which can be used to help track the explain snapshot information. You may also wish to remove explain snapshots. The snapshots can be removed from the explain tables by selecting **Statement → Remove** after highlighting the entry to be removed.

The Visual Explain output displays a hierarchical graph representing the components of an SQL statement. Each part of the query is represented as a graphical object. These objects are known as *nodes*. There are two basic types of nodes:

- *OPERATOR* nodes indicate an action that is performed on a group of data.
- *OPERAND* nodes show the database objects on which an operator action takes place. An operand is an object that the operators act on. These database objects are usually tables and indexes.

There are many operators that can be used by the DB2 optimizer to determine the best access plan. Some of the operators used by Visual Explain are shown in Fig. 12–28.

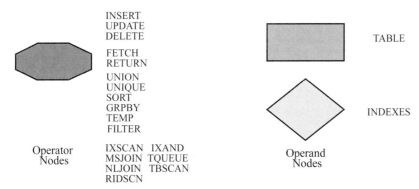

Fig. 12–28 *Operators and operands displayed in Visual Explain*

These operators indicate how data is accessed (IXSCAN, TBSCAN, RIDSCN, IXAND), how tables are joined internally (MSJOIN, NLJOIN), and other factors, such as if a sort will be required (SORT). More information about the operators can be found using Visual Explain Online Help.

The objects shown in a Visual Explain graphic output are connected by arrows showing the flow of data from one node to another. The end of an access plan is always a RETURN operator.

The access plan shown in Fig. 12–29 is a simple SQL statement: SELECT * FROM BILLW.CANDIDATE. In this example, there are two operators and a single operand. The operand is the BILLW.CANDIDATE table, and the operators include a table scan (TBSCAN) and a RETURN operator.

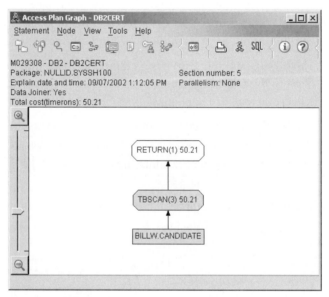

Fig. 12–29 *Visual Explain: Graphical access plan for SQL statement*

Generating explain data for an SQL statement is the only way to analyze the access plan determined by the DB2 optimizer.

Each node, shown in an access plan graph, has detailed information that can be accessed by double-clicking the node or by choosing the **Show details** option from the **Node** menu item.

To display the details of the table scan operation, select the **TBSCAN** operator node and then select **Show details** from the **Node** menu item. The information about the TBSCAN operation, shown in the access plan, is displayed in Fig. 12–30.

Fig. 12–30 *Visual Explain: Operator details*

This window contains several different sections:

- Cumulative costs - Contains information about the estimated cumulative costs calculated using the statistics stored in the system catalog tables.
- Cumulative properties - Contains information about the table, columns, and so forth used to satisfy the query.
- Input arguments - Contains information about the input arguments that affect the behavior of the operator.

It is also possible to examine the detailed information about the operands. Select a operand node and then select **Show statistics** from the **Node** menu item.
Fig. 12–31 shows operand details for the BILLW.CANDIDATE table.

Fig. 12–31 *Visual Explain: Detailed statistics information for an operand*

Detailed information for operand nodes shows the table or index statistics, including table space information, the number of columns, and the number of rows in the object. Fig. 12–31 shows the explained and current statistics from the system catalog tables. These statistics are used by the DB2 optimizer to determine the access plan. Fig. 12–31 shows that there were no statistics gathered for the BILLW.CANDIDATE table.

When the optimizer has no statistics to work with for a table, or if the statistics for a table indicate that the cardinality of the table is relatively small, then the optimizer itself will attempt to calculate the cardinality of the table. The optimizer does this by using certain factors, including the average column length of the table and the number of pages used by the table.

Current statistics are the key to good access plans. If DB2 is not aware of the characteristics of objects involved in a query, it may not be able to generate a good access plan. To ensure the latest statistics are available for the optimizer, a DB2 utility must be used. This utility is called RUNSTATS. Here is an example of gathering statistics for the BILLW.CANDIDATE table.

```
RUNSTATS ON TABLE BILLW.CANDIDATE
            WITH DISTRIBUTION AND DETAILED INDEXES ALL
```

Statistics for the BILLW.CANDIDATE table are stored in the system catalog tables. After running the RUNSTATS utility, rebind the packages against the database and re-explain the SQL statement. You will note that the values for the current statistics have changed, and probably the total cost of the access plan generated would change too. Fig. 12–32 shows that the updated BILLW.CANDIDATE statistics have changed.

Fig. 12–32 *Visual Explain: Table statistics after RUNSTATS*

When determining the access plan for dynamic SQL statements, the DB2 optimizer always uses the current statistics. For a static SQL statement, DB2 uses the statistics available at BIND time (when the package was created). To ensure that current statistics are used with static SQL statements that were compiled before the statistics were updated, the packages must be recreated. This can be accomplished using the REBIND command.

In Fig. 12–33, the total cost for the SQL statements is not the same in both cases. They differ because different statistics were used by DB2 when the explain snapshot was captured.

Monitoring and Tuning

Fig. 12–33 *Visual Explain: List of explained statements*

In our example, the difference of the total cost of the explained queries is very small. This is because the DB2 optimizer estimates some statistics for tables if the statistics have not been gathered. Therefore, the default statistics were quite close to the actual statistics, hence, the similar total costs. The statistics are estimated based on the number of pages in the tables, row length, and so on. Due to the dynamic nature of databases, the estimated, or catalog, statistics may be very different than what the database really looks like. In these cases, the access plan chosen by DB2 may be inefficient.

Please refer to "Maintaining Data" on page 493 for detailed information about the RUNSTATS and REBIND commands.

 Note: Updated statistics become critical as your SQL statements grow in complexity.

Visual Explain can be used to see the decisions that the optimizer made for sorting. In Fig. 12–34, you can see that an index was used to provide the ordered result from the BILLW.CANDIDATE table.

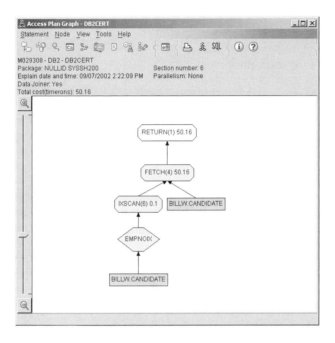

Fig. 12–34 *Sort request satisfied by an index*

The sort heap is used for each application sort request. The DB2 optimizer may decide to attempt to perform a nonoverflowed piped sort. However, if there is not enough available memory to allocate another sort heap at run time, then the sort may be performed using a temporary table instead.

There is a database manager parameter that is used to control the total amount of memory allocated for sorting on the DB2 server. The parameter is called SHEAPTHRES. The SHEAPTHRES parameter should be set to the maximum amount of memory for all sort heaps allowed to be allocated at any given time.

As already explained, if intra-partition parallelism is enabled, a sort operations can be processed in parallel, and it can be a private sort or a shared sort, which uses memory from two different memory sources. The size of the shared sort memory area is statically predetermined (and not preallocated) at the time of the first connection to a database based on the value of SHEAPTHRES. The size of the private sort memory area is unrestricted.

The SHEAPTHRES parameter is used differently for private and shared sorts.

For private sorts, this parameter is an instance-wide soft limit on the total amount of memory that can be consumed by private sorts at any given time. When the total private-sort memory consumption for an instance reaches this limit, the memory allocated for additional incoming private-sort requests will be considerably reduced.

For shared sorts, this parameter is a database-wide hard limit on the total amount of memory consumed by shared sorts at any given time. When this limit is reached, no further shared-sort memory requests will be allowed (until the total shared-sort memory consumption falls below the limit specified by SHEAPTHRES).

The Visual Explain output shown in Fig. 12–35 shows a sort operator. If the detailed information for the sort operator is displayed, the type of sort and the columns involved are shown. Accompanying snapshot information could be used to determine if the sort operation was piped or non-piped. Note that there are two relational table scan operators. The first table scan is reading the base table BILLW.CANDIDATE, and the second table scan is reading from a temporary sort table.

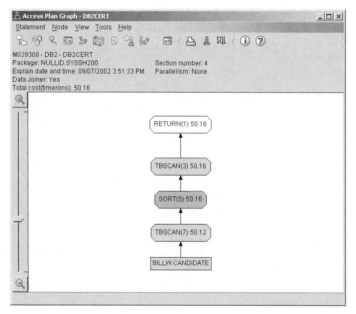

Fig. 12–35 *Visual Explain with sort operator*

There are a number of sorting-related performance variables that can be monitored using the DB2 Snapshot Monitor. These parameters include:

- *Percentage of overflowed sorts* - This variable can be monitored to determine if the optimizer is attempting to use a sort heap and fails. If the percentage is high, consider increasing the SORTHEAP and/or SHEAPTHRES values.

- *Percentage of piped sorts accepted* - This variable can be monitored to determine if piped sorts are being chosen but not accepted by the optimizer. If the percentage is low, consider increasing the SORTHEAP and/or SHEAPTHRES.

As with the buffer pool allocation, it is important to allocate as much memory as possible to the sort heap (and set the threshold accordingly) without over-allocating memory and causing memory paging to occur.

Guidelines on Using Explain Output

There are a number of ways in which analyzing the explain data can help you to tune your queries and environment. For example:

- *Are indexes being used?* Creating appropriate indexes can have a significant benefit on performance. Using the explain output, you can determine if the indexes you have created to help a specific set of queries are being used. In the explain output, you should look for index usage in the following areas:
- Join Predicates
- Local Predicates
- GROUP BY clauses
- ORDER BY clauses
- The select list

  You can also use the Explain Facility to evaluate whether a different index can be used instead of an existing index or no index at all. After creating a new index, collect statistics for that index using the RUNSTATS command and recompile your query. Over time, you may notice, through the explain data, that instead of an index scan, a table scan is now being used. This can result from a change in the clustering of the table data. If the index that was previously being used now has a low cluster ratio, you want to:

- Reorganize your table to cluster the data according to that index.
- Use the RUNSTATS command to update the catalog statistics.
- Recompile the query (bind or rebind).
- Reexamine the explain output to determine whether reorganizing the table has affected the access plan.
- *Is the type of access appropriate for the application?* You can analyze the explain output and look for types of access to the data that, as a rule, are not optimal for the type of application being executed. For example:

Online Transaction Processing (OLTP) Queries

OLTP applications are prime candidates to use index scans with range-delimiting predicates because they tend to return only a few rows that are qualified using an equality predicate against a key column. If your OLTP queries are using a table scan, you may want to analyze the explain data to determine the reasons why an index scan was not used.

Read-Only Queries

The search criteria for a *read-only* type query may be vague causing a large number of rows to qualify. If the user usually looks only at a few screens of the output data, she may want to try to ensure that the entire answer set need not be computed before some results are returned. In this case, the goals of the user are different from the basic operating principle of the optimizer, which attempts to minimize resource consumption for the entire query, not just the first few screens of data.

For example, if the explain output shows that both merge scan join and sort operators were used in the access plan, the entire answer set will be materialized in a temporary table before any rows are returned to the application. In this case, you can attempt to change the access plan by using the OPTIMIZE FOR clause on the SELECT statement. In this way, the optimizer can attempt to choose an access plan that does not produce the entire answer set in a temporary table before returning the first rows to the application.

The Index Advisor

The *Index Advisor* is an administrative tool that provides assistance in the designing of indexes on tables. It is useful in the following situations:

- Finding the best indexes for a problem query
- Finding the best indexes for a set of queries (work load) subject to resource limits that are optionally applied
- Testing out an index on a workload without having to create the index

There are two concepts associated with this facility: *workload* and *virtual indexes*.

A work load is a set of SQL statements (SELECT, INSERT, UPDATE, DELETE) that DB2 has to process over a given period of time. The information in the workload is concerned with the type and frequency of the SQL statements over a given period of time. The index advisor uses this workload information in conjunction with the database information to recommend indexes. The goal of the advising engine is to minimize the total workload cost.

Virtual indexes are indexes that do not exist in the current database schema. These indexes could be either recommendations that the facility has made or indexes that are being proposed to create but wish to model the effect using the advisor facility.

The advisor facility uses two tables that are extensions to the EXPLAIN tables:

- ADVISE_WORKLOAD -This table is where you describe the workload to be considered. Each row in the table represents an SQL statement and is described by an associated frequency. There is an identifier called WORKLOAD_NAME for each workload that is a field in the table. All SQL statements that are part of the same workload, should have the same WORKLOAD_NAME.

- ADVISE_INDEX - This table stores information about recommended indexes. Information is placed into this table by the SQL compiler, the db2advis command (DB2 Index Advisor Command), or manually using SQL statements.

By setting the CURRENT EXPLAIN MODE special register to RECOMMEND INDEXES, the ADVISE_INDEX table will be populated when the EXPLAIN function is invoked.

When the CURRENT EXPLAIN MODE special register is set to EVALUATE INDEXES, the ADVISE_INDEX table will be used as input into the EXPLAIN process, reading the virtual index definitions and using them in the EXPLAIN process as if they were real indexes.

The DB2 Index Advisor can be invoked using the DB2ADVIS command or by invoking it from the Control Center. This example connects to the DB2CERT database and recommends indexes for each table referenced by the queries in the input file. The maximum allowable time for finding a solution is 3 minutes.

```
DB2ADVIS - d db2cert -f sql.in -t 3
```

Configuring Database Resources

Monitoring database activity should be performed with a purpose in mind. The purpose of monitoring may be to achieve greater concurrency or to reduce the amount of disk access wait time. Another key purpose of monitoring database activity is to provide input for configuring various DB2 (instance) and database parameters to optimize memory utilization and increase performance.

Some of the key DBM and DB configuration parameters and how they relate to each other will be examined. Some of these parameters are used to determine the size of the memory allocated for each DB2 instance, database, or application.

 Note: A SHOW DETAILS option has been added to the GET DATABASE and GET DATABASE MANAGER CONFIGURATION commands that will list both the current value and the value that will be used at the next instance start or database activation.

One of the most important factors affecting database performance is the size of each buffer pool in the database. When you create or alter a buffer pool, you have to set the size of each one. If you set the size to minus 1, then the default size is used, which is specified by the BUFFPAGE parameter in the database configuration file. Each buffer pool is the data cache between the applications and the physical disk. You can place your data in separate buffer pools by specifying a buffer pool for a particular table space. Also, it is possible for multiple table spaces to use one buffer pool.

If there were no buffer pools, then all database activity would result in disk access. If the size of each buffer pool is too small, the buffer pool hit ratio will be low, and the applications will wait for disk access activity to satisfy SQL queries. If one or more buffer pools are too large, memory on the server may be wasted. If the total amount of space used by all buffer pools is larger than the physical memory available on the server, then operating system paging (disk activity) will occur. Accessing a buffer pool that has been paged out to disk is inefficient.

If you create your own buffer pools in addition to the default buffer pool IBMDEFAULTBP, you must be careful how you allocate space for each one. There is no point in allocating a large buffer pool to a table space containing a large number of small, rarely used tables and a small buffer pool to a table space containing a large, frequently accessed table. The size of buffer pools should reflect the size of tables in the table space and how frequently they are updated or queried.

The DB2 optimizer will utilize the different buffer pools to achieve the best query performance. There is a parameter that provides the optimizer with information regarding the average number of active applications (AVG_APPLS). This parameter is used by the optimizer to determine how much of each buffer pool may be used for each application.

DB2 allows the addition, alteration, and dropping of buffer pools without stopping database activity. With the ability to change buffer pool allocations and update configuration parameters online, memory usage can be customized to specific tasks. For example, if you have a prime shift memory allocation that is optimized for query performance (a large buffer pool), a script can be executed to optimize memory usage for a load operations during the time reserved for batch operations. The script would:

- Reduce the buffer pool size
- Increase the utility and sort heap
- Run loads with the configuration optimized for load
- Return parameters to prime shift values when the loads have completed

The buffer pool analyzer is a graphical tool that collects detailed and summary data regarding buffer pool usage and can provide recommendations on buffer pool size and thresholds. It can also simulate buffer pool performance so the administrator can anticipate the impact of changes to the environment.

Fig. 12–36 *Buffer pool analyzer*

 Note: Buffer pool allocations and the altering of database manager and database configuration parameters that affect memory can now be changed online while DB2 is running.

Another memory block shared at the database level is called the database heap (DBHEAP). There is one database heap per database, and the database manager uses it on behalf of all applications connected to the database. It contains control block information for tables, indexes, table spaces, buffer pools, and so forth.

 Note: DB2 allows certain DBM (INSTANCE_MEMORY) and DB (DATABASE_MEMORY, MAXAPPLS) configuration parameters to be set to AUTOMATIC, thereby allowing the database to select the values of these parameters.

There are many I/O caches that can be configured, including a log file cache (LOGBUFSZ) and a system catalog table cache (CATALOGCACHE_SZ). The log buffer is used as a buffer for writing log records to disk. Every transaction involves writing multiple log records. To optimize disk write performance, the writes are buffered in memory and periodically flushed to disk. The catalog cache is used to store the system catalog tables in memory. As an SQL statement is compiled or referenced, the database object information needs to be verified. If the information is in memory, then there is no need to perform disk activity to access the data. The package cache (PCKCACHESZ) is used to reduce the need to reload access plans (sections) of a package. This caching can improve performance when the same section is used multiple times within a program.

Note: The access plans are cached for static and dynamic SQL statements in the package cache.

Record blocking is a distributed caching technique used to send a group of records across the network to the client instead of a single record at a time. The decrease in network traffic increases application performance and allows for better network throughput. The records are blocked by DB2 according to the cursor type and bind parameter. If the optimizer decides to return the query output in blocks, the amount of data in each block is determined by the ASLHEAPSZ parameter.

The application heap (APPLHEAPSZ) contains a number of memory blocks that are used by DB2 to handle requests for each application.

The sort heap (SORTHEAP) determines the maximum number of memory pages that can be used for each sort. The sort heap area is allocated in the agent private memory if intra-partition parallelism is disabled. However, if intra-partition parallelism is enabled, a sort operation is processed in parallel, and the sort heap area is allocated in the agent private memory or the database global memory depending on which type of sort, a *private sort* or a *shared sort*, is performed. For a private sort, a sort heap area is allocated independently for each parallel agent in the private agent memory. For a shared sort, a sort heap area is allocated in the database global memory, and each parallel agent shares this sort heap. The SORTHEAP parameter is used by the optimizer to determine if the sorting can be performed in memory or on disk. DB2 will always attempt to perform the sort in memory.

The SHEAPTHRES parameter is used to control the amount of memory that can be allocated for sort heaps in a DB2 server.

One of the key performance parameters that affects the amount of memory used on the DB2 server as a data cache (database level) will now be modified. The default buffer pool size can be updated to 200 MB using the following command:

```
UPDATE DB CFG FOR db2cert USING BUFFPAGE 50000
```

Allocating at least half of the physical memory on a machine to buffer pool space is usually a good starting point when adjusting the size of buffer pools. This assumes a dedicated DB2 database server and a single database active at any given time. For example, to effectively use a database server with 400 MB of RAM, the total size of all the buffer pools could amount to 200 or 300 MB.

Any modification to the database configuration file will not be effective until all applications using the database are disconnected. The subsequent database connection will use the new database configuration parameters. If you change the DBM (instance) configuration parameters, the new values will not be effective until the instance has been stopped and restarted.

The size of the memory used to perform record blocking will now be modified. The memory area used for record blocking is known as the application support layer heap (ASLHEAPSZ). The following command would set the record blocking to be 200 KB in size (the units are 4 KB).

```
UPDATE DATABASE MANAGER CONFIGURATION USING ASLHEAPSZ 50
```

Any changes to the database manager configuration will not take effect until the instance is stopped and restarted except default database monitor switch parameters, such as DFT_MON_BUFPOOL, DFT_MON_LOCK, DFT_MON_SORT, DFT_MON_TABLE, DFT_MON_UOW, and DFT_MON_STMT.

In this example, when the instance is restarted, records will be sent across the network from the DB2 server to the application in 200 KB blocks (likely more than a single row). If the average row length were 1 KB, then 200 records would be returned in a single block of data (assuming more than 200 records are in the final result table).

Note: Record blocking occurs for remote and local DB2 client applications.

DB2 Universal Database also provides graphical tools that enable you to configure DB2 easily. The Configuration Advisor is a tool that asks you to define what you want to use the database for: to define size requirements and certain country spe-

Monitoring and Tuning

cific information. Then, using your input as a guideline, the Advisor tunes certain parameters to better fit your needs in DB2. Right-click on a database icon in the Control Center window and select Configuration Advisor. This will bring up the Configuration Advisor window as shown in Fig. 12–37.

Fig. 12–37 *Configuration Advisor*

The various tabs in the Advisor panel indicate the range of questions that the Advisor might ask. Once the Advisor has been filled in, you can go to the Results panel and see the new values of the parameters. In complex environments, the Advisor may not be able to make all the changes that are needed, so you may want to review the different parameters to see what has been changed and left unchanged. Fig. 12–38 gives an idea of what the Results panel might look like. You do not need to apply the changes immediately in the Advisor. Instead, you can save a command to make the result come into effect as a script file, which can be run later from the Task Center.

Note: The AUTOCONFIGURE command invokes the Performance Configuration Wizard for a given database. There are options available when using AUTOCONFIGURE that assists you to define values for several database manager and database configuration parameters that can improve transaction or query performance.

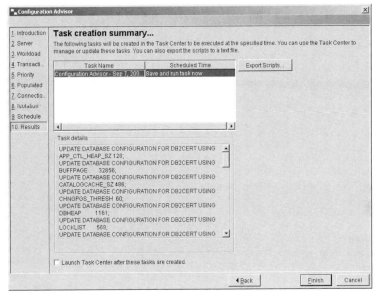

Fig. 12–38 *Configuration Advisor - Results panel*

Another tool provided by DB2 is a user interface to the database manager and database configuration files. Using the Control Center, you can configure either the database manager or each database, using online help to guide you along.
Fig. 12–39 shows how you can configure the DB2CERT database from the Control Center. The configuration tool also provides hints for each database configuration parameter.

Fig. 12–39 *Configure database using Control Center*

Configuring Intra-Partition Parallelism

Intra-partition parallelism in DB2 can be enabled using the INTRA_PARALLEL DBM configuration parameter. To enable intra-partition parallelism in DB2, you would issue the following command:

```
UPDATE DBM CFG USING INTRA_PARALLEL YES
```

Note: The default value for the INTRA_PARALLEL parameter is YES in an SMP machine and NO in a uniprocessor machine.

If the degree of parallelism is set to -1, then the optimizer will decide the degree of parallelism for each SQL query. For instance, on a four-way SMP machine, a simple insert statement will gain no advantage from being run in parallel across the CPUs, so using the -1 setting will result in this type of statement running on only one CPU (a degree of parallelism of 1).

Setting the DBM configuration parameter MAX_QUERYDEGREE to 2 in a uni-processor machine environment could improve I/O performance slightly. This is because the uni-processor may not have to wait for input or output tasks to complete before working on a new query, thus improving the performance of I/O bound applications.

Embedded SQL applications and CLI applications can override the default degree of parallelism with various options. The following table gives a brief overview of the parameters and options that can enable parallelism in DB2

Table 12–2 *DB2 Parallelism Parameters*

Parameter	Values
INTRA_PARALLEL (Database Manager Configuration)	• YES/NO. • Defaults to NO on uni-processor machine. • Defaults to YES on SMP machine. • If changed, packages already bound will automatically be rebound at next execution.
MAX_QUERYDEGREE (Database Manager Configuration)	• -1 (ANY), 1-32767. • Defaults to -1 - Allows optimizer to choose degree of parallelism based on cost. • No SQL executed on a database in this instance can use a degree of parallelism higher than this value.

DFT_DEGREE (Database Configuration)	• -1 (ANY), 1-32767.
	• Defaults to 1 (no parallelism).
	• Provides the default value for:
	  • CURRENT DEGREE special register.
	  • DEGREE bind option.
	  • Maximum for any SQL in this database.

CURRENT DEGREE (Special Register for dynamic SQL)	• -1 (ANY), 1-32767. • Sets degree of parallelism for dynamic SQL. • Defaults to DFT_DEGREE.
DEGREE (precompile or bind option for static SQL)	• -1 (ANY), 1-32767. • Sets degree of parallelism for static SQL. • Defaults to DFT_DEGREE. • To change: PREP STATIC.SQL DEGREE 2.

Monitoring and Tuning

Table 12–2 *DB2 Parallelism Parameters (Continued)*

Parameter	Values
RUNTIME DEGREE (SET RUNTIME DEGREE command)	• -1 (ANY), 1-32767. • Sets degree of parallelism for running applications. • To change (setting degree to 4 for the application whose handler number is 100): `SET RUNTIME DEGREE FOR (100) to 4` • Only affects queries issued after SET RUNTIME is executed.
DB2DEGREE (CLI configuration file)	• -1 (ANY), 1-32767. • Default is 0. • Sets degree of parallelism for CLI applications. • CLI application issues a SET CURRENT DEGREE statement after database connection.

The maximum query degree of parallelism for an active application is specified using the SET RUNTIME DEGREE command. The application can set its own runtime degree of parallelism by using the SET CURRENT DEGREE statement. The actual runtime degree used is the lower of:

• MAX_QUERYDEGREE DBM configuration parameter
• Application runtime degree
• SQL statement compilation degree

More information on parallelism support in DB2 Universal Database can be found in the *DB2 UDB V8.1 Administration Guide*.

Performance Tuning Scenario

A straightforward DB2 performance tuning scenario will now be examined. A database application user telephones you because he or she has observed that around 2:00 p.m every day the application is much slower than at other times. The response is slow, and sometimes the user has to wait to obtain database requests.

You assume that this problem occurs because there are many applications accessing the database around 2:00 p.m. So, you decide to use the Snapshot Monitor to gather information from that time frame. The first resources you decide to monitor are the buffer pool activity and the number of lock escalations. You will obtain this information if snapshots are captured before, during, and after 2:00 p.m and the output compared. Snapshots are taken every 30 seconds for a period of time.

You notice that the buffer pool hit ratio decreases below 50 percent, the number of lock escalations increases, and the average lock wait time is increasing around 2:00 p.m.

You decide to capture a snapshot of the currently active applications for the DB2CERT database. The DB2 command LIST APPLICATIONS, as shown below, is actually a database monitor snapshot for applications. You can also list and force off applications using the Control Center.

```
LIST APPLICATIONS FOR DATABASE db2cert
```

The LIST APPLICATIONS command will list all of the currently active applications connected to the database as shown below.

```
Auth Id  Application   Appl.   Application Id                   DB       # of
         Name          Handle                                  Name     Agents
-------  -----------   ------  -----------------------------   -------  ------
BILLW    db2bp.exe     51      *LOCAL.DB2.020621152850         DB2CERT  1
BILLW    DB2CC.EXE     53      09030177.0449.020621153153      DB2CERT  1
BILLW    DB2BP.EXE     58      09030177.044F.020621154423      DB2CERT  1
RNICOL   db2bp.exe     59      09030173.04D5.020621154801      DB2CERT  1
RNICOL   db2bp.exe     60      09030173.04D7.020621154834      DB2CERT  1
DB2USER  DB2CERT2.EXE  61      09030180.04E3.020621154925      DB2CERT  1
```

Fig. 12–40 *Output of LIST APPLICATIONS command*

You note that DB2USER, the user who was complaining about performance, was using the DB2CERT2 application shown as the last line in the output.

Taking snapshots based on locks for each of the other applications, you note that the DB2USER user has a large number of row locks allocated and is using most of the locking memory as defined by the LOCKLIST database parameter.

Snapshots are then taken based on statements for the APPL_ID
*LOCAL.DB2.020621152850. It is discovered that the application is performing a
large number of inserts on the TEST table.

You decide to increase the amount of memory allocated for locks because lock
escalation occurs when an application starts exhausting the available lock list.

The lock memory is defined in the database configuration file. The value can be
modified using the CLP, the Command Center, or the Control Center. The CLP
command to obtain the current database configuration settings is:

```
GET DATABASE CONFIGURATION FOR db2cert
```

Some of the important database configuration parameters are shown in Fig. 12–41.
The first step for resolving the locking problem is to increase the size of the
LOCKLIST and the value for MAXLOCKS. You can issue the following CLP command
to perform the update:

```
UPDATE DB CFG FOR db2cert USING LOCKLIST 250 MAXLOCKS 30
```

```
Degree of parallelism                        (DFT_DEGREE) = 1
Default query optimization class           (DFT_QUERYOPT) = 5
Database heap (4KB)                              (DBHEAP) = 1200
Catalog cache size (4KB)                  (CATALOGCACHE_SZ) = 64
Log buffer size (4KB)                          (LOGBUFSZ) = 8
Utilities heap size (4KB)                  (UTIL_HEAP_SZ) = 5000
Buffer pool size (4KB)                         (BUFFPAGE) = 1000
Extended storage segments size (4KB)      (ESTORE_SEG_SZ) = 16000
Number of extended storage segments      (NUM_ESTORE_SEGS) = 0
Max storage for lock list (4KB)                (LOCKLIST) = 100

Max appl. control heap size (4KB)         (APP_CTL_HEAP_SZ) = 128

Sort list heap (4KB)                           (SORTHEAP) = 256
SQL statement heap (4KB)                       (STMTHEAP) = 2048
Default application heap (4KB)                (APPLHEAPSZ) = 128
Package cache size (4KB)                       (PCKCACHESZ) = (MAXAPPLS*8)
Statistics heap size (4KB)                   (STAT_HEAP_SZ) = 4384
Percent. of lock lists per application         (MAXLOCKS) = 10

Changed pages threshold                    (CHNGPGS_THRESH) = 60
Number of asynchronous page cleaners       (NUM_IOCLEANERS) = 1
Number of I/O servers                      (NUM_IOSERVERS) = 3
Sequential detect flag                         (SEQDETECT) = YES
Max number of active applications              (MAXAPPLS) = 40
Average number of active applications          (AVG_APPLS) = 1
Group commit count                             (MINCOMMIT) = 1

Max DB files open per application              (MAXFILOP) = 6
```

Fig. 12–41 *Database configuration parameters*

You may also decide to change the average number of active applications to match the database activity. The AVG_APPLS parameter will affect the usage of each buffer pool as determined by the optimizer. Since there were only five applications using the database according to the LIST APPLICATIONS command, set the value to 8 (allow a few extra connections). The following CLP command will modify the AVG_APPLS parameter:

```
UPDATE DB CFG FOR db2cert USING AVG_APPLS 8
```

After all these modifications, you should create new application packages (to create new access plans for any static SQL). Use the REBIND command to update the package information. You can also use the DB2RBIND utility to take care of this.

Now you should verify that the changes were beneficial. In this example, you should determine whether the lock escalations occur the next day and verify that the user (DB2USER) is obtaining acceptable response time. Remember that most performance problems must be addressed within the application or the database design itself.

Monitoring and Tuning

Diagnostics and Problem Determination

DB2 Universal Database offers a range of tools that can be used to determine the cause of problems or errors in the DB2 system. Potential problems include:

- Operating-system-specific
- Hardware- or I/O-specific
- Application-specific
- Communications-specific

In a complex environment, such as a distributed DB2 database system or a high-volume OLTP database system, there is a possibility that problems could occur. You need tools to analyze anything that might be characterized as an error. In more serious cases, you may want to determine the cause of a system crash. This kind of trouble-shooting needs to be done as quickly and efficiently as possible.

Error Messages and SQL Codes

DB2 Universal Database has a large number of error codes that explain the possible problems within the database system. This means DB2 can report on problems within a database but also on problems within any of the tools and functions that are supplied with DB2.

These messages are divided into a few different categories. Each message has an error code associated with it. The prefix of the error code dictates what category the error code falls under:

- ADM - Administration Notification messages
- ASN - DB2 Replication Support messages
- CCA - Configuration Assistant messages
- CLI - CLI/ODBC application messages
- CLP - Command Line Processor messages
- DBA - Control Center or DBA Utility messages
- DBI - DB2 Installation messages
- DWC - Data Warehouse Center messages
- DXX - XML Extender messages
- GSE - Spatial Extender messages
- ICC - Information Catalog Center messages
- SAT - DB2 Satellite Edition messages
- SPM - Syncpoint Manager messages
- SQJ - DB2 embedded SQL in Java (SQLJ) messages
- SQL - SQL messages

Because the DB2 environment can be complex, there are a large number of error messages. During installation and setup of DB2, administrators may encounter some DBI, DBA, and CCA messages as they become accustomed to the new system. Another example might be users running adhoc queries against a DB2 database. They could receive SQL errors because of inaccurate SQL syntax or because they were not granted access to certain tables. If you have the specific code associated with an error, you can view the error message text in two ways: first, by consulting the *DB2 Messages Reference*, which details all the error codes in DB2; Second, by querying the code using the CLP or Command Center:

```
DB2 ? SQL0818
```

If an SQL statement fails, you receive an SQL error code as well as an SQLSTATE code. The SQLSTATE code is a standard code based on the ISO/ANSI SQL92 standard. It is unchanged across all the members of the DB2 Family, including RDBMSs on host systems. The SQL error codes may be unique to DB2 Universal Database for Linux, Windows, and UNIX.

The SQL codes can be in two formats: a negative code (or in the format SQLxxxxN) or positive code (or in the format SQLxxxxW). The *negative* codes signify SQL *errors*, and the *positive* codes signify SQL *warnings* (a zero SQL code means that the SQL completed successfully).

Sometimes the SQL codes contain reason codes within the error message text. These reason codes usually provide more detailed information to supplement the message text. Some examples of reason codes include operating system return codes and communications protocol return codes. The *DB2 UDB V8.1 Messages Reference* provides some detail on common return codes. Sometimes, however, it may be necessary to consult other system documentation.

When using the Administration tools that come with DB2, the Journal records any messages that are returned to the user. For example, if you try to use the Control Center to access the DB2CERT database while an offline backup is in progress, a pop-up dialog box will inform you that the database is in use. This message is then recorded in the Journal. Fig. 12–42 gives an example of the messages logged by the Journal.

Monitoring and Tuning

Fig. 12–42 *Messages in the journal*

Diagnostic and Service Logs

DB2 will allow you to log most administrative tasks within the system. There are diagnostic log files for each DB2 instance, a diagnostic log for the Administration Tools that come with DB2, a report log for the DB2 Governor, and logs to document DB2 installation. The focus will be on the diagnostic logs for each DB2 instance.

DB2 will not log any Data Definition Language (DDL) statements or Data Manipulation Language (DML) statements. DB2 *will* log different administrative tasks, such as activating databases, backing up databases, starting and stopping DB2, or starting DB2 communications support.

These kinds of messages, when logged by DB2, are known as *informational* messages. However, in a trouble-shooting scenario, the messages that you will be looking for are *error* and *warning* messages. This is also known as *First Failure Data Capture (FFDC)* information. FFDC information is diagnostic information about an error that is captured automatically by the DB2 Administration Server when the error occurs. This information captured by the DB2 Administration Server FFDC includes:

- Administration notification logs - When significant events occur, DB2 writes information to the administration notification log. The information is intended for use by database and system administrators. Many notification messages provide additional information to supplement the SQLCODE that is provided. The type of event and the level of detail of the information gathered are determined by the NOTIFYLEVEL configuration parameter. On Windows, administration notification messages are written to the event log.

- Dump files - Sometimes, when a DB2 process or thread fails and signals an error, it will also log extra information in external binary dump files. These files are more-or-less unreadable and are intended for DB2 Customer Service personnel.

- Trap files - DB2 creates a trap file if an operating system trap/segmentation violation/exception occurs.

 Note: The log previously known as the db2alert.log has been removed and the alerts are now written to the administration notification and diagnostic logs.

The FFDC information is logged in the directory specified by the DIAGPATH database manager configuration parameter. FFDC information is logged separately for each DB2 instance and is logged for both DB2 Server instances and DB2 Administration Server. The default DIAGPATH value is null at instance creation time. By default, the diagnostic files are written to the instance directory (in the db2dump subdirectory in UNIX platforms).

The DIAGPATH parameter is a database manager configuration parameter, so you could change it in the Control Center by right-clicking on the appropriate instance and clicking on **Configure**. You could also use the CLP or Command Center:

```
UPDATE DBM CFG USING DIAGPATH 'C:\NEWDIAGPATH'
```

The level of diagnostic information, DIAGLEVEL, is also a database manager configuration parameter. The DIAGLEVEL parameter can be set to the following values:

- 0 - No administration notification messages captured. (This setting is not recommended).

- 1 - Severe errors only. Only fatal and unrecoverable errors are logged. To recover from some of these conditions, you may need assistance from DB2 service.

- 2 - All errors. Conditions are logged that require immediate attention from the system administrator or the database administrator. If the condition is not resolved, it could lead to a fatal error. Notification of very significant, non-error activities (for example, recovery) may also be logged at this level. This level will capture Health Monitor alarms.

- 3 - All errors and warnings. Conditions are logged that are non-threatening and do not require immediate action but may indicate a non-optimal system. This level will capture Health Monitor alarms, Health Monitor warnings, and Health Monitor attentions. This is the default.
- 4 - All errors, warnings, and informational messages.

The default DIAGLEVEL is usually sufficient for normal DB2 operation. However, during the initial set-up of DB2, or when errors are occurring, the DIAGLEVEL could be updated to 4 in order to gather as much information as possible: Note that you must set *notifylevel to a value of 2 or higher for the Health Monitor to send any notifications to the contacts defined in its configuration.*

```
UPDATE DBM CFG USING DIAGLEVEL 4
```

Tracing Problems in DB2 Universal Database

Sometimes problems occur in DB2 or applications using DB2, and the FFDC information is not sufficient to determine the source of the problem. At this point, DB2 Customer Service may ask the DBA to run traces against the application, against the CLI/ODBC/JDBC driver, or against the database itself.

Here is the syntax of the DB2TRC command:

Tracing or debugging the DB2 application is primarily a task for the application developer who created the program. DB2 embedded SQL programs provide extensive error-reporting functions using the SQLCA structure. This allows application developers to monitor their code executing against DB2.

Tracing against DB2 itself is somewhat similar to CLI/ODBC/JDBC tracing. You specify where you want the trace output to go and then turn on tracing. Tracing also has a significant performance impact on DB2. However, you have some flexibility when tracing inside DB2. You can filter what you want to monitor. You can specify how large a memory buffer you wish to use to hold trace information. You can specify how many DB2 errors the trace retains. Tracing against DB2 can be started with the **db2trc** command. You have to specify certain options to gather the trace information. You take a DB2 trace in four steps:

- Switch on tracing (DB2TRC ON).
- Dump the trace output (DB2TRC DMP).
- Switch off tracing (DB2TRC OFF).
- Format the trace output (DB2TRC FLW or DB2TRC FMT).

Using the FLW option, you can specify that you would like the trace output formatted in order of DB2 thread/process. Using the FMT option, you can specify that you want the trace output formatted in chronological order. When switching on tracing, you can specify some additional options:

Monitoring and Tuning

- -m - Mask the particular record types you wish to trace.
- -e - Specify a limit to the number of DB2 errors retained by the trace.
- -r - Specify a limit to the size of trace records.
- -s or -f - Specify whether the trace output should be held in shared memory or written directly to a file.
- -l or -i - Specify the size of the memory buffer in which the trace output is stored. The -l option will retain the last records of the trace. The -i option will retain the initial records.

After you have used the DB2TRC DMP command and the DB2TRC OFF command, you can format the trace output. You execute the DB2TRC FMT command, for example:

```
C:\SQLLIB\BIN> db2trc fmt mytrace.dmp mytrace.out
Trace wrapped      :YES
Size of trace      :3996054 bytes
Records in trace   :39450
Records formatted  :39450
```

Fig. 12–43 *DB2TRC command*

A trace file formatted with the DB2TRC FMT command might look something like the excerpt in Fig. 12–44.

```
14719    DB2 fnc_retcode   SW- query graph      sqlnq_ftb::new (1.33.60.55)
         pid 138; tid 117; cpid 139; time 7951153; trace_point 254
         return_code = 000000 = 0

14720    DB2 fnc_entry     SW- query graph      sqlnq_ftb::sqlnq_ftb (1.30.60.56)
         pid 138; tid 117; cpid 139; time 7951153; trace_point 0
         called_from 0081F618

14721    DB2 cei_entry     oper_system_services sqlogmblk (1.20.15.82)
         pid 138; tid 117; cpid 139; time 7951153; trace_point 0
         called_from 10047AE9

14722    DB2 cei_data      oper_system_services sqlogmblk (1.25.15.82)
         pid 138; tid 117; cpid 139; time 7951153; trace_point 1
         4c05 9601 8c00 0000 0000 0000           L...........
```

Fig. 12–44 *Example of DB2 trace records*

For more information on tracing in DB2 Universal Database, please refer to the *DB2 Information Center.*

CLI/ODBC/JDBC Trace Facility

DB2 CLI and DB2 JDBC trace file analysis can benefit application developers in a number of ways. First, subtle program logic and parameter initialization errors are often evident in the traces. Second, DB2 CLI and DB2 JDBC traces may suggest ways of better tuning an application or the databases it accesses. For example, if a DB2 CLI trace shows a table being queried many times on a particular set of attributes, an index corresponding to those attributes might be created on the table to improve application performance. Finally, analysis of DB2 CLI and DB2 JDBC trace files can help application developers understand how a third party application or interface is behaving.

The DB2 CLI and DB2 JDBC drivers offer comprehensive tracing facilities. By default, these facilities are disabled and use no additional computing resources. When enabled, the trace facilities generate one or more text log files whenever an application accesses the appropriate driver (DB2 CLI or DB2 JDBC). These log files provide detailed information about:

- The order in which CLI or JDBC functions were called by the application

- The contents of input and output parameters passed to and received from CLI or JDBC functions the return codes and any error or warning messages generated by CLI or JDBC functions

DB2 CLI and DB2 JDBC Trace Configuration

The configuration parameters for both DB2 CLI and DB2 JDBC traces facilities are read from the DB2 CLI configuration file db2cli.ini. By default, this file is located in the \sqllib path on the Windows platform and the /sqllib/cfg path on Linux or UNIX platforms. You can override the default path by setting the DB2CLIINIPATH environment variable. On the Windows platform, an additional db2cli.ini file may be found in the user's profile (or home) directory if there are any user-defined data sources defined using the ODBC Driver Manager. This db2cli.ini file will override the default file.

To view the current db2cli.ini trace configuration parameters from the command line processor, issue the following command:

```
GET CLI CFG FOR SECTION COMMON
```

For example, the following command issued from the command line processor updates the db2cli.ini file and enables the JDBC tracing facility:

Monitoring and Tuning

```
UPDATE CLI CFG FOR SECTION COMMON USING jdbctrace 1
```

Note: Tracing a CLI/JDBC application will slow down the application's performance considerably. Also, a large amount of data is written to the output trace file and may use up a large amount of disk space.

DB2 CLI Trace Options and the db2cli.ini File

When an application using the DB2 CLI driver begins execution, the driver checks for trace facility options in the [COMMON] section of the db2cli.ini file. These trace options are specific trace keywords that are set to certain values in the db2cli.ini file under the [COMMON] section.

The DB2 CLI trace keywords that can be defined are (see the *DB2 V8 Information Center* for further detail):

- `TRACE=0|1` - enables or disables tracing
- `TRACEFILENAME=0 | <any positive integer>` - specifies how often trace information is written to the DB2 CLI trace log file.
- `TRACEPATHNAME=<fully_qualified_trace_path_name>` - specifies where all DB2 CLI trace information is to be written. There is no default path to which DB2 CLI trace output log files are written, and the path specified must exist at application execution time (the DB2 CLI driver will not create the path).
- `TRACEFLUSH=0 | <any positive integer>` - specifies how often trace information is written to the DB2 CLI trace log file.
- `TRACEREFRESHINTERVAL=0 | <any positive integer>` - any value greater than 0 causes the DB2 CLI trace facility to reread the `TRACE` and `TRACEPIDLIST` keywords from the db2cli.ini file at the specified interval (every n seconds).
- `TRACECOMM=0|1` - enable tracing of communications between the client and server (CLI functions processed completely on the client and server, number of bytes sent and received with the server, and time spent communicating between the client and server).
- `TRACETIMESTAMP=0|1|2|3` - specifies the addition of various timestamp information with trace records.
- `TRACEPIDTID=0|1` - specifies to add process and thread ID information to be included in the trace.
- `TRACEPIDLIST=<no value> | <pid1,pid2, pid3,...>` - restricts which pro-

cess ID values the CLI traces will generate.

- TRACETIME=0|1 - specifies to calculate the elapsed time between CLI function calls and returns will be calculated and included in the DB2 CLI trace.

- TRACESTMTONLY=0|1 - 0 specifies trace information for all DB2 CLI function call swill be written to the DB2 CLI trace log file, 1 specifies only information related to SQLExecute() and SQLExecDirect()function calls will be written to the log file. This trace option can be useful in determining the number of times a statement is executed in an application.

An example db2cli.ini file trace configuration using these DB2 CLI keywords and values is:

```
[COMMON]
TRACE=1
TRACEFILENAME=\TEMP\CLITRACE.TXT
TRACEFLUSH=1
```

The output form the DB2 CLI trace is a sequence of CLI/ODBC API calls. The following example demonstrates what the ODBC trace output would look like for an unsuccessful connection attempt to a DB2 database.

```
SQLAllocHandle( fHandleType=SQL_HANDLE_ENV, hInput=0:0, phOutput=&12d1d5c
)

SQLAllocHandle( phOutput=0:1 )
    <--- SQL_SUCCESS    Time elapsed - +1.000000E-002 seconds

SQLSetEnvAttr( hEnv=0:1, fAttribute=SQL_ATTR_ODBC_VERSION,
vParam=2,cbParam=0)
    ---> Time elapsed - +0.000000E+000 seconds

SQLSetEnvAttr( )
    <--- SQL_SUCCESS    Time elapsed - +0.000000E+000 seconds

SQLAllocHandle( fHandleType=SQL_HANDLE_DBC, hInput=0:1, phOutput=&12d1d4c
)
    ---> Time elapsed - +0.000000E+000 seconds

SQLAllocHandle( phOutput=0:1 )
    <--- SQL_SUCCESS    Time elapsed - +0.000000E+000 seconds

SQLGetInfo( hDbc=0:1, fInfoType=SQL_DRIVER_ODBC_VER, rgbInfoV-
alue=&12d1e30, cbInfoValueMax=12, pcbInfoValue=&128324 )
    ---> Time elapsed - +0.000000E+000 seconds

SQLGetInfo( rgbInfoValue="03.00", pcbInfoValue=5 )
    <--- SQL_SUCCESS    Time elapsed - +0.000000E+000 seconds

SQLDriverConnect( hDbc=0:1, hwnd=11:1402, szConnStrIn="DSN=DB2CERT;",
cbConnStrIn=-3, szConnStrOut=&12d1e50, cbConnStrOutMax=256, pcb-
ConnStrOut=&129130, fDriverCompletion=SQL_DRIVER_COMPLETE_REQUIRED )
    ---> Time elapsed - +0.000000E+000 seconds
( DBMS NAME="DB2/NT", Version="08.01.0000", Fixpack="0x21010104" )
( StmtOut="SET CURRENT DEGREE 'ANY'" )
( COMMIT=0 )

SQLDriverConnect(
szConnStrOut="DSN=DB2CERT;UID=janeway;PWD=******;DB2DEGREE=ANY;LOBMAXCOLU
MNSIZE=1048575;LONGDATACOMPAT=1;DBALIAS=DB2CERT;PATCH1=131072;", pcb-
ConnStrOut=121 )
    <--- SQL_SUCCESS    Time elapsed - +1.502000E+000 seconds
( DSN="DB2CERT" )
( UID="janeway" )
( PWD="******" )
( DB2DEGREE="ANY" )
( LOBMAXCOLUMNSIZE="1048575" )
( LONGDATACOMPAT="1" )
( DBALIAS="DB2CERT" )
( PATCH1="131072" )
```

Fig. 12–45 *Example of a CLI/ODBC trace*

DB2 JDBC Trace Options and the db2cli.ini File

When an application using the DB2 JDBC driver begins execution, the driver also checks for trace facility options in the db2cli.ini file. As with the DB2 CLI trace options, DB2 JDBC trace options are specified as keyword/value pairs located under the [COMMON] section of the db2cli.ini file.

The DB2 JDBC trace keywords that can be defined are:

- `JDBCTRACE=0|1` - enables or disables tracing
- `JDBCTRACEPATHNAME=<fully_qualified_trace_path_name>` - specifies where all DB2 JDBC trace information is to be written. There is no default path to which DB2 JDBC trace output log files are written, and the path specified must exist at application execution time.
- `JDBCTRACEFLUSH=0 | <any positive integer>` - specifies how often trace information is written to the DB2 JDBC trace log file.

An example db2cli.ini file trace configuration using these DB2 JDBC keywords and values is:

```
[COMMON]
JDBCTRACE=1
JDBCTRACEPATHNAME=\TEMP\JDBCTRACE\
JDBCTRACEFLUSH=1
```

Enabling DB2 JDBC tracing does not enable DB2 CLI tracing. Some versions of the DB2 JDBC driver depend on the DB2 CLI driver to access the database. Consequently, Java developers may also want to enable DB2 CLI tracing for additional information on how their applications interact with the database through the various software layers. DB2 JDBC and DB2 CLI trace options are independent of each other and can be specified together in any order under the [COMMON] section of the db2cli.ini file.

DB2 CLI Driver Trace Versus ODBC Driver Manager Trace

It is important to understand the difference between an ODBC driver manager trace and a DB2 CLI driver trace. An ODBC driver manager trace shows the ODBC function calls made by an ODBC application to the ODBC driver manager. In contrast, a DB2 CLI driver trace shows the function calls made by the ODBC driver manager to the DB2 CLI driver on behalf of the application.

An ODBC driver manager might forward some function calls directly from the application to the DB2 CLI driver. However, the ODBC driver manager might also delay or avoid forwarding some function calls to the driver. The ODBC driver

Monitoring and Tuning

manager may also modify application function arguments or map application functions to other functions before forwarding the call on to the DB2 CLI driver.

Reasons for application function call intervention by the ODBC driver manager include:

- The Microsoft cursor library will map calls such as SQLExtendedFetch() to multiple calls to SQLFetch() and other supporting functions to achieve the same end result.

- ODBC driver manager connection pooling will usually defer SQLDisconnect() requests (or avoid them altogether if the connection gets reused).

For these and other reasons, application developers may find an ODBC driver manager trace to be a useful complement to the DB2 CLI driver trace.

For more information on capturing and interpreting ODBC driver manager traces, refer to the ODBC driver manager documentation. On the Windows platforms, refer to the Microsoft ODBC 3.0 Software Development Kit and Programmer's Reference, also available online at: http://www.msdn.microsoft.com/.

DB2 CLI Driver, DB2 JDBC driver, and DB2 traces

Internally, some versions of the DB2 JDBC driver make use of the DB2 CLI driver for database access. For example, the Java getConnection() method may be internally mapped by the DB2 JDBC driver to the DB2 CLI SQLConnect() function. As a result, Java developers might find a DB2 CLI trace to be a useful complement to the DB2 JDBC trace.

The DB2 CLI driver makes use of many internal and DB2 specific functions to do its work. These internal and DB2 specific function calls are logged in the DB2 trace. Application developers will not find DB2 traces useful, as they are only meant to assist IBM Service in problem determination and resolution.

DB2 CLI Driver and DB2 JDBC traces and CLI or Java Stored Procedures

On all workstation platforms, the DB2 CLI and DB2 JDBC trace facilities can be used to trace DB2 CLI and DB2 JDBC stored procedures.

Most of the DB2 CLI and DB2 JDBC trace information and instructions mentioned previously is generic and applies to both applications and stored procedures equally. However, unlike applications which are clients of a database server (and typically execute on a machine separate from the database server), stored procedures execute at the database server. Therefore, the following additional steps must be taken when tracing DB2 CLI or DB2 JDBC stored procedures:

- Ensure the trace keyword options are specified in the db2cli.ini file located at the

DB2 server.

If the TRACEREFRESHINTERVAL keyword is not set to a positive, non-zero value, ensure all keywords are configured correctly prior to database startup time (that is, when the db2start command is issued). Changing trace settings while the database server is running may have unpredictable results. For example, if the TRACEPATH-NAME is changed while the server is running, then the next time a stored procedure is executed, some trace files may be written to the new path, while others are written to the original path. To ensure consistency, restart the server any time a trace keyword other than TRACE or TRACEPIDLIST is modified.

Trouble-shooting Information

Extensive information on problem determination in DB2 can be found in the *DB2 Information Center*. Also, there are a number of readme files, technical hints and tips, as well as online DB2 publications available in the DB2 Technical Library on the World Wide Web. The DB2 Technical Library is located at: `http://www.software.ibm.com/data/db2/library`.

Summary

DB2 agents are represented by threads in Windows and processes in Linux and UNIX operating environments. While the DB2 process model usually has one coordinating agent represent a client or application connection to DB2, the connection concentrator improves performance by allowing multiple client connections to be handled by each coordinating agent. Important database manager and database configuration parameters were reviewed and their effect on performance.

The Health Center is part of IBM's autonomic computing strategy to have complex systems able to self-manage and self-tune itself. Health indicators are used by the Health Monitor to evaluate specific aspects of database manager or database performance. Health indicators measure either a finite set of distinct states or a continuous range of values to determine whether the state is healthy or unhealthy. If the change in the state is determined to be unhealthy, an alert can be issued in response. Health Monitor information can be accessed through the Health Center, Web Health Center, the Command Line Processor, or APIs.

There are two types of monitors available to analyze database activity, the Snapshot and Event Monitor. The Snapshot Monitor provides point-in-time information regarding resource usage. Many of the elements returned from a snapshot are counters and high-water marks. An Event Monitor is defined through the Control Center or by using a DDL statement. Once activated, the monitored events can be written to SQL table, a file, or to a named pipe.

The DB2 optimizer is one of the most advanced in the relational database industry. The optimizer will generate an access plan during query compilation. Access plans are stored in the system catalog tables for static SQL applications. Access plans for dynamic SQL statements are generated at query execution time and stored in memory.

To gain an understanding of the access plan (strategy) chosen by the DB2 optimizer, the Explain Facility may be used. The Explain Facility will populate relational tables with detailed information for the SQL statements. These tables can then be queried to determine the plan information regarding index usage and other database resources. There is a snapshot column in the explain tables that is used to store a graphical representation of the access plan. This graphical version of the plan can be examined using Visual Explain.

Diagnostics and problem determination information is provided in DB2. This information comes in the form of SQLCODE, and SQLSTATE codes, CLI/JDBC and DB2 traces, and other First Failure Data Capture (FFDC) information.

P A R T 4

Developing Applications

C H A P T E R 13

Application Development Overview

- ◆ DEVELOPMENT ENVIRONMENT
- ◆ PROGRAMMING INTERFACES

*A*pplications represent the interface to the database, and as a DB2 Universal Database administrator, you may have to provide support to developers when they write applications that access the database. DB2 does not have its own programming language. Instead, it allows data to be manipulated using interfaces that pass SQL statements. It also provides an Application Programming Interface for managing and administering the database.

A DB2 application can perform specific queries or process well-defined transactions. An application that performs transaction processing is sometimes referred to as an Online Transaction Processing (OLTP) application. An application that performs ad hoc queries is sometimes referred to as a Decision Support System (DSS) or Online Analytical Processing (OLAP) application. DB2 can be used as the database server for both types of applications.

In this chapter, we will explore the DB2 application development environment, become familiar with many of the options available for developing DB2 applications, and examine some common features of DB2 applications.

DB2 Application Development Environment

You can develop applications at a DB2 server or a client. You can develop and test applications that run on one operating system and access databases on the same or a different operating system. For example, you can create an application that runs on the Windows operating system but accesses a database on a UNIX platform such as AIX. Once you have developed your applications, you can distribute them to other systems, where they can be executed using the DB2 runtime client component that is included in all DB2 products.

To supplement or extend client applications, DB2 programming can also involve development of components that run on the server either as parts of the database manager or as separate modules.

Software Requirements

Before developing applications for DB2, the following products need to be installed and configured:

- Non-DB2 application development utilities, including a compiler or interpreter
- DB2 Universal Database, installed locally or remotely
- DB2 Developer's Edition including the Application Development client

The Application Development client is included in the DB2 UDB database and can also be used to develop applications.

Non-DB2 Application Development Utilities

DB2 allows for application development through a variety of programming languages and third-party application development tools. You must ensure that the proper programming tools and products are installed on each of the development machines. For example, if you are planning to develop an application using a programming language like C, C++, COBOL, or FORTRAN, you need to have the appropriate compilers for creating application modules such as executables and libraries. For Java programs, you need the Java Development Kit (JDK). To develop REXX applications, you need to have REXX support installed, which includes a runtime interpreter. Third-party or ODBC application development environments such as Lotus Notes and Microsoft Visual Basic have their own requirements.

Note: DB2 will not enhance features for FORTRAN and REXX beyond the level of support for these languages in DB2 Universal Database Version 5.2.

Because each compiler or development tool has different attributes, you may need to configure it for use with DB2. Instructions for setting up development tools and a list of supported compilers is provided in the *DB2 UDB V8 Application Development Guide.*

DB2 Universal Database

The database server can either be installed on the same system where the application is being developed or on a remote machine. Generally, if the database is to be accessed by a single developer, it may as well reside on the same system where the application is being developed. When many developers need to access a database, a common database server may be more suitable.

Most of the time, the database location for development purposes is chosen based on convenience and may not be its final location. This is because the location and platform of the database server has little influence over the application development process on the client. For example, if the database were moved from a development platform of DB2 on Windows 2000 to a production platform of DB2 on AIX, it is unlikely that the application would require any changes. However, you may need to bind the application to the new database. We will discuss the bind process in more detail later.

DB2 provides a sample database that you require for running the supplied sample programs. The sample database can be created using the db2samp1 command or through the First Steps tool found in the DB2 folder. You may use the sample database for development purposes or choose to create a customized database. A database can be created using the Control Center, Command Center, Command Line Processor (CLP) or a script. A database can only be created by a user with SYSADM or SYSCTRL privileges. Upon creating the database, the user who created the database will be the DBADM (by default). This user can then grant privileges to other users who can create database objects and populate them with data to be used for development purposes.

Once you have successfully created a database and all of its objects, you should verify that your environment has been set up properly by establishing a connection to the database. You can test the connection to the database using the DB2 CLP, Command Center, Configuration Assistant, or the Control Center.

Application
Development

DB2 Application Development Client (DB2 ADC)

The DB2 ADC provides tools (such as precompilers) and required files (such as DB2 library and header files) needed to develop applications that access DB2 databases using an embedded SQL or DB2 CLI interface. It also contains sample programs that use all of the supported DB2 programming interfaces. The DB2 ADC comes as part of the DB2 Developer's Edition products and the DB2 UDB database servers.

The Personal Developer's Edition (PDE) product provides for the application development needs of a single user on Windows 32-bit operating systems and Linux. The DB2 Universal Developer's Edition (UDE) provides for the application development needs of one or more users on all DB2-supported platforms. When there are multiple developers in the development environment, additional licenses permit developers to share the programming libraries and precompilers.

The DB2 ADC is unique for each *client* development platform. For example, suppose you have been asked to develop an embedded SQL application that would allow a Windows user to access a DB2 database on an AIX server. The user needs a Windows application. You would require the DB2 Software Developer's Kit for Windows to develop the application. Note that the developer's kit is available for free from the DB2 UDB web site: `www.software.ibm.com/data/db2/udb`.

You do not need the DB2 Software Developer's Kit for developing JDBC programs. Developing applications through many end-user and ODBC tools also does not require the DB2 SDK.

DB2 Programming Interfaces

There are many programming methods available to a DB2 application developer. These include:

- Embedded SQL - Static and dynamic
- Call Level Interface (CLI), Open Database Connectivity (ODBC)
- Java Interfaces - JDBC, SQLJ
- Native DB2 Application Programming Interfaces (APIs)
- Microsoft Data Objects - ADO, RDO, DAO, ADO.NET
- Other interfaces, third-party, and ODBC end-user tools

Why are there so many different programming methods? Each programming method has its unique advantages. We will examine each of the methods and provide examples of their advantages and disadvantages.

Embedded SQL

SQL (Structured Query Language) is the database interface language used to access and manipulate data in DB2 databases. You can embed SQL statements in your applications, enabling them to perform any task supported by SQL, such as retrieving or storing data.

An application in which you embed SQL statements is called a host program. A programming language that you compile, and in which you embed SQL statements, is called a host language. The program and language are defined this way because they host or accommodate SQL statements. Using DB2, you can code your embedded SQL applications in the C/C++, COBOL, FORTRAN, Java (SQLJ), and REXX programming languages.

There are two types of embedded SQL statements: static and dynamic. These are discussed in the following sections.

Static Embedded SQL

Static SQL statements are ones in which the SQL statement type and the database objects accessed by the statement, such as column names, are known prior to running the application. The only unknowns are the data values the statement is searching for or modifying. The database objects being accessed must exist when a static embedded application module is bound to the database. The development process involves the combination of SQL with a third-generation programming language. When the embedded SQL program is executed, it uses predefined SQL statements that have been bound to the database as application packages. Thus, the access plan to data is retained in the database in a ready-to-execute package.

There are many performance benefits to having ready-to-execute database logic stored within the database. Static embedded SQL programs have the least runtime overhead of all the DB2 programming methods and execute faster. The package is in a form that is understood by the database server. However, as you might have guessed already, this method of developing applications is not the most flexible because every SQL statement that the end-user executes needs to be known and understood during the development process.

The transactions are grouped into packages and stored in the database. The SQL statements are embedded within programming modules. The programming modules, which contain embedded SQL statements, must be precompiled. The modified programming modules, created by the precompiler, are then compiled and linked to create the application. During the precompile phase, the SQL statements are analyzed and packages are created. We will examine all of the steps for creating static embedded DB2 applications in the next chapter.

Static applications for DB2 can be coded using C/C++, Java, COBOL, or FORTRAN. DB2 provides support for static SQL statements in Java programs using the SQLJ (Embedded SQL for Java) standard. REXX cannot be used for static SQL.

Generally, static statements are well suited for high-performance applications with predefined transactions. A reservation system is a good example of such an application.

Fig. 13–1 *SQL statements prepared during application development*

Advantages

- Ready-to-use packages may be optimal for faster execution
- Use programming skills in COBOL, C/C++, or FORTRAN

Disadvantages

- Must define SQL statements during development
- Requires precompiling

Dynamic Embedded SQL

Dynamic SQL statements are those statements that your application builds and executes at runtime. An interactive application that prompts the end-user for key parts of an SQL statement, such as the names of the tables and columns to be searched, is a good example of dynamic SQL. The application builds the SQL statement while it is running and then submits the statement for processing.

Dynamic embedded SQL, as shown in Fig. 13–2 on page 766, still requires the precompile, compile, and link phases of application development. The binding or selection of the most effective data access plan is performed at program execution time, as the SQL statements are *dynamically prepared*. Choosing the access path at program execution time has some advantages and some drawbacks.

The database objects being accessed must exist when a static embedded application module is bound to the database. Dynamic embedded SQL modules do not require that these database objects exist when the application is precompiled. However, the database objects must exist at runtime.

An embedded static SQL programming module will have its data access method determined during the static bind phase, using the database statistics available at bind time. An embedded dynamic SQL programming module will have its data access method determined during the statement preparation and will utilize the database statistics available at query execution time.

Therefore, there is no need to rebind dynamic embedded SQL programming modules to the database following a collection of database statistics. The database statistics are collected when the RUNSTATS command is issued. The results are stored in the system catalog tables. There is, of course, a query execution time overhead to choose the access path, since each dynamically prepared SQL statement must be optimized.

In Fig. 13–2, the development steps for embedded dynamic SQL program modules are shown. Using embedded dynamic SQL statements does not remove the precompile phase of development, but it does provide the execution of dynamic SQL statements.

Source code for Dynamic embedded SQL. Languages: C/C++, COBOL, FORTRAN	Modified Source Code with DB2 calls. Ready to Compile / Link	Package Stored in the Database during BIND. Access path chosen during execution
PRECOMPILE	**COMPILE /LINK**	**BIND / EXECUTE (DYNAMIC)**

Fig. 13–2 *SQL statements prepared during application execution*

Generally, dynamic SQL statements are well suited for applications that run against a rapidly changing database where transactions need to be specified at runtime. An interactive query interface is a good example of such an application.

Advantages

- Current database statistics are used for each SQL statement.
- Database objects do not have to exist before runtime.
- They are more flexible than static SQL statements.

Disadvantages

- Since SQL statements are optimized at runtime, they may take more time to execute.

Call Level Interface and ODBC

The DB2 Call Level Interface (CLI) is a programming interface that your C and C++ applications can use to access DB2 databases. DB2 CLI is based on the Microsoft Open Database Connectivity Standard (ODBC) specification and the X/Open and ISO Call Level Interface standards. Because DB2 CLI is based on industry standards, application programmers who are already familiar with these database interfaces may benefit from a shorter learning curve. Many ODBC applications can be used with DB2 without any modifications. Likewise, a CLI application is easily ported to other database servers.

DB2 CLI is a dynamic SQL application development environment. However, instead of embedding the SQL statements, your application passes dynamic SQL statements as function arguments to the database using C/C++ Application Programming Interfaces (APIs) provided with DB2. The necessary data structures used to communicate between the database and the application are allocated transparently by DB2.

Because the SQL statements are issued through direct API calls, CLI programs are not precompiled. Also, CLI applications use common access packages provided with DB2; hence, there is no need to bind the program modules separately. You only need to bind the DB2 CLI packages once to each database you want to access using any DB2 CLI or ODBC applications on a client.

Many differences exist between developing an embedded SQL application module and developing a CLI module. Since an application is usually composed of a number of program modules, the modules can use different DB2 programming techniques. It can be beneficial to use different DB2 programming interfaces in a single application.

The CLI application development environment is shown in Fig. 13–3.

Ready to compile source containing database access APIs. SQL statements passed as API (Function) arguments.	All CLI packages bound once (No application Bind). Access path chosen during execution.
COMPILE /LINK	**EXECUTE /DYNAMIC**

Fig. 13–3 *Application development using CLI or ODBC*

Advantages

- Precompiler *not* required
- Binding an application package to the database *not* required
- Current database statistics used
- Can store and retrieve sets of data
- Can use scrollable and updatable cursors
- Easy porting to other database platforms

Disadvantages

- Must have C/C++ programming skills
- Dynamic binding can result in slower query execution

Java Interfaces (JDBC and SQLJ)

DB2 provides support for many different types of Java programs including applets, applications, servlets, and advanced DB2 server-side features. Java programs that access and manipulate DB2 databases can use the Java Database Connectivity (JDBC) API and Embedded SQL for Java (SQLJ) standard. Both of these vendor-neutral SQL interfaces provide data access to your application through standardized Java methods. The greatest benefit of using Java regardless of the database interface is its *write once, run anywhere* capability, allowing the same Java program to be distributed and executed on various operating platforms in a heterogeneous environment without recompiling. And since the two Java database interfaces supported by DB2 are industry open standards, you have the added benefit of using your Java program against a variety of database vendors.

For JDBC programs, your Java code passes *dynamic* SQL to a JDBC driver that comes with DB2. DB2 executes the SQL statements through JDBC APIs and the results are passed back to your Java code. JDBC is similar to DB2 CLI because JDBC uses dynamic SQL and you do not have to precompile or bind a JDBC program.

With DB2 SQLJ support, you can build and run SQLJ programs that contain *static* embedded SQL statements. Since your SQLJ program contains static SQL, you need to perform steps similar to precompiling and binding. Before you can compile an SQLJ source file, you must translate it with the SQLJ translator to create native Java source code. After translation, you need to create the DB2 packages using the DB2 for Java profile customizer (db2profc). Mechanisms contained within SQLJ rely on JDBC for many tasks like establishing connections.

Choosing between SQLJ and JDBC for your Java program involves many of the same considerations and tradeoffs as for static versus dynamic embedded SQL in other languages. SQLJ may be beneficial because static SQL can be faster. Java programs containing embedded SQL can also be subjected to static analysis of SQL statements for the purposes of syntax checking, type checking, and schema validation. On the other hand, not all data objects to be accessed may be known before execution, requiring JDBC for dynamic SQL. A Java programmer can create a powerful application by including both static and dynamic constructs with ease since SQLJ shares environment and state information with JDBC.

Table 13–1 *Differences Between JDBC and SQLJ*

JDBC	SQLJ
SQL via API calls	SQL is embedded
Dynamic SQL	Static SQL
Precompiling not required	Translate SQLJ and create packages

Advantages

Java programs written for DB2 offer:

- Increased portability to other database systems and operating platforms
- Easy access to databases across the Internet from multiple client platforms
- Representation of the NULL state built into Java types
- Object-oriented application development and data access model

Disadvantages

- Must have Java programming skills
- Can be slower since Java is interpreted

Native DB2 APIs

DB2 supplies native Application Programming Interfaces (APIs), which can be used to directly manipulate DB2 instances and databases. They are also called administrative or database manager APIs. Some tasks, such as performing a backup of a database, must be coded using these APIs. There is no method of embedding an SQL statement to perform this operation because the BACKUP DATABASE command is not part of SQL.

The DB2 APIs are provided in many programming languages, including C/C++, COBOL, and FORTRAN. Information is exchanged between the application and database using special data structures. If the source program module contains only DB2 APIs, there is no need to precompile, and a database package is not created.

The native DB2 APIs are not directly used for coding SQL statements on their own. The native APIs rely on embedded SQL or CLI to perform OLAP/OLTP and are generally used in conjunction with these interfaces to provide administrative or database management functions. For example, the function `sqlaintp()` is commonly used to retrieve the complete text for a DB2 error message, so an embedded SQL application can then display the error message to the end-user. The DB2 APIs are grouped by functional category (see Table 13–2). For details on using these APIs, see the *DB2 UDB V8.1 API Reference*.

Table 13–2 *Types of Native (Administrative) DB2 APIs*

Backup/Recovery	Database Monitoring
Database Control	Operational Utilities
Database Manager Control	Data Utilities
Database Directory Management	General Application Programming
Client/Server Directory Management	Application Preparation
Network Support	Remote Server Utilities
Database Configuration	Table Space Management
Node and Nodegroup management	

Advantages

- Enables advanced features of DB2 (e.g., table space administration)
- No precompiling or binding required

Disadvantages

- Requires host language compiler/linker
- Can be more difficult to implement
- Cannot issue SQL statements
- Not easily ported to other database servers

Note: SNAPSHOT table functions were introduced in DB2 Version 8.1 to allow the user to access information on DB2 system objects without using API calls. This is particularly useful for the Java developer who does not have to use JNI (Java Native Interface) to call these API functions. For more information on these functions, see "SNAPSHOT Table Functions" on page 413.

Microsoft Data Objects (DAO, RDO, ADO, OLE-DB)

You can write Microsoft Visual Basic and Microsoft Visual C++ applications that conform to the Data Access Object (DAO) and Remote Data Object (RDO) specifications. These applications interface with DB2 using DB2's ODBC (CLI) driver. DB2 also supports ActiveX Data Object (ADO) applications via the OLE:ODBC bridge, or a native OLE DB driver for DB2.

ActiveX Data Objects (ADO) allow you to write an application to access and manipulate data through an OLE DB provider. The OLE DB API was designed by Microsoft to allow data access to a much broader set of data providers than are available through ODBC. The primary benefits of ADO are high speed, ease of use, low memory overhead, and a small disk footprint.

Remote Data Objects (RDO) provide an information model for accessing remote data sources through ODBC. RDO offers a set of objects that make it easy to connect to a database, execute queries and stored procedures, manipulate results, and commit changes to the server. It is specifically designed to access remote ODBC relational data sources and makes it easier to use ODBC without complex application code. It is a primary means of accessing a relational database that is exposed with an ODBC driver.

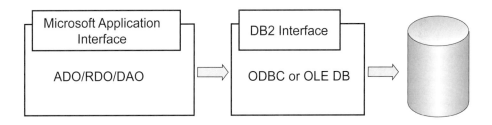

Fig. 13–4 *Applications using Microsoft data objects*

Microsoft Visual Basic is a widely used tool that permits development of rich featured applications using a variety of data access models including ADO, DAO, and RDO.

Advantage

- Provide standardized programming model independent of data source

Disadvantage

- Data objects available on Microsoft Windows platforms only

DB2 .NET Provider Support

Users who need to use .NET features to access DB2 have two options:

- Open Database Connectivity (ODBC) .NET Data Provider
  OLE-DB.NET Data Provider

  The ODBC .NET and OLE-DB .NET providers are available directly from Microsoft and will allow your application to communicate with DB2 using ODBC or OLE-DB calls. The bridge drivers are currently not certified to run with DB2 UDB, but a number of customers have used them successfully in their development environment.

  To download this provider, check the Microsoft download site:

  `http://msdn.microsoft.com/downloads/`

- Native DB2 .NET Data Provider

  The initial release of DB2 UDB Version 8.1 does not include a native .NET driver. However, Version 8.1.2 (fixpak 2) delivers the .NET provider along with tighter integration with the Microsoft Visual Studio .Net development environment. A native driver will have better performance than using the ODBC .NET provider and support more DB2 features. Check on the DB2 website for availability of this driver:

  `http://www.software.ibm.com/data/udb`

Other Interfaces and Tools

There are numerous third-party application building tools and end-user applications that interface with DB2 using one or more programming methods described previously. However, many of these tools and applications provide their own front-end data access methods, making the underlying interface to the database transparent to application developers and end-users. This can provide a simpler alternative to developing applications than using a high-level programming language.

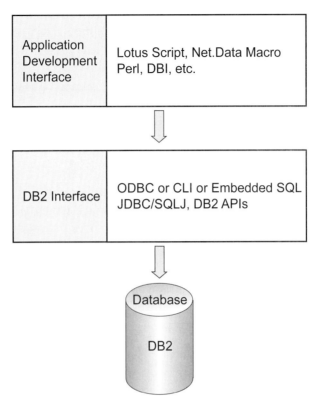

Application Development

Fig. 13–5 *Application development using other interfaces*

ODBC Tools

There might be cases where you need to perform a basic task, such as querying the database, developing reports, and analyzing data. ODBC end-user tools such as Lotus Notes and Microsoft Access can assist in creating applications to perform these tasks. With Lotus products, you can develop applications using LotusScript, a full-featured, object-oriented programming language that comes with a wide array of objects, events, methods, and properties, along with a built-in program editor.

Net.Data

Net.Data enables development of Web applications for Internet and intranet access to DB2 data. It provides an interface between the Web server and DB2 client code, allowing end-users to access DB2 using just their Web browsers on their workstations. It can run on the Web server machine as a common gateway interface (CGI) application or exploit Web server interfaces (APIs) and FastCGI to provide better performance. Net.Data supports client-side processing as well as server-side processing with languages such as Java, REXX, Perl, and C++. It provides conditional logic and a rich macro language. Net.Data uses CLI as the default back-end for connecting to DB2. Besides DB2, it also supports access to other data sources such as Oracle, Sybase, Informix, DRDA-enabled data sources, ODBC data sources, flat files, and Web registry data.

 Note: Net.Data support stabilized in DB2 Version 7.2, and no enhancements for Net.Data support are planned for the future.

Perl DBI

Perl DBI is an application programming interface that provides database access for the Perl language. Like ODBC, Perl DBI provides a standardized database interface independent of the actual database being used. DB2 supports the Perl Database Interface (DBI) specification for data access through the DBD::DB2 driver. This driver works in conjunction with the DBI to access DB2 via CLI. The ability to access DB2 from a Perl environment is particularly useful for database testing and maintenance scripts on UNIX platforms and Windows. Perl applications are also commonly used for writing CGI scripts for Web access.

PHP

PHP can be used as a method to access DB2 from web-based applications. PHP is a server-side, HTML-embedded, cross-platform scripting language. It supports DB2 access using the Unified-ODBC access method, in which the user-level PHP communicates to DB2 using ODBC calls. Unlike standard ODBC, with the Unified-ODBC method, communication is directly to the DB2 CLI layer, not through the ODBC layer.

Each of the third-party products mentioned in this section has its own benefits and drawbacks. Some common features are described below.

Advantages

- Quick access to data using a simple or graphical interface
- Faster way for developing relatively simple applications
- Development skills reusable with other data sources
- Provide abstraction over low-level data access details

Disadvantages

- Sometimes unsuitable for complex applications
- May not be able to access certain DB2 features and functions

Summary

DB2 supports applications on a wide variety of operating platforms and numerous methods of coding the applications.

Applications can contain embedded SQL or be coded using standard APIs like CLI, ODBC, and JDBC. Applications can also be developed using other interfaces such as Perl DBI and ActiveX Data Objects. There are many IBM and non-IBM products like Net.Data and Visual Basic, and end-user tools such as Lotus Notes and Microsoft Access, which make the process of application development faster and easier.

Depending on the type of application, one or more programming techniques can be used. DB2 allows applications to be developed that use many popular programming languages including C/C++, COBOL, FORTRAN, Java, and REXX. The DB2 Software Developer's Kit (SDK) included with DB2 Personal Developer's Edition (PDE) and DB2 Universal Developer's Edition (UDE) provides support for developing DB2 applications using these programming languages.

Application Development

Development Considerations

- ◆ PACKAGES
- ◆ BINDING
- ◆ CLI & ODBC SETTINGS
- ◆ JDBC & SQLJ SETTINGS
- ◆ SQL STORED PROCEDURE BUILDER

Embedded SQL programming was introduced in the previous chapter. Even though many of the alternatives to embedded SQL programming offer faster and easier ways to develop applications, it is nevertheless useful to understand and know how to program using embedded SQL. Static statements offer great performance benefits and are only possible through embedded SQL. If you are migrating applications from mainframes such as S/390 or using COBOL, you may prefer embedded SQL.

A precompiler for a variety of programming languages is provided with the DB2 Development Kits (Personal and Universal). The precompiler is used to convert embedded SQL statements into a series of Application Programming Interface (API) requests (as was discussed in the previous chapter).

Embedded SQL Overview

Fig. 14–1 on page 779 illustrates the steps involved in building an embedded SQL application. These are as follows:

1. Create source files that contain programs with embedded SQL statements.

2. Connect to a database, then precompile each source file.

   The precompiler converts the SQL statements in each source file into DB2 run-time API calls to the database manager. The precompiler also produces an access package in the database and, optionally, a bind file, if you specify that you want one created. We will discuss packages and bind files in the following sections.

3. Compile the modified source files (and other files without SQL statements) using the host language compiler.

4. Link the object files with the DB2 and host language libraries to produce an executable program.

5. Bind the bind file to create the access package if this was not already done at precompile time or if a different database is to be accessed.

6. Run the application. The application accesses the database using the access plan in the package.

Creating Packages

A *package* is a database object that contains optimized SQL statements. A *package* corresponds to a single source programming module and, *sections* corresponds to the SQL statements contained in the source program module.

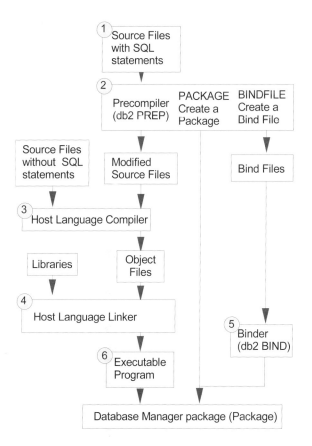

Fig. 14–1 *Process for creating embedded SQL applications*

A programming module that contains embedded *static* SQL statements requires precompiling, during which time the precompiler generates a package (by default). This package contains a number of sections that correspond to embedded SQL statements. A section is the compiled form of an SQL statement. While every section corresponds to one statement, every statement does not necessarily have a section. An optimized *access plan* will be stored in the section. The package can be stored directly in the database, or the data needed to create a package can be stored in a bind file. Creating a bind file and bind it in a separate step is known as *deferred binding*.

A program module that contains embedded *dynamic* SQL statements has an associated package and sections, but in this case, the sections are used as placeholders for the SQL statement that will be dynamically prepared. There are no access plans stored in the sections because they are in embedded static SQL modules.

Like views and tables, packages have an associated schema name. The fully qualified name of a package is SCHEMA-NAME.PACKAGE-NAME.

In most cases, application developers use deferred binding. Deferred binding
requires a two-step process:

1. Creating a bind file (which contains information to create a package)

2. Binding the package bind file to the database

Let's examine these steps. First, we need to create a bind file. The bind file is generated by the precompiler when the appropriate option is specified. The precompiler can be invoked with the PREP or PRECOMPILE command using the Command
Center or the Command Line Processor (CLP).

The precompiler input is always a source programming module with embedded
SQL statements. Each DB2-supported programming language has its own precompiler provided with the DB2 Software Developer's Kit. The file extension of the
source program module is used to determine which precompiler (e.g., C, C++,
COBOL, FORTRAN) will be invoked.

In Table 14–1, the input host language source file extensions and the modified
source file output extensions are provided. The examples in this book are written in
C. Therefore, the cmbedded SQL program files are named program-name.sqc, and
the precompiler output files are named program-name.c. The name of the source
module is important, because the precompiler will use this as the name of the package unless otherwise specified.

Table 14–1 *Precompile File Extensions*

Host Language	File Extension (Input - Source)	File Extension (Output - Modified Source)
C	.sqc	.c
C++ (case sensitive - AIX)	.sqC	.C
C++ (case insensitive - Windows)	.sqx	.cxx
COBOL - Use TARGET and/or OUTPUT options to use other extensions	.sqb	.cbl
FORTRAN (UNIX)	.sqf	.f
FORTRAN (Windows)	.sqf	.for

If you issue these DB2 commands/statements:

```
CONNECT TO DB2CERT USER DB2CERT USING DB2
PRECOMPILE PROG1.SQC
CONNECT RESET
```

then you would create an application package called DB2CERT.PROG1 in the
DB2CERT database. This package would contain a lot of information about the
embedded SQL statements, apart from the host variable values required to execute
the embedded SQL statements that are contained in the file prog1.sqc. There are
additional steps required before you have an executable application. All database
objects specifically referenced (tables, views, etc.) must exist during the precompile phase because in this example deferred binding is not being used. The other
inconvenient aspect of not creating a separate bind file is that the entire database
would need to be provided, along with the application to the end-user, since the
package only exists in the database. The data needed to create the package is not
contained in a separate bind file in this example.

Let's look at an example of deferred binding with the DB2 commands/statements:

```
CONNECT TO DB2CERT USER DB2CERT USING DB2
PRECOMPILE PROG1.SQC BINDFILE
CONNECT RESET
```

This example demonstrates the use of the precompiler option BINDFILE. This
option is used to generate an output file that contains all of the data needed to create the package for the source module. By using this option, this data is stored in a
file called prog1.bnd. You can change the name of the output bind file, but in this
example, we did not rename the bind file. To avoid confusion between source program modules, bind files, and package names, try to avoid renaming any of these
objects. If you want to create the package using a different name, use the option
PACKAGE USING <PACKAGE-NAME>. If you want to create the package using a different schema name, use the option COLLECTION <SCHEMA-NAME>.

The name of the package is determined when the prog1.bnd file is bound to the
database. If the same user were to bind this package, the name of the package
would be DB2CERT.PROG1. If the database objects do not exist during precompile,
only warnings will be generated, and the bind file is created. (Object existence and
authentication SQL codes are treated as warnings instead of as errors.) The BIND

command verifies the existence and access privileges of database objects and will only be successful once the required objects are present.

> **Note:** Database objects referenced in embedded static SQL programs must exist in the database during package creation (PRECOMPILE without BINDFILE option or BIND) unless the DEFERRED_PREPARE option is set to YES.

For each source program module containing embedded static SQL statements, a corresponding package must exist in the database. Assume that we are creating an application that accesses two different DB2 databases. The objects referenced in the application must exist in the database for the package to be created successfully. Therefore, we will develop the application using two different program modules. Each program module or source file represents a database package. If we keep the SQL statements for each database in separate packages, the bind will be successful. We can then compile and link the program modules together into a single executable.

Any PRECOMPILE error messages will be reported to the display or to a message file. The error message file can be specified using the MESSAGES option when issuing the PRECOMPILE command. It is recommended to send the messages to an output file so you can examine the file to determine the cause of the errors. Errors during precompile could include invalid host variable definitions and incorrect SQL statements.

When precompiling, you can also determine whether the SQL embedded in the program conforms to different syntaxes and standards. For example, you can check to see if the application works against DB2 for OS/390, or is ISO/ANS SQL92 compliant. This is done using the LANGLEVEL, SQLFLAG, and SQLRULES options when precompiling the program.

It is important to remember that an embedded dynamic SQL programming module does have associated packages but does *not* contain access plans or executable sections. For example, suppose an SQL program contains four static SQL statements and two dynamic SQL statements in a single source module. There would be four SQL sections (each with an access plan) created and stored in the database within a single package.

Binding Applications

The most common method of binding in application development is *deferred binding*. When deferred binding is used, the information about the SQL statements is stored in the bind file created by the precompile process. This bind file must be bound against the database to create a package. Once the package exists in the database, there is no longer any need to bind the application.

The SQL statements from the bind file are examined during the bind process, and the current database statistics are used to determine the best method of data access. At this point, an access plan is chosen by the DB2 optimizer. This access plan is then stored in the database system catalog tables. An access plan is *only* created for static embedded SQL statements. Embedded dynamic SQL statements have a package and a section number assigned, but there is *no* access plan created until the statement is executed.

The bind process needs to be performed following each successful precompile of the application source modules. When the bind file is created, a timestamp is stored in the package. The timestamp is sometimes referred to as a *consistency token*. This same timestamp is also stored in the database when the bind is completed and is used to ensure that the resulting application executes the proper SQL statement.

The modified source module (output from the precompile) will attempt to execute the SQL statements by package name and section number. If the required package and section are not found, the following message will be returned:

```
SQL0805N Package 'pkgschema.pkgname' was not found.
SQLSTATE=51002
```

Note: The SQLERROR(CONTINUE) and VALIDATE(RUN) bind options, in previous releases only available with DB2 Universal Database for OS/390, are now available for the DB2 Universal Database family. This allows you to port your DB2 Universal Database for OS/390 applications that make use of these options to the rest of the DB2 Universal Database family.

If the required package and section exist in the database system catalogs, the timestamp is then checked. If the timestamp in the application executable does not match the timestamp stored in the system catalog tables in the database, the following message is returned:

```
SQL0818N A TIMESTAMP CONFLICT OCCURRED.
SQLSTATE=51003
```

To avoid this problem, you can use the VERSION option during the precompilation step. The VERSION option allows multiple packages that share both the schema and package-id to co-exist in the system catalogs. This option will allow you to introduce and test a new version of a package on the system without affecting users of the existing version of the package. The support of the version option will allow ongoing package maintenance to occur without interruption of end-user access to the system. The PREP, BIND, REBIND and DROP PACKAGE facilities have been enhanced to support package versioning.

Authorization Considerations for Static SQL

If the package does not yet exist in the database, the user who issues the BIND must have BINDADD authority for the database or be a member of a group that has this authority. The user must also have one of these privileges: IMPLICIT_SCHEMA on the database (if the schema name of the package does not exist) or CREATEIN on the schema (if the schema name does already exist). The person who binds the package by default becomes the package owner, unless the OWNER keyword is specified during the BIND. In addition, since static statements execute with privileges of the package owner authorization ID, that userid must also have the proper privileges for all of the referenced objects in the SQL statements referenced in the bind file information. These privileges must be explicitly granted to the user binding the packages or to PUBLIC. If the privileges are granted to a group of which the user is a member but are not granted explicitly to the user, the bind will fail.

Unqualified database objects in embedded static SQL programs are by default qualified with the userid of the package owner. Alternatively, you may specify the QUALIFER keyword during the BIND to indicate the qualifier name for unqualified objects in static SQL statements.

Table 14–2 summarizes the behavioral characteristics of static SQL with respect to authorization ID used for statements and the qualifier for unqualified database objects depending on whether the OWNER and QUALIFIER options are used during the BIND:

Table 14–2 *Static SQL - Authorization and Qualifier Summary*

BIND Keyword	Authorization ID	Qualification Value for Unqualified Objects
OWNER and QUALIFIER NOT specified	ID of the user binding the package	ID of the user binding the package
OWNER specified	ID of the user specified in OWNER bind option	ID of the user specified in OWNER bind option
QUALIFIER specified	ID of the user binding the package	ID of the user specified in the QUALIFIER bind option
OWNER and QUALIFIER specified	ID of the user specified in OWNER bind option	ID of the user specified in the QUALIFIER bind option

Once the package exists in the database, any person with EXECUTE privilege on the package can issue any of the SQL statements contained in the package, even if the individual does not have explicit privilege on the database object. This is a feature of embedded static SQL program modules. It allows end-users access to a portion of data contained in a table without defining a view or column-level privileges.

Authorization Considerations for Dynamic SQL

Unlike static SQL, dynamically prepared statements can be made to execute under the authorization ID of either the user that binds the package (the package owner) or the user who executes the application, depending on which option is used for the DYNAMICRULES keyword during the bind.

Under DYNAMICRULES RUN (the default), the person who runs a dynamic SQL application must have the privileges necessary to issue each SQL statement (it specifies that the authorization ID of the user executing the package is to be used) as well as the EXECUTE privilege on the package. The privileges may be granted to the user's authorization ID, to any group of which the user is a member, or to PUBLIC. With DYNAMICRULES RUN, the person binding the application only needs the BINDADD authority on the database, if the program contains no static SQL.

When using the DYNAMICRULES BIND option, authorizations and privileges required are similar to static SQL. That is, the user that binds a dynamic SQL application (the authorization ID of the package owner) must have BINDADD authority as well as the privileges necessary to perform all the dynamic and static SQL statements in the application. The user that runs the application inherits the privileges associated with the package owner authorization ID and therefore only needs the EXECUTE privilege on the package.

Note: If you bind packages with DYNAMICRULES BIND, and have SYSADM or DBADM authority or any authorities that the user of the package should not receive, consider explicitly specifying OWNER to designate a different authorization ID. This prevents the package from automatically inheriting SYSADM, DBADM, or other unnecessary privileges on dynamic SQL statements from the userid that binds the application.

The authorization ID privileges and qualifier values used for DYNAMICRULES RUN and BIND options are summarized in Table 14–3:

Table 14–3 *Dynamic SQL - Authorization and Qualifier Summary*

DYNAMICRULES Option	Authorization ID	Qualification Value for Unqualified Objects
RUN (default)	ID of user executing package	Owner's authorization ID whether or not the owner is explicitly specified. It can be superseded by the CURRENT SCHEMA special register.
BIND	The implicit or explicit value of OWNER bind option	The implicit or explicit value of the QUALIFIER bind option.

Examining Packages and Timestamps

We have briefly discussed packages and timestamps. Let's examine how we can verify that the bind file and the packages in the database match. When the BIND command is successful, a single entry in the system catalog view SYSCAT.PACKAGES is created. There are a number of columns defined for this table. We will not go into a complete explanation here, but let's look at the timestamp column. The timestamp associated with a package is actually stored in the column named UNIQUE_ID. If you were to successfully issue the command:

```
bind db2look.bnd messages msg1.out
```

the SYSCAT.PACKAGES view would have a new entry for this bind file with the package name DB2LOOK and the package schema as your authorization user ID. Any error or warning messages would be written to the file called msg1.out. To examine the timestamp contained in the db2look.bnd file, there is a utility provided with DB2 called db2bfd.

Here is an example of the output of the db2bfd tool:

```
db2look.bnd:  Header Contents

Header Fields:

Field           Value
-----           -----
releaseNum      0x800
Endian          0x4c
numHvars        435
maxSect         99
numStmt         468
optInternalCnt  4
optCount        10


Name                  Value
------------------    -----
Isolation Level       Uncommitted Read
Creator               "NULLID  "
App Name              "DB2LOOK "
Timestamp             "5AEWWXKS:2002/10/23 22:22:04:56"
Cnulreqd              Yes
Sql Error             No package
Block                 Block All
Validate              Bind
Date                  Default/local
Time                  Default/local


*** All other options are using default settings as specified by the server ***
```

Note that the timestamp is encoded as 5AEWWXKS and the decoded timestamp is also shown. This timestamp is the exact time when the PRECOMPILE command was used to generate the bind file.

To confirm that this bind file (db2look.bnd) has been bound to the database, issue this SQL statement once connected to the database:

```
select pkgschema, pkgname, unique_id
from syscat.packages
where pkgname = 'DB2LOOK'
```

The output of this SQL statement should contain a single row result with a UNIQUE_ID matching the bind file, as shown here:

```
PKGSCHEMA   PKGNAME   UNIQUE_ID
---------   -------   ---------
NULLID      DB2LOOK   5AEWWXKS
```

The UNIQUE_ID contained in the bind file matches this value. Therefore, you know that this bind file has been successfully bound to the database.

Binding Utilities

The CLP is a dynamic SQL application that is provided with DB2. The packages associated with the utilities, like the DB2 CLP, are included in the sqllib directory, in the bnd subdirectory.

The bind files associated with the DB2 CLP and utilities are found in a list file called db2ubind.lst.

Specifically, the bind files associated with the DB2 CLP are: db2clpcs.bnd, db2clprr.bnd, db2clpur.bnd, db2clprs.bnd, and db2clpnc.bnd.

> **Note:** Each of the CLP bind files is created with different isolation levels. This allows a user the ability to change the isolation level when using the CLP utility, using the CHANGE ISOLATION LEVEL command.

These bind files must have been bound to the database you wish to access using the DB2 Command Center, the DB2 CLP or the Configuration Assistant (CA).

> **Note:** To bind the DB2 utilities (e.g., CLP, IMPORT, EXPORT) issue the command: bind @db2ubind.lst blocking all.

To bind a number of packages using a single BIND command, add the "@" character in front of the source filename. When this character is encountered, DB2 will assume that the file contains a list of bind files and is not a bind file itself.

Blocking

Record blocking is a feature of DB2 Universal Database that reduces data access time across networks when an application is retrieving a large amount of data. The record blocking is based on cursor type and the amount of storage allocated on the DB2 server to perform record blocking. Cursors are used in applications to manipulate multirow result sets from a DB2 server.

The DBM configuration parameter known as ASLHEAPSZ specifies the amount of memory used to buffer data on the server for applications requesting multiple data records. For applications executing on remote clients, the buffer is specified by the DBM configuration parameter known as RQRIOBLK.

You can think of record blocking as data retrieval caching. The record blocking options are described in Fig. 14–4. Usually, you would specify BLOCKING ALL for applications that perform many queries. An *ambiguous cursor* is a cursor that has been defined without any reference to its intended usage in an SQL statement. As we will see, all cursors are defined using a SELECT statement. They are used in a SELECT, DELETE, or UPDATE statement.

The default blocking option for static embedded applications is BLOCKING UNAMBIG. The default blocking option for CLI applications and the CLP is BLOCKING ALL.

Table 14–4 *Record Blocking Options*

BLOCKING <option>	Record Blocking Behavior
UNAMBIG	All cursors except those specified as FOR UPDATE are blocked.
ALL	Ambiguous cursor are blocked.
NO	No cursors are blocked.

Record blocking affects the way you, as an application developer, declare your cursors within your application. The more specific you are with your cursor declaration, the more likely DB2 will use record blocking appropriately. If record blocking is enabled, the cache is allocated when the cursor is opened. It is deallocated when the cursor is closed. Therefore, to avoid wasting memory resources on the server, avoid keeping cursors open if they are no longer required.

 Note: All cursors used for dynamic SQL statements are assumed to be ambiguous.

 Development Considerations

Support for CLI and ODBC Programming

We have been discussing static and dynamic SQL statement processing by embedding the SQL statements in an application module. A precompile or preparation stage is required to map these SQL statements to DB2 API calls. We are required to manipulate SQLDA data structures to handle dynamic SQL. This can become quite complex and, more importantly, are not easily ported to various database vendors. An alternative method of developing database applications using callable SQL interfaces has become a popular technique of creating powerful yet highly portable applications.

A callable SQL interface involves invoking APIs (also referred to as functions or function calls in this chapter) that allow the developer to access database information directly; therefore, there is no need for precompiling the application and there is no database-specific language to learn. One such callable SQL interface is Microsoft's Open Database Connectivity (ODBC). There are slightly different callable SQL interface standards known as Call Level Interface (CLI) as defined by groups such as X/Open and ISO.

DB2 has its own CLI which is based on the X/Open, ISO, and ODBC standards. The focus of the discussion here will be application development using DB2 CLI. We will also cover ODBC briefly but will not go into too much detail because the two standards are very similar.

All of the SQL statements are dynamically prepared and executed using CLI or ODBC. The programming techniques and runtime environment for CLI are quite different than those for embedded SQL. We will discuss many of these differences.

Embedded Dynamic Versus Call Level Interface

Developing an application using CLI is different than using embedded SQL techniques. So before we examine how to code CLI applications, let's examine some of the key differences.

The DB2 CLI environment is different from embedded SQL in the following ways:

- No explicit cursors are required.
- There is no precompile stage.
- No application level packages created. There is a set of CLI packages that is bound once for all CLI applications.
- No COMMIT/ROLLBACK statement is used to control transaction processing. An API called SQLEndTran() is used to commit or rollback a transaction.
- No SQLDA data structure is required.

- No SQLCA data structure is used because the errors are analyzed using SQLSTATES and return codes though special error-handling APIs.
- No host variables are used in SQL statements; parameter markers are used instead.

The differences listed above are important to understand before attempting to develop CLI applications. There are some unique features provided with CLI that are not available in an embedded SQL environment including:

- Manipulation of multiple rows of data at a time (array fetch/insert)
- The ability to have bidirectional (scrollable) cursors
- Easier to query the system catalog tables because there are predefined APIs to query system catalog table resources

ODBC Versus CLI

The ODBC and CLI standards overlap in many areas. They are both based on a set of APIs that access data sources using programs written in the C/C++ programming language. The initial ODBC standard was based on an early version of the X/Open CLI standard, and they have evolved over the years.

The ODBC standard is based on levels of conformance. The DB2 ODBC driver currently conforms to ODBC level 3.51. This includes all core, level 1, and level 2 functions. As the ODBC standard continues to evolve, so may DB2's ODBC conformance.

The DB2 product provides both a CLI driver and an ODBC driver. In the CLI environment, the application communicates directly with the CLI driver. In an ODBC environment, the ODBC Driver Manager provides the interface to the application. It also dynamically loads the ODBC driver for the necessary database server that the application connects to. It is the driver that implements the ODBC function set, with the exception of some extended functions implemented by the Driver Manager. Fig. 14–2 illustrates the relationship between the application and DB2 in both the ODBC and CLI environments.

Development Considerations

Fig. 14–2 *DB2 CLI versus ODBC*

A DB2 CLI application does not require the ODBC driver or the ODBC driver manager to operate. The advantage of coding an ODBC application is the ease of portability. Also, the application can access more than one database vendor product. Therefore, you could develop an application that accesses data from multiple database vendor products quite simply with the ODBC interface. The DB2 CLI driver can only access DB2 Family data sources.

 Note: The installation of the ODBC driver is *only* required if ODBC applications are being executed. To run CLI applications, only the DB2 runtime client needs to be installed. It includes the DB2 CLI driver.

Setting Up the CLI Environment

There are several steps involved in setting up a DB2 CLI environment. All of the CLI APIs are contained in a static library. These are the names of the libraries on the various DB2 development operating systems:

- The DB2 CLI library on Windows platforms is called db2cli.lib.
- The DB2 CLI library on UNIX platforms is called libdb2.a or libdb2.so.

Before we attempt to develop an application, we must ensure that the following steps have been performed successfully:

- The DB2 Software Developer's Kit must be installed.
- The database being accessed is cataloged properly. If the database is remote, a node must also be cataloged.
- DB2 CLI bind files must be bound to the database.
- Configure the CLI environment using the Configuration Assistant or edit the db2cli.ini file directly. It is important to remember to examine the CLI environment settings in the db2cli.ini file or by using the Configuration Assistant. These settings affect the execution behavior of all CLI applications executing on the system.

CLI Bind Files

The bind files required for CLI applications will be automatically bound when the first CLI application connects to the database. If CLI applications from multiple systems connect to a database, the CLI packages from each client platform and unique build level (fixpak level) need to be bound to the database. The bind may not be successful if the user does not have BINDADD authority on the database. Therefore, the database administrator may be required to bind the necessary bind files manually using the DB2 BIND command or the Configuration Assistant (CA). Each of the supported DB2 servers use different bind files (Table 14–5).

Table 14–5 *CLI Bind List Files*

Bind File	DB2 Server
db2cli.lst	DB2 Universal Database (OS/2, Windows, UNIX)
ddcsvm.lst	DB2 for VM (SQL/DS)
ddcsvse.lst	DB2 for VSE (SQL/DS)
ddcsmvs.lst	DB2 for OS/390 (MVS/ESA)
ddcs400.lst	DB2 for OS/400

Development Considerations

For example, to manually bind the CLI packages from a DB2 Command Window on Windows against a DB2 for AIX database, you would issue the following command after connecting to the database:

```
DB2 BIND @DB2CLI.LST MESSAGES DB2CLI.MSG GRANT PUBLIC
```

Likewise, if the DB2 database resides on S/390, you could use this command:

```
DB2 BIND @ddcsmvs.lst BLOCKING ALL SQLERROR CONTINUE
MESSAGES MVSBIND.MSG GRANT PUBLIC
```

Configuring CLI

Usually it is not necessary to modify the DB2 CLI configuration file (db2cli.ini). It is important to understand that the file exists and may require small modifications. Some of the reasons for modifying the CLI configuration file include:

- Increase CLI application performance
- Change default CLI behavior
- Enable workarounds for specific applications

The db2cli.ini file is located in the sqllib/cfg directory of the instance owner in UNIX environments, in the sqllib directory for Windows 32-bit operating systems, or the sqllib/win directory for 16-bit Windows environments.

```
; Comment Goes Here
[DB2CERT]
CURSORHOLD=0
TNXISOLATION=4
DEFERREDPREPARE=1
DB2DEGREE=4
PATCH1=2
```

Fig. 14–3 *Example db2cli.ini configuration*

An example db2cli.ini file is shown in Fig. 14–3. There are many more options that can be specified in the CLI configuration file, but these options were selected because they can dramatically affect an application's execution environment. The keywords and values shown here may not be applicable to your environment.

The first line is a comment about this section of the file. Multiple databases may be configured in this file. The second line contains the database alias name in brackets, [DB2CERT]. The DB2CERT database can still be accessed from a DB2 CLI application without an entry in the db2cli.ini file, but if there is no section for the DB2CERT database, all of the default values for the parameters will be used. This may not be desirable.

The five lines below the database name contain keywords and corresponding values. The supported keywords are defined in the *DB2 UDB V8.1 Call Level Interface Guide and Reference*, but let's examine the keywords defined in Fig. 14–3 and explain them in Table 14–6.

Table 14–6 *Configuring a DB2 CLI Environment*

Keyword	Meaning
CURSORHOLD	0 = cursor no hold (the cursors are destroyed when the transaction is committed) 1 = cursor hold (default) The default value of this keyword is 1. This means that the cursors are maintained across units of work. This is quite different from embedded SQL since all cursors exhibit the cursor without hold behavior unless the DECLARE CURSOR statement includes the phrase WITH HOLD.
TXNISOLATION	1 - Uncommitted Read 2 - Cursor Stability (default) 4 - Read Stability 8 - Repeatable Read 32 - No Commit (DB2 for OS/400 only) This keyword identifies the isolation level used for concurrency.
DEFERREDPREPARE	0 = Deferred Prepare is not used. 1 = Deferred Prepare is used (default). Defers sending the PREPARE request until the corresponding execute request is issued. The two requests are then combined into one command/reply flow (instead of two) to minimize network flow and to improve performance.
DB2DEGREE	0-32767/ANY (Default is 0) Sets the degree of parallelism for the execution of SQL statements.
PATCH1 PATCH2	The keywords Patch1 and Patch2 are used for work-arounds to known problems when using certain applications or environments. In our example, we used PATCH1=4 to map timestamp values to date values. To use multiple Patch1 values, simply add the values together to form the keyword value. For example, if you want the patches 1, 4, and 8, then specify PATCH1=13. Unlike PATCH1, to specify multiple patches for PATCH2, the values are specified in a comma delimited string, for example PATCH2="7,15".

The DB2 CA or ODBC Administrator Tool on the Windows platform allows you to configure the CLI environment without editing the db2cli.ini file directly. The interface is easy to use and explains each parameter that can be modified:

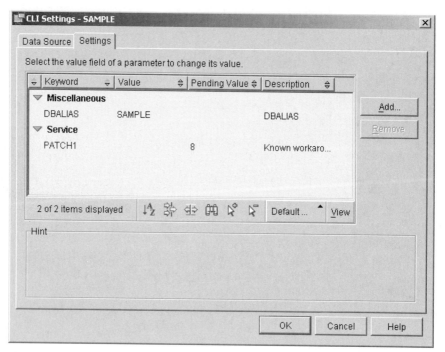

Fig. 14–4 *CLI/ODBC settings panel in the Configuration Assistant*

Accessing a DB2 Database via ODBC

To access a DB2 database from ODBC, the following are required on the DB2 client where the ODBC application executes:

- DB2 runtime client or server must be installed. If the database is on a remote DB2 system, it should be cataloged correctly and be accessible for connecting to.
- The ODBC Driver Manager must be installed.
- An ODBC driver for DB2 must be installed and registered with the ODBC driver manager.
- The DB2 database must be registered as an ODBC data source with the driver manager.

There must be an ODBC driver manager installed on the computer where the ODBC application has been installed. For all Microsoft operating systems, the ODBC driver manager is provided by Microsoft.

The IBM DB2 ODBC driver or another ODBC driver for DB2 must be installed and registered. The Microsoft ODBC driver manager and the DB2 ODBC driver are automatically installed on Windows 32-bit platforms during DB2 installation as long as the ODBC component, highlighted by default, is not unchecked. The DB2 ODBC driver is also registered with the driver manager during installation of DB2 on Windows platforms. On Windows platforms, you can run the Microsoft ODBC Administrator from the Control Panel to verify that "IBM DB2 ODBC Driver" is shown in the list. On UNIX platforms, the DB2 ODBC driver and databases available through it are specified using '.odbc.ini' and '.odbcinst.ini' files in the home directory of the user running the ODBC application. Note that the files start with a '.'.

The database must be identified to the ODBC driver manager as an available data source. The data source can be made available to all users of the system (a system data source) or only to the current user (a user data source). On Windows, you can register the data source with the driver manager using the CA, as shown in Fig. 14–5. Databases configured though the CA are selected as system ODBC data sources by default, unless you explicitly uncheck the selection. For non-Windows platforms, this is accomplished by using the appropriate ODBC Administration tool or by configuring the driver manager manually.

Development Considerations

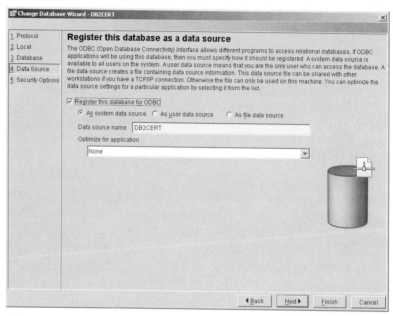

Fig. 14–5 *Database properties*

ODBC Development Considerations

For ODBC application development, you must obtain an ODBC Software Development Kit.

The steps of binding of CLI packages and customizing CLI using db2cli.ini or CA are also applicable to ODBC applications that will access DB2 data sources. These steps are performed in the same way as for CLI applications.

Support For Java Programming

DB2 supports many types of Java programs. Applets and applications are two main types of Java programs. Before explaining how to code applets and applications for DB2, let's first examine these two types.

Java applications rely on the DB2 client code to connect to the DB2 database. You start your application from the desktop or command line, like any other application. The DB2 JDBC driver handles the JDBC API calls from your application. These calls to the DB2 JDBC driver are translated to DB2 CLI calls via Java native methods. The JDBC driver uses the CLI driver on the client to communicate the requests to the server, receives the results, and passes them to the Java application. Thus an application requires at least the DB2 runtime client code to be installed where the application executes.

Fig. 14–6 *Java applications for DB2*

Java applets do not require any DB2 client code to be installed on the system where they execute. You need only a Java-enabled Web browser on the client machine to run your applet. Typically, you would embed the applet in a HyperText Markup Language (HTML) page. When you load your HTML page, the browser downloads the Java applet to your machine, which then downloads the Java class files and DB2's JDBC driver. When your applet calls the JDBC API to connect to DB2, the JDBC driver establishes a separate network connection with a DB2 JDBC applet server residing on the Web server. The JDBC server communicates with the database via the DB2 CLI driver and sends the results back to the client through the separate connection.

Fig. 14–7 *Java applets for DB2*

DB2 also supports user-defined functions and stored procedures written in Java.

Java programs that access DB2 databases can do so using JDBC or SQLJ interfaces. The JDBC API allows you to write Java programs that make dynamic SQL calls to databases. SQLJ extends JDBC to support embedded static SQL. The next few sections deal with coding Java programs for DB2 using JDBC and SQLJ.

JDBC Programming

If your DB2 application or applet uses JDBC, you need to familiarize yourself with the JDBC specification and understand how to call JDBC APIs to access a database and manipulate data in that database. Here we introduce some commonly used terms and constructs to help you better understand JDBC programs for DB2.

DB2's JDBC Drivers

DB2 JDBC drivers are installed during the installation of DB2 client or server code. DB2 provides an *app* driver: COM.ibm.db2.jdbc.app.DB2Driver. You would use this driver for *applications* that run on machines where DB2 (client or server) is installed. DB2 also comes with a *net* driver:
COM.ibm.db2.jdbc.net.DB2Driver. You would use this driver when your Java program executes on a machine that does not have DB2 installed, that is, for running applets. The class files for the drivers are packaged in db2java.zip.

The JDBC classes are found in the java.sql package.

Note: The type 3 driver, formerly known as the "net" driver, is deprecated. DB2 Java applets should be migrated to the type 4 driver.

SQLJ Programming

SQLJ source files contain embedded static SQL statements. Even though we covered static embedded SQL in the previous chapter, we will discuss Embedded SQL for Java (SQLJ) separately in this section. This is because Java differs from the traditional host languages like C and also because SQLJ uses JDBC as a foundation for such tasks as connecting to databases and handling SQL errors.

SQLJ programs use JDBC as the runtime interface with DB2; however, any static SQL statements require the application packages to exist in the database before executing the programs. The interaction between SQLJ programs and DB2 is shown in Fig. 14–8.

Fig. 14–8 *SQLJ's interface with DB2*

Because SQLJ applications and applets access the database through DB2's JDBC support, they require the JDBC classes (java.sql.*), and DB2's JDBC driver classes contained in db2java.zip. The SQLJ translator that replaces embedded SQL statements in the SQLJ program uses classes in sqlj.zip (in the sqllib/java directory). However, the interfaces and classes in sqlj.zip are not required for executing the program. To execute SQLJ programs, the SQLJ runtime classes (sqllib/java/runtime.zip) are needed to authenticate and execute any SQL packages that were bound to the database at the precompiling and binding stage.

DB2 Development Center

In DB2 Version 8, the Development Center replaces the Stored Procedure Builder. The Development Center provides an easy-to-use interface for developing routines such as stored procedures and user-defined functions (UDFs).

The Development Center provides a single development environment that supports the entire DB2 family ranging from the workstation to z/OS. You can launch the Development Center as a stand-alone application from the DB2 Universal Database program group or from a DB2 Universal Database center, such as the Control Center, the Command Center, or the Task Center.

With the Development Center, you can:

- Create, build, and deploy Java and SQL stored procedures
- Create, build, and deploy user-defined functions:
  - SQL table and scalar UDFs
  - UDFs that read MQSeries messages
  - UDFs that access OLE DB data sources
  - UDFs that extract data from XML documents
- Debug SQL stored procedures using the integrated debugger
- See the contents of the server for each database connection that is in your project or that you have explicitly added to the Server View. You can also view and work with other database objects such as tables, triggers, and views.
- Export and import routines and project information.

The Development Center also provides a DB2 development add-in for each of the following development environments:

- Microsoft Visual C++
- Microsoft Visual Basic
- Microsoft Visual InterDev

With the add-ins, you can access the features of the Development Center and other DB2 centers from the Microsoft development environment, making it easy to develop and incorporate stored procedures and UDFs.

A sample Development Center screen is found in Figure 14–9.

Fig. 14–9 *DB2 Development Center*

Note: The DB2 Development Center assists you with creating the part of the stored procedure that runs on the database server. You must write the client application separately.

Development Considerations

Summary

The process of creating static embedded SQL program modules was discussed in this chapter. By embedding SQL statements into a programming language, we can manipulate the data contained in a DB2 database. The programming modules containing the SQL statements must be converted from SQL statements to DB2 library APIs. This step is known as the precompilation step, since it is always performed before the programming module is compiled and linked.

This chapter also discussed CLI, ODBC, and JDBC development and what steps are required to develop and execute programs using these interfaces.

Finally, we introduced the DB2 Development Center. This tool can be used to develop, test, and debug user-defined functions and stored procedures.

Development SQL

- ◆ USER-DEFINED FUNCTIONS
- ◆ USER-DEFINED STRUCTURED DATATYPES
- ◆ SYNONYM AND ALIAS
- ◆ COMMIT AND ROLLBACK
- ◆ SQL PROCEDURAL LANGUAGE

*T*his chapter will cover some of the additional SQL features that are included in DB2 that are primarily intended for developers. User-defined functions (UDFs) and user-defined structured datatypes can be used for enhancing the functions and datatypes available in DB2. SYNONYM, ALIAS, COMMIT, and ROLLBACK are used within programs for controlling the access to objects and determining changes in the database. Finally, the SQL Procedural Language (SQL PL) is introduced for its use in triggers, user-defined functions, and for SQL statements.

User-Defined Functions

User-defined functions (UDFs) form the basis of *Object-Relational* extensions to the SQL language along with user-defined types (UDTs) and LOBs. Fundamentally, a database function is a relationship between a set of input data values and a result value. DB2 Universal Database comes with many built-in functions; however, it is possible to create your own column, scalar, and table functions.

There are three types of functions:

- Column
- Scalar
- Table

Column functions take in a set of data values and derive a single result. For example, to determine the average score of all tests taken:

```
SELECT AVG(SCORE) FROM TEST_TAKEN
```

Column functions such as AVG, SUM, and COUNT are detailed in the *DB2 UDB V8.1 SQL Reference*.

Scalar functions take in one value and return another value. For example, to look at all tests taken since 1996:

```
SELECT * FROM TEST_TAKEN
          WHERE YEAR(DATE_TAKEN) > 1996
```

The third type of function, a table function, can only be used in the FROM clause of an SQL statement. It returns columns of a table, resembling a regular created table.

There are a large number of functions built-in to DB2 and can be found in the *DB2 UDB V8.1 SQL Reference*.

In DB2, you can create your own functions (which can be scalar or table functions). A UDF can be written in a high-level programming language such as C, C++, Java, SQL PL, or you can use a single SQL statement.

You can also create a user-defined function based on another UDF or built-in function. This concept is similar to *overloading* classes in object-oriented programming. This is called a *sourced* function. A UDF that you write from scratch is called an *external* function.

Note: In a Windows environment, as part of the Microsoft Object Linking and Embedding (OLE) architecture, DB2 can act as an OLE Automation Controller. Through this mechanism, DB2 can invoke methods of OLE automation objects as external UDFs.

External UDFs, once written and generated as dynamically loadable libraries or classes, must be registered with the database. The `congrat` function shown in Fig. 15–1 is registered using the CREATE FUNCTION statement.

```
CREATE FUNCTION congrat(VARCHAR(30),VARCHAR(40))
        RETURNS CLOB(1K)
        EXTERNAL NAME 'congrat.a!congrat'
        LANGUAGE C
        PARAMETER STYLE DB2SQL
        DETERMINISTIC
        FENCED
        NO SQL
        NO EXTERNAL ACTION
        DISALLOW PARALLEL;
```

Fig. 15–1 *Registering a user-defined function*

Sourced UDFs are registered in the same way, simply by specifying the *parent* source function. This example allows us to create an AVG function for the SCORE data type:

```
CREATE FUNCTION AVG (SCORE)
        RETURNS SCORE
        SOURCE  SYSIBM.AVG(DECIMAL);
```

These CREATE FUNCTION statements place an entry for each UDF in the view SYSCAT.FUNCTIONS. You can view the UDFs registered with the database in the Control Center.

Development SQL

With DB2, you can also create a third type of user-defined function called a *table function*. A table function is a UDF that returns a table to the SQL statement that calls it. This means that a table function can only be referenced in the FROM clause of a SELECT statement. The table function provides a means of including external data in SQL queries. Table functions can read non-DB2 data, for instance, a file on the operating system, tabularize it, and return the data to DB2 as a result set that can subsequently be treated like any other table. For example, the APPFORM table function in the next example takes in a candidate application form, processes it, and returns the data in an appropriate format to be inserted in the CANDIDATE table (except for the candidate ID, which is generated):

```
CREATE FUNCTION appform(VARCHAR(30))
RETURNS TABLE (LNAME VARCHAR(30),FNAME VARCHAR(30),
               INITIAL CHAR(1), HPHONE PHONE,
               WPHONE PHONE, STREETNO VARCHAR(8),
               STREETNAME VARCHAR(20),
               CITY VARCHAR(20),
               PROV_STATE VARCHAR(30),
               CODE CHAR(6), COUNTRY VARCHAR(20))
EXTERNAL NAME 'tbudf!appform'
LANGUAGE C
PARAMETER STYLE DB2SQL
NO SQL
DETERMINISTIC
NO EXTERNAL ACTION
FINAL CALL
DISALLOW PARALLEL
CARDINALITY 20;
```

Fig. 15–2 *User-defined table function - appform*

If we wanted to insert a new candidate into the CANDIDATE table based on his or her application form, we could use the following SELECT statement:

```
INSERT INTO CANDIDATE
   SELECT SUBSTR(GENERATE_UNIQUE(),1,9) AS CID,
          LNAME, FNAME, INITIAL,
          HPHONE, WPHONE,
          STREETNO, STREETNAME, CITY,
          PROV_STATE, CODE, COUNTRY
   FROM appform('D:\DOCS\NEWFORM.TXT');
```

Note: DB2 also provides table functions for accessing data from OLE DB providers. This allows you to incorporate data into your DB2 database or application from a wide variety of relational and non-relational data sources including Oracle, Microsoft SQL Server, and Microsoft Access.

User-defined functions are like any other database object in DB2, meaning that each UDF has a schema name associated with it. Ideally, each UDF is fully qualified when it is called. However, this can be quite difficult and can limit the flexibility of SQL queries. The alternative is to use the special register CURRENT FUNCTION PATH. DB2 uses this path to resolve unqualified function references. The path in this case is not a list of directories, but a list of schema names such as "SYSIBM", "SYSFUN" or "DB2CERT". SYSFUN is the schema used for built-in UDFs. Note that the authorities needed to create UDFs are the same as those required to create stored procedures.

For more information on the various types of UDFs and the parameters used in the CREATE FUNCTION statement, please refer to the *DB2 UDB V8.1 Application Development Guide: Building and Running Applications.*

SQL-Bodied Scalar Functions

The previous examples referred to user-defined functions and table functions that used a programming language such as C, C++, SQL PL, or Java to create the logic associated with the function. An alternative method of creating these functions is through the use of SQL statements.

```
CREATE FUNCTION BONUS(salary int, bonus_percent int)
   RETURNS INT
   LANGUAGE SQL CONTAINS SQL
   RETURN
     (
     salary * bonus_percent / 100
     );
```

Fig. 15–3 *User-defined function - BONUS*

The CREATE FUNCTION statement allows the use of a single SQL statement to calculate the value to be returned. The BONUS function takes the salary value and calculates the bonus based on a percentage rate. This function could now be used in an SQL statement to calculate the bonus for an employee:

```
VALUES bonus(30000,10);

1
-----------
        3000
```

Fig. 15–4 *Using the BONUS function*

This function could be used anywhere in an SQL statement where a normal function could be used. Figure 15–5 illustrates how the BONUS function could be used as part of an INSERT statement.

```
UPDATE EMPLOYEE
  SET BONUS_PAY = BONUS(EMPLOYEE.SALARY, 10);
```

Fig. 15–5 *Advanced use of the BONUS function*

The body of the function can only consist of one SQL statement and no form of logic is allowed. However, the SQL language does include the CASE statement, so this can allow for a limited form of logic. The BONUS function is modified in Figure 15–6 to return different bonus values depending on the salary level.

```
CREATE FUNCTION BONUS(salary int, bonus_percent int)
   RETURNS INT
   LANGUAGE SQL CONTAINS SQL
   RETURN
     (
     CASE
       WHEN salary <= 20000 then salary / bonus_percent
       WHEN salary <= 30000 then salary / bonus_percent / 2
       WHEN salary <= 40000 then salary / bonus_percent / 4
       ELSE 0
     END
     );
```

Fig. 15–6 *BONUS function - Additional logic*

The following SQL shows the result from four different salary values:

```
VALUES BONUS(20000,10), BONUS(30000,10), BONUS(40000,10),
BONUS(50000,10);

1
-----------
       2000
       1500
       1000
          0
```

Fig. 15–7 *Using the BONUS function*

Note that the limitation of one SQL statement per function body only applies if the return statement is used. A developer can use SQL procedural statement (SQL PL) statements to add additional logic to a user-defined function. See the section on "SQL Procedural Language" on page 825.

SQL-Bodied Table Functions

User-defined table functions can also be written using a single SQL statement. This gives the user the capability of creating a table UDF without the need to write a program in C, C++, or Java.

The table UDF can only access database tables as part of the definition, so it is not as flexible as an external UDF. The example in Fig. 15–8 creates a table UDF that returns records from the TEST_TAKEN table where the test scores are between two values.

```
CREATE FUNCTION GET_MARKS(
     begin_range INT,
     end_range   INT)
  RETURNS TABLE(cid    CANDIDATE_ID,
               number TEST_ID,
               score  SCORE)
  LANGUAGE SQL READS SQL DATA
  RETURN
    SELECT CID, NUMBER, SCORE FROM TEST_TAKEN
       WHERE
           INTEGER(SCORE) BETWEEN
                 begin_range AND end_range;
```

Fig. 15–8 *GET_MARKS table function*

Note the extensive use of user-defined types in this example. The function takes two SCORE arguments that represent the range of marks that we want to retrieve from the table. This table function can now be used as part of a select statement. The SQL in Fig. 15–9 retrieves the list of candidates who scored between 60 and 70 percent on their test.

```
SELECT * FROM TABLE(GET_MARKS(60,70)) AS MARKS

CID NUMBER SCORE
--- ------ -----------
111 500            65
111 502            67
```

Fig. 15–9 *GET_MARKS table function usage*

In order to use the table function, the SQL statement must make use of the TABLE clause with the table function imbedded within it. In addition, the resulting table must be named with the AS clause.

The table that is returned via the table function can also have additional SQL predicates applied to it. For instance, the SQL could have been modified to only return those marks for test number 500:

```
SELECT * FROM TABLE(GET_MARKS(60,70)) AS MARKS
   WHERE NUMBER = TEST_ID('500');

CID NUMBER SCORE
--- ------ -----------
111 500            65
111 502            67
```

Fig. 15–10 *GET_MARKS table function usage with additional logic*

The table UDF can be used in situations where the developer wants to dynamically control the rows being returned to a user. A view definition could have been created to return information about the TEST_TAKEN table, but the definition would have been static. For instance, the following view definition would return exactly the same result:

```
CREATE VIEW GET_MARKS AS (
    SELECT CID, NUMBER, SCORE FROM TEST_TAKEN
        WHERE
            INTEGER(SCORE) BETWEEN 60 AND 70;
```

Fig. 15–11 *GET_MARKS as a VIEW*

However, it will only return the scores between 60 and 70. In contrast, the table UDF can use variables to change the rows that are returned.

More information on user-defined table definitions can be found in the *DB2 UDB V8.1 SQL Reference* and how to develop these functions using a high-level language are found in the *DB2 UDB V8.1 Application Development Guide: Building and Running Applications*.

Structured Datatypes

Structured datatypes (or sometimes referred to as abstract datatypes) is extended to table definitions. The structured datatype is similar to the typed tables discussed in "Advanced SQL" on page 343. However, these datatypes are used within the definition of the table itself, rather than being used to define tables.

For instance, our DB2CERT database contained information about the candidates taking the test. The original definition for the table is shown in Figure 15–12.

```
CREATE TABLE CANDIDATE
  (CID              CANDIDATE_ID     NOT NULL,
   LNAME            VARCHAR(10)      NOT NULL,
   FNAME            VARCHAR(8)       NOT NULL,
   INITIAL          CHAR(1),
   HPHONE           PHONE,
   WPHONE           PHONE,
   STREETNO         VARCHAR(8),
   STREETNAME       VARCHAR(15)      NOT NULL,
   CITY             VARCHAR(10)      NOT NULL,
   PROV_STATE       VARCHAR(10)      NOT NULL,
   CODE             CHAR(6)          NOT NULL,
   COUNTRY          VARCHAR(10)      NOT NULL,
   CERT_DBA         CHAR(1) NOT NULL WITH DEFAULT,
   CERT_APP         CHAR(1) NOT NULL WITH DEFAULT,
   PRIMARY KEY (CID)
  );
```

Fig. 15–12 *Table definition for the CANDIDATE table*

A number of UDTs were used in the definition of this table. For instance, a UDT called CANDIDATE_ID was created to represent a unique identifier for this individual. Further down the table definition, a number of fields were created for storing the address information of the candidate in the table. These multiple fields could be combined into one structured datatype definition as shown in Figure 15–13.

```
CREATE TYPE ADDRESS_TYPE AS
  (
  STREETNO      VARCHAR(8),
  STREETNAME    VARCHAR(15),
  CITY          VARCHAR(10),
  PROV_STATE    VARCHAR(10),
  CODE          CHAR(6),
  COUNTRY       VARCHAR(10)
  )
MODE DB2SQL WITH FUNCTION ACCESS INSTANTIABLE;
```

Fig. 15–13 *Creating structured datatype*

Now that the definition has been created, we can use it as part of the table creation:

```
CREATE TABLE CANDIDATE
  (CID          CANDIDATE_ID      NOT NULL,
  LNAME         VARCHAR(10)       NOT NULL,
  FNAME         VARCHAR(8)        NOT NULL,
  INITIAL       CHAR(1),
  HPHONE        PHONE,
  WPHONE        PHONE,
  ADDRESS       ADDRESS_TYPE NOT NULL,
  CERT_DBA      CHAR(1) NOT NULL WITH DEFAULT,
  CERT_APP      CHAR(1) NOT NULL WITH DEFAULT,
  PRIMARY KEY (CID))
```

Fig. 15–14 *Creating CANDIDATE table with the address structure*

The use of structured datatypes can help simplify the definitions of tables that have many common elements. This will also make it much easier to develop applications that use object-oriented techniques. Your structured datatypes can contain other structured datatypes as well as UDTs within them.

There are a number of administrative changes that you need to be aware of when using these datatypes in the definition of the table. The first change is how elements are inserted into a table. The relational model always assumes that a column contains one value. Because of this restriction, a number of new operators were required to allow structures to be inserted into tables. For instance, the INSERT command needs to know how to insert a structure.

To illustrate the use of these new operators, we will create a new table with a structured datatype of COMPENSATION.

```
CREATE TYPE COMPENSATION AS
  (
  SALARY      INT,
  BONUS       INT,
  COMMISSION  INT
  )
MODE DB2SQL WITH FUNCTION ACCESS INSTANTIABLE;
```

Fig. 15–15 *Creating COMPENSATION datatype*

The COMPENSATION structure contains three elements that make up a person's pay. This structure will be used in the creation of an EMPLOYEE table.

```
CREATE TABLE EMPLOYEE
  (
  NAME  CHAR(10),
  PAY   COMPENSATION
  )
```

Fig. 15–16 *Creating EMPLOYEE table with COMPENSATION datatype*

At this point we need to insert some information into the EMPLOYEE table. To insert values into the PAY column, we use the COMPENSATION constructor (similar to a casting function):

```
INSERT INTO EMPLOYEE VALUES (
'Shirley',
COMPENSATION()..SALARY(30000)..BONUS(1000)..COMMISSION(3000)
)
```

Fig. 15–17 *Inserting a structure into the EMPLOYEE table*

The COMPENSATION constructor indicates to DB2 that the fields following it make up part of the structure and the double-dot "`..`" notation combines the elements. The values needed to be cast as a COMPENSATION type since the PAY column is defined as a COMPENSATION type.

Fortunately for the developer, you can also generate a PAY SQL-bodied function that makes the syntax more readable.

```
CREATE FUNCTION PAY(A INT, B INT, C INT)
   RETURNS COMPENSATION
   LANGUAGE SQL
   RETURN(
      COMPENSATION()..SALARY(A)..BONUS(B)..COMMISSION(C)
   );
```

Fig. 15–18 *Creating PAY constructor*

Now the SQL for inserting the structure can be simplified:

```
INSERT INTO EMPLOYEE VALUES
(
'Katrina',PAY(40000,2000,6000)
)
```

Fig. 15–19 *Using PAY function to insert a structure*

After the data has been inserted into the table, you must use the ".." notation to extract the individual elements of the structure. When you define your structured datatype, DB2 generates a number of functions that allow you to extract the values without using the double-dot notation. The two statements found in Figure 15–20 generate identical results:

```
SELECT NAME, PAY..SALARY, PAY..BONUS, PAY..COMMISSION
   FROM EMPLOYEE;

SELECT NAME, SALARY(PAY), BONUS(PAY), COMMISSION(PAY)
   FROM EMPLOYEE;

NAME          2            3            4
----------  -----------  -----------  -----------
SHIRLEY        30000         1000         3000
KATRINA        40000         2000         6000
```

Fig. 15–20 *Selecting information from the EMPLOYEE table*

When displaying structures, DB2 does not generate column names as in the case of regular column types. The user must supply column names through the use of the AS keyword in the SELECT list.

The structure elements can also be used in the where clause and in any part of the SQL that uses column information. For instance, the previous SQL could be modified to return only those employees who have a salary >= 30000 and a bonus and commission that do not exceed 5000 in value.

```
SELECT NAME, PAY..SALARY, PAY..BONUS, PAY..COMMISSION
   FROM EMPLOYEE
WHERE
   SALARY(PAY) >= 30000 AND
   (BONUS(PAY) + PAY..COMMISSION <= 5000);

NAME          2            3            4
----------  -----------  -----------  -----------
SHIRLEY          30000         1000         3000
```

Fig. 15–21 *Selecting information from the EMPLOYEE table with logic*

Figure 15–21 illustrates the use of the double-dot notation and the casting functions against the same structure.

Finally, the developer or DBA needs to create some transform functions for DB2 so that it can handle SELECT commands that do not explicitly name the columns in the select list. The following SQL statement will generate an error:

```
SELECT * FROM EMPLOYEE;

SQL20015N  A TRANSFORM GROUP "DB2_PROGRAM" IS NOT DEFINED
   FOR DATA TYPE "DB2CERT.COMPENSATION".  SQLSTATE=42741
```

Fig. 15–22 *Error when selecting without column names*

DB2 does not know how to represent the PAY structure found within the EMPLOYEE table. In order to make a SELECT * work, two steps need to be taken. First, a UDF needs to be created that returns the contents of the structure as one value. This value must be a simple type, not a structure. For instance, we could create a function that returns the value of each field in the PAY structure as a string of values. The SQL in Figure 15–23 returns the PAY structure as a character string.

```
CREATE FUNCTION SHOW_PAY (P COMPENSATION)
    RETURNS VARCHAR(25)
    LANGUAGE SQL
    RETURN '(' ||
            RTRIM(CHAR(P..SALARY)) || ',' ||
            RTRIM(CHAR(P..BONUS)) || ',' ||
            RTRIM(CHAR(P..COMMISSION)) ||')' ;

SELECT NAME, SHOW_PAY(PAY) FROM EMPLOYEE;

NAME         2
----------   ------------------------
SHIRLEY      (30000,1000,3000)
KATRINA      (40000,2000,6000)
```

Fig. 15–23 *SHOW_PAY function for displaying PAY column*

After this function is defined, we need to create a transform for this column so that DB2 knows how to handle it in a select statement.

```
CREATE TRANSFORM FOR COMPENSATION
    DB2_PROGRAM
        ( FROM SQL WITH FUNCTION SHOW_PAY(COMPENSATION)) ;
```

Fig. 15–24 *Transform function for COMPENSATION type*

Once the transform is defined, the PAY column can be used in a select list without worrying about the structure underneath.

```
SELECT * FROM EMPLOYEE;

NAME         PAY
----------   ------------------------
SHIRLEY      (30000,1000,3000)
KATRINA      (40000,2000,6000)
```

Fig. 15–25 *Transform function for COMPENSATION type*

Since the PAY column can now be represented as a single value, DB2 places the column heading at the top of the results.

When creating transforms for columns, the developer or DBA should understand how a user would interpret the column. The transform function that was defined previously represents the PAY column as a character string. This may seem odd to a user who expects to see a single value being returned from the database. A more-intuitive definition would be to have the SHOW_PAY function calculate the actual employee PAY by summing the columns together. The SQL in Figure 15–26 creates a function that returns the sum of the three PAY elements.

```
CREATE FUNCTION SHOW_PAY (P COMPENSATION)
      RETURNS INT
      LANGUAGE SQL
      RETURN P..SALARY + P..BONUS + P..COMMISSION ;

SELECT NAME, SHOW_PAY(PAY) FROM EMPLOYEE;

NAME           2
----------  -----------
SHIRLEY          34000
KATRINA          48000

SELECT * FROM EMPLOYEE;

NAME         PAY
----------  -----------
SHIRLEY          34000
KATRINA          48000
```

Fig. 15–26 *Alternative function for displaying PAY column*

The advantage of creating a function like SHOW_PAY that returns a single value is that it can now be used in a regular SQL statement to select records based on the total pay of the individual. For instance, the following SQL statement will return only those employees who have a total pay greater than 45000.

```
SELECT * FROM EMPLOYEE
   WHERE SHOW_PAY(PAY) > 45000;

NAME         PAY
----------  -----------
KATRINA          48000
```

Fig. 15–27 *Alternative function for displaying PAY column*

User-defined structured datatypes and user-defined functions are powerful features within DB2. A development group can create common structures and routines to be used within the database. That can lead to better control of data definitions as well as to encourage more code reuse through the use of UDFs.

Schemas and Aliases

In this section, we will discuss two database objects, schemas and aliases, which have not been discussed in detail in the previous chapters.

Schema

A schema is a database entity that represents a collection of named objects within a DB2 database. The schema name is actually part of the fully qualified name of the object being accessed. When database objects are being defined using the SQL CREATE <db object> statement, a qualifier or schema-name should be provided in the name of the database object.

Schemas may be explicitly created using the CREATE SCHEMA statement with a one user specified as the owner. If the user Bert wanted to create tables with a schema called DB2, the DBADM could use the Control Center to create the schema for BERT or use the following statement. Since BERT owns the schema, he can create objects within the schema.

```
CREATE SCHEMA DB2 AUTHORIZATION BERT
```

Schema names are associated with many database objects, including tables, views, indexes, and packages. For application development purposes, the table, view, and package objects are of primary interest because indexes cannot be directly referenced in SQL DML statements (INSERT, UPDATE, DELETE). If the creator of a database object does not include the schema name in the database object definition, then the object will be created using the creator's authorization ID (assuming IMPLICIT_SCHEMA has not been revoked for the creator).

For example, assume that a user called MARK created a table using the statement: CREATE TABLE TABLE1 (C1 CHAR(3)). The complete name of the database object would be MARK.TABLE1, and the application would have to specify the entire name.

 Note: Avoid using unqualified table or view names in SQL statements.

In Fig. 15–28, the schema for the table called TEST is DB2CERT. If you refer to this table in an embedded SQL application, you should reference the table using its fully qualified name, DB2CERT.TEST. Failure to include the schema name can result in unexpected behavior.

In an embedded SQL application, unqualified database objects are qualified with the authorization ID of the person who performed the BIND command to bind the application package to the database. In a dynamic SQL application, unqualified database objects are qualified with the authorization ID of the person who is executing the statement. This difference is a major consideration during application development because it affects the required data access privileges.

The fully qualified name of a database object must be unique within the database. Thus, from the previous example, another table can exist with the name TEST, if the schema name is something other than DB2CERT.

```
create table db2cert.test (
    number        test_id      not null,
    name          varchar(30)  not null,
    type          char(1)      not null,
    avgscore      score        not null,
    cutscore      score        not null,
    length        minutes      not null,
    totaltaken    integer      not null,
    totalpassed   integer      not null,
    constraint primary key(number))
```

Fig. 15–28 *Creating a table specifying a schema*

Alias

An alias can be used to refer to a table within the database. If an application contains SQL statements that access tables based on an alias, then the alias can be defined to represent different tables without modifying the application. An alias can be created for a table or another alias.

For example, assume a user named DANA created a table called PRICES, and a user named AUSTIN created a table called PRICES. These tables reside in the same database and are named DANA.PRICES and AUSTIN.PRICES. Suppose you are asked to develop an application that would access both of these tables and produce summary reports. Also assume that you are using an embedded SQL technique. Your application would require two sets of queries, one for each schema name: DANA and AUSTIN. This is not a good programming technique and is prone to error. For instance, if you find a problem with one of the SQL statements, you may forget to make the corresponding change in the statement that accesses the other table. An alias can be used as the target table name for the SQL statements in your application. If the referenced object in your application is an alias, it can be defined to represent the table DANA.PRICES or AUSTIN.PRICES.

Let's create the alias objects that could be used in the example scenario.

```
CREATE ALIAS DB2CERT.PRICES FOR DANA.PRICES
OR
CREATE ALIAS DB2CERT.PRICES FOR AUSTIN.PRICES
```

The application could be developed referencing the table object as DB2CERT.PRICES. The application would then access whichever table has been defined as the source for the DB2CERT.PRICES alias. There can only be one definition for the DB2CERT.PRICES alias at any given time within the database. You could not create the DB2CERT.PRICES alias twice, for example. However, the same alias name could be used in different databases.

Another example of using aliases involves creating multiple aliases for the same source table or view. Assume that the database object was called DB2CERT.PRICES, and we wanted to allow the users ANDREW and GEOFF to issue the following SQL statement from the CLP:

```
SELECT * FROM PRICES
```

The SELECT statement did not explicitly qualify the table name by using the table's schema name. Since the CLP interface is an embedded dynamic SQL interface, the table is implicitly qualified with the current authorization IDs. The target table for this query would be ANDREW.PRICES and GEOFF.PRICES. These are two different tables. However, the goal of the SELECT statement was to access the data in the DB2CERT.PRICES table. Create two aliases to provide the desired results:

```
CREATE ALIAS ANDREW.PRICES FOR DB2CERT.PRICES
CREATE ALIAS GEOFF.PRICES FOR DB2CERT.PRICES
```

If you were not the user ANDREW, and you tried to create the alias ANDREW.PRICES, you would require CREATE_IN authority in the schema ANDREW, or DBADM or SYSADM authority to create the alias ANDREW.PRICES in the schema. Once you create the alias ANDREW.PRICES, the privileges on the referenced table or view (in this case, `DB2CERT.PRICES`) are used to determine if access is granted to users on `ANDREW.PRICES`.

COMMIT and ROLLBACK

A program must establish a connection to the target database server before it can run any executable SQL statements. This connection identifies both the authorization ID of the user who is running the program and the name of the database server against which the program is run. After the connection has been established, the program can issue SQL statements that manipulate data (`SELECT`, `INSERT`, `UPDATE`, or `DELETE`), define and maintain database objects (`CREATE`, `ALTER`, or `DROP`), and initiate control operations (`GRANT`, `REVOKE`, `COMMIT`, or `ROLLBACK`). These statements are considered as parts of a transaction. A transaction is a sequence of SQL statements (possibly with intervening program logic) that the database manager treats as a whole. An alternative term that is often used for transaction is unit of work. To ensure the consistency of data at the transaction level, the system makes sure that either all operations within a transaction are completed or none are completed.

A transaction begins implicitly with the first executable SQL statement and ends with either a `COMMIT` or a `ROLLBACK` statement or when the program ends. In some DB2 programming interfaces, you do not issue the `COMMIT` or `ROLLBACK` SQL statements explicitly, but instead employ APIs or object methods to end transactions that result in a commit or a rollback. A commit makes the changes performed during the current transaction permanent, and a rollback restores the data to the state it was in prior to beginning the transaction.

To properly end a program, it must perform these steps:

- End the current transaction (if one is in progress) by explicitly issuing either a `COMMIT` statement or a `ROLLBACK` statement.
- Release the connection to the database server by using the `CONNECT RESET` statement or the appropriate function or method for your programming interface.
- Clean up resources used by the program. For example, free any temporary storage.

Developers can also create intermediate `SAVEPOINTS` within their SQL so that they can selectively `ROLLBACK` to a prior point in their code. This feature allows for greater flexibility when working with modular code and stored procedures.

SQL Procedural Language

The SQL procedural language (SQL PL) consists of SQL control statements that allow the structured query language to be used in a manner similar to writing a program in a programming language like C++ or Java. SQL control statements provide the capability to control the logic flow, declare and set variables, and handle warnings and exceptions. Some SQL control statements can also include other nested SQL statements.

While SQL PL was originally designed as a stored procedure language, it can so be used in the body of a routine, trigger, or a dynamic compound statement.

SQL PL blocks contain the following control statements, along with any SQL that might be required:

- DECLARE
- SET assignment statement
- FOR statement
- GET DIAGNOSTICS statement
- IF statement
- ITERATE statement
- LEAVE statement
- RETURN statement
- SIGNAL statement
- WHILE statement

A SQL PL block can issue most SQL statements, except for the following:

- CREATE any object other than indexes, tables, or views
- DROP any object other than indexes, tables, or views
- FLUSH EVENT MONITOR
- REFRESH TABLE
- RENAME TABLE, RENAME TABLESPACE
- REVOKE
- SET INTEGRITY

A description of all of the SQL PL control statements are described in the following sections.

BEGIN ATOMIC Statement

All SQL PL statement blocks must start with the BEGIN ATOMIC statement and end with a corresponding END statement. The SQL statements found between these keywords are interpreted as SQL PL control statements. Outside of this block, these keywords will cause an SQL error. To run a series of commands as a stand-alone block of SQL, make sure that you use a different SQL delimiter instead of the semi-colon. The semi-colon is used as a statement terminator in SQL PL so you will need to use a different character to delimit multiple commands within your script or commands. The following figure contains a set of SQL that will execute as part of a SQL PL block (Fig. 15–29):

```
CONNECT TO DB2CERT@
DROP TABLE TEST@
CREATE TABLE TEST (NUMBER INT)@

BEGIN ATOMIC
  DECLARE I INT DEFAULT 1;
  WHILE I <= 10 DO
    INSERT INTO TEST VALUES(I);
    SET I = I + 1;
  END WHILE;
END@

SELECT * FROM TEST@
QUIT@
```

Fig. 15–29 *SQL PL commands in a file*

Note how in the previous example that each command is terminated with a "@" sign. To execute this SQL as part of a script, the CLP command must be modified to allow the use of the dollar sign as a delimiter. Assuming the name of this file was called SQLBLOCK.DB2, the following command will execute this SQL (Fig. 15–30):

```
DB2 -td@ -v -f SQLBLOCK.DB2
```

Fig. 15–30 *Using a @ sign as a delimiter*

While the SQL PL can command a variety of SQL commands, a SELECT statement will not be returned to the calling program (either CLP or an application) as a open cursor that records can be fetched from. From a user perspective, issuing a SELECT statement within a BEGIN ATOMIC block will not return a result set, while outside of the block it will. For instance, if the SQL PL in figure 15–29 was modified to place the SELECT statement outside the control block, no result set would be returned when you issued the DB2 command (Figure 15–31):

```
CONNECT TO DB2CERT@
DROP TABLE TEST@
CREATE TABLE TEST (NUMBER INT)@

BEGIN ATOMIC
  DECLARE I INT DEFAULT 1;
  WHILE I <= 10 DO
    INSERT INTO TEST VALUES(I);
    SET I = I + 1;
  END WHILE;
  SELECT * FROM TEST;
END@

QUIT@
```

Fig. 15–31 *SQL PL with no output*

Normally you would use SQL PL blocks to apply complex logic to INSERT, UPDATE, and DELETE statements. If you do need to see the results of these statements, you must issue the SELECT outside the scope of the SQL PL block. However, you can use a SELECT statement within an SQL PL block to calculate values, find values, or for any other purpose other than to display results.

For user-defined functions, the RETURN statement is replaced with the BEGIN ATOMIC block (Figure 15–32):

```
CREATE FUNCTION TAX_PAYMENT(SALARY INT) RETURNS INT
  LANGUAGE SQL READS SQL DATA
  BEGIN ATOMIC
    ... SQL PL ...
  END
```

Fig. 15–32 *SQL PL for a user-defined function*

The same is true for a trigger definition where you can now replace a single SQL statement with a block of SQL PL (Figure 15–33):

```
CREATE TRIGGER CHECK_TAXES NO CASCADE BEFORE
  INSERT ON EMPLOYEE_WAGES REFERENCING NEW AS X
  FOR EACH ROW MODE DB2SQL
  BEGIN ATOMIC
    ... SQL PL ...
  END
```

Fig. 15–33 *SQL PL for a trigger*

Development SQL

SQL PL can extend the capabilities of triggers and user-defined functions within a DB2 database, as well as giving the developer and DBA more flexibility in the types of SQL scripts that they can create. The following sections describe in more detail the syntax that is allowed in SQL PL command blocks. For a more detailed discussion of SQL PL in the use of stored procedures, please refer to the *DB2 Universal Database Version 8.1 Application Development Certification Guide.*

DECLARE Statement

The DECLARE statement is used to specify which variables will be used within the SQL PL block as well as error handling definitions. The basic structure of the DECLARE statement is (Figure 15–34):

```
DECLARE SQL-VARIABLE-NAME DATA-TYPE DEFAULT NULL
                                    DEFAULT DEFAULT-VALUES

DECLARE CONDITION-NAME CONDITION FOR SQLSTATE VALUE ...
```

Fig. 15–34 *DECLARE statement*

The variable name can be any valid SQL identifier and contain any SQL data type, including user-defined datatypes and structured types. Along with the definition, the user can include a default value for the variables. Users should take care in not creating variables that conflict with DB2 special register names or column names that my be returned as part of a FOR loop. The following figure lists some valid DECLARE statements (Figure 15–35):

```
DECLARE PAY DECIMAL(15,2) DEFAULT 10000.00;
DECLARE SALARY COMPENSATION;
```

Fig. 15–35 *DECLARE examples*

Note that only one variable can be defined per DECLARE statement. In addition to defining the variables that will be used in the SQL PL block, the DECLARE statement can also be used to assign a symbolic name to a specific SQL error code. This declaration is only used for simplifying coding within the SQL PL block and does not give the block of code any error handling capability. For more details on how these error codes are handled, see the section on the SIGNAL command.

SET Statement

The SET command is used to assign values to declared variables, or to columns in a table in a trigger definition. Many program languages drop the requirement of using a SET statement when assigning variables, but this is a mandatory clause in the SQL PL language.

A variable can be assigned any one of the following values:

- a constant
  ```
  SET BONUS = 5000.00;
  ```
- the contents of another variable or a parameter from the function arguments
  ```
  SET PAY = EMPLOYEE_SALARY;
  ```
- the result of a calculation
  ```
  SET PAY = EMPLOYEE_SALARY + BONUS + COMMISSION * 1.53;
  ```
- result of an SQL statement that returns only one value
  ```
  SET PAY = SELECT SALARY FROM EMPLOYEE WHERE EMPNO = 5;
  ```
- the NULL value
  ```
  SET PAY = NULL;
  ```
- the default value, based on the definition of the variable
  ```
  SET PAY = DEFAULT;
  ```
- the contents of a special register
  ```
  SET USERID = USERID;
  SET TODAY = CURRENT DATE;
  ```

The same rules that apply to SQL statements are used to determine the way that calculations are performed on variables, including operator precedence and casting to other datatypes. Multiple assignments can be performed in one SET statement as illustrated in the following example (Figure 15–36):

```
SET PAY = 10000.00; SET BONUS = 1500.00;

SET PAY = 10000.00, BONUS = 1500.00;

SET (PAY, BONUS) = (10000.00, 1500.00);

SET (PAY, BONUS) =
    SELECT (PAY, BONUS) FROM EMPLOYEE WHERE EMPNO = '000010';
```

Fig. 15–36 *SET statement*

The last form of the SET statement is very useful when retrieving columns values via a SELECT statement.

IF/THEN/ELSE Statement

SQL PL contains a number of logical constructs that allow the user to modify processing based on the outcome of some test. There are three forms of the IF statement:

- IF THEN/END IF block

    The logic within the IF THEN/END IF block is executed when the condition found within the IF statement is TRUE. If the value is not TRUE, processing continues after the END IF statement.

- IF THEN/ELSE/END IF block

    The IF THEN/ELSE/END IF is similar to the IF statement, except that if the condition found within the IF statement is true, processing will continue until the ELSE statement is found, and then skip down to the END IF statement. If the condition is FALSE, processing continues from the ELSE statement to the END IF statement.

- IF THEN/ELSEIF/ELSE/END IF block

    Although SQL PL control statements lack the CASE statement, this limitation can be overcome through the use of IF THEN/ELSEIF logic. The ELSEIF is a convenient short form of having multiple IF THEN/ELSE IF THEN blocks of code. When the IF statement is evaluated and the result is FALSE, the processing jumps down to the next ELSEIF block. If this ELSEIF is false, then processing will continue with the next ELSEIF block in the list and so on until one of the ELSEIF blocks is true. If none of the sections is true, processing will go to the final ELSE clause. This structure lets you handle multiple conditions and allow for a final section of logic that catches errors that were not handled in previous code.

The example shown in figure 15–37 shows all three types of IF statements. The logic within the IF statement can contain any valid SQL that will result in a TRUE or FALSE value. Boolean expressions that include the standard comparison operators are allowed (<,=,>,<>,<=,>=,NOT), along with SQL statements that result in a true or false value.

```
IF (COMMISSION > 30000) THEN
    BONUS = COMMISSION / 100;
END IF;

IF (PAY + BONUS + COMMISSION > 100000) THEN
    SALARY = 0.90 * (PAY + BONUS + COMMISSION);
ELSE
    SALARY = PAY + BONUS + COMMISSION;
END IF;

IF (SALARY > 100000) THEN
    TAX_RATE = 0.50;
ELSEIF (SALARY > 70000) THEN
    TAX_RATE = 0.40;
ELSEIF (SALARY > 50000) THEN
    TAX_RATE = 0.30;
ELSE
    TAX_RATE = 0.10;
END IF;
```

Fig. 15–37 *IF statement*

The previous example uses only boolean expression to determine whether or not a condition was TRUE or FALSE. In addition to regular expression operators, the user can also include SQL statements to determine how processing should continue. A few simple examples illustrate the use of SQL in IF statements.

- Using SQL operators to check values

  Instead of using complex comparison statements, a user can take advantage of the SQL syntax available to them and use that instead.

  ```
  IF (SALARY BETWEEN 10000 AND 90000) THEN ...
  IF (DEPTNO IN ('A00','B01','D11')) THEN ...
  ```

- Check for NULL values

  ```
  IF (SALARY IS NULL) THEN ...
  ```

- Check for the existence of values within a table

  ```
  IF (EXISTS (SELECT * FROM EMPLOYEE)) THEN ...
  IF ((SELECT COUNT(*) FROM EMPLOYEE) > 0) THEN ...
  ```

- Check for values based on a SELECT statement

  ```
  IF (EMP.SALARY < (SELECT AVG(SALARY) FROM EMPLOYEE)) THEN ...
  ```

In summary, the IF statement gives the user a large degree of flexibility in modifying the behavior of their code. The additional power of SQL can also be used as means of controlling the logic within the IF statement.

WHILE Statement

The WHILE statement gives the user the ability to loop within a section of code until the while condition is no longer met. A WHILE statement has the following format (Figure 15–38):

```
LABEL:
  WHILE condition DO
    ... SQL PL ...
  END WHILE LABEL;
```

Fig. 15–38 *WHILE statement*

The condition field within the WHILE clause is identical to the IF statement. You can use either boolean expressions or SQL operators to generate a TRUE or FALSE value. If the calculated value is FALSE, processing will skip all of the logic within the WHILE block and start execution of the first statement after the END WHILE keyword.

The LABEL field is optional for a WHILE statement and can be used to uniquely identify this block of code. The LABEL consists of a unique name that follows the same naming conventions as an SQL column. If LABEL is specified for a WHILE statement, it must be placed on the END WHILE statement as well.

A sample WHILE statement is shown below (Figure 15–39):

```
BEGIN ATOMIC
  DECLARE COUNT INT DEFAULT 5;

  WHILE COUNT > 0 DO
    INSERT INTO DEPARTMENTS VALUES 'F'|| RTRIM(CHAR(COUNT));
    SET COUNT = COUNT - 1;
  END WHILE;
END
```

Fig. 15–39 *WHILE example*

FOR Statement

Users familiar with other programming languages may expect the FOR statement to work in a similar fashion. However, the FOR statement is not intended to be used for executing program logic "n" number of times depending on a loop counter, but rather for executing logic on the rows being returned as the result of a SELECT statement. The syntax of the FOR statement is found in figure 15–40.

```
LABEL:
   FOR row_label AS select statement DO
      ... SQL PL ...
   END FOR LABEL;
```

Fig. 15–40 *FOR statement*

The LABEL field is optional for a FOR statement and can be used to uniquely identify this block of code. The LABEL consists of a unique name that follows the same naming conventions as an SQL column. If LABEL is specified for a FOR statement, it must be placed on the END FOR statement as well.

The ROW_LABEL is similar to a FOR label but it is used to identify the row of data being returned by the SELECT statement. For example, the following block of code selects data from the EMPLOYEE table based on BONUS data (Figure 15–41):

```
SET TOTAL_BONUS = 0;
FOR emp AS SELECT * FROM EMPLOYEE WHERE BONUS > 1000 DO
   SET TOTAL_BONUS = TOTAL_BONUS + emp.BONUS;
END FOR;
```

Fig. 15–41 *FOR statement example*

When using FOR loops, a user should not declare variables that my conflict with columns being returned in the SELECT statement. In the event that the column name is already defined as a variable, you will end up getting error messages referring to invalid use of a variable in assignment statements. This is caused by DB2 trying to assign values to a variable that is considered part of a row, rather than to the variable you DECLARED at the beginning. The result set names take precedence over DECLARED variables. This problem does not occur with multiple nested FOR statements that may have the same column names since each answer set will have a different row label.

When results are returned as part of the FOR statement, each column can be accessed either through the direct column name, or through the row label. It is better to use the explicit row label and column name together to avoid ambiguity when trying to modify (or debug) the code at a later date.

Development
SQL

ITERATE Statement

The ITERATE statement is used to cause processing to continue from the beginning of a FOR or WHILE loop. This is used in circumstances where the record does not match a certain criteria and the logic needs to get the next record and start processing over again.

The ITERATE statement must have a label supplied as an argument, so any FOR or WHILE statement that is being used with this function must have a corresponding label associated with it. Users should be cautious in the use of the ITERATE statement in a WHILE loop to ensure that any variable found in the loop logic is incremented or decremented before iterating! A sample use of an ITERATE statement is found below (Figure 15–42):

```
SET TOTAL_BONUS = 0;
CHECK_BONUS:
FOR EMP AS SELECT * FROM EMPLOYEE DO
  IF (EMP.BONUS > 1000) THEN
     SET TOTAL_BONUS = TOTAL_BONUS + EMP.BONUS;
  ELSE
     ITERATE CHECK_BONUS;
  END IF;
END FOR CHECK_BONUS;
```

Fig. 15–42 *ITERATE statement*

LEAVE Statement

The LEAVE statement compliments the ITERATE statement in FOR and WHILE loops. In the event that the user needs to get out of a loop, the LEAVE statement can be used to transfer processing to the first statement after the END that terminates this loop.

LEAVE statement require that a label be supplied as an argument, so any FOR or WHILE statement that you want to exit from must have a label supplied. The following SQL PL will stop processing of records if the maximum bonus for all employees is exceeded (Figure 15–43):

```
SET TOTAL_BONUS = 0;
ADD_BONUS:
FOR EMP AS SELECT * FROM EMPLOYEE DO
  SET TOTAL_BONUS = TOTAL_BONUS + EMP.BONUS;
  IF (TOTAL_BONUS > 10000) THEN
    LEAVE ADD_BONUS;
  END IF;
END FOR ADD_BONUS;
```

Fig. 15–43 *LEAVE statement*

RETURN Statement

The RETURN statement is used to exit out of a function and return a value. The RETURN statement is not supported in SQL PL command blocks or in triggers. If a return code is required then the SIGNAL command should be used instead.

The RETURN statement has a single argument which can be a constant, a variable, a SELECT statement that returns a single value, or the NULL value. Table functions can return multiple rows in the form of a SELECT statement.

The following function returns the cube of a input value (Figure 15–44):

```
CREATE FUNCTION CUBEIT(CUBE INT) RETURNS INT
   LANGUAGE SQL READS SQL DATA
   BEGIN ATOMIC
     DECLARE CUBE_NUMBER INT DEFAULT 0;
     SET CUBE_NUMBER = CUBE * CUBE * CUBE ;
     RETURN CUBE_NUMBER;
   END
```

Fig. 15–44 *RETURN statement*

SIGNAL Statement

In the event that something abnormal happens during the processing of your SQL PL code, you may want to use the SIGNAL command to alert the application of the problem. The SIGNAL command has the following formats (Figure 15–45):

```
SIGNAL SQLSTATE value SET MESSAGE_TEXT='...';
SIGNAL condition SET MESSAGE_TEXT='...'
```

Fig. 15–45 *SIGNAL statement*

The first form of the SIGNAL command requires that you know the SQLSTATE that you want to raise. For instance, SQLSTATE '02000' indicates that no records were found. The SET MESSAGE_TEXT keyword allows you to return diagnostic information back to the calling application so that additional error handling can be done. There are a variety of ways that this function can be used. An initial SELECT statement may return may valid rows, but none may match the criteria required by the function. In this event, an SQLSTATE '02000' may be a valid error to send back to the calling application.

In other cases, the user may want to set up specific error codes that they want to use to signify errors that are generated by a function, and not the SQL code itself. For these types of error codes, users should consider using SQLSTATEs that start with

7, 8, 9, and I through Z. These ranges are not used by DB2 and are available for user-defined errors.

The original CUBEIT function is modified in the following example to raise an error when the number is too big to cube (Figure 15–46):

```
CREATE FUNCTION CUBEIT(CUBE INT) RETURNS INT
  LANGUAGE SQL READS SQL DATA
  BEGIN ATOMIC
    DECLARE CUBE_NUMBER INT DEFAULT 0;
    IF (CUBE_NUMBER > 10000) THEN
      SIGNAL SQLSTATE '98000'
        SET MESSAGE_TEXT = 'NUMBER TOO BIG TO CUBE!';
    END IF;
    SET CUBE_NUMBER = CUBE * CUBE * CUBE ;
    RETURN CUBE_NUMBER;
  END
```

Fig. 15–46 *SIGNAL example*

The results of an invalid cube value are show in figure 15–47:

```
VALUES CUBEIT(600);

1
-----------
SQL0438N  APPLICATION RAISED ERROR WITH DIAGNOSTIC TEXT:
"NUMBER TOO BIG TO CUBE!".  SQLSTATE=98000
```

Fig. 15–47 *SIGNAL results*

As an alternative to placing SQLSTATE codes throughout an application, the user can declare symbolic names for SQLSTATES. This is accomplished in with the DECLARE statement. The following example declares the bad cube number SQL-STATE with the symbolic name of TOOBIG (Figure 15–48):

```
CREATE FUNCTION CUBEIT(CUBE INT) RETURNS INT
  LANGUAGE SQL READS SQL DATA
  BEGIN ATOMIC
    DECLARE CUBE_NUMBER INT DEFAULT 0;
    DECLARE TOOBIG CONDITION FOR SQLSTATE '98000';
    IF (CUBE > 500) THEN
      SIGNAL TOOBIG
        SET MESSAGE_TEXT = 'NUMBER TOO BIG TO CUBE';
    END IF;
    SET CUBE_NUMBER = CUBE * CUBE * CUBE ;
   RETURN CUBE_NUMBER;
  END
```

Fig. 15–48 *SIGNAL with DECLARE statement*

Instead of signalling an error based on the exact SQLSTATE, the program can now just use the symbolic name (TOOBIG) to raise the error. Note that the message text must still be set where the error is raised, rather than in the declare section.

GET DIAGNOSTICS Statement

The GET DIAGNOSTICS statement is used within an SQL PL trigger or block (not function) to return the number of records that were affected by an UPDATE, INSERT, or DELETE statement. The syntax of the GET DIAGNOSTICS command is found below (Figure 15–49):

```
GET DIAGNOSTICS VARIABLE = ROW_COUNT;
```

Fig. 15–49 *GET DIAGNOSTICS statement*

The VARIABLE referenced in the statement is a declared variable that will contain the number of rows that were affected by the previous SQL statement. The following SQL will raise an SQLSTATE when no records are updated as part of an UPDATE command (Figure 15–50):

```
BEGIN ATOMIC
  DECLARE REC_COUNT INT DEFAULT 0;
  UPDATE EMPLOYEE
     SET BONUS = 10000
     WHERE EMPNO = '000000';
  GET DIAGNOSTICS REC_COUNT = ROW_COUNT;
  IF (REC_COUNT = 0) THEN
     SIGNAL SQLSTATE '75000'
        SET MESSAGE_TEXT = 'NO EMPLOYEES FOUND';
  END IF;
END
```

Fig. 15–50 *GET DIAGNOSTICS example*

SQL PL Example

The following SQL shows SQL PL being used in stored procedures, triggers, and user-defined functions. The example will not only illustrate the level of procedural complexity that you can now have in all of these SQL features, but also how portable the language is across all of these environments.

The system that is being designed consists of two simple tables. The EMPLOYEE table contains information on all employees within a company, including their personal information and salary. Along with the salary is a tax field that indicates how much tax the individual needs to pay a year, based on their current salary.

The tax amount in the EMPLOYEE table is calculated from a TAX_RATE table that contains tax percentages based on incremental amounts of salary. This table contains the following data (Table 15–1):

Table 15–1 *Taxation table*

Salary Ranges	Tax Percentage
First 10000	10
Second 10000	15
Next 30000	20
Anything Left	30

Tax is calculated in increments, where the first 10000 is taxed at 10%, the next amount (to 20000) at 15% and so on until we have the final taxation amount. For example, someone earning 35000 a year would pay the following amount:

tax = (10000)*.10 + (10000)*.15 + (15000)*.20 = 5500

The table definition for the TAX_RATE table is found in figure 15–51.

```
CREATE TABLE TAX_RATE
   (
   TAX_BRACKET    INT NOT NULL,
   INCOME_AMOUNT  INT NOT NULL,
   TAX_PCT        DECIMAL(5,2) NOT NULL
   );
INSERT INTO TAX_RATE VALUES
   (1,10000,0.10),
   (2,10000,0.15),
   (3,30000,0.20),
   (4,0,0.30);
```

Fig. 15–51 *TAX_RATE table definition*

Processing of the tax rate information is based on the following logic:

1. Set the tax payable to zero and the remaining salary to the current salary

2. Set the current tax bracket to one

3. Set the taxable amount equal to the lesser of the taxable income amount or the remaining salary. If the taxable income amount is zero then the taxable amount becomes the remaining salary.

4. Add the taxable amount times the tax percentage into the tax payable

5. Subtract the taxable amount from the remaining salary

6. If the remaining salary is not zero, go to the next tax bracket and repeat from step 3

In order to make sure the tax brackets are in the proper order, the TAX_RATE table must be sorted in ascending sequence. Otherwise, it may be possible to get the wrong tax bracket being selected first and generating incorrect results.

This TAX_PAYMENT calculation can be implemented in a number of ways. The first approach is to create a user-defined function that will calculate the tax and have it included as part of an INSERT statement. The code for this TAX_PAYMENT function can be found in figure 15–52.

Development SQL

```
CREATE FUNCTION TAX_PAYMENT(SALARY INT) RETURNS INT
  LANGUAGE SQL READS SQL DATA
  BEGIN ATOMIC
    DECLARE REMAINDER INT DEFAULT 0;
    DECLARE TAX_INCR  INT DEFAULT 0;
    DECLARE TAX_PAID  INT DEFAULT 0;
    DECLARE TAX_RANGE INT DEFAULT 0;
    DECLARE TAXABLE   INT DEFAULT 0;

    IF (SALARY <= 0) THEN
        SIGNAL SQLSTATE '75000'
          SET MESSAGE_TEXT = 'BAD SALARY';
    END IF;

    SET TAX_PAID = 0;
    SET REMAINDER = SALARY;

L1: FOR TAX_RATES AS
      SELECT * FROM TAX_RATE ORDER BY TAX_BRACKET ASC DO
        SET TAX_RANGE = TAX_RATES.INCOME_AMOUNT;
        IF (TAX_RANGE = 0) THEN
            SET TAX_RANGE = REMAINDER;
        END IF;
        IF (TAX_RANGE >= REMAINDER) THEN
            SET TAX_INCR = REMAINDER * TAX_RATES.TAX_PCT;
            SET TAX_PAID = TAX_PAID + TAX_INCR;
            LEAVE L1;
        ELSE
            SET TAX_INCR = TAX_RANGE * TAX_RATES.TAX_PCT;
            SET TAX_PAID = TAX_PAID + TAX_INCR;
            SET REMAINDER = REMAINDER - TAX_RANGE;
        END IF;
      END FOR L1;
      RETURN TAX_PAID;
  END
```

Fig. 15–52 *TAX_PAYMENT function*

After this function is created, a user can reference this function in any SQL statement. The VALUES clause can be very useful in testing the functionality of a new user-defined function (Figure 15–53):

```
VALUES TAX_PAYMENT(35000)

1
-----------
       5500
```

Fig. 15–53 *Sample TAX_PAYMENT calculation*

This function can now be used as part of an INSERT statement to update the tax payable for an employee. Assume that the EMPL (employee) table has the following simple design (Figure 15–54):

```
CREATE TABLE EMPL
   (
   EMPNO    INT NOT NULL,
   SALARY   INT NOT NULL,
   TAX      TNT NOT NULL
   );
```

Fig. 15–54 *EMPLOYEE table*

To insert records into this table with the proper tax value, the SQL would look similar to this (Figure 15–55):

```
INSERT INTO EMPL VALUES
   (1, 50000, TAX_PAYMENT(50000)),
   (2, 30000, TAX_PAYMENT(30000)),
   (3, 64000, TAX_PAYMENT(64000));

SELECT * FROM EMP;

EMPNO          SALARY       TAX
-----------  -----------  -----------
         1        50000         8500
         2        30000         4500
         3        64000        12700
```

Fig. 15–55 *Inserting records into the EMPLOYEE table*

Since we have placed the tax payment calculation into a function, every SQL INSERT or UPDATE statement will require that this function be used. This is probably not the best way to implement this logic since it is possible that a user may forget to use this function. Another approach would be to use this logic within a trigger statement. A trigger will get fired on every INSERT or UPDATE statement and we can guarantee that this logic is used. Figure 15–56 shows the TAX_PAYMENT function moved into the body of an INSERT trigger.

```
CREATE TRIGGER CHECK_TAXES
  NO CASCADE BEFORE
  INSERT ON EMPL
  REFERENCING NEW AS X
  FOR EACH ROW MODE DB2SQL
  BEGIN ATOMIC
    DECLARE REMAINDER INT DEFAULT 0;
    DECLARE TAX_INCR  INT DEFAULT 0;
    DECLARE TAX_PAID  INT DEFAULT 0;
    DECLARE TAX_RANGE INT DEFAULT 0;
    DECLARE TAXABLE   INT DEFAULT 0;

    IF (SALARY <= 0) THEN
        SIGNAL SQLSTATE '75000'
          SET MESSAGE_TEXT = 'BAD SALARY';
    END IF;

    SET TAX_PAID = 0;
    SET REMAINDER = X.SALARY;

L1: FOR TAX_RATES AS
      SELECT * FROM TAX_RATE ORDER BY TAX_BRACKET ASC DO
        SET TAX_RANGE = TAX_RATES.INCOME_AMOUNT;
        IF (TAX_RANGE = 0) THEN
            SET TAX_RANGE = REMAINDER;
        END IF;
        IF (TAX_RANGE >= REMAINDER) THEN
            SET TAX_INCR = REMAINDER * TAX_RATES.TAX_PCT;
            SET TAX_PAID = TAX_PAID + TAX_INCR;
            LEAVE L1;
        ELSE
            SET TAX_INCR = TAX_RANGE * TAX_RATES.TAX_PCT;
            SET TAX_PAID = TAX_PAID + TAX_INCR;
            SET REMAINDER = REMAINDER - TAX_RANGE;
        END IF;
      END FOR L1;
      SET X.TAX = TAX_PAID;
  END
```

Fig. 15–56 _TAX_PAYMENT in a trigger body_

The only changes that had to made to the logic (other than defining a trigger instead of a function) was the substitution of REMAINDER = X.SALARY at the beginning of the logic and SET X.TAX = TAX_PAID instead of a RETURN statement at the end.

If the INSERT statements are run again (without the TAX_PAYMENT function) the following results would be returned (Figure 15–57):

```
INSERT INTO EMPL VALUES
  (1, 50000, 0),
  (2, 30000, 0),
  (3, 64000, 0);

SELECT * FROM EMPL;

EMPNO          SALARY        TAX
-----------  -----------  -----------
          1        50000         8500
          2        30000         4500
          3        64000        12700
          1        50000         8500
          2        30000         4500
          3        64000        12700
```

Fig. 15–57 *Inserting records into the EMPLOYEE table with triggers*

The good news is that the trigger had the same effect as the function! This trigger could have been simplified by making use of the existing TAX_PAYMENT function. The following trigger definition replaces all of the logic with a call to the TAX_PAYMENT function (Figure 15–58):

```
CREATE TRIGGER CHECK_TAXES
  NO CASCADE BEFORE
  INSERT ON EMPL
  REFERENCING NEW AS X
  FOR EACH ROW MODE DB2SQL
  BEGIN ATOMIC
    SET X.TAX = TAX_PAYMENT(X.SALARY);
  END
```

Fig. 15–58 *TAX_PAYMENT function in a trigger*

Issuing the INSERT statements will result in exactly the same results as before. Finally, the logic within the TAX_PAYMENT function can also be placed into a stored procedure. The stored procedure would look similar to the following code (Figure 15–59):

Development SQL

```
CREATE PROCEDURE INSERT_WAGES
    (
    I_EMPNO INT,
    I_SALARY INT
    )
    LANGUAGE SQL MODIFIES SQL DATA
  BEGIN ATOMIC
    DECLARE REMAINDER INT DEFAULT 0;
    DECLARE TAX_INCR  INT DEFAULT 0;
    DECLARE TAX_PAID  INT DEFAULT 0;
    DECLARE TAX_RANGE INT DEFAULT 0;
    DECLARE TAXABLE   INT DEFAULT 0;

    IF (I_SALARY <= 0) THEN
        SIGNAL SQLSTATE '75000'
          SET MESSAGE_TEXT = 'BAD SALARY';
    END IF;

    SET TAX_PAID = 0;
    SET REMAINDER = I_SALARY;

L1: FOR TAX_RATES AS
        SELECT * FROM TAX_RATE ORDER BY TAX_BRACKET ASC DO
          SET TAX_RANGE = TAX_RATES.INCOME_AMOUNT;
          IF (TAX_RANGE = 0) THEN
             SET TAX_RANGE = REMAINDER;
          END IF;
          IF (TAX_RANGE >= REMAINDER) THEN
             SET TAX_INCR = REMAINDER * TAX_RATES.TAX_PCT;
             SET TAX_PAID = TAX_PAID + TAX_INCR;
             LEAVE L1;
          ELSE
             SET TAX_INCR = TAX_RANGE * TAX_RATES.TAX_PCT;
             SET TAX_PAID = TAX_PAID + TAX_INCR;
             SET REMAINDER = REMAINDER - TAX_RANGE;
          END IF;
      END FOR L1;
      INSERT INTO EMPL VALUES (I_EMPNO, I_SALARY, TAX_PAID);
    END
```

Fig. 15–59 *TAX_PAYMENT in a stored procedure*

This stored procedure would be called from an application program and it would INSERT the record into the table, along with calculating the proper tax payment. Before implementing this stored procedure, it would probably be beneficial to drop the INSERT trigger since it will be repeating the same logic on the tax column as the stored procedure would!

In summary, SQL PL can be extremely powerful for a developer, user, or DBA to create sophisticated logic within a number of SQL objects. The code is extremely portable and can be easily moved between different objects without much effort.

SQL PL in Stored Procedures

SQL PL can also be used in the body of DB2 stored procedures, but they differ from SQL PL control statements in a number of aspects.

- SQL PL stored procedures support the following extensions which are not permitted in triggers, UDFs, or SQL statements:

  - ALLOCATE CURSOR, ASSOCIATE LOCATORS, CALL

    SQL PL control statements currently are restricted from calling stored procedures. This is the reason why the ALLOCATE and ASSOCIATE statements are not supported in control statements. It is anticipated that this restriction will be lifted in a future release of DB2.

  - PREPARE, DESCRIBE, OPEN, FETCH

    No cursor processing is allowed in the body of a SQL PL block. The FOR control statement can be used to loop through a answer set.

  - CONNECT, DISCONNECT, SET CONNECTION

    The body of a SQL PLSQL PL block cannot change the current connection.

  - SAVEPOINT, COMMIT, ROLLBACK

    SQL PL blocks cannot set savepoints or rollback work, but they are able to COMMIT work if this is the last statement of the block.

  - CASE, GOTO, LOOP, REPEAT statements

    Most of these control statements can be simulated using a combination of IF and WHILE statements. Although this may make for more complex logic, it doesn't reduce the capability of SQL PL.

  - procedure compound statement

    A SQL control statement is already part of a procedure compound statement, and nesting of these structures is not supported.

  - RESIGNAL

    SQL PL blocks can signal errors, but the ability to resignal to a different error is not supported.

  - INSERT, UPDATE, DELETE

    SQL PL used within a user-defined function (UDF) has the added restriction that it cannot issue any data modification commands. Triggers and SQL PL statements run as SQL commands can modify data. External UDFs written in C, C++, or Java can update data within the scope of the program.

- SQL PL currently requires a C compiler and the SQL PL is compiled into an executable program which is stored for further execution.

For more information on SQL PL as a stored procedure language, either refer to the *DB2 UDB V8.1 SQL Reference*, or the *DB2 SQL Procedural Language for Linux, UNIX and Windows* book from Prentice Hall.

Summary

In this chapter, we have examined additional SQL features used in DB2 application development.

User-defined functions allow a developer to extend the types of functions used within DB2 and allow for the sharing of common routines between users and application developers.

User-defined structured datatypes can be used to create common structures in database tables and allow for tighter control of datatypes in table definitions.

Schemas and aliases can be used to simplify application development and to reduce confusion when accessing objects in a database.

The Commit and Rollback commands provide a way of ensuring transaction integrity within the database.

Finally, the SQL PL language has been introduced as a way of extending the capabilities of triggers, user-defined functions, and SQL commands.

Appendices

DB2 UDB V8.1
Certification Test Objectives

This appendix provides the test objectives for the following exams:

- DB2 UDB V8.1 Family Fundamentals (700)
- DB2 for Linux, UNIX, and Windows Database Administration (701)
- DB2 for Linux, UNIX, and Windows Advanced DBA (704)

How does one certify? There are three basic steps:

1. Understand certification test objectives.

2. Review study guides or take an education course. Then assess your knowledge by taking a free assessment exam at certify.torolab.ibm.com

3. Register and take the certification exam.

For more information on IBM Data Management skills programs please visit:

www.ibm.com/software/data/education.html

Detailed information on the IBM Professional Certification program including the DB2 Universal Database certification exams can be found at:
http://www.ibm.com/certify.

Experience with DB2 Universal Database Version 8.1 is the best route to preparing for the DB2 UDB V8.1 certification exams. This certification guide is intended to be used alongside your day-to-day use of DB2 UDB V8.1 while preparing for the exams.

DB2 UDB Certification Levels

There are five job roles and three levels of certified solution expert associated with the DB2 UDB product in the distributed environment. The following diagram lists the exam numbers and the corresponding certification level associated with it.

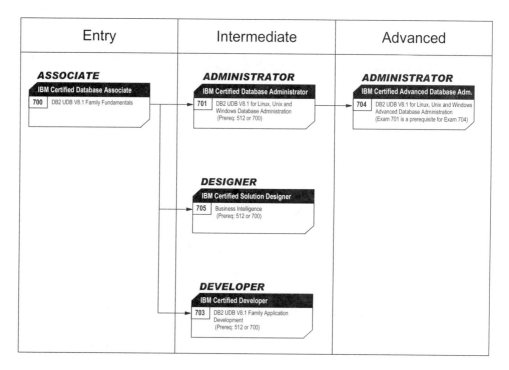

These certification levels are accurate at time of publication, but additional exams may be added to these levels over time. For more information on the certification levels, please refer to the IBM certification site: http://www.ibm.com/certify.

DB2 UDB V8.1 Family Fundamentals (700)

IBM certification in DB2 UDB V8.1 Fundamentals requires an in-depth knowledge of basic SQL, DML, DDL, and an understanding of Database Objects (tables, views, etc.). Further, a basic understanding of the concepts and features of DCL, database creation, data types, stored procedures, programming, components and packaging, protocols supported, installation of products, GUI tools, CLP, basic isolation levels, and import/export is required.

Below are listed the primary objectives which the DB2 UDB V8.1 Fundamentals exam covers. These objectives are listed here to assist you in your preparation for the DB2 UDB V8.1 Fundamentals exam, which is a critical component toward any DB2 UDB V8.1 certification.

To prepare for this exam, Chapters 1 - 8 should be completed. This will give you a good base toward your exam preparation and together with your experience with DB2 UDB V8.1, should prepare you for the DB2 UDB V8.1 Fundamentals (700) test.

I. Planning

- Knowledge of DB2 UDB products (client, server, etc.)
- Knowledge of DB2 tools
- Knowledge of Datawarehouse and OLAP concepts
- Knowledge of non-relational data concepts (extenders, etc.)

II. Security

- Ability to distinguish between authorities and privileges
- Knowledge of different privileges

III. Accessing DB2 UDB Data

- Ability to identify and locate DB2 UDB servers
- Ability to use the DB2 UDB tools to access and manipulate DB2 UDB objects
- Ability to use DB2 UDB tools to create basic DB2 UDB objects

IV. Working with DB2 UDB Data

- Knowledge of transactions
- Given a DDL SQL statement, knowledge to identify results
- Given a DML SQL statement, knowledge to identify results
- Given a DCL SQL statement, knowledge to identify results
- Ability to use SQL to SELECT data from tables
- Ability to use SQL to SORT or GROUP data
- Ability to use SQL to UPDATE, DELETE, or INSERT data
- Ability to call a procedure

V. Working with DB2 UDB Objects

- Ability to demonstrate usage of DB2 UDB data types
- Given a situation, ability to create table
- Knowledge to identify when referential integrity should be used
- Knowledge to identify methods of data constraint
- Knowledge to identify characteristics of a table, view or index

VI. Data Concurrency

- Knowledge to identify factors that influence locking
- Ability to list objects on which locks can be obtained
- Knowledge to identify characteristics of DB2 UDB locks
- Given a situation, knowledge to identify the isolation levels that should be used

DB2 for Linux, UNIX, and Windows Database Administration (701)

Certification Information

The certification role of IBM Certified Solutions Expert requires an in-depth knowledge of DB2 UDB Data Movement, Recovery, Utilities, Configuration, and Authorization and Privileges.

Listed below are the primary objective coverage areas in the DB2 UDB V8.1 Database Administration test, which is required to obtain this certification role. They are listed here to assist you in your preparation toward this certification.

To prepare for this exam, Chapters 9 - 12 should be completed. A good knowledge of the material covered in Chapter 1 - 8 is also required. This will give you a good base toward your exam preparation and together with your significant experience with DB2 UDB V8.1, should prepare you for the DB2 for Linux, UNIX, and Windows Database Administration (701) test.

I. DB2 Server Management

- Ability to configure/manage DB2 instances (e.g. scope)
- Knowledge of DB2 authentication
- Knowledge of DB2 authorizations
- Ability to set user and/or group privileges
- Knowledge of the DB2 force command
- Ability to configure client/server connectivity
- Ability to schedule jobs
- Ability to configure client server connectivity using DISCOVERY
- Skill in interpreting the Notify log

II. Data Placement

- Ability to create a database
- Skill in discussing the use of schemas
- Skill in discussing the various table space states
- Ability to create and discuss the characteristics of an SMS tablespace
- Ability to create and discuss the characteristics of a DMS tablespace
- Ability to create and manipulate the various DB2 objects

III. Database Access

- Ability to create DB2 Tasks using the GUI tools
- Knowledge of the creation and management of indexes
- Ability to create constraints on tables (e.g., RI, Informational, Unique)
- Ability to create views on tables
- Skill in examining the contents of the System Catalog tables
- Ability to use GUI Tools to access DB objects
- Knowledge of how to enforce data uniqueness

IV. Monitoring DB2 Activity

- Ability to obtain/modify database manager configuration information
- Ability to obtain/modify database configuration information
- Ability to capture EXPLAIN/VISUAL EXPLAIN information
- Skill in analyzing EXPLAIN/VISUAL EXPLAIN information (sortheap, buff-page, degree)
- Ability to identify the functions of the DB2 Governor and Query Patroller
- Ability to obtain and modify DB2 registry variables
- Ability to capture snapshots
- Ability to create and activate event monitors
- Ability to Identify output from the Health Center

V. DB2 Utilities

- Ability to use EXPORT utility to extract data from a table
- Ability to use IMPORT utility to insert data into a table
- Ability to use the LOAD utility to insert data into a table
- Knowledge to identify when to use IMPORT vs. LOAD
- Ability to use the REORG, REORGCHK, REBIND and RUNSTATS utilities
- Ability to use DB2Move and DB2Look
- Knowledge of the functionality of the DB2 Advisors
- Ability to use the DB2 Control Center

VI. Backup and Recovery

- Ability to perform database-level and table space level BACKUP & RESTORE
- Knowledge to identify and explain issues on index recreation
- Knowledge of database logging
- Knowledge of crash recovery
- Knowledge of version recovery
- Knowledge of Roll Forward recovery

Certification Information

DB2 for Linux, UNIX, and Windows Advanced DBA (704)

Those who pass this exam are considered experts with proven skills in administering an enterprise-class database environment. They are senior members of the database administration team and manage mission critical systems and applications.

Advanced DB2 administration techniques can be found in the new Advanced DBA Certification Guide and Reference for DB2 UDB v8 for Linux, Unix and Windows, 1st edition, by Dwaine Snow and Thomas Phan, ISBN: 0-13-046388-4.

I. Advanced Administration

- Ability to design table spaces
- Ability to create table spaces
- Ability to manage table spaces
- Ability to design buffer pools
- Ability to create buffer pools
- Ability to manage buffer pools
- Ability to exploit intra-parallelism
- Ability to exploit inter- parallelism
- Ability to design and configure federated database access
- Ability to manage distributed unit of work

II. High Availability

- Ability to develop a logging strategy
- Ability to use advanced backup features
- Ability to use advanced recovery features
- Ability to implement a standby database (log shipping, replication, failover, fault monitor)

III. Performance and Scalability

- Identify and use configuration parameters that affect database system performance
- Identify and use DB2 registry variables that affect database system performance
- Knowledge of query optimizer concepts
- Ability to manage and tune memory and I/O
- Ability to analyze performance problems
- Ability to manage a large number of users and connections
- Ability to partition large amounts of data for performance
- Ability to manage the number of partitions in a database
- Ability to create and manage multi-dimensional clustered tables
- Ability to determine the more appropriate index

IV. Networking & Security

- Ability to configure a partitioned database on multiple servers
- Ability to manage connections to host systems
- Ability to identify and resolve connection problems
- Knowledge of external authentication mechanisms
- Ability to implement data encryption

APPENDIX B

CD-ROM Installation

The accompanying CD-ROM contains a copy of DB2 UDB Personal Edition V8.1.2 for Windows. This product is provided in "Try and Buy" mode. Once the product has been installed, it will continue to operate for 180 days. To use this software past the 180-day period requires a DB2 license, which is not provided.

DB2 Installation

To install DB2 for Windows, perform the following steps:

- Insert CD-ROM.
- If the installation does not automatically start, use the file manager to execute X:\SETUP.EXE (where X is the drive letter of your CD drive).

If you are installing on a Windows NT/2000/XP/2003 workstation, you must be an administrator. This username must belong to the Administrators group and must comply with SQL naming standards.

Documentation

Two sets of documentation are provided on the CD. The documentation can be found in the following directories:

- DB2-PDF

  The documentation in this directory contains the manuals in PDF (Adobe Acrobat Reader) format. The README.TXT file contains the titles of the documents and their corresponding file name in this directory.

  To obtain the Adobe Acrobat Reader, please go to the Adobe product website:

  http://www.adobe.com/products/acrobat/

- DB2-HTML

  The DB2-HTML directory contains all of the documentation in HTML format. To view the documentation you need to use either Internet Explorer or Netscape Navigator. Use your browser to view the file called INDEX.HTM and the browser will display the main DB2 Information Center screen:

You can access the documentation from this screen, as well as search for keywords across all of the documentation.

DB2DEMO

The DB2DEMO program is included on the CD-ROM in the DB2DEMO directory. The DB2DEMO program allows you to try out various features of DB2 without having to write any code.

One of the shortcuts created in the DB2DEMO folder is the DB2 UDB V8 Certification Examples icon. By clicking on this icon, you will be able to try out many of the features found within the Certification Guide. Help for this program can be found from within the product itself, or by using a browser to view the INDEX.HTM file in the DB2DEMO directory that was created as part of the installation process.

Installation File

The DB2DEMO installation program consists of only one file that contains the executable along with all of the supporting files required to run the program. The file is found in the DB2DEMO directory on the CD:

- DB2DEMOSETUP.EXE - Installation program for the DB2DEMO program

Before beginning the installation, make sure that you have about 40M of disk space available (half of this is temporary space that will be released when the installation is complete).

Setup and Installation of the Program

From within the directory that you found the DB2DEMOSETUP program (either the CD-ROM or on your hard drive), you double-click your left mouse button on this file name, or execute it from a command line:

```
X:\DB2DEMO\db2demosetup.exe
```

After clicking on the DB2DEMOSETUP program, there will be some temporary messages displayed while the program unpacks some files:

CD-ROM Contents

When the files have been unpacked. you will be presented with the first installation screen:

Make sure that you have exited any programs that may be currently running (just to be on the safe side) and the hit NEXT to continue on to the next step.

The next screen gives you the copyright and legal information for the program. Please read it and select YES to continue:

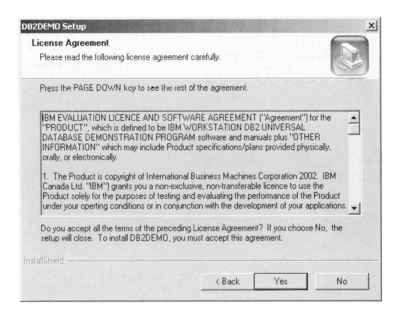

The next screen that appears is the directory screen:

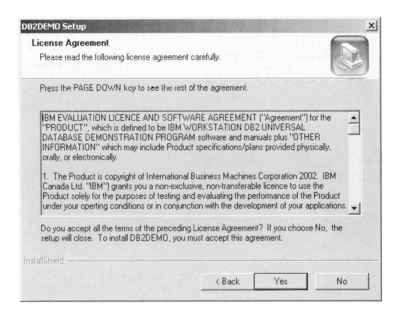

Select a drive and directory to place the DB2DEMO program into. By default, the name of the directory is called DB2DEMO and it is placed on the C: drive. Use the Drives and Directories list boxes to change the value of the field to point to the installation directory you want.

When you are ready to go, hit the NEXT button. At this point in time, the installation program will ask you for the Program Group that the DB2DEMO program will be placed into:

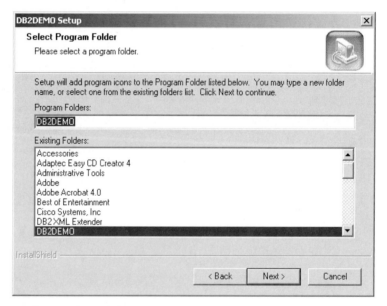

Once you have selected the group name, the program will confirm the installation information:

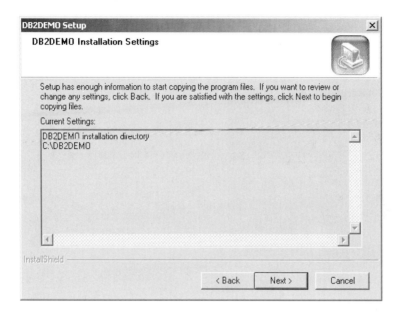

Once you hit the continue button, the program will begin copying files:

When copying is complete, the final dialog box will be displayed:

Depending on which operating system you were installing on, you may be asked to reboot the machine, or be given an option to try out the demo program or look at the additional README information that is supplied with the program. You can also start up DB2DEMO by going into the DB2DEMO group and selecting the DB2DEMO icon:

Advanced Installation

The SAMPLE database can be installed on any server supported by DB2 UDB. The program that creates that sample database is called DB2SAMPL and can be found in the sqllib\bin directory on your server.

When you install the database on a different machine, you still need to use the DB2DEMO program on Windows 2000 or Windows XP, but the data will be on the server instead of the local machine.

In order to install this on a different server, you need to be very familiar with DB2 commands and the security of the machine you are working on. The steps required to run this demo against a different server are:

1. Install DB2 on the server operating system

2. Create a privileged userid that can administer the DB2 system

3. Create the sample database on the system

4. Create a userid on this system that can be used to connect from the remote system

5. Set up the Windows client so that the SAMPLE database has been catalogued properly.This includes installing the DB2 Client Application Enabler code on the workstation. Without this code, the demonstration program cannot run.

Once the installation is complete, you should be able to run the DB2DEMO program from the client and connect to the remote SAMPLE database.

Special Notes for Windows 98/Me Users

DB2 UDB Version 8.1 supports Windows XP/2000/NT/2003 users. Earlier releases also supported Windows 95/98/Me which required special handling from a security perspective. Note that Windows 95 is no longer supported in DB2 Version 8.1, but continues to be supported for DB2 Version 7.2.

DB2 UDB requires that you be logged on with a username before anything can be done in the database. Usually this is not a problem with Windows NT/2000/XP since you must logon before getting to your desktop. The situation is not that straightforward in Windows 95/98/Me. You might have a logon panel if you are connecting to a network. You can bypass this logon however, and still get your desktop! What this means is that for some of you have never identified yourself with a userid to the system.

When DB2 starts up, either with a DB2START command or any of the other system commands, it first determines if you have identified yourself to the system. If not, it will look at the DB2LOGON information to determine what your userid should be. In the majority of cases, you will have not issued a DB2LOGON, and so the commands will fail. If you find that commands are failing, you may want to issue the DB2LOGON command and enter a userid and password before issuing any DB2 commands. The userid and password can be any value you like, as long as DB2 has something to work with.

The DB2DEMO program looks to see if you are logged on as a user. If you are not logged on, the program will create a default logon with a userid of DB2DEMO and with a password of DB2DEMO. You can see if this has occurred after the program has

CD-ROM Contents

started by looking at the system variables by issuing a %DUMPVARS command. This will display all of the variables in the system, and USERID and PASSWORD should be displayed in this list.

If you find yourself outside of the demonstration program having problems using DB2, you may want to issue the DB2LOGON command. The db2logon command simulates a user logon. The format of the db2logon command is:

```
db2logon userid /p:password
```

The user ID that is specified for the command must meet the DB2 naming requirements:

- It can be a maximum of 30 characters (bytes) in length.
- It cannot be any of the following: USERS, ADMINS, GUESTS, PUBLIC, LOCAL, or any SQL reserved word that is listed in the SQL Reference.
- It cannot begin with: SQL, SYS or IBM
- Characters can include:
    - A through Z (Windows 95 and Windows 98 support case-sensitive user IDs)
    - 0 through 9
    - @, #, or $

Uninstalling the Demonstration

To uninstall the DB2DEMO program, use the Add/Delete panel within the Services group to delete the application:

Select the DB2 Demonstration program and the various files will be deleted. The directory may not be deleted if you have personalized any of the files.

Support

We've tried to think of everything, but occasionally things go wrong. If you have a problem with the demonstration code, please send us a note with your email address, name, and a description of the problem. We can be reached at baklarz@yahoo.com or quapla00@hotmail.com.

Index

Symbols

.NET Provider Support 772

A

access path 710
access plan 710, 779
Administration notification logs 744
Advanced SQL 343
alias 298, 301, 822–824
Analyzing Data's Physical Organization
  REORGCHK 562
APIs
  description 769
application
  static embedded 764
applications
  dynamic embedded (description) 765
AS clause 300
ASLHEAPSZ 788
asterisk, use of 285
atomicity 425
ATTACH command 81
attributes 272
Audit
  Audit facility 180
  Buffering audit log writes 180
  Configuring the audit facility 181
  Extracting the audit log 182
  Flushing the audit buffer 182
  Handling audit facility errors 181
  Looking at the current configuration 181
  Pruning the audit log 183
  Starting the audit facility 181
  Stopping the audit facility 183
Audit Facility Administrator 702, 704
Authentication
  Authentication types at the client 140
  Authentication types at the gateway 143
  Authentication types at the server 139
  CLIENT 139
  default 151
  SERVER 139
  SERVER_ENCRYPT 139
  Setting the Authentication Type 151
Authorities 152

  BINDADD 784
  DBADM 155
  SYSADM 154
  SYSCTRL 154
  SYSMAINT 154
Autostart, Event monitor option 698

B

Backup Domain Controller 172
BDC 172
BETWEEN 307
BIND
  Explain options 715
  options (PACKAGE USING) 781
  output 129
  OWNER 784
  QUALIFIER 784
bind file
  display contents (db2bfd) 786
BINDADD 163
binding
  applications 783
  deferred 779
  multiple bind files 788
  record blocking 788
  utilities 128, 788
Block Indexes 248
Block Map 250
Buffer Pools 196
Built-in data type 191
Built-in Functions 301

C

caching
  system catalogs 732
Candidate Dimensions 251
cartesian product 291
CASE expression 314
  advanced 375
  use in functions 376
CAST expression definition 289
CAST function definition 289
casting functions 214
CATALOG_NOAUTH 151
cell 247
CHECK clause 231
check pending state 231
child table 295

W

X